OBJECTIVE GENETICS, BIOTECHNOLOGY, BIOCHEMISTRY AND FORESTRY

Second Edition

OBJECTIVE GENETICS, BIOTECHNOLOGY, BIOCHEMISTRY AND FORESTRY

Second Edition

V. K. KHANNA
Former Professor
Department of Genetics and Plant Breeding
College of Agriculture
G.B. Pant University of Agriculture & Technology
Pantnagar, Uttarakhand
&
Former Professor & Chairman
School of Crop Improvement and Dean
College of PG. Studies
Central Agricultural University
Barapani, Meghalaya

I.K. International Pvt. Ltd.
NEW DELHI

Published by
I.K. International Pvt. Ltd.
4435-36/7, Ansari Road, Daryaganj
New Delhi-110 002 (India)
E-mail: info@ikinternational.com
Website: www.techsarworld.com

ISBN: 978-93-90620-66-1

Published/Printed by Krishan Makhijani for I.K. International Pvt. Ltd., 4435-36/7, Ansari Road, Daryaganj, New Delhi-110 002

Dedicated to

My Beloved Parents

Shri Chander Prakash Khanna

and

Smt. Nirmala Khanna

PREFACE TO THE SECOND EDITION

I am happy to know that a large number of teachers and students are using this book for teaching or learning for the preparations of competitive examinations such as Agricultural Research Services of ICAR, National Eligibility Test, and Civil Services Examinations, etc. Also, the entrance tests for admission to many universities have a combination of objective and subjective questions. These days, for a lot of jobs in the universities or banks or in the private sector, questions are asked in relation to agriculture, where a knowledge of Genetics, Plant Breeding, Tissue Culture and Biotechnology has become important. Due to environmental issues the science of forestry has really picked up and due to infections and their control it has become important to know about how vaccines are produced and how they give us immunity against viruses and other microbes, for which we need to study biotechnology and biochemistry as well.

One has to really know the subject well to be able to find the correct answer in the multiple-choice questions. These questions also give an opportunity to learn and understand the subject better. This book will help the examinees screen and select the deserving candidates easily.

There are no books in the market which deal with objective type questions on so many subjects as in this book which has questions on Genetics & Plant Breeding, Tissue Culture, Biotechnology, Biochemistry and Forestry. All these subjects are related with each other in the sense that undergraduates study courses on these and the postgraduates of Genetics and Plant Breeding take Biotechnology as a minor subject whereas Biotechnology students take Biochemistry or Genetics and Plant Breeding as a minor subject.

I am grateful to a large number of teachers and students who have given me the feedback and their suggestions which have been useful for making improvement in this second addition. I have not kept Plant Breeding as a separate chapter but put the related questions under the chapter "General" which also has many related questions on various subjects. The questions about different Genetics topics are under separate chapters and also there are separate chapters on Tissue Culture, Biotechnology, Biochemistry and Forestry. There is a big increase in the number of questions as compared to the First edition of this book.

You will also find the glossaries of Genetics, Tissue Culture, Biotechnology, Biochemistry and Forestry in this book. There is information about the Nobel Prize, list of Nobel laureates in various subjects including peace prize and also those recipients who were born in India. Then, there is the list of state agricultural universities in India and a lot more.

I am always open to suggestions from the readers and would welcome them as that would help in further improvement of the book.

V. K. KHANNA

PREFACE TO THE FIRST EDITION

In most of the competitive examinations such as Agricultural Research Services of Indian Council of Agricultural Research, National Eligibility Test (NET), State Eligibility Test and Civil Services Examination, etc. objective type questions are asked. Also, the entrance tests for admission to many universities are totally objective. To test the capabilities of the students in different courses, many universities have a combination of objective and subjective questions.

In most of the books, the objective type questions judge the student on the basis of their ability to memorize, because of the way they are formulated. It is important to be able to remember the year of historical events, the scientists involved and who named what to make one remember the landmark contributions of the people on a particular subject. Along with those kinds of questions, majority of the questions in this book have been designed to assess the candidate's understanding of the subject. It is perhaps for the first time in an Indian book where questions have four to six choice statements which are to be understood to find the right answer. One has to think and remember what one has learnt to be able to answer these questions. If the candidate has only surface knowledge, then he would find it difficult to answer. Moreover, with these kinds of questions, students would learn a lot more of the subject. I am sure that after reading this book, the examinees would make use of these questions to assess the students' intelligence and they would be able to screen students much more easily.

There are some books on objective type questions on the subject of Plant Breeding and a few on Genetics but there is hardly any book which deals with Tissue Culture, Biotechnology, Biochemistry and Forestry. All these subjects are related as many postgraduate students of Genetics and Plant Breeding take Biotechnology as a minor subject whereas those of Biotechnology take Biochemistry or Genetics or Plant Breeding as a minor subject. Also, undergraduates in agricultural universities study courses on all these subjects including Forestry. All the students studying any of these subjects should have in-depth knowledge to be successful in competitive examinations, subject tests, entrance examinations and the interviews.

A large number of students and teachers have interacted with me and given their suggestions which encouraged me to write a book of this kind. I am sure this book is going to be useful to students, teachers and examiners. Since I have chosen many related subjects, I have put the plant breeding questions related to genetics in a chapter named 'General'. Likewise, I have put all the questions on tissue culture, biotechnology, biochemistry and forestry under single separate chapters and tried to cover most of the important topics.

In this book, I have also added the glossaries of genetics, tissue culture, biotechnology, biochemistry, and forestry. Along with that, there is brief note about Nobel Prize, list of Nobel laureates in physiology, chemistry and peace and those who are Indian or India born. This is followed by State Agricultural Universities in India, merits and awards given by ICAR, institutions and centers under ICAR and a lot of more information.

I thank Mr. Ganesh Joshi for his help in typing and correcting the proofs along with my Ph.D. students, Payal, Rishika and Maninder.

I am highly appreciative of the understanding and support from my wife Indu and my daughter Roshni. I am grateful to my parents and my uncle, Dr. P. K. Seth and aunty Mrs. Chandana Seth for their love and encouragement.

Suggestions for improving the book are welcome.

V. K. KHANNA

THE AUTHOR

V. K. Khanna has 39 years of experience of teaching and conducting research on wide-hybridization, genetics and biotechnology. He has guided 76 students for their MSc and PhD theses and published 175 research papers in Indian and foreign journals of repute. He has also presented 193 research papers in conferences/symposia/workshops in India and abroad, a few of them being lead papers including a key-note addresses in an international conference. He has been the Chairman/Co-Chairman in many national and international conferences. He has also published 57 popular articles and written 15 books and laboratory manuals and 3 book chapters. He has visited various universities abroad and presented his research work in conferences in Australia, USA, Germany, Taiwan, Singapore and Philippines and also visited universities and research stations in U.K., the Netherlands, Russia and Thailand. He was a Fellow of the Food and Agricultural Organization (FAO) of the United Nations. He has worked on molecular markers and genetic transformation at the University of Queensland, Australia. He was a member of the editorial board and reviewing committee of some Indian and foreign journals. He was a member of the National Review Committee on Genetic Manipulation in the Department of Biotechnology, Government of India. He got a patent (2008) with the National Research Development Corporation, New Delhi for "Gamma Kafirin gene promoter of *Sorghum bicolor* with minimum essential regulatory motifs for temporal and spatial expression of genes". He has taught 21 PG and 8 UG courses. He has been the PI of 14 research projects and Co-PI of one. Dr. V. K. Khanna has been the recipient of many awards including the Best Paper Awards and the Best Teacher Award. He has worked as Joint Director Research; in charge of Govt. notified Seed Testing Laboratory, in-charge; Pantnagar Centre of Plant Genetic Resources; Additional Coordinator Admissions; Acting Registrar; Acting Dean of College of Agri Business Management at G. B. Pant University of Agriculture & Technology, Pantnagar. Later, he joined as Professor, Biotechnology and Chairman, School of Crop Improvement and in-charge Dean at College of Post Graduate Studies, Central Agricultural University, Barapani, Meghalaya from where he retired in July, 2019 at the age of 70 years.

CONTENTS

Section-II
ANSWERS

Section-III
APPENDICES

SECTION-I

QUESTIONS

1
General

MULTIPLE-CHOICE QUESTIONS

MOLECULES

1. **Which of the following is not true of hydrocarbons?**
   (a) Phospholipids have hydrocarbon tails
   (b) Octane is a hydrocarbon
   (c) Many hydrocarbons are used in living systems
   (d) Hydrocarbons are insoluble in water
   (e) Only hydrogen atoms are used to complete the valence requirements of carbon

2. **Many biological molecules have functional groups that alter the chemical reactivity of the molecule. Which of the following is not a functional group?**
   (a) Hydroxyl group
   (b) Ethylene group
   (c) Aldehyde group
   (d) Carboxyl group
   (e) Carbonyl group

3. **Which of the following is not a fundamental property of carbon?**
   (a) Carbon-containing molecules are stable
   (b) Carbon-containing molecules form stereo-isomers
   (c) Carbon-containing molecules are diverse
   (d) Carbon has a valence of 4
   (e) Carbon atoms are most likely to form ionic bonds with one another

4. **Which of the following sequences correctly illustrates the hierarchical nature of cellular structures, from smallest to largest?**
   (a) Organic molecules, macromolecules, organelles, supramolecular structures, cells
   (b) Organelles, organic molecules, supramolecular structures, macromolecules, cells
   (c) Organic molecules, macromolecules, supramolecular structures, organelles, cells
   (d) Macromolecules, organic molecules, supra-molecular structures, organelles, cells
   (e) Organic molecules, supramolecular structures, macromolecules, organelles, cells

5. Why do polar substances such as sodium chloride (NaCl) dissolve so readily in water?

(a) The sodium ions repel the partial negative end of the water dipole
(b) NaCl is a very dry powder, and the water is able to soak into the salt
(c) The partially charged ends of the water molecules are able to surround the oppositely charged salt ion
(d) Spheres of hydration form between the water and the ions
(e) Both (c) and (d)

6. While fishing, a biology student makes the following observations:

Water spiders appear to be able to walk on the surface of the water.

Flat rocks may be made to skip across the water.

Which of the following properties of water explain these observations?

(a) Water is an excellent solvent
(b) Water molecules create spheres of hydration around solute molecules
(c) Water molecules are cohesive
(d) Water molecules are often associated *via* hydrogen bonds
(e) Both (c) and (d)

7. Which of the following is not true of the polymerization of macromolecules?

(a) The polymer chain has usually two ends
(b) Macromolecules are synthesized by the stepwise addition of a monomer
(c) The monomer is usually activated by the coupling of the monomer to a carrier
(d) Often the energy needed for polymerization is supplied by ATP
(e) Water is used to join the monomers of the macromolecules

8. The term *amphipathic* describes the characteristic of some molecules, which have

(a) two polar regions
(b) only a single polar region
(c) both a polar and a nonpolar region
(d) no polar regions
(e) two nonpolar regions

9. Which of the following amino acids is a nonpolar (hydrophobic) amino acid?

(a) Lysine (b) Valine
(c) Aspartate (d) Tyrosine
(e) Serine

10. Which of the following is a disaccharide?

(a) Glucose (b) Lactose
(c) Fructose (d) Galactose
(e) None of the above

11. Which of the following has the greatest number of glycosidic bonds?

(a) Glucose (b) DNA
(c) Amylose (d) Vitamin A
(e) Triacylglycerol

12. Which of the following is not a steroid?

(a) Testosterone (b) Cortisol
(c) Aldosterone (d) Estradiol
(e) Epinephrine

13. Which of the following statements is not true of the amino acids?

(a) Only around 20 amino acids are used in protein synthesis
(b) All amino acids exist in two stereoisomeric forms
(c) Amino acids have an N-terminus, C-terminus, and R groups
(d) There are more than 60 different kinds of amino acids present in the cell
(e) The R group of amino acids differs from one amino acid to another

14. Which of the following three letter symbols represents an amino acid that is polar and uncharged?

(a) Gln (b) Asp
(c) Ala (d) His
(e) Pro

15. A(n) _____ is composed of tetrameric protofilaments

(a) microtubule
(b) extracellular matrix
(c) microfilament
(d) bacteriophage
(e) intermediate filament

16. Which of the following is true of an asymmetric carbon atom?

(a) Asymmetric carbon atoms create stereoisomers
(b) Methane has an asymmetric carbon
(c) Molecules may have only one asymmetric carbon atom
(d) Only amino acids have asymmetric carbon atoms
(e) A carbon with hydrogens attached at two locations is usually asymmetric

17. Which of the following is true of glycolipids?

(a) Glycolipids are usually found on the exterior surface of the plasma membrane
(b) Usually more than 10 sugar units are attached to the glycolipid
(c) Fructose and sucrose are often part of glycolipids
(d) Laurate is a glycolipid
(e) Thudicum discovered glycolipids in the late sixteenth century

18. Which of the following does not represent the correct pairing of the three-letter abbreviation with the one-letter abbreviation of an amino acid?

(a) Arg-A (b) Glu-E
(c) Met-M (d) Pro-P
(e) Phe-F

19. Which of the following is true of fatty acids?

(a) Fatty acids with 24 carbons are most common
(b) Saturated fatty acids have no double bonds between carbons
(c) Fatty acids are synthesized by the stepwise addition of three carbon units
(d) Unsaturated fatty acids are usually branched
(e) Laurate is an unsaturated fatty acid

20. Which of the following is not a structural polysaccharide?

(a) Chitin
(b) Glycogen
(c) Cellulose
(d) Peptidoglycan

21. The technique that allows various proteins to be differentiated based on size, once the proteins have been denatured, is

(a) SDS PAGE
(b) liposome formation
(c) freeze fracture technique
(d) PCR
(e) RFLP

22. Biologically, which of the following is the least important characteristic of water?

(a) Water typically contains isotopes of hydrogen
(b) Water is a good solvent
(c) Water has a temperature stabilizing capacity
(d) Water molecules have numerous hydrogen bonds
(e) Water molecules are polar

23. Which is an organic compound found in most cells?

(a) Glucose (b) Water
(c) Sodium chloride (d) Oxygen gas

24. Which are the four most abundant elements in living cells?

(a) Carbon, oxygen, nitrogen, sulphur
(b) Carbon, oxygen, hydrogen, nitrogen
(c) Carbon, oxygen, sulphur, phosphorus
(d) Carbon, sulphur, hydrogen, magnesium

25. Which pair of compounds can be classified as inorganic?

(a) Nucleic acids and minerals
(b) Proteins and water
(c) Water and salts
(d) Nucleic acids and proteins

26. Which formula represents an organic compound?

(a) $Mg(OH)_2$ (b) NaCl
(c) $C_{12}H_{22}O_{11}$ (d) NH_3

27. Water molecules enter plant epidermal cells by

(a) osmosis
(b) active transport
(c) translocation
(d) transpiration

28. Which of the following is not found in the blood?

(a) Fibrinogen (b) Glucose
(c) Urea (d) Glycogen

29. Which one of the pH listed below represents the strongest base?

(a) 7 (b) 10
(c) 13 (d) 15

30. Covalent bonds result from

(a) the sharing of equal numbers of electrons by two atoms
(b) the exchange of equal numbers of electrons by two atoms
(c) the combination of two atoms of the same valence
(d) the sharing of unequal numbers of electrons by two atoms

31. An element having 8 protons, 8 neutrons, and 8 electrons would weigh ______ daltons

(a) 8 (b) 32
(c) 24 (d) 16

32. Atomic number is equal to the number of ______ in the nucleus of the atom

(a) electrons (b) protons
(c) neutrons (d) positrons

33. Which of the following pH values represents the greatest concentration of H^+ ions?

(a) 4 (b) 10
(c) 2 (d) 7
(e) 12

34. Which of the following pH values represents the strongest acid?

(a) 4 (b) 10
(c) 2 (d) 7
(e) 12

35. Of the following elements, which is the least common in living organisms?

(a) Sodium (b) Oxygen
(c) Hydrogen (d) Nitrogen
(e) Carbon

36. With respect to galactose, glucose is

(a) a stereoisomer (b) a structural isomer
(c) not an isomer (d) not related

37. Which of the following is not a lipid?

(a) Chitin (b) Terpenes
(c) Steroids (d) Prostaglandins
(e) Unsaturated fat

38. Glucose is a

(a) protein (b) disaccharide
(c) nucleic acid (d) monosaccharide
(e) starch

39. Triacylglycerol contains fatty acids and
(a) glucose (b) glycogen
(c) glycerol (d) guanine
(e) an amino group

40. In the formation of a macromolecule, what type of reaction would join two subunits together?
(a) Hydrophobic reaction
(b) Hydrolysis reaction
(c) Dehydration reaction
(d) Denaturation reaction

41. Assuming they all had the same number of carbon atoms, which of the following has the most C-H bonds?
(a) An unsaturated fat
(b) A polyunsaturated fat
(c) A polysaccharide
(d) A saturated fat

42. Why is cellulose so difficult for most animals to digest?
(a) They don't have the proper enzyme to break the bonds between subunits
(b) Cellulose is made up of chitin, which is indigestible
(c) The bonds holding cellulose subunits together are extremely strong
(d) There are many hydrogen bonds holding the subunits together

43. What happens during the hydrolysis reaction?
(a) Protein coils into its secondary structure
(b) The bond between two subunits of a macro-molecule is broken
(c) Saturated fats become unsaturated
(d) A bond is formed between two subunits of a macromolecule
(e) Water breaks ionic bonds

44. Which of the following is not a disaccharide?
(a) Sucrose (b) Maltose
(c) Lactose (d) Amylose
(e) None of the above

45. The general term for a large molecule made up of many similar subunits is
(a) polymer (b) functional group
(c) peptide (d) helix
(e) pectin

46. Dehydration and hydrolysis reactions involve removing or adding ______ to macromolecule subunits
(a) C and O (b) CH and NH_2
(c) C and H (d) COOH and H
(e) OH and H

47. The empirical formula for carbohydrates is
(a) $(CHO)^2$ (b) $(CH_20)_n$
(c) $2(CHO)_n$ (d) $(C_2HO)_n$
(e) $(C_nH_nO_n)^2$

48. Which type of macromolecule carries out catalysis in biological systems?
(a) Proteins called enzymes
(b) Carbohydrates called starch
(c) Lipids called steroids
(d) Nucleic acids called RNA
(e) Carbohydrates called sugars

49. Molecules that have the same chemical formula but different molecular structures are called
(a) isotopes
(b) ions
(c) structural isotopes
(d) isomers
(e) both (a) and (c)

50. A hydrocarbon is said to be saturated if
(a) one end of the molecule is hydrophilic while the other end is hydrophobic
(b) it has one or more double bonds between carbon atoms
(c) it contains more than one functional group
(d) each internal carbon atom is covalently bonded to two hydrogen atoms
(e) its functional groups include at least one aromatic ring

51. An individual has been infected with a particular retrovirus. In order for the latent virus DNA to be inherited by subsequent generations of this individual, it must be found

(a) at a point early in childhood
(b) in stem cells
(c) in germ line cells
(d) in all cells simultaneously
(e) in somatic cells

52. Carbon dioxide generally enters the plant through pores called

(a) mesophyll (b) cuticle
(c) nucleopores (d) bacteriopores
(e) stomata

53. The Latin phrase *omnis cellulae cellula* refers to a cellular principle. Which of the following statements is the best translation of this phrase?

(a) All cells arise only from preexisting cells
(b) The cell is the basic unit of structure
(c) Tissues are composed of similar cells
(d) All organisms consist of one or more cells
(e) Cells are generally found in clusters

54. Which scientist is credited with coining the term "cell" from the Latin *cellulae*?

(a) Robert Hooke
(b) Robert Brown
(c) Theodor Schwann
(d) Antonie van Leeuwenhoek
(e) Matthias Schleiden

55. Which is not a main feature of the cell theory?

(a) Cells arise only by the division of existing cells
(b) The cell is the unit of function of all living things
(c) Each cell is surrounded by a membrane
(d) The cell is responsible for the function of all living things

56. If a solution outside a cell is more concentrated so that the cell loses water to its environment, the external solution is said to be ______ to the cell contents

(a) hypertonic (b) in equilibrium
(c) isotonic (d) hypotonic

57. Which mechanism requires energy?

(a) Facilitated diffusion
(b) Osmosis
(c) Diffusion
(d) Active transport

58. Osmosis is a process that

(a) involves the movement of particles from saturated solutions
(b) moves water molecules from an area of higher concentration to an area of lower concentration, using energy
(c) involves the active transport of dissolved solids
(d) continues until the medium on each side of the membrane has become hypertonic
(e) equalizes the concentration of particles by the movement of water molecules

59. Which of the following is a phototroph?

(a) A mushroom
(b) Bacteria growing on decomposing matter
(c) An earthworm
(d) A tree
(e) All of the above

60. Which of the following units is used to measure energy?

(a) Joule (b) Watt
(c) Meter (d) Both a and b

61. When scientists use the scientific method, they use terms to indicate their degree of certainty. Which of the following terms conveys the least degree of certainty?

(a) Law
(b) Theory
(c) Hypothesis
(d) Both hypothesis and theory
(e) Both theory and law

62. __________ lower the energy needed to initiate a chemical reaction in a living cell

(a) Enzymes (b) Nucleotides
(c) Carbohydrates (d) Proteins
(e) Amino acids

63. The "gap" in Darwin's theory of evolution was his inability to

(a) explain the basis of variation
(b) explain migration
(c) observe large populations
(d) observe variation
(e) no gaps existed

64. The science of genetics is concerned with

(a) the distribution of heritable characteristics in populations
(b) the transmission of traits
(c) the origin of heritable differences
(d) the expression of genetic information
(e) all of the above are correct

65. Every nucleus in a eukaryotic organism contains the same amount of DNA, with the exception of nuclei in the

(a) fibroblasts (b) neurons
(c) muscle cells (d) gametes
(e) epidermal cells

66. The steps of the "scientific method," in the correct order, are

(a) collect data, interpret results, test the hypothesis, make observations, design experiments
(b) make observations, collect data, interpret results, test the hypothesis, design experiments, draw conclusions
(c) make observations, formulate the hypothesis, design experiments, collect data, interpret results, draw conclusions
(d) design experiments, draw conclusions, collect data, interpret results, make observations, test the hypothesis
(e) none of the above

67. Approximately ______ % of the world's production of fats and oils comes from plants

(a) 15 (b) 25
(c) 45 (d) 75
(e) 95

68. The mutant allele *r* is expressed as red leaves in autotetraploid poinsettia plants. The proportion of red plants expected in the progeny of the cross of Rrrr x RRrr is

(a) 1/36 (b) 1/24
(c) 1/12 (d) 1/6
(e) 1/3

69. Differential distribution of substances in the egg most typically results in

(a) differences in gene expression which may establish a pattern in the embryo as the cells divide
(b) amplification of specific genes during development
(c) development of polyploid tissues
(d) loss of specific genes during development
(e) dominance of genes derived from the father

70. A gene showing codominance

(a) has both alleles independently expressed in the heterozygote
(b) has one allele dominant to the other
(c) has alleles tightly linked on the same chromosome
(d) has alleles expressed at the same time in development
(e) has alleles that are recessive to each other

71. *Arabidopsis* is advantageous for plant genetic research because

(a) it is commercially important as a food crop
(b) it is an endangered species
(c) it is the closest to humans of any existing plant
(d) it is a small plant with a small genome size that can be raised inexpensively
(e) it is a close relative of corn, and results with this species can be applied to problems in corn

72. A threshold trait is one which

(a) is expressed on a continuous scale (such as blood pressure)
(b) is present in a few discrete classes, but is influenced by both genetics and the environment (such as diabetes)
(c) is caused by only a single gene, with no environmental influence
(d) is present in a very low frequency in the population
(e) is associated with superior survival of the heterozygote

73. Twin studies in humans are useful because

(a) they allow more refined estimates of chromosome location to be made
(b) twins have a greater likelihood of being heterozygous
(c) they allow improved expression of genes
(d) cloning of genes is facilitated by the presence of extra copies
(e) they allow genetic as opposed to environmental influences on variation in a trait to be estimated

74. The pH of human blood is slightly basic. Which of the following is most likely to be the pH of the human blood?

(a) 10.6 (b) 7.4
(c) 6.4 (d) 4.6

75. The preformation theory was proposed by

(a) Bateson
(b) Lamarck
(c) Sutton and Boveri
(d) Swammerdam and Bonnet

76. The germplasm theory was proposed by

(a) Weismann (b) Darwin
(c) Boveri (d) Lamarck

77. The theory of acquired characters was given by

(a) Lamarck (b) Wolff
(c) De Vries (d) Darwin

78. The theory of epigenesis was proposed by

(a) Darwin (b) Bateson
(c) Wolff (d) De Vries

79. The theory which has universal acceptance is

(a) pangenesis (b) epigenesis
(c) preformation (d) germplasm

80. The first artificial plant hybrid was produced by

(a) Koelreuter (b) Bateson
(c) Thomas Fairchild (d) Mendel

81. Fairchild's mule was produced from a cross between

(a) sweet william and carnation
(b) sweet william and petunia
(c) carnation and daffodil
(d) daffodil and petunia

82. Koelreuter carried out hybridization experiments in

(a) carnation (b) tobacco
(c) xerbera (d) chrysanthemum

83. The first step in genetic improvement of a plant species is

(a) domestication
(b) germplasm collection
(c) selection
(d) distribution

84. Vilmorin successfully used progeny test for the improvement of

(a) triticale (b) maize
(c) bajra (d) sugarbeet

85. Genetic basis of pure lines or pure line theory was proposed by

(a) Nilsson-Ehle (b) Bateson
(c) Johannsen (d) None of them

86. Johannsen proposed the pure line theory based on his work on

(a) french bean (b) lima bean
(c) field bean (d) none of the above

87. In most of the breeding programmes, the main aim is to develop a variety with

(a) high yielding ability
(b) disease resistance
(c) insect resistance
(d) improved quality

88. Improved gluten strength is an important quality trait for

(a) rice (b) jowar
(c) ragi (d) wheat

89. Generally, pulses are deficient in

(a) methionine and lysine
(b) tryptophan and methionine
(c) tryptophan and lysine
(d) lysine

90. Generally, cereals are deficient in

(a) lysine (b) tryptophan
(c) proline (d) isoleucine

91. The modern wheat varieties are

(a) photoinsensitive
(b) thermoinsensitive
(c) photo-and thermo-sensitive
(d) photo-and thermo-insensitive

92. Development of determinate varieties is not desirable in

(a) pigeon pea (b) cotton
(c) sugarcane (d) mung bean

93. The name of first Agricultural Research Institute established in India was

(a) Imperial Agricultural Research Institute
(b) National Agricultural Research Institute
(c) Indian Agricultural Research Institute
(d) Central Agricultural Research Institute

94. The Imperial Agricultural Research Institute was renamed as the Indian Agricultural Research Institute in the year

(a) 1945 (b) 1952
(c) 1947 (d) 1960

95. Semi-dwarf wheat varieties were initially developed by Norman E. Borlaug at

(a) CIMMYT (b) ICARDA
(c) IARI (d) ICRISAT

96. The 'Father of green revolution' is

(a) B.P. Pal (b) M.S. Swaminathan
(c) N.E. Borlaug (d) M.S. Randhawa

97. The first agricultural university in India was established at

(a) Ludhiana (b) Pantnagar
(c) Pusa (d) Hisar

98. The botanical name of Indian cane is

(a) *Saccharum barberi*
(b) *Saccharum sinense*
(c) *Saccharum robusta*
(d) *Saccharum officinarum*

99. Tropical noble canes were not successful in India mainly due to their

(a) poor yield
(b) susceptibility to low winter temperatures in North India
(c) sensitivity to high summer temperatures
(d) low sucrose yield

100. The term nobilization is related to

(a) maize (b) sugarcane
(c) soybean (d) rice

101. The world's first high yielding semi-dwarf aromatic rice variety is

(a) Texamati (b) Taraori basmati
(c) Pusa basmati 1 (d) None of these

102. The first Director General and Vice-President of Indian Council of Agricultural Research was

(a) Dr. B.P. Pal
(b) Dr. M.S. Swaminathan
(c) Dr. M.S. Randhawa
(d) Dr. D.P. Singh

103. The Indian Society of Genetics and Plant Breeding was founded by

(a) T.S. Venkataraman
(b) M.S. Swaminathan
(c) C.A. Barber
(d) B.P. Pal

104. The term 'green revolution' was coined by

(a) M.S. Swaminathan
(b) N.E. Borlaug
(c) William Goud
(d) M.S. Randhawa

105. G.B. Pant University of Agriculture and Technology was established in

(a) 1958 (b) 1960
(c) 1962 (d) 1964

106. Agricultural Research Service was initiated due to the efforts of

(a) M.S. Swaminathan
(b) M.S. Randhawa
(c) B.P. Pal
(d) Jawahar Lal Nehru

107. The prefix Co in the names of sugarcane varieties stands for

(a) College (b) Coimbatore
(c) Combodia (d) Cochin

108. Jute Technological Research Laboratory was established in 1938 at

(a) Rawalpindi (b) Dacca
(c) Barrackpur (d) Calcutta

109. International Rice Research Institute was established at Los Banos, Phillippines in the year

(a) 1960 (b) 1956
(c) 1958 (d) 1972

110. International Centre for Maize and Wheat Improvement was established at el Baton, Mexico in

(a) 1959 (b) 1969
(c) 1979 (d) 1966

111. International Centre for Tropical Agriculture was established in 1967 at

(a) Palmira (Colombia)
(b) Ibadan (Nigeria)
(c) Addis Ababa (Ethiopia)
(d) Nairobi (Kenya)

112. The National Seeds Corporation was established in the year

(a) 1960 (b) 1968
(c) 1964 (d) 1963

113. International Centre for Genetic Engineering and Biotechnology was established in

(a) 1977 (b) 1987
(c) 1992 (d) 1981

114. Tarai Development Corporation was established in

(a) 1960 (b) 1968
(c) 1979 (d) 1969

115. The term 'yellow revolution' is related to the production of

(a) oilseeds (b) fruits
(c) vegetables (d) yellow flowers

116. Staggered planting means sowing of two strains

(a) at different dates
(b) at different locations
(c) in alternate rows
(d) in different fields

117. Technology Mission on Oilseeds was launched by the Government of India in

(a) 1980 (b) 1989
(c) 1984 (d) 1986

118. World Trade Organisation came into existence on

(a) 21 January, 1990 (b) 1 January, 1995
(c) 12 January, 1996 (d) 1 January, 1994

119. The headquarters of WTO is located at

(a) Rome (b) Washington
(c) Tokyo (d) Geneva

120. 'Texamati' rice was patented by which US company?

(a) Monsanto (b) Pfizer
(c) Ricetek (d) Delta-Pine land

121. *Triticale* is a

(a) man made cereal
(b) usually diploid species
(c) usually hexaploid species
(d) both a and c

122. In 1983, late blight of potato was inadvertently introduced in India from

(a) China (b) Europe
(c) Sri Lanka (d) Mexico

123. Plant introduction consists of

(a) procurement and quarantine
(b) cataloguing and evaluation
(c) multiplication and distribution
(d) all of these

124. In 1940, bunchy top of banana was inadvertently introduced into India from

(a) Ceylon (b) Malaya
(c) Burma (d) China

125. Germplasm is also called

(a) gene pool (b) gene bank
(c) gene collection (d) genetic resource

126. The Royal Botanic Gardens is located at

(a) Kew (England)
(b) Brisbane (Australia)
(c) Washington (USA)
(d) Alberta (Canada)

127. Gene bank is best maintained as

(a) DNA bank (b) field bank
(c) explant bank (d) seed bank

128. Rice flower has how many stamens?

(a) 6 (b) 3
(c) 2 (d) 4

129. Cleistogamy promotes

(a) cross-pollination (b) sterility
(c) self-pollination (d) none of the above

130. The National Seeds Corporation was established in

(a) 1960 (b) 1967
(c) 1963 (d) 1947

131. The first artificial hybrid was produced by

(a) Joseph Koelreuter
(b) Thomas Fairchild
(c) Bateson
(d) Mendel

132. The first artificial plant hybrid was produced through a cross between

(a) two *Nicotiana* species
(b) two *Tabacum* species
(c) two varieties of maize
(d) sweet william and carnation

133. Botanical name of carnation is

(a) *Dianthus caryophyllus*
(b) *Dianthus barbatus*
(c) *Dianthus robusta*
(d) *Dianthus aestivum*

134. Bread wheat has somatic chromosome number of

(a) $2n = 14$ (b) $2n = 28$
(c) $2n = 56$ (d) $2n = 42$

135. Noblized canes represent which of the following?

(a) Interspecific hybridization
(b) Introgressive hybridization
(c) Intervarietal hybridization
(d) Both a and b

136. *Raphanobrassica* is promising as a

(a) forage crop (b) vegetable crop
(c) root crop (d) fruit crop

137. Parthenocarpy occurs in

(a) pineapple (b) citrus
(c) fig (d) all of the above

138. Hybrid varieties were first exploited in

(a) onion (b) watermelon
(c) sunflower (d) maize

139. India was the first country to develop hybrid varieties in which crop?

(a) Rice (b) Cotton
(c) Sunflower (d) Maize

140. India is the second country, after China, in the world to have developed hybrids in

(a) sunflower (b) cotton
(c) rice (d) sugarcane

141. The methods of membrane transport that do not require protein channels or carriers are

(a) osmosis (b) diffusion
(c) phagocytosis (d) exocytosis
(e) all of the above

142. In India, the crop in which a hybrid variety was the first to be developed is

(a) maize (b) bajra (pearl millet)
(c) jowar (sorghum) (d) sunflower

143. Among the given parameters, which are the examples of morphological parameters involved in drought tolerance?

(a) Earliness, wax content and awns
(b) Leaf rolling, hairs and increased grain weight
(c) Reduced leaf area, colour of leaf and root system
(d) All of the above

144. Among the given hormones, which of the following is a stress hormone?

(a) Abscisic acid (b) Cytokinin
(c) Auxin (d) Gibberellin

145. The actual geographical area of the world that is under cultivation is

(a) 10.1% (b) 18.2%
(c) 10.6% (d) 12.6%

146. The potentially arable geographical area in India is

(a) 11.6% (b) 15.6%
(c) 18.6% (d) 13.6%

147. In which of the following, stomata open only during night?

(a) Xerophytes
(b) Mesophytes
(c) Succulents showing CAM
(d) All of the above

148. Among the plants given below, which one is the example of a C4 plant?

(a) Maize (b) Sorghum
(c) Sugarcane (d) All of the above

149. One gram of nitrogen is present in how many grams of protein?

(a) 6.25 (b) 4.25
(c) 5.25 (d) 3.25

150. Prolonged consumption of only sorghum causes

(a) dwarfism (b) pellagra
(c) mental retardation (d) hypertension

151. Soybean protein is deficient in

(a) isoleucine (b) lysine
(c) cysteine (d) methionine

152. Maize is deficient in

(a) methionine (b) isoleucine
(c) tryptophan (d) none of the above

153. Distant crosses may fail due to

(a) inability of pollen to germinate
(b) failure of the pollen tubes to grow
(c) degeneration of endosperm
(d) all of the above

154. In case of sorghum, dark brown seeds are associated with

(a) high protein content
(b) poor starch quality
(c) low tannin content
(d) high tannin content

155. In pearl millet, white kernel is associated with

(a) higher carotenoids
(b) higher crude protein
(c) both (a) and (b)
(d) higher lysine content

156. In fodder maize, yellow kernel colour is associated with

(a) higher crude protein content
(b) lower crude protein content
(c) higher fibre content
(d) lower fibre content

157. In fodder maize, brown midrib is associated with

(a) lower lignin content
(b) higher tannin content
(c) greater digestibility
(d) more yield

158. In carrot, deep orange root colour is associated with

(a) higher lycopene content
(b) lower lycopene content
(c) higher β-carotene content
(d) lower β-carotene content

159. Which oil contains an antioxidant?

(a) Sesame (b) Sunflower
(c) Soybean (d) Mustard

160. Hormones are composed from many classes of molecules. Hormones are not found in which of the following categories of substances?

(a) Proteins (b) Peptides
(c) Nucleic acids (d) Steroids

161. Into which of the following acids is glucose broken down in the first stage of carbohydrate metabolism?

(a) Pyruvic acid
(b) Lactic acid
(c) Hydrochloric acid
(d) Citric acid

162. Who is considered the father of taxonomy?

(a) Mendel (b) Bateson
(c) Tshermak (d) Linnaeus

163. The process by which an amino acid losses its amino group is called

(a) hydration (b) deamination
(c) oxidoamination (d) dehydration

164. Which of the following plants produce endosperm following fertilization?

(a) Wheat (b) Canola
(c) Pine (d) Both (a) and (b)
(e) Both (a) and (c)

165. Which of the following correctly explains how a favourable genetic trait can increase in frequency in a population?

(a) Lamarck's principle
(b) Natural selection
(c) Adaptive radiation
(d) Genetic recombination
(e) Segregation of alleles

166. Which of the following is a sulphur containing amino acid?

(a) Lysine (b) Serine
(c) Cystine (d) Leucine

167. Prions are

(a) recently discovered organelles in bacteria
(b) a single or double strand of nucleic acid wrapped in a protein coat
(c) naturally occurring glycoprotein that take two forms
(d) none of the above

168. Which of the following is not a property of life?

(a) Molding or adapting to one's environment
(b) Regulating materials that enter or leave the system
(c) Responding to stimuli
(d) Maintaining a relatively constant internal condition
(e) Reproducing, passing hereditary material to the next generation

169. Which of the following gases is least likely to have existed in the early atmosphere of the earth?

(a) NH_3 (b) CO_2
(c) N_2 (d) H_2O
(e) O_2

170. Which of the following was not a source of energy on the early earth?

(a) Lightning
(b) Ozone
(c) Ultraviolet radiation
(d) Volcanic eruptions
(e) All of the above were a source of energy

171. Within our own solar system, the most likely candidate for having life on it is

(a) Moon (b) Jupiter
(c) Venus (d) Sun
(e) Europa, a moon of Jupiter

172. Approximately, what percentage of today's atmosphere is oxygen?

(a) 21% (b) 73 %
(c) 1% (d) 50 %
(e) 13%

173. Which gas in today's atmosphere shields us from ultraviolet radiation?

(a) Ozone (b) Nitrogen
(c) Oxygen (d) Carbon dioxide
(e) Carbon monoxide

174. Which of the following is not a characteristic of all living organisms?

(a) Reproduction
(b) Heredity
(c) Metabolism
(d) Movement from place to place
(e) All of the above are characteristics of all living organisms

175. The oxygen that is present in our atmosphere comes primarily from the

(a) eruption of volcanoes
(b) breakdown of ozone
(c) breathing of animals
(d) photosynthesis of plants, algae, and bacteria
(e) none of the above

176. Which of the following is not a characteristic of the first cells?

(a) Heterotroph
(b) Single-celled
(c) Genome composed of RNA
(d) Anaerobic
(e) Prokaryotic

177. What is the yield of chemical energy, on average, for every gram of carbohydrate and of fat that is utilized?

(a) 4 kcal each
(b) 9 kcal each
(c) 4 kcal and 9 kcal, respectively
(d) 9 kcal and 4 kcal, respectively
(e) 40 kcal and 90 kcal, respectively

178. The sodium-potassium pump passes

(a) more Na+ out than K+ in
(b) K+ out and Na+ in on a one-for-one basis
(c) Na+ out and K+ in on a one-for-one basis
(d) K+ and Na+ in the same direction

179. A phospholipid has

(a) a phosphate group in place of one fatty acid
(b) phosphate groups in place of two fatty acids
(c) phosphate groups in place of three fatty acids
(d) a phosphate group in place of a carbon in glycerol
(e) none of the above

180. A net gain of water tends to occur

(a) in a hypo-osmotic solution from an iso-osmotic solution
(b) in an iso-osmotic solution from a hyper-osmotic solution
(c) in a hyper-osmotic solution from a hypo-osmotic solution
(d) in a hypo-osmotic solution from a hyper-osmotic solution
(e) in one iso-osmotic solution from another iso-osmotic solution of the same composition

181. Red blood cells have a characteristic concave shape because of

(a) spectrin
(b) dextrin
(c) haemoglobin
(d) hemocyanin
(e) iron

182. By a mechanism called cotransport

(a) sugar moves down its concentration gradient, while sodium moves up its concentration gradient
(b) sodium moves outward against its concentration gradient, while sugar moves inward down its concentration gradient
(c) sugar and sodium move inward down their concentration gradient
(d) sodium moves inward down its concentration gradient, while sugar moves inward up its concentration gradient
(e) sodium and sugar move outward against their concentration gradient

183. Cystic fibrosis results from defective ion channels for

(a) Na^+ (b) Cl^-
(c) Ca^{++} (d) ClO_3^-
(e) H^+

184. Fluidity of phospholipid bilayer is increased by

(a) double bonds between carbon atoms in the fatty acid tails
(b) steroid lipids at certain temperatures
(c) poor alignment of the fatty acids' tails
(d) cholesterol at certain temperatures
(e) all of the above

185. In each cycle, the sodium-potassium pumps transfer

(a) two potassium ions in and two sodium ions out
(b) one sodium ion out and one potassium ion in
(c) three sodium ions out and two potassium ions in
(d) one potassium ion out and two sodium ions in
(e) three sodium ions in and two potassium ions out

186. ______ are transported by a particular carrier or pass through a particular channel

(a) All water-soluble ions or molecules
(b) Certain water-soluble molecules or ions
(c) All insoluble molecules or ions
(d) Certain insoluble ions or molecules
(e) Only the smallest molecules or ions

187. Equilibrium is reached in an aqueous solution when

(a) random motion stops
(b) water molecules and dissolved molecules are moving at the same rate
(c) the dissolved molecules or ions are equally distributed throughout the solution
(d) molecular motion stops
(e) there are the same number of water molecules as dissolved molecules

188. Substances transported by facilitated diffusion

(a) move passively through specific channels from an area of greater concentration to one of lower concentration
(b) are limited to solvents
(c) must have movements coupled to those of other substances
(d) may flow to a region of higher concentration by the expenditure of energy
(e) are restricted to only one direction through the membrane

189. In a lipid bilayer, the lipids have

(a) their water repelling heads facing inward
(b) their water repelling tails facing inward
(c) their hydrogen bond forming heads facing inward
(d) their hydrogen bond forming tails facing inward
(e) no relationship to water

190. A lipid bilayer is held together by

(a) surface tension
(b) double bonds in their fatty acid tails
(c) the attraction of the phospholipid heads to each other
(d) hydrogen bonding with water
(e) the electrostatic attraction of phosphate groups for each other

191. The sodium-potassium pump establishes concentration gradients

(a) of higher sodium concentrations inside the cell and higher potassium concentrations outside the cell
(b) of sodium and potassium, but the area of their concentrations (inside or outside) depends on the needs of the cell
(c) of higher potassium concentrations inside the cell and higher sodium concentrations outside the cell
(d) of ATP inside the cell where it is needed
(e) by pumping sodium outside the cell and potassium is cotransported out as well

192. In cotransport processes, sugars can be brought into the cell against their concentrations gradients

(a) because ATP powers the pump that brings them in
(b) because they follow sodium ions into the cell that are traveling down their concentration gradients
(c) because they follow potassium in through the sodium-potassium pump
(d) through endocytosis
(e) by all of the processes listed above

PLANT REPRODUCTION

193. In the angiosperm life cycle, which of the following is not a member of the sporophyte generation?

(a) Carpel (b) Anther
(c) Pollen (d) Ovary

194. A number of megaspores degenerate after being produced by the meiosis of the megaspore mother cell. That number is

(a) 4 (b) 3
(c) 2 (d) 1

195. A plant that flowers in its second year of growth and then dies is

(a) a biennial (b) a semi-annual
(c) an annual (d) a perennial

196. Which of the following flowering arrangements promotes self-pollination?

(a) Monoecious (b) Dioecious
(c) Dichogamous (d) None of the above

197. If a flower is to be pollinated by moths, it should be

(a) red (b) blue
(c) purple (d) orange
(e) yellow

198. Plants that produce only ovules or pollen are called

(a) monoecious (b) monogamous
(c) dichogamous (d) dioecious
(e) bigamous

199. If a flower is to be pollinated by bees, it should be

(a) red (b) white
(c) blue (d) green
(e) orange

200. Plants producing both staminate and pistilate flower on the same plant are said to be

(a) monoecious (b) dioecious
(c) heteroecious (d) dichogamous
(e) polyoecious

201. A trend in floral evolution is

(a) bilateral symmetry
(b) spiral symmetry
(c) radial symmetry
(d) lateral symmetry
(e) asymmetry

202. Genetic self-incompatibility tends to increase

(a) pollen dispersal (b) inbreeding
(c) pollination (d) isolation
(e) outcrossing

203. Many genes are known that affect both leaves and

(a) petals (b) stamens
(c) sepals (d) carpels
(e) corollas

204. If a flower is to be pollinated by birds, it should be

(a) blue (b) white
(c) yellow (d) red
(e) green

205. Self-pollination can occur in which of the following?

(a) Dichogamous plants
(b) Dioecious plants
(c) Pistillate plants
(d) Staminate plants
(e) None of the above

206. Which of the following is the largest irrigation canal in India?

(a) Buckingham canal
(b) Sirhind canal
(c) Indira Gandhi canal
(d) Sutlej Yamuna Link canal

207. Coating urea with which of the following has been found to increase the yield of crops?

(a) Lime (b) Ash
(c) Neem oil (d) Eucalyptus oil

208. Kharif crops are harvested in

(a) March – April
(b) May – June
(c) June – July
(d) October – November

209. Which one of the following is known as a pseudocereal?

(a) Wheat (b) Barley
(c) Horse gram (d) Quinoa

210. What kind of soil is treated with gypsum to make it suitable for cropping?

(a) Aluvial
(b) Water-logged
(c) Acidic
(d) Soil with excessive clay content

211. What is 'slash and burn agriculture'?

(a) Method of sugarcane agriculture
(b) Process of deforestation
(c) Agriculture without irrigation
(d) Jhum cultivation

212. The nitrogen present in the atmosphere is

(a) of no use to plants
(b) injurious to plants
(c) directly utilized by plants
(d) utilized through microorganisms

213. For which of the following black soil is not very suitable?

(a) Cotton (b) Wheat
(c) Groundnut (d) Potato

214. Which of the following is grown mainly on mountain slopes?

(a) Paddy (b) Tea
(c) Groundnut (d) Potato

215. Which acid is used in the production of fertilizers?

(a) Nitric acid (b) Hydrochloric acid
(c) Sulphuric acid (d) Acetic acid

216. Which one of the following is generally found in sedimentary rocks?

(a) Basalt (b) Silica
(c) Shale (d) Magnesium

217. Which of the following rocks is different from others?

(a) Marble (b) Gypsum
(c) Sandstone (d) Limestone

218. Which Indian state has no horticultural university?

(a) Himachal Pradesh
(b) Andhra Pradesh
(c) Karnataka
(d) Jammu & Kashmir

219. Scientific name of wild mango is

(a) *Mangifera sylvatica*
(b) *M. indica*
(c) *M. rubenica*
(d) *M. foetida*

220. Highest percentage of nitrogen is found in

(a) urea
(b) aqueous ammonia
(c) ammonium sulphate
(d) DAP

221. Olericulture is a science of study of

(a) fruits
(b) vegetables
(c) flowers
(d) ornamental horticulture

222. Which type of nitrogen fertilizer is suitable for water-logged soil?

(a) Zinc sulphate
(b) Ammonium sulphate
(c) Zinc phosphate
(d) Potassium nitrate

223. Red colour in onion is caused due to the presence of

(a) zinc (b) sulphur
(c) iron (d) anthocyanin

224. The leading areca nut producing state in India is

(a) Kerala (b) Karnataka
(c) Meghalaya (d) Andhra Pradesh

225. The actual location or place where an organism lives is called

(a) habitat (b) ecosystem
(c) niche (d) biome

226. Which of the following does not have any enzyme in its cells?

(a) Lichen (b) Virus
(c) Bacteria (d) Algae

227. From which organism is penicillin obtained?

(a) Amoeba (b) Virus
(c) Protozoa (d) Fungi

228. Which of the following is responsible for the red colour of tomato?

(a) Capsaicin (b) Carotene
(c) Anthocyanin (d) Lycopene

229. Penicillin inhibits synthesis of bacterial

(a) cell wall (b) protein
(c) RNA (d) DNA

230. Dropsy is a disease caused by the adulteration in

(a) ghee (b) arhar dal
(c) mustard oil (d) turmeric powder

231. Which one of the following organic acid is abundant in grapes, tamarind and banana?

(a) Acetic acid (b) Citric acid
(c) Lactic acid (d) Tartaric acid

232. Which of the following organisms is dependent on saprophytic mode of nutrition?

(a) *Agaricus* (b) *Ulothrix*
(c) *Riccia* (d) *Cladophora*

233. Which one of the following elements is essential for the formation of chlorophyll in plants?

(a) Calcium (b) Iron
(c) Magnesium (d) Potassium

234. Carbohydrate is a nutrient stored in both plants and animals in the form of

(a) cellulose and galactose, respectively
(b) starch and glycogen, respectively
(c) starch and glucose, respectively
(d) cellulose and glycogen, respectively

235. Which of the following plant is able to absorb most of the pollutant in water?

(a) Mango (b) Coconut
(c) *Hydrilla* (d) *Eichhornia*

236. The bio-fertilizer used as a supplementary food for the cattle especially for milking bovines is

(a) *Azolla* (b) *Rhizobium*
(c) *Azospirillium* (d) *Azotobactor*

237. A natural phenomenon that becomes harmful due to pollution is

(a) global warming
(b) ecological balance
(c) greenhouse effect
(d) desertification

238. Which of the following is a Saprotroph?

(a) Man (b) Pigeon
(c) Mushroom (d) Algae

239. Which of the following moisture content is considered safe for storage?

(a) 15% (b) 14%
(c) 16% (d) 17%

240. Combination of which of the following is known as gluten?

(a) Lysine + Glutelin
(b) Gliadin + Lysine
(c) Gliadin + Glutelin
(d) Glutelin + Glutelin

241. Yellow colour in turmeric is due to the presence of

(a) boron (b) curcumin
(c) iron (d) potassium

242. In maize plants

(a) silk appears first
(b) tassels appear first
(c) both silk and tassel appear at the same time
(d) none of these

243. Red delicious is a variety of

(a) mango (b) guava
(c) papaya (d) apple

244. The colour of tomato is due to the presence of

(a) carotene (b) lycopin
(c) xanthophyll (d) anthocyanin

245. Whiptail is the disorder of cauliflower due to the deficiency of

(a) zinc (b) boron
(c) molybdenum (d) potassium

246. Asexual reproduction includes

(a) autogamy (b) allogamy
(c) amphimixis (d) apomixis

247. In India wheat gene bank is located at

(a) IARI, New Delhi (b) Ludhiana
(c) Uttar Pradesh (d) Karnal

248. Stomata open at night in

(a) C4 plants (b) C3 plants
(c) CAM plants (d) All plants

249. The shoot and fruit borers, jassids, spider mites and leaf rollers are the major pests of which of the following vegetable crops?

(a) Tomato (b) Okra
(c) Cucumber (d) Peas

250. Which state has more area under chillies cultivation amongst the following states?

(a) Nagaland
(b) Andhra Pradesh
(c) Manipur
(d) Tamil Nadu

251. Tea production is maximum in which of the following countries?

(a) China (b) United Kingdom
(c) India (d) Sri Lanka

252. Which fruit crop has the longest area in India?

(a) Banana (b) Mango
(c) Papaya (d) Guava

253. Which crop is affected by Tobacco caterpillar?

(a) Jute (b) Sugarcane
(c) Sugarbeet (d) Maize

254. Sugarcane + potato is an intercropping system of

(a) autumn season (b) spring season
(c) zaid season (d) rainy season

255. Which crop requires maximum amount of nitrogen?

(a) Potato (b) Wheat
(c) Barley (d) Sugarcane

256. First dwarf variety of paddy developed in India is

(a) Jaya (b) Govind
(c) Saket-4 (d) Narendra-97

257. Which of the following cakes is not edible?

(a) Mustard cake (b) Castor cake
(c) Sesame cake (d) Groundnut cake

258. Kinnow is the hybrid variety of

(a) citrus (b) orange
(c) mandarin (d) lemon

259. Cauliflower belongs to the family

(a) Poacae (b) Malvaceae
(c) Cruciferae (d) Leguminaceae

260. The main reason of Irish Famine in potato was

(a) late blight disease
(b) bacterial blight disease
(c) blast disease
(d) ear cockle disease

261. Salt tolerant crop is

(a) Cowpea (b) Field pea
(c) Garlic (d) Turmeric

262. Pulses fit well in the cropping system as they are

(a) short duration crops
(b) long duration crops
(c) disease resistant crops
(d) moisture stress resistant crops

263. The first K. V. K. (Krishi Vigyan Kendra) in India was established in

(a) Bombay (b) Port Blair
(c) Pondicherry (d) Assam

264. The first product of photosynthesis in C3 plants is

(a) pyruvic acid
(b) succinic acid
(c) phospho-glyceric acid
(d) oxalo-acetic acid

265. Line breeding is a type of

(a) inbreeding (b) outbreeding
(c) natural breeding (d) none of these

266. Main function of bio-fertilizer is to increase

(a) chemical process
(b) physiological process
(c) biological process
(d) photosynthesis process

267. Majority of cultivated rice varieties have high degree of resistance against

(a) false smut (b) brown spot
(c) leaf scald (d) sheath rot

268. Widely grown field crop in the world is

(a) rice (b) wheat
(c) maize (d) sorghum

269. Which crop absorbs arsenic more readily than other crops?

(a) Rice (b) Pulses
(c) Sugarcane (d) Cotton

270. Which Oomycete is used as a biocontrol agent?

(a) *Pythium oligandrum*
(b) *P. bigurcatum*
(c) *P. insidiosum*
(d) *P. acrogynum*

271. First cultivated plant apart from wheat is

(a) maize (b) rice
(c) barley (d) potato

272. Generally post-harvest disease is caused by

(a) bacteria (b) fungus
(c) both (a) and (b) (d) virus

273. Quality protein maize was developed by ______ gene

(a) Opaque-3 (b) Opaque-1
(c) Opaque-2 (d) Opaque-4

274. ______ is world leader in wheat production:

(a) USA (b) China
(c) Australia (d) Argentina

275. ______ is the world leader in rice production

(a) China (b) India
(c) Indonesia (d) Philippines

276. ______ is the world leader in pulse production

(a) India (b) China
(c) Pakistan (d) Russia

277. The bone is the natural reservoir for

(a) fluorine (b) water
(c) calcium (d) iron

MARK TRUE OR FALSE (T/F)

1. Pollination by insects depends on the random movement of insects from flower to flower
2. In angiosperms, the male gametophyte contains a single sperm that unites with the egg to produce the seed
3. Science is based on evidence rather than consensus
4. Scientists seek facts, but sometimes the best they can do are theories
5. Homologous structures in different species may serve different functions
6. Domestication is the process of bringing a wild sp. under human management

7. Petunia was the first artificial plant hybrid produced
8. Koelreuter belonged to Sweden
9. Baking quality is important for breeders in barley
10. Increased tillering is related to dwarfness in wheat
11. Aflatoxin is present in Khesari dal
12. ICAR was known as Imperial Council of Agricultural Research till 1945
13. Chowdhary Ram Dhan produced 'Veeri' wheat varieties
14. Borlaug was awarded Nobel Peace Prize in 1970
15. The number of Agricultural Universities in India is 30
16. *Saccharum barberi* is the tropical noble cane
17. Indian canes are high yielding
18. There are two Central Agricultural Universities in India
19. The All India Coordinated Maize Improvement Project was started in Collaboration with CIMMYT, Mexico
20. Taraori Basmati has a large grain size
21. Varalaxmi is the first cotton hybrid released in India
22. B.P. Pal was the first secretary of ICAR
23. China stands first in the development of hybrid rice in the world
24. N.E. Borlaug coined the word green revolution
25. Breeder seed has to be 100% pure
26. Foundation seed can be 98% pure
27. White tag is issued for breeder seed
28. Yellow tag is issued for foundation seed
29. Blue tag is issued for certified seed
30. The hexaploid wheat endosperm has 63 chromosomes
31. Apogamy is the development of embryo from synergids
32. The centre of origin of potato is Central America
33. Deletion can result in Pseudodominance
34. Translocation can result in 'Bar eye' in *Drosophila*
35. In an artificial seed, a gel encloses a zygotic embryo
36. Sutton and Boveri gave the chromosomal theory of inheritance
37. A wild type is always a dominant character
38. Seed protein content is a threshold character
39. Speciation begins with allopatric races
40. Xenia is the effect of pollen genotype on the endosperm
41. The pathogen reproduction rate reduces in horizontal disease resistance
42. Broken seed of ¾ size with intact embryo is classified as defective
43. Breeder seed has the lowest genetic purity
44. Foundation seed is produced from nucleus seed
45. The costliest seed is the nucleus seed
46. Maize is a C4 plant
47. Cotton belongs to the family "Malvaceae"
48. Karnal bunt of wheat is a bacterial disease
49. Metaxenia is observed in date palm
50. A plant that flowers in its second year of growth and then dies is a biennial plant
51. The process of double fertilization is unique to gymnosperms
52. The ovule ultimately matures into a fruit
53. Both glycoside and peptide linkages result from dehydration synthesis
54. Glycogen, starch, and cellulose are all polymers of glucose
55. Hydrolysis of one molecule of a triglyceride to glycerol and fatty acids yields two molecules of water

56. India is the largest producer of ginger in the world
57. Sri Lanka is the largest producer of tea in the world
58. The largest producer of sugarcane in the world is Brazil
59. India is the largest producer of garlic in the world
60. The largest producer of papaya in the world is India
61. Mustard is a commercial crop in India
62. Madhya Pradesh produces the largest quantity of pulses in India
63. NAFED is the agency responsible for procurement, distribution and storage of food grain production in India
64. The Agriculture Ministry determines the minimum support price of crops for India
65. Yellow vein mosaic is a disease of okra

2
Natural Selection, Genetics and Evolution

MULTIPLE-CHOICE QUESTIONS

1. **The spotted touch-me-not, a flowering plant, has seed pods that burst open when touched and forcefully eject their seeds. Such an adaptation is favorable because it**
   (a) aids in the dispersal of the species
   (b) attracts insects that aid in pollination
   (c) prevents germination within the seed pod
   (d) can cause genetic changes to occur
2. **According to Darwin's theory of evolution, differences between species may be the result of**
   (a) the disuse of body structures
   (b) the transmission of acquired characteristics
   (c) natural selection
   (d) mutagenic agents
3. **Two nucleotide sequences found in two different species are almost exactly the same. This suggests that these species**
   (a) are evolving into the same species
   (b) contain identical DNA
   (c) may have similar evolutionary histories
   (d) have the same number of mutations
4. **The theory that evolutionary change is slow and continuous is known as**
   (a) punctuated equilibrium
   (b) geographic isolation
   (c) speciation
   (d) gradualism
5. **The concept that species have changed over long periods of time is known as**
   (a) ecology
   (b) embryology
   (c) spontaneous generation
   (d) organic evolution
6. **The study of homologous structures in mature organisms provides evidence for the evolutionary relationships among certain groups of organisms. Which field of study includes this evidence of evolution?**
   (a) Comparative cytology
   (b) Biochemistry
   (c) Geology
   (d) Comparative anatomy

7. The diagram below represents a section of undisturbed layers of a sedimentary rock in New Delhi, and shows the location of fossils of several closely related species. According to currently accepted evolutionary theory, which is the most probable assumption about species A, B, and C?

→ Surface of ground

Species A
Species B and A
Species B
Species C

(a) Species B is more abundant than species C
(b) Species C existed before species B
(c) Species A and B are genetically identical
(d) Species B descended from species A

8. Which group of organisms is believed to be among the earliest to evolve on earth?

(a) Arthropods (b) Coelenterates
(c) Protozoans (d) Reptiles

9. Which concept was not included in Charles Darwin's theory of natural selection?

(a) Survival of the fittest
(b) Struggle for existence
(c) Overproduction of offspring
(d) Punctuated equilibrium

10. According to the heterotroph hypothesis, the first life on earth was able to

(a) synthesize its food from inorganic compounds
(b) feed upon carbohydrates produced by autotrophs
(c) feed upon available nutrients in the environment
(d) carry on photosynthesis instead of respiration

11. Darwin's theory of evolution is not based on the concept of

(a) use and disuse of organs
(b) mutations
(c) natural selection
(d) a and b above

12. The biochemical analysis of different chlorophyll pigments in plants would be most useful in determining

(a) how plants reproduce asexually
(b) how plants pass favorable traits to their offspring
(c) why some plants produce haemoglobin
(d) which plants might have a common ancestor

13. The structural similarities between the flippers of whales and the arms of humans are used to show that the

(a) human species began life in the oceans
(b) human species and whales have a common ancestry
(c) whales are older than the human species
(d) whales evolved from the human species

14. Homologous structures among animals provide evidence for evolution in that these structures are

(a) different in different animals, but are modifications of the same basic structure
(b) similar in function, but of different basic structure
(c) all shown in the fossil record
(d) all produced by the same gene

15. Darwin spent 5 years sailing around the world on the

(a) H.M.S. Species
(b) H.M.S. Beagle
(c) H.M.S. Evolution
(d) H.M.S. Tortoise

16. Darwin explained his theory of evolution in a book called

(a) *On the Origin of Species*
(b) *The Principles of Population*
(c) *Survival of the Fittest*
(d) *Around the World in Eighty Days*

17. Which of the following did not help Darwin formulate his theory of evolution?

(a) Fossil evidence that species had changed over time
(b) Closely related species on oceanic islands
(c) Belief that the earth was several thousand years old
(d) Evidence of artificial selection in domestic animals
(e) All of the above did help Darwin

18. Structures that have the same evolutionary origin even though they may now have different structures or functions are said to be

(a) endemic (b) analogous
(c) homologous (d) immutable
(e) homogeneous

19. Who wrote an essay on population growth that helped Darwin formulate his theory of evolution?

(a) Hooper
(b) Walters
(c) Alfred Russel
(d) Thomas Malthus
(e) Wallace

20. Which of the following pairs are analogous structures?

(a) The front leg of a horse and a human arm
(b) The front leg of a frog and a bat wing
(c) The wing of a bird and a bat wing
(d) The front flipper of a porpoise and a human arm
(e) The wing of a bird and a butterfly wing

21. Of the following biological levels of organization, which represents the smallest or lowest level?

(a) Organs (b) Populations
(c) Cells (d) Organisms
(e) Tissues

22. According to Darwin's theory of evolution

(a) all individuals have an equal chance of surviving and reproducing
(b) species are immutable
(c) tortoises are the modern descendents of glyptodonts
(d) all of the above
(e) none of the above

23. Charles Darwin was best known in the 19th century for

(a) creating the idea of evolution
(b) creating the idea of uniformitarianism
(c) making the idea of evolution acceptable for scientists and the educated general public
(d) all of the above

24. Which of the following statements is true about Charles Darwin?

(a) He believed that evolution was due to inheritance of acquired characters
(b) He supported Lamarck's explanation of how evolution occurred
(c) He understood that the variation that exists in natural populations of plants and animals is the result of repeated mutations
(d) None of the above

25. The theory of evolution by natural selection was independently developed by

(a) Charles Lyell and James Hilton
(b) Charles Lyell and Charles Darwin
(c) Charles Darwin and Alfred Wallace
(d) Erasmus and Lamarck

26. Darwin and Wallace theory of evolution by natural selection failed to explain how

(a) nature operates to reduce variation in a population every generation
(b) new genetic varieties can appear in a population every generation
(c) both (a) and (b)
(d) neither of the above

27. Which is a major concept located in Lamarck's theory of evolution?

(a) Change is the result of the survival of the fittest
(b) Body structure can change according to the action of the organisms
(c) Population size decreases the rate of evolution
(d) Artificial selection is the basis of evolution

28. According to Darwin's theory of natural selection, individuals who survive are the ones best adapted for their environment. Their survival is due to

(a) possessions of adaptations developed through use
(b) possessions of inherited adaptations that maximize fitness
(c) lack of competition within the species
(d) choices made by plant and animal breeders

29. An adaptation is an inherited characteristic that can be

(a) physical or behavioural
(b) physical or geographical
(c) acquired during the organism's lifetime
(d) the result of artificial selection

30. Charles Darwin called the adaptability of an organism to survive and reproduce in its environment

(a) diversity (b) fitness
(c) adaptation (d) evolution

31. Which of the following phrases best describes the result of natural selection?

(a) The natural variations found in all populations
(b) Unrelated but similar species living in different locations
(c) The changes in the inherited characteristics of populations
(d) The struggle for existence undergone by all living things

32. The number and locations of bones of many fossil vertebrates are similar to those in living vertebrates. Most biologists would probably explain this fact on the basis of

(a) the needs of the organisms
(b) a common ancestor
(c) the struggle for existence
(d) the inheritance of acquired traits

33. Which phrase best defines evolution by natural selection?

(a) An adaptation of a species to its environment
(b) A sudden replacement of one population by another
(c) Changes in the species as it becomes more perfect
(d) A process of change in species over time

THE ORIGIN AND EARLY HISTORY OF LIFE

34. The earliest cellular life forms appear to have been

(a) viruses
(b) one-celled plants
(c) one-celled animals
(d) bacteria

35. Scientists generally agree that the first molecules, which were formed as life, evolved were

(a) proteins
(b) RNA
(c) peptides and nucleic acids
(d) none of the above

36. Which of the following organisms alive today is likely to be most similar to the first life forms that evolved on the earth?

(a) Methane-producing bacteria
(b) Cyanobacteria
(c) Algae
(d) Dinosaurs
(e) Humans

37. The oldest fossils found so far date back to the

(a) cambrian Period
(b) archean Era
(c) phanerozoic Era
(d) proterozoic Era

38. Multicellular fossils appear at the beginning of the

(a) proterozoic era
(b) precambrian period
(c) archean era
(d) phanerozoic era
(e) cambrian period

39. Which of the following traits evolved most recently?

(a) Prokaryotic cells (b) Eukaryotic cells
(c) Multicellularity (d) Photosynthesis
(e) Heredity

40. According to the scientific theory of the origin of life on earth, life arose spontaneously from inanimate chemicals. Do scientists think that this process is still going on on our planet today?

(a) Yes, it probably is
(b) No, because conditions on earth have changed and are no longer conducive to spontaneous evolution of life
(c) None of the above is correct
(d) (a) and (b) are correct

41. Which of the following possible explanations of the origin of life on earth allows testable hypotheses to be constructed?

(a) Evolution
(b) Spontaneous origin
(c) Extra-terrestrial origin
(d) All of the above
(e) None of the above

42. The endosymbiotic theory explains

(a) the origin of all organelles in eukaryotic cells
(b) how bacterial cells can invade eukaryotic cells and cause diseases
(c) how mitochondria and chloroplasts originated from free-living cells
(d) how eukaryotic cells consume food
(e) none of the above

GENETICS AND EVOLUTION

43. Allopatric speciation involves the formation of new species

(a) from populations that live in the same geographic region
(b) from individuals who have undergone sexual isolation first
(c) from populations that live in different geographic regions
(d) in all of these ways
(e) in none of these ways

44. Which one of the following statements is correct?

(a) The Holarctic Region is marked by vampire bats
(b) The Ethiopian Region is marked by bears
(c) The Neotropical Region is marked by foxes
(d) The Australian Region is marked by orang-utan
(e) None of the above is correct

45. Which of the following is not a prezygotic reproductive isolating mechanism?

(a) Populations live in the same regions but occupy different habitats
(b) Cross-fertilization is prevented or restricted by differences in reproductive structures
(c) Populations live in the same region but are sexually mature at different times
(d) Hybrids are sterile because gonads develop abnormally
(e) None of the above

46. The founder-flush theory of quantum speciation suggests that

(a) genetic flushing rids populations of all but the most dominant type
(b) founders are flushed out into the open and therefore face stronger selection pressures
(c) species can be started by a single individual
(d) speciation is a process with a gradual and even tempo
(e) none of the above

47. Protein polymorphism arises from the fact that

(a) alleles of genes can encode proteins with different amino acid composition
(b) gene loci encode identical gene products
(c) mutations can be silent
(d) the genetic code is degenerate
(e) none of the above

48. Examination of many different loci have shown that

(a) most gene loci have many variant alleles at the nucleic acid level
(b) most gene loci have two variants at the nucleic acid level
(c) alleles at each locus are completely conserved between individuals in a species
(d) most gene loci have only one nucleic acid variant, occasionally two, and rarely more than two
(e) none of the above

49. Selectionists generally believe that

(a) enzyme or protein polymorphism is often associated with adaptation to certain environmental conditions
(b) mutations leading to amino acid substitutions are almost uniformly bad
(c) enzyme polymorphisms exist in such high frequencies because all polymorphic genes are usually subject to strong selection pressures
(d) all of the above
(e) none of the above

50. Theodore Dobzhansky and colleagues in their study of *Drosophila pseudoobscura* found that

(a) reproductive isolation preceded generation of races
(b) genetic differences were largely quantitative
(c) only one "race" of *D. pseudoobscura* could be found prior to speciation
(d) all of the above
(e) none of the above

51. Comparison of the protein product encoded by the insulin gene showed that

(a) the protein is widely different in other mammals
(b) the protein is same in different mammals
(c) the protein has only recently evolved, so it is completely identical in mammals
(d) all of the above
(e) none of the above

52. Based on comparison of human and chimpanzee genomes, humans and chimpanzees have been shown to share no common ancestor

(a) humans being in the same taxonomic family might be justified
(b) humans being in a different taxonomic family than chimpanzees is supported
(c) all of the above
(d) none of the above

53. What is the view that the earth was shaped primarily by rapid and violent events?

(a) Actualism
(b) Catastrophism
(c) Neptunism
(d) Plutonism
(e) Uniformitarianism

54. What is a fossil?

(a) A remnant of ancient life
(b) An animal body part
(c) Any buried old object
(d) Any old object

55. What is the half life of Uranium-235?

(a) 0.7 billion years (b) 1.3 billion years
(c) 18 billion years (d) 4.5 billion years
(e) 49 billion years

56. Which of the following isotopes decays by electron capture?

(a) Carbon-14 (b) Potassium-40
(c) Rubidium-87 (d) Uranium-235
(e) Uranium-238

57. Which of the following was not used by Darwin as an evidence for evolution?

(a) Domestic animal variation
(b) Embryological similarities
(c) Genetic similarities
(d) Morphological similarities
(e) Rudimentary organs

58. Which of the following may be a case of inheritance of acquired characters?

(a) Aging effects
(b) Giraffe necks
(c) Immune response
(d) Large muscles
(e) Vestigial organs

59. The effects of natural selection may be countered by

(a) gene flow (b) genetic drift
(c) mutation (d) inbreeding

60. In relation to natural selection, evolution is the

(a) process (b) outcome
(c) mechanism (d) purpose

61. Kimura's theory that opposed natural selection was the

(a) natural theory
(b) nearly neutral theory
(c) neutral theory
(d) adaptive theory

62. Scientists generally agree that heterozygous advantage is

(a) rare (b) frequent
(c) pervasive (d) none of the above

63. The occurrence of large or small beak sizes among seed cracker birds in the absence of medium-sized beaks is an example of

(a) directional selection
(b) stabilizing selection
(c) disruptive selection
(d) none of the above

64. Even though sickle-cell anemia is usually fatal to homozygous individuals, the disease persists because

(a) gene therapy has alleviated the condition
(b) the disease is carried on a dominant allele
(c) individuals with one allele for sickle-cell anemia are resistant to malaria
(d) a combination of all of the above
(e) none of the above

65. Sickle-cell trait in humans is a classic example of

(a) how mutations can lead only to tragic outcomes
(b) why outbreeding is important
(c) the superior fitness seen in heterozygotes
(d) how every organism is an integrated gene complex

66. For a man living in India, which genotype would be the most advantageous to have?

(a) Homozygous for the sickle cell allele
(b) Heterozygous for the sickle cell allele
(c) Homozygous for the normal haemoglobin allele
(d) It doesn't matter; all are equally advantageous

67. For a man living in central Africa, which genotype would be the most advantageous to have?

(a) Homozygous for the sickle cell allele
(b) Heterozygous for the sickle cell allele
(c) Homozygous for the normal haemoglobin allele
(d) It doesn't matter; all are equally advantageous

68. Sickle cell anemia is caused by a change in the amino acid sequence of the two beta chains in the haemoglobin molecule. How many amino acids have been changed in each beta chain compared to normal haemoglobin?

(a) 1 (b) 5
(c) 10 (d) Hundreds
(e) Thousands

69. Mating with relatives is called

(a) inbreeding (b) out crossing
(c) random mating (d) wide hybridization
(e) polymorphic

70. The random loss of alleles in a population is called

(a) mutation
(b) selection
(c) genetic drift
(d) electrophoresis
(e) gene flow

71. Which of the following factors is most likely to contribute to gene flow between populations?

(a) Random mating (b) Migration
(c) Mutation (d) Genetic drift
(e) Inbreeding

72. In the Hardy-Weinberg equation, the term 2pq represents the frequency of the

(a) dominant homozygotes
(b) recessive homozygotes
(c) dominant alleles
(d) recessive alleles
(e) heterozygotes

73. A scientist measures the circumference of acorns in a population of oak trees and discovers that the most common circumference is 2 cm. What would you expect the most common circumference(s) to be after 10 generations of stabilizing selection?

(a) 2 cm
(b) Greater than 2 cm or less than 2 cm
(c) Greater than 2 cm and less than 2 cm
(d) Can't tell from the information given

74. Refer to the above question, but this time answer what you would expect after 10 generations of disruptive selection

(a) 2 cm
(b) greater than 2 cm or less than 2 cm
(c) greater than 2 cm and less than 2 cm
(d) can't tell from the information given

75. Refer to the same question, but this time answer what you would expect after 10 generations of directional selection

(a) 2 cm
(b) greater than 2 cm or less than 2 cm
(c) greater than 2 cm and less than 2 cm
(d) can't tell from the information given

76. How common is genetic polymorphism in natural populations?

(a) Essentially all loci are polymorphic
(b) Essentially no loci are polymorphic
(c) Depending on the species, all loci are polymorphic or none are
(d) Depending on the species, more or less than half the loci are polymorphic

77. What per cent of a typical human's loci is heterozygous?

(a) 2% (b) 5%
(c) 37% (d) 55%
(e) 76%

78. Why is genetic polymorphism important for evolution?

(a) Individual variability provides the raw material for natural selection to act on
(b) Genes cannot mutate unless they are polymorphic
(c) Only heterozygous individuals are selected in natural populations
(d) The Hardy-Weinberg equilibrium is less likely to be disturbed in polymorphic populations
(e) None of the above; genetic polymorphism is not important for evolution

79. In a population of flowers, the frequency of the allele for red flowers was 0.8. What was the frequency of the white allele—the only other allele for flower colour?

(a) 0.8 (b) 0.4
(c) 0.6 (d) 0.2
(e) 0.1

80. Referring to the above question, what is the frequency of homozygous red flower plants in the population?

(a) 0.04 (b) 0.16
(c) 0.32 (d) 0.48
(e) 0.64

81. Referring to the same question, what is the frequency of homozygous white flower plants in the population?

(a) 0.04 (b) 0.16
(c) 0.32 (d) 0.48
(e) 0.64

82. Referring to the same question, what is the frequency of plants in the population that are heterozygous for flower colour?

(a) 0.04 (b) 0.16
(c) 0.32 (d) 0.48
(e) 0.64

83. What is the ultimate source of genetic variability?

(a) Mutation
(b) Migration
(c) Genetic drift
(d) Nonrandom mating
(e) Selection

84. The movement of new genes into a population as a result of migration or hybridization is called

(a) founder principle (b) selection
(c) gene flow (d) bottleneck effect
(e) adaptation

85. A virus killed most of the Penguins in the Indian Ocean (e.g., dropped the population from 6000 to 500). In an effort to help preserve the species, scientists caught 30 Penguins and used them to start a new population in the northwest Pacific Ocean. Which of the following factors would most likely have the least impact in this new population?

(a) Founder effect
(b) Random mating
(c) Genetic drift
(d) Bottleneck effect

86. Inbreeding
(a) increases the rate of mutation
(b) increases the proportion of homozygous individuals in a population
(c) never occurs in plants
(d) all of the above
(e) none of the above

87. The theory of population genetics and how evolution occurs includes all but which one of the following
(a) mating must be random
(b) the size of the population is small
(c) there is no influx of genes from other populations.
(d) no genotype has selective advantage over the other

88. Using the Hardy-Weinberg Principle, which expression represents the frequency of the homozygous recessive genotype?
(a) p^2 (b) 2 pq
(c) q^2 (d) q

89. Which statement most accurately reflects what population geneticists refer to as "fitness"?
(a) Fitness is the measure of an organism's adaptability to various habitats
(b) Fitness reflects the number of mates each individual of the population selects
(c) Fitness refers to the relative health of each individual in the population
(d) Fitness is a measure of the contribution of a genotype to the gene pool of the next generation

90. The fact that the majority of human newborns weigh around 3 kg is reflective of
(a) directional selection
(b) stabilizing selection
(c) disruptive selection
(d) none of these is correct

91. Organisms that are least likely to experience extinction over the long term are most likely to be found in
(a) areas inhabited by humans
(b) very stable habitats
(c) deserts
(d) islands

92. Which one of the following would cause the Hardy-Weinberg principle to be inaccurate?
(a) The size of the population is very large
(b) Individuals mate with one another at random
(c) Natural selection is present
(d) There is no source of new copies of alleles from outside the population
(e) None of the answers is correct

93. The lack of allele variation in the Indian tiger population is an example of
(a) mutations
(b) founder effect
(c) artificial selection
(d) bottleneck effect
(e) out crossing

94. Which one of the following populations would most quickly lead to two groups with few shared traits?
(a) A population with disruptive selection
(b) A population with directional selection
(c) A population with stabilizing selection
(d) A population with no selection
(e) None of the above

95. Human chromosome banding patterns match most closely those of
(a) chimpanzees (b) monkeys
(c) gorillas (d) orangutans

96. A 60-base sequence of DNA found in the genome of many species that controls body formation is called
(a) conserved gene (b) cytochrome C
(c) molecular clock (d) homeobox

97. What genetic information can be used to trace material lineage?

(a) X-chromosome
(b) Y-chromosome
(c) Nuclear genes
(d) Mitochondrial genes

98. Which genetic information can be used to trace paternal lineage?

(a) X-chromosome
(b) Y-chromosome
(c) Nuclear genes
(d) Mitochondrial genes

99. Several species of ______ lived from 2-4 million years ago and walked upright

(a) *Dryopithecus* (b) *Australopithecus*
(c) *homo* (d) *hablo*

100. ______ made tools out of bone and stone, used fire, and dwelled communally in caves

(a) *Dryopithecus* (b) *Australopithecus*
(c) *Homo erectus* (d) *Homo habilis*

101. Animals ancestral to humans are called

(a) hominoids
(b) hominids
(c) bipedals
(d) this animal is, as yet, unidentified

102. The term "eugenics" was coined by

(a) Sir Ronald Fisher
(b) Francis Galton
(c) Charles Davenport
(d) Adolf Hitler

103. One difference between humans and chimps that might stem from a single gene is

(a) language
(b) opposable thumbs
(c) hairiness
(d) size of frontal lobes

104. Genes in the same order on chromosomes in different species are

(a) conserved (b) syntenic
(c) hybridized (d) none of the above

105. The force that initiates evolution is

(a) variation (b) mutation
(c) extinction (d) adaptation

106. ______ is a vestigial organ

(a) Intestinal villi
(b) Papillae
(c) Vermiform appendix
(d) None of the above

107. Example of a homologous organ

(a) the arm of a human, wing of a bird
(b) wing of an insect, wing of a bird
(c) leg of a dog, leg of a spider
(d) none of the above

108. Which condition can be explained by Lamarckism?

(a) How giraffes got their long neck
(b) How humans lost their tail
(c) How humans became bipedal
(d) All of the above

109. ______ was considered a missing link between reptiles and the birds

(a) Archaeopteryx (b) Pteranodon
(c) Avimimus (d) Caudipteryx

110. The oldest mineral discovered so far is ______ which dates back to 4.4 billion years

(a) iron (b) zircon
(c) cadmium (d) silicon

111. On the origin of species was written by

(a) Charles Darwin
(b) Ludmila Kuprianova
(c) Mikhail A. Fedonkin
(d) Ithuhbuna Lawraga

112. Which of the following does not tend to promote speciation?

(a) Founder effect
(b) Reproductive isolation
(c) Natural selection
(d) Gene flow

113. In "survival of the fittest", the fittest organisms are

(a) the ones that can run the fastest
(b) the best adapted to their environment
(c) the ones that can produce the most offspring
(d) the largest organisms

114. Natural selection occurs because organisms within a particular species have

(a) fewer offspring than are able to survive
(b) the ability to pass on the characteristics acquired over their lifetime
(c) the ability to change colour to suit the background
(d) variation due to differences in their genes

115. The tendency of the population to remain in genetic equilibrium may be disturbed by

(a) random mating
(b) lack of migration
(c) lack of mutations
(d) lack of random mating

116. A baby has been born with a tail. It is the case exhibiting

(a) atavism
(b) mutation
(c) retrogressive evolution
(d) metamorphosis

117. Homologous organisms indicate the

(a) convergent evolution
(b) parallel evolution
(c) common descendent
(d) natural selection

118. One of the important consequences of geographical isolation is

(a) random creation of new species
(b) no change in the isolated fauna
(c) preventing speciation
(d) speciation through reproductive isolation

119. De Vries gave his mutation theory on organic evolution while working on

(a) *Oenothera lamarckiana*
(b) *Pisum sativum*
(c) *Drosophila melanogaster*
(d) *Althea roses*

MARK TRUE OR FALSE (T/F)

1. A person with sickle cell trait, having one S allele and one normal, will be resistant to malaria and eventually develop sickle cell anemia
2. Evolution by natural selection works best on a population having no variation
3. According to Darwin's theory of evolution, evolution occurs through natural selection operating on populations in ecosystems
4. Mutation is a relatively unimportant source of variation and is not the foundation for evolution
5. Mutations tend to have little effect on the allele frequency in a population
6. The effects of genetic drift are most apparent in small populations
7. Inbreeding increases the proportion of homozygous individuals in a population
8. The rate of DNA hybridization reflects the degree of evolutionary relatedness
9. Different genes evolve at different rates
10. Isolating mechanisms prevent gene exchange
11. Geographically separated populations are called sympatric populations
12. Gene exchange between populations in the same geographic locality is prevented in allopatric populations

13. Seasonal isolation means that potential mates do not meet because they flourish in different seasons
14. When either sperm or egg is destroyed because of the interspecific cross, it is called zygotic mortality
15. The hybrid has normal viability but is reproductively sterile when there is zygotic mortality
16. Amino acid positions on a protein that shows changes during the same particular revolutionary period have been called covarions
17. 5 S RNA is present in animal mitochondria
18. Evolution and natural selection are the same thing
19. Evolution is the gradual unfolding of organisms from pre-existing organisms through change since the beginning of life
20. Organic evolution is the evolution of non-living organisms
21. The forelimbs of a bird and a human being are called homologous organs
22. Homologous organs develop in a similar fashion
23. The wings of a bird and an insect are developmentally similar
24. Analogous organs are structurally same and perform similar functions
25. Biogenetic law was proposed by Haeckel
26. During the embryonic development of any organism, its complete evolutionary history is repeated
27. Biogenetic law states that 'ontogeny recapitulates phylogeny'
28. Nictitating membrane of human beings is not a vestigial organ
29. Vermiform appendix is functional among the herbivore ruminant mammals
30. Archaeopteryx bears a number of features, which are found in reptiles
31. The book 'Philosophie zoologoque' was written by Linnaeus
32. Weismann supported Lamarck's theory of acquired characters
33. Darwin observed nature during his voyage on the ship, H.M.S. Beagle
34. Synthetic theory of evolution is the most accepted theory
35. Genetic drift connects microevolution to macroevolution because species originate at random
36. Natural selection is the survival of the fittest
37. The response to natural selection is fastest in small populations
38. Darwin's view of genetics was correct
39. All evolutionary change is reversible
40. Weismann's separation of a transitory soma from a continuous and enduring germline was founded on the observation of the behavior of chromosomes during meiosis
41. Population genetics and quantitative genetics are important for the understanding of evolution because they provide a quantitative description of change in the genetic composition of populations, which is the basic element of evolutionary change
42. The commonest types of life cycle are sexual haploids and asexual diploids
43. The spread of an advantageous allele in a population is characterized by slow change when the allele is rare, rapid change at intermediate frequencies, and again slow change when the allele is common
44. The rate of spread is generally faster in a haploid than a diploid population
45. Sexual (as opposed to asexual) reproduction accelerates the spread of the allele
46. Fitness-related traits have on an average lower heritability than morphological traits
47. A heritability of body weight of 0.2 means that body weight is determined for 20% by genetic factors and for 80% by environmental factors

48. The rate of change estimated from the fossil record is slower than the rate of change observed in artificial selection experiments
49. The main evolutionary relevant difference between sexual and asexual reproduction is that asexual organisms are mainly haploid, while sexual organisms are mainly diploid
50. Zygotes are always diploid, so the position in the life cycle where meiosis occurs determines whether the adults are haploid (the haplontic life cycle) or diploid (the diplontic life cycle)
51. Natural selection changes populations and not individuals
52. Natural selection increases diversity between populations of a species
53. Males of many species are brightly coloured to dominate over a female
54. For natural selection to act on a population the population needs to contain genetic variations
55. Natural selection can create new traits
56. Natural selection occurs with one individual
57. Natural selection does not select organisms, it selects traits that are beneficial
58. Thomas Malthus predicted that the human population would grow faster than the resources needed to sustain it
59. Darwin proposed that the selective use or disuse of an organ led to a change in the organ that was then passed on to the offspring
60. Genetic drift is the change in the allele frequency of a population as a result of natural selection rather than choice events
61. If a habitat contains 20 animal and 20 plant species, it is called biodiversity
62. Species is the lowest category of classification
63. Fauna refers to the total number of plants found in a specific region at a particular time
64. The essential building blocks of life include carbohydrates, proteins, water and nucleic acids
65. Cyanobacteria cannot fix atmospheric nitrogen
66. Butterworts are insectivorous plants
67. A virus cannot grow and divide
68. *Volvox* has diplontic life cycle
69. Cyanobacteria are classified under Kingdom Monera
70. The fleshy stem of onion is an edible part

3
General Genetics

MULTIPLE-CHOICE QUESTIONS

BLOOD GROUPS

1. The term "Cytogenetics" was coined by

(a) Bateson
(b) Sutton
(c) Morgan
(d) Chatton

2. A man with blood group O and a woman with group A have one child with group A and a second child with group O. Which one of the following is incorrect?

(a) The father is $I^O I^O$
(b) The mother is $I^A I^A$
(c) The first child is $I^A I^O$
(d) The second child is $I^O I^O$
(e) The mother is $I^A I^O$

3. A person with blood group AB has

(a) anti-A antibodies in the blood
(b) anti-B antibodies in the blood
(c) both anti-A and anti-B antibodies in the blood
(d) has neither anti-A nor anti-B antibodies in the blood
(e) no antigens on the surface of the red cells

4. What are the possible offspring from a type A mother and a type AB father?

(a) A, B, AB, and O (b) A, B, and AB
(c) A and AB (d) A only

5. Which of the following systems would be most important in determining maternal-fetal compatibility?

(a) Rh blood group
(b) ABO blood group
(c) MHC class I molecules
(d) MHC class II molecules
(e) MHC class III molecules

6. In a disputed paternity case, the following blood groups were identified

Mother	Group AB
Baby	Group A
Mr Ram	Group O
Mr Sham	Group AB

Which combination of the following statements is correct?

(i) the genotype of the baby could be $I^A I^A$ or $I^A I^O$
(ii) Mr Ram could be the father

(iii) Mr Sham cannot be the father
(iv) neither man could be the father
(v) either man could be the father

(a) i and ii; (b) ii and iii;
(c) iii and iv; (d) i, ii and v;
(e) ii, iii and iv

7. In man, ABO blood group was first discovered by

(a) Landsteiner (b) Muller
(c) Benzer (d) Davidson

8. A maternity case involves an infant with type AB blood. Four women claim to be the mother. You be the judge, as far as the blood type evidence allows

(a) the woman with type A blood could not be the mother
(b) the woman with type AB blood could not be the mother
(c) the woman with type O blood could not be the mother
(d) the woman with type B blood could not be the mother
(e) all four women could be the mother

9. A mother who has blood type AB has a child who is also AB. The potential father has blood type O. A well informed geneticist concludes that

(a) it is very likely
(b) he cannot be the father
(c) he might, but it is unlikely
(d) he or any other male of blood type O is the father
(e) no conclusion can be drawn

10. A woman with type A blood has a child with type A blood. Which of the following men could not be the father of this child?

(a) A (b) B
(c) AB (d) all could be the father

11. The genotypes of a husband and wife are I^AI^B x I^Ai. Among the blood types of their children, how many different genotypes and phenotypes are possible?

(a) 2 genotypes; 3 phenotypes
(b) 3 genotypes; 4 phenotypes
(c) 4 genotypes; 4 phenotypes
(d) 3 genotypes; 3 phenotypes
(e) 4 genotypes; 3 phenotypes

12. Vijay has type A blood, but his mother has type B blood. His wife, Indu, has type B blood, but her father had type A blood. What is the probability that the little Vijay will have type O blood?

(a) 100% (b) 50%
(c) 25% (d) 0%
(e) cannot be determined from the information given

13. A man with blood type A, whose mother had blood type O, marries a woman of blood type B, whose father was blood type O. The chances of this couple's having a child with blood type O are

(a) 25% (b) 50%
(c) 75% (d) 100%
(e) 0 %

14. A person with blood type AB can receive blood from a person of

(a) any other ABO type
(b) only AB (c) only O
(d) either A or B

15. Two parents with blood types A and O have a child who has type O blood. What is the chance that their next child will be type A?

(a) 0 (b) 1/2
(c) 1/4 (d) 1

16. A person who has type O blood has

(a) A antigens on the cell surface
(b) B antigens on the cell surface
(c) both A and B antigens on the cell surface
(d) no surface antigens

17. The antigens for ABO and Rh blood groups are present on

(a) plasma (b) white blood cells
(c) red blood cells (d) platelets

18. What are the two blood tests?

(a) Rh and ABB (b) ABO and Rh
(c) ABO and Rn (d) ABC and Rh

19. Which is the rarest blood group?

(a) AB negative (b) AB positive
(c) O negative (d) O positive

20. Who discovered blood groups?

(a) Thomas Cooley
(b) Karl Landsteiner
(c) Camilla Golgi
(d) Ernst Haecker

21. Rh group was discovered in

(a) 1930s (b) 1940s
(c) 1950s (d) 1960s

22. If the blood group of an individual is A, then the antibodies present are

(a) anti B antibodies
(b) anti A antibodies
(c) anti O antibodies
(d) anti OA antibodies

23. Which blood type can be transfused to the individual whose blood type is unknown?

(a) AB positive
(b) AB negative
(c) O positive
(d) O negative

24. In determining phenotype of ABO system

(a) O is dominant over A
(b) B is dominant over A
(c) O is recessive
(d) A is dominant over O

25. On what basis is the blood type classified?

(a) Antigen and antibody
(b) Haemoglobin content
(c) Rhesus factor
(d) Oxygen content

26. How many blood types exist including the positive and negative factors?

(a) 3 (b) 4
(c) 8 (d) 6

27. If the blood of two different groups is mixed together, what problem is observed?

(a) Coagulation
(b) Agglutination
(c) Thrombus formation
(d) Embolism

28. Which blood type is a universal donor?

(a) O^- (b) O^+
(c) AB^- (d) AB^+

29. If the person has AB^- blood, who all can donate the blood to him?

(a) A^+, B^-, O^-, AB^+
(b) A^-, B^-, O^+, AB^+
(c) A^+, B^+, O^+, AB^-
(d) A^-, B^-, O^-, AB^-

30. In the ABO blood system you normally can be type

(a) A (b) B
(c) ABO (d) A, B, AB, or O

31. Blood type O may be solely given to people with ______ type of blood.

(a) AB and A only (b) O and B only
(c) A and B only (d) A, B, AB, and O

32. Red blood cells that do not contain either A or B antigens on their surface are normally found in person with blood type

(a) A (b) AB
(c) B (d) O

33. Which of the following is true about Anti D?

(a) It causes haemolysis with prominent schistocyte formation
(b) It is primarily the IgG isotype rather than IgM
(c) It does not react with D positive cells treated with dithiothreitol (DTT)
(d) None of the above

34. Bombay blood group is characterised by the absence of

(a) H gene (b) both A and B gene
(c) A gene (d) B gene

35. The serum of an individual with B blood group contains

(a) anti A and anti B antibodies
(b) anti A antibodies
(c) anti B antibodies
(d) anti D antibodies

36. If the blood group of a person is A then, the antibodies present in that person's blood is

(a) anti OA antibodies
(b) anti O antibodies
(c) anti A antibodies
(d) anti B antibodies

37. The antigens for ABO and Rh blood groups are present

(a) on WBC's (b) on platelets
(c) on RBC's (d) in plasma

38. Under which circumstances will an antigen-antibody reaction occur?

(a) A person with type O blood is given type A blood
(b) A person with type A blood is given type O blood
(c) A person with type AB is given type O blood
(d) A person with type AB is given type B blood

39. If one of your parents is blood type A and the other is type B, which of the following blood types would you likely be?

(a) O (b) AB
(c) A or B (d) Any

40. An individual's blood type is determined by

(a) environment (b) genetics
(c) both environment and genetics
(d) your children's blood type

41. The Rh factor determines what part of the blood type

(a) + or -
(b) the number of antigens
(c) the number of antibodies
(d) agglutination

EPISTASIS

42. The gene having masking effect is called

(a) modifier gene (b) epistatic gene
(c) hypostatic gene (d) pleiotropic gene

43. The gene whose effect is masked is called

(a) hypostatic gene (b) epistatic gene
(c) pleiotropic gene (d) none of these

44. Epistasis is also known as

(a) intergenic interaction
(b) interlocus interaction
(c) interallelic interaction
(d) all of these

45. In recessive epistasis, F_2 phenotypic ratio is modified to

(a) 9:3:4 (b) 12:3:1
(c) 15:1 (d) 9:6:1

46. Complementary epistasis modifies F_2 phenotypic ratio into

(a) 12:3:1 (b) 9:3:3:1
(c) 9:6:1 (d) 9:7

47. Simple epistasis modifies F_2 phenotypic ratio into

(a) 9:7 (b) 12:3:1
(c) 13:3 (d) 12:4

48. Duplicate epistasis modifies F_2 phenotypic ratio into

(a) 13:3 (b) 9:7
(c) 12:3:1 (d) 15:1

49. What ratio of phenotypes would you expect if you cross a heterozygous Pea comb chicken to a heterozygous Rose comb chicken?

(a) 9 walnut: 3 rose: 3 pea: 1 single
(b) 1 walnut: 1 rose: 1 pea: 1 single
(c) 3 walnut: 1 single
(d) 3 rose: 1 pea

50. Which of the following events is least likely to occur in a cross involving epistasis by both genes?

(a) A monohybrid has a different phenotype from either of the two parents
(b) Two lines of true breeding white parents produce purple flowered offspring
(c) A 9:3:3:1 ratio of F_2 phenotypes is seen
(d) All of these are likely to be seen in epistatic interactions

51. Coat colour in dogs depends on the action of at least two genes. At one locus, a dominant epistatic inhibitor of coat colour pigment (I–) prevents the expression of colour alleles at another independently assorting locus, thereby producing white coat colour. When the recessive condition exists at the inhibitor locus (ii), the alleles of the second locus will be expressed, ii B– producing black and iibb producing brown. When dihybrid white dogs are mated, what would be the phenotypic ratio in the offspring?

(a) 12:3:1 (b) 9:7
(c) 9:3:3:1 (d) 3:1
(e) 1:2:1

52. In a rare blood type referred to as the Bombay phenotype, individuals are unable to attach the A or B antigens to their red blood cells. Individuals that are homozygous recessive for gene "H" have the Bombay phenotype and their blood type is type "O" regardless of their ABO genotype. This is an example of

(a) multiple alleles
(b) overdominance
(c) environmental influence
(d) epistasis

53. Colour of chickens is determined by interacting loci: AA or Aa give white, aaBB or aaBb give coloured, and aabb produces white. What are the phenotypic frequencies of the offspring from a cross between two fully heterozygous chickens?

(a) 15 white : 1 coloured
(b) 13 white : 3 coloured
(c) 12 white : 4 coloured
(d) 9 white : 7 coloured
(e) none of the above

54. The relationship of the h and H genes affects the expression of the ABO blood type in the following ways: genotype HH or Hh, AB produces blood type AB while genotype hh, AB produces blood type O. This is an example of

(a) complete dominance
(b) codominance
(c) incomplete dominance
(d) epistasis

55. The Bombay phenotype is a result of ______ interacting genes and is an example of

(a) 2, complete dominance
(b) 2, incomplete dominance
(c) 3, incomplete dominance
(d) 2, epistasis

56. Two unlinked loci affect mouse hair colour. CC or Cc mice are agouti. Mice with genotype cc are albino because all pigment production and deposition of pigment in hair is blocked. At the second locus, the B allele (black agouti coat) is dominant to the b allele (brown agouti coat). A mouse with a black agouti coat is mated with an albino mouse of genotype bbcc. Half of the offspring are albino, one quarter are black agouti, and one quarter are brown agouti. What is the genotype of the black agouti parent?

(a) BBCC (b) BbCc
(c) bbCC (d) BbCC
(e) BBcc

57. Two unlinked loci affect mouse hair colour. AA or Aa mice are agouti. Mice with genotype aa are albino because all pigment production is blocked, regardless of the phenotype at the second locus. At the second

locus, the B allele (agouti coat) is dominant to the b allele (black coat). What would be the result of a cross between two agouti mice of genotype AaBb?

(a) 4 agouti: 4 black: 8 albino

(b) 9 agouti: 3 black: 3 albino: 1 grey

(c) 9 agouti: 3 black: 4 albino

(d) 8 agouti: 4 black: 4 albino

58. Coat colour of mice is determined by interacting loci: bb gives albino, A–B– gives agouti (an alternating light and dark combination), and aaB– gives black. What are the phenotypic frequencies of the offspring from the dihybrid (a cross between two double heterozygotes, i.e., a cross between two AaBb)?

(a) 15 agouti: 1 albino

(b) 9 agouti: 3 black: 4 albino

(c) 9 agouti: 4 black : 3 albino

(d) 12 agouti: 3 black : 1 albino

(e) 3 black: 1 albino

59. If a classic 9:3:3:1 ratio was altered to a 13:3 ratio, what type of epistatic gene interaction would be responsible?

(a) Recessive epitasis

(b) Dominant and recessive epistasis

(c) Duplicate recessive epistasis

(d) Duplicate dominant epistasis

(e) None of the above

60. ______ is when one character is affected by two or more gene pairs and a variety of phenotypic ratios appear, depending on the type and degree of interaction between the gene pairs

(a) Penetrance (b) Expressivity

(c) Epistasis (d) Disjunction

(e) Pleiotropism

61. When you cross different lines of spherical squash, the progeny are disk-shaped:

spherical P = aaBB × AAbb

disc F_1 = AaBb

What phenotypes would you expect to be exhibited in the progeny if you were to cross an F_1 disk-shaped individual (AaBb) with a long individual (aabb)?

(a) all disk (b) disk and sphere

(c) disk, sphere, and long

(d) all sphere (e) all long

62. What sort of ratio of phenotypes would you expect with epistasis?

(a) 9:3:3:1 (b) 3:1

(c) 1:1 (d) 15:1

63. An F_2 generation in which the phenoypic ratio of the offspring is 9:7 is usually due to

(a) codominance (b) epistasis

(c) dominance (d) recessiveness

(e) additive alleles

64. In swine, when a pure-breeding red is crossed with a pure-breeding white, the F_1 are all red. However, the F_2 shows 9 red, 1 white and 6 of a new colour—gray. The gray phenotype is most likely determined by

(a) complementary alleles of two different genes.

(b) a heterozygote of the alleles determined red and white

(c) recessive epistasis

(d) the presence of a dominant allele at either of the two loci, and red is determined by the dominant allele of both loci.

65. Epistasis

(a) may be caused by the presence of homozygous `recessives at one gene pair

(b) may be caused by the presence of a dominant allele at a gene pair

(c) may be in only one direction, from one particular gene pair to another

(d) may be in both directions when one gene pair is mutually epistatic to the other

(e) all of the above are correct

66. The 9 (agouti): 3 (black) : 4 (albino) ratio for mouse coat colour is an example of

(a) complete dominance at both gene pairs, but one gene, when homozygous recessive, is epistatic to the other
(b) complete dominance at both gene pairs, but either recessive homozygote is epistatic to the effects of the other gene
(c) complete dominance at both gene pairs, but one gene, when dominant, is epistatic to the other
(d) complete dominance at both gene pairs, but either gene, when dominant, is epistatic to the other

67. When there is complete dominance at one gene pair, partial dominance at the other; first gene, when homozygous recessive, is epistatic to the second gene, then the F_2 ratios of phenotypes would be

(a) 13 : 3 (b) 9 : 6 : 1
(c) 7 : 6 : 3 (d) 6 : 3 : 3 : 4

68. Which of the following statements is true?

(a) A 9:3:3:1 ratio of F_2 phenotypes never indicates gene interaction
(b) When each gene pair affects a different character, a 9:3:3:1 ratio of F_2 phenotypes indicates epistasis
(c) When each gene pair affects the same character, a 9:3:3:1 ratio of F_2 phenotypes may indicate epistasis
(d) All the above statements are wrong

69. If there is partial or codominance at both gene pairs, then the F_2 phenotypic ratio would be

(a) 6:3:3:2:1:1
(b) 7 : 4 : 3 : 2
(c) 11 : 5
(d) 1 : 2 : 1 : 2 : 4 : 2 : 1 : 2 : 1

70. In case of two-gene interaction, the gene which is masking the expression of another gene is called ______ And the gene whose expression is masked is called

(a) dominant, recessive
(b) recessive, dominant
(c) epistatic, hypostatic
(d) hypostatic, epistatic

71. Epistatic is the interaction between ______ genes

(a) 2 (b) 4
(c) 8 (d) 16

72. What is the dihybrid phenotypic ratio for recessive epistasis in an F_2 generation

(a) 9 : 3 : 3 : 1 (b) 9 : 6 : 1
(c) 9 : 3 : 4 : 1 (d) 9 : 3 : 4

73. In mouse agouti locus is hypostatic to pigment development locus. If C is for pigment development, and A is for agouti, and recessive alleles in agouti locus give black colour and recessive in pigment locus gives white colour, what will be the phenotype of A/- c/c and a/a C/c?

(a) Agouti, white (b) Black, agouti
(c) Black, black (d) White, white

74. The cross between a black mouse and a white mouse

(a) cannot give a black mouse
(b) cannot give a white mouse
(c) cannot give a agouti mouse
(d) can give all combinations

75. Which one of the following has dominant allele in both loci?

(a) Black (b) Agouti
(c) Albino (d) White

76. Coat colour in Labrador receiver is controlled by epistasis. B specifies black pigment, b is for brown pigment (recessive) and E locus determines the expression of B locus. Which one of the following is wrong?

(a) bb EE gives yellow
(b) Bb EE gives black
(c) bb Ee gives brown
(d) BB EE gives black

77. In case of dominant epistasis which of the following will have the same expression, when A is the epistatic locus?

(a) A/a B/b and a/a B/b
(b) A/A b/b and A/A B/B
(c) a/a b/b and A/a b/b
(d) a/a b/b and B/B

78. Dominant epistasis ratio with A as epistatic gene 12:3:1 corresponds to

(a) A/- B/- : A/- b/b : a/a B/-
(b) a/a B/- : a/a b/b : a/a b/-
(c) A/A B/- : A/- B/- : a/a b/b
(d) A/- -/- : a/a B/- : a/a b/b

79. Which one of the following is not the case of epistasis?

(a) Full colour in mouse
(b) Fruit colour in summer squash
(c) Fruit shape in summer squash
(d) Coat colour in Labrador

80. Which of the following is incorrect about greying of coat colour of horse?

(a) The greying is a case of dominant epistasis
(b) The colour of the fur and skin gradually turns grey
(c) The G/G and G/g shows greying
(d) Coat colour of horse with G/- combination will grey irrespective of what was its colour to start with

81. In case of summer squash, the W locus shows dominant epistasis over the Y locus. W locus develops white colour while Y/- gives yellow and y/y gives green. If you cross a yellow and a green summer squash you cannot get

(a) yellow (b) green
(c) white (d) you can get all

82. In case of summer squash which of the following is not right?

(a) The W allele produces a white substance
(b) A white substance is converted to yellow when dominant Y allele is present
(c) The transformation of white substance to yellow is via green intermediate
(d) The green intermediate has combination at the Y locus y/y

83. Flower colour in sweet pea shows duplicate epistasis. If purple colour is dominant what is the F_2 ratio?

(a) 15 : 1 (b) 9 : 7
(c) 3 : 1 (d) 9 : 3: 4

84. Which of the following condition in recessive duplicate epistasis will give the odd phenotype?

(a) A/- B/- (b) A/- b/b
(c) a/a B/- (d) a/a b/b

85. Choose the off one out in case of duplicate recessive epistasis

(a) A/A b/b (b) A/A B/B
(c) A/a B/b (d) A/a B/-

86. If you are selfing purple flower in sweet pea, you will get

(a) purple flower on every occasion
(b) white flower on every occasion
(c) may be white or purple flower
(d) a blend of white and purple flower

87. Selfing a white flower of sweet pea would give a

(a) white flower only
(b) equal probability of white or purple
(c) more white flowers than purple
(d) purple flowers only

88. In sweet pea a white substance is first converted to a ______ substance by first gene and then to a ______ substance by second gene to give a purple flower

(a) yellow, purple (b) green, purple
(c) purple, yellow (d) white, yellow

89. Shepherd's purse has two shape heart and which is narrow. If you cross a true breeding heart to a true breeding narrow, F_1 will give

(a) heart (b) narrow
(c) a mixture of heart or narrow
(d) disc shaped

90. The 15/16 of the duplicate dominant epistasis does not correspond to

(a) A/a B/b (b) A/A b/b
(c) a/a B/b (d) a/a b/b

91. You crossed two heart shaped Shepherd's purse which is heterozygous at one locus and homozygous recessive at the other gene locus, what would be the ratio of heart shaped and narrow in F_1?

(a) All heart (b) All narrow
(c) 3:1 (d) 15: 1

PENETRANCE AND EXPRESSIVITY

92. Siamese cat colouration is due to

(a) nutritional effects
(b) position effects
(c) gene suppression
(d) genetic background
(e) temperature effects

93. Penetrance refers to

(a) range of phenotypic expression in an individual
(b) extent of genotypic expression in an individual
(c) extent of phenotypic expression in an individual
(d) range of phenotypic expression in a population
(e) extent of phenotypic expression in a population

94. A penetrant gene will produce its effect in

(a) 50% individuals
(b) 25% individuals
(c) 75% individuals
(d) 100% individuals

95. A semi-lethal allele is an example of which of the following extensions of Mendelian genetics?

(a) Incomplete dominance
(b) Incomplete penetrance
(c) Variable expressivity
(d) Overdominance

96. In soybeans, resistance to sudden death syndrome (SDS) is inherited as a dominant condition. In some cases, individuals that are not resistant to SDS (but whose parents were) can pass the trait to their progeny. This is an example of which of the following?

(a) Overdominance
(b) Incomplete penetrance
(c) Incomplete dominance
(d) Variable expressivity

97. Neurofibromatosis is a condition in humans that is generally inherited in a dominant fashion. Assuming that this disorder is 90% penetrant, what is the chance that a single child born to a father with neurofibromatosis and a mother known not to carry the mutation will have the disorder?

(a) 90% (b) 50%
(c) 45% (d) 5%

98. In a group of fruit flies homozygous for an allele that causes a reduced number of thoracic bristles, you notice that the number of bristles varies from about half the normal to only a few bristles. This is an example of which of the following?

(a) Incomplete dominance
(b) Overdominance
(c) Incomplete penetrance
(d) Variable expressivity

99. Some people with polydactyly have an extra toe; others have an extra finger. This situation is an example of a trait that is

(a) incompletely penetrant
(b) variably expressed
(c) both a and b
(d) neither a nor b

100. Expressivity is the

(a) number of genes contributing to an expressed phenotype
(b) strength of phenotype expressed in individuals of a known genotype
(c) number of phenotypes expressed due to a known genotype
(d) proportion of individuals of a known genotype expressing a phenotype
(e) none of the above

101. Some people with polydactyly have an extra toe; others have an extra finger. This situation is an example of a trait that is

(a) completely penetrant
(b) variably expressed
(c) both a and b
(d) neither a nor b

102. A gene is identified that confers great athletic ability. A family of 10 children is identified in which all 10 children carry this gene. However, only three of the children exhibit great athletic ability, four have slightly better than average athletic ability, and three have average athletic ability. What does this tell you about the expressivity of this gene?

(a) 100% expressivity
(b) <100% expressivity
(c) 1% expressivity
(d) You cannot tell anything about the expressivity from this information

103. The percentage of individuals with a given genotype who exhibit the phenotype associated with that genotype is called

(a) penetrance (b) expressivity
(c) incomplete dominance
(d) co-dominance (e) lethality

104. An individual with a homozygous genotype for a particular phenotype ______ expresses the phenotype

(a) always (b) never
(c) sometimes (d) unknown relation

105. It is known that homozygous dominant gene for a type of cone gives brown colour. The formation of cones with brown, yellow colour expresses ______ and white expresses the

(a) penetrance, expressivity
(b) expressivity, genotype
(c) genotype, phenotype
(d) expressivity, penetrance

106. Which of the following the incorrect option about penetrance?

(a) If penetrance is 100% all recessive genotypes show one phenotype
(b) If penetrance is 100% the expressivity is 100%
(c) If penetrance is 100% all the heterozygotes have similar phenotype
(d) If penetrance is 100% all the dominant genotypes have a different phenotype from recessive

107. If the gene is non-penetrant then which of the following is not right?

(a) The pedigree chart will not express the defecting phenotype in that individual
(b) The person's children are not likely to express that phenotype
The expressivity is 0 %
The genotype here did not make its proper phenotypic expression

108. Which of the following trait shows only variation in expressivity?

(a) Brachdactyly
(b) Osteoporosis imperfectica
(c) Pea seed colour
(d) Polydactyly

109. Neurofibilomatosis varies in

(a) penetrance
(b) expressivity
(c) both penetrance and expressivity
(d) it is 100 % penetrant and expressive

110. The genes that Mendel worked with were

(a) variable in penetrance and expressivity
(b) variable in penetrance only
(c) variable in expressivity only
(d) 100% penetrance with 100% expressivity

LETHAL ALLELES

111. In *Aurea*, a type of snapdragon, only ______ carrying dominant genes live

(a) homozygous (b) homozygote
(c) heterozygote (d) heterozygous

112. The ______ mouse is lethal

(a) homozygous white
(b) homozygous black
(c) heterozygous agouti
(d) homozygous, yellow

113. Which of the following is not true for yellow mice?

(a) The homozygous yellow mice die
(b) A normal mice crossed to yellow mice will always give normal probabilities of F_1
(c) In yellow mice the yellow colouring allele is under the control of Raly promoter
(d) The homozygous mouse dies as the yellow allele is produced in excess

114. The lethal mutation that is seen in the yellow mice is due to ______ mutation

(a) insertion (b) deletion
(c) non-sense (d) frame shift

115. Which one of the following is not true for Tay Sach's disease?

(a) It causes death in heterozygotes
(b) Death occurs within 2-3 years of life
(c) HEXA gene is affected
(d) Central nervous system is affected

116. A person homozygous for lethal allele

(a) always dies
(b) always expresses the phenotype
(c) may not express the phenotype
(d) will have severe abnormalities

117. Huntington's disease affects individuals carrying the gene starting from the age of

(a) 10 (b) 20
(c) 30 (d) none of these

GENERAL

118. Geneticists calculate the ______ of a trait, or the degree to which it is inherited, as the percentage of pairs in which both twins express the trait

(a) heritability
(b) coefficient of relationship
(c) concordance
(d) empiric risk

119. Can a child have darker skin than either of his parents?

(a) Yes (b) No
(c) No basis for determination
(d) Both (a) and (b) are possible

120. Human height is an example of a (an) ______ trait

(a) autosomal (b) sex-linked
(c) epistatic (d) polygenic

121. Heritability is a measurement that estimates the proportion of

(a) genetic variation in a group that can be attributed to phenotype
(b) phenotypic variation in an individual that can be attributed to genes
(c) phenotypic variation in a group that can be attributed to genes
(d) none of the above

122. In humans, obesity has a heritability of 0.75. Expression of weight gain is

(a) inherited from a parent 75% of the time
(b) solely dependent on the inheritance of weight gain genes
(c) strongly influenced by the environment
(d) dependent on the inheritance of genes and the influence of the environment

123. The risk of recurrence of a trait based on known incidence in a population refers to

(a) the empiric risk
(b) the correlation coefficient
(c) heritability (d) concordance

124. The correlation coefficient between identical twins for body weight was calculated to be 0.42. What is the heritability of body weight?

(a) 0 (b) 0.21
(c) 0.42 (d) 0.84

125. The correlation coefficient between fraternal twins for body weight was calculated to be 0.42. What is the heritability of body weight?

(a) 0 (b) 0.21
(c) 0.42 (d) 0.84

126. A correlation coefficient of 1.0 indicates

(a) a perfect inverse relationship
(b) a very poor relationship
(c) no relationship between variables
(d) a perfect direct relationship

127. Characteristics shared by adopted children and their biological parents are mostly ______ while their similarities with adoptive parents reflect ______ influences

(a) environmental, heritable
(b) genetic, environmental
(c) genetic, heritable
(d) plastic, immutable

128. Assume that three pairs of alleles with no environmental modification control height in humans. In this model, each dominant allele contributes four inches to a base height of four feet. What is the range of heights possible in this population?

(a) 0 - 2 feet (b) 4 - 5 feet
(c) 2 - 4 feet (d) 4 - 6 feet

129. Following question 128, if a woman of the minimal height specified marries a man of intermediate height, what is the maximum height their child could achieve?

(a) 3 feet (b) 4 feet
(c) 5 feet (d) 6 feet

130. In general, empiric risk for an individual increase with

(a) the severity of the disorder
(b) the number of affected family members
(c) how closely related the person is to affected individuals
(d) all of the above

131. A higher heritability would be found for a trait in a population that is

(a) homozygous for genes affecting the trait
(b) in a uniform environment
(c) heterozygous for genes affecting the trait
(d) in a heterogeneous environment

132. Given that eye colour is controlled by two pairs of genes, what are the genotypes of the lightest-eyed parents who could produce a child with medium brown eyes?

(a) AABB x aabb (b) AAbb x aaBB
(c) AaBb x Aabb (d) Aabb x Aabb

133. Association studies

(a) make use of SNP mapping
(b) relate sequence patterns to the probability of developing a particular disorder
(c) are more powerful than heritability studies
(d) all of the above are true in regard to association studies

134. Siblings share ______ % of their genes, fraternal twins share ______ %, and identical twins share ______ % of their genes (on average)

(a) 50, 50, 50 (b) 50, 100, 100
(c) 100, 100, 100 (d) 50, 50, 100

135. A woman with phenotypically normal parents has two brothers with Duchenne muscular dystrophy. She experiences mild muscle weakness in her legs. Which of the following mechanisms is most likely to be directly involved?

(a) Germline mosaicism
(b) Skewed inactivation
(c) Mutation near the pseudoautosomal region of the Y-chromosome
(d) New mutation in this woman
(e) Nondisjunction of her mother's X chromo-somes

136. The exon trapping technique is used

(a) to identify coding sequence within a DNA sequence
(b) to provide new primers for a PCR reaction
(c) to identify promoter regions of genes
(d) to test for cross-species conservation of DNA sequence
(e) to provide probes for Northern blot analysis

137. Somatic cell gene therapy is feasible for which of the following diseases?

(a) Spina bifida
(b) Cystic fibrosis
(c) Alcoholism
(d) Adenosine deaminase (ADA) deficiency
(e) (b) and (d)

138. Which of the following is not currently a candidate for gene therapy?

(a) Cystic fibrosis
(b) Adenosine deaminase deficiency
(c) Lung cancer
(d) Bipolar affective disorder
(e) AIDS

139. Fluorescence *in situ* hybridization (FISH)

(a) does not involve radioactivity
(b) offers better resolution than standard *in situ* hybridization
(c) is sometimes used with interphase chromo-somes
(d) (a), (b), and (c)
(e) (a) and (c)

140. The *in situ* hybridization technique does not involve the use of

(a) cloned probes (b) X-ray film
(c) complementary base pairing
(d) gene product expression
(e) metaphase chromosomes

141. Which of the following can be used to determine the physical locations of genes?

(a) Radioactive *in situ* hybridization
(b) Fluorescence *in situ* hybridization
(c) Somatic cell hybridization
(d) Cytogenetic analysis of deletions and translocations
(e) All of the above

142. In genetic screening, sensitivity refers to

(a) the proportion of true negatives detected by the test
(b) the proportion of true positives detected by the test
(c) the demonstration of a compassionate attitude
(d) the positive predictive value of the test
(e) none of the above

143. Which of the following are advantages of direct genetic diagnosis over indirect genetic diagnosis?

(a) Recombination does not cause diagnostic errors
(b) PCR techniques can be used
(c) Information from other family members is not needed
(d) Direct diagnosis can be performed in the prenatal period
(e) (a) and (c)

144. Now suppose you do have a reasonable candidate locus for the disease you are studying. Which of the following would be least likely to contribute useful information?

(a) DNA sequencing
(b) Single-stranded conformation polymorphism (SSCP) analysis
(c) Northern blotting
(d) Denaturing gradient gel electrophoresis (DGGE)
(e) Chromosome karyotype

145. Suppose you are attempting to find a disease-causing gene, and you have identified a number of families in which the disease is transmitted. If you have no knowledge of the gene product and no reasonable candidate locus, which of the following would be the first technique you would be most likely to use?

(a) Linkage analysis
(b) DNA sequencing
(c) Single strand conformation polymorphism (SSCP) analysis
(d) Denaturing gradient gel electrophoresis (DGGE)
(e) Fluorescence *in situ* hybridization

146. Disadvantages of using allele-specific oligonucleotides for genetic diagnosis include

(a) part of the gene's DNA sequence must be known
(b) other family members affected with the disorder must also be studied
(c) a different oligonucleotide must be used for each disease-causing mutation
(d) the mutation must occur at a restriction site
(e) (a) and (c)

147. Which of the following is not true of genetic diagnosis using fetal cells in the maternal circulation?

(a) PCR is used to amplify DNA from the fetal cells
(b) The procedure involves no risk to the foetus
(c) The procedure involves virtually no risk to the mother
(d) The procedure is more accurate than amnio-centesis
(e) FISH analysis can be used to detect aneuploidy in the fetal cells

148. In one gene mapping technique, denatured DNA from metaphase chromosomes is hybridized with a radioactively labeled probe. This DNA is then exposed to film to reveal the approximate chromosomal location of the DNA in the probe. Which technique does this best describe?

(a) Southern blotting
(b) *in situ* hybridization
(c) Somatic cell hybridization
(d) Fluorescence *in situ* hybridization
(e) Single strand conformation polymorphism (SSCP) analysis

149. When a colour blind man marries a woman pure for normal colour vision, it is probable that one of the following situations may result. It is probable that

(a) all the children will be colour blind
(b) all the grandchildren will be colour blind
(c) only the sons will be colour blind
(d) half the grandsons will be colour blind

150. The quickest way to produce homozygous breeding lines from heterozygous parents is through

(a) half-seed techniqueb)doubled haploids
(c) introgression
(d) aneuploidy
(e) protoplast fusion

151. Which of the following pairs of species best demonstrate the c-value paradox?

(a) *Arabidopsis* and rice
(b) Rice and maize
(c) Rice and poplar
(d) Wheat and maize
(e) Rice and wheat

152. Which of the following methods would give you the most precise and accurate information about where and when a given gene is expressed?

(a) *in situ* hybridization
(b) DNA microarray
(c) Protein microarray
(d) Reporter gene fusion including introns
(e) Reporter gene fusion including UTR

153. Continued self-fertilization in a population of plants heterozygous for a character would normally result in which of the following?

(i) A decrease in the percentage of recessive homozygotes
(ii) An increase in trhe percentage of dominant homozygotes
(iii)A decrease in the numbers of recessive homozygotes
(iv)A reduction of heterozygotes by 50% in each generation
(a) I and ii; (b) I and iii; (c) ii only; (d) ii and iv; (e) iv only

154. Appearance of an inherited phenotype at progressively earlier age in successive generations illustrates

(a) dosage compensation
(b) genetic expressivity
(c) position effect
(d) genetic imprinting
(e) genetic anticipation

155. A human pedigree may give us information on

(a) how a gene is inherited
(b) the type of mutation that caused a specific genetic trait
(c) how the mutation occurred
(d) the protein product of a mutated gene
(e) where the gene is located on a chromosome

156. What type of experiment can be done to differentiate between a homozygous dominant and a heterozygous genotype for a dominant trait?

(a) Chi-square test (b) Test cross
(c) Punnett square (d) Human pedigree analysis

157. Who gave the term "genetics"?

(a) Mendel, 1865 (b) Bateson, 1905
(c) Wilson, 1910 (d) Tackholm, 1922

158. Who gave the term "mitosis"?

(a) Farmer and Moor, 1905
(b) Levitsky, 1924
(c) Waldeyer, 1888
(d) Flemming, 1882

159. Who gave the term "meiosis"?

(a) Farmer and Moor, 1905
(b) Mendel, 1865
(c) Flemming, 1882
(d) Navashin, 1922

160. Who gave the term "chromosome"?

(a) Waldeyer, 1888
(b) Heitz, 1928
(c) Morgan and Catell, 1912
(d) Muller, 1940

161. Who gave the term "ideogram"?

(a) Navashin, 1922 (b) Wilson, 1910
(c) Randolph, 1928 (d) Bateson, 1902

162. Who gave the term "karyotype"?

(a) Wilson, 1896 (b) Levitsky, 1924
(c) Waldeyer, 1903 (d) Rhoades, 1952

163. Who gave the term "telomere"?

(a) Muller, 1940 (b) Heitz, 1928
(c) Flemming, 1882 (d) Randolph, 1928

164. Who gave the term "euchromatin and heterochromatin"?

(a) Muller, 1940 (b) Heitz, 1928
(c) Bridges, 1917 (d) Navashin, 1922

165. Who gave the term "crossing over"?

(a) Waldeyer, 1888
(b) Heitz, 1928
(c) Morgan and Catell, 1912
(d) Muller, 1940

166. Who gave the term "heterogametic"?

(a) Wilson, 1910 (b) Heitz, 1928
(c) Bridges, 1917 (d) Bateson, 1902

167. Who gave the term "ploidy"?

(a) Tackholm, 1922 (b) Strasburger, 1910
(c) Muller, 1940 (d) Wilson, 1896

168. Who gave the term "aneuploids"?

(a) Strasburger, 1910 (b) Randolph, 1928
(c) Tackholm, 1922 (d) Bridges, 1917

169. Who gave the term "deficiency"?

(a) Bridges, 1917 (b) Randolph, 1928
(c) Flemming, 1882 (d) Muller, 1940

170. Who gave the term "amphidiploid"?

(a) Tackholm, 1922 (b) Heitz, 1928
(c) Bridges, 1917 (d) Navashin, 1927

171. Who gave the term "β-chromosome"?

(a) Randolph, 1928 (b) Tackholm, 1922
(c) Bridges, 1917 (d) Heitz, 1928

172. Who gave the term "allelomorph"?

(a) Mendel, 1865 (b) Bateson, 1902
(c) Wilson, 1910 (d) Heitz, 1928

173. Who gave the term "gynandromorphy"?

(a) Goldschmidt, 1915
(b) Fol, 1891
(c) Waldeyer, 1903
(d) Wilson, 1910

174. Who gave the term "satellite"?

(a) Bridges, 1917 (b) Tackholm, 1922
(c) Randolph, 1928 (d) Navashin, 1912

175. Who gave the term "centromere"?

(a) Waldeyer, 1903 (b) Rhoades, 1952
(c) Bridges, 1917 (d) Muller, 1940

176. Who gave the term "allele"?

(a) Mendel, 1865 (b) Bateson, 1902
(c) Bridges, 1917 (d) Johannsen, 1909

177. Who gave the term "multiple allele"?

(a) Morgan, 1914
(b) Montogomery, 1902
(c) Brown, 1931
(d) Bridges, 1917

178. Who gave the term "polyploidy"?

(a) Kihara and Ono, 1926
(b) Navashin, 1927
(c) Tackholm, 1922
(d) Strasburger, 1910

179. Who gave the term "apomixes"?

(a) Winkler, 1906 (b) McClintock, 1951
(c) Janssens, 1909 (d) Stern, 1932

180. Who gave the term "character"?

(a) Mendel, 1865 (b) Bridges, 1917
(c) Bateson, 1907 (d) Benzer, 1903

181. Who gave the term "cistron"?

(a) Benzer, 1957 (b) Cooper, 1941
(c) Crick, 1963 (d) Stern, 1936

182. Who gave the term "epistasis"?

(a) Mendel, 1865 (b) Morgan, 1912
(c) Bateson, 1907 (d) Brown, 1931

183. Mendel's results were rediscovered independently in 1900 by

(a) De Vries (b) Correns
(c) Tschermak (d) all of them

184. The term "molecular biology" was first used by

(a) Astbury (b) Crick
(c) Mendel (d) Benzer

185. The terms "eukaryotes" and "prokaryotes" were coined by

(a) Bateson (b) Benzer
(c) Chatton (d) Boveri

186. *The Journal of Genetics* was founded by

(a) Johannsen
(b) Bateson and Punnett
(c) Watson and Crick
(d) Sutton and Boveri

187. Dominance refers to

(a) intra-allelic interaction
(b) intra-locus interaction
(c) intragenic interaction
(d) all of these

188. Manifold effects of a gene refer to

(a) penetrance (b) pleiotropy
(c) isoalleles (d) expressivity

189. Pleiotropy was first reported by

(a) Morgan (b) Plate
(c) Bateson (d) Sears

190. The modifier gene was first observed by

(a) Muller (b) Bridges
(c) Bateson (d) Boveri

191. Side effects of a gene are studied by using

(a) inbred lines (b) isogenic lines
(c) pure lines (d) none of these

192. Isogenic lines differ from each other for

(a) one locus (b) several loci
(c) two loci (d) none of these

193. The term "multiple allele" was coined by

(a) Sturtevant (b) Morgan
(c) Correns (d) De Vries

194. The term "isoallele" was first used by

(a) Morgan (b) Muller
(c) Benzer
(d) Stern and Schaeffer

195. The parallel behaviour of chromosomes and genes was established in 1903 by

(a) Boveri
(b) Bateson and Punnett
(c) Morgan
(d) Sutton and Boveri

196. The gene was divided into recon, cistron, and muton by

(a) Muller (b) Benzer
(c) Morgan (d) Bateson

197. The largest unit within the gene is

(a) cistron (b) muton
(c) intron (d) recon

198. The smallest unit within a gene is called

(a) intron (b) cistron
(c) recon (d) muton

199. Genes with intervening sequences are known as

(a) jumping genes (b) overlapping genes
(c) isogenes (d) split genes

200. Genes which code for more than one protein are called

(a) split genes (b) selfish genes
(c) overlapping genes (d) cistrons

201. Defective copies of normal genes refer to

(a) selfish genes (b) pseudo genes
(c) jumping genes (d) mutons

202. A repetitive DNA sequence with no obvious function is called

(a) selfish gene (b) overlapping gene
(c) split gene (d) cistron

203. Jumping genes were first discovered by

(a) Benzer (b) Muller
(c) Morgan (d) McClintock

204. McClintock was awarded Nobel prize for discovery of jumping genes in

(a) 1953 (b) 1964
(c) 1993 (d) 1983

205. Overlapping genes were first discovered by

(a) Benzer *et al.* (b) Khurana
(c) Korenberg (d) Barrell *et al.*

206. Terms "introns" and "exons" were coined by

(a) Jacob (b) Gibert
(c) Davidson (d) Khurana

207. The term "selfish gene" was first used by

(a) Baltimore (b) Crick
(c) Jacob (d) Gilbert

208. The term "transposon" was coined by

(a) Gilbert (b) Hedges and Jacob
(c) Jacob and Monod d) Muller

209. The term "RNA splicing" was coined by

(a) Baltimore (b) Cairns
(c) Sears (d) Berget *et al.*

210. Berget *et al.* coined the term RNA splicing in

(a) 1967 (b) 1987
(c) 1957 (d) 1977

211. The term "gene silencing" was first used by

(a) Temin (b) Bateson
(c) Morgan (d) Ohno

212. Split gene was first reported in

(a) *Drosophila* (b) garden pea
(c) *E. coli* (d) chickens

213. Terms "exons" and "introns" are related to

(a) overlapping genes (b) split genes
(c) isogenes (d) jumping genes

214. In split gene, coding sequences are called

(a) introns (b) cistrons
(c) recons (d) exons

215. In split gene, non-coding sequences are known as

(a) exons (b) introns
(c) mutons (d) cistrons

216. The first case of intragenic recombination was reported in

(a) bee (b) datura
(c) *Oenothera* (d) *Drosophila*

217. Genes that keep on changing their position within the chromosome and between chromosome of the same genome are called

(a) jumping genes
(b) transposable elements
(c) transposons
(d) none of these

218. Selection provides an opportunity to isolate the most desirable genotype from a

(a) homogenous population
(b) heterogeneous population
(c) homozygous population
(d) heterozygous population

219. Mass selection is always based on

(a) genotype (b) progeny test
(c) heritability (d) phenotype

220. The first semidwarf wheat varieties developed in India were Kalyan Sona and Sonalika. They were developed through

(a) mutagenesis
(b) hybridization followed by selection
(c) primary introduction
(d) selection in introduced material

221. The source of reduced height (*rht*) genes used in wheat breeding is

(a) Norin 10
(b) Tom Thumb
(c) Norin 10 and Tom thumb
(d) Dee-geo-woo-gen

222. Dee-geo-woo-gen is a rice variety belonging to the group

(a) *Indica* (b) *Javanica*
(c) *Africana* (d) *Japonica*

223. Taichung Native 1 was developed in

(a) China (b) Taiwan
(c) Japan (d) IRRI, Philippines

224. Jaya and Ratna rice varieties contain the dwarfing gene from

(a) Dee-geo-woo-gen
(b) spontaneous mutation
(c) induced mutation
(d) Norin 8

225. IR 8 variety of rice was developed at

(a) CRRI, Cuttack (b) Taiwan
(c) Japan (d) IRRI, Philippines

226. The first cotton hybrid was developed by

(a) Munshi Singh (b) Phundan Singh
(c) K.N. Kadapa (d) C.T. Patel

227. The first pigeonpea hybrid was based on

(a) cytoplasmic male sterility
(b) genetic male sterility
(c) cytoplasmic-genetic male sterility
(d) chemical hybridizing agent

228. The first cotton hybrid released in India was

(a) H6 (b) NH4
(c) Varalaxmi (d) H4

229. The first commercial hybrid bajra was developed by

(a) D.S. Athwal (b) K.S. Gill
(c) B.R. Murty (d) K.R. Sarkar

230. In case of wheat, *Rht* 1 and *Rht* 2 genes for reduced plant height are derived from

(a) Tom Thumb (b) Norin 8
(c) Norin 10 (d) Kalyan Sona

231. Varalaxami cotton hybrid is derived from the cross between

(a) *G. hirsutum* x *G. hirsutum*
(b) *G. hirsutum* x *G. barbadense*
(c) *G. barbadense* x *G. barbadense*
(d) *G. herbaceum* x *G. herbaceum*

232. DUS criterion requires the following in case of a new variety

(a) distinct from other varieties of the same crop
(b) consists of uniform individuals
(c) stable in performance
(d) all of a, b and c

233. Hybrid seed production in jowar and bajra is based on

(a) A, B and R lines (b) A and R lines
(c) B and R lines (d) A and B lines

234. In India, which of the following gener-ation system of multiplication is followed for seed production?

(a) Breeder Seed – foundation seed – certified seed
(b) Nucleus seed – foundation seed – certified seed
(c) Breeder seed – foundation seed – registered seed
(d) Nucleus seed – registered seed – certified seed

235. A two line system of hybrid seed production is based on

(a) A and B lines (b) A and R lines
(c) B and R lines
(d) A line and B or R line

236. Breeder seed has genetic purity of

(a) 98% (b) 100%
(c) 95% (d) 99%

237. Foundation seed has the minimum genetic purity of

(a) 95% (b) 99.5%
(c) 90% d) 98%

238. Tag of which colour is issued for breeder seed?

(a) Yellow/golden (b) Blue
(c) Green (d) White

239. Thermo – and photo-sensitive genetic male sterility systems were first developed in

(a) maize (b) rice
(c) soybean (d) barley

240. Tag of which colour is issued for foundation seed?

(a) Yellow (b) Blue
(c) Red (d) White

241. The maximum heterosis is likely to be manifested in a

(a) single cross (b) three-way cross
(c) double topcross (d) double cross

242. Heterosis due to dominance gene effects is best exploited by

(a) synthetic varieties
(b) composite varieties
(c) hybrid varieties
(d) open-pollinated varieties

243. Tag of which colour is issued for certified seed?

(a) Yellow (b) Blue
(c) Green (d) Red

244. The quickest method for developing an improved variety is by

(a) primary introduction
(b) mass selection
(c) secondary introduction
(d) domestication

245. Cytoplasmic-genetic male sterility is used commercially to produce hybrid seed in

(a) sunflower and jowar
(b) jowar and maize
(c) bajra and cotton
(d) all of the above

246. Vilmorin practised individual plant selection in sugarbeet based on

(a) testcross performance
(b) topcross test
(c) polycross test
(d) progeny test

247. Purity of existing pureline varieties can be maintained by regular

(a) pureline selection (b) pedigree selection
(c) mass selection (d) recurrent selection

248. Purelines can be used

(a) as varieties
(b) as parents in hybridization
(c) for studies on mutation
(d) for all of the above purposes

249. Pureline selection has been the most commonly used method in the early stages of improvement of

(a) cross-pollinated crops
(b) self-pollinated crops
(c) often cross-pollinated crops
(d) both b and c

250. Self-pollinated crops evolved from an ancestor that was

(a) cross-pollinated
(b) self-pollinated
(c) often self-pollinated
(d) often cross-pollinated

251. The bulk method is suitable for handling the segregating generations of

(a) cereals and oilseeds
(b) cereals and grain legumes
(c) smaller millets and oilseeds
(d) all of the above

252. Bulk method can be used for

(a) isolation of homozygous lines
(b) mass selection for certain traits
(c) providing natural selection to change the composition of populations
(d) All of the above

253. Isogenic lines are easily produced by which breeding method?

(a) Backcross (b) Pedigree
(c) SSD (d) Bulk

254. Leaf rust resistance in wheat (*T. aestivum*) has been transferred from

(a) *Triticum monococcum*
(b) *Aegilops speltoides*
(c) *T. timopheevii*
(d) All of the above

255. The idea of multiline varieties was first suggested in 1952 by

(a) Borlaug (b) Briggs
(c) Knowels (d) Jenson

256. Segregating generations from crosses of self-pollinated crops can be handled according to

(a) pedigree method
(b) backcross method
(c) mass-pedigree method
(d) all of the above

257. Which is not correct about pure lines?

(a) They become genetically variable with time
(b) The chief cause of genetic variation within purelines is mutation
(c) They are not found in cross-pollinated species
(d) Mass selection is routinely practised to maintain their purity

258. A desirable cross should have

(a) high mean yield
(b) high genetic variance
(c) high mean yield and high genetic variance
(d) high mean yield, high genetic variance and high genetic advance under selection

259. Self- and often cross-pollinated crops show considerable

(a) inbreeding depression
(b) heterosis and additive variance
(c) additive variance
(d) heterosis

260. In a random mating population, gene and genotype frequencies will be the same generation after generation if there is no

(a) selection and migration
(b) selection and mutation
(c) selection and random drift
(d) all of the above

261. Whether a population is at equilibrium or not can be easily determined using a

(a) t-test (b) z-test
(c) X^2-test (d) F-test

262. Populations of cross-pollinated crop species are highly

(a) heterozygous and heterogeneous
(b) heterozygous and homogeneous
(c) homozygous and heterogeneous
(d) homozygous and homogeneous

263. Among the given breeding methods, which one is the oldest method of selection?

(a) Recurrent selection
(b) Ear-to-row selection
(c) Mass selection
(d) Mass-pedigree selection

264. The development of a new variety usually takes

(a) 4-5 years (b) 10-12 years
(c) 15-17 years (d) 7-8 years

265. Selection for simply inherited traits is started from

(a) F_2 (b) F_4
(c) F_5 (d) F_3

266. For accurate genetic studies, which emasculation method will be suitable?

(a) Self-incompatibility
(b) Male sterility
(c) Hand emasculation
(d) Hot water treatment

267. In cases of distant hybridization, chromosome elimination has been reported in certain interspecific crosses in

(a) *Nicotiana* (b) maize x wheat
(c) *Hordeum* (d) all of the above

268. Chromosome number of plants can be doubled by

(a) tissue culture (b) nitrous oxide
(c) colchicine (d) all of the above

269. In *T. aestivum*, gene Ph is present on chromosome

(a) 5A (b) 2B
(c) 5D (d) 5B

270. Asexually propagated crops are

(a) mostly perennial
(b) highly heterozygous
(c) generally polyploidy
(d) all of the above

271. Faculative apomixis occurs in

(a) mango (b) litchi
(c) citrus (d) both (a) and (c)

272. A chimera will be maintained by which of the following?

(a) Apomixis
(b) Somatic embryogenesis
(c) Cutting, budding and grating
(d) Adventitious shoot regeneration

273. Which estimates of heterosis is of commercial or practical value?

(a) Average heterosis
(b) Heterobeltiosis
(c) Economic heterosis
(d) Luxuriance

274. Overdominance hypotheis was independently proposed in 1908 by

(a) Shull and Hull (b) Hayes and Smith
(c) Beal and Shull (d) East and Shull

275. Heterosis can be fixed by

(a) vegetative propagation
(b) apomixis
(c) balanced lethal system
(d) all of the above

276. When a single cross hybrid is crossed with an open-pollinated variety, it is termed as

(a) topcross (b) testcross
(c) double topcross (d) three-way cross

277. Which of the following genetic male sterility systems is the most convenient to use?

(a) Genetic
(b) Cytoplasmic
(c) Temperature-sensitive genetic
(d) Cytoplasmic-genetic

278. Which male sterility system is the most general in its application, i.e., can be applied to any material?

(a) Genetic
(b) Cytoplasmic
(c) Cytoplasmic-genetic
(d) chemically induced

279. Which of the following were the earliest to be used to exploit heterosis?

(a) Double crosses
(b) Varietal crosses
(c) Inbred x variety crosses
(d) Single crosses

280. The concept of gene-for-gene relationship between host and pathogen was proposed by

(a) Van der Plank (b) Browning
(c) Marshall (d) Flor

281. In case of disease, score 0 indicates

(a) lack of disease symptom
(b) resistance
(c) lack of pathogen reproduction
(d) lack of contact

282. The terms "vertical" and "horizontal" resistance were introduced by

(a) Browning (b) Van der Plank
(c) Flor (d) Marshal

283. Rust is a

(a) soil-borne disease
(b) air-borne disease
(c) seed-borne disease
(d) insect transmitted disease

284. Epidemics are of common occurrence in the case of

(a) soil-borne fungi
(b) seed-borne fungi
(c) viral diseases
(d) air-borne fungi

285. A minor disease today may become a major disease tomorrow due to

(a) changes in crop varieties
(b) changes in pathogen
(c) changes in agricultural practices
(d) all of the above

286. Disease resistance is a function of

(a) host genotype
(b) environment
(c) host and pathogen genotypes
(d) pathogen genotype

287. A variety is called tolerant to a disease if it shows, compared to the susceptible control, a

(a) noticeably lower disease score
(b) lower reproduction rate of pathogen
(c) significantly lower reduction in yield at the same level of disease symptoms
(d) a lower rate of disease spread

288. The major disease resistance (R) genes usually encode proteins, which act by

(a) interfering with pathogen infection
(b) interfering with pathogen establishment
(c) interfering with pathogen reproduction
(d) activating other genes that produce hypersensitive response

289. Which of the following does not concern vertical resistance?

(a) Phytoalexins
(b) Vertifolia effect
(c) Reduced reproduction rate
(d) Hypersensitive response

290. Which of the following does not concern horizontal resistance?

(a) Immunity
(b) Polygenic control
(c) Reduced reproduction rate
(d) Race-nonspecificity

291. Which is the main reason for disease epidemics?

(a) Narrow genetic base
(b) Low horizontal resistance
(c) Introduction of a new pathogen
(d) Large acreage under single varieties

292. *Opaque*-2 and *Opaque*-7 are mutants of

(a) maize (b) wheat
(c) sorghum (d) barley

293. In case of *Brassica campestris,* erucic acid content in seed is governed by

(a) one pair of genes
(b) two pairs of genes
(c) three pair of genes
(d) polygenes

294. Fine structure analyses of the *rII* region of T4 bacteriophage suggested that genes are best defined as fundamental and indivisible units of

(a) structure—recombination occurs between whole genes only
(b) change—mutation occurs as changes in whole genes (alleles) only
(c) function—complementation occurs between whole gene products only
(d) all of the above
(e) (a) and (b) only

295. A high concentration pair wise infection with *rII* mutant T4 phage forms rare plaques of *E. coli K* (not due to reversion). The lysate from these rare plaques is then plated at low concentration on *E. coli K* and is expected to form plaques

(a) never (b) rarely
(c) ½ of the time (d) always
(e) with an unknown probability, there is not enough information given

296. Dominant alleles are always

(a) wild type (b) neomorphic
(c) rare (d) expressed
(e) mutant

297. The component(s) of phenotypic variation illustrated by these norms of reaction is (are)

(a) phenotype + genotype
(b) genotype
(c) genotype x environment interaction
(d) environment
(e) genotype + environment

298. The Sutton-Boveri theory states that genes are located on chromosomes and is supported by observations that chromosomes and genes both

(a) assort independently in mitotic cells
(b) duplicate during the S-phase of cell cycle
(c) occur in diploids
(d) segregate equally into gametes
(e) all of the above

299. "Hereditary factors" is an old name for

(a) DNA
(b) transforming units
(c) genes
(d) chromosomes
(e) all of the above

300. What single information would most help in predicting genotypic frequencies of the progeny resulting from a cross?

(a) The number of chromosomes
(b) The allelic relationship, i.e., dominance, incomplete dominance, codominance
(c) The frequency of the various possible parental phenotypes
(d) The parental gametes
(e) The parental phenotypes

301. A man learns that both his parents had Huntington's disease, which is caused by a dominant autosomal allele. What is the chance that he will have the disease?

(a) 0% (b) 25%
(c) 50% (d) 75%
(e) 100%

302. An environmentally caused trait that appears to be inherited is called a (an)

(a) pleiotropic gene (b) penetrant gene
(c) expressed gene (d) phenocopy

303. Two albino individuals marry and start a family. Their first child is normal in pigmentation. Is infidelity suspected and why/why not?

(a) Yes, albinism is recessive and neither parent carries a pigment gene
(b) No, albinism is dominant therefore at least one of the parents is a carrier
(c) No, each parent has a different allele causing his or her albinism (genetic heterogeneity)
(d) Cannot be determined from the limited information given

304. A woman who carries the CF gene and her homozygous normal husband have a child with CF. How can this occurrence be explained?

(a) Heteroplasmy
(b) Uniparental disomy
(c) Genomic imprinting
(d) None of the above; infidelity is the only plausible explanation

305. The alleles determining human ABO blood types are an example of

(a) incomplete dominance
(b) polygenes
(c) sex linkage
(d) all of the above
(e) none of the above

306. In familial hypercholesterolemia, individuals homozygous for the allele causing the disorder completely lack receptors on liver cells that take up cholesterol from the blood stream. Heterozygotes have one-half the number of receptors, while individuals homozygous for the normal allele are phenotypically normal. This is an example of

(a) complete dominance
(b) codominance
(c) incomplete dominance
(d) epistasis

307. In humans, the dominance relationship between the A and B alleles of the ABO blood group gene is an example of

(a) complete dominance
(b) codominance
(c) incomplete dominance
(d) epistasis

308. A situation where each allele produces a protein that can be detected in the heterozygote is called

(a) penetrance
(b) expressivity
(c) incomplete dominance
(d) co-dominance
(e) lethality

309. Alleles that are both expressed in a heterozygote are

(a) completely dominant
(b) codominant
(c) incompletely dominant
(d) epistatic

310. The fundamental units of life are

(a) genes (b) alleles
(c) chromosomes (d) cells

311. Our closest relative, according to karyotypes is the

(a) mouse (b) domestic cat
(c) gorilla (d) chimpanzee

312. A couple seeks testing and counseling after they have a child with cystic fibrosis. Testing reveals that the mother is a carrier, but the father is not. How can these results be explained?

(a) The man tested is not the biological father
(b) A mutation altered the child's normal allele
(c) Uniparental disomy (from the mother)
(d) All are possible explanations, additional testing is needed

313. A geneticist crosses a plant with red flowers to a plant with white flowers. The offspring include plants with red flowers (1/4), pink flowers (1/2), and white flowers (1/4). Which allele is dominant?

(a) Red
(b) White
(c) Neither, they are incompletely dominant
(d) Neither, they are codominant

314. Consider the cross AaBb x AaBb. If the alleles for both genes exhibit incomplete dominance, what phenotypic ratio is expected in the resulting offspring?

(a) 1:1:1:1 (b) 9:3:3:1
(c) 3:6:3:1:2:1 (d) 1:2:1:2:4:2:1:2:1

315. Consider the cross AaBb x AaBb. If trait A exhibits complete dominance and trait B exhibits codominance, what phenotypic ratio is expected in the offspring?

(a) 1:1:1:1 (b) 9:3:3:1
(c) 3:6:3:1:2:1 (d) 1:2:1:2:4:2:1:2:1

316. Which of the following is the best example of overdominance?

(a) Two lines of true breeding white parents produce purple flowered offspring
(b) Two lines of true breeding tomatoes that are susceptible to *Verticillium* wilt (a fungal infection) produce 3 offspring that are resistant to verticillium wilt
(c) Two true breeding lines, one tall and one short, produce offspring of medium height
(d) Two true breeding lines, one tall and one short, produce all tall offspring

317. Coat colour of horses can be Cremello (almost white), Palomino (golden coat with lighter mane and tail), or Chestnut (brown). Among these phenotypes, Palomino never breeds true. Cremello and Chestnut always breed true when they are mated with other horses of the same coat colour. What is the simplest explanation for these relationships?

(a) Multiple alleles
(b) Epistasis
(c) Codominance
(d) Inactivation of the X-chromosome
(e) Lyon hypothesis

318. The study of the way individual traits are transmitted from one generation to the next is called

(a) ecology
(b) genetics
(c) cell biology
(d) homology
(e) analogy

319. A genetic disorder caused by a dominant allele is

(a) sickle-cell anemia
(b) PKU
(c) Tay-Sachs disease
(d) hemophilia (royal)
(e) Huntington's disease

320. With codominance, a likely ratio resulting from a monohybrid cross would be

(a) 3:3 (b) 1:2:2:4
(c) 1:2:1 (d) 9:3:3:1
(e) 3:1

321. Marfan Syndrome, a dominant single-gene defect, is characterized by lens dislocation, long limbs, spindly fingers, a caved-in chest, and a weakened aorta. This is an example of a (an) ______ trait

(a) multifactorial (b) pleiotropic
(c) incompletely dominant
(d) phenocopy

322. Early ideas about heredity include

(a) traits can be masked in some generations
(b) traits were segregated among progeny
(c) alleles do not influence each other
(d) traits are transmitted directly
(e) not all copies of a factor are identical

323. Which of the following represents a testcross?

(a) Ww x WW (b) ww x Ww
(c) Ww x Ww (d) WW x WW
(e) None of the above

324. A genetic disorder caused by a dominant allele is

(a) sickle-cell anemia
(b) PKU (c) Tay-Sachs disease
(d) hemophilia (e) Huntington disease

325. Monozygotic twins are used in human heritability studies because

(a) they are genetically identical
(b) they are raised together in the same environment
(c) environmental effects are not important for the expression of their genotypes
(d) monozygotic twins are genetically similar in the same way siblings are; however, they share the same womb
(e) they are not used in human heritability studies

326. Which of the following are mismatched?

(a) QTLs = RFLPs
(b) RFLPs = DNA markers
(c) QTLs = more than one loci
(d) Discontinuous variation = QTLs
(e) Cosegregation = genetic mapping

327. The genotype of an individual is not always reflected in the phenotype. This may be due to which of the following?

(a) Epistasis
(b) Dominance
(c) Incomplete dominance
(d) All the answers suggest ways in which the genotype may not be observed in the phenotype

328. Genetic anticipation refers to the phenomenon which shows

(a) dominant disorders that affect the victim later in life
(b) an increase in severity of symptoms and a decrease in the age of onset as it is passed through the family
(c) a disorder that affects only individuals from a specific ethnic group
(d) an increase in the number of mutations on a single chromosome over time

329. Green colour blindness in humans is a sex-linked recessive trait. In a family, the daughter has normal vision, whereas the son is colour blind. One can realistically surmise that

(a) the mother was heterozygous for colour blindness
(b) the father was heterozygous for colour blindness
(c) the father was homozygous for colour blindness
(d) the mother, most probably, was colour blind
(e) the father, most probably, was colour blind

330. The idea of unit factors of inheritances was not obvious because

(a) the religious view of fixity of species would not allow it
(b) early plant breeders were not systematic in their record keeping
(c) "The Origin of Species" by Darwin had not yet been published
(d) DNA had not been discovered
(e) early plant breeders did not make as many hybrids as Mendel

331. A dominant lethal allele can exist in a population

(a) only if the gene is expressed after sexual maturity
(b) only if it is recessive
(c) only if it is heterozygous
(d) only if it is on a sex chromosome
(e) only if it expresses an enzyme

332. Bread wheat arose under human cultivation through a process of

(a) interspecific hybridization
(b) acquired inheritance
(c) spontaneous generation
(d) pangenesis
(e) epigenesis

333. Of the four main genetic capabilities, the one explained by the central dogma is

(a) mutation
(b) storage
(c) pangenesis
(d) replication
(e) expression

334. In the Punnett's square, the way it is used in Klug and Cummings, the rows and columns represent

(a) the distribution of the phenotypes
(b) heterozygotes
(c) homologous sets of chromosomes
(d) possible gametic genotypes
(e) sex chromosomes

335. In guinea pigs, the following alleles of an autosomal locus affecting coat colour are listed in descending order of dominance

C (black) > c^k (sepia) > c^d (cream) > c^a (albino)

A cross between black male and sepia female produced litters having 14 black, 8 sepia, and 6 albino progeny. What are the exact genotypes of the parents with regard to this locus?

(a) CC male x c^kc^k female
(b) Cc^d male x c^kc^d female
(c) Cc^k male x c^kc^a female
(d) Cc^a male x c^kc^a female
(e) CC male x c^kc^a female

336. The coat colours of mice are known to be governed by a multiple allelic series in which the allele A^y, when homozygous, is lethal early in embryonic development but produces yellow colour when in heterozygous condition with other alleles. Agouti (mousy colour) is governed by the A allele, and black by the recessive <u>a</u>. The dominance hierarchy is as follows: A^y > A > <u>a</u>. The following phenotypic ratio is expected in the viable F_1 from the cross A^yA x A^y<u>a</u>.

(a) 1:1:1 (b) 1:1
(c) 3:1 (d) 2:1
(e) None of the above

337. How many different genotypes could be formed by the multiple allelic series in the above question?

(a) 8 (b) 6
(c) 4 (d) 3
(e) None of the above

338. The following equations, $P(pw_{11} + qw_{12})/w$ and $p^2w_{11} + 2pqw_{12} + q^2w_{22}$, respectively, are used to estimate

(a) multiple allelic frequency and average fitness
(b) recurrence frequency of alleles and average fitness
(c) average fitness and quantitation of interacting gene pairs
(d) average fitness and recurrence frequency of alleles
(e) quantitation of interacting gene pairs and multiple allelic frequency

339. For a long time, human eye colour was thought to be controlled by a single gene: brown (B), dominant over blue (<u>b</u>). Using this assumption, can brown-eyed parents have a blue-eyed child?

(a) Yes (b) No
(c) Not enough information given to determine correct answer
(d) Only in certain Caribbean populations

340. If you roll a dice three times, what is the probability of obtaining three "fours" in succession?

(a) 1/6 (b) 1/32
(c) 1/64 (d) 3/64
(e) 1/216

341. In a family of 5 children, what is the probability that there will be 1 boy and 4 girls?

(a) 1/32 (b) 5/32
(c) 9/32 (d) 11/32
(e) 15/32

342. Consider a family for which the pedigree shows that one parent is a carrier for a recessive trait and the other displays the trait, i.e., Aa_x aa. In families with 2 children, how often would we expect that both children will exhibit the recessive trait?

(a) 1/2 (b) 1/4
(c) 1/8 (d) 1/16
(e) None of the above

343. The term that describes the develop-ment of an individual without fertili-zation is

(a) pleiotropism
(b) parthenogenesis
(c) gyrandromorphism
(d) exconjugation
(e) none of the above

344. What is the probability of getting a boy in a subsequent birth if in the first 4 births there were all girls?

(a) 1/2 (b) 1/3
(c) 1/4 (d) 1/5

345. Metabolic diseases are usually the result of a(n)

(a) lethal gene that is recessive
(b) lethal gene that is dominant
(c) nondisjunction of sex genes
(d) codominant alleles
(e) incomplete dominance such as in snapdragons

346. The position of a gene on a chromosome is known as the gene's

(a) centromere (b) phenotype
(c) genotype (d) expression
(e) locus

347. A very dark skinned individual is mated with a light skinned individual. The F_1 individuals are all intermediate in skin colour. The skin colour of F_2 individuals is variable; there are individuals as dark as the dark parent and as light as the light parent, with many other individuals showing many graduations in skin colour between the two extremes. What is the most likely mode of inheritance for skin colour?

(a) Pleiotropy
(b) Multiple alleles
(c) Complementary genes
(d) Epistasis
(e) Multiple gene inheritance

348. Pleiotropism is the condition of

(a) a single gene having multiple effects
(b) interaction of multiple alleles
(c) a single gene being influenced by several traits
(d) a trait that is not expressed for several generations
(e) multiple gene inheritance

349. Theoretically, if a female hemophiliac married a normal male, what percentage of their male offspring would be expected to have hemophilia?

(a) 100% (b) 50%
(c) 25% (d) 0%

350. A man with red-green colour blindness marries a woman who is neither colour blind nor a carrier for this trait. Which statement would best describe their probable offspring?

(a) All of their sons would be colour blind
(b) All of their children would be colour blind
(c) Fifty per cent of their sons would be colour blind
(d) Fifty per cent of their daughters would be colour blind
(e) None of their children would be colour blind, but all of their daughters would be carriers

351. Parents heterozygous for a recessive allele are called

(a) carriers (b) codominant
(c) hybrids (d) true-breeding
(e) pleiotropic

352. If a F_1 plant that is heterozygous for 5 independently assorting genes is selfed (crossed with itself), how many unique genotypes are possible in the F_2?

(a) 32 (b) 125
(c) 243 (d) 1024

353. A situation in which an organism has both haploid and diploid stages would be called

(a) multiple alleles
(b) alternation of generations
(c) codominance
(d) incomplete dominance
(e) hemizygosity

354. Typical phenotypic ratios resulting from epistatic interactions in a monohybrid cross would be

(a) 9:3:3:1, 1:2:1 (b) 1:1:1:1, 2:1
(c) 9:3:4, 9:7 (d) 3:1, 1:2:1
(e) none of the above

355. The percentage of individuals with a given genotype who exhibit the pheno-type associated with that genotype is called

(a) penetrance
(b) expressivity
(c) incomplete dominance
(d) codominance
(e) lethality

356. A situation in which an allele causes inviability when present in two doses is called

(a) penetrance
(b) expressivity
(c) incomplete dominance
(d) codominance
(e) lethality

357. Which of the following statements about a lethal allele is not correct?

(a) Lethal alleles are always recessive
(b) Lethal alleles may have a late age of onset
(c) Lethal alleles may be caused by mutations in essential genes
(d) Lethal alleles may affect one individual differently than another

358. Mating type refers to

(a) the number of sex chromosomes in a eukaryotic cell
(b) a system in which haploid fungal cells fuse only with fungal cells with a different complement of allele
(c) the gametes of a plant that undergo alternation of generation
(d) the gametophytes of a flowering plant
(e) the sporophytes of a flowering plant

359. The following coat colours are known to be determined by alleles at one locus in horses

Palomino = golden coat; Cremello = almost white; Chestnut = brown.
The following table gives the ratios obtained in matings of the above varieties
(a) Cremello x Cremello—all Cremello
(b) Chestnut x Chestnut—all Chestnut
(c) Cremello x Chestnut—all Palomino
(d) Palomino x Palomino—¼ Chestnut, ½ Palomino, ¼ Cremello

Based on these data, what are the genotypes of each type of horse?

(a) AA = Chestnut; Aa = Cremello; aa = Palomino
(b) AA = Cremello; Aa = Chestnut; aa = Palomino
(c) AA = Palomino; Aa = Cremello; aa = Chestnut
(d) AA = Palomino; Aa = Chestnut; aa = Cremello
(e) AA = Chestnut; Aa =Palomino; aa = Cremello

360. In chickens, the dominant allele *Cr* produces the creeper phenotype (having short legs). However, the creeper allele is lethal in the homozygous condition. If two creepers are mated, what proportion of the living progeny will be creepers?

(a) 1/4 (b) 1/2
(c) 3/4 (d) 1/3
(e) 2/3

361. In the purple penguin, a series of alleles occurs at the *p* locus on an autosome. All alleles affect the colour of the feathers. p^d = dark-purple; p^m = medium-purple; p^l = light-purple; p^{vl} = very pale-purple. The order of dominance is $p^d > p^m > p^l > p^{vl}$. If a light-purple female (heterozygous for very pale-purple), is crossed to a dark-purple male (heterozygous for the medium-purple), the ratio of phenotypes expected among the baby penguins would be

(a) 2 dark: 1 medium: 1 light
(b) 1 dark: 1 medium
(c) 1 dark: 1 medium: 1 light: 1 very pale
(d) 1 medium: 1light
(e) 2 dark: 1 light: 1 very pale

362. The drug ______ was used to treat morning sickness between 1957 and 1961. Unfortunately, babies born to mothers, who used this drug, had incomplete or missing legs and arms

(a) lithium (b) diethylstilbestrol
(c) penicillamine (d) thalidomide

363. Birth defects can result from a (an) ______ or ______. However, only the latter is transmitted to future generations

(a) environmental intervention, malfunctioning gene
(b) malfunctioning gene, environmental intervention
(c) acquired characteristic, environmental intervention
(d) malfunctioning gene, acquired characteristic

364. The occurrence of affected individuals in every generation in a family suggests ______ trait

(a) an autosomal dominant
(b) an autosomal recessive
(c) either dominant or recessive
(d) sex-linked

365. Which of the following crosses is a test cross?

(a) Unknown x AA
(b) Unknown x Aa
(c) Unknown x aa
(d) Unknown x unknown

366. Two phenotypically normal individuals have an affected child. What can we conclude about the parents?

(a) They both carried the disease allele
(b) They are not the parents of the child
(c) They are affected
(d) No conclusions can be drawn

367. The geneticist ______ has compiled a compendium of human genetic traits called Mendelian Inheritance in Man

(a) Gregor Mendel (b) Hermann Muller
(c) Victor McKusick (d) John Hopkins

368. If relatives are married to each other, their children have a much higher risk of getting affected by a (an) ______ condition

(a) environmental (b) dominant
(c) recessive (d) undetected

369. Consider a group of 100 individuals (50 couples), all of whom carry a recessive disease allele. If 200 children were born to these couples, what percentage of the children would, theoretically, be carriers like their parents?

(a) 0 (b) 25
(c) 50 (d) 75

370. A group of genes or DNA sequences that are inherited together on the same chromosome is called a

(a) haplotype (b) genotype
(c) heteroplast (d) phenotype

371. Progeny that exhibits a mixing of maternal and paternal alleles on a single chromosome are

(a) parentals (b) recombinants
(c) haplotypes (d) mixed groups

372. Which of the following has the highest protein content?

(a) Oat (b) Ragi
(c) Wheat (d) Bajra

373. Which of the following has the highest fat content?

(a) Rice (b) Bajra
(c) Maize (d) Oat

374. *Triticum durum* is known as

(a) bread wheat (b) macaroni wheat
(c) club wheat (d) none of these

375. *Triticum compactum* is known as

(a) bread wheat (b) macaroni wheat
(c) club wheat (d) none of these

376. *T. aestivum* is known as

(a) bread wheat (b) macaroni wheat
(c) club wheat (d) none of these

377. Which of the following has the highest protein content?

(a) Bread wheat (b) Macaroni wheat
(c) Club wheat (d) None of these

378. The principles of SRI method are

(a) rice field soil is kept moist and anaerobic condition is minimized
(b) rice field soil is kept saturated and anaerobic condition is maximized
(c) 21 days old seedlings are transplanted with just three leaves
(d) both (b) and (c)

379. Heart rot disease in sugarbeet is caused due to the deficiency of

(a) boron (b) calcium
(c) iron (d) potassium

380. The green revolution has mainly been successful for

(a) rice (b) maize
(c) wheat (d) corn

MARK TRUE OR FALSE (T/F)

1. You would expect individuals with type B blood to produce the anti-B antibody
2. One gene can have multiple effects on an organism
3. In some cases, the type of dominance relationship observed depends on how the phenotype is defined
4. For alleles that display incomplete dominance, the phenotypic ratio expected in the F_2 generation of a monohybrid cross would be the same as the genotypic ratio
5. For genes, which have multiple alleles, the relationships between those alleles can be a variety of types of dominant/ recessive relationships
6. Lethal alleles violate the rules of Mendelian inheritance
7. Epistasis is a genetic condition in which certain alleles of one locus can alter the expression of alleles of a different locus
8. Mitomycin C is an antibiotic
9. Normal adult haemoglobin (Hb A) consists of two á and two ã (gamma) chains
10. Severe anaemia at birth is a feature of Alpha-thalassaemia
11. The mutation in sickle-cell disease consists of a deletion
12. The common mutation in á-thalassaemia consists of a deletion
13. The mutational mechanism in ä, â-thalassaemia consists of a deletion
14. The Philadelphia chromosome **is** a product of a reciprocal translocation
15. Mendel was born in 1820
16. The first Agricultural University in India is PAU, Punjab
17. Sugarcane flowers and sets seed in Shahjahanpur in U.P.
18. IRRI was established in Philippines in 1960
19. Breeding for resistance to major diseases sometimes leads to increased susceptibility to minor diseases
20. Generally, pulses are deficient in lysine
21. Barber is famous for his work on sunflower
22. Dee-geo-woo-gen is a variety of Mexican wheat
23. WTO is located in Geneva
24. White colour tag is used for Foundation seed
25. Foundation seed has the maximum genetic purity of 95%
26. The Central Agricultural University is located at N. Delhi

27. The first artificial plant hybrid was produced by Fairchild in 1717
28. Semi-dwarf wheats were first developed by Swaminathan
29. World's first high yielding dwarf aromatic rice variety is Jasmine
30. Aruna variety of Castor was developed through mutation
31. Triticale is developed from the cross between wheat and rye
32. In India introduction of sugarcane propagules from Fiji is prohibited
33. In 1900, potato moth came in India from Italy
34. Recalcitrant seeds are produced by mango
35. Genetic drift is also called genetic erosion
36. In 1940, bunchy top of banana was inadvertently introduced into India from Malaya
37. The world's collection of coffee germplasm is maintained at Kenya
38. Flag smut of wheat came to India from Mexico
39. Litchi and loquat were introduced into India from China
40. Adventive embryos occur naturally in guava
41. Monoecious condition occurs in the case of coconut
42. Pin x Thrum results in a compatible mating
43. Sporophytic incompatibility is found in *Brassica*
44. In gametophytic system, self-incompatibility is eliminated by double pollination
45. In facultative apomixis, sexual reproduction also occurs along with apomixis
46. In chasmogamy, flowers do not open at all
47. Apomixis can be used for the fixation of heterosis
48. The sporophytic system has been exploited for hybrid production in *Brassica*
49. During transfer of a restorer gene, CMS line is used as the female parent
50. Self incompatibility is easy to use in the production of hybrid seed
51. Genotypic variance cannot be calculated from replicated data
52. The concept of partial diallel was developed by Kempthorne
53. The characters that show continuous variation are qualitative characters
54. When a gene influences the expression of more than one character, it is known as epistasis
55. The gene whose expression is masked by another gene is known as hypostatic
56. Tendency of two genes to be inherited together is known as independent assortment
57. Linkage between two dominant genes is known as coupling phase
58. Standard deviation is the square root of variance
59. Cultivar is the cultivated variety of a plant species
60. Selection is essentially based on genotype of plants
61. Generally, pureline selection is used to maintain the purity of purelines
62. A complex cross is also called a convergent cross
63. Random drift occurs in large populations
64. Most of the oil in maize seed is found in the seed coat
65. The concept of progeny test was developed by Vilmorin
66. Norin 12 has contributed Rht 1 gene for reduced height in wheat
67. Pseudoalleles are present in a complex locus
68. The experimental evidence for the existence of multiple factors was given by East
69. Maleic hydrazide is used as a hybridizing agent in crops
70. Mitomycin C inhibits DNA synthesis
71. Mitomycin C inhibits RNA and protein synthesis

72. Mitomycin C requires NADPH for it to become active
73. In some cases, the type of dominance relationship observed depends on how the phenotype is defined
74. An individual's ABO blood type is normally determined by the inheritance of 1 or 3 possible alleles (A, B, or O) from each parent
75. Human blood types in the ABO blood group are based on a series of enzyme controlled reactions
76. When typing blood a positive reaction helps you deduce what blood type the sample is
77. The person having antigen B on surface of RBC's has blood group B
78. The antigens for ABO and Rh blood groups are present in plasma
79. The serum of a person with B blood group contains anti-A antibodies
80. AB blood group is the universal donor
81. When typing blood a positive reaction shows clumping
82. Bombay phenotype (Oh) individuals do not have anti-O antibodies
83. The formed elements of the blood are suspended in a pale somewhat yellow fluid is known as serum
84. Those proteins that contribute to the viscosity of the blood and help maintain a consistent pH in the blood are known as "globulin" proteins
85. The gamma globulins are well known as "antibody" molecules which are produced in the immune system
86. Red blood cells have no nucleus; instead they are filled with the red pigment "haemoglobin"
87. The red blood cell appears as a biconvex disk
88. When RBC's are suspended in solutions that contain excessive amounts of solute, the cells "swell" in a process called crenation
89. When RBC's are placed in a solution that contains no solute, they tend to burst in a process known as "haemolysis"
90. Red blood cell formation goes on in the red bone marrow by a process called erythropoiesis
91. The haemoglobin molecule consists of "four" chains of polypeptides
92. When carbon monoxide enters red blood cells it binds "weakly" to the haemoglobin molecule
93. I have type AB positive blood. My dad could be type O positive
94. I have type O positive blood. I have A, B, and Rh antibodies
95. Blood type is determined by the antigens
96. Haemoglobin is a protein inside RBC's
97. The most common blood group in USA is O positive
98. The rarest blood group in USA is AB negative
99. White blood cells help the blood clot and the platelets help to fight infections
100. Expressivity depends on penetrance
101. Expressivity may be thought of as a result of different degrees of function of the protein encoded by the gene
102. Epistasis is the interaction between two genes producing a new phenotype
103. Epistasis can produce a ratio of 12:3:1
104. If you cross two different strains of white flower you may get a purple flower in a sweet pea plant
105. Lethal alleles can only be recessive
106. Dominant lethal alleles are quickly removed from the pool while the recessive ones remain

4

Microscopy

MULTIPLE-CHOICE QUESTIONS

MULTIPLE CHOICE QUESTIONS

1. **Which of the following microscopic methods has the greatest magnification?**
   (a) Single lens simple video microscopy
   (b) Phase-contrast microscopy
   (c) Scanning electron microscopy
   (d) Fluorescence microscopy
   (e) Dark field microscopy
2. **Which of the following can be viewed only by electron microscopy?**
   (a) Viruses (b) Bacteria
   (c) Nuclei (d) Mitochondria
   (e) Frog eggs
3. **Which type of microscopy has the greatest resolving power?**
   (a) Fluorescence
   (b) Phase-contrast
   (c) Electron
   (d) Confocal scanning
   (e) Digital video
4. **Which microscope can magnify objects hundreds of thousands of times?**
   (a) Electron microscope
   (b) Stereoscopic microscope
   (c) Compound microscope
   (d) Phase-contrast microscope
5. **Which has lenses that are not made of glass?**
   (a) Electron microscope
   (b) Compound microscope
   (c) Hand lens
   (d) Stereoscopic microscope
6. **Which device regulates the amount of light entering a microscope?**
   (a) Nosepiece (b) Eyepiece
   (c) Body tube (d) Diaphragm
7. **The part of the microscope that contains the objectives is the**
   (a) eyepiece (b) nosepiece
   (c) stage (d) ocular

8. Which is the part of the microscope you look into?

(a) Ocular (b) Nosepiece
(c) Body tube (d) Diaphragm

9. Which of the following is true of a nanometer?

(a) A nanometer is one millionth of a millimeter
(b) A nanometer is one millionth of a meter
(c) A nanometer is about the size of a common bacterial cell
(d) The nanometer is the most common measurement used in measuring whole cells
(e) None of the above

10. Which of the following is closest to a micrometer in size?

(a) The length of a gene
(b) The width of a mRNA molecule
(c) A human erythrocyte
(d) *E. coli*
(e) Tubulin protofilaments

11. The limit of resolution can best be defined as

(a) twice the wavelength of light
(b) the distance that an object must be moved to be distinguished from its background
(c) the distance that two objects must be apart in order to be distinguished as separate objects
(d) the solvent that must be available to remix a solution
(e) all of the above

12. Which of the following is not true of electron microscopy (EM)?

(a) It can be used to examine the movement of flagella
(b) The limit of resolution for EM is about 0.1-0.2 nm
(c) It came to be used extensively in the early 1950's
(d) It uses heavy metals as stains
(e) Electrons replace light in the electron microscope

13. Scanning electron microscopy (SEM) is especially suited

(a) to creat a sense of depth
(b) to examine internal cellular structure
(c) to observe living specimens
(d) both (a) and (c)
(e) choices (a), (b), and (c)

14. In a photomicrograph that had been magnified 3500 times, an organelle measured 12 mm. What was the actual length?

(a) 3.4 μm (b) 34 μm
(c) 420 μm (d) 0.42 μm
(e) 0.042 μm

15. Cell objects smaller than 0.2 μm can be observed

(a) by naked eyes
(b) by an optic microscope
(c) by an electron microscope
(d) by a proton microscope

16. Which of the following will most likely give the best 3-D resolution of a weed pollen grain?

(a) Bright-field microscope
(b) Scanning electron microscope
(c) Dark field microscope
(d) Transmission electron microscope

17. In a light microscope, light rays are focused by glass

(a) mirrors (b) prisms
(c) lenses (d) spheres

18. To focus the beam of electrons, an electron microscope uses

(a) lenses (b) electrons
(c) lasers (d) electromagnets

19. In which electron microscope the electrons pass through the specimen?

(a) Transmission (b) Scanning
(c) Light (d) Optical

20. In which electron microscope the electron beam is passed back and forth across the surface of the specimen?

(a) Transmission (b) Light
(c) Scanning (d) Optical

21. The images formed by the electron microscope are called

(a) photoelectron micrograph
(b) SEM
(c) photomicrograph
(d) photograph

22. The ability to distinguish between two objects as separate items is referred to as

(a) magnifying power of the microscope
(b) distinguishing power of the microscope
(c) focusing power of the microscope
(d) resolving power of the microscope

23. The actual size of an object that appears to be 5 cm when it is magnified 1000 times is

(a) 5 cm (b) 50 nm
(c) 5 μm (d) 50 μm

24. An object that is actually 30 nm long appears to be 90 μm when magnified

(a) 30 times (b) 3000 times
(c) 5000 times (d) 300 times

25. Of the following, which instrument is most commonly used to observe the external features of a grasshopper's abdomen?

(a) Ultracentrifuge
(b) Microdissection instrument
(c) Dissecting microscope
(d) Electron microscope

26. To study the structure of phloem and xylem tissue, a student could prepare and observe sections using a/an

(a) microscope
(b) centrifuge
(c) incubator
(d) triple beam balance

27. A student observed a *Paramecium* under the low power objective of a microscope (100 X) and then under high power (400 X). The image of the *Paramecium* under low power, compared to the image of the same *Paramecium* under high power, would be

(a) smaller and in a darker field of view
(b) smaller and in a brighter field of view
(c) larger and in a darker field of view
(d) larger and in a brighter field of view

28. Of the following microscopes, which one can resolve the smallest objects?

(a) Brightfield
(b) Phase-contrast
(c) Darkfield
(d) Transmission electron microscope

29. A microscope with a 10 X ocular lens and a 43 X objective lens would yield a magnification of what power?

(a) 43 (b) 430
(c) 10 (d) 4300

30. Why are virtually all microbiological dyes known as basic dyes?

(a) Because the basic nature of the molecule is needed for the molecule to penetrate the cell wall
(b) Because the bacterial cell has an excess of negatively charged groups and basic dyes contain positively charged ionizable groups
(c) Because basic dyes are needed to neutralize the amino and nucleic acids
(d) Because no other types of dye will bind to the capsule of the cell

31. Which stain would be the best to make the structures of cheek epithelial cells easier to observe?

(a) Iodine (b) Methyl red
(c) Phenolphthalein (d) Methylene blue

32. The use of immersion oil makes it possible to increase quantitatively which of the following?

(a) Wavelength of light
(b) Size of the real image
(c) Resolving power
(d) Numerical aperture

33. The electron microscope has been particularly useful in studying bacteria, because

(a) electrons can penetrate tough bacterial cell walls
(b) bacteria are so small
(c) bacteria move so quickly that they are hard to photograph
(d) with few organelles present, bacteria are distinguished by differences in individual macromolecules

34. Roshni would like to film the movement of chromosomes during cell division. Her best choice for a microscope would be a

(a) light microscope, because of its resolving power
(b) transmission electron microscope, because of its magnifying power
(c) scanning electron microscope, because the specimen is alive
(d) transmission electron microscope, because of its great resolving power
(e) light microscope, because the specimen is alive

35. Some human cells divide approximately every 24 hours. You do some experiments to show that the G_1 and S phases take up half of the cycle time. Further microscopic observations demonstrate that the mitotic phase is one hour long. How long does the post-synthesis "gap" take in this case?

(a) 1 hour (b) 6 hours
(c) 9 hours (d) 11 hours
(e) 23 hours

36. Which of the following will give the best 3-D resolution of a live protozoan?

(a) Bright field microscopy
(b) Scanning electron microscopy
(c) Normarsky microscopy
(d) Transmission electron microscopy

37. Circle of least confusion is most directly associated with what lens aberration?

(a) Spherical aberration
(b) Coma
(c) Astigmatism
(d) Curvature of field

38. A camera gives a life-size picture of a flower when the lens is 20 cm from the film. What should be the distance between lens and the film to photograph a flock of birds high overhead?

(a) 10 cm (b) 20 cm
(c) 5 cm (d) 40 cm

39. If 30 eyepiece divisions on the ocular micrometer = 0.70 μm in the stage micrometer, what is 1 eyepiece division in μm?

(a) 2.300 μm (b) 23.000 μm
(c) 0.023 μm (d) 42.800 μm
(e) 4.280 μm

40. A cell was observed under a microscope using a 10 X ocular lens and a 40 X objective lens. The cells appeared to have a width of 24 mm. If the same ocular lens but a 10 X objective lens was used, what would be the width of the cells?

(a) 96 mm (b) 24 mm
(c) 6 mm (d) 12 mm

41. Which of the following types of optics would provide the greatest contrast and best reveal the sub-cellular structural detail for observing the bacterial cell?

(a) Bright field (b) Dark field
(c) Phase-contrast (d) Fluorescence

42. When the oil-immersion lens is used

(a) light rays are scattered, so unnecessary background material is not seen
(b) light rays are concentrated by minimizing refraction to increase clarity
(c) objects are held in place on the microscopic slide
(d) magnification of the objects is increased about ten-fold

43. The best type of microscopy to detect motility is

(a) phase-contrast
(b) bright field
(c) confocal laser scanning microscopy
(d) differential interference contrast

44. In magnetotactic bacteria, magnetite forms intracellular inclusion bodies. The best type of microscopy to observe the magnetite inclusions might be

(a) differential interference contrast (DIC)
(b) phase-contrast
(c) scanning electron microscopy
(d) confocal laser scanning microscopy

45. In considering the instrumentation for cytofluorimetry (flow cytometry) and FACS, which of the following is true?

(a) The stream of solution containing cells is passed through a capillary tube of 20 micrometers diameter in order to get cells passing the detector one at a time
(b) If one needs to perform 5 colour fluorescence analyses, one must have an instrument which has 5 lasers
(c) Side scattered light is detected at right angles to the incident laser light and at right angles to the stream of cells
(d) In FACS, droplets containing cells are deflected into tubes by a magnetic field applied across the stream of droplets

46. To investigate the internal structure of a cell by transmission electron microscope, the sample should be prepared using one of the following techniques

(a) ultramicrotomy and ultra thin sectioning
(b) ultramicrotomy and semi-sectioning
(c) paraffin or cryostat sectioning
(d) ion-beam milling

47. Refraction in a compound light microscope is minimized by which one of the following?

(a) Achromatic objective lenses
(b) Use of immersion oil
(c) Numerical aperture of the objective lens used
(d) Simple staining of the bacterial smear

48. The ability to see fine detail (resolution) would be best (i.e., smallest numerical value of R) under which one of the following sets of conditions?

(a) Shortest wavelength of illumination and smallest numerical aperture
(b) Shortest wavelength of illumination and largest numerical aperture
(c) Longest wavelength of illumination and smallest numerical aperture
(d) Longest wavelength of illumination and largest numerical aperture

49. The position of the focal point of the light coming from the light source relative to the position of the specimen is controlled by which one of the following parts of a compound light microscope?

(a) Iris diaphragm (b) Fine focusing knob
(c) Abbe condensor (d) Stage micrometer

50. Although he did not produce the first microscope, which one of the following persons is given the most credit for refining microscope lenses to such a quality that he was the first to visualize "microorganisms"?

(a) Kepler (b) Galileo
(c) Hooke (d) van Leeuwenhoek

51. Resolution by any microscope is ultimately limited by the

(a) curvature of the lenses
(b) wavelength of the light
(c) light intensity
(d) lens aberrations

52. Assuming all other factors to be the same, electron microscopes have greater resolving power than light microscopes because

(a) the wavelength of electrons is much longer than the wavelength of visible light
(b) electron microscopes have more lenses
(c) because the beams in electron microscopes overlap creating a clearer picture
(d) because the wavelengths in visible light are longer than with electrons
(e) because electron microscopes are compound microscopes

53. When the power of ocular lens is 10 X, the magnification is

(a) 30 times (b) 20 times
(c) 200 times (d) 2000 times

54. Which of the following light is suitable for getting maximum resolution?

(a) Red (b) Green
(c) Blue (d) Orange

55. All the following are components of compound microscope except

(a) stage clips (b) fine adjustment
(c) electron gun (d) binocular eyepiece

56. Resolving power of an instrument can be increased by

(a) using an illumination of longer wavelength and by decreasing the NA
(b) using an illumination of longer wavelength and by increasing the NA
(c) using an illumination of shorter wavelength and by increasing the NA
(d) using an illumination of shorter wavelength and by decreasing the NA

57. Which of the following is best suited to get the surface view of an object?

(a) SEM (b) TEM
(c) Both (a) and (b)
(d) Compound microscope

58. The resolving power of unaided human eye is

(a) 1 cm (b) 100 micrometre
(c) 200 nanometre (d) 400 nanometre

59. Which of the following is used to visualize live cells?

(a) SEM
(b) TEM
(c) Phase contrast microscope
(d) All of these

60. The refractive index of air is

(a) 0.50 (b) 0.75
(c) 1.00 (d) 1.25

61. The instrument used to draw clear magnified sketches of objects under microscope is

(a) compound microscope
(b) light microscope
(c) camera lucida
(d) camera attached stereomicroscope

62. Which of the following is true of dark field microscopy?

(a) Adding disc called 'stop' to the condenser will make bright field to dark field
(b) The stop disc prevents the entry of light from the central field and object is illuminated with beam of light
(c) The light gets reflected from the sides of the specimen and appears bright in dark background
(d) All of these

63. Which of the following can produce a virtual image which is always smaller than the object?

(a) A plane mirror (b) A convex lens
(c) A concave lens (d) A concave mirror

64. Which part of the compound microscope helps in gathering and focusing light rays on the specimen to be viewed?

(a) Eyepiece lens (b) Objective lens
(c) Condenser lens (d) Magnifying lens

65. What is the minimum distance for the eye to focus on any object?

(a) 11 cm (b) 25 cm
(c) 32 cm (d) 42 cm

66. Resolving power of a microscope is a function of

(a) wavelength of the light used
(b) numerical aperture of the lens system
(c) refractive index
(d) wavelength of light used and numerical aperture of lens system

67. The greatest resolution in light microscopy can be obtained with

(a) longest wavelength of visible light used
(b) an objective with minimum numerical aperture
(c) shortest wavelength of visible light used
(d) shortest wavelength of visible light used and an objective with the maximum numerical aperture

68. Oil immersion objective lens has an NA value of

(a) 0.65 (b) 0.85
(c) 1.33 (d) 1.00

69. In fluorescence microscopy, which of the following performs the function of removing all light except the blue light?

(a) Exciter filter (b) Barrier filter
(c) Dichroic mirror (d) Mercury arc lamp

70. Total magnification is obtained by

(a) magnifying power of the objective lens
(b) magnifying power of the eyepiece
(c) magnifying power of the condenser lens
(d) magnifying power of both the objective lens and eyepiece

71. In light microscopy, which of the following is used as a fixative prior to staining technique?

(a) Osmic acid (b) Glutaraldehyde
(c) Heat
(d) Osmic acid, glutaraldehyde, heat

72. In phase contrast microscopy, the rate at which light enters through the objects is

(a) constant
(b) inversely proportional to their refractive indices
(c) directly proportional to their refractive indices
(d) exponentially related to their refractive indices

73. Which part of the light microscope controls the intensity of light entering the viewing area?

(a) Coarse adjustment screw
(b) Fine adjustment screw
(c) Diaphragm
(d) Condenser lens

74. What would you see using a dark-field microscope on bacteria that transmit light without reflecting it into the objective lens?

(a) Dark bacteria on a bright background
(b) Bright bacteria on a bright background
(c) Bright bacteria on a dark background
(d) Fluorescent bacteria on a dark background

75. How does ultraviolet light microscopy use fluorescence to make images?

(a) Objects absorb invisible UV light and emit visible light to make images
(b) Objects absorb invisible UV light and emit nothing
(c) Objects transmit UV light without absorbing it
(d) Objects fluoresce only when visible light strikes them

76. If you wish to change an immunofluorescence stain so it stains a different type of microorganism than it did before, what would you do?

(a) Use a different type of microscope
(b) Switch from epifluorescence to transmitted fluorescence
(c) Change the dye from a fluorescent to a non-fluorescent dye
(d) Change to a different type of fluorescent dye

77. Scanning electron microscopy is most often used to reveal

(a) surface structures
(b) Internal structures
(c) both surface and internal structures simultaneously
(d) either surface or internal structures, but not simultaneously

78. You were given a specimen of an active, motile microorganism, which of the following types of microscopy would be most effecting in visualizing the live microbe?

(a) Bright-field microscopy
(b) Dark-field microscopy
(c) Fluorescence microscopy
(d) Phase-contrast microscopy

79. The instrument that produces a bright image of the specimen against a dark background is called a (n) ______ microscope

(a) phase-contrast (b) transmission
(c) scanning electron (d) dark field

80. The microscope that exposes specimens to UV and forms an image with the resulting light emitted at a different wavelength is called a ______ microscope

(a) phase-contrast
(b) dark-field
(c) scanning electron
(d) transmission electron

81. Which of the microscopes given below forms images in visible light?

(a) Bright-field (b) Dark-field
(c) Fluorescence (d) (a) and (b)

82. What do phase-contrast and dark-field microscopes have in common?

(a) They increase contrast between the specimen and their surroundings without staining
(b) They make specimens appear bright on a dark background
(c) They make specimens fluorescence
(d) They make specimens visible that refract light away from the objective

83. Which of the following microscopes is usually good for use on unstained specimens?

(a) Phase-contrast (b) Flourescence
(c) Bright-field (d) Scanning electron

MARK TRUE OR FALSE (T/F)

1. The microscopes of van Leeuwenhoek were compound microscopes
2. Microscopes can enlarge the image of large objects
3. The naked eye is able to distinguish between two points 0.1 cm apart
4. Resolving power of a microscope and its limit of resolution are same
5. The objective lens in a microscope produces a magnified real image
6. An eyepiece in a microscope produces a magnified virtual image
7. An eyepiece in a microscope has the resolving power
8. Parfocal microscope means that the focus does not change when the objective is changed
9. While using a microscope, eyeglasses need not be worn unless one has severe astigmatism
10. A lens is a glass with two curved surfaces
11. A double convex lens is a diverging lens

12. Chromatic aberration in a lens is very difficult to correct
13. When spherical aberration is present in a lens, the image may be fuzzy
14. Numerical aperture of a microscope increases with magnification
15. Greater magnification improves the quality of the final image
16. Numerical aperture is normally increased by decreasing the focal length
17. As the numerical aperture increases, the working distance decreases
18. The depth of field increases sharply with increasing numerical aperture
19. The image formed by the lens is known as a real image if it can be focused on a screen
20. A virtual image is inverted
21. Resolving power of a microscope is the minimum distance between two points in order that they may be discriminated as such
22. As the limit of resolution increases, the resolving power decreases
23. The limit of resolution of human eye is about 1000 microns
24. Human eye is most sensitive to green light
25. For phase-contrast microscopy, the samples should be absorbent
26. Iris diaphragm is not an optical part of the microscope
27. All modern microscopes are parfocal and parcentral
28. Oil immersion lens should be wiped clean with chemicals
29. Parcentral indicates that the center of the field does not change when the objective is changed
30. Always use the coarse adjustment when you are using the high power lens
31. One should look through the monocular microscope with both the eyes open
32. When lenses fail to bring all rays from a given point on an object to a unique focus, it is called an aberration
33. Refraction is the change of direction of a ray of light while passing obliquely from one medium into another in which the speed of transmission differs
34. The limit of resolution of a light microscope is 1.0 microns
35. Wavelength of infrared radiation is less than white light
36. The ocular micrometer is used to calibrate the stage micrometer
37. Dark-field microscopy is used to study details of the structure of aquatic organisms such as protozoa and small crustaceans
38. In phase-contrast microscopy, the differences in transmission and phase can be converted into intensity differences
39. Electromagnetic theory considers light to be associated with variations in electric and magnetic fields
40. In a phase-contrast microscope, the amplitude of light is related to colour intensity
41. In a phase-contrast microscope, if the two light waves are completely in phase, less light is seen
42. In the above microscopy, if the two waves are out of phase, nothing is seen
43. The principle behind phase-contrast microscopy lies in further retardation of indirect waves
44. In phase-contrast microscopy, the sample should be absorbent
45. Collagen and chlorophyll show natural fluorescence
46. Fluorescent dyes have been used for the investigation of chromosome behavior with the fluorescent microscope

47. Acridine orange gives a green fluorescence with RNA
48. It is possible to visualize yeast DNA with fluorescence microscopy
49. Interference microscope is more versatile than the phase-contrast microscope
50. By the use of interference microscope, it is possible to measure the dry weight of the object
51. Polarizing microscopy is used for analyzing indirectly the mitotic spindle
52. Resolution of the transmission electron microscope is poorer than that of the scanning electron microscope
53. Electron microscopes can normally examine only dried specimens
54. Transmission electron microscope is monochromatic
55. The earliest and simplest microscope was the magnifying glass
56. Of the different types of microscopes available for scientific use only the polarizing microscope is not applicable for the examination of forensic specimens
57. The mechanical system of a microscope is composed of six parts
58. Most forensic work will require a 10 × eyepiece with a 4 ×, 10 ×, 20 ×, or 45 × objective
59. The magnification of a microscope with a 10 × eyepiece and a 10 × objective will be 1000 ×
60. The polarizing microscope is best used for forensic microscopy requiring a side-by side comparison
61. The stereomicroscope is the most frequently used and versatile microscope found in the crime laboratory
62. Light that is confined to a single plane of vibration is said to be plain-polarized and requires special means to detect it
63. With the development of the scanning electron microscope, a forensic analyst can view a particle under a microscope while at the absorption spectrum
64. Low power shows more area than high power
65. When moving the slide towards the left, the objects viewed through the microscope will move towards the left
66. There is less depth of focus under high power compared to observing under low power
67. The diaphragm is used to adjust the amount of light entering the microscope
68. All objects in different depths appear in focus at the same time
69. High power has more detail than low power
70. Objects viewed under the microscope appear upside down and inverted
71. Observers see about ten times more width under low power than under high power

5

Cell and Cell Structure

MULTIPLE-CHOICE QUESTIONS

1. **A reproductive cell capable of forming a new individual by itself is a**
   (a) zygote (b) gamete
   (c) sporangium (d) spore
   (e) none of these

2. **Eukaryotic cells can be distinguished from prokaryotic cells, because**
   (a) only prokaryotic cells are motile
   (b) only eukaryotic cells oxidize organic molecules under aerobic conditions
   (c) only eukaryotic cells have a nuclear envelope
   (d) only eukaryotic cells have a mechanism for exchanging genetic information
   (e) none of the above

3. **The gram stain classifies bacteria on the basis of their**
   (a) motility
   (b) cell wall structure
   (c) ribosomal structure
   (d) ability to transfer genes among one another
   (e) possession of spores

4. **Which of the following organelles contains the enzymes needed to synthesize ATP in the presence of oxygen?**
   (a) Mitochondria
   (b) Golgi body
   (c) Endoplasmic reticulum
   (d) Nucleus

5. **Which structure includes all of the others?**
   (a) Nucleolus (b) Nucleus
   (c) Chromosomes (d) Genes

6. **Most cell membranes are composed principally of**
   (a) DNA and ATP
   (b) proteins and lipids
   (c) chitin and starch
   (d) nucleotides and amino acids

7. **Which structure is usually present only in animal cells?**
   (a) Vacuole (b) Cell wall
   (c) Nucleus (d) Centriole

8. Normally, in the process of osmosis, the net flow of water molecules into or out of the cell depends upon differences in the

(a) concentration of water molecules inside and outside the cell
(b) concentration of enzymes on either side of the cell membrane
(c) rate of molecular motion on either side of the cell membrane
(d) rate of movement of insoluble molecules inside the cell

9. Sodium ions are "pumped" from a region of lower concentration to a region of higher concentration in the nerve cells of humans. This process is an example of

(a) diffusion (b) passive transport
(c) osmosis (d) active transport

10. Endoplasmic reticulum (ER) consists of flattened sacs called

(a) ribosomes (b) cisternae
(c) golgi apparatus (d) vesicles

11. Which of the following endoplasmic reticulum has ribosomes on its surface?

(a) Smooth (b) Hard
(c) Rough (d) Soft

12. Which of the following endoplasmic reticulum does not have ribosomes on its surface?

(a) Soft (b) Smooth
(c) Hard (d) Rough

13. The ribosomes of eukaryotic cells are known as the

(a) 80 S type (b) 8 S type
(c) 800 S type (d) 80 N type

14. The ribosomes of eukaryotic cells are important in

(a) exocytosis (b) autolysis
(c) protein synthesis (d) transport

15. Glycoproteins are formed in the

(a) ribosomes
(b) golgi apparatus
(c) endoplasmic reticulum
(d) mitochondria

16. Potentially harmful enzymes are isolated within

(a) ribosomes (b) vesicles
(c) cisternae (d) lysosomes

17. Of the following features, which is characteristic of prokaryotic cells?

(a) Circular DNA
(b) Endoplasmic reticulum
(c) Mitochondria
(d) Nucleolus

18. The organelles involved in enzyme synthesis are

(a) smooth ER (b) ribosomes
(c) lysosomes (d) golgi bodies

19. A typical differential centrifugation run would yield organelle fractions in the following order

(a) nuclear fraction → mitochondrial fraction → microsomal fraction
(b) microsomal fraction → mitochondrial fraction → nuclear fraction
(c) mitochondrial fraction → nuclear fraction → microsomal fraction
(d) microsomal fraction → nuclear fraction → mitochondrial fraction

20. In a plasma membrane, which of the following provides a general barrier to the movement of molecules?

(a) Lipids (b) Proteins
(c) Carbohydrates (d) All of these

21. Lichens are composed of

(a) algae and bacteria (b) algae and moss
(c) algae and fungi (d) moss and fungi

22. While studying a cell with an electron microscope, a scientist notes the following: numerous ribosomes, a well-developed endoplasmic reticulum, chloroplasts, and a cell wall. Which of the following could be the source of this cell?

(a) A fungus (b) An animal
(c) A bacteriumd) A virus
(e) A plant

23. A cell has a defect that results in the loss of its ability to regulate the passage of water, food and wastes into and out of the cell. In which of the following cell structures is this defect most likely to be located?

(a) Ribosomes
(b) Chloroplasts
(c) Cell membrane
(d) Endoplasmic reticulum

24. Homologous chromosomes are not necessarily identical in their

(a) overall size
(b) centromere placement
(c) arm ratio
(d) placement of genes
(e) alleles

25. Every nucleus in a eukaryotic organism contains the same amount of DNA, with the exception of nuclei in the

(a) epidermal cells (b) muscle cells
(c) gametes (d) neurons
(e) fibroblasts

26. All of the following are cellular organelles in a eukaryotic cell except the

(a) mitochondria
(b) endoplasmic reticulum
(c) plasma membrane
(d) nucleus

27. The haploid chromosome number of the horse is n=16. How many autosomes are there in the zygote?

(a) 14 (b) 15
(c) 16 (d) 30

28. Nucleoplasm is also called

(a) karyolimph (b) karyoplasm
(c) a and b above (d) none of these

29. According to the Denver Classification, a chromosome with its centromere located very close to, but not on the end of the chromosome is

(a) telocentric (b) acrocentric
(c) metacentric (d) subcentric
(e) submetacentric

30. In the diagram below, the acrocentric chromosome is

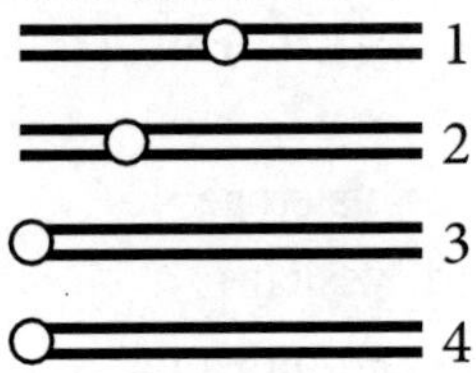

(a) chromosome 1
(b) chromosome 2
(c) chromosome 3
(d) chromosome 4
(e) none of those shown

31. To enter or leave a cell, substances must pass through

(a) a microtubule (b) the golgi apparatus
(c) a ribosome (d) the nucleus
(e) the plasma membrane

32. Bacterial cells are prokaryotic; in comparison to a typical eukaryotic cell, they would

(a) be smaller
(b) have a smaller nucleus
(c) lack a plasma membrane
(d) have fewer internal membranous compartments
(e) have a greater variety of organelles

33. You would expect a cell with an extensive golgi apparatus to

(a) make a lot of ATP
(b) secrete a lot of material
(c) move actively
(d) perform photosynthesis
(e) store large quantities of food

34. Which of the following correctly matches an organelle with its function?

(a) Mitochondrion . . . photosynthesis
(b) Nucleus . . . cellular respiration
(c) Ribosome . . . manufacture of lipids
(d) Lysosome . . . movement
(e) Central vacuole . . . storage

35. Of the following organelles, which group is involved in manufacturing substances needed by the cell?

(a) Lysosome, vacuole, ribosome
(b) Ribosome, rough ER, smooth ER
(c) Vacuole, rough ER, smooth ER
(d) Smooth ER, ribosome, vacuole
(e) Rough ER, lysosome, vacuole

36. A cell has mitochondria, ribosomes, smooth and rough ER, and other parts. Based on this information, it could not be

(a) a cell from a pine tree
(b) a grasshopper cell
(c) a yeast (fungus) cell
(d) a bacterium
(e) actually, it could be any of the above
(f) their organelles are small and tightly packed together

37. Cell fractionation is the most appropriate procedure for preparing ______ for study

(a) isolated cells which are normally found tightly attached to neighbouring cells
(b) cells without a functional cytoskeleton
(c) isolated organelles
(d) the basic macromolecules
(e) bone and other similar cells which are situated within a mineral framework

38. Which of the following clues would tell you whether a cell is prokaryotic or eukaryotic?

(a) The presence or absence of a rigid cell wall
(b) Whether or not the cell is partitioned by internal membranes
(c) The presence or absence of ribosomes
(d) Whether or not the cell carries out cellular metabolism
(e) Whether or not the cell contains DNA

39. The glycosidic linkage present in the xylan is

(a) α $(1 \rightarrow 4)$ (b) β $(1 \rightarrow 4)$
(c) β $(1 \rightarrow 3)$ (d) β $(1 \rightarrow 3)$

40. Para crystalline cortex of microfibrils contains

(a) hemicellulose (b) glucose
(c) cellulose
(d) cellulose and hemicellulose

41. Genes are present in

(a) chromosomes (b) peroxisomes
(c) ribosomes (d) glyoxysomes

42. Type of structural proteins found in the cell wall is

(a) nucleoprotein (b) glycoprotein
(c) enzymes (d) chromoprotein

43. The organelle found only in plant cell is

(a) peroxisomes (b) mitochondria
(c) glyoxisomes (d) microtubules

44. The cell was first discovered by

(a) Robert Hooke (b) Flemming
(c) Lamarck (d) Johannsen

45. Plastids are absent in

(a) bacteria (b) viruses
(c) animals (d) all of the above

46. In green plants, photosynthesis takes place in

(a) leucoplasts (b) chloroplasts
(c) chromoplasts (d) all of these

47. The seat of control of the cell is

(a) mitochondria (b) chloroplasts
(c) nucleus (d) all of the above

48. Mitochondria are the sites of oxidation of

(a) lipids (b) proteins
(c) carbohydrates (d) all of the above

49. Endoplasmic reticulum is associated with the synthesis of

(a) glycogen (b) lipids
(c) protein (d) all of the above

50. Digestive enzymes of the cell are present in

(a) nucleolus b) ribosomes
(c) lysosomes d) none of the above

51. In a cell, packaging of food materials takes place in

(a) chloroplasts (b) golgi bodies
(c) mitochondria (d) nucleolus

52. Lysosomes originate from

(a) nucleolus (b) chromosomes
(c) Golgi bodies (d) ribosomes

53. Pinching in of fluids by a unicellular organism is the process called

(a) phagocytosis (b) osmosis
(c) pinocytosis (d) exocytosis
(e) facilitated diffusion

54. Which is true of eukaryotic cells?

(a) Evolved more recently than prokaryotic cells
(b) They lack membrane bound organelles
(c) Lack a nuclear membrane
(d) Lack DNA

55. What is the function of chloroplasts?

(a) Protein synthesis (b) Photosynthesis
(c) Respiration (d) Movement

56. Which structure is found only in plant cells or algae?

(a) Endoplasmic reticulum
(b) Mitochondria (c) Nucleus
(d) Lysosome (e) Plastid

57. Cilia and flagella are most similar in structure to

(a) basal bodies (b) ribosomes
(c) mitochondria (d) chloroplasts
(e) endoplasmic reticulum

58. Which organelle sometimes merges with food vacuoles and functions in chemical hydrolysis?

(a) Lysosomes (b) Chloroplasts
(c) Nucleus (d) Mitochondria
(e) Ribosomes

59. A structure commonly found in animal cells, but rarely in plant cells is the

(a) golgi apparatus (b) centriole
(c) nucleus (d) mitochondria
(e) endoplasmic reticulum

60. Which cell organelle contains the chromosomes?

(a) Golgi apparatus (b) Nucleus
(c) Lysosome (d) Mitochondria

61. Certain types of lymphocytes (white blood cells) in the lymph nodes ingest bacteria and debris. This function most likely occurs by

(a) exocytosis (b) passive transport
(c) phagocytosis (d) pinocytosis
(e) facilitated transport

62. Which cell structure is known as the power house of the cell?

(a) Nucleus
(b) Mitochondria
(c) Vacuole
(d) Endoplasmic reticulum

63. In plants, the plastids which store lipids are called

(a) leucoplasts (b) scale scars
(c) golgi bodies (d) chloroplasts
(e) chromoplasts

64. According to the fluid mosaic model of the plasma membrane, proteins are

(a) spread out in a continuous layer over both membrane surfaces
(b) located in the hydrophilic area of the membrane
(c) oriented in a random manner throughout the membrane
(d) embedded in the lipid bilayers
(e) capable of leaving the membrane and dissolving in the solution of the external environment

65. Use the information below and your knowledge of biology to answer the following two questions, which follow the reading passage.

Each student in a biology laboratory received two solutions. One solution was distilled water. The other was a salt solution with concentrations of salts slightly greater than that of a living cell. The solutions were labeled X and Y, respectively. The students were instructed to place some fresh-water protozoans in each of the solutions and to identify the solutions on the basis of their observations. The protozoans in solution X shriveled. Those in solution Y swelled up and burst. These results indicate that

(a) solution X was salt water
(b) solution Y contained killer protozoans
(c) solution Y was salt water
(d) solution X was distilled water
(e) solution X was tap water

66. In the above example, the protozoans in solution X shriveled because

(a) an antagonistic substance was placed into the solution
(b) their membranes were more permeable to the passage of water than the organisms in Y
(c) osmotic pressure failed to operate
(d) a disproportionate amount of water diffused from the protozoans
(e) golgi bodies in the test organisms lost their function

67. Which structure is chiefly responsible for the rigidity of the plant cell?

(a) Cell membrane (b) Cell wall
(c) Nucleolus (d) Nucleus

68. In pond water, protozoans pump out excess water by means of their

(a) pellicle (b) trichocyst
(c) cell membrane (d) contractile vacuole
(e) pseudopodia

69. Which is a major function of the mitochondria?

(a) Assembling proteins such as enzymes
(b) Carrying out respiratory activity
(c) Duplicating the chromosomes needed for cell division
(d) Absorbing light in photosynthesis
(e) All of the above are major functions

70. Which is involved directly in synthesis of proteins as well as transport within the cell?

(a) Ribosomes
(b) Golgi bodies
(c) Rough endoplasmic reticulum
(d) Smooth endoplasmic reticulum
(e) Vacuoles

71. A dominant organelle in cells heavily involved in lipid synthesis is the

(a) ribosome
(b) lysosome
(c) smooth endoplasmic reticulum
(d) mitochondria
(e) contractile vacuole

72. The golgi apparatus would be most prominent in cells that

(a) do not divide
(b) are biggest in size
(c) contain no mitochondria
(d) actively secrete substances
(e) none of the above

73. A gland cell capable of producing large quantities of protein hormone would most likely have well developed

(a) cilia
(b) centrioles
(c) rough endoplasmic reticulum
(d) smooth endoplasmic reticulum
(e) lysosomes

74. Which substance would normally have the least difficulty crossing a cell membrane?

(a) Water (b) Protein
(c) Carbohydrate (d) Salt
(e) There would be little difference in any of the above

75. Which process requires the chemical energy of the cell?

(a) Diffusion (b) Facilitated diffusion
(c) Osmosis (d) Bulk flow
(e) None of the previous

76. Normally, the cytoplasm of the cell does not contain

(a) chloroplasts (b) mitochondria
(c) ribosomes (d) lysosomes
(e) chromosomes

77. A cell membrane is

(a) permeable (b) semi-permeable
(c) impermeable (d) none of these

78. Which organelle is responsible for the master control of the cell?

(a) Mitochondria (b) Ribosome
(c) Golgi apparatus (d) Nucleus

79. Which of the following are not components of the cell membrane?

(a) Cell surface markers
(b) Transmembrane proteins
(c) Interior protein network
(d) Plasmodesmata

80. To cross the cell membrane, water must

(a) squeeze between phospholipid molecules
(b) pass through aquaporins
(c) be transported at the expense of ATP
(d) be moved by a cotransport system

81. If a cell's contents are greatly hypoosmotic to the surrounding environment, the cell will probably

(a) expand (b) become isotonic
(c) burst (d) shrivel

82. Exocytosis is a process by cells which

(a) pass substances out of the cell in vesicles
(b) pass substances out of the cell through the membrane by osmosis
(c) release substances directly into the extracellular fluid through a pore
(d) release substances directly into the extracellular fluid through a pit
(e) identify substances in the environment

83. Clathrin-coated pits are used to

(a) extrude bulk fluids from the cell
(b) allow desired molecules directly into the cytoplasm
(c) pass wastes in vesicles to the outside.
(d) pass information into adjacent cells
(e) bring desired substances from the environment into the cell in vesicles

84. A lipid bilayer

(a) permits water-soluble molecules to pass through it
(b) facilitates the passage of water-soluble molecules through it
(c) inhibits the passage of water-soluble substances through it
(d) actively transports water-soluble molecules through it
(e) is indifferent to the passage of water molecules through it

85. A cell is recognized by other tissue members as "self" by its surface

(a) glycolipids (b) phosphate groups
(c) glycoproteins (d) ketoglutaric acids
(e) glycocarbohydrates

86. A cell engaged in phagocytosis must be

(a) engulfing a live organism
(b) acquiring a liquid
(c) engulfing a dead organism
(d) transporting bulk dissolved nutrients
(e) transporting bulk solid material

87. A, B, and O blood groups are marked by surface

(a) glycoproteins (b) glycolipids
(c) glycocarbohydrates (d) glycerol
(e) gluterates

88. Threonine, an amino acid, and arabinose, a monosaccharidem, cross the cell membrane down their concentration gradients by

(a) diffusion (b) endocytosis
(c) phosphorylation (d) facilitated diffusion
(e) osmosis

89. A contractile vacuole is an organelle that pumps excess water out of many freshwater protozoan cells. A freshwater protozoan was placed in solution A and observed to form contractile vacuoles at a rate of 10 per minute. The same protozoan was then placed in solution B and observed to form contractile vacuoles at a rate of 3 per minute. Based on this information, which of the following statements is correct?

(a) Solution A is hyperosmotic to solution B
(b) Solutions A and B are isosmotic
(c) Solution B is hyperosmotic to solution A
(d) Solutions A and B are isosmotic to the protozoan cell
(e) Both a and b

90. The membrane transport mechanism used when an amoeba engulfs a bacterial cell is called

(a) exocytosis
(b) pinocytosis
(c) facilitated diffusion
(d) active transport
(e) phagocytosis

91. Continuing from the previous question, once the bacterial cell has been digested, the amoeba will dispose of indigestible materials by which of the following processes?

(a) Facilitated diffusion
(b) Through gated channels in membrane proteins
(c) Exocytosis
(d) Active transport
(e) By any of the above processes

92. Basic structural and functional unit of the human body is

(a) protein (b) the cell
(c) tissue (d) the organ
(e) the organ system

93. The watery medium that surrounds a cell is called

(a) cytosol (b) protoplasm
(c) extracellular fluid (d) cytoplasm
(e) a colloidal gel

94. Functions of the cell membrane include all of the following, except

(a) separation of the cytoplasm from the extracellular fluid
(b) regulation of exchange of materials with the extracellular environment
(c) sensitivity to changes in the concentration of certain substances in the extracellular fluid
(d) identifying foreign substances and cells
(e) structural support

95. The plasma membrane

(a) is composed of a bilayer of proteins
(b) is composed of a bilayer of lipids
(c) is composed of only carbohydrate molecules
(d) is a complex combination of carbohydrates and proteins
(e) is a complex combination of carbohydrates and lipids

96. Which of the following is not a function of membrane proteins?

(a) Binds to ligands
(b) Regulates the passage of ions
(c) Acts as carrier molecules for various solutes
(d) Acts as anchors or stabilizers for the cell membrane
(e) Produces energy

97. Functions of the glycocalyx include

(a) lubricating and protecting the cell membrane
(b) identifying the cell for the immune system
(c) acting as receptors for hormones
(d) all of the above
(e) (b) and (c) only

98. Each of the following is an example of a nonmembranous organelle, except

(a) lysosomes
(b) cilia
(c) centrioles
(d) ribosomes
(e) cytoskeleton

99. Components of the cytoskeleton may include all of the following, except

(a) microfilaments
(b) intermediate filaments
(c) microtubules
(d) thick filaments

100. Most of the ATP required to power cellular operations is produced in the

(a) ribosomes
(b) endoplasmic reticulum
(c) nucleus
(d) mitochondria
(e) golgi apparatus

101. The components of ribosomes are formed by

(a) the endoplasmic reticulum
(b) golgi complexes
(c) lysosomes
(d) mitochondria
(e) nucleoli

102. Synthesis of lipids takes place in the

(a) ribosomes
(b) rough endoplasmic reticulum
(c) smooth endoplasmic reticulum
(d) golgi apparatus
(e) mitochondria

103. Which of the following consists of a network of intracellular membranes with attached ribosomes?

(a) Rough endoplasmic reticulum
(b) Smooth endoplasmic reticulum
(c) Mitochondria
(d) Nucleoli
(e) Golgi apparatus

104. Renewal or modification of the cell membrane is a function of the

(a) microtubules
(b) mitochondria
(c) rough endoplasmic reticulum
(d) ribosomes
(e) golgi apparatus

105. Vesicles containing enzymes that neutralize toxins such as alcohol are

(a) lysosomes (b) peroxisomes
(c) centrosomes (d) endosomes
(e) toxisomes

106. When activated, lysosomes function in
(a) formation of new cell membranes
(b) synthesis of proteins
(c) digestion of foreign material
(d) synthesis of lipids
(e) cell division

107. The complex structures of DNA and protein found in the cell nucleus are
(a) nucleoplasm (b) chromosomes
(c) histones (d) nucleases
(e) mitochondria

108. Which endoplasmic reticulum modifies and packages newly synthesized proteins?
(a) The ribosomal reticulum
(b) The proteosomes reticulum
(c) The raised reticulum
(d) The smooth reticulum
(e) The rough reticulum

109. The cell membrane includes
(a) integral proteins
(b) glycolipids
(c) phospholipids
(d) all of the above
(e) a and c only

110. Extracellular fluid serves as
(a) a storage area
(b) a reserve area
(c) a component of the phospholipid bilayer
(d) a transport medium
(e) a transport medium with large storage capacity

111. Tubulin is a
(a) carbohydrate that assembles into filamentous tubes (microtubules)
(b) lipid that assembles into filamentous tubes (microtubules)
(c) protein that assembles into filamentous tubes (microtubules)
(d) protein that forms the fluid portion of the cytosol
(e) lipid that forms the fluid portion of the cytoplasm

112. Endocytosis is a
(a) method for transporting substances across the cell membrane
(b) method for metabolizing within the cytosol
(c) form of anabolism
(d) manner in which lysosomes are formed
(e) method for synthesizing products

113. Peroxisomes
(a) contain enzymes that break down hydrogen peroxide
(b) absorb and break down fatty acids, generating hydrogen peroxide in the process
(c) are the same organelle as lysosomes
(d) (a) and (b)
(e) none of the above

114. Some cells contain large numbers of mitochondria while others have relatively few or none. This suggests that
(a) cells with large numbers of mitochondria are short-lived
(b) cells with large numbers of mitochondria have a high energy demand
(c) cells with small numbers of mitochondria have a high energy demand
(d) cells with large numbers of mitochondria have a low energy demand
(e) some cells are older than others

115. A mature red blood cell lacks a nucleus. Thus, it
(a) can repair itself rather readily
(b) is malformed
(c) is normal, but its function will be impaired
(d) will be a long-lived cell
(e) cannot repair itself and will disintegrate within a few months

116. Histones are found in
(a) nucleoli (b) mitochondria
(c) lysosomes (d) vesicles
(e) cisternae

117. White blood cells engulfing disease-causing bacteria illustrate

(a) pinocytosis (b) endocytosis
(c) exocytosis (d) phagocytosis
(e) receptor-mediated endocytosis

118. Microtubules have the following functions?

(a) They form structural components of organelles
(b) They regulate the exchange of waste products with ECF
(c) They provide a mechanism for changing the cell shape
(d) All of the above
(e) Both a and c

119. Each of the following is a function of smooth endoplasmic reticulum, except

(a) removal and storage of calcium ions
(b) modification of protein products
(c) synthesis of steroid hormones
(d) synthesis of triglycerides in liver cells
(e) detoxification of drugs in liver cells

BACTERIA

120. An infectious disease, which is becoming a concern due to the emergence of acid-fast, antibiotic-resistant forms of the pathogen, is which one of the following?

(a) Cholera (b) Tuberculosis
(c) Malaria (d) Whooping cough

121. The "tangy" acidic taste common to most yogurts is due to the production of lactic acid by which one of the following microorganisms?

(a) *Lactobacillus acidophilus*
(b) *Streptococcus mutans*
(c) *Thiobacillus thiooxidans*
(d) *Helicobacter pylori*

122. Strictly anaerobic bacteria are not able to

(a) obtain energy from organic compounds
(a) survive
(b) convert hydrogen peroxide (H_2O_2) to non-toxic forms
(c) grow in thioglycollate broth (in a sealed container)

123. Which one of the following types of bacteria would have gram-positive spherical-shaped cells arranged in chains longer than 2 cells per chain?

(a) *Neisseria meningitidis*
(b) *Staphylococcus epidermitis*
(c) *Streptococcus pyogenes*
(d) *Streptococcus pneumoniae*

124. The tissue destruction characteristic of gas gangrene is caused by which of the following bacteria?

(a) *Streptococcus pyogenes* (also known as "flesh-eating" bacteria)
(b) *Clostridium tetani*
(c) *Clostridium perfringens*
(d) *Staphylococcus epidermitis*

125. Which of the following is the most common sexually-transmitted disease (STD) in the US, and is caused by a bacterium that changes its cell size during its life cycle (resulting in a smaller form called an elementary body and a larger form called a reticulate body)?

(a) Syphilis (caused by *Treponema pallidum*)
(b) Gonorrhea (caused by *Neisseria gonorrhoeae*)
(c) Genital warts
(d) The STD caused by members of the genus *Chlamydia*

126. Which one of the structural components of a bacterial cell listed in a–d would be important to consider in every one of the following:

members of the genus ***Clostridium*** AND autoclaving AND anthrax as a bioweapon AND botulism (a form of food-borne disease)

(a) cell wall
(b) cell membrane
(c) endospore
(d) O-specific side chain of the gram-negative outer membrane

127. Which of the following is a rather easily visible difference, after a laboratory staining procedure, between *Neisseria meningitidis* (also called meningococcus) and *Streptococcus pneumoniae*, two bacteria that cause bacterial meningitis?

(a) Cell shape
(b) Gram reaction
(c) Cell arrangement
(d) Presence or absence of an endospore

128. *Streptococcus mutans* has a capsule, is able to cleave sucrose (table sugar) into glucose and galactose, can polymerize glucose into dextran, and produces large amounts of lactic acid from glucose. Thus, it is quite likely that this bacteria is involved in

(a) strep throat
(b) rheumatic fever
(c) production of cavities (dental caries)
(d) production of yogurt

129. Most bacteria obtain energy from the oxidation of which of the following?

(a) Organic compounds
(b) Inorganic compounds
(c) Sunlight
(d) Nitrates and nitrites when converted to ammonia

130. The bacterium, which is an example of a thermophile from which a very important heat-resistant enzyme is obtained that is used in the polymerase chain reaction (PCR), is which of the following?

(a) *Thermus aquaticus*
(b) *Thiobacillus thiooxidans*
(c) *Helicobacter pylori*
(d) *Lactobacillus acidophilus*

131. A few students are having difficulty separating their two unknown samples using the streak plate method, because one of the unknown samples may be a bacterium that has the ability to move within the very thin layer of water on the surface of the agar using a cell-wall associated structure known as a (hint: spirillum-shaped cells would have this structure, but spirochete-shaped cells would not)

(a) pilus
(b) peptidoglycan
(c) flagellum
(d) group translocation protein

132. The genus *Diplococcus* is no longer used, and has been replaced by which one of the following genera?

(a) *Neisseria* (b) *Streptococcus*
(c) *Staphylococcus* (d) *Coccobacillus*

133. Which of the following types of bacteria does not have a cell wall (very rare among the bacteria) and causes a form of pneumonia often called "atypical" pneumonia?

(a) *Mycobacterium* (b) *Streptococcus*
(c) *Mycoplasma* (d) *Streptomyces*

134. The size of most typical bacterial cells is measured using which of the following dimensions?

(a) Millimeters (b) Micrometers
(c) Nanometers (d) Angstroms

135. Penicillin remains one of the most widely used and most effective antibiotic. It is able to interefere with the production of which of the following structures found in most procaryotic cells that is not found in human cells?

(a) endoplasmic reticulum
(b) cell walls
(c) double-stranded DNA
(d) 16 S ribosomal subunits

136. The intracellular, extrachromosomal circular pieces of DNA found in many bacteria are known as

(a) nucleoids (b) plasmids
(c) Taq polymerases
(d) *Coccobacilli* dsDNA

137. Acid-fast bacteria would have which of the following appearances after a gram stain?

(a) Blue/Violet (b) Red/Pink
(c) Yellow (d) Colourless

138. Poly-beta-hydroxybutyrates are an example of a bacterial inclusion body. They have been commercially exploited to make which one of the following?

(a) Water-resistant garments used in a microbiology laboratory
(b) Biodegradable plastics
(c) Clothes that resist staining
(d) Antibiotics

139. Stomach ulcers, once thought to be caused by diet and/or stress, are now known to be caused almost exclusively by which one of the following bacteria?

(a) *Lactobacillus acidophilus*
(b) *Streptococcus mutans*
(c) *Helicobacter pylori*
(d) *Clostridium botulinum*

140. The "rigidity" of a bacterial cell wall is most often associated with which of the following biochemical characteristics?

(a) The number of cross-linkages between peptidoglycans (which are repeating units of N-acetylmuramic acid and N-acetylglucosamine)
(b) The lipid content
(c) The presence or absence of teichoic acids
(d) The per cent of polysaccharide in the cell wall

141. An Hfr strain of *E. coli* contains

(a) a vector of yeast or bacterial origin, which is used to make many copies of a particular DNA sequence
(b) a bacterial chromosome with a human gene inserted
(c) a bacterial chromosome with the F factor inserted
(d) a human chromosome with a transposable element inserted
(e) a bacterial chromosome with a phage inserted

142. A lytic viral cycle is usually the result of infection by a(n)

(a) prophage (b) virulent phage
(c) temperate phage (d) antiphage

143. A virus that incorporates its DNA into the DNA of its host organism is a

(a) virulent phage (b) prophage
(c) lytic phage (d) none of these

144. A phage is a

(a) virus that can infect bacteria
(b) virus that can infect humans
(c) small bacterial cell that needs to live inside another cell
(d) virus that shares its DNA with its host cell

145. Bacteria that contain recombinant plasmids can be easily isolated because they

(a) are larger than recombinant bacteria
(b) are resistant to certain antibiotics
(c) grow much faster than non-recombinant bacteria
(d) are smaller than non-recombinant bacteria

146. In Gram-positive bacteria, the cell membrane becomes invaginated and folded to form structures called

(a) flagella (b) plasmid
(c) mesosomes (d) peroxisomes

147. Recombinant bacteria have been used to produce

(a) human growth hormone
(b) vaccines (c) insulin
(d) all of these

148. Viruses are exceptions to the cell theory, but they have some characteristics of living things. Which among the following is one of those characteristics?

(a) They are made up of many specialized cells
(b) They contain genetic material
(c) They reproduce by mitosis
(d) They contain chlorophyll

149. The bacterial cell wall is composed of

(a) a phospholipid matrix
(b) a lipoprotein
(c) a polymer of sugars
(d) chitin
(e) a structural protein

150. A Gram-negative bacterium is enclosed by

(a) a single thick wall
(b) a single thin wall
(c) a double thick wall
(d) a double thin wall
(e) no wall, just a plasma membrane

151. The cytoplasm of a bacterium

(a) is supported by the cytoskeleton
(b) is supported by microtubules
(c) is supported by keratin
(d) has no internal support structure
(e) is supported by folds in the interstitial membrane

152. A Gram-positive bacterium is stained ______ by the Gram stain

(a) pink (b) purple
(c) blue (d) green
(e) red

153. Bacterial ribosomes

(a) are unable to synthesize proteins in the presence of tetracycline
(b) are larger than eukaryotic ribosomes
(c) have the same RNA contents as eukaryotic ribosomes
(d) contain the same forms of proteins as eukaryotic ribosomes

154. Plasmids are best thought of as

(a) escaped fragments of eukaryotic DNA
(b) excised portions of bacterial chromosomes
(c) self-replicating RNA
(d) escaped pieces of mitochondrial DNA

155. Some bacteria form a thick-walled ______ in response to poor nutrient conditions

(a) endospore (b) capsule
(c) sheath (d) pilus
(e) autospore

156. Bacteria normally contain their genome in

(a) a nucleoid region (b) an endospore
(c) a plasmid (d) a pilus
(e) a heterospore

157. Which of the following is a product for which bacteria are not employed?

(a) Bread (b) Cheese
(c) Lactic acid (d) Antibiotics
(e) Turpentine

158. Plant diseases such as citrus canker are caused by

(a) *Enterobacteria* (b) *Actinomyces*
(c) *Rickettsia* (d) *Spirochaetes*
(e) *Pseudomonads*

159. A major portion of the world's natural gas reserves were produced by

(a) primitive protists (b) anaerobic fungi
(c) actinomyces (d) ancient viruses
(e) archaebacteria

160. In 1997, ______ was the leading cause of death by a single infectious agent worldwide

(a) TB (b) smallpox
(c) cholera (d) diphtheria
(e) plague

161. Genetic recombination occurs in bacteria through the transfer of

(a) vili (b) plasmids
(c) endospores (d) autospores
(e) gametes

162. Gram-negative bacteria are resistant to the Gram stain because of the presence of a large ______ in an outer membrane layer

(a) glycoprotein (b) polymer
(c) lipopolysaccharide d)polysaccharide
(e) lipoprotein

163. Cell division in bacteria takes place mainly by

(a) conjugation (b) binary fission
(c) sporulation (d) fragmentation
(e) mitosis

164. Organisms that obtain their energy by oxidizing inorganic chemical sources are called ______

(a) photoautotrophs (b) chemoautotrophs
(c) detritivores (d) heterotrophs

165. Which of the following statements is (are) true about the cyanobacteria?

(a) Cyanobacteria appeared about 3 billion years ago
(b) Cyanobacteria produce methane
(c) The presence of cyanobacteria increased the concentration of free oxygen
(d) Both a and c are correct
(e) Both a and b are correct

166. Which of the following are characteristics of bacterial cells?

(a) Bacterial cells are prokaryotes
(b) Bacterial cells do not have an organized nucleus
(c) Bacterial cells have a cell wall
(d) Bacterial cells have a ring of double-stranded of DNA
(e) All of the above are true

167. When exposed to harsh conditions, some bacteria form

(a) capsules (b) endospores
(c) pili (d) flagella
(e) a cell wall

168. Which one of the following statements is not true about bacteria and eukaryotes?

(a) Eukaryotes are generally larger than bacteria
(b) Bacteria lack internal compartmentalization
(c) Both types of organisms reproduce by mitosis
(d) Bacteria are fundamentally single-celled
(e) The flagella of bacteria are less complex than those of eukaryotes

169. All of the following diseases are caused by bacteria except

(a) plague (b) yellow fever
(c) typhus (d) cholera
(e) tuberculosis

170. The methanobacteria, halobacteria, and sulfobacteria are included in which bacterial group?

(a) Blue-green algae (b) Archaebacteria
(c) Eubacteria (d) Cyanobacteria
(e) All of the above

171. Which non-toxic, fast growing cyanobacterium is cultivated in tanks as a protein-rich animal feed?

(a) *Stigonema* (b) *Spirulina*
(c) *Nostoc* (d) *Oscillatoria*

172. The early earth was a harsh environment, and present day organisms that could possibly have survived that type of environment are

(a) eukaryotic organisms
(b) archeabacteria
(c) early plants called blue-green algae
(d) protobionts
(e) eubacteria

173. In prokaryotes, genetics recombination can occur by

(a) conjugation (b) transduction
(c) transformation (d) all of the above

174. Which of the following is not characteristic of a prokaryote?

(a) Cell wall (b) DNA
(c) Nucleus (d) Plasma membrane

175. Prokaryotes reproduce

(a) sexually (b) by binary fission
(c) by conjugation (d) all of the above

176. Sex pilus is used to exchange DNA between bacteria during

(a) conjugation (b) transformation
(c) transduction (d) binary fission

177. Endospores

(a) are a means of reproduction
(b) can survive for hundreds of years
(c) cannot be killed
(d) all of the above

178. Many prokaryotes have accessory rings of DNA called ______, which are often used as vectors for genetic engineering

(a) fimbriae (b) nucleoids
(c) plasmids (d) ribosomes

179. The primary source of genetic variability in prokaryotes is

(a) mutations (b) transduction
(c) conjugation (d) transformation

180. Facultative anaerobes

(a) require a constant supply of oxygen
(b) grow in the presence or absence of oxygen
(c) die in the presence of oxygen
(d) none of the above

181. Gram-negative and Gram-positive bacteria

(a) stain differently with Gram stain
(b) have different amounts of peptidoglycan in their cell walls
(c) both (a) and (b)
(d) neither (a) nor (b)

182. The cell walls of prokaryotes are distinguished by the presence of

(a) chitin (b) peptidoglycan
(c) silica (d) cellulose

183. Bacteria that photosynthesize and are common in fresh water, soil and moist surfaces are

(a) archaea (b) cyanobacteria
(c) commensals (d) all of the above

184. Cyanobacteria are able to fix nitrogen with their

(a) endospores (b) chloroplasts
(c) heterocysts (d) nuclei

185. The ______ are believed to be responsible for first introducing oxygen into the primitive atmosphere

(a) green sulfur bacteria
(b) cyanobacteria
(c) purple bacteria
(d) methanogens

186. Gram negative bacteria

(a) appear pink when stained with gram stain
(b) have a thick layer of peptidoglycan in their cell wall
(c) do not get stained with gram stain
(d) both (a) and (b)

187. Cyanobacteria have symbiotic relationships with

(a) liverworts (b) corals
(c) fungi (d) all of the above

188. Antibiotics

(a) selectively kill bacteria
(b) should be used whenever someone feels sick
(c) only kill the disease causing bacteria
(d) all of the above

189. Which of the following is a problem associated with antibiotic therapy?

(a) Misuse of antibiotics increases the number of antibiotic resistant strains
(b) People can die if given an antibiotic to which they are allergic
(c) The use of antibiotics can prevent natural immunity from occurring
(d) All of the above

190. Which of the following is not a true statement about the kingdom Protista?

(a) It is an artificial grouping
(b) Its members are placed there as a matter of convenience
(c) Although diverse, the group represents a closely related group evolutionarily
(d) It contains unicellular, colonial, and multicellular groups

191. Up to a point, successive generations of diatoms

(a) are smaller
(b) are larger
(c) remain the same size
(d) are produced sexually

192. Which of the following is not a group used in the text to classify protists?

(a) Mastigophora (b) Sarcodina
(c) Sporozoans (d) Diatoms
(e) molds

193. Malaria results from a mosquito injecting the ______ of *Plasmodium* into the human bloodstream

(a) sporocyst (b) glycoprotein coat
(c) merozoites (d) gametocytes
(e) sporozoites

194. All of the following belong to the kingdom Protista except

(a) viruses (b) fungi
(c) sporozoans (d) sarcodines
(e) protozoa

195. The green alga, ______, has recently been investigated as a food source in several nations

(a) *Volvox* (b) *Prochloron*
(c) *Chlamydomonas* (d) *Spirogyra*
(e) *Chlorella*

196. During the conjugation of the ciliate, *Paramecium*, ______ are exchanged

(a) macronuclei (b) heterocysts
(c) zoogonia (d) micronuclei
(e) stigmas

197. The chloroplasts of ______ algae contain phycobilins

(a) green (b) red and green
(c) red (d) green and brown
(e) brown

198. The algae are subdivided into three groups according to

(a) the type of meiosis in their life cycle
(b) the structure of their cell walls
(c) the kind of chlorophyll they contain
(d) the size of their multicellular structures
(e) none of the above

199. Viruses always have at least

(a) an outer capsid
(b) a cell wall
(c) an inner core of nucleic acid
(d) both (a) and (c)

200. Viruses are described as non-living because they

(a) don't metabolize
(b) aren't organized on a cellular level
(c) don't respond to stimuli
(d) all of the above

201. Which of the following characteristics of living things do viruses have?

(a) Metabolism
(b) Cellular organization
(c) Evolution
(d) Independent reproduction

202. Which of the following is correctly matched?

(a) Tobacco mosaic virus – plants
(b) Hepatitis virus – brain cells
(c) Bacteriophages – spleen cells
(d) Rabies virus- fish

203. A virus relies on the host's ______ for its own reproduction

(a) enzymes (b) ribosomes
(c) tRNA and ATP (d) all of the above

204. Which of the following produces cells that carry a copy of the latent viral DNA?

(a) The lysogenic cycle
(b) The lytic cycle
(c) None of the above
(d) Both (a) and (b)

205. In the ______ cycle, viral replication occurs immediately and viruses are released after lysozyme disrupts the cell wall

(a) lytic (b) lysogenic
(c) none of the above (d) both (a) and (b)

206. RNA animal viruses that have a DNA stage are called

(a) bacteriophages (b) retroviruses
(c) viroids (d) phages

207. Prions

(a) are disease causing proteins
(b) are believed to cause Creutzfeldt–Jakob disease
(c) have been linked to mad cow disease
(d) all of the above

208. Disease causing naked strands of RNA are called

(a) prions (b) viroids
(c) bacteriophages (d) retroviruses

209. The prokaryotes include

(a) bacteria (b) archaea
(c) viruses (d) both (a) and (b)

210. Who discovered cell in 1665?

(a) Robert Hooke (b) Robert Crook
(c) David Thomson (d) Marie Francois

211. Name the organelle which serves as a primary packaging area for molecules that will be distributed throughout the cell?

(a) Mitochondria (b) Golgi apparatus
(c) Vacuole (d) Plastids

212. Name the outermost boundary of the cell

(a) Plasma membrane
(b) Cytoplasm
(c) Nuclear membrane
(d) None of the above

213. Name the process in which the ingestion of material by the cells is done through the plasma membrane

(a) Egestion (b) Diffusion
(c) Osmosis (d) Endocytosis

214. Which among the following sentences is not correct about the organelles?

(a) They are found in all eukaryotic cells
(b) They are found in multicellular organisms
(c) They coordinate to produce the cell
(d) They are small sized and mostly internal

215. Name the process in which the passage of water goes from a region of higher concentration to a region of lower concentration through a semi-permeable membrane?

(a) Diffusion (b) Osmosis
(c) Both (a) and (b) (d) Neither (a) nor (b)

216. Name an organism which contains single chromosome and cell division occurs through fusion or budding?

(a) Eukaryotes (b) Prokaryotes
(c) Bacteria (d) Primitive organism

217. Name the process in which the membrane of a vesicle can fuse with the plasma membrane and exude its contents to the surrounding medium?

(a) Exocytosis (b) Endocytosis
(c) Osmosis (d) Diffusion

218. The jelly-like substance present inside the cell is known as

(a) cytoplasm (b) ectoplasm
(c) nucleoplasm (d) protoplasm

219. Blue-green algae are

(a) prokaryotes (b) eukaryotes
(c) both (a) and (b) (d) neither (a) nor (b)

220. The powerhouse of a cell is called

(a) cell wall (b) mitochondria
(c) ribosomes (d) nucleus

221. The seat of control of a cell is

(a) nucleus (b) cell wall
(c) cytoplasm (d) mitochondria

222. Protoplasm found inside the nucleus is known as

(a) amyloplast (b) nucleoplasm
(c) cytoplasm (d) elaioplasm

223. Prokaryotic genetic system has

(a) DNA but no histones
(b) both DNA and histones
(c) neither DNA nor histones
(d) either DNA or histones

224. What do prokaryotic cells lack?

(a) Cell membrane
(b) Cytoplasm
(c) Cell wall
(d) Membrane-bound nucleus

225. Lampbrush chromosomes are seen in

(a) prophase (b) mitotic metaphase
(c) mitosis (d) meiotic prophase

226. Which one of the following is not considered a part of the endomembrane system?

(a) Vacuole (b) Lysosome
(c) Golgi complex (d) Peroxisome

227. Animal cells differ from plant cells in possessing

(a) plastid (b) golgi body
(c) vacuole (d) centrosome

228. Which of the following organelle has a single membrane?

(a) Mitochondria (b) Nucleus
(c) Spherosomes (d) Chloroplast

229. Ribosomes were discovered by

(a) Golgi (b) Palade
(c) Porter (d) De Robertis

230. Plasma membrane is made of

(a) proteins and lipids
(b) proteins, nucleic acids and lipids
(c) proteins and carbohydrates
(d) proteins, lipids and carbohydrates

231. Polyribosomes are aggregates of

(a) only RNA
(b) peroxisomes
(c) ribosomes and rRNA
(d) several ribosomes held together by string of mRNA

232. Cell wall shows

(a) complete permeability
(b) semi-permeability
(c) differential permeability
(d) impermeability

233. Which one is apparato reticolare?

(a) Microfilaments
(b) Golgi bodies
(c) Microtubules
(d) Endoplasmic reticulum

234. An outer covering membrane is absent over

(a) plastid (b) mitochondrion
(c) nucleolus (d) golgi bodies

235. Lysosomes are rich in

(a) nucleic acids (b) hormones
(c) carbohydrates (d) hydrolytic enzymes

236. Microtubules are absent in

(a) flagella (b) centrioles
(c) spindle fibres (d) mitochondria

237. Nucleoproteins are synthesized in

(a) cytoplasm (b) nuclear envelope
(c) nucleoplasm (d) nucleolus

238. The animal cells are interconnected by

(a) cell walls (b) desmosomes
(c) plasma membrane (d) plasmodesmata

239. Polytene chromosomes are found due to

(a) mitosis (b) endomixes
(c) endomitosis (d) meiosis

240. r- RNA is synthesized by

(a) cytoplasm (b) golgi bodies
(c) nucleolus (d) nucleus

241. Cristae are associated with

(a) mitochondria (b) cytoplasm
(c) vacuole (d) ribosomes

242. Glycocalyx is associated with

(a) cell wall (b) plasma membrane
(c) nucleus (d) ribosomes

243. Histone octamer contains

(a) 8 types of histones
(b) 5 types of histones
(c) 6 types of histones
(d) 8 types of four different types

244. Detoxification of lipid drugs and other harmful compounds in ER is carried out by

(a) Cytochrome P 450 (b) Cytochrome B
(c) Cytochrome D d) Cytochrome F

245. Sodium and potassium pumps are examples of

(a) passive transport (b) plasmolysis
(c) active transport (d) osmosis

246. Cell theory is not applicable to

(a) virus (b) microorganisms
(c) fungi (d) algae

247. Digestive enzymes are present in

(a) liposomes (b) lysosomes
(c) ribosomes (d) mitochondria

248. Which among the following is known as a mitoplast?

(a) Mitochondria without outer membrane
(b) Mitochondria without inner membrane
(c) Mitochondria without membrane
(d) Another name for mitochondria

249. Cell drinking is

(a) exocytosis (b) endocytosis
(c) pinocytosis (d) phagocytosis

250. Amyloplasts store

(a) fats (b) proteins
(c) lipids (d) starch

251. Centrioles take part in the formation of

(a) cell plate (b) spindle
(c) nucleus (d) centrosomes

252. Semiautonomous organelle in the cell is

(a) peroxisomes
(b) chloroplast
(c) endoplasmic reticulum

253. The membrane around the vacuole is called

(a) cytoplast (b) tonoplast
(c) amyloplast (d) elaioplast

254. Microfilaments are composed mainly of a protein called

(a) actin (b) tubulin
(c) myosin (d) chitin

255. Experiments demonstrating the importance of the nucleus in controlling the growth of the cell was performed in

(a) starfish (b) *acetabularia*
(c) *neurospora* (d) leucocytes

256. Which of the following is associated with the structure of Golgi complex?

(a) Cristae (b) Cisternae
(c) Annuli (d) Polyps

257. The subunits of prokaryotic ribosomes are

(a) 60 S + 40 S (b) 70 S + 30 S
(c) 60 S + 30 S (d) 50 S + 30 S

258. Plant cell wall is mainly composed of

(a) cellulose (b) starch
(c) protein (d) lipid

259. Smooth endoplasmic reticulum is the site of

(a) protein synthesis
(b) carbohydrate synthesis
(c) amino acid synthesis
(d) lipid synthesis

260. In higher plants, the shape of the chloroplast is

(a) discoid (b) cup shaped
(c) girdle shaped (d) ribbon shaped

261. Assembly of two subunits 40 S and 60 S of the ribosome is

(a) 100 S unit (b) 80 S unit
(c) 70 S unit (d) 90 S unit

262. Oxysomes are ATP synthases present on

(a) outer nuclear membrane facing cytoplasm
(b) outer mitochondrial membrane facing cytoplasm
(c) inner mitochondrial membrane facing matrix
(d) inner mitochondrial membrane facing cytoplasm

263. Autophagy and heterophagy are processes associated with the function of

(a) nucleus (b) microbodies
(c) lysosomes (d) mitochondrion

264. Which of the following organelles is involved in lipid metabolism?

(a) Golgi apparatus (b) Peroxisomes
(c) SER (d) RER

265. Arrange in correct order the function of each organelle

(i) ribosomes
(ii) Chloroplast
(iii) Golgi apparatus
(iv) Mitochondrion

(a) i. Protein synthesis ii. Organic molecule synthesis iii.Secretory centre iv. Beta oxidation
(b) i. Protein synthesis ii. Beta oxidation iii. Secretory centre iv. Organic molecule synthesis
(c) i. Protein synthesis ii. Secretory centre iii. Beta oxidation iv. Organic molecules synthesis
(d) i. Protein synthesis ii. Seretory centre iii. Organic molecules synthesis iv. Beta oxidation

266. Which of the following organelles contain coding DNA?

(a) Chloroplast and nucleus
(b) Chloroplast, mitochondrion and nucleus
(c) Chloroplast, mitochondrion, ribosomes and nucleus
(d) Chloroplast, mitochondrion, ribosomes, RER and nucleus

267. The organelle that helps in penetration of sperm into egg during fertilization is

(a) nucleus (b) peroxisome
(c) mitochondrion (d) lysosome

268. Glyoxysomes are organelles involved in

(a) conversion of amino acids to proteins
(b) conversion of fatty acids to carbohydrates
(c) conversion of amino acids to carbohydrates
(d) conversion of fatty acids to lipids

269. Hydrogen peroxide clearance inside the cell is carried out by the

(a) glyoxysome with enzyme isocitrate lyase
(b) peroxisome with enzyme catalase
(c) glyoxysome with enzyme catalase
(d) peroxisome with enzyme amino oxidase

270. The grafting experiment of Hammerling established the role of nucleus in heredity. The experimental material was

(a) *Chlorella* (b) *Acetabularia*
(c) *Chara* (d) *Scendesmus*

271. Nuclei are absent in

(a) red blood cells and bacterium
(b) red blood cells only
(c) red blood cells, sieve cells and bacterium
(d) none of these

272. Which of the following statement is true regarding the size of nucleus?

(a) The size of the nucleus is directly proportional to that of the cytoplasm
(b) The size of the nucleus depends on the total cell volume
(c) The size of the nucleus depends on the chromosome number or ploidy level of the cell
(d) All of these

273. Nucleus has

(a) DNA only
(b) DNA and protein only
(c) DNA, RNA and proteins
(d) None of these

274. Nuclear membrane is in continuous connection with

(a) SER (b) RER
(c) Golgi apparatus (d) Lysosomes

275. The protein network that lines the inner side of nuclear membrane is called

(a) nucleolus (b) nuclear matrix
(c) nuclear lamina (d) nuclear proteins

276. The number of nuclear pores depends on the

(a) size of the cell
(b) transcriptional activity of the cell
(c) DNA content of the cell
(d) all of these

277. The most important function of nuclear envelope is to

(a) regulate nucleo-cytoplasmic traffic
(b) protect genetic material
(c) prevent the entrance of active ribosomes into the nucleus
(d) synthesis of r-RNAs

278. The DNA protein ratio in chromatin is

(a) 3:1 (b) 2:1
(c) 1:1 (d) 4:1

279. Nucleolus is a prominent acidophilic spherical bodies in the nucleus. Its function is

(a) RNA synthesis
(b) DNA synthesis
(c) histone synthesis
(d) ribosomal subunit synthesis

280. The basic proteins of the nucleus are

(a) nucleo-histones (b) nucleo-protamines
(c) both (a) and (b) (d) none of these

281. The major amino acids in histones are

(a) glutamate and aspartic acid
(b) lysine and arginine
(c) arginine, lysine and histidine
(d) histidine

282. The light stained diffused region of chromatin is known as

(a) heterochromatin (b) euchromatin
(c) chromatin (d) none of these

283. Steroid hormones have receptors predominantly on

(a) cell surface
(b) cytoplasm
(c) both cell surface and cytoplasm
(d) inside nucleus only

284. The major interaction responsible for stabilizing plasma membrane is

(a) hydrophilic interactions
(b) covalent bonds
(c) ionic bonds
(d) hydrophobic interactions

285. The organelles involved in protein transport are

(a) ER and Golgi
(b) ER and mitochondria
(c) Golgi and mitochondria
(d) lysosomes and Golgi

286. The role of carbohydrates in cell membrane is

(a) cell adhesion
(b) cell-cell recognition
(c) assisting transport across cell membrane
(d) cell storage reserve

287. All hormones can cross plasma membrane except

(a) estrogen (b) insulin
(c) progestrone (d) thyroxine

288. The major biochemical responsible for selective uptake of materials across membrane is

(a) carbohydrate (b) protein
(c) lipids (d) phospholipids

289. All the following substances pass through cell membrane except

(a) oxygen (b) water
(c) carbon dioxide (d) hydrogen ions

290. At physiological pH increase in cholesterol level

(a) increases fluidity
(b) decreases fluidity
(c) no change in fluidity
(d) none of the above

291. The longer the fatty acid chain, fluidity of the lipid bilayer

(a) increases
(b) decreases
(c) no change in fluidity
(d) none of the above

292. The inner leaflets of erythrocytes have

(a) sphingomyelin and phosphatidylcholine
(b) phosphatidylserine and phosphatidylethanolamine
(c) sphingomyelin and phosphatidylserine
(d) phosphatidylserine and phosphatidylcholine

293. Lipid bilayer is

(a) hydrophilic
(b) hydrophobic
(c) hydrophilic and hydrophobic
(d) depends on the surrounding medium

294. Which of the following membrane has the largest amount of proteins?

(a) Erythrocyte membrane
(b) Myelin sheath membrane
(c) Inner mitochondrial membrane
(d) Outer mitochondrial membrane

295. High lipid content is a characteristic of

(a) erythrocyte membrane
(b) myelin sheath membrane
(c) inner mitochondrial membrane
(d) outer mitochondrial membrane

296. The distribution of intrinsic proteins in the cell membrane is

(a) symmetrical (b) asymmetrical
(c) random (d) uniform

297. In cell membranes, carbohydrates in glycoproteins or glycolipids are oriented

(a) towards outside
(b) towards inside
(c) towards outside and inside
(d) randomly distributed

298. The plasma membrane is impermeable to all molecules except

(a) glucose (b) ATP
(c) urea (d) K^+

299. The erythrocyte glucose transporter is an example of

(a) simple diffusion
(b) active diffusion
(c) facilitated diffusion
(d) ion driven active transport

300. Which of the following transport induces conformational change in protein?

(a) Simple diffusion
(b) Active diffusion
(c) Facilitated diffusion
(d) Ion driven active transport

301. Na^+ glucose transporter is an example of

(a) facilitated diffusion
(b) ATP driven active transport
(c) symport (d) antiport

302. Clathrin coated pits are associated with

(a) phagocytosis (b) pinocytosis
(c) receptor mediated endocytosis
(d) exocytosis

303. Which of the following is a semi-autonomous organelle?

(a) Mitochondrion
(b) Chloroplast
(c) Both (a) and (b)
(d) Mitochondrion, chloroplast and ribosomes

304. Who coined the term mitochondrion?

(a) Kolliker (b) Flemming
(c) Altman (d) Benda

305. Myocardial muscle cells have numerous large mitochondria called

(a) myocardial mitochondrion
(b) mitosomes
(c) myosomes
(d) sarcosomes

306. The number of mitochondria in a cell depends on

(a) pH of the cell
(b) shape of the cell
(c) both (a) and (b)
(d) functional state of the cell

307. Which of the following statements are true about mitochondria?

(a) Mitochondria has two envelopes
(b) Outer membrane has porin channels
(c) Inner membrane is not permeable
(d) All of these

308. Cristae are

(a) the membraneous infoldings of the outer membrane of mitochondria
(b) the jelly like central matrix of mitochondria
(c) the membraneous infoldings of the inner membrane of mitochondria
(d) enzymes located on the inner mitochondrial membrane

309. F_0-F_1 particles meant for ATP synthesis are present on

(a) outer mitochondrial membrane attached to the cytosolic or C face
(b) outer mitochondrial membrane attached to the matrix or M face
(c) inner mitochondrial membrane attached to the matrix or M face
(d) inner mitochondrial membrane attached to the cytosolic or C face

310. Which of the following stains is used to visualise mitochondrion?

(a) Janus green (b) Acetocarmine
(c) Haematoxylin (d) Orange G

311. Which of the following is the histochemical marker for mitochondrial inner membrane?

(a) Monoamine oxidase
(b) Cytochrome oxidase
(c) Malate dehydrogenase
(d) Adenylate kinase

312. Mitoplasts are

(a) mitochondria without membranes
(b) mitochondria without outer membrane
(c) mitochondria without inner membrane
(d) mitochondrial plastids

313. The inner membrane of the mitochondria is usually highly convoluted forming a series of infolding known as

(a) thylakoids (b) lamellae
(c) cristae (d) grana

314. Oxysomes of F_0-F_1 particles occur on

(a) thylakoids
(b) mitochondrial surface
(c) chloroplast surface
(d) inner mitochondrial membrane

315. Select the wrong statements from the following.

(a) Both chloroplast and mitochondria contain an inner and outer membrane
(b) Both chloroplast and mitochondria have an internal compartment, the thylakoid space bound by the thylakoid membrane
(c) The chloroplasts are generally much larger than mitochondria
(d) Both chloroplast and mitochondria contain DNA

316. Which of the following statements regarding mitochondrial membrane is not correct?

(a) The outer membrane resembles a sieve
(b) The enzymes of the electron transfer chain are embedded in the outer membrane
(c) The outer membrane is permeable to all kinds of molecules
(d) The inner membrane has no role to play

317. In mitochondria, cristae act as sites for

(a) protein synthesis
(b) phosphorylation of flavoproteins
(c) breakdown of molecules
(d) oxidation reduction reaction

318. Mitochondrial inner membrane is rich in phospholipid

(a) Cardiolipin
(b) Phosphatidyl inositol
(c) Phosphatidyl serine
(d) Phosphatidyl choline

319. All the statements are true except

(a) mitochondria are called the powerhouses of the cell
(b) mitochondrial DNA is called mt DNA
(c) mitochondria is the site of oxidative phosphorylation and Krebs cycle
(d) mitochondria is the site of Calvin cycle

320. Which of the following is not a function of mitochondrion?

(a) Electron transport chain and associated ATP production
(b) Glycolysis and associated ATP production
(c) Fatty acid breakdown
(d) Thermogenesis

321. mt DNA is

(a) simple, double stranded linear DNA molecule
(b) simple, single stranded linear DNA molecule
(c) simple, single stranded circular DNA molecule
(d) simple, double stranded circular DNA molecule

322. The inner mitochondrial membrane has

(a) NADH dehydrogenase complex
(b) b-c 1 complex
(c) cytochrome oxidase complex
(d) all of these

323. Which of the following is called the "traffic police" of the cell?

(a) Lysosome b) SER
(c) Golgi apparatus d) RER

324. In 1873, Camillo Golgi discovered Golgi apparatus in Purkinje cells (nerve cells). Which is the stain that he used to visualise Golgi apparatus?

(a) Janus green b) Silver stain
(c) Orange G d) Haemotoxylin

325. Dictyosomes are

(a) Golgi apparatus of plant cells
(b) Golgi apparatus of plant cells and lower invertebrates
(c) Golgi apparatus of plant cells, lower invertebrates and animal cells
(d) Golgi apparatus like structure in prokaryotes

326. The simplest unit, the saucer-like closed compartments of Golgi apparatus is called

(a) tubule (b) vesicle
(c) crista (d) cisterna

327. GERL region is

(a) Golgi + RER + SER + lysosomes + vesicles association involved in packaging and sorting of cellular materials
(b) Golgi + SER + RER + lumen of cytoplasm association involved in packaging and sorting of cellular materials
(c) Golgi + ER + lysosome association involved in packaging and sorting of cellular materials
(d) None of these

328. Histochemical localisation of Golgi is by staining with

(a) Bismarck red (b) Fast green
(c) Osmium tetroxide (d) Acetocarmine

329. Which of the following organelle is involved in cell plate formation?

(a) SER (b) RER
(c) Lysosome (d) Golgi apparatus

330. The functions of Golgi apparatus include all except

(a) GA is the sorting centre of the cell
(b) GA is involved in post-translational modification
(c) GA is involved in secretory protein synthesis
(d) GA is involved in cell plate formation

331. Which of the following statements are true regarding Golgi apparatus?

(a) GA has polarity
(b) Cis-face is located close to either nucleus or translational ER
(c) Trans-face is located near plasma membrane
(d) All of these

332. Which of the following organelle is located near the nucleus and contains a collection of flattened membrane bound cisternae?

(a) Nucleus (b) Centriole
(c) Mitochondrion (d) Golgi apparatus

333. Golgi complex was first recognised in

(a) blood cell (b) root cell
(c) nerve cell (d) shoot cell

334. Besides giving out secretory vesicles, the Golgi apparatus is also concerned with the formation of

(a) nucleus (b) plastids
(c) nucleolus (d) lysosomes

335. Zone of "exclusion" is associated with

(a) nucleus (b) nucleolus
(c) nucleoplasm (d) golgi complex

336. Golgi apparatus is absent in

(a) higher plants
(b) yeast
(c) bacteria and blue-green algae
(d) none of these

337. Acid phosphatase is the cytochemical marker for

(a) cis-region of GA
(b) trans-region of GA
(c) GERL region
(d) median region of GA

338. Golgi apparatus is often seen associated with

(a) mitochondria (b) RER
(c) lysosome (d) none of these

339. Which of the following organ is called the "sorting centre" of the cell?

(a) RER (b) SER
(c) GA (d) Lysosome

340. Function of Golgi apparatus in animal cells include

(a) sorting and packaging
(b) exocytosis of melanin granules
(c) exocytosis of thyroxin hormone
(d) all of these

341. Which of the following statements are incorrect regarding ER?

(a) The adipose tissue has both SER and RER
(b) Plasma cells have RER only
(c) RBC lacks both RER and SER
(d) Hepatocytes have both RER and SER

342. Which of the following organelles have a continuous connection with nuclear membrane?

(a) Golgi apparatus (b) Lysosomes
(c) RER (d) SER

343. In RER, ribosomes are located on

(a) the cytoplasmic side
(b) the luminal side
(c) both (a) and (b)
(d) all throughout

344. SER is involved in

(a) phospholipid biosynthesis and detoxification reaction
(b) phospholipid biosynthesis and protein synthesis
(c) protein synthesis
(d) phospholipid biosynthesis

345. SERs in retinal cells are called

(a) sarcoplasmic reticulum
(b) retinal reticulum
(c) myeloid bodies
(d) amyloid bodies

346. The functions of RER include

(a) protein synthesis and detoxification
(b) protein synthesis and post-translational modification
(c) protein synthesis and phospholipid biosynthesis
(d) protein synthesis only

347. Which of the following statements are true regarding endoplasmic reticulam?

(a) ER provides structural framework to the cell
(b) ER acts as an intracellular transporting system
(c) SER is involved in the synthesis of lipids
(d) all of these

348. Rough ER is called rough because of

(a) rough texture of the surface
(b) surface is studded with membrane proteins
(c) surface is studied with ribosomes
(d) All of these

349. RER is involved in the synthesis of

(a) membrane proteins and secretory proteins
(b) different proteins of the cell
(c) membrane proteins, secretory proteins and lysosomal proteins
(d) membrane proteins, secretory proteins and nuclear proteins

350. Which of the following organelle is involved in xenobiotic detoxification?

(a) Golgi (b) Lysosome
(c) SER (d) RER

351. Protein glycosylation occurs in the

(a) lumen of mitochondrion
(b) lumen of rough ER
(c) lumen of smooth ER
(d) lumen of lysosomes

352. Ribophorins are

(a) transmembrane glycoproteins on RER
(b) transmembrane glycoproteins on SER
(c) luminal proteins on RER
(d) luminal proteins on SER

353. Which of the following organelle is called "the perinuclear dense bodies"?

(a) Lysosome (b) Nucleolus
(c) Peroxisome (d) All of these

354. Lysosomes are present in all except

(a) muscle cells (b) acinar cells
(c) erythrocytes (d) hepatocytes

355. Which is the enzyme used as a marker for the lysosomes?

(a) Pyruvate dehydrogenase
(b) Phospholipase
(c) Acid phosphatase
(d) Succinate dehydrogenase

356. The pH of lysosome is

(a) neutral
(b) acidic
(c) basic
(d) depends on the cell type

357. The staining technique used to locate lysosome is

(a) Janus Green staining
(b) Bismarck stain
(c) Gomori stain
(d) Osmium tetraoxide

358. Liposomal factions are isolated by

(a) electrophoresis
(b) ultra-centrifugation
(c) both (a) and (b)
(d) sucrose density gradient centrifugation

359. The acidic pH of lysosome is due to

(a) deposition of waste materials
(b) presence of hydrolytic enzymes which have an acidic optimum pH
(c) presence of anabolic enzymes which have an acidic optimum pH
(d) all of these

360. Which of the following organelle is called the "suicidal bags of the cell"?

(a) Lysosomes
(b) Lysosomes and Golgi
(c) Lysosomes and ER
(d) Lysosomes and mitochondria

361. Which of the following is the function of lysosomes?

(a) Autophagy (b) Autolysis
(c) Digestion (d) All of these

362. During protein targeting, lysosomal proteins are tagged with

(a) sialic acid
(b) KDEL sequence
(c) mannose-6-phosphate
(d) glycolipids

363. Which of the following is not a disease associated with lysosome malfunctioning?

(a) Tay-Sachs disease (b) I-cell disease
(c) Pompe's disease (d) Marfan syndrome

364. Lysosomes are involved in

(a) extracellular digestion
(b) intracellular digestion
(c) both (a) and (b)
(d) none of these

365. Lysosomes involved in extracellular digestion are present in

(a) cardiac cells (b) sperm
(c) zygote (d) all of these

366. The acidic pH in the lysosome is maintained by

(a) GTP dependent proton pump in the lumen
(b) ATP dependent proton pump on the membrane
(c) HCl in lysosome
(d) All of these

367. Lysosomal membrane is rich in

(a) cardiolipin (b) sialic acid
(c) sterols (d) all of these

368. Which of the following cells lacks cytoskeleton?

(a) Eukaryotic plant cell
(b) Prokaryotic bacterial cells
(c) Both (a) and (b)
(d) Prokaryotic cells and eukaryotic animal cells

369. Cytoskeletons are chemically

(a) nucleoprotein filaments
(b) nucleoprotein filaments and lipids
(c) ribonucleoprotein filaments
(d) protein filaments

370. The existence of cytoskeleton was first postulated by

(a) Strausburger (b) Kolitzoff
(c) Meischer (d) Crick

371. The cytoskeleton consists of

(a) microtubules
(b) microfilaments
(c) intermediate filaments
(d) all of these

372. Microtubules are made up of

(a) flagellin (b) desmin
(c) tubulin (d) actin and myosin

373. Which of the following is a myosin associated protein

(a) 'tus' protein (b) 'tau' protein
(c) 'rho' protein (d) G protein

374. The microtubule assembly is inhibited by

(a) colchicine (b) vincristine
(c) vinblastine (d) all of these

375. The microfilaments are made up of

(a) actin (b) actin and tubulin
(c) desmin (d) vimetin

376. Microfilaments are involved in

(a) cyclosis
(b) amoeboid movements
(c) furrow formation during cell division
(d) all of these

377. The intermediate filament present in nail and hair is type I IF protein made of

(a) lamins (b) vimetins
(c) keratins (d) tubulins

378. Which of the following is a microfilament inhibitor?

(a) Aspirin (b) Cinchonine
(c) Colchicine (d) Cytochalasin -B

379. Chromosome movement during cell division is regulated by

(a) microtubules
(b) microfilaments
(c) intermediate filaments
(d) all of these

380. Which of the following statements are true?

(a) Intermediate filaments are resistant to colchicine and cytochalasin-B
(b) Microtubules are made up of tubulins
(c) Microtubules are made up of actin
(d) All of these

381. Cilia and flagella of eukaryotic cells are made up of

(a) keratin (b) tubulin
(c) lamin (d) desmin

382. Which of the following is the most heterogenous type of cytoskeletal filament?

(a) Microtubules
(b) Microfilaments
(c) Intermediate filaments
(d) None of these

MARK TRUE OR FALSE (T/F)

CELL AND CELL STRUCTURE

1. The net movement of uncharged, polar molecules across a semipermeable membrane from a low concentration to a high concentration occurs by facilitated diffusion.
2. Mitochondria are the main site of protein synthesis
3. Mitochondria have DNA arranged in circles
4. In mitochondria, the inner membrane contains the enzymes needed for Kreb's cycle
5. Mitochondria contain a bilayer membrane
6. Mitochondria contain DNA that is inherited exclusively from the mother
7. The genes for HLA are on chromosome No. 6
8. HLA is a multiple allelic system
9. The inheritance of HLA alleles follow a codominant Mendelian system
10. The HLA proteins are found inside the cell
11. HLA B37 is associated with ankylosing spondylitis
12. Chloroplasts mainy produce proteins
13. A karyotype may be prepared from chorionic villi cells of the foetus
14. A karyotype helps in the diagnosis of chromosome disorders
15. A karyotype is made from cells arrested at telophase of mitosis
16. A karyotype from a Patau syndrome patient shows an extra chromosome No. 18
17. A karyotype helps in the identification of the Philadelphia chromosome in chronic myeloid laeukemia
18. In classical haemophilia A, carriers may show clinical features
19. In Duchenne muscular dystrophy, carriers never produce affected males if the husband is normal
20. In cystic fibrosis, a mating between carriers has a 25% risk of producing an affected child
21. Carrier states are seen in achondroplasia
22. Certain carrier states can be detected using DNA studies

BACTERIA

23. Gram-positive bacteria have an outer membrane that stains purple
24. Because the peptidoglycans wall of Gram-positive bacteria is covered by an outer (lipopolysaccharide) membrane, they are more resistant to the action of most antibiotics than Gram-negative bacteria
25. Most bacterial cells have two chromosomes
26. Some bacteria are unable to grow in the presence of oxygen
27. Since prokaryotes are haploid, mutations are immediately subjected to natural selection
28. Bacteria (Domain Bacteria) are the more common type of prokaryote
29. All photosynthetic bacteria produce oxygen during photosynthesis
30. The kingdom Protista is the most diverse in the domain Eukarya

31. If an organism is capable of photosynthesis, it belongs to the plant kingdom
32. One characteristic that sets the Protists apart from the rest of the kingdoms is their small size
33. Diatoms have intricate double shells made up of calcium carbonate
34. Viruses are not able to multiply outside a living cell
35. Viruses can be seen with a light microscope
36. Bacteriophages are viruses that parasitize bacteria
37. Viruses do not display any characteristics of living things
38. Human immunodeficiency virus (HIV) is a retrovirus
39. A naked virus lacks a membranous envelope
40. Viruses have both DNA and RNA
41. Some viruses are cancer causing
42. Viruses are not susceptible to antibiotics, so antibiotics should not be taken when you have a cold or the flu
43. Viral DNA does not change, so vaccinations are effective for your entire lifetime
44. Spindle fibres in cells are made up of pectin
45. To observe G-banding on chromosomes, fluorescent microscopy is required
46. The R-bands are located in the zones that do not fluoresce with quinacrine mustard, that is, they are between the Q-bands
47. The amount of DNA per haploid nucleus is called C value
48. Chromosomal DNA along with histones and non-histones form a nucleoprotein fibre
49. Histones are acidic proteins carrying a net negative charge at physiological pH
50. A nucleosome is much larger than a chromomere

6
Cell Division

MULTIPLE-CHOICE QUESTIONS

1. In the cell cycle, the resting phase is called

(a) interphase (b) prophase
(c) metaphase (d) telophase

2. Assume that a cell has 50 units of DNA at G_1 of interphase. How many units of DNA would a cell at prophase of mitosis contain?

(a) 25 (b) 50
(c) 100
(d) Cannot be determined

3. Assume that a cell has 50 units of DNA at G_1 of interphase. How many units of DNA would a cell at telophase of mitosis contain?

(a) 25 (b) 50
(c) 100
(d) Cannot be determined

4. The G_0 phase is

(a) the checkpoint before G_1
(b) the state of most cells in an animal body
(c) another name for interphase
(d) a permanent state of all body cells

5. In the life cycle of a human cell, each chromosome contains two chromatids by the end of the ______ phase

(a) C (b) G_1
(c) G_2 (d) M
(e) S

6. Replication of the genome occurs in the ______ phase of the cell cycle

(a) C (b) G_1
(c) G_2 (d) M
(e) S

7. The amount of DNA in the nucleus doubles from what is called a 2C amount, present in a diploid cell immediately after mitotic division, to the 4C amount, present at the end of the ______ phase

(a) S (b) G_1
(c) G_2 (d) M

8. DNA synthesis occurs during the ______ phase of the cell cycle

(a) gap 1 (G_1) (b) gap 2 (G_2)
(c) S (d) mitosis

9. A flowering plant has somatic chromosome number of 40. How many chromatids will be present at G_1?

(a) 0 (b) 20
(c) 40 (d) 80

10. A flowering plant has somatic chromosome number of 40. How many chromatids will be present at G_2?

(a) 0 (b) 20
(c) 40 (d) 80

11. A flowering plant has a somatic chromosome number of 40. The number of centromeres at prophase in one somatic cell would be

(a) 40 (b) 80
(c) 80 (d) none
(e) 80

12. In the cell cycle, the resting phase is divided into three parts. The production of proteins takes place during

(a) first growth (G_1)
(b) synthesis
(c) second growth (G_2)
(d) nuclear division phase

13. DNA is replicated in the cell during

(a) cytokinesis phase
(b) synthesis (S) phase
(c) nuclear division phase
(d) second growth (G_2) phase

14. Organelles grow and divide in the cell during

(a) synthesis phase
(b) cell division
(c) nuclear division
(d) synthesis phase second growth (G_2)

15. When does DNA synthesis occur during the cell cycle?

(a) G_1 (b) G_2
(c) G_0 (d) S

16. Cells which no longer divide (such as certain specialized cells found in the human brain) remain in which phase of the cell cycle?

(a) Prophase (b) S Phase
(c) G_0 Phase (d) G_1 Phase

17. The purpose for check points in the cell cycle is to

(a) cause cells to grow out of control leading to cancers
(b) stop mitosis to prevent chromosome duplication
(c) stop DNA synthesis to prevent chromosome duplication
(d) pause the cell cycle until all the necessary building blocks are synthesized
(e) give geneticists something else to study

18. A diploid cell has 40 units of DNA at G_1 of interphase. How many units of DNA are present in the cell after meiosis I?

(a) 10 (b) 20
(c) 40 (d) 80

19. A diploid cell has 40 units of DNA at G_1 of interphase. How many units of DNA are present in a gamete?

(a) 10 (b) 20
(c) 40 (d) 80

20. Mitosis is controlled at the ______ checkpoint

(a) C (b) G_1
(c) G_2 (d) M
(e) S

21. DNA replication is controlled at the ______ checkpoint

(a) C (b) G_1
(c) G_2 (d) M
(e) S

22. The primary growth phase of a cell is the

(a) G_0 (b) G_1
(c) G_2 (d) M
(e) S

23. Preparations for genome separation are made in the ______ phase

(a) C (b) G_1
(c) G_2 (d) M
(e) S

24. The cell cycle is controlled in most cells by

(a) time, after a certain length of time the cell divides
(b) a series of checkpoints
(c) the completion of one phase, which triggers the beginning of the next
(d) cell size, when the cell reaches a certain size, it divides
(e) different cells exhibit different control strategies, any of the 4 above can be found in eukaryotic organisms

25. Cell growth is controlled at the ______ checkpoint

(a) C (b) G_1
(c) G_2 (d) M
(e) S

26. A cleavage furrow forms in animal cells during

(a) C (b) G_1
(c) G_2 (d) M
(e) S

27. Which factors do not influence cell division?

(a) Crowding (b) Growth hormones
(c) Cyclins
(d) All of the above influence cell division

28. Which statement best describes a difference between cell division in plant and animal cells?

(a) In animal cells, cytoplasmic division is accomplished by a groove formation
(b) In plant cells, cytoplasmic division is accomplished by a centromere division
(c) In plant cells, centrosomes have a distinct role in spindle formation, while in animal cells centrosomes do not function during cell division
(d) In animal cells, replication of chromosomes occurs during the nondividing phase, while in plant cells replication occurs when the nuclear membrane disintegrates

29. A replicated chromosome consists of two very long strands of identical chromosomal material called

(a) telomeres (b) chromatids
(c) centromeres (d) genes

30. Which of the following events do not occur during interphase?

(a) Chromatin condenses
(b) Protein synthesis
(c) Organelles replicate
(d) DNA replication

31. Chromosome condensation during mitosis involves

(a) disappearance of the nuclear membrane
(b) production of a solenoid fibre
(c) the disappearance of nucleosomes
(d) contraction of the spindle fibres
(e) extensive DNA synthesis

32. Chromosomes are thin strands about

(a) 50 μm long (b) 1 μm long
(c) 100 μm long (d) 25 μm long
(e) 75 μm long

33. Chromosomes are made up of two strands called

(a) centrioles (b) centromeres
(c) chromosomes (d) chromatids

34. The strands in the above question are joined at a point called

(a) spindle (b) chromatid
(c) centromere (d) chromosome

35. Chromosomes are made up of DNA, RNA and three types of proteins. These proteins are called

(a) histones (b) scaffold proteins
(c) polymerases (d) nucleosomes

36. The proteins, as in the above question, hold the DNA in position. These proteins having enzymatic function are called

(a) histones (b) polymerases
(c) scaffold proteins (d) nucleosomes
(e) polymerases

37. The proteins having a structural function are

(a) histones (b) polymerases
(c) scaffold proteins (d) nucleosomes

38. Mitosis is also called

(a) homotypic division (b) somatic division
(c) equational division(d) all of these

39. The term "equational division" was first used by

(a) Weismann (b) Flemming
(c) Strasburger (d) none of these

40. In plants, mitosis occurs in

(a) root tip (b) leaf base
(c) stem tip (d) all of these

41. Chromosomes become shorter and thicker during

(a) prophase (b) anaphase
(c) telophase (d) metaphase

42. Chromosomes move towards opposite pole during

(a) interphase (b) anaphase
(c) metaphase (d) prophase

43. In mitosis, chromosomes are arranged at equatorial plate during

(a) early prophase (b) early metaphase
(c) late metaphase (d) late prophase

44. Nucleolus disappears at the end of

(a) prophase (b) anaphase
(c) telophase (d) metaphase

45. Nucleolus reappears at the end of

(a) prophase (b) anaphase
(c) telophase (d) metaphase

46. In ______, chromosomes align down the center of the cell, held by the spindle

(a) prophase (b) metaphase
(c) anaphase (d) telophase

47. During ______, replicated chromosomes condense, the spindle forms, and the nuclear membrane breaks down

(a) prophase (b) metaphase
(c) anaphase (d) telophase

48. In ______, centromeres part and one set of chromosomes is pulled to each end of the cell

(a) prophase (b) metaphase
(c) anaphase (d) telophase

49. During anaphase of the mitosis

(a) DNA recombines
(b) sister chromatids move to opposite poles
(c) the nuclear membrane disappears
(d) RNA replicates
(e) DNA content essentially doubles

50. During prophase of mitosis

(a) DNA recombines
(b) sister chromatids move to opposite poles
(c) the nuclear membrane disappears
(d) RNA replicates
(e) DNA content essentially doubles

51. The longitudinal halves of a chromosome that have undergone replication are known as

(a) centrosomes (b) chromatids
(c) chaismata (d) centromeres

52. A flowering plant has somatic chromosome number of 40. How many centromeres will be present at prophase in one somatic cell?

(a) 0 (b) 20
(c) 40 (d) 80

53. A flowering plant has somatic chromosome number of 40. How many chromatids will be present at prophase in one somatic cell?

(a) 0 (b) 20
(c) 40 (d) 80

54. A flowering plant has somatic chromosome number of 40. How many kinetochores will be present at prophase?

(a) 0 (b) 20
(c) 40 (d) 80

55. Chromatin material in eukaryotes is uncoiled during

(a) telophase (b) anaphase
(c) interphase (d) prophase
(e) metaphase

56. A plant has the chromosome number $2n = 2x = 16$. Which of the following is untrue?

(a) There are eight chromosomes in each telophase nucleus at mitosis
(b) The zygote has 16 chromosomes
(c) The pollen grains have 8 chromosomes
(d) All of the chromosomes have centromeres
(e) The species is diploid

57. Nuclear division occurs when the nucleus divides to give two cells by

(a) metaphase (b) meiosis
(c) mitosis (d) cytokinesis

58. Nuclear division is followed by cell division also known as

(a) cytokinesis (b) mitosis
(c) meiosis (d) synthesis

59. The fusion of gametes resulting in the doubling of the number of chromosomes is known as

(a) mitosis (b) syngamy
(c) telophase (d) anaphase

60. Regarding mitosis and cytokinesis, one difference between higher plants and animals is that in plants

(a) the spindles contain cellulose microfibrils in addition to microtubules, whereas animal spindles do not contain microfibrils
(b) sister chromatids are identical, whereas in animals they differ from one another
(c) a cell plate begins to form at telophase, whereas in animals a cleavage furrow is initiated at that stage
(d) chromosomes become attached to the spindle at prophase, whereas in animals, chromosomes do not become attached until anaphase
(e) spindle poles contain centrioles, whereas spindle poles in animals do not contain centrioles

61. In prokaryotes, just before the cell divides, the two daughter genomes are attached side by side to the

(a) cell membrane (b) replication origin
(c) centromeres (d) equatorial plate
(e) kinetochore

62. The spindle forms in the phase

(a) C (b) G_1
(c) G_2 (d) M
(e) S

63. ______ begins when pairs of sister chromatids align in the center of the cell

(a) anaphase (b) interphase
(c) metaphase (d) prophase
(e) telophase

64. The condensation of the chromosome portion containing the rRNA genes causes the disappearance of the

(a) nucleus (b) aster
(c) centriole (d) tubulin
(e) nucleolus

65. A nuclear envelope forms around each set of sister chromatids in

(a) anaphase (b) interphase
(c) metaphase (d) prophase
(e) telophase

66. The centromeres move towards the poles in

(a) anaphase (b) interphase
(c) metaphase (d) prophase
(e) telophase

67. One cycle of mitosis gives rise to

(a) two haploid cells
(b) four haploid cells
(c) four diploid cells
(d) two diploid cells

68. Each chromosome replicates to produce two sister chromatids in

(a) anaphase (b) interphase
(c) metaphase (d) prophase
(e) telophase

69. In plant cytokinesis, cellulose is laid down forming

(a) a middle lamella
(b) a cell plate
(c) cell walls
(d) a plasma membrane
(e) a cleavage furrow

70. Microtubules grow from the poles to kinetochores of each chromatid during

(a) anaphase (b) interphase
(c) metaphase (d) prophase
(e) telophase

71. Just prior to cell division, the diploid human body cell contains ______ chromatids

(a) 23 (b) 46
(c) 69 (d) 92
(e) 122

72. Which of the following statements about mitosis is incorrect?

(a) The daughter nuclei are genetically identical to the parent nucleus
(b) Chromosomes separate during anaphase due to the interaction of polar microtubules from opposite poles pushing against each other
(c) Chromosomes separate during anaphase when the kinetochore microtubules shorten as they depolymerize
(d) Chromosomes move to the metaphase plate using motor proteins, a kind of kinesin, attached to spindle fibres
(e) The centrosomes organize the microtubules of the spindle fibres

73. Besides colchicines, which one of the following induces chromosome doubling?

(a) Acenaphthene (b) 8-hydroxyquinoline
(c) Nitrous acid (d) All of the above

74. Which of the following terms is not related to mitosis?

(a) Gametes (b) Chromosomes
(c) DNA replication (d) Somatic cells
(e) All are related

75. Which phase of mitosis is associated with chromosomes alignment at the center of the cell and centromeres dividing?

(a) Interphase (b) Prophase
(c) Metaphase (d) Anaphase
(e) Telophase

76. Which phase of mitosis is associated with the formation of nuclear envelope?

(a) Interphase (b) Prophase
(c) Metaphase (d) Anaphase
(e) Telophase

77. Which phase of mitosis is associated with the separation of chromatids?

(a) Interphase (b) Prophase
(c) Metaphase (d) Anaphase
(e) Telophase

78. During cell division, which structure forms as a network of protein cables?

(a) Spindle (b) Aster
(c) Kinetochore (d) Centromere
(e) Chromatid

79. Chromosome condensation during mitosis involves

(a) disappearance of the nuclear membrane
(b) production of a solenoid fibre
(c) the disappearance of nucleosomes
(d) contraction of the spindle fibres
(e) extensive DNA synthesis

80. For a diploid plant with 24 chromosomes

(a) the basic chromosome number is $x = 6$
(b) the gametic number is $n = 12$
(c) the number of chromosomes in the pollen nuclei is 6
(d) the number of chromatids in a diplotene nucleus is 24
(e) the root meristem cell has 48 chromosomes

81. During meiosis

(a) two identical cells are produced
(b) the chromosome number stays the same
(c) chromosomes are not involved
(d) the chromosome number is doubled
(e) the chromosome number is reduced by half

82. Which is not correct regarding nondisjunction?

(a) May fail to separate maternal chromatids from one another or paternal chromatids from one another
(b) May fail to separate maternal from paternal chromatids
(c) May lead to Down syndrome
(d) Separates maternal from paternal chromatids
(e) Occurs more frequently in human females over age 35

83. How many different gametes can be formed from the genotype AABBCCDdEe?

(a) 2 (b) 2^4
(c) 3^2 (d) 2^2
(e) 4^2

84. How many tetrads are found in meiotic prophase in an organism with a diploid number of 12?

(a) 4 (b) 6
(c) 18 (d) 24
(e) 12

85. How many dyads move to each pole during the first meiotic anaphase in an organism with a haploid number of 6?

(a) 24 (b) 6
(c) 3 (d) 12
(e) None at anaphase

86. During meiosis

(a) the chromosome number is doubled
(b) chromosomes are not involved
(c) two identical cells are produced
(d) the chromosome number stays the same
(e) the chromosome number is reduced by half

87. Human sperm and egg formation (gametes) differ from one another in which of the following way?

(a) Timing of gamete formation
(b) Polar body formation
(c) Site of gamete production
(d) All of these statements refer to differences between human sperm and egg formation

88. Nuclear division occurs when the nucleus divides to give four cells by

(a) meiosis (b) mitosis
(c) metaphase (d) cytokinesis

89. Meiosis reduces the

(a) diploid number of chromosomes
(b) haploid number of chromosomes
(c) homologous number of chromosomes
(d) zygote number of chromosomes

90. Meiosis reduces the number of chromosomes to

(a) diploid number
(b) homologous number
(c) zygote number
(d) haploid number

91. During prophase I of meiosis I, which substage is characterized by the ap-pearance of chiasmata between paired homologs?

(a) leptotene (b) zygote
(c) pachytene (d) diplotene
(e) diakinesis

92. In animals, meiosis results in the formation of

(a) genes (b) chromosomes
(c) gametes (d) homologous pairs

93. In plants, meiosis results in the formation of

(a) gametes (b) zygotes
(c) spores (d) sporophytes

94. The random assortment of chromosomes takes place during

(a) prophase I (b) metaphase I
(c) anaphase I (d) telophase I

95. The separation of linked genes takes place due to

(a) shuffling (b) crossing over
(c) fusing (d) separating

96. The separation of linked genes takes place during

(a) prophase I (b) telophase I
(c) metaphase I (d) anaphase I

97. If the amount of DNA in a mammalian cell in early prophase is 4 units, what is the amount of DNA in the same cell at anaphase I of meiosis?

(a) 1 unit (b) 2 units
(c) 4 units (d) 8 units

98. What is non-disjunction in meiosis I?

(a) Homologs do not separate at prophase I
(b) Homologs separate, but only one goes to a pole; the other stays at the metaphase plate
(c) Sister chromatids do not separate from each other properly in meiosis I
(d) A segment of one chromatid breaks off of a chromosome during disjunction
(e) More than one of the above is non-disjunction

99. A process that occurs during meiosis but not during mitosis is

(a) anaphase (b) complementation
(c) cytokinesis (d) synapsis
(e) centromere division

100. The stage of meiosis prophase I characterized by thick, fully synapsed chromosomes is

(a) leptotene (b) zygotene
(c) pachytene (d) diplotene
(e) diakinesis

101. The stage of meiosis in which chromosomes pair and cross over is

(a) prophase I (b) metaphase I
(c) prophase II (d) metaphase II
(e) anaphase II

102. If the human female were to produce 400 eggs during her lifetime, the number of primary oocytes from which these would arise would be

(a) 400 (b) 100
(c) 200 (d) 800

103. Which of the following do mitosis and second division of meiosis have in common?

(i) Genetically identical material passes to each pole
(ii) A 'resting phase' (interphase) always occurs before the division commences
(iii) Both chromosomes of an homologous pair lie at the equator during metaphase
(iv) Chromatids separate during anaphase

(a) i and iii (b) ii and iv
(c) iii and iv (d) iii only
(e) iv only

104. If the human female were to produce 400 eggs during her lifetime, from how many secondary oocytes would these eggs arise?

(a) 23 (b) 200
(c) 400 (d) 1200

105. If the human female were to produce 400 eggs during her lifetime, a maximum of how many polar bodies would you expect to find in such a female?

(a) 23 (b) 200
(c) 400 (d) 1200

106. If the human female were to produce 400 eggs during her lifetime, while observing one of these primary oocytes, how many bivalents would you expect to find?

(a) 23 (b) 46
(c) 92 (d) 0

107. Meiosis is also called

(a) heterotypic division
(b) segregational division
(c) reduction division
(d) all of these

108. In plants, meiosis takes place in

(a) anthers (b) ovaries
(c) stem tip (d) a and b above

109. Meiosis provides opportunities for

(a) crossing over (b) segregation
(c) recombination (d) all of these

110. Daughter cells produced by meiosis are different from mother cell in

(a) shape
(b) chromosome number
(c) size
(d) all of these

111. The term "meiotic drive" was first used by

(a) Flemming
(b) Sandler and Novitski
(c) Strasburger
(d) Whitman

112. The term "synaptonemal complex" was first used by

(a) Strasburger (b) Moses
(c) Flemming (d) none of these

113. Synaptonemal complex develops during

(a) pachytene (b) diplotene
(c) diakinesis (d) zygotene

114. Crossing over occurs during

(a) pachytene (b) zygotene
(c) diplotene (d) leptotene

115. Separation of homologous chromosomes begins during

(a) leptotene (b) diplotene
(c) diakinesis (d) pachytene

116. Chromosomes look like bivalent during

(a) leptotene (b) diplotene
(c) diakinesis (d) pachytene

117. In mitosis, division of cytoplasm is called

(a) cytokinesis (b) diakinesis
(c) karyokinesis (d) none of these

118. Oocytes can be frozen in liquid nitrogen. At which phase of the cell cycle are these cells at the time of freezing?

(a) Meiosis, metaphase I
(b) Meiosis, metaphase II
(c) Mitosis, metaphase
(d) Meiosis or mitosis, interphase

119. Which of the following could be a potential drawback to freezing oocytes?

(a) Loss of chromosomal material
(b) Retention of a polar body
(c) Delicate nature of the cell
(d) All of the above

120. Oogenesis (egg cell formation) occurs in the ovary, where the oogonia enlarge greatly to form primary oocytes. Which of the following below correctly desi-gnates the total chromosome content of each primary oocyte?

(a) N (b) 2N
(c) 3N (d) 4N

121. The plant of bread wheat has 42 chromosomes, thus

(a) during meiosis there will be 21 chromosomes going to each pole
(b) during meiosis there will be 42 pairs of chromosomes
(c) during mitosis there will be 21 chromosomes going to each pole
(d) during mitosis there will be 14 chromosomes going to each pole
(e) during mitosis there will be 7 chromosomes going to each pole

122. Chromosomes that contain the same sets of genes and pair up in meiosis I are called

(a) homologous (b) heterologous
(c) complementary (d) non-disjunctive
(e) parallel

123. Which stage of prophase I of meiosis is characterized by the initiation of active pairing?

(a) Leptotene (b) Zygotene
(c) Pachytene (d) Diplotene
(e) Diakinesis

124. Which stage of prophase I of meiosis is characterized by the initiation of chromosomal "thickening"?

(a) Leptotene (b) Zygotene
(c) Pachytene (d) Diplotene
(e) Diakinesis

125. Which stage of prophase I of meiosis is characterized by fully compacted chromosomes ready to begin metaphase?

(a) Leptotene (b) Zygotene
(c) Pachytene (d) Diplotene
(e) Diakinesis

126. Which of the following processes occurs in meiosis but not mitosis?

(a) Cell division
(b) Separation of homologous centromeres to opposite poles
(c) Chromation formation
(d) Chromosome condensation (shortening)
(e) Pairing of homologs

127. A diploid cell containing eight chromosomes undergoes meiosis. How many chromosomes are present in the cell after meiosis I?

(a) 2 (b) 4
(c) 8 (d) 16

128. A diploid cell containing eight chromosomes undergoes meiosis. How many chromosomes are present in the cell after meiosis II?

(a) 2 (b) 4
(c) 8 (d) 16

129. Before birth, female's oocytes are

(a) not present
(b) arrested in prophase I of meiosis
(c) arrested in prophase II of meiosis
(d) arrested in prophase of mitosis

130. Meiosis II proceeds in a female's oocyte

(a) prior to birth
(b) monthly after puberty
(c) upon ovulation
(d) upon fertilization

131. Genetic variability arises during meiosis from

(a) crossing over
(b) independent assortment
(c) random alignment of chromosomes at metaphase
(d) all of the above

132. How many sets of chromosomes are present in a primary oocyte and the polar body derived from it?

(a) 2, 1 (b) 2, 2
(c) 1, 2 (d) 1, 1

133. Which of the following statements about gamete formation is false?

(a) In females, most of the cytoplasm concentrates in one huge cell
(b) In males, meiosis produces four similarly shaped sperms
(c) Spermatogenesis takes months
(d) Oogenesis is completed prior to birth

134. Are the sister chromatids of a chromo-some necessarily identical at the begin-ning of metaphase I of meiosis?

(a) Yes, sister chromatids are always identical structures
(b) Yes, only homologous chromosomes differ from each other
(c) No, crossing over could generate differences
(d) Maybe, it varies from cell division to cell division

135. Meiosis not only halves the number of chromosomes, but also introduces genetic variation through the fusion of gametes at

a) prophase b) metaphase
c) gametogenesis d) fertilization

136. Chromatids coiling in the meiotic and mitotic division is

(a) plectonemic in both
(b) paranemic in both
(c) paranemic in mitosis and plectonemic in meiosis
(d) plectonemic in mitosis and paranemic in meiosis

137. When there is an increase in the conden-sation of chromatin during the process of cell division

(a) heterochromatin increases
(b) euchromatin increases
(c) differentiation of euchromatin and heterochromatin decreases
(d) differentiation of euchromatin and heterochromatin increase

138. ______ is the number of DNA in the chromosome at the G_2 stage of the cell cycle

(a) 1 (b) 2
(c) 3 (d) 0

139. The longest stage in the cell cycle is

(a) interphase (b) anaphase
(c) metaphase (d) none of the above

140. The ______ stage implies the exit of cells from the cell cycle

(a) S (b) G_1
(c) G_2 (d) G_0

141. Synapsis is defined as the pairing of

(a) acentric chromosomes
(b) non-homologous chromosomes
(c) any chromosomes
(d) homologous chromosomes

142. Mitosis can be observed in

(a) polyploid individual
(b) diploid individual
(c) haploid individual
(d) all of these

143. Cyclin is associated with

(a) leptospirosis (b) glycolysis
(c) cyclosis (d) mitosis

144. Synthesis of RNA and proteins takes place in

(a) M phase (b) S phase
(c) G_1 phase (d) G_2 phase

145. Crossing over occurs between

(a) two daughter nuclei
(b) two different bivalents
(c) non-sister chromatids of bivalents
(d) sister chromatids of bivalents

146. Replication of centriole occurs in

(a) interphase
(b) prophase
(c) metaphase
(d) anaphase

147. Colchicine arrests which of the following stages of cell division?

(a) Anaphase (b) Telophase
(c) Interphase (d) Metaphase

148. Amitosis is shown by

(a) *Euglena* (b) *Syllis*
(c) hydra (d) bacteria

149. Name the protein which holds two sister chromatids

(a) Securin (b) Separase
(c) Cohesin (d) APC

150. Which of the following microtubule pulls the chromosomes towards pole?

(a) Astral (b) Polar
(c) Kinetochore (d) Centrioles

151. Spindle fibre is attached to the chromosome by a process known as

(a) congression (b) binding
(c) alignment (d) search and capture

152. What is congression?

(a) Attachment of microtubule to chromosomes
(b) Attachment of two sister chromatids
(c) The endpoint of the spindle pole
(d) The midpoint of two spindle poles

153. During oogenesis the cell that is fertilized by a sperm to become an egg is

(a) primary spermatocyte
(b) secondary oocyte
(c) primary oocyte
(d) secondary spermatocyte

154. A bivalent consists of

(a) two chromatids and one centromere
(b) four chromatids and two centromeres
(c) two chromatids and two centromeres
(d) four chromatids and four centromeres

155. A change in the amount of yolk and its distribution in the egg will affect

(a) fertilization
(b) formation of zygote
(c) pattern of cleavage
(d) number of blastomeres produced

156. Chiasmata are first seen in

(a) pachytene (b) zygotene
(c) leptotene (d) diplotene

157. Balbiani rings occur in

(a) autosome
(b) heterosome
(c) lampbrush chromosome
(d) polytene chromosome

158. Which of the following statements regarding cyclin-dependent protein kinase is not correct?

(a) Their activity is regulated by cyclins
(b) They can change the activity of proteins involved in the progression of cells through cell cycle
(c) Their activity fluctuates during cell cycle
(d) Each type of cell contains one specific form

159. Which of the following statements regarding cyclins is not correct?

(a) They can become linked to ubiquitin
(b) They catalyze the phosphorylation of proteins
(c) They contain specific amino acid sequence that targets them for proteolysis
(d) They are activated and degraded during cell cycle

160. Ubiquitin is a

(a) protein kinase
(b) protease
(c) component of the electron transport system
(d) protein that tags another protein for proteolysis

161. Cdk 2/cyclin E functions in

(a) G/M transition (b) G_2
(c) M (d) G_1/S transition

162. Cyclin dependent kinases which control progression through cell cycle check points are totally activated by which of the following?

(a) Binding to cyclin, plus phosphorylation by a Cdk activating protein kinase
(b) Binding to cyclins
(c) Phosphorylation by Cdk activating protein kinase
(d) Phosphorylation by a tyrosine kinase

163. At the end of each phase of cell cycle cyclins activating Cdks in that phase are inactivated irreversibly by

(a) multiple phosphorylations
(b) de-phosphorylation
(c) ubiquitinylation
(d) destabilizing by proteolysis in a proteasome

164. At which cell cycle check point, cell cycle is halted if cell's DNA is damaged?

(a) $G_1 - S$ (b) $S - G_2$
(c) $G_2 - M$ (d) $G_0 - G_1$ meiosis

165. Which of the following occurs in but not in mitosis?

(a) Attachment of spindle fibres to kinetochore
(b) Replication of DNA prior to start of cell division
(c) Separation of sister chromatids at anaphase
(d) Pairing of homologous chromosomes at metaphase plate

166. Passage of a cell through stages of cell cycle is controlled by a protein kinase that phosphorylates many different proteins at appropriate times

(a) Cdk activating kinase
(b) Cyclin-dependent kinase
(c) Cyclins
(d) Tyrosine kinase

167. The active cyclin-CDK complex regulates the cell cycle through

(a) cleavage of specific proteins
(b) methylation of specific proteins
(c) dephosphorylation of specific proteins
(d) phosphorylation of specific proteins

168. Which of the following cell sequence correctly describes the cell cycle?

(a) S - G_2 - M - Cytokinenins - G_1
(b) M - G_1- G_2 - Cytokinesis
(c) G_1- G_2 - M - Cytokinesis
(d) Cytokinesis - Mitosis - G_1- G_2

169. Which of the following cyclin-CDK complex initiates the degradation of nuclear membrane during the cell cycle?

(a) Cyclin D-CDK_4
(b) Cyclin E-CDK_2
(c) Cyclin A-CDK_4
(d) Cyclin B-CDK_1

170. Which of the following statement is true?

(a) CDKs are inactive in the absence of a partner cyclin
(b) CDK is not necessary to regulate the cell cycle checkpoints
(c) In Eukaryotes only the Cyclin and many CDKs are present
(d) Cyclin possesses catalytic activity in the presence of GTP

171. The first cyclin produced in the cell cycle, in response to extracellular signals is

(a) Cyclin C (b) Cyclin B
(c) Cyclin A (d) Cyclin D

172. Which of the following is not an actual cell cycle checkpoint?

(a) M checkpoint (b) G_1 checkpoint
(c) S checkpoint (d) Spindle checkpoint

173. Spindle assembly checkpoint operates at the

(a) end of metaphase
(b) end of anaphase
(c) beginning of anaphase
(d) end of G_2 phase

MARK TRUE OR FALSE (T/F)

1. At the end of cell division, each daughter cell has the same number of chromosomes but half the amount of DNA that the parent cell had when it was in G_2 of the cell cycle
2. Chromosome replication takes place during interphase
3. Cytokinesis takes place during metaphase
4. Normal human cells can go on dividing indefinitely
5. Following telophase in animal cells, a cell plate begins to form

6. Bacteria divide through a process called binary fission
7. In meiosis II, whole chromosomes separate
8. In spermatogenesis, meiosis begins at puberty
9. Exchange of paternal and maternal DNA takes place in meiosis II
10. Anaphase lag leads to numerical chromosome aberrations
11. Pairing of X and Y chromosomes in spermatogenesis is end to end
12. Phenylketonuria is caused by nondisjunction
13. Sickle cell disease is caused by non-disjunction
14. Down's syndrome is caused by non-disjunction
15. Patau's syndrome is caused by non-disjunction
16. Edward's syndrome is caused by non-disjunction
17. Synteny is the presence of genes on the same chromosome
18. Isochromosome are chromosomes which are identical to each other
19. Heteroplasmy is the presence of two or more different populations of mitochondria within a cell
20. Genoscopy is when similar genotypes manifest as different phenotypes
21. There are 23 pairs of autosomes in normal human beings
22. Chromosome 21 is the shortest chromosome
23. Chromosome 21 is acrocentric
24. Chromosome 21 is in the A group of chromosomes
25. Chromosome 21 carries the gene for growth hormone
26. Chromosome 21 trisomy causes Down's syndrome
27. In the Y chromosome, the long arm is referred to as the p arm
28. In the Y chromosome, the long arm has variable length
29. In the Y chromosome, the long arm demonstrates fluorescence with quinacrine
30. In the Y chromosome, the short arm contains gene for testicular formation
31. Fragile Y chromosome is associated with mental retardation
32. Heterochromatin contains a highly repetitive sequence of DNA
33. Heterochromatin is the inert segment of the chromosome adjacent to the centromere
34. Heterochromatin may be lost without harmful effect in obertsonian translocation
35. Heterochromatin is tightly coiled during the interphase
36. Heterochromatin makes up the p arm of the acrocentric chromosomes
37. In the human cell cycle, cell division occurs in the S phase
38. In the human cycle, G_1 precedes mitosis
39. In the human cycle, DNA synthesis occurs in G_0
40. In the human cycle, vincristine acts on the M phase
41. In the human cycle methotrexate acts on the S phase
42. Karyotype can be obtained from sperm
43. Karyotype can be obtained from chorionic villi
44. Karyotype can be obtained from retinoblastoma cells
45. Karyotype can be obtained from red blood cells
46. Karyotype can be obtained from bone marrow cells
47. DNA in a nucleus becomes 4C at the end of S phase
48. Bread wheat has 28 chromosomes in its somatic cells
49. DNA replication takes place during mitosis
50. A flowering plant has somatic chromosome number of 40.The number of chromatids at G_1 in one somatic cell would be 40
51. A flowering plant has somatic chromosome number of 40.The number of chromatids at G_2 in one somatic cell would be 40

7
Mendelism

MULTIPLE-CHOICE QUESTIONS

1. **Gregor Mendel was most influential in which field of biology?**
   (a) Cytology
   (b) Genetics
   (c) Bacterial transformation
   (d) Chromatography
   (e) Biochemistry

2. **Mendel's unit factors in pairs are most accurately known to be**
   (a) two alleles on a paternal and a maternal homologue
   (b) identical alleles on homologous chromosomes
   (c) two maternal chromatids
   (d) two alleles on nonhomologous chromosomes
   (e) one maternal and one paternal chromatid

3. **______ refers to the specific characteristics displayed by an organism**
   (a) genotype (b) mutation
   (c) phenotype (d) genes

4. **Genes with different information at the same locus are called**
   (a) chromosome
   (b) homologs
   (c) plasmids
   (d) alleles

5. **A linear sequence of DNA nucleotides that provides the genetic information for a single characteristic is a**
   (a) chromosome (b) plasmid
   (c) gene (d) base pair

6. **When genes are passed on from parent to offspring, which of the following events has taken place?**
   (a) Horizontal gene transfer
   (b) Transduction
   (c) Vertical gene transfer
   (d) Retrograde gene transfer

7. The dwarf bean *Phaseolus vulgaris* is self-pollinating and exists as a number of pure-breeding homozygous lines. Which one of the following is the correct explanation for variation in seed size within lines?

(a) Environmental variation
(b) Genetic equilibrium
(c) Mutation
(d) Hybrid vigour
(e) Wobble

8. An organism has a diploid number of 12. On the basis of segregation and independent assortment, how many different types of gametes can be formed?

(a) 12 (b) 2
(c) 212 (d) 1
(e) 64

9. Normal parents have a Tay-Sachs child. Tay-Sachs is a recessive condition. What is the probability that their next child will be normal?

(a) 0.67 (67%) b) 0.75 (75%)
(c) 0.25 (25%) d) 0.00 (0%)
(e) 1.0 (100%)

10. The term "phenotype" refers to the ______ of an individual

(a) breeding pattern
(b) number of chromosomes
(c) number of genes
(d) genetic constitution
(e) appearance of a characteristic or trait

11. If you have a dominant disorder in a diploid organism, which two genotypes would express the same phenotype?

(a) Homozygous dominant and homozygous recessive
(b) Homozygous dominant and heterozygous
(c) Homozygous recessive and heterozygous
(d) None of the above

12. Which is not correct regarding non-disjunction?

(a) May fail to separate maternal from paternal chromatids
(b) Separates maternal from paternal chromatids
(c) May lead to Down syndrome
(d) Occurs more frequently in human females over age 35
(e) May fail to separate maternal chromatids from one another or paternal chromatids from one another

13. How many different gametes can be formed from the genotype AABBCCDdEe?

(a) 2^2 (b) 2^4
(c) 2 (d) 4^2
(e) 3^2

14. In a typical monohybrid cross, genotypic ratio in F_2 will be

(a) 1 : 2 : 1 (b) 3 : 1
(c) 2 : 1 : 1 (d) 1 : 1

15. In case of a dihybrid cross, how many types of gametes will be produced by F_1?

(a) 4 (b) 2
(c) 9 (d) 16

16. In a monohybrid cross, phenotypic ratio in F_2 is

(a) 1 : 1 (b) 2 : 1
(c) 3 : 1 (d) 1 : 1 : 1 : 1

17. In a trihybrid cross, how many types of gametes will be formed in F_1?

(a) 4 (b) 8
(c) 16 (d) 27

18. When two animals of genotype CcRrBb are mated, and assuming independent segregation, what proportion of their offspring will be CCrrBb?

(a) 1/2 (b) 1/8
(c) 1/16 (d) 1/32
(e) 1/64

19. Which of the following is a characteristic of a recessive human disease for which both parents are heterozygous?

(a) Some of the offspring may have the disease
(b) All of the offspring will have the disease
(c) None of the offspring can have the disease
(d) The trait will be seen in every generation
(e) The trait will only be seen in children born in a leap year

20. When the F_1 generation of a monohybrid cross are allowed to self-fertilize, the observed ratio of dominant to recessive phenotypes in the F_2 should be

(a) 2:1 (b) 4:1
(c) 3:2 (d) 3:1
(e) 3:4

21. In certain animals, black coat (B) is dominant over white (b). An F_2 family from the cross BB x bb showed six animals with black coats. Which one of the following is the correct reason for the lack of any white-coated animals in the F_2?

(a) The phenotype of the recessive homozygote could not be recognized
(b) Mutation (c) Sampling error
(d) Crossing over (e) Recombination

22. An individual heterozygous for two pairs of alleles (AaBb) produces four kinds of gametes. Which one of the following is true if the two genes are unlinked?

(a) The gametes carry either AA or BB
(b) The gametes are all either AB or ab
(c) There is no independent segregation
(d) There is an excess of AB + ab over Ab + aB
(e) The proportions are ¼ AB + ¼ Ab + ¼ aB + ¼ ab

23. Mendel's discovery that characteristics are inherited due to transmission of hereditary factors resulted from his

(a) careful microscopic examinations of genes and chromosomes
(b) dissections to determine how fertilization occurs in pea plants
(c) breeding experiments with many generations of fruit flies
(d) analysis of the offspring produced from many pea plant crosses

24. How did Mendel's work support the chromosome theory of inheritance?

(a) The behaviour of chromosomes during meiosis correlated with Mendel's principle of inheritance
(b) Mendel's work matched with the continuous variation theory
(c) Mendel's statistical evidence of gene segregation indicated the involvement of chromosomes
(d) The trait that Mendel studied was known to lie on chromosomes

25. Manx cats have no tails. Their phenotype is determined by a single gene with two alleles, normal and Manx. Crosses between Manx cats yield ratios of 2 Manx: 1 normal. This ratio suggests that

(a) the Manx allele is recessive
(b) it is an example of codominance
(c) it is an example of lethal gene
(d) it is a sex-linked gene
(e) Manx cats are homozygous for the Manx allele

26. In humans, right-handedness is dominant over left handedness and the gene is autosomal. A right-handed man, whose father was left-handed, married a left-handed woman. Which one of the following statements is true?

(a) The man was heterozygous; his father was homozygous
(b) The man was homozygous; his father was heterozygous
(c) The man was homozygous and his wife was heterozygous
(d) The man and his wife were both heterozygous

27. The feature of silky feathers in show fowl is caused by a recessive allele. A pure breeding bird with normal feathers was crossed with a bird with silky feathers and all the offspring were normal. The offspring was then allowed to interbreed. Which of the following statements would be true about the F_2 generation?

(i) The expected ratio of normal to silky would be 3:1
(ii) Half of the F_2 birds would be heterozygous
(iii) All males would be silky
(iv) A quarter of the F_2 birds would be homozygous
(v) Some of the normal birds would be pure breeding

(a) i, ii and iii (b) ii, iii and iv
(c) iii, iv and v (d) i, ii and v
(e) ii, iv and v

28. Mendel's results were rediscovered independently in 1900 by

(a) De Vries (b) Correns
(c) Tschermak (d) all of them

29. Mendel discovered laws of inheritance working with

(a) hawkweed (b) garden pea
(c) barley (d) *Drosophila*

30. How many characters did Mendel study in garden pea?

(a) Three (b) Seven
(c) Six (d) Five

31. Mendel coined the terms

(a) factors (b) recessive
(c) dominant (d) all of these

32. The term "reciprocal cross" was coined by

(a) Bateson (b) Boveri
(c) Morgan (d) Mendel

33. A cross of F_1 with its homozygous recessive parent is called

(a) hybrid cross (b) test cross
(c) top cross (d) reciprocal cross

34. Mendel presented his results in the meeting of Natural History Society of Brunn in

(a) 1865 (b) 1855
(c) 1885 (d) 1866

35. Mendel's results were published in the

(a) *Journal of Heredity*
(b) *Journal of Genetics*
(c) *Proceedings of Natural History Society of Brunn*
(d) None of these

36. Mendel's results were first published in

(a) English (b) German
(c) Russian (d) French

37. Mendel died in

(a) 1865 (b) 1894
(c) 1864 (d) 1884

38. Mendel had good background of

(a) plant breeding (b) geography
(c) mathematics (d) history

39. Mendel failed to confirm his findings when he worked with

(a) maize (b) hawkweed
(c) sea urchin (d) *Drosophila*

40. Mendel was born in

(a) Germany (b) Holland
(c) Czeckoslovakia (d) Austria

41. Mendel's results were rediscovered by

(a) De Vries (b) Tschermak
(c) Correns (d) all of these

42. Mendel's results were rediscovered in

(a) 1900 (b) 1898
(c) 1928 (d) 1865

43. Johannsen coined the terms

(a) genotype (b) gene
(c) phenotype (d) all of these

44. Terms "genotype" and "phenotype" were coined by

(a) Mendel (b) Johannsen
(c) Boveri (d) Bateson

45. Johanssen coined the terms "genotype" and "phenotype" working with

(a) chickpea (b) *Drosophila*
(c) cow pea (d) common bean

46. How many laws of inheritance were given by Mendel?

(a) Two (b) Four
(c) One (d) Three

47. For all the seven characters in garden pea, Mendel always observed

(a) incomplete dominance
(b) linkage
(c) codominance
(d) complete dominace

48. In his studies, Mendel did not observe

(a) lethality (b) linkage
(c) codominance (d) all of these

49. Mendel explained his results with the help of

(a) physics (b) mathematics
(c) cytology (d) none of these

50. Deviations from Mendel's results include

(a) incomplete dominance
(b) multiple alleles (c) lethal genes
(d) pleiotropic genes (e) codominance
(f) epistasis (g) all of these

51. Expression of both alleles in F_1 refers to

(a) partial dominance (b) codominance
(c) overdominance
(d) incomplete dominance

52. Mendel's idea that pairs of characters separate during gamete formation is called the law of

(a) particulate inheritance
(b) dominance
(c) segregation
(d) independent assortment

53. The allele that masks the effects of the other is ______ and the masked allele is

(a) homozygous, heterozygous
(b) homozygous, recessive
(c) dominant, recessive
(d) dominant, incomplete

54. What is the most common outcome in the F_2 generation of a cross between a tall plant and a dwarf plant?

(a) 1 tall : 1 dwarf (b) 3 tall : 1 dwarf
(c) 1 tall : 2 medium : 1 dwarf
(d) All tall

55. Two carriers of albinism have four children. One of their children is albino and the remaining three are normally pigmented. What is the probability that their next child will be albino?

(a) 0 % (b) 25 %
(c) 75 % (d) 100 %

56. Kathy's brother has cystic fibrosis. Her husband has no family history of cystic fibrosis. What is the chance that Kathy's child will inherit this disease?

(a) 1/2 x 1/2 = 1/4 (b) 1/3 x 1/2 = 1/6
(c) 2/3 x 1/4 = 1/6 (d) 2/3 x 1/2 = 1/3

57. The occurrence of affected individuals in every generation in a family suggests ______ trait

(a) an autosomal dominant
(b) an autosomal recessive
(c) either dominant or recessive
(d) sex-linked

58. Which of the following is an example of a dihybrid cross?

(a) AaBb x aabb (b) AaBb x AaBb
(c) aabb x AABB (d) aabb x aabb

59. Which of the following phenotypic results are expected from a dihybrid cross?

(a) 1:1:1:1 ratio
(b) 9:3:3:1 ratio
(c) All dominant for both traits
(d) All recessive for both traits

60. Mendel's law of ______ states that a random assortment of maternally and paternally derived chromosomes in meiosis results in gametes that have different combinations of these genes

(a) particulate inheritance
(b) dominance
(c) segregation
(d) independent assortment

61. Mendel's laws are explained by

(a) chromosome behavior in mitosis
(b) chromosome behavior in meiosis
(c) cytokinesis in mitosis and meiosis
(d) Mendel's laws have not been explained

62. Which genotype is normally not found in a gamete?

(a) AB (b) Ab
(c) aa (d) ab

63. Which of the following crosses is a test cross?

(a) Unknown x AA
(b) Unknown x Aa
(c) Unknown x aa
(d) Unknown x unknown

64. Two phenotypically normal individuals have an affected child. What can we conclude about the parents?

(a) They both carried the disease allele
(b) They are not the parents of the child
(c) They are affected
(d) No conclusions can be drawn

65. The geneticist ______ has compiled a compendium of human genetic traits called Mendelian Inheritance in Man

(a) Gregor Mendel (b) Hermann Muller
(c) Victor McKusick (d) John Hopkins

66. Relatives who have children together have a much higher risk of having children affected by a (an) ______ condition

(a) environmental (b) dominant
(c) recessive (d) undetected

67. Consider a group of 100 individuals (50 couples), all of whom carry a recessive disease allele. If 200 children were born to these couples, what percentage of the children would, theoretically, be carriers like their parents?

(a) 0 (b) 25
(c) 50 (d) 75

68. In the cross AaBb x aabb, what percentage of the offspring is expected to show a completely dominant phenotype?

(a) 0 (b) 25
(c) 50 (d) 100

69. Consider the cross AaBb x AaBb. If the alleles for both genes exhibit complete dominance, what genotypic ratio is expected in the resulting offspring?

(a) 1:1:1:1 (b) 9:3:3:1
(c) 3:6:3:1:2:1 (d) 1:2:1:2:4:2:1:2:1

70. Can independent assortment be demonstrated in a monohybrid cross?

(a) Yes, you can observe random distribution of alleles into gametes
(b) Yes, you can observe random assortment of genes into gametes
(c) No, you must observe genes that are on the same chromosome
(d) No, you must examine the transmission of two or more genes

71. The ______ rule of probability is useful in calculating the risk that certain individuals will inherit a particular genotype

(a) product
(b) summation
(c) additive
(d) none of the above is correct

72. Advantages of using the garden pea for Mendel's experiments included all listed below except

(a) true-breeding varieties were scarce
(b) he could expect to observe segregation of traits among the offspring
(c) they have relatively short generation time
(d) sex organs of the pea are enclosed within the flower

73. Pea plants can

(a) self-pollinate, but are not self-compatible
(b) self-fertilize
(c) only cross-fertilize
(d) reproduce without pollination

74. In Mendel's F_2 generation, one out of four plants had white flowers because

(a) the trait is sex-linked
(b) both parents were heterozygous purple
(c) one parent was homozygous recessive
(d) both parents were heterozygous white

75. Mendelian inheritance may be difficult to analyze because of all of the following except

(a) formation of Barr bodies
(b) pleiotropic effects
(c) continuous variation
(d) epistasis

76. In the F_2 generation, the 3:1 ratio is really a disguised

(a) 1:2:1 (b) 2:1:1
(c) 1:1:2 (d) 4:0
(e) 4:1

77. The ratio often referred to the Mendelian ratio is

(a) 1:3:3:1 (b) 9:7
(c) 1:3:1 (d) 1:1
(e) 3:1

78. When Mendel crossed pure-breeding purple and white flowered pea plants, the dominant to recessive ratio in the F_1 generation was

(a) 3:1 (b) 4:0
(c) 4:1 (d) 5:1
(e) 9:3:3:1

79. In Mendel's F_2 generation of the purple and white flower crossing, the dominant to recessive ratio was

(a) 1:3:1 (b) 3:1
(c) 1:1 (d) 9:7
(e) 9:3:3:1

80. Which of the following represents a testcross?

(a) Ww x WW (b) ww x Ww
(c) Ww x Ww (d) WW x WW
(e) none of the above

81. An individual who has two similar alleles is said to be

(a) homozygous
(b) heteromologous
(c) homologous
(d) heterozygous
(e) diplozygous

82. Which of the following represents a dihybrid?

(a) WWSs (b) WwSS
(c) WwSs (d) WWss
(e) wwSs

83. Where two alternatives for a trait are tall and short, and tall is dominant, the genotype of a heterozygous individual would be expressed as

(a) sS (b) ss
(c) SS (d) Ss
(e) tall

84. The appearance resulting from a given gene combination is referred to as the

(a) genotype (b) phenotype
(c) phototype (d) alleleotype
(e) stereotype

85. Compared to previous geneticists, the unique characteristic of Mendel's work was

(a) keeping records of numbers of different progeny
(b) choosing the garden pea for his experiment
(c) producing hybrids
(d) studying more than one generation
(e) crossing true-breeding plants

86. The two alternatives for a trait are red and white, and red is dominant. However, white is the most common trait. What is the genotype of a homozygous dominant individual?

(a) RR (b) rr
(c) WW (d) ww
(e) red

87. Where the two alternatives for a trait are broad and narrow, and broad is dominant, the phenotype of a homozygous dominant individual would be expressed as

(a) BB (b) nn
(c) Bn (d) NN
(e) broad

88. What is the phenotype of a fruit fly whose genotype is g^+g^+vsvs (where g = gray body and vs = vestigial wings; wild type = black body and normal wings)?

(a) Gray body; vestigial wings
(b) Gray body; normal wings
(c) Black body; vestigial wings
(d) Black body; normal wings

89. In garden peas, height is determined by a single gene with tall being dominate to short. If two heterozygous plants are crossed, what proportion of the tall progeny will be homozygous dominant?

(a) 3/4 (b) 2/3
(c) 1/2 (d) 1/3
(e) 1/4

90. In the cross MMnn x mmNN, what proportion of the resulting F_1 would be homozygous dominant for both genes?

(a) None (b) 1/16
(c) 3/16 (d) 9/16
(e) all

91. In humans, pointed eyebrows are dominant to smooth eyebrows and widow's peak (downward pointed frontal hairline) is dominant to continuous hairline. What phenotypic ratio would you expect in the offspring from a cross between an individual heterozygous for both genes and an individual homozygous recessive for both genes?

(a) 9:3:3:1 (b) 9:3:4
(c) 1:1:1:1 (d) 1:2:1:2:4:2:1:2:1
(e) 9:7

92. In case of monohybrid cross, incomplete dominance gives this phenotypic ratio in F_2

(a) 1 : 1 b) 3 : 1
(c) 2 : 1 d) 1 : 2 : 1

93. A ratio of 12:3:1 is most characteristic of a cross involving

(a) 1 gene pair (b) 2 gene pairs
(c) 3 gene pairs (d) 4 gene pairs
(e) none of the above

94. A mother who has a blood type AB has a child who is also AB. The potential father has blood type O. A well-informed geneticist concludes that

(a) he cannot be the father
(b) he might be the father, but it is unlikely
(c) he is very likely be the father
(d) he or any other male of blood type O could be the father
(e) no conclusion can be drawn

95. The genotype of an individual is not always reflected in the phenotype. This may be due to which of the following?

(a) Epistasis
(b) Dominance
(c) Incomplete dominance
(d) All the answers suggest ways in which the genotype may not be observed in the phenotype

96. A father with myotonic dystrophy has three daughters who are all carriers of the mutant allele and two sons who are unaffected non-carriers. The three daughters have six sons of which four are affected and two are not, and four daughters of which two are carriers and two are not. What type of mutation is suggested from this description?

(a) Autosomal dominant
(b) Autosomal recessive
(c) Sex-linked dominant
(d) Sex-linked recessive
(e) Y-linked

97. Some mutations have been found that are expressed differently depending on the sex of the parent the gene is passed through. This is called

(a) sex-linked inheritance
(b) penetrance
(c) imprinting
(d) heterozygous
(e) incomplete dominance

98. A recessive mutation was discovered in a small island population (1000). The mutation was observed in the heterozygous state, but never in the homozygous state. What is the possible explanation for this observation?

(a) Only individuals with opposite alleles at this locus reproduced
(b) The recessive allele is lethal in a homozygous state
(c) The heterozygous state is "fixed" in this population
(d) The population size is too small to give an explanation for this phenomena

99. Green hair is inherited in the following way. All daughters of a green-haired father have green hair. Children of green-haired mothers and normal fathers are all normal. The best conclusion is that

(a) the gene is an autosomal dominant
(b) the gene is an X-linked recessive, and the females are the heterogametic sex
(c) the gene is an X-linked recessive, and males are the heterogametic sex
(d) the gene is an X-linked dominant, and the males are the heterogametic sex
(e) none of the above, their hair was dyed at birth

100. In a cross involving polygenic inheritance, only 2/125 of the offspring (F_2) were as extreme as one of the P_1 parents. How many gene pairs are involved?

(a) Two (b) One
(c) Five (d) Four
(e) Three

101. In a cross involving polygenic inheritance where three gene pairs control plant height, the shortest and tallest plants are 6 and 24 cm, respectively. What height will all F_1 plants display if homozygous 12 cm and 24 cm plants are crossed?

(a) 9 cm (b) 21 cm
(c) 15 cm (d) 12 cm
(e) 18 cm

102. Assume that a single gene has two alleles. In a diploid organism, how many possible genotypes are there?

(a) 2 (b) 3
(c) 4 (d) 6
(e) 8

103. Assume that a single gene has three alleles. In a diploid organism, how many possible genotypes are there?

(a) 2 (b) 3
(c) 4 (d) 6
(e) 8

104. "Hereditary factors" is an old name for

(a) DNA (b) transforming units
(c) genes (d) chromosomes
(e) all of the above

105. To determine whether or not the genes are linked, you should perform a/an

(a) test cross
(b) conjugation test
(c) restriction analysis
(d) complementation test
(e) ordered analysis

106. You want to know whether height in giraffes is a Mendelian trait. When true-breeding tall and short giraffes are crossed, they produce only tall F_1 giraffes. When these are bred among themselves, 12.5% of the F_2 are short, suggesting that height in giraffes is probably

(a) influenced by 1 gene
(b) influenced by 2 genes
(c) influenced by 3 genes
(d) influenced by 4 genes
(e) a quantitative trait

107. A dihybrid cross that gives rise to progeny in a 15:1 phenotypic ratio implies

(a) linked duplicate dominant genes
(b) one gene with semi-dominance
(c) two unlinked genes with co-dominant alleles
(d) recessive epistasis of two unlinked genes
(e) none of the above

108. What would be the frequency of AABBCC individuals from the mating of two AaBbCc individuals?

(a) 1/64 (b) 1/32
(c) 1/16 (d) 1/8
(e) 3/16 (f) 1/4

109. The phenomenon of "independent assortment" refers to

(a) expression at the same stage of development
(b) unlinked transmission of genes in crosses resulting from being located on different chromosomes, or far apart on the same chromosome
(c) association of an RNA and a protein implying related function
(d) independent location of genes from each other in an interphase cell
(e) association of a protein and a DNA sequence implying related function

110. Mendel's law of segregation, as applied to the behavior of chromosomes in meiosis, means that

(a) pairing of homologs will convert one allele into the other, leading to separation of the types
(b) alleles of a gene separate from each other when homologs separate in meiosis I, or in meiosis II if there is a single crossover between the gene and the centromere
(c) genes on the same chromosome will show 50% recombination
(d) alleles of a gene will be linked and passed on together through meiosis

111. The allele associated with sickle cell anemia apparently reached a high frequency in some human populations due to

(a) random mating
(b) superior fitness of heterozygotes in areas where malaria was present
(c) migration of individuals with the allele into other populations
(d) a high mutation rate at that specific gene
(e) genetic drift

112. A cross between two true breeding lines, one with dark blue flowers and one with bright white flowers, produces F_1 offspring that are light blue. When the F_1 progeny are selfed, a 1:2:1 ratio of dark blue to light blue to white flowers is observed. Which genetic phenomenon is consistent with these results?

(a) Epistasis
(b) Incomplete dominance
(c) Codominance
(d) Inbreeding depression
(e) Random mating

113. Which of the following is an example of codominance in genetic traits?

(a) A tall pea plant and a short pea plant produce tall pea plants
(b) An orange cat and a black cat produce an orange and black kitten
(c) A blue-eyed man and a brown-eyed woman produce a blue-eyed child
(d) A colour-blind woman and a man with normal vision produce a colour-blind son

114. What ratios typically result from crosses dealing with a single genetic locus?

(a) 9:3:3:1, 1:2:1
(b) 1:1:1:1, 1:4:6:4:1
(c) 3:1, 1:1, 1:2:1
(d) 9:7, 12:3:1
(e) 15:1, 1:2

115. In *Drosophila*, the recessive alleles for brown and scarlet eyes (resulting from two independent genes) interact so that the double homozygous recessive is white. A pure-breeding brown and pure breeding scarlet are crossed. What proportion of the F_2 will be white?

(a) 1/4 (b) 3/4
(c) 1/16 (d) 7/16
(e) 9/16

116. Given a two allele, one loci system in which the frequency of genotype *Aa* is 0.25, a frequency of genotype *aa* of 0.50, and *A* is dominant to *a*, then what is the frequency of the phenotype associated with allele *A*? What is the frequency if instead *A* is recessive to *a*?

(a) 0.25, 0.25
(b) 0.25, 0.50
(c) 0.50, 0.25
(d) 0.50, 0.50
(e) None of the above

117. Is a cross between an AABb individual and an AaBB individual capable of producing a dihybrid? If so, how many of the progeny would expect to be dihybrids? Possible bonus question: If you allowed random mating within a population containing 40% AABb individuals and 60% AaBB individuals, what fraction of the progeny would you expect to be dihybrids (the answer to this bonus question is not included among the multiple choice answer below)?

(a) No
(b) Yes, 10%
(c) Yes, 25%, 12%
(d) Yes, 50%
(e) Yes, 75%
(f) Yes, 80%
(g) None of the above

118. Two Mexican hairless dogs are crossed. What ratio of hairy: hairless dogs is expected in the offspring generation?

(a) 3 hairless, one hairy
(b) 3 hairy, one hairless
(c) 2 hairless, one hairy
(d) Cannot be predicted

119. A modified Mendelian ratio is represented by

(a) 9:3:3:1
(b) 1:3:1
(c) 3:1
(d) 9:7
(e) 1:1

120. Early ideas about heredity include

(a) traits can be masked in some generations
(b) traits were segregated among progeny
(c) alleles do not influence each other
(d) traits are transmitted directly
(e) not all copies of a factor are identical

121. A ratio of 12:3:1 is most characteristic of a cross involving

(a) 1 gene pair
(b) 2 gene pairs
(c) 3 gene pairs
(d) 4 gene pairs
(e) none of the above

122. A pea plant is heterozygous for both seed shape and seed colour. S is the allele for the dominant, spherical shape characteristic; s is the allele for the recessive, dented shape characteristic. Y is the allele for the dominant, yellow colour characteristic; y is the allele for the recessive, green colour characteristic. What will be the distribution of these two alleles in this plant's gametes?

(a) 50% of gametes are Sy; 50% of gametes are sY
(b) 25% of gametes are SY; 25% Sy; 25% sY; 25% sy
(c) 50% of gametes are sy; 50% of gametes are SY
(d) 100% of the gametes are SsYy
(e) 50% of gametes are SsYy; 50% of gametes are SSYY

123. When does a phenotype ratio of 9:3:3:1 occur?

(a) The genes reside on the same chromosome
(b) Genes on the same chromosome might be linked. If we assume linked genes, and that the heterozygotes are F_1-hybrids from true breeding parents, the offspring would be predicted to occur in a 3:1 ratio of spherical, green- to dented, yellow-seeded plants.
(c) Each gene contains two mutations
(d) The gene pairs assort independently during meiosis
(e) Only recessive traits are scored
(f) None of the above

124. Which of the following genetic crosses would be predicted to give a phenotypic ratio of 9:3:3:1?

(a) SSYY x ssyy (b) SsYY x ssyy
(c) SsYy x SsYy (d) SSyy x ssYY
(e) ssYY x ssyy

125. The gametes of a plant of genotype SsYy should have the genotypes

(a) Ss and Yy (b) SY and sy
(c) SY, Sy, sY, and sy
(d) Ss, Yy, SY and sy
(e) SS, ss, YY, and yy

126. Which of the following genotypes would you not expect to find among the offspring of a SsYy x ssyy test cross

(a) ssyy (b) SsYy
(c) Ssyy (d) ssYy
(e) SsYY

127. The expected phenotypic ratio of the progeny of a SsYy x ssyy test cross is

(a) 9:3:3:1 (b) 3:1
(c) 1:1:1:1 (d) 1:2:1
(e) 3:1:1:3

128. In a dihybrid cross, AaBb x AaBb, what fraction of the offspring will be homozygous for both recessive traits?

(a) 1/16 (b) 1/8
(c) 3/16 (d) 1/4
(e) 3/4

129. Following a SsYy x SsYy cross, what fraction of the offspring is predicted to have a genotype that is heterozygous for both characteristics?

(a) 1/16 (b) 2/16
(c) 3/16 (d) 4/16
(e) 9/16

130. In a dihybrid cross, SsYy x SsYy, what fraction of the offspring will be homozygous for both traits?

(a) 1/16 (b) 1/8
(c) 3/16 (d) 1/4
(e) 3/4

131. In Mendel's experiments, the spherical seed character (SS) is completely dominant over the dented seed character (ss). If the characters for height were incompletely dominant, such that TT are tall, Tt are intermediate and tt are short, what would be the phenotypes resulting from crossing a spherical-seeded, short (SStt) plant to a dented-seeded, tall (ssTT) plant?

(a) All the progeny would be spherical-seeded and tall
(b) 1/2 would be spherical-seeded and of intermediate height; 1/2 would be spherical-seeded and tall
(c) All the progeny would be spherical-seeded and short
(d) You cannot predict the outcome
(e) All the progeny would be spherical-seeded and of intermediate height

132. Compare these two of the Mendel's postulates: segregation vs. independent assortment

(a) segregation involves longitudinal division, while independent assortment involves reductional division
(b) Mendel observed the chromosomal basis for segregation, but could not see the basis for independent assortment
(c) both segregation and independent assortment involve unit factors in the cells
(d) both segregation and independent assortment require two or more genes
(e) either segregation or independent assortment result in a 9:3:3:1 phenotypic ratio

133. A single gene has four alleles. In a diploid organism, how many possible genotypes are there involving this gene?

(a) 12 (b) 6
(c) 10 (d) 8
(e) 4

134. Two genes each have two alleles. In a diploid organism, how many possible genotypes are there?

(a) 3 (b) 4
(c) 6 (d) 8
(e) 9

135. Two genes each have two alleles, one dominant and the other recessive. In a diploid organism, what is the maximum possible number of phenotypes?

(a) 3 (b) 4
(c) 6 (d) 8
(e) 9

136. An autosomal gene is one that is located on a chromosome other than a sex chromosome, therefore

(a) it is sex-linked (b) it is X-linked
(c) it shows Mendelian patterns of segregation
(d) it does not show Mendelian patterns
(e) it is only expressed in the male

137. Mendel's fourth postulate was independent assortment, which is observed

(a) when two genes are tightly linked on the same chromosome
(b) with monohybrids
(c) when two genes are distantly linked or on different chromosomes
(d) only in peas
(e) during mitosis

138. Consider the following dihybrid cross in the garden pea (*Pisum sativum*): W = allele for round, w = allele for wrinkled, G = allele for yellow, g = allele for green. What would be the phenotypic ratio if you crossed a yellow, round parent (heterozygous for both gene pairs) with a green, wrinkled parent?

(a) 1:1:1:1 (b) 3:1
(c) 1:2:1
(d) all progeny would be yellow and round
(e) none of the above

139. If two individuals with the following genotype were crossed, AaBbCCDdEe, what would be the possible number of different phenotypes produced in their progeny?

(a) 4 (b) 8
(c) 16 (d) 32
(e) None of the above

140. Which reason was not used by Mendel to choose the garden pea (*Pisum sativum*) as an experimental organism?

(a) Annual
(b) Easily fertilized
(c) Easily grown
(d) Well-defined characteristics

141. Which conclusion could not be attributed to Gregor Mendel?

(a) Two inherited factors govern each trait
(b) Each human carries a number of lethal alleles
(c) One factor comes from each parent
(d) In the heterozygous condition, one allele for a trait may mask the expression of the other allele for the trait
(e) Only one of the two possible factors from a parent can be passed on to each offspring

142. The expression of a gene in an individual is termed the

(a) genotype of the individual
(b) incomplete dominance in the individual
(c) linked gene
(d) locus
(e) phenotype of the individual

143. Only one of the two possible alleles from each parent is passed on to each offspring is a statement of the

(a) law of dominance
(b) law of segregation
(c) law of independent assortment
(d) law of incomplete dominance
(e) law of disjunction

144. A typical phenotypic ratio for a dihybrid cross is

(a) 9:1 (b) 3:4
(c) 9:3:3:1 (d) 1:2:1:2:1
(e) 6:3:3:6

145. In the fruit fly *Drosophila*, the allele for normal body (B) is dominant over the allele for hair body (b), and the allele for normal leg (L) is dominant over the allele for short leg (l). A cross is performed between a homozygous normal body/homozygous short fruit fly and a heterozygous normal body/heterozygous normal leg fruit fly.

What ratio of the progeny of this cross is hybrid normal body and hybrid normal leg?

(a) 1/16 (b) 2/16
(c) 4/16 (d) 6/16
(e) 8/16

146. What ratio of the progeny of this cross would appear normal bodied and normal legged?

(a) 1/16 (b) 2/16
(c) 4/14 (d) 6/16
(e) 8/16

147. A dihybrid cross SS tt x ss TT is made in which S is dominant, but there is no dominance between T and t. Assuming independent assortment, how many phenotypic classes are expected in F_2?

(a) 2 (b) 3
(c) 4 (d) 5
(e) 6

148. In the ABO blood system in humans, if a person of type B blood has children with a person of type AB blood, what blood types could their children have?

(a) Type AB, type A, and type B
(b) Type B and type AB
(c) Type AB, type A, type B, and type O
(d) Type A and type B

149. A gene for corn has two alleles, one for yellow kernels and one for white kernels. Cross pollination of yellow corn and white corn results in ears of corn that have an approximately even mix of yellow and white kernels. Which term best describes the relationship between the two alleles?

(a) Genetic recombination
(b) Codominance
(c) Incomplete dominance
(d) Chimerism

150. Suppose that in barley plants, the alleles for tall stalks is dominant over short stalks and the allele for wide leaves is dominant over thin leaves. What would be the best way to determine the genotype of a barley plant with a tall stalk and wide leaves?

(a) Perform a test cross with a barley plant that has a tall stalk and thin leaves
(b) Perform a test cross with a known heterozygous barley plant
(c) Perform a test cross with a barley plant that has a short stalk and thin leaves
(d) Perform a test cross with a barley plant that has a tall stalk and wide leaves

151. In a cross of AaBb × AaBb, what fraction of the offspring can be expected to express one of the two dominant alleles, but not both?

(a) 9/16 (b) 1/2
(c) 3/8 (d) 3/16

152. If two genes experience independent assortment, which assumption is most likely true?

(a) They are located in close proximity on the same chromosome
(b) Crossing over between the genes does not occur
(c) The genes are located on different chromosomes or are far apart on the same chromosome
(d) The expression of one gene does not affect the expressions of the other

153. A cross between two pea plants with genotypes PpLl and PpLl results in an F_1 generation that is 25% PPLL, 50% PpLl, and 25% ppll. Which reason most likely explains why other possible genotypes are not present?

(a) The genes underwent independent assortment
(b) The loci of the genes are close together
(c) The loci of the genes are on different chromosomes
(d) Crossing over occurred between chromosomes

154. The X linked recessive trait of colour blindness is present in 5% of males. If a mother who is a carrier and father who is unaffected plan to have two children, what is the probability the children will both be male and colour blind?

(a) 50% (b) < 1%
(c) 25% (d) 6.25%

155. In Labrador retriever, the allele for black coat colour (B) is dominant to the allele for brown coat colour (b). However, if a Labrador has two copies of the recessive allele for a pigment-depositing gene E, it can only have yellow coat. In a cross of two doubly heterozygous black Labradors (BbEe x BbEe), what fraction of the next generation would one expect to be yellow?

(a) 3/16 (b) 1/8
(c) 1/16 (d) 1/4

156. In pea plants, the allele for tall stalks (T) is dominant over allele for short stalks (t). Suppose a cross between a tall pea plant and a short pea plant produces 43 tall offspring and 47 short offspring, if one of the tall offspring is crossed with one of the short offspring, what ratio of genotypes would be most likely in their offspring?

(a) 1 TT : 2 Tt : 1 tt (b) 3 Tt : 1 tt
(c) All Tt (d) 1 Tt : 1 tt

MARK TRUE OR FALSE (T/F)

1. The model for the dihybrid cross of heterozygotes predicts a phenotypic ratio of 9:3:3:1
2. A trait caused by a recessive autosomal allele will result in a pedigree that shows affected individuals having at least one affected parent
3. A dominant phenotype is the most common expression of a particular gene in a population
4. According to Mendel, each human carries a number of lethal alleles
5. According to Mendel, two inherited factors govern each trait
6. Mendel said that one factor comes from each parent
7. Mendel reported that in the heterozygous condition, one allele for a trait may mask the expression of the other allele for the trait
8. Mendel said that only one of the two possible factors from a parent can be passed onto each offspring
9. The expression of a gene in an individual is termed the phenotype of the individual
10. The expression of a gene in an individual is also termed the incomplete dominance in the individual
11. Only one of the two possible alleles from each parent is passed on to each offspring is a statement of the law of independent assortment
12. A typical phenotypic ratio for a dihybrid cross is 9:3:3:1
13. Metabolic diseases are usually the result of a lethal gene that is recessive
14. In the fruit fly, *Drosophila*, the allele for normal body (B) is dominant over the allele for hair body (b), and the allele for normal leg (L) is dominant over the allele for short leg (l). A cross is performed between a homozygous normal body/homozygous short fruit fly and a heterozygous normal body/heterozygous normal leg fruit fly. The ratio of the progeny of this cross that is hybrid normal body and hybrid normal leg would be 6/16
15. The ratio of the progeny of the above cross that would appear normal bodied and normal legged is 8/16
16. Most genes are probably pleiotropic
17. The phenotypic ratio of 1:2:1 is characteristic of the F_2 of a monohybrid cross where dominance is lacking
18. The closer two linked genes are on a chromosome, the more frequently crossing over will occur between them
19. Crossing over involves the exchange of parts between nonhomologous chromosomes
20. Down syndrome is also known as trisomy-21 because it results from a nondisjunction involving chromosome-21
21. Any change in the nitrogenous base sequence of an organism's DNA is called a (n) mutation
22. Resistance to malaria is found in any individual that is a (n) non-carrier for sickle cell anemia
23. A picture of the chromosomes of an organism is called a (n) idiotype
24. Red hair and freckles are associated with individuals having linked genes
25. Hemophilia is a condition in which the blood of individuals homozygous for the condition fails to clot properly
26. When a carrier for red-green colour blindness is crossed with a diseased male, 25% per cent of the male offspring is colour blind
27. When two heterozygous tall pea plants are crossed, 25% per cent of the offspring is short
28. The trait expressed in a cross between two contrasting alleles for the same characteristic is said to be codominant
29. A body chromosome is called a (n) somatic chromosome
30. The point on a chromosome where a gene is found is called its linkage

31. If two gray Andalusian fowl are crossed, 50% per cent of the offspring of this cross will be gray
32. In the cross in the above question, 50% per cent of the offspring of this cross will be black
33. Only one of the two possible alleles from each parent is passed onto the offspring for a trait. This is known as Mendel's Law of Independent assortment
34. The test cross involves crossing a pure recessive with a homozygous dominant or heterozygous individual to determine its genotype
35. Non-disjunction is the general term, which describes when a pair of homologous chromosomes fails to separate during meiosis
36. Mendel's seven genes were present on seven different chromosomes
37. Blixt (1975) has pointed out that two of the genes probably lie on chromosome 1, and three on chromosome 4
38. Linked genes that are distantly separated on their chromosomes will segregate more or less independently
39. All the dihybrid crosses were carried out by Mendel
40. Mendel was born in 1822
41. Mendel was born in an educated family
42. Mendel did his experiments in a university
43. Garden pea is a self-fertilizing plant
44. Character and trait mean the same thing
45. Hybrid form of seed shape in garden pea can be observed in the first year of experiment
46. Height of the plant can also be observed in the first year of experiment
47. In garden peas, the gray seed coat always produced white flowers
48. The agent responsible for each character was called a 'factor' by Mendel
49. A cross between any two parents produces a hybrid
50. Principle of segregation means that a hybrid produces two types of individuals
51. An individual that is recessive at one gene pair need not be so at another
52. The phenotype refers to biological appearance excluding chemical and behavioural attributes
53. We can determine the genotype of an individual by knowing its phenotype
54. Plants are crossed with a homozygous recessive plant in a test cross. If they are crossed with a homozygous dominant plant, same result would come
55. Top cross and test cross are the same
56. Pedigree studies are very easy in human beings
57. Independent assortment can be studied only in a dihybrid cross
58. Testing genotype of dihybrid is easier by selfing than with a test cross
59. Different kinds of gametes produced by F_1 heterozygotes is given by 2^n
60. Different kinds of genotypes in F_2 is given by 4^n
61. Different kinds of F_2 genotypes that are homozygous is given by 2^n
62. Mendel demonstrated that variability among the F_2 could be traced to original variability in the first parental cross
63. According to Mendel, factors changed among the offspring
64. Mendel talked about continuous variation
65. Mendel could not get proper results while explaining his results to Nageli, as poor soil resulted in poor germination
66. Pea shows apomixes
67. Mendel used letter symbols indicating which factors represent the normal appearance
68. Model for the dihybrid cross of heterozygotes predicts a phenotypic ratio of 9:3:3:1

8

Sex Determination and Sex Linkage

MULTIPLE-CHOICE QUESTIONS

1. In *Drosophila*, sex is determined by the

(a) ratio of the number of X chromosomes to the number of autosomes
(b) ratio of the number of Y chromosomes to the number of autosomes
(c) ratio of the number of X chromosomes to the number of sets of autosomes
(d) presence or absence of the Y chromosome
(e) ratio of the number of Y chromosomes to the number of sets of autosomes

2. The primary sex ratio in humans

(a) is possibly affected by the lower mass of the Y chromosome
(b) is probably about 1.2 to 1.6
(c) may vary in different ethnic groups according to secondary sex ratio findings
(d) is higher than the secondary sex ratio
(e) all answers are true

3. The effect of Barr body formation in mammals is that

(a) females are mosaics for heterozygous X-linked genes
(b) males are mosaics for heterozygous autosomal genes
(c) males are mosaics for hemizygous X-linked genes
(d) females are mosaics for homozygous X-linked genes
(e) females are mosaics for heterozygous autosomal genes

4. In maize, there are mutant genes that confer male sterility to all of the offspring of the female parent carrying this genotype. This genetic information is not found on any of the chromosomes that make up the maize genome. This type of inheritance is called

(a) extrachromosomal inheritance
(b) transgenic inheritance
(c) pseudoinheritance
(d) biparental inheritance

5. Sex linkage was first discovered in

(a) maize (b) *Drosophila*
(c) garden pea (d) grasshoppers

6. **Colour blindness in man is governed by a recessive gene which is located on**
   (a) X-chromosome (b) Y-chromosome
   (c) autosomes (d) all of these

7. **In a human male cell, non-disjunction occurs in anaphase I for the sex chromosomes, but no chromosomes are lost in the process. What are the karyotypes of the sperm produced from this cell?**
   (a) 23, X 23, Y
   24, XY 22
   (b) 23, X 23, Y
   24, XX 22
   (c) 24, XX 23, YY 24, XX
   23, YY
   (d) 47, XXY 47, XYY
   (e) It is impossible to tell. It would depend on what type of egg each sperm fertilized

8. **w/Y male flies are crossed with heterozygous females and only 3 F_1 progeny result. The probability that all of them will be affected females is**
   (a) 0% (b) <1%
   (c) 12.5% (d) 25%
   (e) 100%

9. ***X*-linked genes typically encode proteins important for**
   (a) specifying gender
   (b) reproductive behavior
   (c) gametogenesis
   (d) all of the above
   (e) all biological processes

10. **A mammal with the genotype XO will be**
    (a) male
    (b) female
    (c) both (intersex)
    (d) androgenous (neither)
    (e) unknown, it depends on the species of mammal

11. **Which of the following would not help to distinguish autosomal dominant from autosomal recessive inheritance?**
    (a) Presence of consanguinity
    (b) Proportion of affected offspring in each mating
    (c) Sex ratio of affected individuals
    (d) Appearance of the disease phenotype in multiple generations of the family
    (e) All of the above

12. **Which of the following is (are) example(s) of a sex-influenced trait?**
    (a) Autosomal dominant breast cancer
    (b) Adenomatous polyposis coli
    (c) Male-pattern baldness
    (d) Cystic fibrosis
    (e) (a) and (c)

13. **When somatic characters are located on sex chromosomes, it is called**
    (a) sex-determination
    (b) sex-linked characters
    (c) complete linkage (d) incomplete linkage

14. **Green colour blindness in humans is a sex-linked recessive trait. In a family, the older son has normal vision, whereas the younger son is colour blind. One can realistically surmise**
    (a) the mother was homozygous for colour blindness
    (b) the father was homozygous for colour blindness
    (c) the father was heterozygous for colour blindness
    (d) the mother most probably was colour blind
    (e) none of the above

15. **Pattern baldness in humans is common in men because**
    (a) it is sex-linked
    (b) it is an example of cytoplasmic (extranuclear) inheritance
    (c) of environmental effects
    (d) of sex-influenced inheritance
    (e) none of the above

16. A trait that appears to be dominant in one sex but recessive in the other is called

(a) a sex-limited trait
(b) a sex-influenced trait
(c) a sex-linked trait
(d) none of the above

17. Which of the following could not be used to describe a sex-limited trait

(a) this term refers to a trait controlled by a gene located on the X or Y chromosomes
(b) this is a trait that occurs more frequently in one sex than another
(c) this is an extreme example of a sex-influenced trait
(d) this trait is likely to be secondary sex characteristics

18. On which of the following chromosomes are sex-linked traits carried?

(a) 13 (b) 18
(c) Y (d) 15
(e) X

19. Hypertrichosis, hairiness of the pinna of the ear, is inherited as a Y-linked recessive in humans. If a man with hypertrichosis marries a normal woman, what type of children may they have?

(a) All of their children of both sexes may have hypertrichosis
(b) All the sons may have hypertrichosis, but none of their daughters
(c) Half of their sons, but none of their daughters may have hypertrichosis
(d) All the daughters have hypertrichosis, but none of their sons
(e) None of their children have hypertrichosis

20. A father with myotonic dystrophy has three daughters who are all carriers of the mutant allele and two sons who are unaffected non-carriers. The three daughters have six sons of which four are affected and two are not, and four daughters of which two are carriers and two are not. What type of mutation is suggested from this description?

(a) Autosomal dominant
(b) Autosomal recessive
(c) Sex-linked dominant
(d) Sex-linked recessive
(e) Y-linked

21. Consider a sex-limited (autosomal) trait where H = hen-feathered and h = cock-feathered (sex-limited to males). In the F_1 generation, a hen-feathered heterozygous male is mated to a hen-feathered heterozygous female. What is the F_2 phenotypic ratio for male progeny?

(a) All cock feathered
(b) 3:1 hen-feathered:cock-feathered
(c) 3:1 cock-feathered:hen-feathered
(d) All hen feathered
(e) None of the above

22. In *Drosophila*, if a white-eyed female (w, sex-linked recessive) is mated to a red-eyed male (wild type, w^+, dominant to white), what will be the eye colour of the male progeny?

(a) All red (b) All white
(c) 1/2 red, 1/2 white
(d) 3:1, white to red ratio
(e) None of the above

23. In humans, males are

(a) homogametic
(b) heterogametic
(c) hermaphroditic
(d) pseudohermaphroditic

24. An affected male and a normal female have four children: two affected daughters and two normal sons. Each of the affected daughters (and their normal husbands) produced affected sons and affected daughters. The couple's normal sons married normal women and had all normal children. What is the most likely mode of inheritance for this trait?

(a) Autosomal dominant
(b) Autosomal recessive
(c) Sex-linked dominant
(d) Sex-linked recessive

25. Male pattern baldness is a ______ trait

(a) sex-linked (b) sex-limited
(c) sex-influenced (d) Y-linked

26. The probability that a male inherited his Y chromosome from his maternal grandfather is

(a) 0% (b) 25%
(c) 50% (d) 100%

27. How many Barr bodies would be observed in the nucleus of an XXY individual?

(a) 0 (b) 1
(c) 2 (d) 3

28. What would be the sex of an XXY individual?

(a) Male (b) Female
(c) Hermaphrodite (d) Mosaic

29. A female whose father was colour blind marries a normal male whose father was also colour blind. What is the probability that their son will be colourblind?

(a) 0% (b) 25%
(c) 50% (d) 75%

30. A female whose father was colour blind marries a normal male whose father was also colour blind. What is the probability that their daughter will be colour blind?

(a) 0% (b) 25%
(c) 50% (d) 75%

31. Sexual identity is determined by the sex chromosome make-up of an individual only

(a) true (b) false
(c) variable (d) basis is unknown

32. A medical condition that arises in the mother during pregnancy is a

(a) sex-linked trait
(b) trait determined by mitochondrial DNA
(c) sex-limited trait
(d) sex-influenced trait

33. Individuals with three copies of most autosomes do not survive. Individuals with an extra X chromosome, however, survive with relatively mild (compared to autosomal abnormalities) consequences. Why?

(a) The X chromosome contains few genes, while autosomes contain a large number
(b) The extra X chromosome(s) are inactivated
(c) The X chromosome determines sex only
(d) None of the above

34. Which of the following genetic conditions is not sex-linked?

(a) Ichthyosis (b) Colour blindness
(c) Sickle-cell anemia (d) (a) and (c)

35. A woman whose brother has hemophilia is concerned about passing this trait to her offspring. What is the risk that she will have a son with hemophilia?

(a) 1/8 (b) 1/4
(c) 1/2 (d) 1

36. Can a male be a carrier for a sex-linked disease?

(a) Yes, if the trait is recessive
(b) Yes, if the male's father and mother were carriers
(c) No, males have only a single copy of sex-linked genes
(d) No way to predict

37. X-inactivation can be used to identify individuals who are

(a) homozygous unaffected
(b) heterozygous
(c) homozygous affected
(d) missing X-linked genes

38. Beard growth in humans is an example of a ______ trait

(a) sex-linked (b) sex-influenced
(c) sex-limited (d) Y-linked

39. Consider a sex-linked recessive trait. Which of the following crosses would produce males and females with different phenotypes?

(a) Homozygous normal female x normal male
(b) Affected female x affected male
(c) Affected female x normal male
(d) Heterozygous normal female x affected male

40. What is the probability that the son of a female carrier of hemophilia and a normal male will be a hemophilic?

(a) Zero (b) 0.25
(c) 0.50 (d) 0.75
(e) 1.00

41. Sex chromosome were first discovered by

(a) Mc Clung (b) Bridges
(c) Bateson (d) Wilson

42. Sex chromosomes were first discovered in

(a) *Drosophila* (b) sea urchin
(c) garden pea (d) grasshoppers

43. Sex chromosomes are also known as

(a) autosomes (b) lysosomes
(c) perixosomes (d) allosomes

44. The X-chromosome was first discovered in 1891 by

(a) Wilson (b) Sutton
(c) Bridges (d) Henking

45. The Y-chromosome was first discovered by

(a) Sutton (b) Mc Chung
(c) Morgan (d) Wilson

46. The term "gynandromorphy" was first used by

(a) Goldschmidt (b) Sutton
(c) Bateson (d) Mc Clung

47. The term "sex-linkage" was coined by

(a) Wilson (b) Boveri
(c) Bridges (d) Morgan

48. The term "sex-linked character" was first used by

(a) Morgan (b) Wilson
(c) Bateson (d) Mc Clung

49. The genic balance theory of sex determination was proposed by

(a) Boveri (b) Morgan
(c) Sutton (d) Bridges

50. The term "sex chromatin" was first used by

(a) Lyon (b) Bridges
(c) Boveri (d) Barr and Bertram

51. The X-hypothesis was proposed by

(a) Barr (b) Boveri
(c) Muller (d) Lyon

52. The term criss-cross inheritance was coined by

(a) Bridges (b) Morgan
(c) Wilson (d) Boveri

53. Sex-linkage was first discovered in

(a) hawkweed (b) grasshoppers
(c) garden pea (d) *Drosophila*

54. Sex-linked genes are located on

(a) X-chromosomes (b) autosomes
(c) Y-chromosomes (d) none of these

55. Barr bodies are also known as

(a) golgi bodies (b) sex chromatin
(c) globules (d) none of these

56. The number of Barr bodies in a cell is always

(a) one less than X-chromosomes
(b) equal to X-chromosomes
(c) one more than X-chromosomes
(d) none of these

57. The number of Barr body in a normal male (XY) is

(a) zero (b) two
(c) three (d) one

58. Holandric genes are present on

(a) X-chromosome (b) autosomes
(c) Y-chromosome (d) none of these

59. The genetic constitution of normal *Drosophila* female is

(a) XX (b) XY
(c) XO (d) XXX

60. In Y chromosome of *Melandrium*, male promoter region is designated as

(a) region Y (b) region III
(c) region IV (d) region II

61. Loss of region I of Y chromosome of *Melandrium* leads to the production of

(a) female plants (b) male sterile plants
(c) bisexual plants (d) all of these

62. In Y-chromosome of *Melandrium*, region IV is known as

(a) male fertility region
(b) pairing region
(c) male sexual region
(d) male promotor region

63. Colour blindness in man is governed by a recessive gene which is located on

(a) X-chromosome (b) autosomes
(c) Y-chromosome (d) none of these

64. The gene which is responsible for hemophilia in man is located on

(a) X-chromosome (b) autosomes
(c) Y-chromosome (d) none of these

65. The genetic constitution of a human with Klinefelter's syndrome is

(a) XYXY (b) XXO
(c) XO (d) XXY

66. The genetic constitution of a human with Turner's syndrome is

(a) YO (b) XXY
(c) XY (d) XO

67. Match SRY with one of the following

(a) Female (b) Male
(c) Autosome (d) None

68. The pattern of sex determination in Protenor bug is

(a) WZ-ZZ (b) XY-XX
(c) XO-XX (d) compound sex

69. Which of the following is male in grasshopper?

(a) XX (b) XY
(c) XO (d) Y

70. The pattern of sex determination in birds is

(a) compound sex (b) XO-XX
(c) XY-XX (d) WZ-ZZ

71. The female in butterflies is

(a) XX (b) XY
(c) XO (d) WZ

72. Which of the following is sterile female in man?

(a) XX (b) XO
(c) XY (d) XXY

73. Which of the following is sterile male in *Drosophila*?

(a) XX (b) XXY
(c) XY (d) None

74. Mutant white eyes in *Drosophila* was discovered by

(a) Carl Correns (b) Calvin Bridges
(c) T. H. Morgan (d) Nilsson Ehle

75. In marine worm *Bonellia*, the sex is determined with the help of

(a) hormones
(b) metabolism
(c) parasite
(d) environmental factors

76. In *Drosophila*, the genic balance mechanism was studied by

(a) Morgan (b) Bridges
(c) Punnet (d) Briggs

77. The relative strength of X chromosomes for femaleness is

(a) 0.5 (b) 0.75
(c) 1.0 (d) 1.5

78. In *Bonellia*, a marine worm, the male develops from a larva that

(a) settles in seawater
(b) attaches to the uterus of the female
(c) settles in the proboscis of a female
(d) secretes a chemical substance

79. Deuteranopia is

(a) red colour blindness
(b) blue colour blindness
(c) green colour blindness
(d) black colour blindness

80. Which chromosomal pair determines sex in *Drosophila*?

(a) I pair (b) II pair
(c) III pair (d) IV pair

81. In which of the following, similar type of sex determination occurs?

(a) Man and birds
(b) Birds and insects
(c) *Drosophila* and honey bee
(d) Man and *Drosophila*

82. In *Bonellia*, the larvae reared in seawater along with female worms develop into

(a) males (b) females
(c) super males (d) super females

83. Which chromosome has no role in sex determination in *Drosophila*?

(a) X (b) Y
(c) Autosomes (d) Both 1 and 2

84. What is the role of the SRY gene in humans?

(a) It initiates the X inactivation process in females
(b) It is located on the X chromosome and causes the X to pair with the Y chromosome during male meiosis
(c) It is located on the Y chromosome and initiates the developmental pathway towards the male phenotype
(d) None of the above answers is correct

85. Which of the following chromosome constitutions would never lead to a viable human baby being born?

(a) XXX (b) XYY
(c) XO (d) YY

86. In species of birds, males are the homogametic sex and females the heterogametic sex. Which of the following is true in sex determination?

(a) The gender of the offspring is determined by the female parent
(b) Male offspring have a ZW chromosome constitution
(c) The gender of the offspring is determined by the male parent
(d) Female and male offspring have the same chromosome constitution

87. In the germ cell-line cell from a human male that is dividing, when do the X and Y chromosomes segregate?

(a) During meiosis
(b) During meiosis I, anaphase
(c) During meiosis II, anaphase
(d) They do not segregate; gametes contain a copy of X and a copy of Y

88. What is the sex chromosome constitution of a male duck-billed Platypus?

(a) XY (b) XO
(c) ZZ (d) XXXXXYYYYY

89. An XXY chromosome constitution produces _____ development in humans and _____ development in fruit flies

(a) female, female (b) male, male
(c) female, male (d) male, female

90. In which of the following phenotypic females do testes develop?

(a) XY with a deletion that removes the SRY gene
(b) XO
(c) XY with the X-linked recessive condition of and both (a) and (b) are correctrogen insensitivity syndrome
(d) Both (a) and (b) are correct

91. A Barr body is a(n)

(a) gene on the X chromosome that is responsible for female development
(b) inactivated X chromosome, visible in the nucleus of a cell that is normally from a female mammal
(c) extra X chromosome in a cell that is the result of non-disjunction
(d) extra Y chromosome in a cell that is the result of non-disjunction

92. What is the apparent purpose for X inactivation in humans and other mammals?

(a) It allows for the levels of expression of genes on the X chromosome to be similar in males and females
(b) It allows for the levels of expression of genes on the autosomes to be similar to the levels of genes on the X chromosomes
(c) It suppresses the expression of genes on the Y chromosome in males
(d) None of the above is correct

93. In which of the following individuals would you expect to find two Barr bodies in their somatic cells?

(a) XX (b) XO
(c) XXX (d) XXY

94. Sex-linked genetically inherited traits

(a) can appear in both males and females
(b) are only found in males
(c) are only found in females
(d) result from premarital sexual intercourse

95. Y-linked traits are inherited

(a) only by females
(b) only by males
(c) by both males and females
(d) only by XYY individuals

96. Harmful X-linked traits are

(a) inherited only from mothers
(b) more numerous than Y-linked ones
(c) more likely to show up in the phenotype of daughters
(d) all are correct

97. Red-green colour blindness is

(a) an X-linked trait
(b) a Y-linked trait
(c) both X and Y linked
(d) not known

98. Men with red-green colour blindness inherited the genes for it from

(a) their mothers
(b) their fathers
(c) either their mothers or fathers
(d) not known

MARK TRUE OR FALSE (T/F)

1. Sex-limited inheritance refers to traits that are located on the X or Y chromosome
2. Y chromosome carries a few loci concerned with metabolism
3. The X chromosome carries the gene for sickle cell anemia
4. The following are true about the offspring of a female carrier of an X-linked recessive disorder and a normal male. Half of their children will be symptomatic

5. Sex chromosomes are known as allosomes
6. Sex chromosomes were first discovered by Montgomery
7. The term "sex-linkage" was coined by Morgan
8. The name "super female" was given by Bridges
9. The X-hypothesis is also known as Lyon's hypothesis
10. The term criss-cross inheritance was given by Morgan
11. Sex-linkage was first discovered by Morgan in *Drosophila*
12. Normal male *Drosophila* has one Barr body
13. Hemophilia is governed by a dominant gene
14. A human with Klinefelter's syndrome has XXY chromosomes
15. In papaya, sex is governed by two genes
16. The term "heterogametic" was coined by Wilson
17. Transformer gene in *Drosophila* was discovered by Sturtevant
18. Transformer gene in *Drosophila* is a dominant gene
19. In the wasp *Bracon hebetor*, the males are haploid and the famales are diploid
20. In the sea worm *Bonnelia*, larvae that are free-swimming and settle on the sea bottom develop into males
21. Large eggs produce females in sea worm *Dinophilus*
22. In the horsetail plant, *Equisetum* sex is affected by environment
23. In muskmelon, the appearance of female flowers is related to the production of ethylene
24. Sex-linkage means the presence of genes related to sex on the X chromosomes
25. In *Drosophila*, the gene for white eyes is present on chromosome number 2
26. Genes present on the X-chromosome in male *Drosophila* are hemizygous
27. In butterflies, the male is the heterogametic sex
28. Colour blindness is a sex-linked character in human beings
29. Bacterial conjugation is often described as a form of sex, although it differs in many respects from eukaryotic sex because conjugation in bacteria generally results in genetic recombination, just as during meiosis in eukaryotes
30. Organisms that can reproduce both sexually and asexually are rare
31. Exclusive sexual or asexual reproduction is relatively rare; in most species, individuals have both options
32. "Anisogamy" means that the male and female gametes are clearly different in size
33. "Anisogamy" means that the males and females are clearly different in morphology and behavior
34. Anisogamy is required for the operation of sexual selection
35. The basis of sexual selection is a difference in initial reproductive investment between males and females
36. The evolutionary maintenance of sexual reproduction is not easy to understand, because it is not clear that the advantages of sex outweigh the disadvantages
37. Sexual recombination can speed up evolution by bringing together beneficial mutations that have arisen in different lines of descent. This advantage of sex is much greater in large than small populations
38. Host-parasite interactions often involve negative frequency-dependent selection
39. Advances in our understanding of the evolution of sex mainly require development of more sophisticated theory

40. Advances in our understanding of the evolution of sex mainly require development of more experimentation
41. A sexual genetic system is more vulnerable to the spread of "selfish" genes, than an asexual system
42. The basic features of sex are shared by all eukaryotic sexual species
43. Y chromosome is the only acrocentric chromosome seen in humans
44. Y chromosome carries the testis determining factor on its short arms
45. Klinefelter's syndrome has two Y chromosomes
46. Y chromosome may be detected in some phenotypic females
47. X-chromosome inactivation normally takes place in males and not in females
48. X-chromosome inactivation is the cause of Y-chromosome being genetically inactive
49. X-chromosome inactivation takes place in humans, so that the same X-chromosome is inactive in all of the cells of the female
50. X-chromosome inactivation occurs in fruit flies but not in mammals
51. X-chromosome inactivation results in genetically turning off of one of the two X-chromosomes in female mammals
52. The X chromosome of the male can be demonstrated in a buccal smear test
53. The X chromosome is not found in the nuclei of all spermatozoa
54. The X chromosome may show an increased fragility in some conditions
55. The X chromosome carries the gene for the Xg blood group
56. The following is true about the offspring of a female carrier of an X-linked recessive disorder and a normal male. Half of their daughters will be symptomatic
57. The following is true about the offspring of a female carrier of an X-linked recessive disorder and a normal male. Half of their sons will be asymptomatic carriers
58. The following is true about the offspring of a female carrier of an X-linked recessive disorder and a normal male. Half of their daughters will be carriers
59. The following is true about the offspring of a female carrier of an X-linked recessive disorder and a normal male. Half of their sons will be symptomatic
60. In relation to sex, maize is a dioceous plant
61. Sexual dimorphism means that sexual differences are clearly evident from external differences
62. In *Bonellia*, if a single worm is reared from the egg in isolation, it develops into a female
63. If newly-hatched worms of *Bonellia* are released in water containing mature females, some worms attach to the proboscis of the female and mature into males
64. In marine mollusk *Crepidula*, if the young animals are reared alone, they become males
65. In *Crepidula*, if young animals are reared in close proximity to an adult, they become females
66. In *Drosophila*, maleness is because of the presence of Y chromosome
67. In *Drosophila*, Y chromosome is important for fertility of males
68. Hemizygous condition is because of the presence of one allele of a gene on autosomes
69. Sex-linkage means that the genes responsible for sex are present on the X and Y chromo-somes
70. In squash bug *Anasa tristis*, females have 21 chromosomes and males have 22 chromosomes
71. In aphids, when females lay unfertilized eggs, these hatch into females only
72. When genes are present on both X and Y chromosomes, the condition is called incomplete sex-linkage

9
Extranuclear Inheritance

MULTIPLE-CHOICE QUESTIONS

1. **How many Barr bodies an abnormal human of the karyotype 49, XXXYY will form?**
   (a) Male and female genotype
   (b) Female genotype
   (c) Female phenotype
   (d) Male phenotype
   (e) Male genotype

2. ***Poky* mutants affect**
   (a) nuclear function
   (b) ribosome function
   (c) chloroplast function
   (d) centriole function
   (e) mitochondrial function

3. **The endosymbiont theory explains the origin of**
   (a) bacteria
   (b) viruses
   (c) chromosomes
   (d) mitochondria
   (e) chromosomes

4. **The molecular genetic components found in mitochondria and chloroplasts are**
   (a) derived from nuclear and organelle DNA
   (b) derived only from organelle DNA
   (c) derived only from nuclear DNA
   (d) derived only from nuclear DNA but regulated by organelle DNA
   (e) derived only from organelle DNA but regulated by nuclear DNA

5. **In *Paramecium*, conjugation between organisms of KK and kk genotypes produces exconjugants that are**
   (a) all kk
   (b) 1/2 KK and 1/2 kk
   (c) all Kk
   (d) 1/4 KK: 1/2 Kk: 1/4 kk
   (e) all KK

6. **Cytoplasmic inheritance is governed by**
   (a) plasma genes (b) extranuclear genes
   (c) cytogenes (d) all of these

7. Plasma genes are present in

(a) chloroplasts (b) mitochondria
(c) a and b above (d) ribosomes

8. First case of cytoplasmic inheritance was reported by

(a) Correns (b) Caspari
(c) Renner (d) Conklin

9. The first case of cytoplasmic inheritance was reported in

(a) corn (b) garden pea
(c) barley (d) four O'clock plant

10. Cytoplasmic inheritance is also known as

(a) organellar inheritance
(b) extrachromosomal inheritance
(c) extranuclear inheritance
(d) all of these

11. Uniparental inheritance refers to

(a) cytoplasmic inheritance
(b) extranuclear inheritance
(c) extrachromosomal inheritance
(d) all of these

12. In maize, cytoplasmic male sterility is governed by

(a) motochondrial genes
(b) ribosomal genes
(c) chloroplast genes
(d) none of these

13. Cytoplasmic DNA replicates in

(a) chloroplasts (b) mitochondria
(c) a and b (d) chromoplasts

14. In *Drosophila*, inheritance of sigma particle is an example of

(a) maternal effect
(b) cytoplasmic inheritance
(c) inheritance of infective particles
(d) all of these

15. In water snail, coiling pattern of shell was reported by

(a) Correns (b) Sturtevant
(c) Welch (d) Caspari

16. In flour moth, maternal effect was reported by

(a) Sturtevant (b) Correns
(c) Ruthsagar (d) Caspari

17. In maize, *iojap* (green and white stripes) leaf colour is controlled by

(a) nuclear genes
(b) mitochondrial genes
(c) chloroplast genes
(d) ribosomal genes

18. Examples of mitochondrial inheritance include

(a) CMS in plants
(b) *petite* in yeast
(c) *pokyness* in *Neurospora*
(d) all of these

19. Examples of plastid inheritance include

(a) leaf colour in four O' Clock plant
(b) leaf colour in zebrina
(c) *iojap* in maize
(d) all of these

20. Only _____ transmit mitochondrial genes. Many mitochondrial disorders are _____, with mitochondria in a cell harboring different alleles

(a) males, heteroplasmid
(b) males, heteromorphid
(c) females, heteromorphid
(d) females, heteroplasmid

21. If you examine a pedigree showing the transmission pattern of a mitochondrial gene mutation, which of the following statements would be false?

(a) Mothers pass the gene to all offspring
(b) Fathers do not transmit the gene
(c) Only females will express the trait
(d) All of the above statements are true

22. Which of the following is not true of a maternal effect gene?

(a) It is located in the nuclear DNA
(b) Maternal genotype affects offspring phenotype
(c) It may control deposition of material into oocytes
(d) It must be located on the X chromosome

23. A pattern of transmission where all offspring have the same phenotype as their mother is consistent with which type of non-Mendelian inheritance?

(a) Maternal effect
(b) Genomic imprinting
(c) Dosage compensation
(d) Extranuclear inheritance

24. Both X-linked genes and extranuclear inheritance produce different results in reciprocal crosses. How can you distinguish between them?

(a) Extranuclear traits can be transmitted from an unaffected mother to an affected son
(b) Extranuclear traits can be transmitted from an affected mother to an affected offspring
(c) Extranuclear traits cannot be transmitted from father to son
(d) None of these

25. For a trait known to be caused by a mitochondrial gene variant, there may be an occasional female that can transmit different phenotypes to her progeny on an apparently random basis. What situation might you suspect?

(a) She is heterozygous for this trait
(b) She displays heteroplasmy for this trait
(c) She displays a low rate of mutation
(d) She is the product of a somatic mutation

26. In *S. cerevisiae,* mutations which cause a segregational petite phenotype

(a) are located in mitochondrial genes
(b) cause mitochondria to have better than normal function
(c) are transmitted according to mendelian rules
(d) prevent growth under all conditions

27. Neutral petite mutations

(a) are an example of extranuclear inheritance
(b) always produce petite progeny when mated to wild type
(c) might be expected to produce normal progeny when mated to a suppressive petite
(d) all of the above

28. Mitochondrial mutations in humans tend to affect some tissues more than others. Which is the most likely explanation?

(a) Some human tissues do not have mitochondria
(b) Some human tissues have higher energy demands than others
(c) Some human tissues can synthesize large amounts of ATP in the absence of mitochondrial function
(d) Heteroplasmy and subsequent segregation often leads to variegated phenotype

29. Symbiotic infective particles

(a) tend to be inherited in an extranuclear pattern
(b) have their own DNA
(c) appear to be similar to viruses in function
(d) all of these

30. Mitochondrial DNA

(a) is circular
(b) contains its own genes for ribosomal RNA
(c) differs in size depending on the organism
(d) all of the above
(e) none of the above

31. Which of the following is true of non-nuclear DNA?

(a) It is found in mitochondria and is maternal in origin
(b) It is found in mitochondria and is paternal in origin
(c) It is found on the Y chromosome and is paternal in origin
(d) (b) and (c) are true
(e) all of the above are true

32. Vibriocin is a bacteriocin specified by bacterial plasmid. It is directed against

(a) *Enterobacterium cloacae*
(b) *Vibrio cholerae*
(c) *E. coli*
(d) none of the above

33. The person(s) who isolated pieces of main-chromosome DNA from *Staphylococcus* and spliced individual pieces into non-conjugal plasmids are

(a) Chang and Cohen (b) Cameron
(c) Davis (d) Brown

34. The popular cloning vectors include

(a) Col EI (b) pSC101
(c) none of the above (d) both a and b

35. Animal ribosomes are 55S with

(a) 16S and 18S rRNA
(b) 16S and 12S rRNA
(c) 20S and 18S rRNA
(d) 20S and 26S rRNA

36. *Neurospora* ribosomes are 80S with

(a) 22S and 15S rRNA
(b) 16S and 18S rRNA
(c) 20S and 26S rRNA
(d) 20S and 28S rRNA

37. *Poky* mutant in *Neurospora* was first isolated by

(a) M. and H. Mitchell (b) Cohen
(c) Caspari (d) Correns

38. Mitochondria from two different parents have the capacity to

(a) fuse
(b) recombine their DNA
(c) cannot fuse
(d) both a and b

39. In higher plants, chloroplasts have distinct

(a) translational components
(b) transcriptional components
(c) none of the above
(d) both a and b

40. Chloroplast DNA of higher plants consist of genes

(a) for rRNAs
(b) for a number of tRNAs
(c) probably for certain ribosomal proteins
(d) all of the above

41. In maternal inheritance, if a cytoplasmic trait is carried solely by the female in a cross

(a) all of the offspring inherit the trait
(b) only females inherit the trait
(c) only males inherit the trait
(d) none of the above is true

42. In maternal inheritance, if a cytoplasmic trait is carried solely by the male in a cross

(a) all of the offspring inherit the trait
(b) only females inherit the trait
(c) only males inherit the trait
(d) none of the offspring inherit it

43. In maternal inheritance

(a) egg cells alone are capable of transmitting cytoplasmic genes to a zygote
(b) sperm cells alone are capable of transmitting cytoplasmic genes to a zygote
(c) both egg cells and sperms are capable
(d) none are capable

44. In *Mirabilis* plant, the leaves on branches may be

(a) fully green
(b) patchy pale-green-to-white
(c) fully pale
(d) all of the above

45. In *Mirabilis* plant, after a cross, if the ovules are derived from variegated branches, the seeds produced give rise to

(a) pure green offspring
(b) pure white offspring
(c) mainly variegated offspring
(d) all of the above

46. In the above example, the variegated ovules contain

(a) normal plastids
(b) abnormal plastids
(c) a mixture of normal and abnormal plastids
(d) none of the above

47. A gene in corn called iojap has been mapped by Rhoades to nuclear linkage group

(a) V (b) VI
(c) VII (d) VIII

48. The endosymbiosis theory was first suggested by

(a) Mahler (b) Raff
(c) Altmann (d) none of the above

49. The plasmid theory was given by

(a) Altmann (b) Mahler
(c) Mahler and Raff (d) Raff

50. A maternally inherited infectious virus known as sigma is found in the cytoplasm of CO_2-sensitive strains of

(a) *Paramecium* (b) *Neurospora*
(c) *Drosophila* (d) maize

51. Kappa particles in *Paramecium* are

(a) Gram-negative (b) Gram-positive
(c) Gram-neutral (d) none of the above

52. The contractile vacuoles in *Paramecium* can be transmitted from one cell generation to the next, independent of the transmission of nuclear genes and cytoplasmic genetic factors, as shown by

(a) Raff
(a) Sonneborn and co-workers
(b) Altmann
(c) None of the above

53. Where is genetic information passed on through extranuclear inheritance not located?

(a) Within animal cells
(b) Within the cytoplasm of the cell
(c) Within the cell nucleus
(d) Within plant cells

54. When does vegetative segregation occur?

(a) Randomly during mitotic cell division
(b) Every third generation in most species of plants
(c) When a species reproduces asexually
(d) During plant reproduction

55. When genetic information is passed through uniparental inheritance, which parent does it usually come from?

(a) Father (b) Mother
(c) Genetic information comes from both parents
(d) Uniparental information only occurs in organisms that reproduce asexually

56. Chloroplasts function to produce

(a) ribosomes (b) energy
(c) sugars (d) vitamins

57. The organelle which functions to transform energy as a result of cellular respiration is called

(a) ribosome (b) nucleus
(c) mitochondria (d) chloroplast

58. Mitochondrial diseases are received from

(a) mother (b) father
(c) in laws (d) environment

59. The transmission of genes that occur outside the nucleus is called

(a) extranuclear inheritance
(b) cytoplasmic inheritance
(c) both (a) and (b)
(d) none of above

60. Extranuclear inheritance commonly occurs in

(a) nucleus
(b) cytoplasmic organelles
(c) ribosomes
(d) cell membrane

61. Kappa particles indicate

(a) nuclear inheritance
(b) cytoplasmic inheritance
(c) mutation
(d) nucleo-cytoplasmic inheritance

62. *Mirabilis jalapa* is a good example of

(a) complete dominance
(b) plastid inheritance
(c) both (a) and (b)
(d) none of the above

63. Cytoplasmic male sterility in maize is manifestation of interaction between

(a) chloroplast and nuclear genes
(b) mitochondrial and nuclear genes
(c) chloroplast and mitochondrial genes
(d) cytoplasmic factors and male sterile genes

64. The two organelles responsible for cytoplasmic inheritance among eukaryotes are

(a) lysosomes and mitochondria
(b) mitochondria and Golgi complex
(c) chloroplasts and mitochondria
(d) chloroplasts and lysosomes

65. After crossing two plants, the progenies are found to be male sterile. The phenomenon is found to be maternally inherited and due to some genes which reside in

(a) nucleus (b) chloroplast
(c) mitochondria (d) cytoplasm

66. Genes for cytoplasmic male sterility in plants are generally located in

(a) mitochondrial genome
(b) in cytosol
(c) chloroplast genome
(d) nuclear genome

67. Which of the following are known as "magical circles"?

(a) plasmids (b) genes
(c) amyloplasts (d) elaioplasts

68. A plasmid

(a) lives together with chromosome
(b) shows dependent assortment
(c) can replicate independently
(d) cannot replicate

69. Hereditary element may be attached to chromosome or found free in cytoplasm is called

(a) microsome (b) diosome
(c) peroxisome (d) episome

70. Plasmids so found in bacteria are

(a) extranuclear DNA
(b) food particles
(c) dead protoplasmic parts
(d) none of the above

71. Plasmids are composed of

(a) folded RNA molecules
(b) single stranded RNA
(c) circular double stranded DNA
(d) none of the above

72. Genes with antibiotic resistance on bacteria are located on

(a) chromosomal DNA
(b) plasmid
(c) RNA
(d) polysome

73. Episome is a

(a) plasmid
(b) part of a chromosome
(c) lysosome
(d) ribosome

74. The hybrid produced by cytoplasmic fusion is called

(a) a sexual hybrid (b) parasexual hybrid
(c) somatic hybrid (d) protoplastic hybrid

75. What is a petite mutant?

(a) Defective mitochondrial function of the yeast
(b) Plastid function mutant
(c) Dwarfism
(d) Maternal effect genes

76. Which of the following is not the type of petite mutant?

(a) Nuclear (b) Neutral
(c) Suppressive (d) Polygene

77. Name the effect which shows the determination of character by the genotype of a female parent?

(a) Cytoplasmic male sterility
(b) Probability
(c) Random mating
(d) Maternal effect

MARK TRUE OR FALSE (T/F)

1. In maternal effect inheritance, the phenotype of the mother determines the genotype of the offspring
2. The mitochondrial genome encodes all proteins required to carry out oxidative phosphorylation
3. In *Chlamydomonas,* mitochondria are inherited from one parent while chloroplasts are inherited from the other
4. Phenotypic effects produced by the egg cytoplasm are known as paternal effects
5. A clear illustration of maternal effect was found in *Ephestia kuhniella* by Conklin
6. In the snail *Limnaea,* those snails which coil to the left are known as dextral
7. The extrachromosomal genetic factors are also known as plasmids
8. The first example of cytoplasmic genes inherited solely through the maternal parent was reported by Correns
9. The name of *Mirabilis jalapa* is six O' Clock plant
10. *Micromonas*, an alga, has only one chloroplast and one mitochondrion
11. Nuclear genetic material has no effect on chloroplast production
12. A wide array of nuclear genes block specific steps in photosynthesis *of Chlamydomonas*
13. The existence of extrachromosomal factors has been demonstrated through differences between non-reciprocal crosses
14. Cytoplasmic genes are absent in *Chlamydomonas*
15. Mutant *petites* were first discovered in *Saccharomyces* by Ephrussi and collaborators
16. Certain strains in yeast showing respiratory deficiency are called *poky*
17. Cytoplasmic DNA is present in kinetoplasts
18. Cytoplasmic DNA replication is conservative
19. Cytoplasmic DNA replication is in phase with DNA replication in the nucleus
20. The formation of chloroplast ribosomes may be affected by nuclear genes
21. In the case of neutral petites, all mitochondrial DNA is absent

22. Conjugation between *Paramecium* having killer and sensitive trait cannot take place
23. In *Paramecium*, the extrachromosomal particle responsible for the *killer* trait is known as *kappa* particle
24. The persistence of *kappa* particle in *Paramecium* does not depend upon any nuclear gene
25. Viruses have been isolated from *kappa* particles
26. Maternal inheritance is the inheritance of genes in (egg) cytoplasmic organelles
27. Maternal effect is when egg proteins and mRNAs affect embryonic development
28. Cytoplasmic DNA is usually circular
29. Renner reported plastid inheritance in maize
30. In *Drosophila*, sigma particle is responsible for CO_2 sensitivity
31. Sinistral coiling in snail is related to right-handed coiling
32. Plasmids represent the smallest bacterial genomes
33. Mitochondrial DNA is the smallest eukaryotic genome known
34. Plasmids that can integrate into or out of the main chromosome are called episomes
35. Plasmids carrying antibiotic resistance genes are known as A plasmids
36. Plasmids which specify proteins are called policins
37. F elements are conjugal plasmids
38. Conjugal plasmids are transmitted from parent to daughter cells in an 'asexual' manner
39. Nonconjugal plasmids may be co-transferred along with conjugal plasmids if both of these elements are present in the same cell
40. The trait of a bacterial plasmid shows no linkage to any marker located in the main chromosome
41. The loss of a plasmid cannot be induced
42. R plasmids can be transmitted from one species to another
43. The Chang-Cohen technique is called DNA cloning
44. Animal ribosomes are small whereas *Neurospora* ribosomes are large
45. Some mitochondrial RNA polymerases are sensitive to the antibiotic rifampicin whereas others are not
46. Because of its large size, mitochondrial DNA is very suitable for mapping studies
47. In yeast cells, the *petite* mutants cannot respire
48. If cells of yeast population are treated with acridine mutagens, 100 per cent of the cells can be converted to the petite state
49. Most petite yeasts carry mutations that exhibit non-Mendelian inheritance
50. In yeast, suppressive petites can carry on mitochondrial protein synthesis

10
Quantitative Genetics

MULTIPLE-CHOICE QUESTIONS

1. **Polygenic inheritance centers on**
   (a) additive alleles and is qualitative
   (b) multiple alleles and is quantitative
   (c) multiple alleles and is qualitative
   (d) epistasis and is qualitative
   (e) additive alleles and is quantitative

2. **Heritability**
   (a) makes people itch
   (b) of white spotting in Fresian cattle is high (95%)
   (c) is the sum of squares of deviation from the mean
   (d) is a variety of *Phaseolus vulgaris*
   (e) only happens at weekends

3. **The quantitative trait locus method does not typically involve**
   (a) estimation of heritability
   (b) linkage analysis
   (c) DNA sequence homology between humans and animal models
   (d) breeding experiments
   (e) gene cloning

4. **Environmental factors most effect the expression of**
   (a) recessive alleles
   (b) multiple alleles
   (c) codominant alleles
   (d) additive alleles
   (e) dominant alleles

5. **Which is not correct about the sporophytic system of self-incompatibility?**
   (a) There are frequent reciprocal differences
   (b) Homozygotes for S allele are a normal part of the system
   (c) Stigma surface is plumose
   (d) An incompatibility group may contain two genotypes

6. **R.A. Fisher divided the genotypic variance into**
   (a) additive and dominance components
   (b) additive and interaction components
   (c) dominance and interaction components
   (d) all of the above

7. **Haymen and Mather partitioned the epistatic component into**
(a) additive x dominance and dominance x dominance
(b) additive x additive and additive x dominance
(c) dominance x dominance and additive x additive
(d) all of the above

8. **Genetic variability can be measured by**
(a) range and variance
(b) standard deviation, and standard error
(c) coefficient of variation and D^2 statistic
(d) all of the above

9. **Mather divided phenotypic variance into**
(a) additive, dominance and epistatic
(b) additive, epistatic and environmental
(c) additive, dominance, epistatic and environmental
(d) additive, dominance and environmental

10. **The D^2 statistic was proposed in 1936 by**
(a) Fisher (b) Mahalanobis
(c) Jinks (d) Mather

11. **The metroglyph analysis was developed by**
(a) Anderson (b) Curnow
(c) Kempthorne (d) Rawlings

12. **On $V_r - W_r$ graph, when the regression line passes through the origin, it indicates**
(a) overdominance
(b) partial dominance
(c) complete dominance
(d) no dominance

13. **Line x tester analysis is a good approach for screening germplasm on the basis of**
(a) GCA and SCA variances
(b) GCA and SCA effects
(c) GCA and SCA variances and effects
(d) *per se* performance of hybrids

14. **In the Finley and Wilkinson model of phenotypic stability analysis, a regression coefficient greater than one indicates**
(a) average stability
(b) below average stability
(c) above average stability
(d) good stability

15. **Which of the following is not correct?**
(a) Coefficient of variation does not have a unit
(b) Variances for different traits can be compared with each other
(c) D^2 statistic is a good technique for determining genetic diversity
(d) Genetic diversity assessed using molecular markers is more reliable than that obtained from yield and yield traits

16. **In case of self-pollinated species, which of the following assumptions of diallel is the most likely to fail?**
(a) Diploid segregation
(b) Absence of epistasis
(c) Homozygosity of parents
(d) Random mating

17. **Path analysis is based on the estimates of**
(a) variance
(b) regression coefficients
(c) coefficients of variation
(d) correlation coefficients

18. **Which one of the following shows severe inbreeding depression?**
(a) Vegetatively propagated crops
(b) Cross-pollinated crops
(c) Self-pollinated crops
(d) Both (a) and (b)

19. An increase in the inbreeding coefficient, F, is likely to result in

(a) reduced likelihood of heterozygotes being present in a population
(b) higher proportion of genes that show linkage
(c) higher proportion of genes with introns
(d) lower level of difference between proteins in two daughter cells
(e) higher level of difference between RNA molecules in two daughter cells

20. Which of the following statements about heritability are true?

(a) Heritability is a measure of the level of gene linkage
(b) It is a measure of inbreeding
(c) It is a measure of proportion of repeated DNA in an organism
(d) It is a measure of the level of heterozygotes in a population
(e) It is a measure of the proportion of variation that is due to genetic causes

21. Heritability is a measure of the parent-offspring relationship in polygenic situations and in situations where individual genetic effects cannot be measured. It is calculated as the

(a) variance divided by the mean
(b) sum of differences between observed and expected, divided by expected
(c) phenotypic variance divided by the environmental variance
(d) genotypic variance divided by the phenotypic variance
(e) phenotypic variance divided by the genotypic variance

22. Environmental factors most affect the expression of

(a) codominant alleles (b) additive alleles
(c) recessive alleles (d) dominant alleles
(e) multiple alleles

23. Polygenic inheritance centers around

(a) epistasis and is qualitative
(b) additive alleles and is quantitative
(c) multiple alleles and is quantitative
(d) additive alleles and is qualitative
(e) multiple alleles and is qualitative

24. In a cross involving polygenic inheritance, only 2/125 of the offspring (F_2) were as extreme as one of the P_1 parents. How many gene pairs are involved?

(a) 3 (b) 1
(c) 4 (d) 5
(e) 2

25. In a cross involving polygenic inheritance where three gene pairs control plant height, the shortest and tallest plants are 6 cm and 24 cm, respectively. What height should all F_1s display if homozygous 12-cm and 24-cm plants are crossed, assuming their environments are the same?

(a) 15 cm (b) 21 cm
(c) 9 cm (d) 12 cm
(e) 18 cm

26. Inheritance of complex traits differs from inheritance of quantitative traits in which of the following ways?

(a) Traits run in families
(b) No clear Mendelian pattern of inheritance is observed
(c) More than one gene is involved
(d) There is no difference

27. Which of the following terms is defined as "a measure of the variation in a phenotype (for a polygenic trait in a given population) due to genetic factors"?

(a) Broad-sense heritability
(b) Narrow-sense heritability
(c) Variance
(d) Biometry

28. Polygenic variation can be assessed through
(a) measures of dispersion
(b) D^2 statistics
(c) metroglyph analysis
(d) all of these

29. Yield components can be determined by
(a) path analysis
(b) correlation analysis
(c) discriminant function
(d) all of these

30. Which of the following biometrical techniques is called Mating design?
(a) Line x tester cross
(b) Partial diallel cross
(c) Diallel cross
(d) All of these

31. Which of the following traits is more sensitive to environmental change?
(a) Polygenic (b) Qualitative
(c) Quantitative (d) a and c above

32. Partial diallel provides information about
(a) gca effects (b) sca variance
(c) gca variance (d) all of these

33. Who developed the concept of line x tester cross analysis?
(a) Kempthorne (b) Mather
(c) Falconer (d) Jinks

34. Which of the following estimates is not possible through generation mean analysis
(a) epistatic variance
(b) dominance variance
(c) additive variance
(d) combining ability

35. Which of the following has specific population adaptation?
(a) Synthetic variety (b) Composite variety
(c) Multiline variety (d) Semi-dwarf wheat

36. The term "homeostasis" was coined in 1954 by
(a) Jinks (b) Falconer
(c) Lerner (d) Kempthorne

37. Stability parameter includes
(a) deviation from regression
(b) regression coefficient
(c) mean yield
(d) all of these

38. Homeostasis is associated with
(a) genetic polymorphism
(b) genetic diversity
(c) heterozygosity
(d) all of these

39. Which of the following types of epistasis is fixable?
(a) Additive x additive
(b) Dominance x dominance
(c) Additive x dominance
(d) All of these

40. Additive genes show
(a) complete dominance
(b) codominance
(c) lack of dominance
(d) overdominance

41. Which of the following is predominant in the natural breeding population?
(a) Dominance variance
(b) Additive variance
(c) Epistatic variance
(d) All of these

42. Selection is not effective for a trait which is governed by
(a) dominance x dominance epistasis
(b) additive x dominance epistasis
(c) dominance variance
(d) all of these

43. The success of genetic advance under selection for a character depends on
(a) selection intensity
(b) heritability of a character
(c) genetic variability
(d) all of these

44. High value of genetic advance indicates that the character is governed by

(a) dominant genes (b) additive genes
(c) epistatic genes (d) none of these

45. Low estimates of narrow sense heritability indicate

(a) epistasis
(b) non-additive gene action
(c) additive gene action
(d) all of these

46. High heritability with high genetic advance indicates

(a) epistatic gene action
(b) dominance action
(c) non-additive gene action
(d) additive gene action

47. Combining ability analysis provides information about

(a) epistasis (b) pleiotropy
(c) gene action (d) none of these

48. Combining ability analysis provides information about

(a) gene action
(b) good specific combinations
(c) good general combinations
(d) all of these

49. The dominance hypothesis of heterosis was first proposed in 1908 by

(a) East (b) Falconer
(c) Davenport (d) Kempthorne

50. Heterosis results due to

(a) epistasis (b) overdominance
(c) dominance (d) all of these

51. Overdominance hypothesis of heterosis was proposed in 1908 by

(a) East and Shull (b) East
(c) Davenport (d) Shull

52. Heterosis is estimated over

(a) better parent (b) mid parent
(c) best local cultivar (d) all of these

53. Traits which show continuous variation are referred to as

(a) Genetic disorders
(b) Phenotypic variation
(c) Quantitative traits
(d) Qualitative traits

54. Which of the following factor does not contribute to quantitative traits?

(a) Polygenes (b) Environmental
(c) Genetic
(d) Carbohydrate content

55. Who explained the multifactorial hypothesis?

(a) Ronald Fisher (b) Darwin
(c) Mendel (d) Nilsson Ehle

56. Which of the following describes the inheritance controlled by cytoplasmic genes?

(a) Extranuclear inheritance
(b) Heritability
(c) Environmental factors
(d) Complex trait

57. Which of the following is not true for cytoplasmic inheritance?

(a) Reciprocal cross is always different
(b) Unequal contribution from male and female gametes
(c) It follows a Mendelian pattern of inheritance
(d) Do not show segregation for traits

58. A QTL

(a) is one of the genes that influences a trait
(b) is a chromosomal region containing genes that influence a quantitative trait
(c) will not contain any genes other than the ones influencing a trait
(d) is a measure of the phenotypic variation in a quantitative trait

59. Flower diameter in sunflowers is a quantitative trait. A plant with 6-cm flowers, from a highly inbred strain is crossed to a plant with 30-cm flowers, also from a highly inbred strain. The F_1 has 18-cm flowers. $F_1 \times F_1$ crosses yield F_2 plants with flowers ranging from 6 to 30 cm in diameter, in approximately 4-cm intervals (6, 10, 14, 18, 22, 26, 30). The number of different genes influencing flower diameter in this plant is

(a) 3 (b) 4
(c) 5 (d) 6

60. Quantitative variation in a trait can be caused by as few as ______ simple Mendelian loci that each have ______ alleles.

(a) 16, 4 (b) 10, 3
(c) 6, 2 (d) 8, 6

61. QTL mapping can tell us which of the following?

(a) The number of loci that influence a quantitative trait
(b) The location of QTL in the genome
(c) The identity of QTL and the proteins they encode
(d) Both the number of loci that influence a quantitative trait and the location of QTL in the genome

62. Which one of the following correctly finishes the statement, "Heritability is ________"

(a) the proportion of variation in a trait, across populations, that is due to genetic variation between the populations
(b) a number that indicates whether natural selection can act on a certain trait
(c) the proportion of variation in a trait that is due to different environments
(d) the proportion of a trait that is due to genes rather than to environment

63. When heritability is calculated using similarities between parents and offspring, an important assumption is

(a) that environments of parents and offspring are independent
(b) that environments of parents and offspring are shared
(c) that the environments of parents and offspring are the same
(d) that heritability is due to genetic variation

64. The response to selection can be calculated as

(a) heritability; selection gradient
(b) selection gradient; relative fitness
(c) heritability; relative fitness
(d) heritability; selection differential

65. It is easier to study polygenic inheritance of characters in plants than in animals because in the plants

(a) matings can be controlled and large number of offspring are obtained
(b) matings cannot be controlled and large number of offspring are produced
(c) matings can be controlled and a small number of offspring can be produced
(d) matings cannot be controlled and a small number of offspring are produced

66. The phenotypic ratio obtained in quantitative inheritance of a dihybrid cross is

(a) 1 : 2 : 1
(b) 1 : 4 : 6 : 4 : 1
(c) 1 : 6 : 15 : 20 : 15 : 6 : 1
(d) 9: 3 : 3 : 1

67. Which of the following is associated with multiple phenotypes?

(a) Epistasis
(b) Pleiotropy
(c) Polygenic inheritance
(d) Mutation

68. Grain colour in wheat is determined by three pairs of polygenes. Following the cross AABBCC (dark colour) × aabbcc (light colour), in F_2 generation what proportion of the progeny is likely to resemble either parent?

(a) None (b) Less than 5 per cent
(c) One-third (d) Half

MARK TRUE OR FALSE (T/F)

1. That genes controlling quantitative traits are transmitted according to Mendelian laws was proposed by Mather
2. The multiple factor hypotheses for inheritance of seed colour in wheat was proposed by Johansson
3. One of the main differences between qualitative and quantitative traits lies in the degree to which they are affected by the environment
4. In 1918, Fisher divided genotypic variance into additive, dominant and recessive components
5. If the heritability of a character is high, selection for it will be difficult
6. Parent-offspring regression upon doubling provides an estimate of heritability
7. The genetic variability for important agronomic traits in most of the crops is mainly due to dominant variance
8. Coefficient of variation is an important measure of variability
9. Total number of crosses to be evaluated in a half diallel with parents is equal to n (n+1)
10. In diallel analysis, the proportion of genes with positive and negative effects in the parents cannot be estimated
11. If epistasis is present, general combining ability component will also include the additive x non-additive interaction component
12. The triallel analysis provides information on epistatic component of the variance also
13. In case of generation mean analysis, three parameter model is used when the nonallelic interactions are present
14. The significance of any of the scaling tests indicates the presence of epistasis
15. If the dominance variance is low, development of hybrid varieties will be beneficial
16. Co-heritability deals with the simultaneous inheritance of many characters
17. Additive and dominance components of genetic variance are estimated from biparental crosses
18. Physiological homoestasis is generally higher in homozygous genotypes than in heterozygous genotypes
19. Polygenes have major effects on the environment
20. The complementary gene action was reported by Nilsson-Ehle
21. Quantitative characters are not affected much by the environment
22. Polygenes show only additive effect
23. Broad sense heritability estimates are valid for segregating generations
24. Meteroglyph analysis has not been used for the analysis of variability in different crops
25. Yield is regarded as a simple character
26. Correlation coefficient analysis does not help in direct selection for yield
27. If reciprocal differences are non-significant, full diallel is not used
28. Epistasis is an example of polygenic trait
29. Heritability estimates the proportion of genetic variation in a group that can be attributed to phenotype
30. Siblings share 50% of their genes
31. Fraternal twins share 100% of their genes
32. Identical twins also share 100% of their genes
33. Expression of weight gain is solely dependent on the inheritance of weight gain genes
34. Intelligence is an example of a multifactorial trait
35. How much heredity and environment influence human traits can be studied by data from dizygotic twins reared apart

36. The concordance tells about the possibility of recurrence of a trait based on known incidence in a population
37. A child cannot have darker skin than either of his parents
38. A very poor relationship is indicated by a correlation coefficient of 1.0
39. In a heterozygous environment, a higher heritability would be found for a trait
40. Heritability studies are less powerful than association studies
41. Biometrical genetics and quantitative genetics are the same
42. Metroglyph analysis does not assess polygenic variation
43. Line x tester design is not a part of mating design
44. Oligogenic characters exhibit discontinuous variation
45. The analysis of D^2 statistics is possible only from replicated data
46. Simple correlation involves many variables
47. Coefficient of determination cannot be obtained directly from multiple correlations
48. Path analysis helps in determining yield components
49. Discriminant function analysis measures the efficiency of various character combinations in plant selection
50. Testing of six parameter model with X^2 test is not possible

11

Cytology and Cytogenetics

MULTIPLE-CHOICE QUESTIONS

1. **The size range of most plant and animal cells is**
   (a) 1-10 nm (b) 1-5 mm
   (c) 10-50 mm (d) 0.1-0.5 mm
   (e) 50-100 mm

2. **Since membranes usually are not permeable to polysaccharides, nucleic acids, and proteins, how are cells able to make use of these molecules?**
   (a) These macromolecules are only incorporated into structures outside the membrane
   (b) Macromolecules are broken down extracellularly, and their subunits diffuse through the membrane
   (c) Macromolecules are digested extracellularly, and their subunits move through transport proteins
   (d) Macromolecules are transported via endocytosis and digested within the cell
   (e) Both (c) and (d)

3. **The cell membrane can be characterized most accurately as**
   (a) permeable to some molecules and impermeable to others
   (b) permeable to only larger molecules
   (c) impermeable to all polar molecules
   (d) permeable to all molecules
   (e) permeable to most small molecules, but impermeable to larger ones

4. **Which of the following is not a function of membranes?**
   (a) Delineation
   (b) Compartmentalization
   (c) Regulation of transport
   (d) Cell-cell communication
   (e) Information storage

5. **A cell membrane is**
   (a) permeable
   (b) semi-permeable
   (c) impermeable
   (d) none of these

6. **Which substance would normally have had the least difficulty crossing a cell membrane?**
   (a) Water
   (b) Protein
   (c) Carbohydrate
   (d) Salt
   (e) There would be little difference in any of the above

7. **You are examining an electron micrograph of cells obtained on the last Martian expedition. Upon closer examination, you notice that there are two dark lines separated by a lightly stained region. These results are similar to the observation of which person's or persons' investigation into membrane structure?**
   (a) Unwin and Henderson
   (b) Gorter and Grendel
   (c) Singer and Nicolson
   (d) Robertson
   (e) Overton

8. **Based on the composition of cell membranes, the most prominent lipids are**
   (a) cholesterol
   (b) phospholipids
   (c) sphingolipids
   (d) both (b) and (c)
   (e) (a), (b) and (c)

9. **According to the fluid mosaic model of the plasma membrane, proteins are**
   (a) spread out in a continuous layer over both membrane surfaces
   (b) located in the hydrophilic area of the membrane
   (c) oriented in a random manner throughout the membrane
   (d) embedded in the lipid bilayers
   (e) capable of leaving the membrane and dissolving in the solution of the external environment

10. **Where would you expect to find an organism possessing a cell membrane with the following composition: large proportions of cholesterol and a predominance of unsaturated fatty acids?**
   (a) Equatorial regions
   (b) Tropical regions
   (c) Frozen wastelands
   (d) Upper levels of an aquatic environment
   (e) Temperate regions

11. **Temperature has a dramatic effect upon cell membranes. This influence can readily make a cell membrane more solid or more fluid in response to the temperature. This is an example of**
   (a) membrane asymmetry
   (b) liquidation
   (c) phase transition
   (d) membrane flexibility
   (e) none of the above

12. **Cell-cell communication in plants takes place via specialized structures called**
   (a) gap junctions (b) plasmodesmata
   (c) desmids (d) cell wall pores
   (e) none of the above

13. **The specific movement of a molecule from one side of a cell to another side of the same cell is known as**
   (a) cellular transport
   (b) intracellular transport
   (c) transcellular transport
   (d) facilitated transport
   (e) passive transport

14. **Communication between animal cells is facilitated by**
   (a) tight junctions (b) plasmodesmata
   (c) gap junctions (d) adhesive junctions
   (e) both (b) and (c)

15. The bacterial cell wall is composed of

(a) a phospholipid matrix
(b) a lipoprotein
(c) a polymer of sugars
(d) chitin
(e) a structural protein

16. Unlike prokaryotes, eukaryotic cell walls are composed of

(a) a carbohydrate matrix cross-linked by short polypeptides
(b) glycolipids and protein fibres
(c) cellulose fibres embedded in a matrix
(d) chitin
(e) proteins and histones

17. A reduction in surface area relative to the volume of a cell limits its size, but some cells have modifications that allow them to be somewhat larger. Which of the following is not one of the modifications that a cell may exhibit in order to overcome a reduction in surface area?

(a) Folding of the membrane
(b) Organelles
(c) Compartmentalization of activities
(d) Cytoplasmic streaming
(e) Production of the cell wall

18. Which structure is chiefly responsible for the rigidity of the plant cell?

(a) Cell membrane (b) Cell wall
(c) Nucleolus (d) Nucleus

19. Lignin is an important component in

(a) bacterial cell walls b) plasmodesmata
(c) fungal cell walls d) tight junctions
(e) secondary plant cell walls

20. The term "cytoplasm" was coined by

(a) Lamarck (b) Strasburger
(c) Flemming (d) Weismann

21. The term "nucleoplasm" was coined by

(a) Strasburger (b) Flemming
(c) Mayer (d) none of these

22. The cytosol is best described as the

(a) internal contents of organelles
(b) area of the cell not occupied by the nucleus
(c) semifluid substance in which organelles are suspended
(d) three dimensional array of interconnected filaments
(e) fluid within the nucleus

23. The smooth endoplasmic reticulum functions in synthesis of

(a) DNA (b) lipids
(c) polysaccharides (d) proteins
(e) all of the above

24. Endoplasmic reticulum is associated with the synthesis of

(a) protein (b) glycogen
(c) lipids (d) all of these

25. The rough ER is so named because it has an abundance of _______ on it

(a) mitochondria (b) lysosomes
(c) golgi bodies (d) ribosomes
(e) vesicles

26. Which is involved directly in synthesis of proteins as well as transport within the cell?

(a) Ribosomes (b) Golgi bodies
(c) Rough endoplasmic reticulum
(d) Smooth endoplasmic reticulum
(e) Vacuoles

27. A dominant organelle in cells heavily involved in lipid synthesis is the

(a) ribosome (b) lysosome
(c) smooth endoplasmic reticulum
(d) mitochondrion (e) contractile vacuole

28. A gland cell capable of producing large quantities of protein hormone would most likely have well developed

(a) cilia
(b) centrioles
(c) rough endoplasmic reticulum
(d) smooth endoplasmic reticulum
(e) lysosomes

29. Which of the following is not a characteristic of prokaryotes?

(a) DNA
(b) Cell membrane
(c) Cell wall
(d) Endoplasmic reticulum

30. Proteins synthesized by the rough ER are

(a) for internal storage
(b) to build more membranes in the cell
(c) to digest food in lysosomes
(d) for internal regulation
(e) exported from the cell

31. Ribosomes that do not anchor on the surface of the rough endoplasmic reticulum during translation most probably

(a) have a defect in ribosomal proteins that allow attachment to the surface
(b) are synthesizing cytoplasmic proteins
(c) do not make the appropriate anchor protein
(d) have a signal peptidase error
(e) all of the above

32. Ribosomes are very old structures found in all organisms (except viruses) from bacteria to humans. As a result, molecular taxonomists are looking at relationships based upon which rRNA sequences?

(a) 16S (b) 18S
(c) 30S (d) Both (a) and (b)
(e) All of the above

33. Ribosomes are made up of ______ subunits

(a) 0 (They are whole.) (b) 2
(c) 3 (d) 4

34. The smooth ER is especially abundant in cells that synthesize extensive amounts of

(a) toxins (b) proteins
(c) enzymes (d) lipids
(e) nucleic acids

35. Enzymes embedded in the membrane of the smooth ER

(a) synthesize lipids
(b) may be used for detoxification
(c) synthesize carbohydrates
(d) mostly are active only when associated with a membrane
(e) all of the above

36. Which organelle sometimes merges with food vacuoles and functions in chemical hydrolysis?

(a) Lysosomes (b) Chloroplasts
(c) Nucleus (d) Mitochondria
(e) Ribosomes

37. Digestive enzymes are contained in

(a) ribosomes (b) plastids
(c) lysosomes (d) all of these

38. Lysosomes originate from

(a) nuclear envelope
(b) endoplasmic reticulum
(c) plastids
(d) golgi bodies

39. Golgi bodies were first discovered in nerve cells of

(a) rabbit (b) cat and owl
(c) monkey (d) rat

40. In a cell, packaging of food material is related to

(a) plastids (b) ribosomes
(c) golgi bodies (d) mitochondria

41. Golgi bodies are associated with packaging of

(a) proteins (b) phospholipids
(c) lipids (d) all of these

42. Glycoproteins and glycolipids assembled in golgi bodies are packaged for distribution in

(a) cisternae (b) lysosomes
(c) peroxisomes (d) liposomes
(e) glyoxysomes

43. The golgi apparatus would be most prominent in cells that

(a) divide rapidly
(b) produce ATP
(c) contain chlorophyll
(d) actively secrete substances
(e) are large and inactive

44. The Golgi apparatus is involved in

(a) transporting proteins that are to be released from the cell
(b) packaging proteins into vesicles
(c) altering or modifying proteins
(d) producing lysosomes
(e) all of the above

45. Which organelle is responsible for the master control of the cell?

(a) Mitochondrion
(b) Ribosome
(c) Golgi apparatus
(d) Nucleus

46. Which of the following is an eukaryotic characteristic?

(a) Cell fission
(b) Little processing of RNA
(c) 70S ribosomes
(d) Membrane-bound nucleus
(e) None of the above

47. Which organelle is round and derives its name from the Latin word for "kernel"?

(a) Nucleus (b) Lysosome
(c) Golgi complex (d) Mitochondrion
(e) Chloroplast

48. Which cell organelle contains the chromosomes?

(a) Golgi apparatus (b) Nucleus
(c) Lysosome (d) Mitochondrion

49. Clusters of rRNA where ribosomes are assembled are called

(a) nuclei (b) cisternae
(c) nucleoli (d) golgi complexes
(e) centrioles

50. The term "nucleolar organizer" was first used by

(a) Mc Clintock (b) Flemming
(c) Strasburger (d) None of these

51. The nuclear membrane functions as a

(a) means of localization of the chromosomes within the cell
(b) selective barrier, allowing certain substances in or out
(c) means of sequestering many of the mRNA processing activities from the cytosol
(d) means of separating nuclear and cytoplasmic constituents
(e) all of the above

52. Which of the following processes would be most likely to occur in the Golgi apparatus?

(a) Detoxification of drugs
(b) Production and packaging of lipids
(c) Glycosylation of proteins
(d) Synthesis of steroids
(e) Synthesis of DNA

53. Which of the following is true of a plant cell?

(a) Plant cells are often much larger than animal cells
(b) Plant cells may contain chloroplasts
(c) Only plant cells have a cell membrane
(d) Chromosomes are found only in plant cells
(e) The plant cell has no cell wall

54. Which organelle has only a single membrane around it?

(a) Peroxisomes (b) Nucleus
(c) Chloroplast (d) Ribosome
(e) Mitochondrion

55. In which of the following cellular respiration occurs?

(a) Ribosome b) Nucleus
(c) Mitochondria (d) Golgi bodies

56. The term "mitochondrion" (Pl. mitochondria) was coined by

(a) Strasburger (b) Benda
(c) Meyer (d) none of these

57. In a cell, the main sites of respiration are

(a) plastids (b) mitochondria
(c) ribosomes (d) none of these

58. Mitochondrial enzymes for oxidative metabolism are

(a) on or within the surface of cristae
(b) located on the outer membrane
(c) in the matrix
(d) floating freely in intermembrane space
(e) in mitochondrial lysosomes

59. Intermediate filaments are

(a) smaller than actin filaments
(b) composed of tubulin
(c) composed of only globular proteins
(d) different in different cell types
(e) none of the above

60. Each nucleosome body is about

(a) 70 Å (b) 110 Å
(c) 140 Å (d) 400 Å

61. Which of the following is the correct order of the levels of DNA packaging in eukaryotic chromosomes?

(a) Chromatin fibre → nucleosome → looped domains → heterochromatin
(b) Heterochromatin → nucleosome → chromatin fibre → looped domains
(c) Nucleosome → looped domains → chromatin fibre → heterochromatin
(d) Nucleosome → chromatin fibre → looped domains → heterochromatin
(e) Chromatin fibre → heterochromatin → nucleosome → looped domains

62. The cells of which of the three domains of life contain ribosomes?

(a) Archaea (b) Bacteria
(c) Eukarya (d) All of the above

63. The term "homologous chromosomes"

(a) refers to replications of the same chromosome
(b) is another name for sister chromatids
(c) must be haploid
(d) means a pair of chromosomes of the same kind, such as sex chromosomes

64. Telomeres are located

(a) at the ends of chromosomes
(b) in mitochondrial DNA
(c) in prokaryotes
(d) none of the above

65. Telomeres are present

(a) in eukaryotes (b) in prokaryotes
(c) in centromere (d) none of the above

66. Telomeres are seen

(a) at the ends of ribosomal RNA
(b) in nuclear DNA
(c) in mitochondrial DNA
(d) in prokaryotes

67. An autosome is

(a) a non-sex determining chromosome
(b) an alternate form of a gene
(c) another term for epistasis
(d) present only in males and is responsible for sex determination
(e) found in mitochondria but not in nuclei

68. Which of the following is not true for histones?

(a) They are rich in basic amino acids
(b) They are associated with the nucleosome
(c) H1, H2, H3 and H4 form the nucleosome core
(d) They are found in the nucleus
(e) H1 functions as a monomer

69. Which of the following is not true about chromosome structure?

(a) A telomere is always on the end of a eukaryotic chromosome
(b) A centromere is always in the middle of a eukaryotic chromosome
(c) A chromatid is a chromosome that has been replicated but has not yet separated from its sister chromatid
(d) The kinetochore is the site of attachment of the centromere to the nuclear spindle apparatus
(e) Heterochromatin is primarily associated with the centromere and telomere regions

70. Homologous chromosomes are those which can be matched by virtue of their similar structure and function within a nucleus. Which chromosomes, making up a genome, do not follow the same characteristics of homology?

(a) Autosomes (b) Sex-chromosomes
(c) Mating types (d) Heterokaryons

71. Chromosome tips, or ______, function as a cellular clock that ticks down as pieces are lost from the very ends

(a) chromatids (b) centromeres
(c) centrioles (d) telomeres

72. A (an) ______ chromosome has its centromere near a tip so that it has one long arm and one very short arm

(a) metacentric (b) submetacentric
(c) acrocentric (d) none of the above

73. This structure emanates from the centromere and contacts the spindle fibres during mitosis

(a) alpha satellite (b) subtelomere
(c) euchromatin (d) kinetochore

74. ______ contains protein-encoding genes

(a) heterochromatin
(b) euchromatin
(c) pericentric inversions
(d) aneuploids

75. Heterochromatic regions at the ends of chromosomes are called

(a) centromeres (b) euchromatin
(c) telomeres (d) satellites

76. The photographic arrangement of chromosomes is called a (an)

(a) karyotype (b) idiogram
(c) anagram (d) chromogram

77. Which of the following cell types is not used to examine chromosomes?

(a) White blood cells
(b) Bone marrow cells
(c) Red blood cells
(d) All of the above can be used

78. Normally the cytoplasm of the cell does not contain

(a) chloroplasts (b) mitochondria
(c) ribosomes (d) lysosomes
(e) chromosomes

79. All mitochondrial genomes analyzed to-date are

(a) circular
(b) linear
(c) less than 50 kb in size
(d) none of the above

80. Which cell structure is known as the powerhouse of the cell?

(a) Nucleus
(b) Mitochondrion
(c) Vacuole
(d) Endoplasmic reticulum

81. Organelles called ______ provide energy from the products of digestion

(a) endoplasmic reticulum
(b) mitochondria
(c) lysosomes
(d) Golgi bodies

82. Diseases resulting from mutations in mitochondrial genes affect

(a) protein synthesis (b) energy acquisition
(c) both (a) and (b) (d) neither a nor b

83. Which is a major function of the mitochondria?

(a) Assembling proteins such as enzymes
(b) Carrying out respiratory activity
(c) Duplicating the chromosomes needed for cell division
(d) Absorbing light in photosynthesis
(e) All of the above are major functions

84. All chloroplast genomes analyzed to-date are

(a) circular
(b) linear
(c) less than 50 kb in size
(d) none of the above

85. All chloroplast genomes analyzed to-date are

(a) linear
(b) less than 50 kb in size
(c) greater than 50 kb in size
(d) none of the above

86. Stroma and grana are parts of

(a) chloroplast (b) leucoplast
(c) chromoplast (d) all of these

87. The term "granum" (Pl. grana) was coined by

(a) Strasburger (b) Meyer
(c) Strugger (d) none of these

88. Within chloroplasts, light is captured by

(a) grana within cisternae
(b) thylakoids within grana
(c) cisternae within grana
(d) grana within thylakoids
(e) none of the above

89. What is the function of chloroplasts?

(a) Protein synthesis (b) Photosynthesis
(c) Respiration (d) Movement

90. Which structure is found only in plant cells or algae?

(a) Endoplasmic reticulum
(b) Mitochondrion (c) Nucleus
(d) Lysosome (e) Plastid

91. In plants, the plastids which store lipids are called

(a) leucoplasts (b) scale scars
(c) golgi bodies (d) chloroplasts
(e) chromoplasts

92. Bacterial genomes are compacted by

(a) histones
(b) other proteins than histones
(c) DNA polymerase
(d) CP proteins

93. Bacterial genomes are compacted by

(a) histones
(b) DNA polymerases
(c) DNA topoisomerases
(d) none of the above

94. Pinching in of fluids by a unicellular organism is called

(a) phagocytosis (b) osmosis
(c) pinocytosis (d) exocytosis
(e) facilitated diffusion

95. Which is true of eukaryotic cells?

(a) Evolved more recently than prokaryotic cells
(b) They lack membrane bound organelles
(c) Lack a nuclear membrane
(d) Lack DNA

96. Cilia and flagella are most similar in structure to

(a) basal bodies (b) ribosomes
(c) mitochondria (d) chloroplasts
(e) endoplasmic reticula

97. A structure commonly found in animal cells, but rarely in plant cells is the

(a) Golgi apparatus
(b) centriole
(c) nucleus
(d) mitochondrion
(e) endoplasmic reticulum

98. Certain types of lymphocytes (white blood cells) in the lymph nodes ingest bacteria and debris. This function most likely occurs by

(a) exocytosis (b) passive transport
(c) phagocytosis (d) pinocytosis
(e) facilitated transport

99. In pond water, protozoans pump out excess water by means of their

(a) pellicle (b) trichocyst
(c) cell membrane (d) contractile vacuole
(e) pseudopodia

100. Only ______ transmit mitochondrial genes. Many mitochondrial disorders are ______ with mitochondria in a cell harboring different alleles

(a) males, heteroplasmic
(b) males, heteromorphic
(c) females, heteromorphic
(d) females, heteroplasmic

101. ______ retain the ability to specialize in particular ways in response to signals

(a) Organelles (b) Eukaryotic cells
(c) Cell membranes (d) Stem cells

102. Plants differ from animals in that plants have

(a) an endoplasmic reticulum
(b) a central vacuole
(c) Golgi complexes
(d) vesicles
(e) organelles

103. Which of the following organelles is found in plant cells but not in animal cells?

(a) Ribosomes
(b) Endoplasmic reticulum
(c) Mitochondria (d) Peroxisomes
(e) None of the above

104. Which of the following organelle can be viewed by a light microscope?

(a) Ribosome
(b) Endoplasmic reticulum
(c) Golgi
(d) Mitochondria

105. Which of the following statement about mitochondria is not true?

(a) Size and shape of mitochondria varies in a cell
(b) Mitochondria in the cell can fuse with one another
(c) Large mitochondria in a cell can split into two
(d) In all cells, one mitochondria will be exceptionally larger than others

106. Nebenkern of insect sperm cells is a modified

(a) nucleus (b) Golgi apparatus
(c) mitochondria (d) centrosome

107. Mitochondria in the human sperm cell are occupied at

(a) sperm head (b) mid piece
(c) sperm tail
(d) no mitochondria in the sperms

108. Which of the following statement is true regarding the membrane system of mitochondria?

(a) Chemical composition of both inner and outer membrane of mitochondria are same
(b) Outer membrane contains more protein/lipid ratio (by weight) than inner membrane
(c) Inner membrane contains more protein/lipid ratio (by weight) than outer membrane
(d) Phospholipids are completely absent on the outer membrane of mitochondria

109. Which of the following membrane lipid constituent can be considered the lipid marker of inner mitochondrial membrane?

(a) Lecithin (b) Cardiolipin
(c) Ceramide (d) Sphingo-ceramide

110. The only place where cardiolipin can be found naturally other than mitochondrial inner membrane is

(a) inner membrane of Golgi apparatus
(b) apoptosome
(c) bacterial plasma membrane
(d) membrane of glyoxysome

111. Which of the following statement regarding the distribution of cholesterol is true in the membrane system of mitochondria?

(a) Cholesterol is completely absent in mitochondrial membrane
(b) Cholesterol is absent in the inner membrane
(c) Cholesterol is present only in the inner membrane
(d) Cholesterol is present in both inner and outer membrane

112. Mitochondrial membrane system processes a variety of porin proteins which allow the passage of selective molecules. Which of the following statement is true regarding the porin protein in the mitochondrial membrane system?

(a) Mitochondrial outer membranes possess porins but they lack the usual beta barrel structure of the usual porins
(b) Both inner and outer mitochondrial membranes possess porin proteins
(c) Only the inner mitochondrial membrane possess porin proteins
(d) Many porin proteins which are structurally similar to the porins of bacterial cells are present in the outer membrane of mitochondria

113. ATP, NAD and CoA can be

(a) freely transported through both outer and inner membranes of mitochondria
(b) freely transported through the outer membrane of mitochondria
(c) freely transported through the inner membrane of mitochondria
(d) cannot be transported freely through outer and inner membranes of mitochondria

114. Cellular organelle(s) involved in the regulation of Ca ions level in the cell are

(a) mitochondria
(b) endoplasmic reticulum
(c) endoplasmic reticulum and mitochondria
(d) mitochondria and vesicles

115. The only enzyme in citric acid cycle (Kreb's cycle) which is attached to the inner mitochondrial membrane is

(a) succinate dehydrogenase
(b) NADPH dehydrogenase
(c) isocitrate dehydrogenase
(d) malate dehydrogenase

116. Which of the following can be used as an enzyme marker for inner mitochondrial membrane?

(a) Succinate dehydrogenase
(b) ATP synthase
(c) Succinyl CoA synthase
(d) Cardiolipin

117. Which of the following is a mobile electron carrier in the mitochondrial electron transport system?

(a) NADH dehydrogenase
(b) FADH dehydrogenase
(c) Ubiquinone
(d) Succinate dehydrogenase

118. Which of the following event is not directly involved with mitochondria?

(a) Apoptosis
(b) ATP synthesis
(c) Controlling cell cycle
(d) Protein degradation

119. Which of the following statement is not true about mitochondria?

(a) Hepatocytes have more than 2000 mitochondria per cell
(b) RBC completely lack mitochondria
(c) Sperm cells of insects completely lack mitochondria
(d) Mitochondrial number may change in each cell of a species

120. Example for autonomous organelle(s)

(a) Mitochondria
(b) Chloroplast
(c) Mitochondria and chloroplast
(d) Chloroplast, mitochondria and Golgi

121. Pick out the odd one

(a) Kearns-Sayre syndrome
(b) Tay-Sachs syndrome
(c) MELAS syndrome
(d) Leber's hereditary optic neuropathy

122. Mitochondrial DNA (mt DNA) is considered one of the best marker tool for population and evolutionary biologists. The reason for this is

(a) mitochondrial DNA undergo spontaneous mutation
(b) mitochondrial DNA can be easily isolated
(c) mitochondrial genes are specific to mt DNA
(d) absence of genetic recombination in mt DNA

123. Cyanide is a mitochondrial toxin. The mechanism of action of cyanide inhibits

(a) NADH dehydrogenase
(b) Succinate dehydrogenase
(c) Cytochrome oxidase
(d) ATP synthase

124. The average thickness of plasma membrane of a eukaryotic cell is

(a) 5 to 10 nm
(b) 5 to 10 Angstrom
(c) 5 to 10 micrometre
(d) 5 to 10 mm

125. Which of the following statement is true regarding the surface tension of plasma membrane?

(a) Surface tension of plasma membrane is more than pure lipid structures
(b) Surface tension of plasma membrane is less than pure lipid structures
(c) Surface tension of plasma membrane and pure lipid structures are same
(d) Plasma membranes do not have surface tension

126. Which of the following statement best describes the chemical composition of plasma membrane?

(a) Plasma membrane is composed of two layers – one layer of phospholipids and one layer of proteins
(b) Plasma membrane is composed of equal number of phospholipids, proteins and carbohydrates
(c) Plasma membrane is bilayers of proteins with associated lipids and carbohydrates
(d) Plasma membrane is bilayers of phospholipids with associated proteins and carbohydrates

127. Which of the following is not the function of plasma membrane?

(a) Intercellular interaction
(b) Responding to external stimuli
(c) Energy transduction
(d) Assisting in chromosome segregation

128. Consider the following statements

(a) The polar portion of cholesterol is facing external to the membrane
(b) Placement of cholesterol molecules in the membrane interfere with the flexibility of lipids
(c) Cholestrol provides stiffness to membrane
(d) Cholestrol is absent in plasma membrane of plants

Which of the above statements are correct?

(a) a, b, c, d, e (b) a, b, c, e
(c) a, c, d, e (d) a, b, c, d

129. Biochemical analysis of plasma membrane sample showed about 20-25% cardiolipin content. Most probably the sample is from

(a) human erythrocytes cell membrane
(b) myelin sheath of nerve cells
(c) mitochondrial inner membrane
(d) mitochondrial outer membrane

130. Glycolipids in plasma membrane are usually located at

(a) outer leaflet of plasma membrane
(b) inner leaflet of plasma membrane
(c) evenly distributed in both inner and outer leaves of plasma membrane
(d) cannot be predicted as it varies according to cell types

131. Which of the following event in a biological membrane would not be energetically favourable and therefore not occur spontaneously?

(a) Rotation of membrane proteins
(b) Rotation of phospholipids
(c) Lateral movements of phospholipids
(d) Flip-flop of phospholipids to the opposite leaflet

132. Malarial parasite uses ______ on the plasma membrane of RBC as a receptor to enter in the cell

(a) band 3 protein (b) glycophorins
(c) spectrin protein (d) ankyrin proteins

133. The carbohydrate content of plasma membrane in eukaryotes is

(a) 2-10% by weight
(b) 20-25% by weight
(c) 30-50% by weight
(d) 60-70% by weight

134. Carbohydrates in the plasma membrane

(a) always face inward to the non-polar portion of membrane
(b) always face outward to extracellular space
(c) always face to the lumen of the cells
(d) directed to all sides in the membrane randomly

135. Enzymes such as desaturase, phospholipase and acetyltransferase are very essential for maintaining the integrity of plasma membranes. These enzymes are involved in

(a) maintaining the bilayer nature of membrane
(b) maintaining the semi-permeability of the membrane
(c) maintaining the fluidity of membrane
(d) maintain the position of trans-membrane proteins in the membrane

136. A person is having the enzyme which adds N-acetylgalactosamine to the ends of glycolipids which determine the blood group. The blood group of the person will be

(a) A (b) B
(c) AB (d) O

137. A person is having the enzyme which adds galactose to the end of glycolipids which determine the blood group. The blood group of the person will be

(a) A (b) B
(c) AB (d) O

138. Red blood cells in the blood repel each other due to

(a) concave shape of RBC
(b) they lack nucleus and other membrane structures
(c) carbohydrate moieties of glycophorin A in RBC membrane contain sialic acid residues
(d) amino acids in the peripheral portion of glycophorin A are negatively charged

139. The main role of carbohydrates in the cell membranes is

(a) adhesion (b) recognition
(c) locomotion (d) reception

140. The fluidity of the plasma membrane increases with the increase in

(a) saturated fatty acids in the membrane
(b) unsaturated fatty acids in the membrane
(c) phospholipid content in the membrane
(d) glycolipid content in the membrane

141. At physiological conditions, cholesterol in the plasma membrane

(a) increases the durability of plasma membrane
(b) increases the permeability of plasma membrane
(c) decreases the durability of plasma membrane
(d) decreases the permeability of plasma membrane

(a) a, b (b) a, c
(c) a, d (d) b, d

142. The molecular basis of MN blood group in humans is the difference in the

(a) amino acid sequence in glycophorin
(b) carbohydrate sequence in glycophorin
(c) folding pattern of glycophorin
(d) distributional pattern of band 3 and glycophorin proteins in the plasma membrane of RBC

143. Which of the following is a cytoskeletal protein?

(a) Glycophorin A (b) Glycophorin B
(c) Spectrin (d) Band 3 protein

144. The length of fatty acid chain in the fatty acids of membrane lipids usually range between

(a) 10-15 carbons (b) 18-20 carbons
(c) 24-30 carbons (d) 28-30 carbons

145. What structural features of a membrane are major contributors to its selective permeability?

(a) Phospholipid bilayer
(b) Trans-membrane proteins
(c) Glycolipids on the outer surface of the membrane
(d) Peripheral membrane proteins on the inside of the membrane

146. Water can pass through the plasma membrane

(a) by simple diffusion only
(b) through aquaporins channel only
(c) by simple diffusion and aquaporins
(d) cannot cross plasma membrane

147. Spherical subunits of eukaryotic chromatin composed of a core particle consisting of an octamer of histones and 146 nucleotide pairs are called

(a) centrosomes (b) polysomes
(c) nucleosomes (d) lysosomes

148. A cell organelle that contains pro-laminar bodies (an aggregation of semi-crystalline lattices of branched tubules) that carry the precursor pigments for chlorophyll is called

(a) etioplast (b) chromoplast
(c) phragmoplast (d) leucoplast

149. Which one of the following is not found in mitochondrial matrix?

(a) Single-stranded DNA
(b) RNA
(c) Double-stranded DNA
(d) Ribosome

150. The Nucleolar Organizer Region (NOR) of humans consists of

(a) chromosomes 13, 14, 15, 21 and 22
(b) chromosomes 13, 14, 15, 21 and 23
(c) chromosomes 13, 14, 15 and 23
(d) chromosomes 14, 15, 16. 21 and 22

151. Which organelles require intact membrane system for ATP synthesis?

(a) Chloroplast and mitochondria
(b) ER
(c) Mitochondria
(d) Chloroplast

152. ABC transporter in plants which are responsible for the detoxification of xenobiotics and prevent oxidative damage is located at

(a) ER (b) plasma membrane
(c) peroxisome (d) tonoplast

153. Acrosome of sperm cell is a modified

(a) lysosome (b) peroxisome
(c) Golgi (d) none of these

154. Lysosomes are known as the 'suicidal bags' because of the

(a) catalytic activity
(b) hydrolytic activity
(c) presence of food vacuole
(d) parasitic activity

155. Select the wrong statement from the following:

(a) both chloroplasts and mitochondria have an internal compartment, the thylakoid space bounded by the thylakoid membrane
(b) both chloroplasts and mitochondria contain DNA
(c) both chloroplasts and mitochondria contain an inner and an outer membrane
(d) the chloroplasts are generally much larger than mitochondria

156. Who discovered the endoplasmic reticulum?

(a) Keith Porter (b) K. Mereschkowsky
(c) G. E. Palade (d) Camillo Golgi

157. In a normal cell, the phosphatidylserine residues

(a) position cannot be predicted, it varies according to cell types
(b) are located at the outer leaflet of plasma membrane
(c) are located at the inner leaflet of plasma membrane
(d) are evenly distributed in both the inner and outer leaves of plasma membrane

158. For the final processing of antigen, macrophages after phagocytosis direct the engulfed material to

(a) proteosome (b) lysosome
(c) peroxisome (d) ER

159. The one and only organism without mitochondria is

(a) monocercomonoides
(b) euglena
(c) amoeba
(d) trypanosoma

160. Among the following, which cell organelle is involved in apoptosis?

(a) Golgi (b) Lysosome
(c) ER (d) Mitochondria

161. The fluid mosaic model of plasma membrane given by Singer and Nicolson is applicable to

(a) both prokaryotic and eukaryotic membranes
(b) only eukaryotic membrane
(c) only to organelle membranes
(d) only to prokaryotic membrane

162. Which of the following types of cells would you expect to contain a high density of cytoplasmic intermediate filaments?

(a) Plant cells (b) Epithelial cells
(c) Sperm (d) Amoeba

163. The average size of 70 S ribosome of prokaryotes is

(a) greater than 250 Angstroms
(b) greater than 200 Angstroms
(c) greater than 303 Angstroms
(d) greater than 290 Angstroms

164. Post-translational modifications take place in

(a) nucleus (b) mitochondria
(c) ER and golgi (d) ER

MARK TRUE OR FALSE (T/F)

1. Since they have chloroplasts for energy production, plant cells lack mitochondria
2. With regard to p53 tumour suppressor gene, it is located on chromosome
3. Located outside the cell membrane of plant cells is plasma membrane
4. Plant cell wall consists of cellulose that gives rigidity to the plant cell
5. Rough membranes having ribosomes in cells, which function in the transport of proteins within the cytoplasm, are golgi bodies
6. Small dense particles attached to endoplasmic reticulum are called ribosomes
7. Boundary of the cell that regulates the flow of materials into and out of the cell is called the cell wall
8. In the cells, microvilli are the foldings of the cell membrane that increase the surface area for absorption
9. The chloroplasts are the sites of chemical reactions to produce the cell's energy in the form of ATP.
10. Parallel membranes in cytoplasm consisting of golgi sacs and golgi vesicles are known as golgi apparatus
11. Plant cell organelles that contain chlorophyll are known as mitochondria
12. In plant cells, chlorophyll is located within parallel stacks of membranes called cisternae
13. Cell junctions between adjacent cell membranes that allow the passage of materials between cells are known as desmosomes
14. Appendages of the cell membrane that move to propel materials past the cell are known as cilia
15. Submetacentric chromosomes have one small and one large arm
16. Centromeric index is the ratio of the short arm length to the total chromosome length
17. Centromere is the secondary constriction of the chromosome
18. The centromere of *Ascaris megalocephala* is diffuse
19. Telomere is the part of chromosome which is near the centromere
20. Generally there are two chromosomes in each nucleus, called nucleolar chromosomes
21. Karyotype of a species is usually not constant
22. A diagram representing chromosomes in which the pair of homologous chromosomes are ordered in a series of decreasing size is called ideogram
23. Direct observation of living cells within the organism is known as vital examination
24. Fixation does not kill the cells
25. DNAse is used for breaking the middle lamella of cells
26. Sodium hydroxide is used to remove heavy oil content in cytoplasm of some cells
27. Colchicine arrests the development of chromosomes, resulting in the separation of chromosomes
28. Fixation checks autolysis or self destruction of cells
29. Ethyl alcohol is a non-precipitant fixative
30. Picric acid is a non-metallic fixative

31. Chromic acid is a metallic fixative
32. Carnoy's fluid has methyl alcohol as one of the components
33. In squash preparation for the study of cell division, the cells are directly spread over a slide prior to fixation
34. If the stain is applied to isolated cells such as blood, the staining is called supravital
35. The colour of a dye is due to auxochromes
36. The example of a basic dye is crystal violet
37. The example of an acidic dye is aniline blue
38. Some basic dyes stain certain cell components a different colour than the colour of the dye. This property is called metachromasia
39. Methyl green is used for staining proteins
40. Pyronin is used for staining DNA
41. Eosin is used for staining proteins
42. Grana are stacks of flattened membraneous sacs present in mitochondria
43. Thylakoids of different grana are connected by stroma lamellae
44. Nucleoli can be stained with methyl green
45. Because its refractive index is similar to that of hyaloplasm, the golgi substance is difficult to observe in living cells
46. Microsomes contain about 50-60% of RNA of the cell
47. With regard to p53 tumour suppressor gene, it encodes 53 k Da protein
48. With regard to p53 tumour suppressor gene, it holds the cell cycle in the G1 phase
49. With regard to p53 tumour suppressor gene, it is stimulated by ionizing radiation
50. With regard to p53 tumour suppressor gene, abnormal gene is associated with childhood tumours

12
Linkage and Recombination

MULTIPLE-CHOICE QUESTIONS

1. Which of the following pertain(s) only to genes located on the same chromosome?

(a) Linkage (b) Synteny
(c) Linkage disequilibrium
(d) Association
(e) (a), (b) and (c)

2. Linked genes

(a) are located near each other on the same chromosome
(b) violate the law of independent assortment
(c) segregate together during meiosis
(d) all of the above
(e) none of the above

3. The term "linkage" was first used by

(a) Bateson (b) Morgan
(c) Mendel (d) Punnett

4. Coupling and repulsion phases of linkage were given by

(a) Morgan (b) Bateson and Punnett
(c) Hutchinson (d) Muller

5. Terms *cis* and *trans* for coupling and repulsion were first used by

(a) Muller (b) Haldane
(c) Bridges (d) Morgan

6. Presence of linkage leads to high frequency of

(a) parental types (b) new combinations
(c) recombinations (d) none of these

7. The term "crossing over" was first used by

(a) Bateson (b) Hutchinson
(c) Muller (d) Morgan and Cattell

8. The chiasmata were first discovered by

(a) Punnett (b) Morgan
(c) Haldane (d) Janssens

9. Crossing over takes place during

(a) leptotene (b) pachytene
(c) diplotene (d) zygotene

10. Normally, crossing over promotes

(a) linkage (b) recombinations
(c) parental types (d) all of these

11. The value of recombinants (%) varies from

(a) 5-10 (b) 0-100
(c) 0-10 (d) 0-50

12. The copy choice theory of crossing over was first proposed by

(a) Morgan (b) Belling
(c) Janssens (d) Muller

13. Terms "interference" and "coincidence" were coined by

(a) Haldane (b) Muller
(c) Janssens (d) Morgan

14. The term "map distance" was coined by

(a) Bateson (b) Morgan
(c) Haldane (d) Bridges

15. Chromosome map is also known as

(a) genetic map (b) linkage map
(c) a and b above (d) none of these

16. The cytological proof of crossing over was first provided by

(a) Morgan (b) Curt Stern
(c) Janssens (d) Bridges

17. In maize, cytological proof of crossing was first provided by

(a) Bridges (b) Muller
(c) Bateson
(d) Creighton and McClintock

18. Chiasma terminalization was first observed by

(a) Bridges (b) Darlington
(c) Janssens (d) Belling

19. Why didn't Mendel find linkage?

(a) All seven genes were on separate chromosomes
(b) Some genes were linked, but they were too close together to crossover
(c) Mendel did detect linkage. He discovered this genetic phenomenon
(d) He didn't execute his crosses correctly, so linkage went undetected
(e) Some genes were linked, but they were too far apart for crossing over to be distinguished from independent assortment

20. Genes A and B are farther apart than genes A and C, all three of which are linked. What cannot be concluded?

(a) B might be between A and C
(b) A might be between B and C
(c) C might be between A and B
(d) more crossovers will occur between A and B than A and C
(e) All four statements may be true

21. People who have red hair usually have freckles. This can best be explained by

(a) linkage
(b) reciprocal translocation
(c) sex-influenced inheritance
(d) non-disjunction
(e) independent assortment

22. New combinations of linked genes are due to

(a) crossing over
(b) independent assortment
(c) mixing of sperm and egg
(d) environmental changes such as temperature extremes
(e) non-disjunction

23. A 50% frequency of recombination means that

(a) the two genes are located on different chromosomes
(b) independent assortment is hindered
(c) abnormal meiosis occurred
(d) the offspring have combinations of traits that match one of the parents
(e) the genes are located on sex chromosomes

24. In the following list, which term is least related to the others?

(a) Recombinants
(b) Karyotype
(c) Linkage map
(d) Genetic recombination
(e) Parental types

25. In the following list, which term is least related to the others?

(a) Sex-linked genes
(b) Duchenne muscular dystrophy
(c) Hemophilia
(d) Wild-type
(e) Colour blindness

26. Progeny that exhibit a mixing of maternal and paternal alleles on a single chromosome are

(a) Parentals (b) Recombinants
(c) Haplotypes (d) Mixed groups

27. The name for a chromosome map unit is

(a) centimorgan (b) centistern
(c) millimendel (d) decibarr
(e) centisutton

28. Linkage analysis

(a) is used on physical mapping
(b) is based on Mendel's laws
(c) can only be used with prokaryotes
(d) none of the above

29. Linkage analysis

(a) is based on recombination frequencies
(b) requires unlinked genes
(c) is used in physical mapping
(d) none of the above

30. Physical mapping

(a) requires large number of organisms
(b) is always based on optical methods
(c) can use DNA fragment libraries
(d) none of the above

31. Physical mapping

(a) can use sequence tagged sites (STSs)
(b) uses polymorphic restriction sites
(c) needs large number of organisms
(d) none of the above

32. Presence of crossing over leads to

(a) new combinations (b) parental types
(c) no change (d) none of these

33. Chromosome map is also known as

(a) genetics map (b) linkage map
(c) a and b above (d) none of these

34. Which one of the following is correct?

(a) Meiosis is the division of the nucleus into two daughter nuclei
(b) Linkage is the association of certain genes in their inheritance
(c) Crossing over is the transfer of pollen from the anther to the stigma
(d) Segregation occurs in prophase of meiosis
(e) Crossing over is the only way in which recombination can occur

35. If Mendel's crosses between tall, spherical-seeded plants and short, dented-seeded plants had produced more than 1/16 short, dented-seeded plants in the F_2 generation, he might have concluded that

(a) the dented seed and short traits are unlinked
(b) he would not have concluded any of the above
(c) all traits in peas assort independently of each other
(d) the spherical seed and tall traits are linked
(e) all traits in peas are linked

36. How did Morgan demonstrate crossing over?

(a) A fly that received only y+w+m+ and ywm chromosomes from her parents was able to transmit different combinations of alleles to her offspring
(b) A fly with a gray body and red eyes (wild type) was able to produce offspring with gray bodies and white eyes
(c) True breeding yellow, white, miniature flies always had yellow, white, miniature offspring
(d) None of these examples demonstrate crossing over

37. What was unique about the chromosomes studied by Creighton and McClintock?

(a) They carried different alleles for two linked genes
(b) They were unable to cross over
(c) These chromosomes were unable to synapse during meiosis I
(d) Physical structures of the chromosomes allowed them to be distinguished from each other

38. You begin to study a novel plant species and discover that this diploid plant has 16 chromosomes. How many linkage groups would you expect to find?

(a) 16 (b) 8
(c) 4
(d) It is impossible to tell from the information provided

39. Given what is known about single, double, and noncrossovers in a three-point map, triple crossovers in a four-point map can be predicted to be

(a) more frequent than single crossovers
(b) less frequent than single crossovers, but more frequent than double crossovers
(c) less frequent than single or double cross-overs
(d) more frequent than noncrossovers
(e) more frequent than double crossovers

40. If the per cent recombination between A and B is 12, A and C is 4, and B and C is 8, then the order of the genes on the chromosome is

(a) A-B-C (b) B-A-C
(c) A-C-B (d) C-B-A

41. Consider the cross AAbb x aaBB. The alleles in the resulting dihybrid are in

(a) coupling (b) repulsion
(c) heteroplasmy (d) none of the above

42. Given the gene sequence ABCDE, crossing over should occur most frequently between

(a) A-B (b) A-C
(c) A-D (d) A-E

43. A plant with the following genotype is testcrossed

$\frac{\mathbf{Ab}}{\mathbf{a\ B}}$

If the two loci were 10 m.u. apart, what proportion of progeny will be aaBb?

(a) 5% (b) 10%
(c) 45% (d) 90%
(e) None of the above

44. In the above, the genotype of one of the P generation parents would be

(a) $\frac{a\ b}{a\ b}$ (b) $\frac{A\ b}{a\ B}$
(c) $\frac{A\ b}{A\ b}$ (d) $\frac{A\ B}{A\ B}$
(e) $\frac{a\ B}{a\ b}$

45. The mutations blistered (bs) and clot (cl) are located on opposite ends of chromosome II in *Drosophila*. A blistered female is crossed with a clot male. The F_1 female is then backcrossed to a blistered clot male. What ratio will be expected in the offspring of the backcross?

(a) 9/16 wild: 3/16 blistered: 3/16 clot: 1/16 blistered, clot
(b) 2/24 wild: 1/4 blistered: 1/4 clot
(c) 1/4 wild: 1/4 clot: 1/4 blistered; 1/4 blistered, clot
(d) 4/10 blistered: 4/10 clot: 1/10 wild: 1/10 blistered, clot
(e) 1/2 blistered: 1/2 clot

46. In which of the following four gene arrangements the greatest number of crossovers will be needed to produce ABCD and abcd gametes?

(a) $\frac{ABcD}{abCd}$ (b) $\frac{aBCd}{AbcD}$
(c) $\frac{AbCd}{aBcD}$ (d) $\frac{ABcD}{abCD}$

47. A LOD score of zero for a recombination frequency of 0.1 indicates

(a) there is no recombination between the disease locus and a marker locus
(b) linkage and non-linkage are equally likely
(c) non-likage is more likely than linkage
(d) linkage is more likely than non-linkage, but only slightly
(e) there is loose linkage between the marker and the disease locus

48. In a two-point map experiment, which is the most characteristic ratio?

(a) 100: 98: 22: 19 (b) 100: 60: 30: 29
(c) 100: 60: 40: 20 (d) 100: 98: 60: 30
(e) None of the above are at all characteristic

49. Genes A and B are linked. You make the following cross AABB x aabb to produce the F_1 generation. You than cross the F_1 to an individual of genotype aabb and observe the following genotypes

AaBb 71; aaBb 31; Aabb 29; aabb 69. What is the recombination frequency between the two loci?

(a) 50% (b) 40%
(c) 30% (d) 20%
(e) 10%

50. Three genes, A, B and C are located on the same chromosome. Recombination occurs between the pairs at following frequencies

A-B 5%; A-C 6%; B-C 11%. What is the correct order of the genes?

(a) ABC (b) CBA
(c) CAB (d) BCA

51. The relative location of 4 genes on a chromosome can be mapped from the following data on crossover frequencies

Genes	Frequency of Crossover
B and D	5%
C and A	15%
A and B	30%
C and B	45%
C and D	50%

Which of the following represents the relative positions of these 4 genes on the chromosomes?

(a) ABCD (b) ADCB
(c) CABD (d) CBAD
(e) DBCA

52. The allele b gives *Drosophila* flies a black body and B gives brown—the wild-type phenotype. The allele wx of a separate gene gives waxy wings and WX gives non waxy—the wild-type phenotype. The allele cn of a third gene gives cinnabar eyes and CN gives red—the wild-type phenotype. A female heterozygous for these three genes is test crossed, and 1000 progeny are classified as follows:

5 brown, non waxy, red
6 black, waxy, cinnabar
69 brown, waxy, cinnabar
67 black, non waxy, red
382 brown, non waxy, cinnabar
379 black, waxy, red
48 brown, waxy, red
44 black, non waxy, cinnabar

The gene locus for the characteristic which lies between the other two gene loci on the chromosome is (which gene is in the middle?)

(a) body colour (b) wing type
(c) eye colour
(d) any one can be in the middle

53. In the above, the map unit distance between the loci for wing type and eye colour is

(a) 10.3 mu (b) 12.2 mu
(c) 12.8 mu (d) 14.7 mu
(e) 25.0 mu

54. In question number 52, the map unit distance between the loci for wing type and body colour is

(a) 10.3 mu (b) 12.2 mu
(c) 12.8 mu (d) 14.7 mu
(e) 25.0 mu

55. In question number 52, the map unit distance between the loci for body and eye colour is

(a) 10.3 mu (b) 12.2 mu
(c) 12.8 mu (d) 14.7 mu
(e) 25.0 mu

56. In question number 52, the coefficient of coincidence of crossovers in the two regions between the extreme loci is

(a) 27.35% (b) 29.56%
(c) 70.40% (d) 70.44%
(e) 72.65%

57. Parent plants with the genotypes AABBCC and aabbcc were crossed, and their F_1 progeny were backcrossed to a homozygous recessive tester. The 1000 backcross progeny had the phenotypic distribution

Phenotype ABC abc AbC aBc Abc aBC ABc abC

Number 190 190 40 40 160 160 110 110

What is the map distance between A and C?

(a) 22 map units b) 30 map units
(c) 32 map units d) 40 map units
(e) 70 map units

58. A mating between two dihybrid individuals yields progeny, which are 16% *AABB*, 8% *AABb*, 1% *AAbb*, 8% *AaBB*, 34% *AaBb*, 8% *Aabb*, 1% *aaBB*, 8% *aaBb*, and 16% *aabb*. Assume no evolution. This is an example of

(a) linkage (b) a Mendelian ratio
(c) selfing (d) non-syntenic loci
(e) none of the above (f) all of the above

59. Consider two recessive alleles (a and b) in humans. Given the following data, determine the distance between the two genes (in map units): AaBb = 206; Aabb = 704; aaBb = 736; aabb = 254

(a) 12:7 (b) 1
(c) 24:2 (d) 28

60. You calculate map distances between genes A, B, and C based on all pairwise dihybrid crosses. When you perform the trihybrid cross to verify your results, you discover that, despite analysis of a very large number of progeny, you have only about half as many double crossover progeny as you expect. Which explanation is the most reasonable?

(a) Your dihybrid cross data are an underestimate of the distance between the more widely separated genes
(b) You are seeing an example of interference
(c) You are seeing an example of random sampling error
(d) None of these

61. What is the convenient way to identify gene order in a trihybrid mapping cross?

(a) Look for double crossover progeny and identify the gene that was flipped relative to parentals
(b) Look for the largest class of single crossovers and the two genes are the ones on the ends
(c) Look for the smallest class of single cross-overs to identify the genes which are closest together
(d) a and b only
(e) All of the above

62. Why is tetrad analysis useful for studying genetics?

(a) Cells within a tetrad are haploid, so genotype is directly reflected in the phenotype
(b) Cells within a tetrad reflect the events of meiosis
(c) Analysis of simple systems can elucidate general rules that apply more broadly
(d) All of the above
(e) None of the above

63. You set up a mapping cross involving two genes in *Aspergillus*, and determine the following percentages of tetrad types: parental ditype 51%, nonparental ditype 49%. What can you say about your genes?

(a) They are closely linked
(b) They are unlinked
(c) They are lethal
(d) They are not expressed in the phenotype

64. You set up a mapping cross involving two genes of interest in *Saccharomyces* and determine the following tetrade types: 8 non-parental ditype; 37 tetratype; 80 parental ditype. What is the most accurate map distance between these two genes?

(a) 18.7 mu
(b) 32.3 mu
(c) 64.6 mu
(d) None of these is accurate

65. There are 4 pairs of chromosomes in *Drosophila*. The linkage groups present in it are

(a) one more than the pair of chromosomes
(b) one less than the pair of chromosomes
(c) four (d) eight

66. Percentage of crossing over is more when

(a) genes are located in a different cell
(b) genes are not linked
(c) linked genes are located close to each other
(d) linked genes are located far apart from each other

67. Repulsion and coupling are two faces of

(a) mutation (b) chiasmata
(c) linkage (d) crossing over

68. If gene frequency between genes a and c is 2%; b and c is 13%; b and d is 4%; a and b is 15%; c and d is 17% and a and d is 19%. The sequence of genes in a chromosome is

(a) a, d, b, c (b) d, b, a, c
(c) a, b, c, d (d) a, c, b, d

69. In a linear chromosome map distance between 4 loci is as follows: a-b is 10%, a-d is 3%, b-c is 4%, and a-c is 6%. The crossover frequency between c and d is

(a) 4-12% (b) 3-6%
(c) 9% (d) 3%

70. Where does the evidence come from that crossing over takes place at a four stranded stage and not at two stranded stage of chromosomes?

(a) Studies on linkage maps of chromosomes of *Drosophila*
(b) Studies of meiosis in maize
(c) 4:4 organization of ascospores in Neurospora
(d) 2 : 2 : 2 : 2 organization of ascospores in Neurospora

71. The inheritance of new combinations of alleles in children results from

(a) puberty (b) recombination
(c) genetic linkage (d) repulsion

72. Linked genes are

(a) located on different chromosomes of the same size and shape
(b) located on the same chromosome
(c) rarely inherited together
(d) located on non-homologous chromosomes

73. Crossing over of parts of chromosomes

(a) has no effect on genetic linkage
(b) usually decreases the number of genetic combinations in a population
(c) can increase the number of genetic combinations in a population
(d) has no effect on genetic combination

74. Crossing over resulting in the inheritance of altered chromosomes by children occurs

(a) during meiosis (b) during mitosis
(c) both of the above (d) embryo formation

75. Linkage ______ as the distance between two genes ______

(a) decreases, decreases
(b) unaffected, decreases
(c) decreases, increases
(d) increases, increases

76. In *Drosophila* males there is complete linkage. What is the reason behind this?

(a) The genes are very closely located
(b) Coupling theory
(c) No synapsis
(d) Unknown reason

77. Linkage results in

(a) formation of more dominant phenotype
(b) formation of more wild phenotype
(c) formation of more parental phenotype
(d) formation of more recombinant phenotype

78. If you suddenly see linkage between two genes that are present in two chromosomes, this can be due to

(a) coupling (b) translocation
(c) inversion
(d) non-homologous end joining

79. Accurate mapping of genes can be done using

(a) two point mapping
(b) three point mapping
(c) single gene mapping
(d) none of the above

80. Recombination occurs in

(a) Single strand stage(b) Two strand stage
(c) Three strand stage (d) Four strand stage

81. Double crossover can involve two, three or four strands at a time. What will be the resultant percentage of recombined genes to normal genes in between when recombination occurred, taking all three types in consideration?

(a) 0% (b) 50%
(c) 70% (d) 90%

82. In animals cytological study of recombination was done by

(a) Barbara McClintock (b) Stern
(c) Creighton (d) Mendel

83. The map distance between genes A and B is 3 units, between B and C is 10 units and between C and A is 7 units. The order of the genes in a linkage map constructed on the above data would perhaps be

(a) A, B, C (b) A, C, B
(c) B, C, A (d) B, A, C

84. Complete linkage has been reported in

(a) Maize (b) Human female
(c) Male *Drosophila* (d) Female *Drosophila*

85. Coupling and repulsion phenomenon was concerned with

(a) crossing over (b) mutation
(c) linkage (d) all of these

86. Linkage prevents

(a) homozygous condition
(b) segregation of alleles
(c) hybrid formation
(d) heterozygous condition

87. Linkage is usually

(a) complete (b) incomplete
(c) intermediate (d) full

88. The ratio obtained by Bateson and Punnet when they test crossed second time between blue long and red round in sweet peas was

(a) 7:1:1:7 (b) 1:1:1:1
(c) 1:7:7:1 (d) 9:3:3:1

89. The scientist who discovered that coupling and repulsion are two aspects of a single phenomenon called linkage is

(a) Bateson (b) Mendel
(c) Morgan (d) Punnet

90. In maize parental and recombinants are produced in the ratio of

(a) 50 : 50 (b) 9 : 7
(c) 1 : 7 : 7 :1 (d) 12 :3 : 1

91. Genes A, B, C, D are located on the same chromosome. The recombination frequencies are as follows: A-B 10%, A-C 25%, A-D 23%, B-C 15%, C-D 48%. What is the most likely order of the genes on the chromosome?

(a) BCAD (b) ACBD
(c) CBAD (d) DBAC

92. Chromosomes and genes share all the following characteristics except that they

(a) are both present in pairs in all diploid cells
(b) both undergo segregation during meiosis
(c) are both copied during the S phase of the cell cycle
(d) both pair up with their homologues during prophase of mitosis

93. The improvement of microscopy techniques in the late 1800s set the stage for the emergence of modern genetics because

(a) it revealed new and unanticipated features of Mendel's pea plant varieties
(b) it allowed biologists to study meiosis and mitosis, revealing the parallels between the behaviour of genes and chromosomes
(c) it allowed scientists to see the DNA present within chromosomes
(d) all of the above are true

94. When Thomas Hunt Morgan crossed his red-eyed F_1 generation flies to each other, the F_2 generation included both red- and white-eyed flies. Remarkably, all the white-eyed flies were male. What was the explanation for this result?

(a) The involved gene was on the X chromosome
(b) The involved gene was on the Y chromosome
(c) The involved gene was on the autosome
(d) Other male specific factors influence eye colour in flies

95. Which of the following statements is (are) true?

(a) The closer two genes are on a chromosome, the higher the probability that a crossover will occur between them
(b) The observed frequency of recombination of two genes that are far apart from each other has a maximum value of 50%
(c) Two of the traits that Mendel studied, i.e., seed colour and flower colour are linked on the same chromosome
(d) Only (b) and (c) are correct

96. How would you explain a testcross involving F_1 dihybrid flies in which more parental-type offspring than recombinant-type offspring are produced?

(a) The two genes are linked
(b) The two genes are unlinked
(c) Recombination did not occur in the cell during meiosis
(d) The testcross was improperly done

97. What does a frequency of recombination of 50% indicate?

(a) The two genes are likely located on different chromosomes
(b) All the offspring have combinations of traits that match one of the two parents
(c) The genes are located on sex chromosomes
(d) Abnormal meiosis has occurred

98. Which of the following is true regarding linkage maps? They

(a) always have a total of 100 map units
(b) can be used to pinpoint the precise physical position of a gene on a chromosome
(c) are a genetic map based on recombination frequencies
(d) require preparation of phenotypes

99. Sturtevant provided genetic evidence of four pairs of chromosomes in *Drosophila* by showing that
(a) there are four major classes of genes in *Drosophila*
(b) *Drosophila* genes cluster into four distinct groups of linked genes
(c) the overall number of genes in *Drosophila* is a multiple of four
(d) the entire *Drosophila* genome has approximately 400 map units

100. Map units on a linkage map cannot be relied upon to calculate physical distances on a chromosome because
(a) the frequency of crossing over varies along the length of the chromosome
(b) the relationship between recombination frequency and map units is different in every individual
(c) physical distances between genes change during the course of the cell cycle
(d) the gene order on the chromosomes is slightly different in every individual

101. A map of a chromosome that includes the positions of genes relative to visible chromosomal features, such as stained bands, is called a
(a) linkage map
(b) physical map
(c) recombination map
(d) cytogenetic map

MARK TRUE OR FALSE (T/F)

1. Every chromosome in a diploid cell comprises a linkage group
2. Map units used in linkage mapping correlate with a specific number of base pairs
3. Crossing over involves the physical exchange of DNA between chromatid
4. If two genes are linked, a double heterozygote will be able to produce only two possible types of gametes
5. Crossing over occurs only within a bivalent
6. Parental phenotypes in the offspring are the most common in a mapping cross
7. Morgan was able to demonstrate linkage of genes to chromosomes because he studied X-linked genes
8. Chi square analysis can help to distinguish between two competing hypotheses
9. Creighton and McClintock's important discovery was that they were able to demonstrate linkage between a translocation and a neighboring gene
10. In linkage mapping, one map unit is equal to one per cent crossover frequency
11. Trihybrid mapping crosses are more accurate than dihybrid mapping crosses
12. You can predict the number of double crossovers in a region accurately if you have a detailed genetic map
13. Unordered tetrad analysis is useful for determining recombination frequencies
14. Double crossovers can occur between multiple chromatids
15. Morgan coined the term "linkage" in 1915
16. Crossing over takes place during diplotene
17. Recombination value varies from 0-50%
18. Jumping genes were first reported in bacteria
19. McClintock reported about jumping genes in 1950
20. Coupling and repulsion terms were given by Stern
21. Linkage maps and chromosome maps means the same thing
22. Crossing over occurs between chromatids of the same chromosome
23. Crossing over involves homologous chromosomes

24. Morgan did not receive Nobel prize
25. Two point test cross is more accurate than a three point test cross
26. In corn, cytological proof of crossing over was provided by Stern
27. In a test cross, linkage provides a high frequency of nonparental types
28. Copy choice theory of crossing over was given by Belling
29. New combinations are produced by crossing over between linked genes
30. The relationship between Mendelian factors and chromosomes was proposed in 1903 by Sutton
31. Drosophila males show complete linkage for only the genes present on sex chromosomes
32. Crossing over takes place at two strand stage
33. In *Drosophila*, the male offspring obtain their X chromosomes only from their mothers
34. Double crossovers are the least in number as compared to single crossovers
35. The ratio of expected frequency of double crossovers to the observed frequency of double crossovers is coincidence
36. Bridges showed that as maternal age increases, crossing over tends to increase
37. Cooler temperatures increase the rate of crossing over
38. Crossing over factors are never present in the cytoplasm
39. In *Drosophila* fed on a high-calcium diet, crossing over between X chromosome genes decreases
40. Crossing over increases in *Drosophila* flies injected with actinomycin D
41. Chiasma is plural and chiasmata is singular
42. Interference in organisms is always negative
43. Linkage of segregating genes of a dihybrid leads to deviations from the test cross ratio of 1:1:1:1
44. Recombination frequencies for particular pairs of linked genes are never stable
45. It is difficult to estimate linkage on the basis of test cross data than on the basis of F_2 data
46. Crossing over takes place at the two strand stage
47. Data from chromosome mapping should be taken from linked gene pairs that are quite close together to get accuracy in crossing over values
48. Two point testcross is better than a three point testcross to obtain good recombination data
49. Double crossover gametes are less than the single crossover gametes
50. Generally, negative interference is found in bacteriophage recombination

13
Chromosomal Aberrations

MULTIPLE-CHOICE QUESTIONS

1. Structural changes in chromosome cause alteration in
(a) phenotype (b) karyotype
(c) fertility (d) all of these

2. Gene sequence is altered by
(a) deletion (b) inversion
(c) duplication (d) all of these

3. Gene number is altered by
(a) duplication (b) inversion
(c) translocation (d) none of these

4. Translocation leads to alteration in
(a) gene number (b) structure of gene
(c) sequence of genes (d) none of these

5. Inversion leads to alteration in
(a) composition of genes
(b) number of genes
(c) sequence of genes
(d) structure of genes

6. Exchange of segments between non-homologous chromosomes refers to
(a) translocation (b) crossing over
(c) transversion (d) inversion

7. Pseudo-dominance is associated with
(a) translocation (b) deletions
(c) inversion (d) transversion

8. The size of chromosome having duplication is
(a) longer than normal
(b) thinner than normal
(c) thicker than normal
(d) shorter than normal

9. Deficiency was first reported by
(a) Morgan (b) Muller
(c) Sturtevant (d) Bridges

10. Bridges first observed deficiency in
(a) *Arabidopsis* (b) corn
(c) datura (d) *Drosophila*

11. Duplication was first reported by

(a) Bridges (b) Morgan
(c) Strutevant (d) Muller

12. Bridges first reported duplication in 1919 in

(a) tobacco (b) garden pea
(c) barley (d) *Drosophila*

13. Inversion was first discovered by

(a) Bridges (b) Sturtevant
(c) Muller (d) Morgan

14. Sturtevant first discovered inversion in

(a) wheat (b) *Drosophila*
(c) barley (d) rats

15. The term "balanced lethal system" was coined by

(a) Bridges (b) Sturtevant
(c) Muller (d) Morgan

16. In *Oenothera,* balanced lethal system was first discovered by

(a) Muller (b) Bridges
(c) Renner (d) Dobzhansky

17. Translocation involves

(a) homologous chromosomes
(b) non-homologous chromosomes
(c) homologous chromatids
(d) all of these

18. Intercalary deletion involves chromosome break at

(a) one point (b) telomere
(c) four points (d) two points

19. Duplication arises due to

(a) chromosomal breakage
(b) unequal crossing over
(c) equal crossing over
(d) none of these

CHANGES IN CHROMOSOME NUMBER

20. Egg and sperm are

(a) monoploid (b) haploid
(c) diploid (d) triploid

21. How many chromosomes does a person with Edward syndrome have?

(a) 45 (b) 46
(c) 47 (d) 48

22. All of the following aneuploids result from female nondisjunction except

(a) Klinefelter syndrome
(b) triplo-X
(c) Turner syndrome
(d) Jacobs syndrome

23. Nondisjunction of chromosome 21 during meiosis II in human females can result in all of the following chromosome complements in a zygote except (assume the oocyte is fertilized by a sperm with a normal chromosome set)

(a) no chromosome 21
(b) euploid for chromosome 21
(c) monosomic for chromosome 21
(d) trisomic for chromosome 21

24. About 90% of trisomy 21 Down conceptions are due to nondisjunction during

(a) meiosis I in the female
(b) meiosis II in the female
(c) meiosis I in the male
(d) meiosis II in the male

25. Consider the following normal sequence of genes: a b c d e f g h. The sequence a b f e d c g h represents a (an)

(a) deletion (b) duplication
(c) inversion (d) translocation

26. Which of the following karyotypes is not possible in the offspring of a translocation carrier (involving chromosomes 14 and 21) and a normal individual?

(a) Deficient 14 or deficient 21
(b) Normal
(c) Translocation Down syndrome
(d) All are possible outcomes

27. A couple seeks testing and counseling after they have a child with cystic fibrosis. Testing reveals that the mother is a carrier, but the father is not. How can these results be explained?

(a) The man tested is not the biological father
(b) A mutation altered the child's normal allele
(c) Uniparental disomy (from the mother)
(d) All are possible explanations, additional testing is needed

28. An individual with the chromosomal description 45, X would be a

(a) normal female
(b) female with Turner syndrome
(c) male with Klinefelter syndrome
(d) cannot be determined

29. In nondisjunction, which parent leads to the sex chromosome aneuploid XYY?

(a) Mother (b) Father
(c) Either parent (d) Both parents

30. The diploid number of chromosomes of garden pea is 2n=14. How many different trisomics could be formed?

(a) 7 (b) 14
(c) 21 (d) 28

31. In a (an) ______, the short arms of two acrocentric chromosomes break, and the long arms join, forming an unusual, long chromosome

(a) Robertsonian translocation
(b) reciprocal translocation
(c) inversion
(d) duplication

32. An individual with two normal sets of autosomes and a single X chromosome has

(a) Down syndrome
(b) Patau syndrome
(c) Turner syndrome
(d) Klinefelter syndrome

33. *Cri-du-chat syndrome is associated with*

(a) a missing chromosome number 5
(b) an additional chromosome number 5
(c) a deletion of the long arm of chromosome number 5
(d) a deletion of the short arm of chromosome number 5

34. The most common autosomal aneuploid is

(a) trisomy 13 (b) trisomy 15
(c) trisomy 18 (d) trisomy 21

35. The term "genome" was coined by

(a) Muller (b) Winkler
(c) Bridges (d) Sturtevent

36. In a genome, each type of chromosome is represented

(a) only once (b) thrice
(c) many times (d) twice

37. Genome analysis was first proposed in 1930 by

(a) Sears (b) Ono
(c) Bridges (d) Kihara

38. Terms "autopolyploidy" and "allopolyploidy" were coined in 1926 by

(a) Sears (b) Kihara and Ono
(c) Winkler (d) Sturtevent

39. Haploids that develop from a normal diploid species are called

(a) monohaploids (b) dihaploids
(c) polyhaploids (d) none of these

40. Substitution haploids are represented as

(a) 2n-1 (b) n-1
(c) n+2 (d) n-1+1

41. An individual lacking one chromosome from the diploid set is referred to as

(a) nullisomic (b) trisomic
(c) disomic (d) monosomic

42. In primary trisomic, the extra chromosome is

(a) isochromosome (b) normal
(c) ring chromosome (d) inverted

43. A nullisomic individual is represented by

(a) 2n – 1 (b) 2n – 2
(c) 2n + 2 (d) none of these

44. Blakeslee in 1921 coined the terms

(a) disomic and monosomic
(b) trisomic and tetrasomic
(c) nullisomic and polysomic
(d) all of these

45. Quasidiploid is represented as

(a) 2n -1-1 (b) 2n+1-1
(c) 2n+2+2 (d) 2n+0+2

46. For the induction of polyploidy, colchicine was first used in 1937 by

(a) Navashin (b) Kihara
(c) Blakeslee (d) Sears

47. *Raphanobrassica* was first developed in 1928 by

(a) Blakeslee (b) Lysenko
(c) Rimpau (d) Karpechenko

48. The first cross between wheat and rye was made in 1890 by

(a) Goodspeed (b) Sears
(c) Mendel (d) Rimpau

49. In tobacco, the new species *Nicotiana digluta* was developed in 1925 by

(a) Bridges (b) Blakeslee
(c) Kihara
(d) Clausen and Goodspeed

50. Hexaploid wheat was first synthesized in 1947 by

(a) Muller
(b) Riley
(c) Borlaug
(d) McFadden and Sears

51. *Raphanobrassica* was first developed in

(a) India (b) USA
(c) Germany (d) Russia

52. In wheat, 5B system was discovered by

(a) Sturtevent (b) Riley and Chapman
(c) Kihara (d) Sears

53. The genetic constitution of *Brassica carinata* is

(a) AACC (b) AABB
(c) BBDD (d) BBCC

54. The genetic constitution of *Brassica nigra* is

(a) BB (b) CC
(c) DD (d) AA

55. Which of the following species of *Brassica* is tetraploid?

(a) *B. nigra* (b) *B. juncea*
(c) *B. campestris* (d) *B. oleracea*

56. Which of the following species of *Brassica* is diploid?

(a) *B. napus* (b) *B. carinata*
(c) *B. juncea* (d) *B. oleracea*

57. Triangle for the origin of tetraploid species of *Brassica* was proposed in 1935 by

(a) Kihara (b) Ono
(c) Sears (d) Nagaharu, U

58. Hexaploid wheat behaves like diploid species due to

(a) 5B system (b) 5A system
(c) 5D system (d) 3D system

59. The progenitor of cultivated cotton is

(a) *Gossypium thurberi*
(b) *G. raimondii*
(c) *G. tomentosa* (d) *G. africanum*

60. Aneuplody refers to

(a) nullisomics (b) polysomics
(c) monosomics (d) all of these

61. One of the features of polyploids in plants is that

(a) they have higher fertility and seed set than regular diploids
(b) their chromosomes pair and disjoin neatly
(c) deleterious dominant alleles are exposed
(d) they do not survive
(e) they have extra whole sets of chromosomes

62. If the diploid chromosome number of an organism is 2n = 16, the octoploid has

(a) 8 (b) 16
(c) 24 (d) 32
(e) 64

63. In dosage compensation

(a) an X chromosome can be inactivated
(b) gene expression can be increased in a single X chromosome
(c) gene expression can be reduced from a pair of X chromosome
(d) all of the above
(e) none of the above

64. Which of the following statements regarding X inactivation in mammals is false?

(a) The process is entirely random
(b) X inactivation may occasionally occur in males
(c) This process ensures a homogenous phenotype in heterozygotes
(d) X inactivation occurs early in embryonic development

65. Monoallelic expression of a gene

(a) occurs when one copy of the gene has been deleted
(b) occurs when one copy of the gene carries a mutation
(c) occurs when the gene is imprinted
(d) is not seen in mammals

66. Klinefelter's syndrome is caused by a nondisjunction resulting in a genotype of

(a) YYY (b) XYY
(c) XXX (d) XXY

67. The genotype of an individual with Turner syndrome is

(a) YO (b) XXY
(c) XYY (d) XO
(e) XXX

68. A disease caused by an autosomal primary nondisjunction is

(a) Turner syndrome (b) Down syndrome
(c) Tay-Sachs disease
(d) Klinefelter syndrome
(e) PKU

69. Which of the following chromosomes, if trisomic, causes the failure of survival of development?

(a) X (b) 21
(c) 11 (d) 18
(e) 15

70. Down syndrome results from

(a) the absence of one chromosome in position 21
(b) the presence of an extra chromosome in position 21
(c) the absence of both chromosomes in position 21
(d) crossing over on the chromosomes in position 21
(e) none of the above

71. Which of the following is not a result of nondisjunction of the sex chromosomes?

(a) Down syndrome
(b) Barr body
(c) Turner syndrome
(d) Klinefelter syndrome
(e) Both (a) and (b)

72. Down syndrome is a human genetic condition involving

(a) a point mutation
(b) polyploidy
(c) polygenic inheritance
(d) an extra autosome
(e) XYY

73. A phenomenon characterized by one part of an animal being a genotypic male and another part of the individual being a genotypic female (2 sexes within one) is called

(a) bivalentism (b) gyandromorphism
(c) pleiotropism (d) hermaphroditism
(e) parthenogenesis

74. One of the features of polyploids in plants is that

(a) they have higher fertility and seed set than regular diploids
(b) their chromosomes pair and disjoin neatly
(c) deleterious dominant alleles are exposed
(d) they do not survive
(e) they have extra whole sets of chromosomes

75. One of the problems of autotetraploids in plants is that

(a) they cannot produce seed
(b) their chromosomes do not pair and disjoin neatly
(c) deleterious recessive alleles are exposed
(d) all of the above
(e) none of the above

76. Potato, coffee and alfalfa are

(a) diploids
(b) allopolyploids
(c) segmental allopolyploids
(d) autopolyploids

77. The cultivated banana is

(a) diploid (b) autotriploid
(c) allotriploid (d) allotetraploid

78. In 1910, the globe mutant of *Datura stramonium* was discovered by

(a) Hugo de Vries (b) Blakeslee
(c) Winge (d) Gates

79. In 1920, Belling demonstrated that the globe mutant of *D. stramonium* was

(a) allopolyploid (b) trisomic
(c) tetrasomic (d) autopolyploid

80. The best source of aneuploids is

(a) autotriploids
(b) haploids
(c) autotetraploids
(d) translocation heterozygotes

81. A full series of nullisomics is available in

(a) tobacco (b) maize
(c) cotton (d) wheat

82. Nullisomic analysis for locating genes on particular chromosomes is restricted to a few highly polyploid species like

(a) wheat (b) alfalfa
(c) potato (d) tobacco

83. Genes suppressing homoeologous pairing in wheat have been located on chromosome

(a) 5A (b) 5D
(c) 2A (d) 5B

84. Colchicine is soluble in

(a) alcohol (b) chloroform
(c) cold water (d) all of the above

85. Among the given concentrations of colchicine, which one is generally used for seed treatment?

(a) 0.01% (b) 0.2%
(c) 0.5% (d) 1.0%

86. Besides colchicine, which one of the following induces chromosome doubling (polyploidization)?

(a) Acenaphathene
(b) 8-hydroxyquinoline
(c) Nitrous oxide
(d) All of the above

87. Autotetraploids show which chromosome configuration at metaphase I?

(a) Qudrivalent (b) Bivalent
(c) Trivalent (d) All of the above

88. Confirmatory evidence on parental species is obtained by

(a) electrophoretic patterns of proteins and enzymes
(b) genomic *in situ* hybridization (GISH)
(c) banding patterns of chromosomes
(d) all of the above

89. Among the following, which is the genomic constitution of bread wheat?

(a) ABD (b) BDR
(c) ADR (d) ABR

90. Genome D of wheat is most probably contributed by

(a) *Triticum tauschii*
(b) *Aegilops cylindrica*
(c) *Aegilops caudata*
(d) *Aegilops ventricosa*

91. A disomic plant would be

(a) diploid (b) allopolyploid
(c) autopolyploid (d) both a and c

92. Which of the following is most commonly used for chromosome substitution?

(a) Pairing between chromosomes of the allopolyploid species and the putative diploid parents
(b) Synthesis of the allopolyploid from the putative parents and comparing its features with those of the allopolyploid
(c) Banding patterns of chromosomes
(d) Protein and enzyme electrophoretic patterns

93. Which of the following is the oldest approach to study the evolution of allopolyploids?

(a) Monosomics (b) Trisomics
(c) Nullisomics (d) All of these

94. The evolution of which of the following is the least clearly known?

(a) *Triticum aestivum* (b) *Nicotiana tabacum*
(c) *Brassica napus* (d) *Brassica juncea*

95. Which of the following is true of chromosome abnormalities?

(a) They are the leading known cause of spontaneous pregnancy loss
(b) In general, monosomics have more severe consequences than trisomics
(c) Most of the aneuploids seen among live births increase with maternal age
(d) None of the above
(e) All of the above

96. A likely explanation for the fact that some 45, X conceptions (Turner syndrome) survive to term is

(a) mosaicism in the foetus
(b) delayed age of onset of the disorder
(c) germline mosaicism in one of the parents
(d) imprinting on the X chromosome
(e) incomplete X inactivation

97. Which of the following will yield the highest recurrence risk for Down syndrome in a family?

(a) 45-year-old mother
(b) 65-year-old father
(c) 5-year-old mother with a previous child with trisomy 21
(d) 20-year-old mother who carries a 21/14 Robertsonian translocation and has had no previous children with Down syndrome
(e) 20-year-old father who carries a 21/14 Robertsonian translocation and has had no previous children with Down syndrome

98. Which of the following would be most likely to produce an imbalance in the amount of essential genetic material in the carrier?

(a) Robertsonian translocation
(b) Paracentric inversion
(c) Pericentric inverison
(d) Reciprocal translocation
(e) Isochromosome

99. In which of the following individuals would you not expect to see a Barr body?

(a) XX male (b) 45, X female
(c) XY female (d) a and b
(e) b and c

100. Which of the following conditions is most compatible with survival to term?

(a) Trisomy 13
(b) Trisomy 18
(c) Monosomy X (45, X Turner syndrome)
(d) Monosomy 21
(d) Trisomy 21

101. A phenotypically normal woman has had two children with trisomy 13. Which of the following scenarios would be least likely to result in this recurrence?

(a) She is a germline mosaic for trisomy 13
(b) She carries a Robertsonian translocation of chromosome 13 to chromosome 14
(c) She carries a Robertsonian translocation of chromosome 21 to chromosome 14
(d) She has had both children in her late 40's
(e) She carries a Robertsonian translocation of chromosome 13 to chromosome 15

102. Which of the following is not a feature of Down syndrome?

(a) Hypotonia (poor muscle tone)
(b) Reduced IQ
(c) Association with elevated maternal age
(d) Increased risk of leukemia
(e) Cleft lip/cleft palate

103. The recurrence risk for trisomy 13 is increased by

(a) advanced paternal age
(b) 13/15 translocation in one of the parents
(c) extensive methylation of chromosome 13
(d) advanced maternal age
(e) b and d

104. Consider a foetus affected with one of the following conditions. For which condition is spontaneous loss during pregnancy most likely?

(a) Down syndrome
(b) Neurofibromatosis type 1
(c) Retinoblastoma
(d) Huntington disease
(e) Trisomy 18

105. Suppose you have established that a disease gene is closely linked to a marker whose location is known. Which of the following would not be useful in defining the disease gene's location?

(a) Testing for unmethylated CG islands
(b) Existence of a chromosome deletion in a patient
(c) Existence of trisomy in a patient
(d) DNA sequencing
(e) Testing for cross-species conservation

106. Which of the following characterize trisomy 21, trisomy 18, and trisomy 13?

(a) Increase risk with advanced maternal age
(b) Hypotonia (decreased muscle tone)
(c) Mental retardation
(d) Increased risk with advanced paternal age
(e) a and c

107. In mice, XO individuals are normal and fertile. When an XO individual is mated with a normal individual, which of the following would you expect to see?

(a) Half the offspring would be male; the other half female
(b) Two-thirds of the offspring would be female; the other one-third male
(c) One-third of the offspring would be female; the other two-thirds male
(d) All of the offspring would be female
(e) All of the offspring would be male

108. Recombination has occurred in a reciprocal translocation heterozygote in the area of translocation. What are the effects on viability of gametes or offspring?

(a) There are no effects on the viability of gametes or offspring
(b) All of the products of recombination will be incorporated into viable gametes, but the offspring made using these gametes will not develop
(c) This recombination will cause the abortion of meiosis in anaphase I. These products will not be recovered in gametes
(d) Half of the products of recombination will be incorporated into viable gametes, but the offspring made using these gametes will not develop. Fertility will be reduced
(e) The original statement is impossible. There is no way to get the recombination described

109. Klinefelter syndrome is

(a) 46, XXY b) 47, XYY
(c) 47, XXY d) 46, XYY
(e) 45, X

110. Each of the following abnormalities involves a 20 megabase region of the long arm of chromosome 5 (5q). Which abnormality is likely to cause more severe disease?

(a) Deletion of the region
(b) Duplication of the region
(c) A balanced translocation involving the region (i.e., in the translocation carrier)
(d) Pericentric inversion
(e) Paracentric inversion

111. Mosaicism is a frequent cause of survival to term in

(a) Down syndrome
(b) trisomy 13
(c) trisomy 18
(d) Klinefelter syndrome (47 XXY)
(e) Turner syndrome (45, X)

112. This phenotype is seen only in males

(a) Down syndrome
(b) trisomy 13
(c) trisomy 18
(d) Klinefelter syndrome (47 XXY)
(e) Turner syndrome (45, X)

113. The leading known cause of mental retardation in the human beings is

(a) Down syndrome
(b) trisomy 13
(c) trisomy 18
(d) Klinefelter syndrome (47 XXY)
(e) Turner syndrome (45, X)

114. Which of the following is not true about chromosome translocations?

(a) They can lead to missing or duplicated chromosome material in the offspring of translocation carriers
(b) They can be helpful in mapping disease-causing genes
(c) They can cause cancer when they occur in somatic cells
(d) They are known to increase with advanced maternal age
(e) b and d

115. An abnormal human of the karyotype 49, XXXYY will form how many Barr bodies?

(a) 3 (b) 4
(c) 2 (d) 5
(e) 1

116. Klinefelter's syndrome and Turner's syndrome are related in which of the following ways?

(a) Result from non-disjunction
(b) Involve an unusual number of X or Y chromosomes
(c) Can be identified by a karyotype
(d) Have 44 autosomes
(e) All of these describe ways in which Klinefelter's syndrome and Turner's syndrome are related

117. Which of the following is not often seen in the individual with Klinefelter syndrome?

(a) Webbed neck
(b) Increasing stature
(c) Diminished IQ (on average)
(d) Sterility
(e) Gynecomastia

118. In which of the following disorders is the extra chromosome contributed in nearly equal proportions by the mother and the father?

(a) 47, XXY (b) Trisomy 21
(c) Trisomy 13 (d) Trisomy 18
(e) 47, XYY

119. In which of the following chromosomal abnormalities is mosaicism most likely to be seen?

(a) Klinefelter syndrome
(b) Down syndrome
(c) XXX syndrome
(d) Turner syndrome
(e) Translocation Down syndrome

120. An individual with three X chromosomes is likely to be

(a) a clinically normal female
(b) an abnormal female
(c) a Turner's individual
(d) a Klinefelter's individual

121. Which of the following is/are characteristic(s) of polyploid plants that may explain the fact that polyploidy has not been a major factor in evolutionary change?

(i) Decreased resistance to disease
(ii) Reduced hardiness
(iii) Lowered fertility
(iv) Reduced height
(a) i only; (b) ii only;
(c) iii only; (d) i and iii;
(e) ii and iii.

122. Recombination has occurred in a pericentric inversion heterozygote in the area of inversion. What are the effects on meiosis and the viability of offspring produced using the gametes?

(a) There are no effects on meiosis or offspring
(b) Meiosis will be normal, but all of the gametes produced from the meiosis will be lethal
(c) Meiosis will be normal, but half of the gametes produced from this meiosis will be lethal
(d) Meiosis will probably stop in anaphase I. If it does finish, all of the gametes produced will be lethal
(e) Meiosis will probably stop in anaphase I. If it does finish, half of the gametes produced will be lethal

123. Gene and centromere (Ÿ) order on a chromosome in *Drosophila* is *a b c (Ÿ) ?d e f*. An inversion that includes genes *b* (Ÿ) *?d* is induced by *X*-irradiation, and a fly with this mutation is then bred with a wild-type fly. The recombinant meiotic products generated when a cross over occurs between *b* and *c* during meiosis in this heterozygote are

(a) a b c d a and f e d (•) c b (•) d f
(b) a b c (•) d a and f e d (•) c b e f
(c) a (•) b c d (•) e f and a d c b e f
(d) a b c (•) d e f and a d (•) c b e f
(e) a b c (•) d e f and a d c (•) b e f

124. Polyploidy refers to

(a) extra copies of a gene adjacent to each other on a chromosome
(b) an individual with complete extra sets of chromosomes
(c) a chromosome which has replicated but not divided
(d) multiple ribosomes present on a single mRNA
(e) an inversion which does not include the centromere

125. X-chromosome inactivation

(a) normally takes place in males but not females
(b) is the cause of the Y chromosome being genetically inactive
(c) takes place in humans, so that the same X chromosome is inactive in all of the cells of a female
(d) occurs in fruit flies but not in mammals
(e) results in genetically turning off one of the two X chromosomes in female mammals

126. Duplication is

(a) an exchange between non-homologous chromosomes, resulting in chromosomes with new genes adjacent to each other
(b) loss of genes in part of a chromosome
(c) an extra copy of the genes on part of a chromosome
(d) a reversal of order of genes on a chromosome
(e) an extra set of chromosomes in an organism

127. The illegitimate recombination event illustrated below will generate

(a) deletions (b) duplications
(c) duplications and deletions
(d) inversions (e) translocations

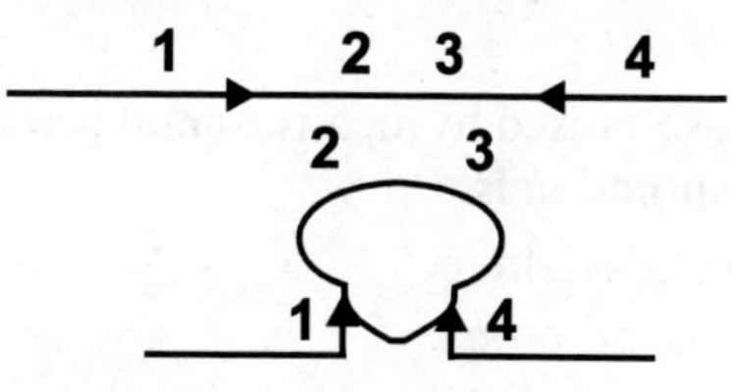

128. Autotriploids can give rise to

(a) aneuploids
(b) Barr bodies
(c) Down syndrome
(d) heterosis

129. The chemical formula of colchicine is

(a) $C_{22}H_{25}O_6N$ (b) $C_{25}H_{22}O_6N$
(c) $C_{22}H_{27}O_8N$ (d) $C_{22}H_{25}O_6N_2$

130. In the DNA sequence below, template strands are black and coding strands are gray. Two chromosome breaks—one between *A* and *B* and the other within the coding sequence of *C*—gives rise to an inversion in which transcription of gene *B* will occur

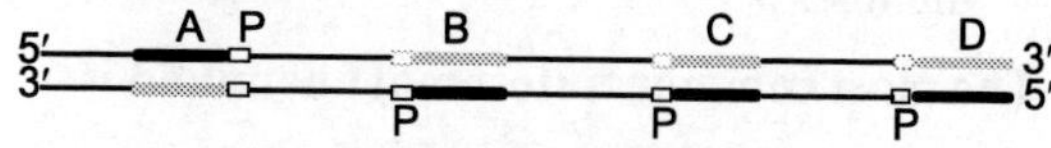

(a) left to right on the lower strand
(b) right to left on the lower strand
(c) left to right on the upper strand
(d) right to left on the upper strand
(e) never, the gene will be disrupted

131. The chromosome form shown below at anaphase of mitosis results from

(a) crossing over
(b) translocation
(c) fusion of the two broken ends of two sister chromatids
(d) nondisjunction
(e) fusion of two chromosomes

132. Which of the following will not cause triploidy?

(a) Fusion of the egg and polar body with subsequent fertilization by sperm cell
(b) Meiotic failure, producing diploid sperm or egg
(c) Dispermy
(d) Mitotic failure in early embryo
(e) (b) and (d)

133. One of the features of polyploids in plants is that

(a) they have higher fertility and seed set than regular diploids
(b) their chromosomes pair and disjoin neatly
(c) deleterious dominant alleles are exposed
(d) they do not survive
(e) they have extra whole sets of chromosomes

134. *Cri-du-chat* syndrome is associated with

(a) a missing chromosome number 5
(b) an additional chromosome number 5
(c) a deletion of the long arm of chromosome number 5
(d) a deletion of the short arm of chromosome number 5

135. The most common autosomal aneuploid is

(a) trisomy 13 (b) trisomy 15
(c) trisomy 18 (d) trisomy 21

136. When chromatids divide along the wrong plane, structures with identical arms called ______ are formed

(a) ring chromosomes
(b) translocations
(c) isochromosomes
(d) satellites

137. In nondisjunction, which parent leads to the sex chromosome aneuploid XYY?

(a) Mother (b) Father
(c) Either parent (d) Both parents

138. An individual with the chromosomal description 45, X would be a

(a) normal female
(b) female with Turner syndrome
(c) male with Klinefelter syndrome
(d) cannot be determined

139. About 90% of trisomy 21 Down conceptions are due to nondisjunction during

(a) meiosis I in the female
(b) meiosis II in the female
(c) meiosis I in the male
(d) meiosis II in the male

140. Consider the following normal sequence of genes: a b c d e f g h. The sequence a b f e d c g h represents a (an)

(a) deletion (b) duplication
(c) inversion (d) translocation

141. Which of the following karyotypes is not possible in the offspring of a translocation carrier (involving chromosomes 14 and 21) and a normal individual?

(a) Deficient 14 or deficient 21
(b) Normal
(c) Translocation Down syndrome
(d) All are possible outcomes

142. How many chromosomes does a person with Edward syndrome have?

(a) 45 (b) 46
(c) 47 (d) 48

143. All of the following aneuploids result from female nondisjunction except

(a) Klinefelter syndrome
(b) triplo-X
(c) Turner syndrome
(d) Jacobs syndrome

144. Klinefelter's syndrome is caused by a nondisjunction resulting in a genotype of

(a) YYY (b) XYY
(c) XXX (d) XXY

145. The genotype of an individual with Turner syndrome is

(a) YO (b) XXY
(c) XYY (d) XO
(e) XXX

146. A disease caused by an autosomal primary nondisjunction is

(a) Turner syndrome
(b) Down syndrome
(c) Tay-Sachs disease
(d) Klinefelter syndrome
(e) PKU

147. Which of the following chromosomes, if trisomic, can cause failure to survive or develop?

(a) X (b) 21
(c) 11 (d) 18
(e) 15

148. Down syndrome results from

(a) the absence of one chromosome in position 21
(b) the presence of an extra chromosome in position 21
(c) the absence of both chromosomes in position 21
(d) crossing over on the chromosomes in position 21
(e) none of the above

149. Which of the following is not a result of nondisjunction of the sex chromosomes?

(a) Down syndrome
(b) Barr body
(c) Turner syndrome
(d) Klinefelter syndrome
(e) both (a) and (b)

150. In a (an) ______, the short arm of two acrocentric chromosomes break, and the long arms join, forming an unusual, long chromosome

(a) Robertsonian translocation
(b) reciprocal translocation
(c) inversion
(d) duplication

151. An individual with two normal sets of autosomes and a single X chromosome has

(a) Down syndrome
(b) Patau syndrome
(c) Turner syndrome
(d) Klinefelter syndrome

152. Which of the following is not true about inversions?

(a) Inverted chromosomes are generally viable
(b) Inversion can cause chromosome breakage
(c) Two strands with an inverted segment will not pair
(d) Inversion including centromere is known as paracentric

153. Consider this sequence A-O-B-C-D-E-F, be a DNA sequence where O is the centromere. Which of the following will be a pericentric inversion?

(a) A-O-B-D-E-F (b) B-O-A-D-E-F
(c) D-B-O-A-E-F (d) A-O-E-D-B-F

154. ______ inversions reduce crossing over in ______

(a) Paracentric, heterozygous
(b) Pericentric, heterozygous
(c) Paracentric, homozygous
(d) Pericentric, homozygous

155. What are the results of pericentric inversion with single crossing over?

(a) Two normal, one dicentric and one acentric chromosome
(b) Two dicentric and 2 acentric chromosomes
(c) Four normal chromosomes with centromere in different positions
(d) Three normal chromosomes, one abnormal acentric chromosome

156. Long pericentric inversions generally do not act as crossover suppressors. Why?

(a) Long stretches of DNA recombination not recognized
(b) Mechanism is different for short and long inversions
(c) Two events of crossing over take place
(d) Crossover product in this is viable

157. Choose the wrong option

(a) Paracentric inversion crossover products are non-viable
(b) Paracentric non-crossover gametes segregate normally
(c) Double crossover in paracentric inversion is lethal
(d) There is genetic imbalance in gametes produced by paracentric inversion crossover

158. In *Drosophila* male there is no crossover suppression due to pericentric inversion as

(a) they have only one set of chromosomes
(b) they always have a double crossover
(c) they never recombine
(d) they do not undergo meiosis

159. Which of the following is an example of inversion?

(a) Chromosome 22 and 9
(b) Chromosome 8
(c) Chromosome 14
(d) Chromosome 3

160. In pericentric inversion, the inversion loop involves ______ strands

(a) 1 (b) 2
(c) 3 (d) 4

161. How will you recognize a terminal deletion from breakage and loss at the terminal end?

(a) Indistinguishable
(b) Terminal break will lead to shorter chromosome than that due to hunk deletion
(c) Terminal break will be sticky
(d) Deletion will be recognized by trans factors

162. What will be the effect of the deletion mutation of a gene at the telomere?

(a) Organism will die
(b) Organism will develop serious hazards due to absence of the gene and its product
(c) Mild effect on the phenotype
(d) No effect

163. You hybridize two cells one of which carries a deletion mutation on chromosome 1. What will you expect to observe?

(a) Buckling of chromatin of first cell
(b) Buckling of chromatin of second cell
(c) Twisting and loop formation between the two chromatins
(d) No observable difference

164. Which of the following is not a possible cause of lethality of individuals carrying a deletion mutation?

(a) Genes that are haplo sufficient do not produce adequate gene product
(b) Genomic imbalance
(c) Unmasking of lethal recessive alleles
(d) Lack of diversity

165. The appearance of a recessive phenotype due to deletion of dominant gene is called

(a) hemi-dominance
(b) pseudo-dominance
(c) imperfect dominance
(d) co-dominance

166. Deletion of a region led to over expression of a gene X. What do you conclude from this observation?

(a) Promoter of gene X is deleted
(b) Part of gene X is mutated
(c) Regulator of gene X is deleted
(d) No effect on gene X or its regulators

167. Yellow colour of mouse is generated by ______ mutation

(a) duplication (b) deletion
(c) inversion (d) translocation

168. Which of the following is not true about the Notch gene in *Drosophila*?

(a) It causes a special indentation of the wing margin
(b) It is expressed in heterozygous form
(c) Notch is lethal in homozygous
(d) Notch is recessive to Facet

169. The likelihood of a child being born with a major genetic defect, such as mental retardation, can often be detected by sampling

(a) the mother's uterus cells
(b) cells from the embryo or the uterus
(c) the father's blood cells
(d) any of the above

170. Which of the following can now be detected by examining a karyotype?

(a) over 3000 genetic defects
(b) an unborn child's gender or sex
(c) both of the above
(d) none of these

171. If there is a family history of genetic disorders, knowing the gender of an unborn child can be important because

(a) male children are more likely to have autosomal defects, which show up in their phenotypes
(b) female children are more likely to have autosomal defects, which show up in their phenotypes
(c) male children are more likely to have X-linked traits, which show up in their phenotype
(d) (a) and (c)

172. Most genetic disorders are due to

(a) gross chromosomal abnormalities such as irregular shapes or number of chromosomes
(b) the gender of an individual
(c) neither of the above
(d) both of the above

173. Which of the following statements is true regarding karyotype analysis?

(a) It is rarely done on the cells of the unborn children because it cannot detect most genetic disorders
(b) It is an important medical tool used in predicting the likelihood that an unborn child will be normal
(c) It is not done any more because human pregnancy has only a small risk of birth defects
(d) None of the above

174. Which of the following statements is true of sex chromosome abnormalities in humans?

(a) They usually have mild effects and are rarely fatal
(b) Most are not gender specific
(c) They cannot be diagnosed before birth
(d) None of the above

175. Male sex chromosome abnormalities can be due to abnormal numbers of ______ chromosomes

(a) X (b) Y
(c) either X or Y (d) none of the above

176. Which of the following statements is incorrect?

(a) Chromosome number is constant within different species in an ecosystem
(b) Chromosome number is constant within different somatic cells of an organism
(c) Chromosome number is constant within individuals in a species in an ecosystem
(d) All of these

177. Long pericentric inversions generally do not act as crossover suppressors. Why?

(a) Crossover product in this is variable
(b) Two events of crossing over take place
(c) Long stretches of DNA recombination not recognized
(d) Mechanism is different for short and long inversions

178. In *Drosophila* male there is no crossover suppression due to pericentric inversion as

(a) they never combine
(b) they have only one set of chromosome
(c) they do not undergo meiosis
(d) they always have double crossover

179. How will you recognize a terminal deletion from breakage and loss at the terminal end?

(a) Terminal break will be sticky
(b) Deletion will be recognized by trans factors
(c) Indistinguishable
(d) Terminal break will lead to shorter chromosome than that due to chunk deletion

MARK TRUE OR FALSE (T/F)

1. A Turner syndrome patient may be male or female
2. The Turner syndrome condition is usually caused by maternal X chromosomal non-disjunction
3. The incidence of X-linked colour blindness amongst Turner syndrome patients is the same as the normal
4. Turner syndrome is associated with cataract
5. In Turner syndrome, peripheral retinal pigmentation is a feature
6. Increase in number of chromosomes occurs in Turner's syndrome
7. Increase in number of chromosomes occurs in fragile-X syndrome
8. Increase in number of chromosomes occurs in Down's syndrome
9. Increase in number of chromosomes occurs in Klinefelter's syndrome
10. Increase in number of chromosomes occurs in Retinoblastoma
11. Turner's syndrome is usually due to non-disjunction in the spermatozoon
12. Half the daughters of a person with Turner's syndrome are affected by the same condition
13. Patients with XXY are infertile
14. All daughters are carriers in X-linked dominant disease
15. The recurrence rate for polygenetic conditions is 1-5%
16. Chromosomal abnormalities are found in achondroplasia
17. Chromosomal abnormalities are found in Cri-du-chat disease
18. Chromosomal abnormalities are found in Patau syndrome
19. In Turner's syndrome, premature cataract is common
20. In Turner's syndrome, the cells contain 45 chromosomes
21. In Turner's syndrome, the offsprings have 50% of them inheriting the disease
22. In Turner's syndrome, there is an increased risk of hypertension
23. In Turner's syndrome, the patient is below the average height
24. In Klinefelter's syndrome, the karyotype is always 47 XXY
25. In Klinefelter's syndrome, the extra chromosome comes from the mother germ cells
26. In Klinefelter's syndrome, there is an increased incidence of lens subluxation
27. In Klinefelter's syndrome, the patient is infertile
28. In Klinefelter's syndrome, there is an increased incidence of breast cancer
29. Down's syndrome has an incidence of 1:700
30. Down's syndrome is associated with the age of the mothers
31. Down's syndrome mosaicism accounts for 2% of all Down's syndrome
32. Down's syndrome is more accurately diagnosed in pregnant woman with amniocentesis than hormonal tests
33. Down's syndrome is associated with congenital glaucoma
34. Retinoblastoma is associated with loss of the short arm of chromosome 13
35. Retinoblastoma is caused by mutation in the growth suppressor gene
36. Retinoblastoma is an autosomal dominant condition
37. Retinoblastoma is sporadic in the majority of unilateral cases
38. Retinoblastoma is inherited in the majority of bilateral cases
39. Turner syndrome is seen only in females

40. Turner syndrome may have one chromosome as an isochromosome
41. Turner syndrome is usually associated with severe mental retardation
42. Turner syndrome patients are usually present with primary amenorrhoea
43. Turner syndrome cannot be detected at birth
44. Fragile X syndrome is due to chromosome aberrations
45. Phenylketonuria is due to chromosome aberrations
46. Cri-du-chat syndrome is due to chromosome aberrations
47. Osteogenesis imperfecta is due to chromosome aberrations
48. Down syndrome is due to chromosome aberrations
49. Diseases associated with HLA-B8 include Sjogren's syndrome
50. Diseases associated with HLA-B8 include multiple sclerosis
51. Diseases associated with HLA-B8 include myasthenia gravis
52. Diseases associated with HLA-B8 include insulin-dependent diabetes mellitus
53. Diseases associated with HLA-B8 include Grave's disease
54. A point mutation that leads to failure of expression of one allele may be because of an isochromosome
55. A chromosome that contains a segment, which has turned upside down and includes the centromere, is a paracentric inversion
56. A chromosome which is made up of the long arms of two acrocentric chromosomes which have fused at their centromeres with loss of the short arms is a Robertsonian translocation
57. A chromosome that has lost material from both ends with fusion of the 'sticky' ends is a ring chromosome
58. Two chromosomes that have exchanged segments without loss or gain of any material result in balanced reciprocal translocation
59. Triploidy in human beings is 69, XXX
60. Tetraploidy in human beings means 92, XXX
61. Tetrasomy in human beings is 48, XXXO
62. The most common chromosome abnormality in first trimester spontaneous miscarriages is trisomy
63. 45, Y karyotypes are not compatible with survival to birth
64. The trisomy karyotype with the mildest effect on human development is 47, XXX
65. Male to male transmission is a key feature of autosomal recessive
66. Trisomics have been reported in tomato
67. The best source of aneuploids are translocation heterozygotes
68 Trisomic analysis can be done to locate genes on particular chromosomes
69. Trisomic analysis has not been done in barley
70. Colchicine does not dissolve in water
71. Tetraploids may not be useful in making distant crosses
72. Apomicts have been reported in *Solanum*
73. Club wheat is known as *Triticum Compactum*
74. *Gossypium barbadense* is an allotetraploid
75. *Brassica juncea* has the genome BBDD
76. It is easy to cross *Brassica campestris* with *B. oleracea*
77. Nullisomics are very suitable for chromosome substitution
78. Autopolyploidy results in late flowering
79. Haploids cannot be obtained by the culture of ovaries
80. Tetraploid sugarbeets produce smaller roots than diploids
81. In many cases, natural alloploids show apomixis

82. Homoeologous chromosomes are likely to pair during meiosis
83. An amphdiploid shows multivalent formation
84. The evolution of *Triticum aestivum* is not clearly known
85. Allopolyploidy does not enable a species to succeed as a crop
86. An amphidiploid behaves like a diploid during meiosis
87. Desynapsis is lack of pairing between homologous chromosomes during meiosis
88. Gigas character is related to a drastic increase in seed formation
89. Autosyndesis is pairing in polyploids between chromosomes contributed by the same parental species
90. Diploidizing system enforces a polyploid to behave like a diploid at meiosis
91. Isochromosomes have both the arms of a chromosome of same length
92. Disomics are polyploids
93. A trisomic having an extra chromosome, which is a translocated chromosome, is called a secondary trisomic
94. A simplex individual is Aaaa
95. Secondary trisomic has an isochromosome as an extra chromosome
96. An individual with the genotype AAAA is a quadriplex
97. Amphimixis means the union of maternal and paternal gametes
98. Tetraploids are the best source of aneuploids
99. Monosomics do not survive in diploid species
100. Tetrasomics form many quadrivalents
101. Aneuploids are useful in the production of substitution lines
102. Colchicine affects dividing as well as non-dividing cells
103. Sweet potato is hexaploid
104. Somatic chromosome number of edible banana is 33
105. For sugarbeets, the optimum level of ploidy is 4 X
106. *Gossypium barbadense* is Asiatic cotton
107. New World cotton is also Gossypium
108. Raphanobrassica has 36 chromosomes
109. The first triticale variety in India was released by G. B. Pant University of Agriculture and Technology, Pantnagar
110. Chromosomal abnormalities are found in myeloid leukaemia
111. Chromosomal abnormalities are found in sickle cell disease
112. Triploidy in human beings is 69, XXX
113. Tetraploidy in human beings means 92, XXX

14

Genetics of Bacteria and Bacteriophages

MULTIPLE-CHOICE QUESTIONS

1. A bacterium containing phage DNA integrated in its chromosome is

(a) lysogenic
(b) avirulent
(c) virulent
(d) prophagic
(e) temperate

2. Plaque assay detects the number of

(a) dental cavities
(b) bacterial prototrophs
(c) bacterial auxotrophs
(d) bacterial viruses
(e) animal viruses

3. Essential genes in viruses can only be studied when they contain

(a) conditional mutations
(b) dominant mutations
(c) no mutations
(d) recessive mutations
(e) all of the above

4. Hfr bacteria

(a) function only as donors in crosses with F^- bacteria and are so called because they result in "high frequency recombination" are correct
(b) are so called because they result in "high frequency recombination"
(c) are derived from F^+ bacteria
(d) function as donors in crosses with F^- bacteria
(e) are so called because they result in "high frequency recombination", and are derived from F^+ bacteria

5. Transduction is

(a) viral-mediated viral recombination
(b) bacterial-mediated bacterial recombination
(c) bacterial-mediated viral recombination
(d) viral-mediated bacterial recombination
(e) none of the above

6. The *lac* repressor is a

(a) DNA molecule (b) RNA molecule
(c) lipid molecule (d) protein molecule
(e) carbohydrate

7. If normal (wild type) repressor is added *in vitro*, which DNA fails to bind the repressor?

(a) $I^- O^+ Z^+$ (b) $I^+ O^+ Z^+$
(c) $I^+ O^c Z^+$ (d) $I^+ O^+ Z^-$
(e) All bind repressor

8. What is the advantage of using IPTG, a gratuitous inducer experimentally? IPTG

(a) is not broken down by the enzyme
(b) is smaller than lactose
(c) is broken down by the enzyme
(d) interacts with DNA
(e) is larger than lactose

9. The *trp* operon is

(a) inducible, but not under either positive or negative control
(b) repressible and under negative control
(c) inducible and under positive control
(d) repressible and under positive control
(e) inducible and under negative control

10. A mutation in the I gene of the *lac* operon directly affects

(a) permease (b) B-galactosidase
(c) the promoter (d) the repressor
(e) the operator region

11. Which of the following is NOT true of a viroid?

(a) Cadang-cadang is a viroid disease of the coconut palm
(b) Viroids affect mostly plants
(c) Its RNA is circular
(d) Viroid possesses about 300-400 nucleotides
(e) Its capsid is quite small

12. Kuru is a degenerative disease of the central nervous system believed to be caused by which type of agent?

(a) Protozoan (b) Bacterium
(c) Prion (d) Virus
(e) Viroid

13. Bacteria do not have organelles. How are they able to carry out photosynthesis?

(a) They use their cell membrane to carry out photosynthesis
(b) 70S ribosomes function as a photosystem
(c) They are parasites of plants that have organelles
(d) They interact in a symbiotic relationship with eukaryotic plants
(e) DNA in the nucleoid captures solar energy

14. How is genetic transfer different from sexual reproduction?

(a) In genetic transfer, genetic material is transferred from one individual to another
(b) In sexual reproduction, genetic material from two individuals is mixed equally
(c) In both processes, the individual donating genetic material retains its original complement of genetic material
(d) None of these

15. Which method of gene transfer involves direct contact between the bacteria?

(a) Conjugation (b) Transduction
(c) Transformation (d) All of these
(e) None of these

16. The end result of F factor-mediated conjugation

(a) is that both strains are F^+
(b) involves transfer of the entire bacterial chromosome
(c) converts the recipient strain to F^+ and the donor to F^-
(d) (a) and (b)
(e) none of the above

17. Which of the following is a description of generalized transduction?

(a) Inaccurate excision of prophage can occasionally remove a small portion of the bacterial chromosome
(b) Random pieces of bacterial DNA can become incorporated into a phage coat
(c) Pieces of bacterial DNA may be released into the culture medium when a cell is lysed
(d) All of these
(e) None of the above

18. How might the function of extracellular endonucleases help protect the bacterium from infection by viruses?

(a) They would prevent the virus from binding to the outside of the bacterial cell
(b) They would destroy the viral coat, so it cannot inject its genetic material
(c) They would cut the viral DNA into small pieces
(d) All of the above
(e) None of the above

19. What do transduction, transformation, and conjugation have in common?

(a) All require presence of an outside factor to facilitate gene transfer
(b) In all three processes, DNA is transferred as a single-stranded molecule
(c) They all transfer large pieces of DNA into recipient cells
(d) All of the above
(e) None of the above

20. In Benzer's intragenic mapping experiments, which events were required to allow the production of infectious phage from rII mutants?

(a) rII mutant strains with mutations in different genes
(b) Homologous recombination between phage
(c) Crossover within the mutant gene, between the mutations
(d) Crossover at one end of the mutant gene, outside the mutation

21. In deletion mapping, mutations can be localized to a region of the gene because

(a) the mutation fails to complement other mutations in the gene
(b) the mutation fails to complement a deletion of a known portion of the gene
(c) the gene sequence can be determined
(d) (a) and (b)
(e) none of the above

22. A key finding of intragenic mapping was

(a) that genes consist of indivisible particles, like beads on a string
(b) that genes do not change over time
(c) that genes can be modified by crossing over and mutation
(d) all of these
(e) none of these

23. Which one of the following is incorrect? A characteristic of the structure of transposons in the Gram-negative bacteria is the presence of

(a) Origin of transfer sequence
(b) Transfer genes next to antibiotic resistance genes
(c) Inverted repeats at the ends
(d) Self-replicating genes
(e) None of the above

24. Which one of the following is incorrect? Exchange of genetic information by transformation

(a) requires sex pili
(b) is restricted to Gram-negative bacteria
(c) is dependent on homologous recombination
(d) none of the above

25. Which one of the following is correct? Insertion sequences are

(a) covalently closed circular DNA
(b) approximately 100 kilobases in size
(c) found only in Gram-positive bacteria
(d) a significant cause of mutations in bacteria

26. Bacteria that possess a natural system for genetic transformation include

(a) *Staphylococcus aureus*
(b) *Helicobacter pylori*
(c) *E. coli*
(d) *Pseudomonas aeruginosa*
(e) *Klebsiella pneumoniae*

27. Which one of the following strains of *E. coli* would be able to conjugate with *E. coli* F^- met^- arg^- $B1^-$ to produce a recombinant that grows on minimal medium supplemented with vitamin B_1?

(a) F^+ met^+ arg^+ $B1^-$ (b) F^+ met^+ arg^+ $B1^+$
(c) Hfr met^- arg^- $B1^+$ (d) Hfr met^+ arg^+ $B1^-$
(e) None of the above

28. Which one of the following strains of *E. coli* would be able to conjugate with *E. coli* F^- trp^- leu^- Lac^- to produce a recombinant that grows on minimal medium with lactose as a sole source of carbon?

(a) F^+ trp^+ leu^- Lac^+ (b) F^+ trp^- leu^+ Lac^+
(c) Hfr trp^+ leu^+ Lac^- (d) Hfr trp^+ leu^+ Lac^+
(e) Hfr trp^- leu^- Lac^+

29. *Trp⁻* mutants (tryptophan auxotrophs) can be isolated from the wild type (*trp⁺*) by

(a) direct plating on a medium containing tryptophan
(b) direct plating on a medium without tryptophan
(c) replica plating from a medium without tryptophan to a medium with tryptophan
(d) replica plating from a medium with tryptophan to a medium without tryptophan

30. Revertants (prototrophs) could be isolated from a population of trp^- mutants by

(a) direct plating on a medium containing tryptophan
(b) direct plating on a medium without tryptophan
(c) penicillin enrichment in a medium which contains tryptophan
(d) penicillin enrichment in a medium lacking tryptophan
(e) two of the above

31. Which reversion in one strain of bacteria is indicated by the results of the experiment?

(a) Streptomycin sensitivity (SMr ——> SMs)
(b) Arginine prototrophy (*arg* ——> *arg⁺*)
(c) Methionine prototrophy (*met⁻* ——> *met⁺*)
(d) All of the above
(e) None of the above

32. Suppose the tetracycline-resistant (Tcr) gene from *Shigella* and the the ampicillin-resistant (Ampr) gene from *S. aureus* are transformed into a strain of *E. coli*, which is sensitive to the two antibiotics. In order to determine if the transformation was successful, what medium should be used to detect the transformants?

(a) Minimal medium with no supplements
(b) Minimal medium plus ampicillin
(c) Minimal medium plus tetracycline
(d) Minimal medium plus ampicillin and tetracycline
(e) None of the above

33. In order to obtain a lysine revertant from strain A (above), the culture should be plated on

(a) minimal glucose medium plus ampicillin
(b) minimal glucose medium plus lysine and phenylalanine
(c) minimal glucose medium plus phenylalanine and tyrosine
(d) minimal glucose medium plus lysine and ampicillin
(e) minimal glucose medium with no supplements

34. Resistance transfer factors (RTFs) in *E. coli* are

(a) insertion elements on the F factor
(b) transmissible plasmids that encode genes for drug resistance
(c) genes that move from place to place on the bacterial chromosome
(d) outer membrane proteins that exclude passage of antibiotics and hydrophobic agents
(e) plasma membrane proteins that mediate the passage of solutes into and out of the cell

35. In the Griffith experiment, the substance present in the suspension of heat-killed virulent cells of *Streptococcus pneumoniae* that, when mixed with living non-virulent cells, transformed them into living virulent cells, was

(a) DNA
(b) capsular material from the virulent cells
(c) mouse phagocytes
(d) RNA
(e) toxin

36. In the Zinder and Lederberg U-tube experiment, DNAase was added to the U-tube to inhibit the process of

(a) translation (b) transformation
(c) lysogeny (d) conjugation
(e) transduction

37. Lys$^+$ revertants (prototrophs) could be isolated from a population of lys$^-$ mutants by

(a) direct plating on a medium containing lysine
(b) direct plating on a medium without lysine
(c) replica plating from a medium without lysine to a medium with lysine
(d) two of the above
(e) none of the above

38. The penicillin enrichment technique is useful when isolating auxotrophic mutants (for example Trp$^-$) because penicillin

(a) prevents the growth of wild type bacteria but not mutants
(b) does not affect eukaryotic cells
(c) kills only the growing bacterial cells, not the mutants in the population
(d) increases the rate of mutation towards auxotrophy
(e) does not affect *E. coli* under the conditions of the procedure

39. Trp$^-$ mutants (tryptophan auxotrophs) can be isolated by

(a) direct plating on medium containing tryptophan
(b) direct plating on medium without tryptophan
(c) replica plating from a medium without tryptophan to a medium with tryptophan
(d) replica plating from a medium with tryptophan to a medium without tryptophan
(e) none of the above

40. During the process of generalized transduction

(a) cell to cell contact is required
(b) a bacteriophage capsid can enclose and transfer any part (gene) of the bacterial chromosome
(c) the transfer of DNA is inhibited in the presence of DNAase
(d) the recipient must be susceptible to infection by the same bacteriophage as the donor
(e) (b) and (d) above

41. A bacterial geneticist mixes together 10^8 cells that require methionine and are ampicillin sensitive, and 10^8 cells that require phenylalanine and tyrosine and are ampicillin resistant. In order to detect whether genetic recombination had occurred between the two strains, it would be best to grow the mixture of cells in

(a) minimal glucose medium with no supplements
(b) minimal glucose medium plus methionine and phenylalanine
(c) minimal glucose medium plus methionine, phenylalanine and tyrosine
(d) minimal glucose medium plus phenylalanine, tyrosine and ampicillin
(e) minimal glucose medium plus ampicillin

42. While these strains grow together, the geneticist (above) plates 10^8 cells of the auxotroph that requires methionine and is ampicillin-sensitive onto minimal glucose medium with no supplements. Approximately, 100 colonies arise on the plate. The geneticist concludes that

(a) the rate of reversion to methionine prototrophy is 10^{-6}

(b) the rate of mutation to ampicillin resistance is 10^{-6}

(c) the combined rate of reversion methionine prototrophy and mutation to ampicillin resistance is 10^{-12}

(d) all of the above

(e) none of the above

43. A bacteriophage is a

(a) bacterium that infects viruses

(b) virus that infects bacteria

(c) viral antibody that lyses bacteria

(d) bacterial antibody that lyses viruses

44. For growth, a mutant bacterium requires that an amino acid not required by the wild parental strain be added to the growth medium. This mutant is an example of a(n)

(a) autotroph

(b) auxotroph

(c) heterotroph

(d) organotroph

45. Lysogeny probably carries a strong selective advantage for the host cell because

(a) it prevents cell lysis

(b) it confers resistance to infection by viruses of the same type

(c) it confers resistance to infection by viruses of a different type (or strain)

(d) all of the above

46. A bacterial geneticist mixes 10^9 cells of *E. coli* strain A that requires lysine and is ampicillin sensitive with 10^9 cells of strain B that requires phenylalanine and tyrosine and is ampicillin resistant. In order to detect whether genetic recombination had occurred between the two strains, it would be best to grow the mixture of cells in

(a) minimal glucose medium plus ampicillin

(b) minimal glucose medium plus lysine and phenylalanine

(c) minimal glucose medium plus lysine and tyrosine

(d) minimal glucose medium plus phenylalanine, tyrosine and ampicillin

(e) minimal glucose medium with no supplements

47. Bacteriophage lambda is a very useful cloning vector in genetic engineering because

(a) it can hold large amounts of DNA

(b) its molecular genetics is well-known

(c) infection of suitable host cells by lambda is more efficient than transformation

(d) all of the above

48. Which of the following traits in not characteristic of Taq polymerase?

(a) Stable at 95°C

(b) Possesses a proof reading function

(c) permits DNA synthesis at high temperatures, thereby increasing specificity

(d) functions at standard atmospheric pressure

49. UV radiation is antimicrobial because

(a) the radiation generates significant amounts of heat within the given cell

(b) the energy present causes breaks in the DNA molecule

(c) the radiation generates magnetic poles, which denature the cellular components

(d) all of the above

50. ______ are applied to living tissue; ______ are used on inanimate objects

(a) Disinfectants/sterilants
(b) Antiseptics/sterilants
(c) Antiseptics/disinfectants
(d) Disinfectants/sterilants

51. The first antibody to contact invading microorganisms was

(a) IgG (b) IgM
(c) IgA (d) IgD

52. The light emitted by luminescent bacteria is mediated by the enzyme

(a) coenzyme Q (b) luciferase
(c) lactose dehydrogenase
(d) carboxylase reductase

53. The vector used in Human Genome project was:

(a) phagemid vector
(b) yeast artificial chromosome
(c) cosmid vector
(d) yeast episomal plasmid

54. Kuru disease in humans is caused by

(a) bacteria (b) viroids
(c) prions (d) mycoplasmas

55. Phagocytic phenomenon was discovered by

(a) Louis Pasteur (b) Alexander Fleming
(c) Metchnikof (d) Robert Koch

56. Hybridoma technique was first discovered by

(a) Kohler and Milstein (b) Robert Koch
(c) 'D' Herelle (d) Landsteiner

57. Griffith (1928) reported the phenomenon of transformation first in

(a) *H. influenzae* (b) *Bacillus species*
(c) *Pneumococci* (d) *E. coli*

58. Hanging drop method for motility study was first introduced by

(a) Robert Koch (b) Louis Pasteur
(c) Jenner (d) Leeuwenhoek

59. Mycoplasmas are bacterial cells that

(a) fail to reproduce in an artificial medium
(b) have a rigid cell wall
(c) are resistant to penicillin
(d) stain well with Gram's stain

60. Rancidity in spoiled foods is due to

(a) lipolytic organisms
(b) proteolytic organisms
(c) toxigenic microbes
(d) saccharolytic microbes

61. Cold like symptoms are caused by

(a) *Pseudomonas*
(b) *E. coli*
(c) *Haemophilus influenza*
(d) *Haemophilus streptococcus*

62. The mode of reproduction which occurs in mycoplasma is

(a) budding (b) bursting
(c) binary fission (d) binary fusion

63. Staining material of Gram-negative bacterium is

(a) fast green (b) haemotoxylin
(c) crystal violet (d) safranin

64. Bacteria that are responsible for fermentation of dairy milk are

(a) *Azotobacter* (b) *Rhizobium*
(c) *Lactobacillus* (d) Hay bacillus

65. The bacterial pili mainly contain

(a) carbohydrates (b) lipids
(c) proteins (d) minerals

66. Role of bacteria in carbon cycle is

(a) photosynthesis
(b) chemosynthesis
(c) breakdown of organic compounds
(d) assimilation of nitrogen compounds

67. Maximum application of animal cell culture technology today is in the production of

(a) insulin (b) interferons
(c) vaccines (d) edible proteins

68. The most infectious food-borne disease is

(a) tetanus (b) dysentry
(c) gas gangrene (d) botulism

69. Intermediate group of pathogen between bacteria and viruses which are intracellular parasites are

(a) mycoplasmas (b) rickettsia
(c) prions (d) virusides

70. Recombination process occurring through the mediation of phages is

(a) conjunction (b) transduction
(c) transformation (d) transfection

71. Majority of the bacteria are

(a) saprophytes (b) symbionts
(c) commensals (d) parasites

72. Attenuation means

(a) killing of the bacteria
(b) inactivation of bacteria
(c) more activating the bacteria
(d) both 1 and 2

73. Gas gangrene bacillus is

a) facultative anaerobe
b) obligate anaerobe
c) facultative aerobe
d) obligate aerobe

74. In Gram-positive bacteria, ratio of RNA to DNA is

(a) 8 : 1 (b) 1 : 2
(c) almost equal (d) none of these

75. How much time is taken by the new DNA to make whole phage particles?

(a) 24 hours (b) 60 minutes
(c) 2 minutes (d) 10-20 minutes

76. When viral genome can become integrated into the bacterial genome, they are known as

(a) temperate phage (b) prophage
(c) bacteriophage (d) episome

77. Which of the following role is performed by a bacteriophage in transduction?

(a) Vector (b) Donor
(c) Recipient (d) Episome

78. How many genes fragments transferred by a bacteriophage contains?

(a) 20 (b) 50
(c) 1 (d) 100

79. When the phage transduces only those bacterial genes adjacent to the prophage in the bacterial chromosome then it is known as

(a) generalized transduction
(b) specialized transduction
(c) restricted transduction
(d) conjugation

80. Which of the following is not true for a bacteriophage?

(a) A very simple structure
(b) Consists of either DNA or RNA
(c) Bacteriophages are viruses
(d) Complex structure that infects bacteria

81. What is the capsid (protective coat) of the bacteriophage made up of?

(a) DNA (b) RNA
(c) Protein (d) Organic acids

82. Which of the following is an example of head and tail bacteriophage?

(a) M 13 (b) Lambda phage
(c) pBR 322 (d) M 16

83. The replication of phage DNA molecule is associated with which step in the infection cycle of a bacteriophage?

(a) First step (b) Second step
(c) Third step (d) Preparation stage

84. What is the reason of instability of phage DNA molecule in the host cell in a lytic cycle?

(a) The huge size of phage DNA
(b) Inability of replicative enzymes
(c) Immediate synthesis of capsid
(d) Lytic cycle inefficiency

85. Which infection cycle is characterized by retention of the phage DNA molecule in the host bacterium for many thousands of cell division?

(a) Lysogenic cycle (b) Lytic cycle
(c) Integrative phase (d) Protein synthesis

86. A specialized transducing virus attacks a healthy bacterial cell. What will be the virulence of the viruses produced by this bacterial cell after infection?

(a) They will be more virulent than original one
(b) No virulence
(c) They will be equally virulent as original one
(d) The virulence will depreciate

87. In which of the following cases will the viral progeny generated retain their infection ability?

(a) A generalized transducing phage affects a normal cell
(b) A specialized transducing phage affects a cell infected by the same virus
(c) A specialized transducing phage will attack a normal cell
(d) A generalized transducing phage will affect a cell with a different viral infection

88. A specialized transducing phage attacking an infected cell with lysogenic stage of the same virus gives rise to

(a) HFR (b) HFT
(c) F′ (d) F

89. Which of the following statements are true about a virion?

(a) Lytic phage
(b) Lysogenic phage
(c) The viral capsid
(d) An infectious and fully formed viral particle

90. Which of the following is the largest virus?

(a) *Megavirus chilensis*(b) Arbo virus
(c) Herpes virus (d) Mumps virus

91. Which of the following statements are true about the capsomeres?

(a) It is an individual unit of the capsid
(b) It is a viral protein for replication
(c) It is a unit of nucleic acid in viruses
(d) All of the above

92. Which of the following has a complex symmetry?

(a) T 4 phage (b) Adenovirus
(c) Influenza virus (d) All of the above

93. Which of the following is a helical virus?

(a) TMV (b) T 4 phage
(c) Pox virus (d) Herpes virus

94. A fully formed infectious viral particle is called

(a) virion (b) viroid
(c) capsid (d) virusoid

95. Which of the following is true about the TMV?

(a) RNA virus (b) DNA virus
(c) Bacteriophage (d) ss DNA or ds DNA

96. The shape of TMV is

(a) rod shaped (b) oval shaped
(c) cuboidal shaped (d) spherical shaped

97. The T2 phage is called

(a) ss DNA phage (b) ss RNA phage
(c) ds DNA phage (d) ds RNA phage

98. Bateriophages that induce bacterial cell lysis are called

(a) viroids (b) lysogenic phages
(c) virulent phages (d) temperate phages

99. Which of the following virus has the smallest genome?

(a) Rabies virus (b) Circovirus
(c) Herpes virus (d) Mimi virus

100. Viral genome inserted into the bacterial DNA is known as

(a) lysogeny (b) prophage
(c) lytic cycle (d) virulent phage

101. Which of the following are the main functions of the capsid?

(a) Determines the antigenic specificity of the virus
(b) Protects genetic material from nuclease attack
(c) Both (a) and (b)
(d) None of these

102. Following is the marker of HIV infection in blood

(a) reverse transcriptase
(b) DNA polymerase
(c) RNA polymerase
(d) none of these

103. Which of the following is the most specific in diagnosis of AIDS?

(a) IHA
(b) Western blot
(c) ELISA
(d) Immuno electrophoresis

104. The Dengue fever virus is

(a) arbo virus (b) echo virus
(c) entero virus (d) orthomyxo virus

105. Main causative organism of chicken pox is

(a) fox virus (b) mumps virus
(c) measles virus (d) none of these

MARK TRUE OR FALSE (T/F)

1. Conjugation involves direct transfer of genetic material from one bacterium to another
2. Hfr strains of bacteria contain F factors that include some genes from the bacterial chromosome
3. Virulent phages generally follow the lysogenic cycle while infecting bacteria
4. In generalized transduction, random bits of the bacterial chromosome are packaged in a phage head
5. Horizontal gene transfer may be mediated via conjugation but not via transduction or transformation
6. Mutations that complement each other are in the same gene
7. Deletion mapping is more efficient but less detailed than fine structure mapping of genes
8. Bacteriophages may be able to infect some strains of bacteria but not others
9. Some *E. coli* cells carry a circular plasmid called the sex factor, F
10. Factor F cannot exist in a free state in the cytoplasm
11. Factor F can be integrated into the circular bacterial chromosome
12. When F is integrated, the bacterial chromosome is transferred linearly to an F^- free cell during conjugation
13. In the nonintegrated state, F cannot pass into F^- free cells during cell conjugation
14. Bacteriophages cannot transfer DNA from one bacterial cell to another
15. During generalized transduction, random chromosome fragments are incorporated into the heads of phages and transferred to other cells by infection
16. DNA from the medium can enter a bacterial cell and integrate into the chromosome, thereby transforming the genotype

17. The different methods of gene transfer in bacteria generate complete diploids that permit the study of recombination and gene interaction
18. Conjugation is a natural union of bacterial cells during which one cell transfers DNA segments to another
19. Transformation is the process by which a bacterial cell can pick up DNA from the environment and incorporate this DNA into its own chromosome
20. Certain phages can occasionally pick up a piece of DNA from one bacterial cell and inject it into another phage, where it can be incorporated into the chromosome. This process is called transduction
21. In conjugation, the gene transfer is partial and unidirectional
22. The donor fragment is called the endogenote
23. The cell containing an endogenote is a partial diploid, or merozygote
24. Wild type bacteria can produce colonies on minimal medium and are called prototrophic
25. Some mutant clones will not grow unless the medium has one or more specific nutrients. They are called auxotropic
26. Wild type bacteria can utilize the sugar, galactose as an energy source
27. In *E. coli*, circular DNA plasmid called the fertility factor (F) is found in all the cells
28. In *E. coli*, fertility factor (F) or the sex factor mean the same thing
29. F^+ cells mean that the F plasmid is present
30. Pili are small proteinaceous tubules that allow the F^- cells to attach to other cells
31. F^+ and F^- cells can conjugate
32. F plasmid can be transferred from F^+ to F^+ cells
33. An IS (insertion sequence) element is a mobile segment of DNA that moves between chromosome and plasmid
34. Hfr and F^+ strains are the same
35. F' can transfer the specific host genes to a recipient (F^-) cell
36. Lederberg and Tatum discovered genetic recombination in bacteria
37. Recombinant frequencies among exconjugants can be used in fine-scale mapping
38. The process of creating a merozygote by an F^+ element is called sexduction
39. Bacteriophage genomes can only be DNA
40. Viral genomes can be single-stranded as well as double-stranded
41. Some RNA phages have segmented genomes, i.e., their genes are carried by a number of different RNA molecules
42. A lytic phage does not kill its host bacterium after initial infection
43. A lysogenic phage can remain quiescent within its host for a substantial period of time
44. *E. coli* phage T2 is one of the best characterized
45. After attachment, the phage infects its DNA genome into the cell through its tail structure
46. During a lytic cycle, the phage genome becomes integrated into the host DNA
47. Lysozyme is the enzyme that causes the bacterium to burst
48. Tobacco mosaic virus has single-stranded linear RNA
49. SV 40 virus has double-stranded linear DNA
50. The viral DNA may be incorporated into the phage head during phage assembly

15
Gene Mutations

MULTIPLE-CHOICE QUESTIONS

1. **A change in a single nucleotide that results in no change in the amino acid sequence of the polypeptide produced is known as**
   (a) frameshift mutation
   (b) silent mutation
   (c) missense mutation
   (d) nonsense mutation
   (e) none of the above

2. **While studying an *E. coli* strain containing a known frameshift mutation, you isolate a mutant in which this frameshift is suppressed. You therefore expect to find which of the following is associated with the suppression? (Assume the frameshift has not been corrected in the coding for the peptide.)**
   (a) Suppressor tRNAs encode an amino acid for a stop signal
   (b) Suppressor tRNAs encode a two-nucleotide anticodon
   (c) Suppressor tRNAs encode a four-nucleotide anticodon
   (d) Both (b) and (c)
   (e) All of the above

3. **A somatic mutation is a change in the DNA that**
   (a) occurs in an ordinary body cell and is not transmitted to the next generation
   (b) occurs in a sex cell and is not transmitted to the next generation
   (c) occurs in all body cells at the same time
   (d) affects the genes associated with sleep
   (e) occurs in any cell and is passed onto the next generation

4. **A researcher has found a very sick mutant *E. coli.* He isolates proteins produced by this mutant. Although the proteins have the right primary sequence at their N termini, many of the proteins are too long. What is wrong with this mutant?**
   (a) Peptidyl transferase is non-functional
   (b) Release factor (RF) is non- functional
   (c) The mutant has a tRNA that can base pair with a stop codon
   (d) The mutant has an altered initiator tRNA
   (e) Elongation factor, G is non-functional

5. **Mutations are errors in DNA that**
   (a) are always harmful
   (b) only occur in the presence of carcinogens
   (c) increase tumour growth
   (d) occur spontaneous at a low rate
   (e) only occur on the X chromosome

6. **Which one of the following is a type of mutation?**
   (a) Transformation
   (b) Nonsense
   (c) Antisense
   (d) Degeneracy
   (e) Wobble

7. ***Drosophila* homozygous for the recessive mutation cu cu were grown at 24° C, and a sample was produced as shown below**

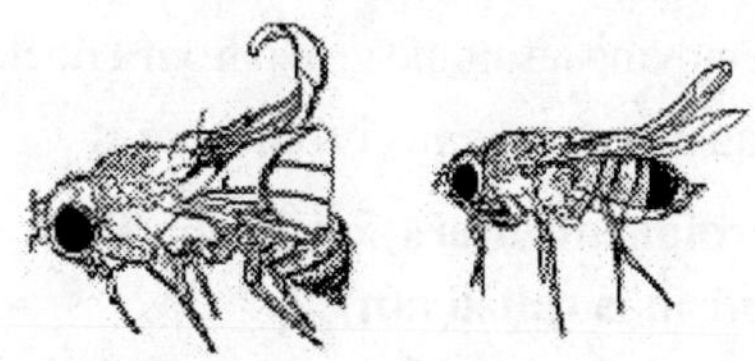

fully curled 30 semi-curled 70
The percentage expressivity for the character is
(a) 60% (b) 70%
(c) 65% (d) 40%
(e) 80%

8. **The fluctuation test of Luria and Delbrück showed that**
   (a) mutation is more random in prokaryotes than eukaryotes
   (b) mutation is more random in eukaryotes than prokaryotes
   (c) phages eat bacteria
   (d) exposure to a phage provokes the occurrence of mutations to phage-resistance in a bacterial population
   (e) exposure to a phage selects pre-existing phage-resistant mutants from a bacterial population

9. **The fluctuation tests done by Luria and Delbruck showed that**
   (a) antibiotics induce the development of resistance in bacteria
   (b) the growth of bacteria fluctuates based on the concentration of antibiotics in the media
   (c) the concentration of antibiotics fluctuates in response to the number of bacteria in a sample
   (d) resistance to antibiotics occurs spontaneously in bacteria

10. **A pure-line mutant strain of *Drosophila* flies with curled wings (cu cu), being kept for teaching, escaped into the hills and despite the cold climate they produced some offspring. These offspring were found to have straight wings. When a sample of them was brought back into the lab, they produced curled-wing progeny. Which of the following explanations for this effect is correct?**
    (a) Mutation
    (b) Change in chromosome number
    (c) Genetic drift
    (d) Temperature-dependent effects on gene expression
    (e) Incomplete dominance

11. **Which of the following mutation types is expected to produce the mildest form of disease?**
    (a) Mobile element insertion
    (b) Frameshift deletion
    (c) Nonsense mutation
    (d) Missense mutation
    (e) Frameshift insertion

12. **Which of the following diseases results from faulty DNA repair?**
    (a) Neurofibromatosis type 1
    (b) Retinoblastoma
    (c) Xeroderma pigmentosum
    (d) Osteogenesis imperfecta
    (e) Hemophilia A

13. Sickle-cell disease is the result of a single nucleotide substitution that produces a single amino acid substitution. This is best described as a

(a) frameshift mutation
(b) nonsense mutation
(c) splice-site mutation
(d) missense mutation
(e) none of the above

14. Which of the following would not tend to raise mutation rates for single-gene disorders in humans?

(a) CG dinucleotides within the gene
(b) Elevated paternal age
(c) Caffeine exposure
(d) Large genes
(e) All of the above are known to raise mutation rates in humans

15. Which of the following is least likely to be seen in a patient with Huntington disease?

(a) Dementia
(b) Affective disorder
(c) New mutation
(d) Delayed age of onset
(e) Loss of motor control

16. A woman with phenotypically normal parents has two brothers with Duchenne muscular dystrophy. She experiences mild muscle weakness in her legs. Which of the following mechanisms is most likely to be directly involved?

(a) Germline mosaicism
(b) Skewed X inactivation
(c) Mutation near the pseudoautosomal region of the Y chromosome
(d) New mutation in this woman
(e) Nondisjunction of her mother's X chromosomes

17. The concept that new varieties of organisms are still evolving is best supported by the

(a) increasing need for new antibiotics
(b) increasing number of individuals in the human population
(c) decreasing number of new fossils discovered in undisturbed rock layers
(d) decreasing activity of photosynthetic organisms due to warming of the atmosphere

18. Mutagens such as 5-bromouracil cause mutations by

(a) substituting for one of the bases normally found in DNA
(b) adding an alkyl group to a nucleotide
(c) removing an amino group from a nucleotide
(d) causing breaks in chromosomes

19. A permanent alteration in the DNA of an organism is called a(n)

(a) mutation (b) hereditary marker
(c) replicon (d) allele

20. Spontaneous mutations

(a) are caused by chemicals such as acridine and caffeine
(b) are caused by physical agents such as ultraviolet light or x-rays
(c) are the result of errors in the base pairing of nucleotides during replication
(d) occur at a rate higher than the rate of induced mutations

21. A DNA mutation that results in no change in protein product produced is termed as

(a) missense mutation
(b) nonsense mutation
(c) silent mutation
(d) frameshift mutation

22. A frameshift mutation occurs when

(a) an adenine is inserted into the DNA sequence of an organism
(b) a thymine replaces a guanine in the DNA sequence of an organism
(c) three new bases are inserted into the DNA strand
(d) three bases are deleted from the DNA strand

23. Pyrimidine dimers are a type of mutation most commonly caused by

(a) alkylating agent (b) deaminating agent
(c) ultraviolet light (d) acridine

24. Photoreactivation

(a) repairs dimers in DNA using an endonuclease
(b) uses light to activate repair enzymes
(c) removes alkylating agents from bases
(d) deaminates bases

25. Organisms that have lost the ability to synthesize a particular enzyme and require certain nutrients to be added to their medium to maintain growth are called

(a) phototrophs (b) auxotrophs
(c) prototrophs (d) autotrophs

26. In fruit flies with the curly wing mutation, the wings will be straight if the flies are kept at 16 degrees Celsius. The most probable explanation for this is that

(a) fruit flies with curly wings cannot survive at high temperatures
(b) the environment influences wing phenotype in these fruit flies
(c) height temperatures increases the rate of mutations
(d) wing length in these fruit flies is directly proportional to temperature

27. Mutations can be considered as one of the raw materials of evolution because they

(a) contribute to new variations in organisms
(b) are usually related to the environment in which they appear
(c) are usually beneficial to the organism in which they appear
(d) usually cause species of organisms to become extinct

28. The process of repetitive replication of a segment of a chromosome is known as

(a) nonsense mutation
(b) missense mutation
(c) gene amplification
(d) frameshift mutation

29. Each of the following chromosome abnormalities involve a 20 megabase region of the long arm of chromosome 5 (5q). Which abnormality is more likely to cause severe disease?

(a) Deletion of the region
(b) Duplication of the region
(c) A balanced translocation involving the region (i.e., in the translocation carrier)
(d) Pericentric inversion
(e) Paracentric inversion

30. Mutations that impact evolution must occur in

(a) somatic cells
(b) brain cells
(c) germline cells
(d) sperm cells

31. Ultraviolet light can cause the formation of double bonds between adjacent pyrimidines, resulting in a formation called

(a) pyrimidine mispairing
(b) pyrimidine-pyrimidine pairing
(c) pyrimidine dimer
(d) pyrimidine pseudopairing

32. Chemical modification of DNA may be caused by

(a) chemicals that resemble DNA nucleotides
(b) chemicals that remove amino acids from adenine to cytosine
(c) chemicals that add hydrocarbon groups to nucleotide bases
(d) all of the above

33. Which of the following would be most likely to produce a pedigree in which there is only one affected individual with no previous family history of the genetic disorder?

(a) Autosomal dominant disease with 80% penetrance
(b) Autosomal recessive disease
(c) Germline mosaicism for an autosomal dominant disease
(d) New mutation for an autosomal dominant disease
(e) X-linked recessive disease

34. When a nucleotide is lost from the normal DNA sequence, it is

(a) deletion
(b) silent substitution
(c) missense substitution
(d) frameshift mutation

35. Some mutations have been found that are expressed differently depending on the sex of the parent the gene is passed through. This is called

(a) sex-linked inheritance
(b) penetrance
(c) imprinting
(d) heterozygous
(e) incomplete dominance

36. A recessive mutation was discovered in a small island population (1,000 people). The mutation was observed in the heterozygous state, but never in the homozygous state. What is the possible explanation for this observation?

(a) Only individuals with opposite alleles at this locus reproduced
(b) The recessive allele is lethal in a homozygous state
(c) The heterozygous state is "fixed" in this population
(d) The population size is too small to give an explanation for this phenomenon

37. A missense mutation involves

(a) a change in the 3′ base of a codon, which, therefore, may be silent or nondetrimental
(b) a change in the first or second base of a codon, which may, therefore, be detrimental
(c) a one-base insertion that changes a codon to a stop codon leading to a truncated protein, which may sometimes be lethal
(d) a deletion following an addition, or an addition following a deletion mutation, which, therefore, negates the first mutation
(e) The ability of a normal gene to cover up the activity of a mutated copy of that gene

38. A nonsense mutation involves

(a) a change in the 3′ base of a codon, which, therefore, may be silent or nondetrimental
(b) a change in the first or second base of a codon, which may, therefore, be detrimental
(c) a one-base insertion that changes a codon to a stop codon leading to a truncated protein, which may sometimes be lethal
(d) a deletion following an addition, or an addition following a deletion mutation, which, therefore, negates the first mutation
(e) The ability of a normal gene to cover up the activity of a mutated copy of that gene

39. Glycosidase is an enzyme involved in DNA repair. This enzyme would be necessary in the repair of the following type of damage to DNA
(a) purine dimer formation
(b) deamination
(c) thymine dimer formation
(d) depurination
(e) none of the above

40. Which one of the following answers represents two mutagens?
(a) Viruses and bacteria
(b) Microwaves and alpha particles
(c) Formaldehyde and beta particles
(d) X-rays and bacteria killed by irradiation of food
(e) Infrared and UV (ultraviolet) radiation

41. The following sequence of DNA bases may be found duplicated in cells, are highly conserved among species, and, when mutated, may lead to abnormal segmental patterns in animals
(a) histone
(b) palindromic
(c) intron
(d) homeobox
(e) heteroduplex

42. An allele that reverses the effect of the mutation of another gene, resulting in a wild-type phenotype is a(n)
(a) activator
(b) repressor
(c) suppressor
(d) dominator

43. Nonsense mutations occur when
(a) The new codon causes an incorrect amino acid to code for an incorrect protein
(b) The loss or gain of 1 or 2 nucleotides that affects the coding for a protein
(c) An alteration in sequence results in a new codon that causes the code to create an incomplete protein
(d) Chromosome break, causing loss of DNA

44. A somatic mutation is a change in the DNA that
(a) occurs in an ordinary body cell and is not transmitted to the next generation
(b) occurs in a sex cell and is not transmitted to the next generation
(c) occurs in all body cells at the same time
(d) affects the genes associated with sleep
(e) occurs in any cell and is passed onto the next generation

45. Suppressor mutations
(a) are not separable from the primary mutation by recombination
(b) can be frameshift mutations
(c) are always indistinguishable from wild type
(d) are often in T→C loops on the tRNA, permitting growth of a wild type polypeptide
(e) never revert

46. A point mutation that leads to substitution of a chemically dissimilar amino acid is called
(a) exact (b) silent
(c) synonymous (d) missense
(e) nonsense

47. Mutations that cannot revert include
(a) silent, neutral, missense and nonsense mutations
(b) lethal, sterile and temperature sensitive mutations
(c) frameshift mutations of 1 base pair
(d) large deletions and insertions
(e) transversions and transitions

48. The two pyrimidines in a DNA strand are
(a) cytosine and adenine
(b) thymine and guanine
(c) cytosine and guanine
(d) cytosine and thymine

49. Spontaneous mutation during DNA replication results when slippage occurs in the

(a) growing strand, causing insertions in the growing strand
(b) template strand, causing insertions in the growing strand
(c) growing strand, causing insertions in the template strand
(d) template strand, causing deletions in the template strand
(e) growing strand, causing deletions in the growing strand

50. Mutations that occur in body cells, which do not go on to form gametes, can be classified as

(a) auxotrophic mutations
(b) somatic mutations
(c) morphological mutations
(d) oncogenes
(e) temperature sensitive mutations

51. A mutation in a codon leads to the substitution of one amino acid with another. What is the name for this type of mutation?

(a) Nonsense mutation
(b) Missense mutation
(c) Frameshift mutation
(d) Promoter mutation
(e) Operator mutation

52. A homeotic mutation is one which

(a) is present in only one form in an individual
(b) substitutes one body part for another in development
(c) results in development of a tumour
(d) is wild type at one temperature and abnormal at another
(e) leads to increased body size in an organism

53. Most new mutations appear to be

(a) beneficial
(b) neutral or deleterious
(c) present in homozygotes rather than heterozygotes
(d) detectable using allozyme studies (protein electrophoresis)
(e) present within pericentric inversions

54. A mutation in which most of the protein coding sequence of the gene is removed is most likely to be which type of allele?

(a) Lethal (b) Dominant
(c) Loss of function (d) Sex-limited

55. Chromosome mutations

(a) are random changes in genes
(b) confer no resistance
(c) are cell organelles
(d) are the sum total of genetic material in the nucleus
(e) are gross changes in the genome, involving the number and the structure of the chromosomes

56. Most reliable studies of mutation in humans are restricted to the novel appearance of

(a) recessive genes
(b) dominant genes
(c) both a and b are true
(d) both a and b are false

57. Pseudogenes are important to evolution because

(a) they are silent genes that have been activated by mutations
(b) they did not exist until recently
(c) they occur entirely within multigene families
(d) mutational changes may convert them to active genes, encoding a protein with different properties
(e) they tend to be transcribed more frequently

58. Double-strand breaks in DNA are lethal to the descendants of

(a) bacteria
(b) fungi
(c) insects
(d) algae
(e) reptiles

59. Slipped mispairing may cause deletions resulting in

(a) single nucleotide substitution
(b) translocations
(c) frameshift mutation
(d) insertion activation
(e) errors in nucleotide choice

60. The primary effect of ultraviolet radiation is the production of

(a) two-stranded breaks in DNA
(a) pyrimidine dimers
(b) base analogue mispairing
(c) isomerization of a base
(d) slipped mispairing

61. Which of the following conditions is caused by a trinucleotide (triplet) repeat expansion?

(a) Cystic fibrosis
(b) Duchenne muscular dystrophy
(c) Huntington disease
(d) *Osteogenesis imperfecta*

62. Gene conversion refers to

(a) a DNA segment being reversed in a chromosome
(b) insertion of a transposon that alters the reading frame
(c) the formation of plasmids from a bacterial genome
(d) single nucleotide substitution caused by a base analogue mispairing
(e) alterations in homologues as mismatch pair errors are corrected

63. Crop improvement can utilize which of the following mutations?

(a) Lethal (b) Sublethal
(c) Subvital (d) Vital

64. The term "mutation" was coined by

(a) Morgen (b) Muller
(c) Stadler (d) De Vries

65. White-eyed mutant in *Drosophila* was first reported in 1910 by

(a) Muller (b) De Vries
(c) Stadler (d) Morgan

66. Which of the following mutagens is a base analogue?

(a) EMS (b) 5 BU
(c) EES (d) MMS

67. Which of the following mutagens is an acridine dye?

(a) EMS (b) 2 AP
(c) Ethidium bromide (d) 5 BU

68. Which are the examples of particulate radiation in the following?

(a) Alpha rays and beta rays
(b) Fast neutrons and thermal neutrons
(c) X-rays and UV rays
(d) Both (a) and (b)

69. Which of the following mutagens is an alkylating agent?

(a) Proflavin (b) EMS
(c) 5 BU (d) Acriflavin

70. 5 bromouracil (5 BU) is

(a) alkylating agent (b) base analogue
(c) acridine dye (d) none of these

71. Ethyl methane sulphonate is

(a) base analogue (b) alkylating agent
(c) hormone (d) acridine dye

72. Frameshift mutagens refer to

(a) alkylating agent (b) radiations
(c) acridine dyes (d) base analogues

73. Muller first used X-rays for induction of mutation in

(a) *Drosophila* (b) barley
(c) datura (d) corn

74. Which are the examples of electromagnetic radiations among the following?

(a) Alpha and beta rays
(b) X-rays and gamma rays
(c) Fast neutrons and thermal neutrons
(d) All of the above

75. The term "muton" was coined in 1957 by

(a) Muller (b) Stadler
(c) Mike (d) Benzer

76. The term "point mutation" was first used by

(a) Morgan (b) Muller
(c) Stadler (d) Bridges

77. Terms "transition" and "transversions" were coined by

(a) Benzer (b) Freeze
(c) Muller (d) Brenner

78. Which are commonly used in mutation breeding as alkylating agents?

(a) Sulphur and nitrogen mustard
(b) Ethylene imine and ethylmethane sulphonate
(c) Methylmethane sulphonate and epoxides
(d) Ethidium bromide and hydroxyl amine

79. A gene that exhibits higher mutation rate than other genes is called

(a) mutator gene (b) mutable gene
(c) hot spot (d) anti-mutator gene

80. With a gene, a unit of mutation is called

(a) hot spot (b) muton
(c) recon (d) cistron

81. Which are the examples of base analogues among the following?

(a) 5-bromouracil and 5-chlorouracil
(b) Acriflavine and proflavine
(c) Ethidium bromide and hydroxyl amine
(d) Sodium azide and nitrous acid

82. For mutation research, Nobel prize was awarded to

(a) Morgan (b) De Vries
(c) Stadler (d) Muller

83. A mutation, which kills more than 50% of the individuals that carry the mutation, is called

(a) lethal (b) sub-vital
(c) vital (d) sub-lethal

84. Which of the following mutagens is less penetrating?

(a) X-rays (b) Beta rays
(c) UV rays (d) Gamma rays

85. Among the given chemical mutagens, which ones are the examples of acridine dyes?

(a) Acriflavine and proflavine
(b) Ethidium bromide and proflavine
(c) Acridine yellow and acridine orange
(d) All of the above

86. Which of the following mutagens is non-particulate?

(a) X-rays (b) Alpha particles
(c) Beta particles (d) Gamma rays

87. Which of the following is not an effect of a mutation?

(a) Prevents a protein from forming
(b) Lowers the amount of a protein
(c) Adds a function to a protein
(d) Any of the above can occur

88. Two healthy people have a child expressing a genetic condition caused by a dominant allele. What can you conclude from this situation?

(a) Infidelity—one parent had to contribute the disease allele
(b) The parents are not free from the disorder—one must be affected
(c) The mutation arose spontaneously in the child
(d) The child is not the biological child of the couple described

89. A point mutation that changes a codon specifying an amino acid into a stop codon is called

(a) missense mutation
(b) nonsense mutation
(c) frameshift mutation
(d) deletion mutation

90. A ______ mutation originates during meiosis, while a ______ mutation originates during mitosis

(a) germinal, somatic
(b) germinal, spontaneous
(c) somatic, germinal
(d) spontaneous, point

91. DNA is repaired by ______ in which a pyrimidine dimer is split

(a) excision repair (b) photoreactivation
(c) mismatch repair (d) proofreading repair

92. Changing the codon AGC to AGA represents a ______ mutation

(a) missense (b) nonsense
(c) frameshift (d) deletion

93. What is the physical basis of mutational hotspots?

(a) Transposons (b) Tautomers
(c) Palindromes (d) Transitions

94. A ______ mutation affects the phenotype only under certain conditions

(a) spontaneous (b) somatic
(c) site-directed (d) conditional

95. A ______ mutation is intentionally caused

(a) spontaneous (b) somatic
(c) site-directed (d) conditional

96. Which of the following genetic diseases results from a mutation that prevents a protein from forming?

(a) Duchenne muscular dystrophy
(b) Hemophilia A
(c) Epidermolysis bullosa
(d) Huntington disease

97. Which of the following genetic diseases results from a mutation that lowers the amount of protein produced?

(a) Duchenne muscular dystrophy
(b) Hemophilia A
(c) Epidermolysis bullosa
(d) Huntington disease

98. Which disease is the result of a somatic mutation?

(a) Retinoblastoma (b) Neurofibromatosis
(c) Down syndrome (d) Huntington disease

99. A spontaneous mutation usually originates as an error in

(a) DNA replication
(b) DNA transcription
(c) translation
(d) reverse transcription

100. The codon for leucine is CUC. How many different amino acids could possibly result from single-base substitutions?

(a) 1 (b) 3
(c) 5 (d) 7

101. A frameshift mutation

(a) replaces one amino acid with another
(b) removes part of the protein
(c) introduces a section of amino acids not normally found
(d) joins two different proteins

102. Which characteristic of the genetic code lowers the likelihood of mutation

(a) universality
(b) degeneracy
(c) triplet
(d) non-overlapping nature

103. Chemicals or other agents that cause birth defects are called

(a) transformers (b) carcinogens
(c) alterations (d) teratogens

104. The International Atomic Energy Agency is located at

(a) Vienna (b) Rome
(c) Tokyo (d) Washington

105. Dominant mutations can be selected in

(a) M1 generation
(b) M2 generation
(c) M3 generation
(d) M2 and M3 generation

106. In the case of plants, which of the following will be the most difficult to identify with reasonable confidence?

(a) Inversion
(b) Translocation
(c) Small deletion or duplication
(d) Cytoplasmic mutation

107. Which chemical was the first to be shown to be mutagenic by Auerbach and Robson?

(a) Nitrogen mustard
(b) Ethylene imine
(c) Ethidium bromide
(d) Ethylmethane sulphonate

108. In case of gene x having two alleles, X and x, which is the appropriate genotype for lethal action if the lethal effect of allele X is recessive?

(a) XX (b) Xx
(c) xx (d) Both a and b

109. Frameshift mutations are produced by base

(a) addition (b) substitution
(c) deletion (d) both (a) and (c)

110. Which one is the most likely to produce a non-functional gene product?

(a) Transversion
(b) Transition
(c) Addition of a base
(d) Addition/deletion of a base

111. Which one is the most optimum dose of a mutagen out of the following?

(a) LD 50
(b) Close to LD 50
(c) Lower than LD 50
(d) Higher than LD 50

112. The largest number of mutant varieties have been developed in

(a) oilseeds (b) cereals
(c) pulses (d) forage crops

113. Which of the following mutagens has given the most number of mutant varieties?

(a) Physical mutagens
(b) Chemical mutagens
(c) Both of them
(d) None of them

114. Although one nucleotide is replaced by another, the resultant amino acid that is produced remains the same in a

(a) deletion
(b) silent substitution
(c) missense substitution
(d) frameshift mutation

115. The substitution of one nucleotide by another results in the formation of a different amino acid in a

(a) deletion
(b) silent substitution
(c) missense substitution
(d) frameshift mutation

116. The type of mutation that causes sickle-cell anaemia is a

(a) deletion
(b) silent substitution
(c) missense substitution
(d) frameshift mutation

117. Diseases resulting from mutations in mitochondrial genes affect

(a) protein synthesis (b) energy acquisition
(c) both (a) and (b) (d) neither (a) nor (b)

118. Mutations are errors in DNA that

(a) are always harmful
(b) occur only in the presence of carcinogens
(c) increase tumour growth
(d) occur spontaneously at a low rate
(e) occur only on the X chromosome

119. A nonsense mutation involves

(a) a regulatory sequence
(b) an AG splice acceptor site
(c) the creation of a different amino acid
(d) the creation of a stop codon

120. Exon skipping is associated with

(a) nonsense mutations
(b) regulatory mutations
(c) RNA processing mutations
(d) silent mutations

121. What is the overall rate at which new mutations arise spontaneously at any given site on the chromosome per round of replication?

(a) $10^{-8} - 10^{-12}$ (b) $10^{-7} - 10^{-9}$
(c) $10^{-6} - 10^{-11}$ (d) $10^{-5} - 10^{-10}$

122. What Is the dinucleotide sequence of microsatellites?

(a) CA (b) AT
(c) CC (d) GC

123. By which process mis(-incorporated base can change into a permanent mutation?

(a) Replication (b) Transcription
(c) Translation (d) Transposition

124. By which enzyme does *E. coli* tag its parental DNA strand?

(a) Methylase (b) Polymerase
(c) Phosphorylase (d) Acetylase

125. Which of the following is not a type of reverse mutation?

(a) Back mutation
(b) Intergenic suppressor mutation
(c) Intragenic suppressor mutation
(d) Missense mutation

126. Which of the following is not true for loss of function mutation?

(a) Usually recessive
(b) Most common mutation
(c) Increases the activity of the gene
(d) Null allelic mutation

127. Name the term given to the type of mutation which depends on the conditions of the environment?

(a) Forward mutation
(b) Reverse mutation
(c) Conditional lethal mutation
(d) Gain of function mutation

128. What is the detection technique of auxotrophs?

(a) Spread plating (b) Replica plating
(c) Streaking (d) Pouring

129. Name the type of mutation in which the cause of mutation is not known?

(a) Spontaneous mutation
(b) Suppressor mutation
(c) Nonsense mutation
(d) Missense mutation

130. Which of the following chemical mutagen affects only replicating DNA?

(a) Acridine dye
(b) Alkylating agent
(c) Deaminating agent
(d) Base analog

131. Transition type of gene mutation is caused when

(a) GC is replaced by TA
(b) CG is replaced by GC
(c) AT is replaced by CG
(d) AT is replaced by GC

132. Gene mutation occurs at the time of

(a) DNA repair
(b) DNA replication
(c) Cell division
(d) RNA transcription

133. The action of ultraviolet radiation on DNA to induce mutation is

(a) formation of thymine dimers
(b) methylation of base pairs
(c) deletion of base pairs
(d) addition of base pairs

134. X-rays cause mutation by

(a) deletion (b) transition
(c) transversion (d) base substitution

135. Which of the following are not ionising radiations?

(a) X rays (b) UV rays
(c) Cosmic rays (d) Alpha rays

136. Cell mutations within a DNA sequence are

(a) unnatural events that are harmful to genetic diversity
(b) unnatural events that always affect the phenotype
(c) natural events that produce genetic diversity
(d) natural events that always affect the phenotype

137. Nonsense mutations occur when

(a) The new codon causes an incorrect amino acid to code for an incorrect protein
(b) The loss or gain of 1 or 2 nucleotides that affects the coding for a protein
(c) An alteration in sequence results in a new codon that causes the code to create an incomplete protein
(d) genes in chromosome mutate and code for incorrect DNA

138. Changes in DNA sequences during replication can lead to

(a) missense mutations
(b) nonsense mutations
(c) aneuploidy
(d) (a) and (b)

MARK TRUE OR FALSE (T/F)

1. Mutations may be recessive because cells can increase the amount of functional protein produced from their remaining normal allele
2. Familial Hypercholesterolemia is produced by a mutation of a dominant gene on the X chromosome
3. Proto-oncogenes regulate the normal cell division
4. Photoreactivation can take place in non-photosynthetic bacteria
5. Frameshift mutations are typically more serious than point mutations
6. Photoreactivation occurs when UV light causes mutations to occur in DNA
7. A mutation can alter the genotype of an organism without altering the phenotype
8. Spontaneous mutations are the result of exposure to mutagens
9. Bacteria that have lost the ability to produce certain nutritional substances are called auxotrophs
10. Prototrophs are nutritional mutations
11. A technique for the screening and detection of nutritional mutations in *Neurospora* was developed by Lederberg
12. Mice and corn appear to have mutation rates of the same order as *Drosophila* and humans

13. Measurement of most ionizing radiation is done in terms of Roentgen units
14. Commonly, mutations show pleiotropy
15. Electromagnetic radiations produce photo-electric effect
16. Pollen grains are not used for mutagen treatment
17. Mutagen treatment reduces fertility and vigour
18. Several spontaneous mutants have been released as varieties
19. Mutations are more frequent in clonal crops
20. UV radiations produce ions
21. Nitroso compounds are used for mutation breeding
22. The primary effect of radiations is to cause ionization
23. Maximum number of varieties have been developed in cereals through hybridization between mutants
24. Mutations produced by changes in the base sequence of a gene are gene mutations
25. Forward mutations are mutations of a wild type to a normal allele
26. The part of a gene that functions as a mutation is a cistron
27. Chimera has different genotypes in its different tissues
28. When a purine is replaced by a pyrimidine, it is called transition
29. Formation of covalent bonds between two bases located within the same DNA strand is known as a dimer formation
30. An allele that has completely lost the function of normal allele is known as a neomorph
31. An allele that has acquired a new function is known as amorph
32. Vital mutations do not reduce the viability of individuals
33. Hypermorph is an allele that functions more efficiently than a normal allele
34. Muller got Nobel prize for his work on mutagenic action of gamma rays
35. Individuals homozygous for recessive lethals die
36. 5-Bromouracil is a base analogue
37. Beta-rays are more penetrative than X-rays
38. X-rays and gamma-rays are electromagnetic radiations
39. UV radiations are produced by UV mercury vapor lamps
40. Free radicals have a very long life
41. Deletions produce frameshift mutations
42. For mutagenesis, plants are irradiated during fruit formation
43. Low wavelength of radiations means low penetration in biological material
44. For polygenic traits, selection for promising mutations is done in M3
45. Mutagenesis is mostly done in cross-pollinated species
46. Transversion is a base substitution
47. Mutations are generally recessive
48. Hydroxylamine is an alkylating agent
49. Cytosine is less sensitive to radiation damage than guanine
50. Only the best variety is selected for mutagenesis
51. During mutation breeding out crossing is a problem
52. Irradiation can be used to break undesirable linkages
53. Mutagenesis is not commonly used in polyploidy species
54. Familial Hyperchloesterolaemia may lead to early coronary heart disease
55. Familial Hypercholesterolemia never arises as a new mutation in a family

56. Familial Hypercholesterolemia in a homozygous state usually leads to a severe form of the disease
57. Familial Hypercholesterolemia is not associated with late maternal age
58. Mutated proto-oncogenes are associated with cancer
59. Gene translocation can transform proto-oncogenes
60. Viral insertion can disrupt normal proto-oncogenes
61. The mutation occurs at a random basis within a genome
62. Detection of mismatches and fidelity of replication is maintained by mutation repair system
63. Mismatch repair system is ATP dependent
64. High level of mutation in the germ cells is acceptable but in somatic cells can be catastrophic
65. All types of mutations are transferable among the generations
66. All mutations are bad
67. Because they arise from a single precursor cell, tumour cells are generally identical

16

Genetic Material (DNA and RNA)

MULTIPLE-CHOICE QUESTIONS

1. **This nucleic acid has a recognition site that allows it to bind to a specific amino acid**
   (a) DNA (b) mRNA
   (c) tRNA (d) rRNA

2. **Which of the following is not a base used in DNA replication?**
   (a) Cytosine (b) Uracil
   (c) Thymine (d) Guanine
   (e) Adenine

3. **Nitrogenous base that occurs in RNA but not in DNA**
   (a) deoxyribose (b) ribose
   (c) uracil (d) cytosine
   (e) thymine

4. **Sugar that occurs in DNA but not in RNA**
   (a) deoxyribose (b) ribose
   (c) uracil (d) cytosine
   (e) thymine

5. **A nitrogenous base that occurs in DNA in equal quantities with guanine**
   (a) deoxyribose (b) ribose
   (c) uracil (d) cytosine
   (e) thymine

6. **Which one of the following is not a nitrogenous base present in nucleic acids?**
   (a) Cytosine (b) Adenine
   (c) Guanine (d) Pyridine

7. **Which one of the following is not the correct nucleotide of cytosine**
   (a) cytosine 5' monophosphate
   (b) cytidine 5' monophosphate
   (c) cytidylic acid
   (d) CMP

8. **The nitrogenous base absent in RNA is**
   (a) uracil (b) adenine
   (c) thymine (d) guanine

9. The increase in absorption at 260 nm during denaturation of DNA is due to

(a) breakdown of DNA
(b) unstacking of bases
(c) removal of phosphate groups
(d) removal of nitrogenous bases

10. Which of the following statements is not true with eukaryotic mRNA?

(a) They are capped at 5' terminus
(b) They are capped at 3' terminus
(c) Poly A tail is present
(d) They are invariably monocistronic

11. Which of the following is not a characteristic of DNA?

(a) Antiparallel
(b) Composed of nucleotides
(c) Complementary
(d) Contains ribose
(e) Double-stranded

12. The DNA of a certain organism has guanine as 40% of its bases. What percentage of its bases would be adenine?

(a) 0% (b) 10%
(c) 20% (d) 30%

13. Nucleosides are made up of

(a) a sugar and a base
(b) sugar, base and a phosphate group
(c) purines and pyrimidines
(d) nucleosomes and histones
(e) none of the above

14. When James Watson and Francis Crick were working on the model for DNA, which main construction constituent did they use in their enlarged, full-sized model?

(a) Wood (b) Metal plastic
(c) Cardboard (d) Stone

15. Cytosine makes up 38% of the nucleotides in a sample of DNA from an organism. What per cent of the nucleo-tides in this sample will be thymine?

(a) 12 (b) 24
(c) 31 (d) 38
(e) It cannot be determined from the information provided

16. A eukaryotic cell lacking telomerase would

(a) be unable to take up DNA from solution
(b) be unable to identify where transcription should begin
(c) have a greater potential to become cancerous
(d) incorporate one extraneous nucleotide for each Okazaki fragment
(e) experience a gradual reduction in length with each replication cycle

17. An RNA molecule folds back upon itself to form a "hairpin" structure held together by a region of base pairing. One segment of the molecule in the paired region has the base sequence 5'-GCAUUGA-3'. What is the base sequence with which this segment is paired?

(a) 5'-UCAAUGC-3'
(b) 5'-GCAUUGA-3'
(c) 5'-TCAATGC-3'
(d) 5'-GCATTGA-3'

18. The sequence of the transcript is 5'-GGUUACAUUC-3'. The sequence of the DNA template would be

(a) 5'-GGUUACAUUC-3'
(b) 5'-GAATGTAACC-3'
(c) 5'-CCAATGTAAG-3'
(d) 5'-CUUACAUUGG-3'

19. If a DNA strand has 10% cytosine, what per cent of its bases is thymine?

(a) 10% (b) 20%
(c) 30% (d) 40%

20. The correct structure of a nucleotide is

(a) phosphate-ribose-adenine
(b) phospholipid-sugar-base
(c) phosphate-sugar-phosphate-sugar
(d) adenine-thymine or guanine-cytosine

21. Genetic information usually flows in one specific direction. Which of the following best represents this flow?

(a) DNA→Protein→RNA

(b) Protein→RNA→DNA

(c) RNA→Protein→DNA

(d) DNA→RNA→Protein

22. Average molecular weight of 1 nucleotide pair is equal to

(a) 200 daltons (b) 330 daltons

(c) 660 daltons (d) 400 daltons

23. A plant useful in the study of plant genomes because of its small genome size is

(a) *Avena sativa*

(b) *Petunia porodii*

(c) *Tulipa* spp.

(d) *Arabidopsis thaliana*

(e) *Pisum sativum*

24. The term "nucleic acid" was first used by

(a) Miescher (b) Mendel

(c) Watson (d) Altmann

25. The term "nucleotide" was coined by

(a) Watson (b) Levene

(c) Benzer (d) Crick

26. For double helical model of DNA, Watson and Crick were awarded Nobel prize in

(a) 1953 (b) 1958

(c) 1960 (d) 1955

27. Which of the following is a single ring structure?

(a) Adenine (b) Cytosine

(c) Guanine (d) All of these

28. Who first reported DNA as genetic material?

(a) Griffith

(b) Hershey and Chase

(c) Benzer

(d) Avery, MacCleod and McCarty

29. How many hydrogen bonds join adenine and thymine in a DNA molecule?

(a) Single (b) Triple

(c) Double (d) All of these

30. How many hydrogen bonds join guanine and cytosine in a DNA molecule?

(a) One (b) Three

(c) Four (d) Two

31. Which of the following nitrogenous bases has double ring structure?

(a) Adenine (b) Cytosine

(c) Uracil (d) Thymine

32. RNA acts as a genetic material in

(a) TMV (b) *E. Coli*

(c) *Neurospora* (d) none of these

33. The term "promiscuous DNA" was coined by

(a) Temin (b) Ellis

(c) Kohne (d) Baltimore

34. The term "repetitive DNA" was first used by

(a) Watson and Crick (b) Jacob and Monod

(c) Britten and Kohne (d) none of these

35. The term "selfish DNA" was first used by

(a) Britten (b) Watson

(c) Wang *et al.* (d) Crick

36. The term "Z-DNA" was coined by

(a) Davidson (b) Britten

(c) Crick (d) Wang *et al.*

37. Transduction was first reported by

(a) Beadle and Tatum

(b) Griffith

(c) Ephrussi

(d) Zinder and Lederberg

38. The term "messenger RNA" was first used by

(a) Benzer (b) Crick

(c) Waston (d) Brenner *et al.*

39. The term "transfer RNA" was coined by

(a) Hoagland *et al.* (b) Watson
(c) Hall *et al.* (d) Brenner *et al.*

40. Who reported that in TMV, RNA is the genetic material?

(a) Conrat and Singer (b) Brenner *et al.*
(c) Hall *et al.* (d) Griffith

41. Semi-conservative replication of DNA was reported in 1957 by

(a) Conrat and Singer (b) Watson
(c) Crick (d) Delbruck and Slent

42. Semi-conservative replication of DNA was confirmed by

(a) Meselson and Stahl (b) Taylor
(c) Cairns (d) all of these

43. Rolling circle model of circular DNA replication was proposed in 1968 by

(a) Cairns (b) Taylor
(c) Watson and Crick (d) Dressler

44. Man has a DNA length per haploid cell of approximately

(a) 10 centimeters (b) 5 meters
(c) 10.1 meters (d) 1.1 meters

45. DNA differs from RNA because

(a) DNA is always double-stranded whereas RNA is always single-stranded
(b) one strand of the DNA doesn't make any sense, whereas both RNA strands make some sense
(c) DNA contains uracil, whereas RNA contains thymine
(d) DNA contains information whereas RNA doesn't
(e) DNA contains deoxyribose, whereas RNA contains ribose

46. In nucleic acids

(a) phosphate is attached to position 1 of the sugar
(b) phosphate is attached to position 2 of the sugar
(c) polymerisation occurs by a condensation reaction involving the 3' phosphate of one nucleotide and the 5' hydroxyl of the other
(d) bases are attached to position 1 of the sugar
(e) bases are attached to position 3 of the sugar

47. Which of the following statements about nucleic acids is true?

(a) DNA and RNA are isomers because they have the same elemental composition
(b) Adenine and guanine are purines
(c) Uracil and thymine are pyrimidines, with each containing two hexagonal rings
(d) The sugar-phosphate backbone is held together by hydrogen bonds
(e) In any sample of DNA, the total amount of adenine plus guanine is equal to the total amount of cytosine plus uracil

48. The two polynucleotide chains in a DNA molecule are like the north and south bound lanes of an interstate because they show

(a) cloverleaf patterns
(b) lots of repair work
(c) a helical structure
(d) antiparallel orientation

49. If the sequence of bases in a section of DNA is TAGGCTAA, what is the corresponding sequence of bases in mRNA?

(a) ATCCGATT (b) TAGGCTAA
(c) AUCCGAUU (d) AATCGGAT

50. A segment of a eukaryotic gene that codes for a specific protein segment is called

(a) an intron (b) an exon
(c) a promoter (d) an operon

51. The difference between a simple tandem array and a compound tandem array is the

(a) frequency of different sequences
(b) direction the sequences face (left or right)
(c) number of different sequences involved
(d) number of repetitions of sequences

52. Bacteriophage genomes can be

(a) DNA only
(b) RNA only
(c) DNA or RNA
(d) none of the above

53. Which of the following is not correct nucleotide of cytosine

(a) Cytosine 5′ monophosphate
(b) Cytidine 5′ monophosphate
(c) Cytidylic acid
(d) CMP

54. The increase in absorption at 260 nm during denaturation of DNA is due to

(a) shining of DNA
(b) unstacking of bases
(c) removal of sugar groups
(d) removal of nitrogenous bases

55. The central dogma of genetics states that

(a) genetics is more important than all other branches of biological sciences
(b) the phenotype is determined entirely by the genotype
(c) information flows from genotype to phenotype
(d) information flows from phenotype to genotype
(e) all organisms are equal

56. Eukaryotic-like (possessing a defined nucleus) cells were obtained from a soil sample. The nucleus was carefully isolated and the chromatin obtained. The fibres had a "beads on a string" appearance, suggesting some type of "histones." Following digestion with micrococcal nuclease, protein removal, and gel electrophoresis, DNA fragments were obtained that were multiples of 280 base pairs in length. Longer incubation with micrococcal nuclease prior to protein removal results in fragments 200 base pairs in length. The amount of DNA that is wrapped around the "core histones" is therefore

(a) 80 base pairs in length
(b) 200 base pairs in length
(c) 360 base pairs in length
(d) 480 base pairs in length
(e) not enough information is given to determine the answer

57. Ribose has five carbon atoms, of which three are asymmetric. What is the maximum number of stereoisomers that may exist for ribose?

(a) 8 (b) 6
(c) 10 (d) 2
(e) 4

58. One reason that prokaryotic genes do not contain introns is that

(a) bacterial proteins are very short and not subject to mutation
(b) integrated viral DNA is not recognized for transcription
(c) due to the short time the bacterium is around as a single organism, a 5′ cap and poly A tail are added immediately for translation to take place
(d) as prokaryotes do not have a nucleus, translation sometimes begins before the transcription has been completed
(e) the introns are cut out during binary fission

59. You and your neighbor have how much difference in DNA sequence?

(a) 0.01% (b) 0.1%
(c) 1% (d) 10%
(e) 25%

60. DNA isolated from *Aspergillus* has an adenine content of 25%. Based upon this information, what is the %G+C within the *Aspergillus* DNA?

(a) 0% (b) 25%
(c) 50% (d) 75%
(e) Answer cannot be determined from this information

61. DNA isolated from cow liver cells contains 28% A; what per cent will be C?

(a) 14% (b) 22%
(c) 28% (d) 36%
(e) 56%

62. Which of the following is true of purines?

(a) Cytosine is a purine
(b) Purines bind readily to deoxyribose, but not ribose
(c) Purines have a double-ringed structure
(d) Adenine's bonding to thymine is stronger than is guanine's to cytosine
(e) Both adenine and thymine are purines

63. Which of the following biological polymers is mismatched with its monomer?

(a) DNA—nucleotide
(b) Cellulose—amino acid
(c) Enzyme—amino acid
(d) Protein—amino acid
(e) Chitin—monosaccharide

64. The ______ model of DNA structure was proposed by ______

(a) gene; Fleming and Pasteur
(b) one gene-one enzyme; Beadle and Tatum
(c) double helix; Watson and Crick
(d) nuclear; Morrison
(e) chromosome; Hotaling

65. The structure of DNA proposed by Watson and Crick was primarily based on the experimental works of

(a) Chargaff and Pauling
(b) Chargaff, Franklin, and Wilkins
(c) Pauling and Franklin
(d) Watson and Franklin

66. The scientist who shared Nobel prize with James D. Watson and F. Crick for the structure of DNA was

(a) Har Govind Khurana
(b) Nirenberg
(c) Maurice Wilkins
(d) Swaminathan

67. Regions of genes that do not code for a protein are called

(a) primers (b) introns
(c) Okazaki fragments (d) exon

68. RNA polymerases use ______ as a template to synthesize ______

(a) RNA, protein (b) RNA, DNA
(c) DNA, RNA (d) DNA, protein

69. In DNA, the base adenine always pairs with the base

(a) guanine (b) cytosine
(c) thymidine (d) adenine

70. In rRNA, the base guanine pairs with the base

(a) guanine and / or cytosine
(b) cytosine and / or thymidine
(c) thymidine and / or guanine
(d) adenine and / or thymidine

71. An mRNA molecule can be broken down into three nucleotide units called

(a) amino acid (b) base
(c) codon (d) anticodons

72. Which nitrogenous base is not normally found in DNA

(a) guanine (b) thymine
(c) uracil (d) adenine

73. RNA is sometimes the genetic material in

(a) viruses (b) animals
(c) yeast (d) bacteria
(e) plants

74. For double-stranded DNA, which is not necessarily true?

(a) C/G = 1
(b) A + G = T + C
(c) A/T = 1
(d) A + C = T + G
(e) A + T = C + G

75. Of the following strands of DNA, in combination with their complement in the form of a double helix, three undergo a hyperchromic shift with a T_m (melting temperature) of about 42 degrees Celsius. One has a T_m of 52 degrees Celsius. Which is that strand?

(a) AAATTTGGGA
(b) TAACTACGAA
(c) TCATGCGATC
(d) CTTAAATTTG
(e) ATTGAGTGTA

BIOLOGICAL SIGNIFICANCE OF DNA-TRANSFORMATION

76. Bacterial transformation was first discovered by

(a) Watson and Crick
(b) Avery, Macleod, and McCarty
(c) Joshua Ryan
(d) Frederick Griffith

77. Avery, MacLeod, and McCarty (1944) demonstrated that DNA was the molecule of heredity by treating heat killed *Streptococcus pneumoniae* S (smooth) strain with DNase, thereby preventing the transfer of "transforming substance" from the killed S strain to the live R (rough) strain when the two were mixed together and injected into mice. Another way that one could demonstrate transformation in bacteria would be to extract DNA from

(a) an ampicillin-sensitive strain and mix with the cells of an ampicillin-resistant strain
(b) a R strain and mix with the cells of a S strain
(c) both S and R strains and mix to allow recombination to take place
(d) a S strain and mix with cells of a R strain
(e) none of the above

78. R type strain of *S. pneumoniae* does not cause pneumonia, because bacterial cells

(a) are surrounded by a polysaccharide capsule
(b) are unable to synthesize a polysaccharide capsule
(c) are undetectable by the immune system
(d) are unable to form colonies

79. In 1928, Frederick Griffith's experiments with *Streptococcus pneumoniae* suggested that

(a) attenuated R (rough) bacteria easily revert to the wild type (virulent)
(b) heat-killed bacteria could somehow "transform" live bacteria
(c) bacteria do not incorporate the DNA of other bacteria
(d) DNA was conclusively the molecule of heredity
(e) all of the above

80. In Griffith's transformation experiments, which of the following did not take place?

(a) Live, smooth pneumococci killed mice
(b) Live, rough bacteria were able to retrieve the DNA dead, encapsulated bacteria and become virulent
(c) DNA was transferred from smooth to rough bacteria by a bacteriophage
(d) Dead, smooth pneumococci had no effect on mice

81. The fact that DNA was responsible for the production of bacterial capsules in Griffith's experiments was discovered by

(a) Avery, MacLeod, and McCarthy
(b) Noah Alan and Joshua Ryan
(c) Watson and Crick
(d) Messelson and Stahl

82. In Griffith's experiments, the "transforming substance" was

(a) RNA
(b) protein
(c) polysaccharides
(d) DNA

83. In an experiment such as Griffith's pneumococcal experiment, which of the following, when injected into a mouse, would result in its death?

(a) Heat killed, smooth pneumococci
(b) Live, rough pneumococci
(c) A mixture of heat killed, smooth pneumococci, and live, rough pneumococci
(d) A mixture of heat killed, rough pneumococci, and live, rough pneumococci

84. Cells able to accept naked DNA from the surrounding medium are said to be

(a) transduction-ready
(b) capable
(c) competent
(d) porated

85. The transfer of DNA between bacteria cells by a virus is

(a) transformation
(b) transduction
(c) transferration
(d) conjugation

86. If, in the transformation experiment of Griffith, a mixture of heat-killed rough bacteria and living rough bacteria were injected into a mouse, it would be expected to

(a) cause transformation
(b) cause transduction
(c) cause transfection
(d) kill the mouse
(e) have no effect on it

REPLICATION AND SYNTHESIS OF DNA

87. Which DNA polymerase in prokaryotes is characteristic of polymerase activity in the 5'—>3' direction and with a processivity of 250 to 1000 nucleotides per second?

(a) DNA polmerase I
(b) DNA polymerase II
(c) DNA polymerase III
(d) No DNA polymerase has this type of specific activity

88. The enzyme responsible for joining Okazaki fragments is

(a) DNA polymerase I
(b) DNA ligase
(c) DNA helicase
(d) DNA gyrase
(e) none of the above

89. All of the following are functions of DNA polymerase in DNA replication except

(a) proofreading each added nucleotide for correct base pairing
(b) initiating a polynucleotide strand
(c) adding deoxyribonucleotides to the 3' end of a growing DNA strand
(d) replacing RNA primers with DNA
(e) reading the DNA template in a 3' to 5' direction

90. The reason why DNA synthesis is discontinuous on the lagging strand resulting in the synthesis of Okazaki fragments can best be described as

(a) the system simply evolved this way for reasons unknown to us
(b) the DNA polymerase can only add nucleotides in a 5' to 3' direction, and since the entire chromosome is not unwound at once, replication must progress away from the *ori* region where the DNA is first unwound
(c) the DNA polymerase can only add nucleotides in a 3' to 5' direction, and since the entire chromosome is not unwound at once, replication must progress away from the *ori* region where the DNA is first unwound
(d) there are multiple *oris* on linear chromosomes; those that are replicated first produce leading strands, while those that are opened later produce lagging strands
(e) it is easier for a cell to regulate gene expression on short pieces of DNA

91. Which of the following is the most reasonable inference from the observation that defects in DNA repair enzymes contribute to some forms of cancer

(a) cancer is generally inherited
(b) mutations generally lead to cancer
(c) cancer cannot occur when DNA repair enzymes work properly
(d) uncorrected changes in DNA can cause some cancers
(e) cancer is caused by environmental factors that damage DNA repair enzymes

92. How does the Watson and Crick model of DNA structure help explain DNA replication?

(a) Deoxyribose sugar always bonds to a nitrogenous base
(b) Precise base pairing allows the base sequence to be copied
(c) Phosphate groups always bond to deoxyribose sugar
(d) The number of purines equals the number of pyrimidines

93. Semi-conservative DNA replication means

(a) the old DNA is completely broken down
(b) the old DNA remains completely intact
(c) each new DNA molecule has half of the old one
(d) only half of the DNA is replicated

94. During replication, DNA is synthesized by

(a) DNA polymerase
(b) RNA polymerase
(c) ribosomes
(d) ribozymes

95. Replication results in the formation of what type of new molecule?

(a) DNA
(b) RNA
(c) Protein
(d) Lipid

96. The enzyme activity absent in DNA polymerase III is

(a) DNA polymerase
(b) 5′ to 3′ exonuclease
(c) 3′ to 5′ endonuclease
(d) primase

97. RNA primer formed during DNA synthesis is removed by

(a) primase
(b) DNA polymerase I
(c) DNA polymerase II
(d) DNA polymerase III

98. The nucleotide involved in DNA synthesis is

(a) ribonucleoside triphosphate
(b) deoxyribonucleoside triphosphate
(c) ribonucleoside monophosphate
(d) deoxyribonucleoside monophosphate

99. Which of the following is used in rolling circle DNA replication, but not in normal cellular DNA replication?

(a) An endonuclease
(b) An exonuclease
(c) Primase
(d) DNA ligase
(e) Helicase

100. In genetics, an origin is

(a) a protein that binds to DNA at the point where replication begins
(b) a protein that binds to DNA at the point where transcription begins
(c) a protein that binds to RNA at the point where translation begins
(d) the point in DNA where transcription starts
(e) the point in DNA where replication starts

101. Which of the following removes only bulky adducts from DNA?

(a) Thymidine dimerase
(b) DNA photolyase
(c) Suicide enzymes
(d) Primer-removal enzymes
(e) DNA methylase

102. Replication of the DNA double helix in which each strand of each daughter molecule is composed partly of the original polynucleotide and partly of new synthesized polynucleotide is known as

(a) conservative replication
(b) dispersive replication
(c) semi-conservative replication
(d) none of the above

103. Why is an RNA primer considered essential during DNA synthesis by DNA polymerase III?

(a) The enzyme requires a free 5'-OH group
(b) The enzyme requires a free 5'-PO_4 group
(c) The enzyme requires a free 3'-OH group
(d) No particular reason; that is simply the observation
(e) The enzyme requires a free 3'-PO_4 group

104. Which molecule serves to destabilize the DNA helix in order to open it up, creating a replication fork?

(a) DNA helicase (b) DNA gyrase
(c) DNA ligase (d) DNA polymerase
(e) SSBPs

105. *In vivo* synthesis of DNA is in

(a) 3' to 5' (b) 5' to 3'
(c) both (d) neither

106. The discovery of Okazaki fragments suggested that DNA synthesis is

(a) continuous (b) 3' to 5'
(c) semiconservative (d) discontinuous
(e) all of the above

107. In the Meselson-Stahl experiment, which mode of replication can be eliminated based on data derived after one generation of replication?

(a) Dispersive
(b) Semiconservative
(c) All three modes
(d) Conservative
(e) None of these three modes

108. In the Meselson and Stahl experiment, *E. coli* was grown for many generations in a medium containing ^{15}N to heavy-label the DNA, and then transferred to a medium containing ^{14}N. Double-stranded DNA was extracted after two generations and separated according to its buoyant density by centrifugation through CsCl. What result was obtained?

(a) One band of medium density only
(b) Two bands, corresponding to DNA, of light and medium density
(c) Two bands, corresponding to DNA, of medium and heavy density
(d) Two bands, corresponding to DNA, of light and heavy density
(e) Three bands, corresponding to DNA, of light, medium and heavy density

ORGANIZATION OF DNA IN GENES AND CHROMOSOMES

109. A unit of heterogenous nuclear RNA is longer than the corresponding mature messenger RNA, because it contains non-coding segments called

(a) introns (b) exons
(c) primasomes (d) histones
(e) none of the above

110. Repetitive DNA

(a) reanneals more quickly than unique sequences
(b) is found in centromeres
(c) is represented by "alu" sequences in humans
(d) is non-coding DNA
(e) all of the above are true

111. The proteins thought to be associated with and essential to the subunit of chromatin are

(a) RNA polymerases
(b) histones
(c) acidic non-histone proteins
(d) DNA polymerase
(e) all of the above

112. The B-globin gene family located on chromosomes 11 in humans consists of 50 kb of DNA. Approximately, how much of the DNA actually codes for globin gene products?

(a) 50% (b) 5%
(c) 100% (d) 75%
(e) 25%

113. The function of "high-copy-number DNA" is

(a) encoding most genes
(b) encoding rRNA
(c) encoding a single gene
(d) encoding tRNA
(e) unknown

114. The function of "low-copy-number DNA" is

(a) encoding most genes
(b) encoding rRNA
(c) encoding a single gene
(d) encoding tRNA
(e) unknown

115. The function of "medium -copy - number DNA" is

(a) encoding most genes
(b) encoding rRNA
(c) encoding a single gene
(d) encoding tRNA
(e) unknown

116. The high-copy-number-DNA in plants

(a) codes for rRNA
(b) codes for proteins required for plant metabolism
(c) are called transposable elements
(d) have no known function
(e) function as enhancers and promoters

117. Which of the following are mismatched?

(a) Simple tandem array—repetitive sequence in the same orientation
(b) Compound tandem array—repetitive sequence in the same orientation
(c) Inverted repeats—repetitive sequence in the opposite orientation
(d) Single-copy gene—sequence is not repeated
(e) All are correctly matched

118. The genome sequencing of rice is important because

(a) the rice genome is very unique and contains genes not found in other plants
(b) the rice genome is very large compared to the DNA of other grains, and so more genes will be identified
(c) it can identify genes associated with disease resistance, growth capacity, etc
(d) it has a rapid life cycle and has many identifiable mutations
(e) all of the above

119. Eukaryotic retrotransposons

(a) encode reverse transcriptase to make DNA from single-stranded RNA
(b) resemble bacterial transposons
(c) encode polymerase to replicate DNA for insertion elsewhere
(d) are also known as short-terminal-repeat (STR)-retrotransposons
(e) do not have the potential to interrupt genes

120. Homology-dependent DNA repair is

(a) based on sequence homology with non-sister chromatids
(b) possible only in prokaryotes
(c) error-free
(d) not observed in terminally differentiated cells (i.e., no longer dividing, e.g., neurons)
(e) involves complex double-stranded chromosome breakage

121. Gene conversion

(a) occurs during crossing over in meiosis
(b) is the change of an allele sequence by DNA repair to the homologous sequence available on a non-sister chromatid
(c) is recombination without the exchange of downstream markers
(d) involves intermediate heteroduplex DNA molecules (hybrid DNA of two non-sister chromatids)
(e) all of the above

122. Bands on polytene chromosomes

(a) are each representative of one or a few genes
(b) allow the identification of individual chromosomes, one from the other
(c) are the basis of cytological map in *Drosophila* and each are representative of one or a few genes
(d) are the basis of cytological map in *Drosophila*
(e) all of the above are correct

123. The C-value Paradox suggests that higher organisms

(a) have more genes than the DNA available to encode them
(b) have less DNA than needed to encode all essential genes
(c) have too few genes to support normal metabolism
(d) synthesize too little RNA to account for all proteins found in cells
(e) have more DNA than needed to encode all essential genes

124. Which one of the following will base pair perfectly with the oligonucleotide 3'-GCATGT-5'?

(a) 3'-CGTACA-5' (b) 5'-CGTACA-3'
(c) 5'-GCATGT-3' (d) 3'-GCATGT-5'
(e) 3'-ACTAGC-5'

125. Which of the following is a difference between duplicational pseudogenes and processed pseudogenes?

(a) Duplicational psuedogenes are associated with DNA that is similar to promoters; processed pseudogenes are not
(b) Duplicational pseudogenes have poly (A) tails; processed pseudogenes do not
(c) Duplicational psuedogenes don't have introns; processed pseudogenes do
(d) Duplicational psuedogenes are the products of reverse transcriptase; processed pseudogenes are not
(e) None of the above is true

126. Which of the following is most abundant in the mammalian genome?

(a) Unique sequence genes
(b) Structural DNA
(c) Multicopy genes
(d) Gene families
(e) Telomere sequences

127. Which of the following would be found in tandem arrays in all organisms?

(a) Origins (b) mRNA genes
(c) tRNA genes (d) rRNA genes
(e) Transcription terminators

128. Topoisomerase is an enzyme that

(a) rejoins broken phosphodiester bonds
(b) transfers bond energy to the growing polypeptide chain during translation
(c) cuts and rejoins DNA backbones
(d) makes RNA primers during DNA replication
(e) breaks DNA hydrogen bonds and unwinds DNA

129. Alternative RNA splicing enables genes to have multiple functions by removing

(a) exons and operators
(b) promoters and enhancers
(c) introns and exons
(d) operaters and promoters
(e) enhancers and introns

130. Chloroplast DNA is

(a) separate from nuclear DNA
(b) coded by the nucleus
(c) paternally inherited
(d) a subset of nuclear DNA
(e) transformed nuclear DNA

131. A characteristic feature of the chloroplast genome is the presence of two

(a) simple tandem arrays
(b) repeat / repeat interspersions
(c) identical inverted repeats
(d) compound tandem arrays
(e) repeat / single-copy interspersions

132. A large inversion of chloroplast DNA is found in the ______ family

(a) castor bean b) sunflower
(c) oats d) *Arabidopsis*
(e) Pea

PROTEIN SYNTHESIS

133. The process of mRNA synthesis from a DNA template is called

(a) translation
(b) transduction
(c) transformation
(d) transcription

134. The process of DNA synthesis from RNA is known as

(a) reverse translation
(b) transcription
(c) reverse mutation
(d) reverse transcription

135. Reverse transcription was first reported by

(a) Watson
(b) Temin and Baltimore
(c) Jacob
(d) Crick

136. Who won Nobel prize for the discovery of reverse transcription?

(a) Temin
(b) Temin and Baltimore
(c) Crick
(d) Baltimore

137. The information carried by DNA is used to create a(n) ______, which then moves to the ribosome for protein synthesis

(a) tRNA (b) rRNA
(c) hnRNA (d) mRNA

138. Messenger RNA

(a) is formed in the 3' to 5' direction
(b) is found only in prokaryote
(c) contains uracil instead of thymine
(d) is synthesized using the enzyme ligase

139. Transcription is the formation of ______ from a ______ template

(a) tRNA, DNA b) mRNA, DNA
(c) mRNA, tRNA d) protein, mRNA

140. The process of ______ results in the synthesis of a new protein

(a) replication
(b) transcription
(c) translation
(d) transversion

141. Which of the following is most closely associated with the removal of tRNA from the P site?
(a) Tu factor
(b) G factor
(c) I factor
(d) Sigma factor
(e) RF factor

142. Which of the following processes does not have a mechanism that checks to make sure that the right monomer is incorporated into the polymer?
(a) Protein synthesis
(b) RNA synthesis
(c) Double-stranded rolling circle DNA synthesis
(d) Normal cellular DNA synthesis
(e) Excision repair DNA synthesis

143. Rho-dependent terminators
(a) require the RNA involved to take on a specific secondary structure before termination can occur
(b) require that a specific protein bind to the RNA and cause termination
(c) require that the RNA be cut before transcription terminates further downstream
(d) occur only on tRNA genes in eukaryotes
(e) more than one of the above is true about Rho-dependent terminators

144. Which of the following is true about rRNA synthesis?
(a) rRNA genes are always in tandem arrays in eukaryotes, but never in tandem arrays in prokaryotes
(b) Pre-rRNA is processed by snRNPs in prokaryotes but not in eukaryotes
(c) The spacers in pre-rRNA are useful as independent RNAs in prokaryotes but not in eukaryotes
(d) Pre-rRNA genes are always transcribed by RNA pol I in eukaryotes, but never transcribed by RNA pol I in prokaryotes
(e) Pre-rRNA is always synthesized in the nucleus, in both eukaryotes and prokaryotes

145. Which of the following is true about sigma factors?
(a) They are made by eukaryotes to regulate synthesis of different mRNAs
(b) They are necessary for prokaryotic RNA polymerase to recognize promoters
(c) They are necessary for prokaryotic RNA polymerase to elongate RNA, but not for promoter recognition
(d) They are involved in the initiation of prokaryotic translation
(e) They are necessary for the elongation of prokaryotic translation, but not for translation initiation

146. The translation process in eukaryotes requires all of the following except
(a) Ribosomes
(b) RNA polymerase
(c) amino charged t RNA
(d) tRNA
(e) IF

147. A certain protein is 60 amino acids long. How many nucleotides are required in DNA to code for this protein?
(a) 60 (b) 120
(c) 180 (d) 240

148. Which statement is not true regarding eukaryotic mRNA?
(a) They are capped at 5′ terminus
(b) They are capped at 3′ terminus
(c) Poly A tail is present
(d) They are invariably monocistronic

149. Prokaryotic mRNAs are synthesized by
(a) RNA polymerase I
(b) RNA polymerase II
(c) RNA polymerase III
(d) primase
(e) none of the above

150. Which statement is incorrect with respect to the technique DNase I footprint analysis?

(a) Protein/DNA binding assay
(b) Bound proteins protect the phosphodiester backbone of DNA from DNase I catalyzed hydrolysis
(c) It is based on a reduced mobility of DNA/ protein complex compared to unbound DNA
(d) DNase I does not affect protein/DNA interaction

151. Once transcribed, eukaryotic mRNA typically undergoes substantial alteration that results primarily from

(a) excision of introns
(b) fusion into circular forms known as plasmids
(c) linkage to histone molecules
(d) union with ribosomes
(e) fusion with other newly transcribed mRNA molecules to form larger translatable units

152. Which one of the following features is characteristic for transcription process?

(a) Conservative
(b) Synthesis of primer
(c) Final product is RNA
(d) Final product is peptide

153. The binding of a Rho protein (hexamer) to a newly synthesized polynucleotide may terminate which important process?

(a) Replication
(b) Transcription
(c) Translation
(d) Post transcriptional processing
(e) Rho proteins play no role in termination

154. When a short segment of single-stranded DNA is exposed so as to serve as the template for the synthesis of RNA from incoming ribonucleoside tri-phosphate molecules (rNTPs), this is characteristic of which phase during transcription in prokaryotes?

(a) Binding (b) Initiation
(c) Elongation (d) Termination

155. The enzyme responsible for attaching the correct amino acid to a particular tRNA is called a(n)

(a) tRNA polymerase
(b) amino acyl tRNA synthetase
(c) anticodon synthase
(d) helicase
(e) telomerase

156. Accuracy in translation of mRNA into polypeptide depends on the specificity in the

(a) binding of ribosomes to mRNA
(b) shape of the A and P sites of the ribosomes
(c) bonding of the anticodon to the codon
(d) attachment of the amino acids to the tRNAs
(e) both (c) and (d) are correct

157. As a ribosome translocates along an mRNA molecule by one codon, which of the following occurs?

(a) tRNA that was in the A site moves into the P site
(b) tRNA that was in the P site moves into the A site
(c) tRNA that was in the P site moves to the E site and is released
(d) tRNA that was in the A site departs from the ribosome
(e) Both (a) and (c) are correct

158. Promoters

(a) include 5' UTR sequences
(b) include consensus sequences for DNA polymerase binding
(c) promote excision of exons from primary transcripts
(d) permit transcription by recognizing inducers and releasing from operator sequences
(e) are essential for gene activity

159. In eukaryotic cells, we sometimes find reverse transcriptase activity, even though the cells are not infected with virus. This activity can be attributed to

(a) infection with small bacteria known as mycoplasma
(b) the presence of viroids
(c) the presence of transposons integrating into polymerase genes
(d) the presence of retrotransposons
(e) a novel viral infection

160. In order to examine mRNA transcripts isolated from cells, one needs to convert a RNA template to DNA. During this conversion, which of the following enzymes is required?

(a) RNA convertase b) DNA polymerase
(c) RNA polymerase d) RNA transcriptase
(e) DNA transcriptase

161. Transfer RNA synthesis and processing uses

(a) an endonuclease
(b) poly(A) polymerase
(c) primase
(d) topoisomerase
(e) more than one of the above

162. Amino acyl tRNA synthetases

(a) attach amino acids together
(b) attach amino acids to ribosomes
(c) attach amino acids to the 5' ends of tRNAs
(d) attach amino acids to the 3' ends of tRNAs
(e) attach amino acids to elongation factor, Tu

163. During translation in eukaryotes, the small ribosomal subunit

(a) initially binds to the mRNA at an AUG codon
(b) associates with the mRNA after binding to a protein bound to the mRNA
(c) binds to the mRNA through basepairing between the medium rRNA and the mRNA
(d) initially binds to the mRNA through basepairing between the tRNA and the mRNAs
(e) binds to the mRNA through basepairing between the large rRNA and the mRNA

164. The process by which proteins are made from RNA is called

(a) translation (b) translocation
(c) transcription (d) transduction
(e) transformation

165. RNA synthesis on a DNA template is called

(a) transfection (b) transformation
(c) translation (d) transduction
(e) transcription

166. The process of tRNA "charging" does not involve

(a) an amino acid (b) rRNA
(c) tRNA (d) ATP
(e) aminoacyl synthetase

167. Areas of a eukaryotic gene that are represented in the final protein product are termed as

(a) cistrons (b) exons
(c) mutons (d) recons
(e) introns

168. Polyribosomes consist of

(a) one mRNA and several ribosomes
(b) several tRNAs
(c) several ribosomes
(d) one mRNA
(e) one mRNA, several tRNAs, and several ribosomes

169. Transcription of ribosomal RNA is primarily the function of

(a) RNA polymerase II
(b) RNA polymerase I
(c) primase
(d) RNA polymerase III
(e) mitochondrial RNA polymerase

170. If you were designing a method to specifically inhibit prokaryotic transcription, but not eukaryotic transcription, interfering with which of the following would work best?

(a) DNase activity
(b) recognition of the promoter region
(c) an intercalating agent
(d) ribosomal binding
(e) RNA polymerase II activity

171. Which of the following activities is not associated with posttranslational processing?

(a) Addition of lipid groups
(b) Specific cleavage of polypeptides
(c) Polyadenylation
(d) Glycosylation
(e) Chaperonin activity

172. Which of the following statements is not true concerning peptidyl transferase?

(a) It requires no outside source of additional energy, such as ATP
(b) It is a ribozyme having catalytic activity
(c) It catalyzes peptide bond formation
(d) It moves the ribosome, so translation continues
(e) It is associated with the large subunit of ribosomes

173. Which of the following is true of transfer RNA?

(a) It is responsible for correct positioning of amino acids in a polypeptide
(b) It serves as the site of protein synthesis
(c) It functions in transcription, translation, and replication
(d) It is an important component of ribosomes
(e) It functions only in replication

174. With regard to translation in prokaryotes, the gene products are often encoded on polycistronic mRNAs. As a result, the quantities of each of the proteins are often graded, such that the first gene has a great deal of protein translated, whereas the last gene has very little. Which of the following features of prokaryotic translation may account for increased production of some products and decreased production of others?

(a) Feedback regulation of ribosomes tells the cell that enough product is made, and ribosomes from such mRNAs dissociate
(b) The different messages have sequences with more or less homology to the Shine Dalgarno sequence; fewer ribosomes binding results in less product
(c) Because transcription and translation in prokaryotes are essentially coupled, there is no gradation in the amount of individual proteins made from a polycistronic message
(d) There is no termination sequence at the end of each gene, so one long protein is made, resulting in equal amounts of products
(e) All of the above

175. An agent that would work well as an antibiotic against prokaryotic infection would target the

(a) mitochondria
(b) 50S large ribosomal subunit
(c) 40S small ribosomal subunit
(d) RNA polymerase II
(e) DNA polymerase

GENETIC CODE

176. Number of codons representing amino acids present in protein is

(a) 20 (b) 24
(c) 64 (d) 61

177. Codons are composed of

(a) triplet sequences of nucleotide bases in mRNA
(b) triplet sequences of nucleotide bases in DNA
(c) triplet sequences of amino acids in polypeptide chains
(d) triplet sequences of deoxyribose sugars in DNA
(e) none of the above

178. An anticodon would be found in/on a(n) ______ molecule

(a) mRNA b) tRNA
(c) gene d) rRNA

179. The coding segments of a stretch of DNA are called

(a) introns b) exons
(c) genes d) chromosome
(e) m RNA

180. An anticodon is found in

(a) r RNA b) t RNA
(c) m RNA d) sense DNA
(e) c and d

181. Which of the following is a sense codon?

(a) UAA b) UGA
(c) AUG d) UAG

182. Degeneracy of genetic code refers to

(a) one amino acid coded by one codon
(b) one amino acid coded by many codons
(c) many amino acids coded by one codon
(d) overlapping codons code for many amino acids

183. The wobble hypothesis involves

(a) rRNA
(b) both mRNA and tRNA
(c) mRNA
(d) tRNA
(e) both mRNA and rRNA

184. Proteins are made from amino acids by the process of

(a) hydration
(b) pinocytosis
(c) active transport
(d) dehydration synthesis

185. Releasing factors recognize

(a) STOP codons of mRNA
(b) STOP signals at the P-site on the ribosome
(c) anticodons of STOP-tRNA
(d) STOP signals at the A-site on the ribosome
(e) STOP anticodons of tRNA

GENE REGULATION

186. The operon model of gene regulation was proposed by

(a) Crick (b) Watson and Crick
(c) Temin (d) Jacob and Monod

187. Jacob and Monod developed the concept of "operon hypothesis" working with

(a) *Drosophila* (b) *E. Coli*
(c) *Neurospora* (d) all of these

188. Who won Nobel prize for operon hypothesis

(a) Baltimore (b) Jacob and Monod
(c) Britten (d) Temin

189. The term "regulator gene" was coined by

(a) Jacob and Monod
(b) Temin
(c) Baltimore
(d) Britten and Davidson

190. In eukaryotes, the operon operator model of gene regulation was proposed by

(a) Jacob
(b) Britten and Davidson
(c) Temin and Baltimore
(d) Monod

191. Gene regulation is also known as the regulation of

(a) gene action (b) protein synthesis
(c) gene expression (d) all of these

192. *Trp* Operon of *E. coli* is under

(a) inducible negative control
(b) inducible positive control
(c) repressible positive control
(d) repressible negative control

193. When is the lactose operon likely to be transcribed?

(a) When there is more glucose in the cell than lactose
(b) When there is more lactose in the cell than glucose
(c) When there is lactose but no glucose in the cell
(d) When the cyclic AMP levels are high within the cell
(e) Both (c) and (d) are correct

194. One of the following is not a kind of mobile genetic element?

(a) Bacteriophage (b) Insertion sequence
(c) Operon (d) Plasmid
(e) Transposon

195. The action of a new drug is unknown, so you test various aspects of eukaryotic cell processes looking for an effect. You notice that the survival of cells exposed to this drug is very low. Further analysis shows that some proteins and mRNAs are much longer than they should be. One hypothesis is that the drug interferes with

(a) transcription termination signals
(b) spliceosome activity
(c) ribosomes
(d) nucleoli
(e) both (a) and (b)

196. Jacques Monod and Francois Jacob deduced the mechanism responsible for the regulation of bacterial gene expression. They are, therefore, responsible for launching the era of

(a) the scientific method
(b) light microscopy
(c) biochemistry
(d) molecular genetics
(e) radioisotopes

197. If the genetic code requires only two nucleotides for incorporation of amino acids, the amino acid sequence using this transcript would be

(a) B-D-B-D-B-D (b) B-B-B-B-B-B
(c) B-D-E-F-G-H (d) B-B-B-D-D-D
(e) B-D-E-B-D-E

198. Release factors of translation recognize the codon

(a) UGA (b) GGA
(c) UUU (d) AUG
(e) GUA

199. DNA methylation may be a significant mode of genetic regulation in eukaryotes. Methylation regulates gene activity by

(a) changing DNA-DNA hydrogen bonding
(b) altering translational activity, especially of highly methylated tRNAs
(c) altering RNA polymerase activity by methylation
(d) altering DNA polymerase activity by addition of methyl groups to glycine residues
(e) adding methyl groups to the cytosine of CG doublets in DNA

200. Which of the following is shared by both prokaryotes and eukaryotes?

(a) RNA splicing (b) Introns
(c) 5′-capping (d) Promoters
(e) 3′-poly A tails

201. Which is not a DNA-binding domain?

(a) Zinc finger
(b) Leucine zipper
(c) Intron-exon-intron
(d) Helix-turn-helix
(e) All of the above are domains that bind to DNA

202. Enhancer elements are found

(a) upstream from the start site
(b) in any of the above regions
(c) none of the above regions; enhancers are environmental agents
(d) within coding sequences
(e) downstream from the start site

203. Regarding enhancers and transcription factors (TFs) and their effect on gene expression

(a) enhancers are cis-activating, while TFs are trans-activating
(b) enhancers are trans-activating, while TFs are cis-activating
(c) both are trans-activating
(d) both are cis-activating
(e) neither are cis or trans-activating; they are repressors

204. The lac repressor is a

(a) DNA molecule (b) protein molecule
(c) lipid molecule (d) RNA molecule
(e) carbohydrate

205. What is the advantage of using IPTG experimentally, a gratuitous inducer? IPTG

(a) is larger than lactose
(b) is broken down by the enzyme
(c) is smaller than lactose
(d) is not broken down by the enzyme
(e) interacts with DNA

206. The trp operon is

(a) inducible and under negative control
(b) inducible, but not under either positive or negative control
(c) repressible and under positive control
(d) repressible and under negative control
(e) inducible and under positive control

207. A mutation in the I gene of the lac operon directly affects

(a) B-galactosidase (b) the operator region
(c) the promoter (d) permease
(e) the repressor

208. Operons

(a) are characteristic of eukaryotic genomes
(b) contain more than one promoter
(c) contain almost no intergeneric sequences
(d) none of the above

209. Operons

(a) are characteristic for eukaryotic genomes
(b) contain more than one gene
(c) contain more than one promoter
(d) contain always similar genes

210. Bacteria are often used for the study of genetic regulatory mechanisms because

(a) they can be grown in large numbers relatively inexpensively
(b) they produce many new generations rapidly
(c) a variety of mutations can be observed in a relatively short time
(d) all of these are true

211. In the *lac* operon system, lactose will be metabolized constitutively at low levels in

(a) $I^+ P^+ O^+ Z^- Y^+$ cells when glucose is present
(b) $I^- P^+ O^+ Z^+ Y^+$ cells when glucose is absent
(c) $Is\ P^+ O^+ Z^- Y^-$ cells when glucose is present
(d) $I^+ P^+ Oc\ Z^+ Y^+$ cells when glucose is absent
(e) $I^- P^+ O^+ Z^+ Y^+$ cells when glucose is present

212. Which of the following factors are not part of the regulatory process that helps to prevent uncontrolled cell growth leading to cancer?

(a) Signal transduction molecules
(b) Growth factors
(c) Growth factor receptors
(d) Nuclear transcription factors
(e) DNA polymerase

MARK TRUE OR FALSE (T/F)

1. DNA is found in herpes virus
2. DNA is found in the nucleosomes
3. DNA is found outside the cell nucleus
4. DNA is replicated in the S phase of the cell cycle
5. DNA duplicates simultaneously in all chromosomes
6. DNA is attached to the 1' position of the sugar ring in one of the four bases
7. In DNA, the bases lie stacked on each other 3.4 A apart
8. During transcription, each daughter DNA contains one newly synthesised strand
9. DNA can be detected with Northern blotting
10. Restriction endonucleases cut the DNA into lengths of about 20 nucleotide base sequences
11. Restriction fragment length polymorphism occurs mainly in the coding region of the DNA
12. Polymerase chain reaction requires the use of DNA polymerase
13. The polymerase chain reaction (PCR) produces multiple copies of DNA
14. PCR requires oligonucleotide primers
15. PCR has a high specificity but low sensitivity
16. PCR requires the use of heat
17. PCR can be used to detect RNA virus
18. Before RNA can be studied by PCR, it has to be translated into complementary DNA
19. Western blotting is used to detect specific protein in a mixture of protein
20. Northern blotting is used to detect DNA sequence
21. Dot blot technique is used to detect the presence of a given sequence of DNA/RNA in the nonfractionated DNA
22. Southern blotting is primarily used to detect DNA sequence
23. Gel electrophoresis is primarily used in both Southern and Northern blottings
24. Mitochondrial DNA is double-stranded
25. Mitochondrial DNA mutates 10 times more frequently than nuclear DNA
26. Each mitochondrion contains about 100 DNA molecules
27. Mitochondrial DNA has no introns
28. Leber's congenital amaurosis is caused by defective mitochondrial DNA
29. About 50% of the nuclear DNA codes for proteins
30. Nuclear DNAs are tightly wrapped around histones to form nucleoprotein complex
31. Introns interrupt the coding sequence
32. Exons are removed during splicing
33. In nuclear DNA, the base pairings are bound together by hydrogen bonds
34. In the DNA structure, the backbone is made up of an alternate molecule of pentose sugar and phosphate
35. In the DNA structure, most coils are left-handed
36. In the DNA structure, there is a terminal hydroxyl group at one end of the chain
37. In the DNA structure, there is a terminal phosphate group at only one end of the chain
38. In the DNA structure, if one chain has -AGG-, the other chain has the sequence -TCC-
39. Cytoplasmic messenger RNA is mainly translated from nuclear DNA

40. Cytoplasmic messenger RNA has a larger molecular weight than heterogeneous RNA
41. Cytoplasmic messenger RNA contains uracil in place of thymidine
42. In cytoplasmic messenger RNA, the sugar moeity is deoxyribose
43. Cytoplasmic messenger RNA is manufactured when the embryo is at the one cell stage
44. Only 1% of the cellular RNA is mRNA
45. Human mRNA is monocistronic
46. Introns are not transcribed into mRNA
47. In mRNA, mutation of the DNA sequence invariably gives rise to a change in the amino acid sequence of the resulting protein
48. RNA polymerase II gives rise to protein encoding mRNA
49. With regard to the DNA structures, adenine (A) and guanine (G) are purine bases
50. In DNA, guanine (G) always pairs with thymidine (T) and adenine (A) with cytosine (C)
51. In DNA, each strand has a pentose-phosphate backbone with projecting bases
52. In DNA, there are 64 possible codons
53. In DNA, each amino acid may be coded by more than one codon
54. Leigh disease is caused by defect in the mitochondrial DNA
55. Kearn-Sayer's syndrome is caused by defect in the the mitochondrial DNA
56. Myotonic dystrophy is caused by defect in the the mitochondrial DNA
57. Okazaki fragments form on the leading strand
58. Leber hereditary optic neuropathy is caused by defect in the the mitochondrial DNA
59. The sperm does not contain mitochondrial DNA
60. Mitochondrial DNA accounts for 10% of total human DNA
61. Mitochondrial DNA encodes protein needed for oxidative phosphorylation
62. Mitochondrial DNA defect results in the formation of red ragged muscle
63. The inheritance of mitochondrial disorder is similar to X-linked disorder
64. Western blotting is used to directly identify DNA
65. Southern blotting is used to directly identify DNA
66. Northern blotting is used to directly identify DNA
67. Polymerase chain reaction (PCR) is used to directly identify DNA
68. Denaturing gradient gel electrophoresis (DGGE) is used to directly identify DNA
69. Introns are segments of DNA that do not code for proteins
70. Transcription refers to the process of DNA synthesis
71. During DNA replication, the leading strand serves as a template for the replication of lagging strands
72. A bacterial chromosome is made up of individual units called Okazaki fragments
73. Vertical gene transfer occurs between cells of the same generation
74. Plant genomes are more complex than other eukaryotic cells at the DNA level but not necessarily at the chromosome level
75. Reverse transcriptase is an enzyme that can make RNA from DNA
76. The polymerase chain reaction is a method of copying fragments of DNA
77. Non-coding sequences of DNA are called exons
78. Repeating sequences of DNA are called core sequences
79. mRNA is formed in the 3' to 5' direction
80. RNA carries no information, only DNA carries biological information

81. Nucleic acids are found only in eukaryotic cells but never in prokaryotic cells
82. The general structure of a nucleotide consists of a glucose molecule, a phosphate sugar and a nitrogenous base
83. There are two types of sugars found in different nucleotides; ribose and deoxyribose
84. Ribose sugars are found on one chain of the DNA molecule, and deoxyribose sugars are found on the other chain of the DNA molecule
85. RNA molecules are always found in cells undergoing protein synthesis
86. Ribose sugars and deoxyribose sugars have the same number of oxygen atoms in their molecular structure
87. RNA molecules are single-stranded
88. DNA molecules always contain the nitrogenous base, thymine
89. DNA nucleotides have more phosphate than RNA nucleotides
90. A DNA molecule has a double helix at one end of the molecule and a single helix at the other end of the molecule
91. RNA molecules are made by copying the sequence of bases along certain selected stretches of the DNA molecule
92. Genetic information is usually held in the sequence of nitrogenous bases along a DNA molecule
93. During cellular division, DNA molecules and the information they contain are copied
94. RNA carries no information, only DNA carries biological information
95. DNA gyrase is a topoisomerase that introduces or removes supercoils in DNA, two at a time
96. The 5'-3' exonuclease activity of DNA polymerase III is essential to eliminate the RNA primers at the 5' end of each Okazaki fragment during DNA replication
97. Watson and Crick described the structure of tRNA
98. A nucleic acid with the base composition 35% adenine, 35% cytosine, 15% thymine and 15% guanine is ssDNA
99. Wobble is both prokaryotic and eukaryotic
100. The most common form of DNA in living things is A-DNA
101. Denaturing a section of DNA introduces negative supercoiling in the double-stranded section
102. 80s ribosomes are prokaryotic
103. Bidirectional DNA replication can occur in both prokaryotes and eukaryotes
104. Helicase denatures DNA sequences
105. Primase can remove supercoiling
106. Topoisomerase makes short RNA sequences
107. DNA Pol III makes leading strand DNA in prokaryotes
108. Okazaki strands are made on the lagging strand
109. Initiation sequence for translation is AUT
110. mRNA has a cloverleaf structure
111. Polysome shows active translation
112. *Ori* is the origin of replication
113. In DNA, the guanine - cytosine bonds are made of two hydrogen bonds
114. The DNA from a single cell is nearly 2 meters long
115. mRNA can be detected with Southern blotting

17

Genetics of Development and Behaviour

MULTIPLE-CHOICE QUESTIONS

1. **The progressive restriction of future developmental capacity is**
   (a) predestination (b) maternal effect
   (c) differentiation (d) transdetermination
   (e) determination
2. **Homeotic mutants in *Drosophila* are those in which**
   (a) a structure is missing
   (b) recombination has taken place
   (c) one structure is replaced with another
   (d) translocations have occurred
   (e) a position-effect is evident
3. **Studies of transdetermination and regeneration have shown that the differentiated state can**
   (a) frequently be reversed
   (b) always be reversed (c) rarely be reversed
   (d) never be reversed (e) not be assessed
4. **What is the term that refers to the regulatory events, which establish a specific pattern of gene activity and developmental fate for a given cell?**
   (a) Determination (b) Gradient regulated
   (c) Lysogen (d) Attenuation
   (e) Differentiation
5. **Which of the following is not a common approach to be taken for the study of behavioural genetics?**
   (a) Identification of behavioural differences between genetic strains of the same species or between closely related species
   (b) Selection of a variant behavioural trait from a genetically heterogeneous population and attempting to transfer the trait to another strain by genetic crosses
   (c) Crossing genetically identical animals together, observing the resulting progeny perform the same behavioural tests, and then examining the brain of each offspring for similarities
   (d) Collection and analysis of inbred strains of organisms with relatively constant genotypes, spontaneous or inbred mutants with behavioural deviations
   (e) None of the above

6. The rat maze-learning studies performed by E.C. Tolman

(a) used an artificial selection approach to generate two lines of rats: "bright maze runners" and "dull maze runners"
(b) the duller rats were more emotional in open-field experiments
(c) involved mating the brightest rats to dullest rats to generate a pure genetic line
(d) showed that selection of a genetic strain superior in all the various components of intelligence is possible
(e) none of the above

7. Drosophila geotaxis experiments carried out by Jerry Hirsch and his colleagues showed that

(a) genes on the second chromosome make the largest contribution to positive geotaxis
(b) there are probably 10-20 major gene loci responsible for variations in geotaxic behavior
(c) selection for positive geotropism is stronger than negative geotropism
(d) geotaxis is under polygenic control
(e) geotaxis is a learned phenomenon, not a genetic one

8. Crossing a drone derived from a cross of bees from the Brown (hygienic) line and the Van Scoy (non-hygienic) line with a purebred Brown queen yields diploid female workers in which of the following ratios

(a) all non-hygienic bees
(b) all hygienic bees
(c) 3 hygienic bees: 1 nonhygienic bee
(d) 1 hygienic bee: 1 uncapping bee: 1 removing bee: 1 non-hygienic bee
(e) none of the above

9. In *E. coli,* chemotactic behavior involves

(a) increased phosphorylation of Che A in the presence of an attractant molecule
(b) only four gene products, but each with several alternatively spliced forms
(c) chemoreceptors clustered at the base of the flagellar motors
(d) short runs followed by long periods of tumbling when a chemical gradient of a chemotactic substance is detected
(e) none of the above

10. The utility of genetic mosaics in *Drosophila* studies include

(a) the ability to localize the primary focus of gene expression
(b) the ability to identify whether the gene product is required in the cell expressing the gene (i.e., is cell autonomous) or is needed by other cells (generally neighbors)
(c) the ability to determine the critical period of gene expression for a mutant phenotype to be averted
(d) the ability to study otherwise lethal alleles
(e) all of the above

11. Which one of the following is not a kind of behavioural mutant that has been found in *Drosophila*?

(a) Savoir-faire, a mutant in which males are unsuccessful in courtship
(b) Sluggish, a mutant that moves slowly
(c) Wiggle, a mutant in which *Drosophila* larvae wiggle through their food
(d) Dunce, a mutant which fails to learn conditioned response
(e) Paralyzed, a mutant that collapses above a critical temperature

12. Huntington disease is

(a) a dominant neurological disease
(b) a trinucleotide-repeat disease
(c) all of the above
(d) a late-onset monogenic disease
(e) none of the above

13. Schizophrenia is

(a) all of the above
(b) a trisomy-based disease
(c) a late-onset monogenic disease
(d) a dominant neurological disease
(e) none of the above

14. In *Drosophila*, the pattern is established

(a) during the production of oocyte
(b) as a result of environmental interactions with the oocyte
(c) during gastrulation
(d) after the embryogenesis has completed
(e) none of these

15. A morphogen

(a) conveys positional information to cells within the embryo
(b) is typically present in similar amounts in all cells
(c) functions only at very low concentrations
(d) all of these
(e) none of these

16. Which of these would be an example of a homeotic phenotype?

(a) The wings are shrunken and useless
(b) The eyes of the fly are brown instead of the normal red
(c) The first abdominal segment has legs
(d) All of these
(e) None of these

17. Homologous genes

(a) are genes that have evolved to have similar sequences
(b) are genes that have similar sequences due to common descent
(c) are genes that have similar functions
(d) are present only in vertebrates

18. In plant development, an organized group of actively dividing stem cells is

(a) unusual
(b) a meristem
(c) a signaling center
(d) only present at the apical tip of each shoot
(e) none of these

19. How is sex determination in *C. elegans* similar to sex determination in *Drosophila*?

(a) In both cases, the end result of the process is either a male or a hermaphrodite
(b) In both cases, alternative splicing is a major mechanism of control of gene activity
(c) In both cases, expression of genes on the X chromosome is reduced in the process of dosage compensation
(d) In both cases, the ratio of X chromosomes to autosomes determines which pathway the individual will follow
(e) None of the above

20. Which of these mechanisms is common to sex determination in *Drosophila*, *C. elegans*, mammals, and plants?

(a) Transcriptional regulation
(b) Alternative splicing
(c) Environmental influences
(d) Y linked genes that determine maleness

21. The most common pattern of sex phenotypes in plants is

(a) monomorphic
(b) hermaphroditic
(c) dioecious
(d) sexually dimorphic

22. Homeotic genes are responsible for

(a) development (b) cell cycle
(c) gene regulation (d) homeostasis

23. The mosaic developmental pattern is always

(a) non-autonomous (b) conditional
(c) regulative (d) autonomous

24. For making transgenic animals in fertilized egg, the best place to insert transgene is

(a) female pronuclei
(b) cleavage cells
(c) male pronuclei
(d) cytoplasm

25. The establishment of the anterior-posterior or dorsal-ventral body axes is called

(a) morphogenesis (b) differentiation
(c) pattern formation d) division

26. Mutations in homeotic genes can lead to what type of developmental defect?

(a) The embryo will develop with every other segment failing to form
(b) The anterior portion of the embryo does not develop
(c) The development of segments will be changed wholesale from their normal identity to that of a different segment
(d) Several adjacent segments will be missing

27. The dorsal mutant in *Drosophila* will result in

(a) effect on anterior-posterior pattern formation
(b) dorsalization of the ventral side
(c) no effect
(d) ventralization of the dorsal side

28. Which statement is correct for capacitation?

(a) Maturation of egg in oviduct after fertilization
(b) Meiotic division in the egg after penetration of sperm
(c) Maturation of spermatozoa in the male body
(d) Maturation of mammalian spermatozoa after entering the oviduct of the female

29. During development, the homing of the cell is mediated by

(a) integrin (b) cadherin
(c) laminin (d) selectin

30. The portion of the *Drosophila* body plan which will produce the wings is called

(a) dorsal side (b) abdomen
(c) thorax (d) telson

31. Organ identity genes are responsible for the correct positioning of floral organs on floral meristem. Mutation in them will lead to

(a) the appearance of organs at incorrect position
(b) no flower
(c) loss of organs from certain whorls
(d) more number of organs in certain whorls

32. The yolky side of an egg is called its

(a) animal side (b) vegetal side
(c) vegetable side (d) vegan side

33. ______ is the process of structural male gamete maturation from already haploid gametes

(a) Spermatogenesis (b) Spermiogenesis
(c) Spermatoformicon (d) All of the above

34. Oocytes that are discarded in the process of oogenesis are called

(a) antigens (b) epitopes
(c) non-polar bodies (d) polar bodies

35. A ______ is an excised piece of leaf or stem tissue used in micropropagation of

(a) micro shoot (b) medium
(c) explant (d) scion

36. The larval epidermis is produced by

(a) clear cytoplasm
(b) yellow cytoplasm
(c) gray vegetal cytoplasm
(d) brown cytoplasm

37. Rate of growth stops and the plants die at a temperature of

(a) 20-30 °C
(b) 10-20 °C
(c) 35-40 °C
(d) None of the above

38. The secondary tissue is added by the

(a) intercalary meristem
(b) vascular cambium
(c) apical meristems
(d) both (a) and (b)

39. Phenomena that some cells evoke a specific developmental response in the other cells is

(a) embryonic influence
(b) embryonic induction
(c) embryonic stimulation
(d) embryonic dominance

40. Effect of auxin diffusing from an apical bud on lateral shoots is known as

(a) promoting effect (b) compensatory effect
(c) inhibitory effect (d) supporting effect

41. Migration of individual cells from the surface into the embryo's interior is known as

(a) ingression (b) involution
(c) invagination (d) delamination

42. During development, if a cell has committed to a particular fate, it is said to be

(a) pluripotent (b) totipotent
(c) determined (d) differentiated

43. Bones of vertebrates are derived from embryonic

(a) ectoderm (b) epiderm
(c) mesoderm (d) endoderm

44. Synthesis of cytoplasm and cell wall material takes place during

(a) maturation (b) cell division
(c) elongation (d) none of the above

45. *Acetabularia* is a kind of

(a) fungus (b) protist
(c) multicellular alga (d) unicellular alga

46. An internal factor that influences growth in plants is

(a) hormone (b) water
(c) nutrition (d) all of the above

47. Stage one in differentiation involves

(a) recognition of apical meristems
(b) formation of embryo
(c) recognition of cambium
(d) production of leaf primordial

48. Oocytes that are discarded in the process of Oogenesis are

(a) antigens
(b) epitopes
(c) polar bodies
(d) non-polar bodies

49. During embryogenesis, the separation of cells into the three individual germ layers first occurs during which of the following?

(a) Neurulation (b) Organogenesis
(c) Gastrulation (d) Cleavage

50. Which of the following defines the process by which the entry of one sperm into an oocyte prevents the other sperms from fertilizing the same egg?

(a) Induction reaction
(b) Determination
(c) Differentiation
(d) Cortical reaction

51. Which germ layer gives rise to the digestive tract?

(a) Endoderm (b) Ectoderm
(c) Epiderm (d) Mesoderm

52. During which stage of embryogenesis formation of primitive streak occurs?

(a) Neurula (b) Morula
(c) Blastula (d) Gastrula

53. During embryogenesis, the process in which a committed cell develops distinctive functions and characteristics is known as

(a) induction (b) differentiation
(c) determination (d) specification

54. The following is a class of proteins that is part of the complex that regulates the central events of the cell cycle

(a) Cyclins (b) Caspases
(c) Tubulins (d) None of these

55. Tumour suppressors include genes whose normal functions are

(a) cell adhesion
(b) activators of apoptosis
(c) c3
(d) d3

56. "Death receptors" are likely to activate

(a) paracrine signals
(b) ubiquitin
(c) cyclin dependent kinase inhibitors
(d) initiator caspases

57. Simple binary fission is found in

(a) paramecium
(b) sponge
(c) euglena
(d) amoeba

58. Paramecium exhibits

(a) Simple binary fission
(b) Transverse binary fission
(c) Longitudinal binary fission
(d) Oblique binary fission

59. Which of the following does not show metamorphosis?

(a) frog (b) housefly
(c) hydra (d) mosquito

60. When the eggs are released from the ovary of frogs they are at the

(a) primary oocyte stage
(b) secondary oocyte stage
(c) ootid stage
(d) matured ova stage

61. The nervous system, epidermis, hair and nails are derivatives of

(a) endoderm
(b) mesoderm
(c) ectoderm
(d) chordomesoderm

62. Development of egg without fertilization is known as

(a) parthenogenesis (b) parthenocarpy
(c) polyembryony (d) paedogenesis

63. Cleidoic eggs are found in

(a) birds (b) mammals
(c) insects (d) molluscs

64. In order to become structurally and functionally a spermatozoan, each spermatid has to undergo a process of differentiation called

(a) spermiation (b) spermiogenesis
(c) spermatogenesis (d) androgenesis

65. In the human female, the primary oocytes remain small without any growth for

(a) 4-5 years (b) 6-8 years
(c) 8-10 years (d) 12-14 years

66. Mammalian placenta is

(a) a cord between mother and foetus
(b) place of attachment in uterus wall where exchange of material between mother and foetus takes place
(c) outer covering of foetus
(d) allantoic part of the uterus

67. If an unfertilized frog's egg is pricked with a micro-needle, it will

(a) die immediately
(b) start dividing
(c) remain undivided
(d) transform into a tadpole at a faster rate

68. In the growing oocyte, the nucleus enlarges in size due to an increase in

(a) proteins (b) nucleoplasm
(c) DNA (d) RNA

69. Which of the following has the capacity to reproduce without fertilization of eggs?

(a) Spider (b) Cow
(c) Honeybee (d) Earthworm

70. Spermatoliosis is a process by which
(a) the spermatids differentiate into spermatozoa
(b) primary spermatocyte is transformed into a secondary spermatocyte
(c) spermatogonia complete multiplication phase
(d) secondary spermatocyte extrudes polar bodies

71. Which of the following do not show parental care over their young ones?
(a) Mammals (b) Lizards
(c) Fowls (d) Bats

72. Meroblastic cleavage is found in
(a) man (b) hen's egg
(c) frog (d) rabbit

73. The substance fertilizin is secreted by
(a) ova
(b) sperm
(c) primary spermatogonia
(d) both (a) and (b)

74. Anti-fertilizin is secreted by
(a) fertilized egg (b) spermatozoa
(c) unfertilized egg (d) egg membranes

75. During cleavage, the embryo
(a) enlarges in size
(b) decreases in size
(c) retains the same size as at the beginning
(d) gradually enlarges in size

76. Morphogenetic movement involves
(a) movement of organs
(b) movement of small cell masses
(c) movement of large cell masses
(d) differentiation of cells

77. A zygote is completely divided into two cells by a cleavage furrow. The cleavage type is
(a) equatorial (b) meroblastic
(c) radial (d) holoblastic

78. Amount of yolk and its distribution are changed in egg. Which one is affected?
(a) Pattern of cleavage
(b) Formation of zygote
(c) Number of blastomeres
(d) Fertilization

79. The function of prostrate gland is
(a) storage of semen
(b) provide motility to sperms
(c) formation of semen
(d) release of hormones

80. Ball-like structure formed after completion of cleavage is
(a) blastulla (b) morulla
(c) gastrulla (d) neural plate

81. Morphogenetic movements take place during
(a) formation of morula (b) blastulation
(c) gastrulation (d) organogenesis

82. Amniotes include
(a) fishes, reptiles and amphibians
(b) amphibians, birds and reptiles
(c) birds, reptiles and mammals
(d) amphibians, reptiles and mammals

83. In organisms, shape of foetus is determined by
(a) organogenesis (b) blastula
(c) morphogenesis (d) reproduction

84. Which is correct about human embryonic development?
(a) Cleavage divisions bring about considerable increase in mass of protoplasm
(b) In the second division, one of the two blastomeres usually divides a little sooner than the second
(c) With more cleavage divisions the resultant blastomere becomes larger and larger
(d) Cleavage divisions result in a hollow ball of cells called morula

85. During cleavage

(a) size of resulting cells decreases
(b) size of resulting cells increases
(c) size of early embryo increases
(d) size of early embryo decreases

86. Development of animal embryo from an unfertilized egg is called

(a) parthenocarpy (b) parthenogenesis
(c) apospory (d) apomixis

87. Middle piece of a mammalian sperm contains

(a) nucleus (b) vacuole
(c) mitochondria (d) centriole

88. Some mature cells cannot undergo division because

(a) their genes have become inactive
(b) they lack centrioles
(c) they have taken up specific function and undergone differentiation
(d) they have lost the ability to divide

89. Which of the following is not an approach typically used in biological psychology to understanding personality?

(a) Repertory grids
(b) Evolutionary
(c) Behavioural genetics
(d) Life history

90. Which of the following is not a measure commonly used in biological personality psychology research?

(a) Cardiovascular activity
(b) Electroencephalogram
(c) Computed tomography
(d) All of these are measures used in biological personality psychology

91. What does "temperament" refer to ?

(a) Individual differences in emotional and behavioural styles evident in young children
(b) Individual differences in emotional and behavioural responses of animals (i.e., animal personality
(c) The factors which influence the development of personality
(d) All of these

92. ______ is the study of the degree to which your observable characteristics (your ______) are the result of the genetic material you have inherited from your parents (your ______). This material is contained in

(a) Phylogenetic inheritance, genotype, phenotype, DNA
(b) Behavioural genetics, phenotype, genotype, DNA
(c) Phylogenetic inheritance, phenotype, genotype, neural transmitters
(d) Behavioural genetics, genotype, phenotype, DNA

93. What is the name typically given to the assessment of the degree of similarity on a particular characteristic between parents and their children, or between siblings, used in behavioural genetics research?

(a) Genetic drift
(b) Proportion of non-shared variance
(c) Heritability estimate
(d) Proportion of shared variance

94. Which of the statements regarding heritability is not true?

(a) Statements about the heritability of individual differences should only be applied to a population, not an individual
(b) Heritability estimates are only applicable to the particular group, time and circumstances it was calculated for
(c) Heritability is an estimate and can be calculated in a number of ways
(d) Heritability is static and unchanging within in a population

95. The idea that you can assess someone's personality by studying their face is called

(a) phrenology (b) physiology
(c) somatology (d) physiognomy

96. The ______ complex is to girls as the ______ complex is to boys

(a) electra, oedipus
(b) oedipus, electra
(c) oral, phallic
(d) phallic, oral

97. The discovery that the heritability of the big five personality traits is around 40% - 50% suggests that

(a) the environment plays no role in personality
(b) genes play no role in personality
(c) the environment plays an important role in personality
(d) the big five traits account for about half of our personality

98. The influence of parents on the personality of their children is

(a) non-existent
(b) weakest in early childhood
(c) strongest in early childhood
(d) consistent across the lifespan

99. What is special about "knockout" mice?

(a) They are very attractive
(b) Their DNA has been modified
(c) They are easy to knockout
(d) They are unusually aggressive

100. The aim of behavioural genetics is to learn about

(a) the extent to which the geneticists can modify people's behaviour
(b) the possibility of eradicating behavioural problems in children
(c) the genetic and environmental influences on human behaviour
(d) the ability of animals to learn language

101. Monozygotic is to ______ twins as dizygotic is to ______ twins.

(a) male, female
(b) female, male
(c) fraternal, identical
(d) identical, fraternal

102. Which of the following would NOT be useful to a behavioural geneticist?

(a) Family studies (b) Case studies
(c) Adoption studies (d) Twin studies

MARK TRUE OR FALSE (T/F)

1. During the early stages of Drosophila development, mitosis is not accompanied by cytokinesis
2. A morphogen is a molecule that controls positional information by controlling cell adhesion
3. Gap genes directly regulated pair-rule genes
4. Homeotic mutations have only been seen in invertebrate species
5. Change in expression of a single gene can lead to major changes in determination or differentiation of a cell
6. Cell differentiation is the process by which cells specialize into their adult form and function
7. In *C. elegans*, the father and the mother of an individual worm could be the same individual
8. Homeosis is the replacement of one body part by another
9. The zygote is totipotent, giving rise to every adult cell type
10. Some fate decisions are made non-autonomously by individual cells
11. The same basic sets of genes identified in Drosophila and the regulatory proteins that they encode are conserved in mammals
12. Subdivision of the embryonic left-right axis results in a series of distinct units called metameres

13. In developmental pathways, regulation is at all possible levels of information transfer between the gene and its active protein product
14. Components of developmental pathways are reutilized extensively in the course of development and are highly conserved within the animal kingdom
15. In Drosophila, individual flies with two X chromosomes and three sets of autosomes (X: A ratio = 0.67) are super males
16. XYY humans are sterile males
17. XXX humans are fertile females
18. Humans who are mosaics of XX and XY tissue generally exhibit a uniform sexual phenotype
19. All of the human mosaics of XX and XY tissue are phenotypically male
20. In Drosophila, anterior development uses localized gene regulators
21. Cell fate is determined by compartments that form by the blastoderm stage
22. Complex loci are extremely large and involved in regulation
23. The early embryo develops differences along the anterior-posterior axis and dorsal-ventral axis
24. The genes that control the early stages of fly development do not code for transcription factors
25. Maternal genes are expressed during oogenesis and act in the oocyte
26. During the first 10 division cycles, nuclei divide in a common cytoplasm
27. In both flies and mammals, many areas of the body display sexually dimorphic characteristics, i.e., these areas differ in males and females
28. In Drosophila, the two sexes have similar pigmentation of the abdomen
29. Every cell lineage in Drosophila makes its own sexual decision
30. In Drosophila, with regard to sexually dimorphic phenotypes, the effects of null mutations in several of the genes in the pathway are to transform males into phenotypic females
31. Each individual human cell makes an independent determination of its sex
32. Sex reversed XX human beings are phenotypic males
33. The sex reversal gene in human beings is present on the Y chromosome
34. In human beings, the testis-determining factor on the Y chromosome and the sex reversal gene are different
35. Genes influence our behaviour
36. It is now believed by scientists that a number of genes are largely responsible for developing a person's intelligence

18
Population Genetics

MULTIPLE-CHOICE QUESTIONS

1. **Which of the following definitions is not correct?**
   (a) Interbreeding refers to consanguinal matings (e.g., those between first cousins)
   (b) A population is a local group belonging to a single species, within which mating is actually or potentially occurring
   (c) Allele frequency refers to the proportion of the alleles (at a given locus) in a population that are a particular allele type
   (d) A gene pool is the set of genetic information carried by all interbreeding members of a population
   (e) Genotype frequency refers to the proportion of people in a population that are of a given genotype

2. **Coefficient of inbreeding**
   (a) measures the frequency with which inbreeding occurs in a particular population
   (b) indicates the difference between expected genotypic frequencies and those observed in an inbreeding population
   (c) indicates the frequency with which an inbred individual will be homozygous due to inheritance from a common ancestor
   (d) all of the above
   (e) none of the above

3. **What affect will inbreeding tend to have on genotypic frequencies in a population?**
   (a) It will increase the frequency of genotypes that produce a dominant phenotype
   (b) It will decrease the frequency of genotypes that produce a dominant phenotype
   (c) It will increase the frequency of homozygous genotypes
   (d) It will increase the frequency of heterozygous genotypes
   (e) It will not have effect on genotypic frequencies

4. All members of an isolated village were genotyped for a particular RFLP. Of the 1000 individuals, 200 were homozygous for the presence of the restriction site, 700 were heterozygous, and 100 were homozygous for its absence. What is the frequency of the "restriction site present" allele, p?

(a) 0.9 (b) 0.55
(c) 0.45 (d) 0.2
(e) None of the above

5. Which of the following is not a condition of the Hardy-Weinberg law?

(a) The population is infinitely large or, in practical terms, is large enough that sampling errors and random effects are negligible
(b) Mating within the population occurs at random with respect to the loci under consideration
(c) There is no selective advantage for any of the genotypes under consideration; all genotypes are equally viable and fertile
(d) No more than one other factor—mutation, migration or random genetic drift—can be acting at one time during the period under study
(e) All of the above are conditions of the Hardy-Weinberg law

6. An X-linked disease (non-lethal) occurs at different frequencies in males and females. While 0.1% of males are affected, and only 0.0001% of females are affected. What is the frequency of the disease allele?

(a) 0.001 (b) 0.1001
(c) 0.000001 (d) 0.1
(e) None of the above

7. A population is in Hardy-Weinberg equilibrium for a gene locus that has four alleles at the following allelic frequencies: a1 (0.1), a2 (0.2), a3 (0.4), and a4 (0.3). What is the expected frequency of the a2a3 genotype?

(a) 0.2 (b) 0.4
(c) 0.08 (d) 0.16
(e) None of the above

8. Which of the following is true about mutations in population genetics?

(a) Mutation is a major force in generating genetic variability, but by itself plays a relatively insignificant role in changing allelic frequencies
(b) Except in situations of Hardy-Weinberg equilibrium, mutation plays a significant role in changing allelic frequencies
(c) Mutation frequencies can be calculated from the frequency of homozygous recessive genotypic class alone
(d) Mutation rate, mu, is equal to the allelic frequency of the recessive allele divided by the initial frequency of the recessive allele
(e) None of the above

9. Which of these might be considered a neutral mutation?

(a) A mutation in the wobble base of a lysine codon of the gene for an essential metabolic protein
(b) A nonsense mutation in gene required for the correct assembly of cytoskeleton
(c) A mutation in an intron splice recognition site in a unique aminoacyltransferase
(d) All of these might be considered neutral mutations
(e) None of these could be considered neutral mutations

10. If 5% of the parents giving rise to the next generation are immigrants and the immigrants are 100% AA while the existing population gene pool is only 20% A, what is the change in the frequency of the A allele after one generation?

(a) –0.8 (b) +0.04
(c) –0.04 (d) –0.24
(e) None of the above

11. Which of the following is not one of the classes of natural selection?

(a) Disruptive selection
(b) Directional selection
(c) Neutral selection
(d) Stabilizing selection
(e) None of the above

12. For a locus, where there are two alleles, B and b, and for which bb is homozygous lethal and BB and Bb have identical fitness, what is the expected allele frequency of b after 10 generations if the frequency of b is 0.1 at generation zero?

(a) 0.0 (b) 0.05
(c) 0.5 (d) 0.1
(e) None of the above

13. If all mating in a population is between first cousins, what is the F value of the resulting generation?

(a) 0.25 (b) 0.1250
(c) 0.0625 (d) 0.0
(e) None of the above

14. Which of the following is not true of linkage disequilibrium?

(a) It is a type of association that involves alleles at linked loci
(b) It can be caused by natural selection
(c) It can be caused by a disease mutation that has arisen recently on a chromosome containing a specific marker allele
(d) It becomes nondetectable after one generation of random mating
(e) It can be used to map genes

15. Which of these is not one of the requirements for the presence of equilibrium in allele frequencies in a population?

(a) Large population size
(b) No new mutations in the gene of interest
(c) No natural selection for the gene of interest
(d) Mate selection based on phenotype of interest
(e) None of these (all are requirements)

16. You have an acquaintance who is extremely self-centered and stubborn. She is currently separated from her fourth husband. All of her husbands have also been self-centered and stubborn. This would be an extreme example of

(a) assortative mating
(b) disassortative mating
(c) inbreeding
(d) all of the above
(e) none of the above

17. In the silver oak trees at Pantnagar University campus, there is a gene controlling leaf shape. The curled allele and the straight allele show incomplete dominance. 52 % of the trees have curled leaves, 12% have straight leaves, and 36% have partially curled leaves. What are the allele frequencies for this gene?

(a) Curled allele = 0.52; straight allele = 0.12; and partially curled allele = 0.36
(b) Curled allele = 0.52 and straight allele = 0.12
(c) Curled allele = 0.721 and straight allele = 0.3464
(d) Curled allele = 0.7 and straight allele = 0.3
(e) None of these is correct

18. In the silver oak trees at Pantnagar University campus, there is a gene controlling leaf shape. The curled allele and the straight allele show incomplete dominance. 52 % of the trees have curled leaves, 12% have straight leaves, and 36% have partially curled leaves. Is this population randomly mating?

(a) Yes
(b) No. There is inbreeding going on
(c) No. There is positive assortative mating going on
(d) No. There is negative assortative mating going on
(e) No. There is no way to determine the type of non-random mating from these data

19. A population geneticist had been studying some animals in a field at Pantnagar University. He had allele and genotype frequencies for genes involved in burrow building for this population. One day the field caught fire. The fire killed 98% of his animals, but preferentially left those, who had the genetically determined urge to dig deeper holes. Compared to "pre-fire" conditions, what would you expect to see in the next generation of animals (after the fire)?

(a) Alleles and genotypes that cause deep burrows will be more abundant
(b) Alleles that cause deep burrows will be more abundant
(c) Genotype frequencies for these genes will be unchanged
(d) Genotypes that cause deep burrows will be more abundant. Allele frequencies for these genes will be unchanged
(e) Neither genotype nor allele frequencies will change
(f) No. There is no way to determine the type of non-random mating from these data

20. A population geneticist had been studying some animals in a field at the University of Delhi. He had allele and genotype frequencies for genes involved in burrow building for this population. One day the field caught fire. The fire killed 98% of his animals, but preferentially left those who had the genetically determined urge to dig deeper holes. Compared to "pre-fire" conditions, what would you expect to see for genes not involved in the ability to survive fire?

(a) For these genes, the population would be unchanged compared to "pre-fire" conditions
(b) There should be a decrease in all allele frequencies and an increase in homozygosity
(c) There should be a decrease in the number of alleles per gene, but genotype frequencies should be unchanged
(d) There should be a general decrease in the number of alleles and the frequency of homozygotes
(e) There should be a general decrease in the number of alleles and the frequency of heterozygotes

21. Why is mutation important in population genetics?

(a) Mutation has a significant effect on allele frequencies by itself
(b) Mutation is a nuisance. It just creates "bad" alleles that get weeded out of the population
(c) Mutation causes genetic drift in small populations
(d) Mutation creates the genetic variation that is needed for populations and species to evolve
(e) Mutation isn't a significant phenomenon in population genetics

22. The likelihood of an individual in a population carrying two specific alleles of a human DNA marker, each of which has a frequency of 0.2, will be

(a) 0.4
(b) 0.32
(c) 0.16
(d) 0.08
(e) 0.02

23. What are the assumptions of Hardy Weinberg equilibrium?

(a) Small population size, random mating, no selection, no migration, no mutation
(b) Large population size, random mating, no selection, no migration, no mutation
(c) Large population size, random mating, heterozygotes survive the best, no migration, no mutation
(d) Large population size, like individuals mate, no selection, no migration, no mutation
(e) Large population size, random mating, no selection, migrants enter from other populations, no mutation

24. If the frequency of males affected with an X-linked recessive condition in a human population is .10 (one in ten), what will be the expected frequency of affected females?

(a) 0.0001 (b) 0.001
(c) 0.02 (d) 0.01
(e) 0.05

25. The following genotypes are found in a population

AA Aa aa
70 50 20
What are the allele frequencies of A and a?

(a) A = 0.86 and a = 0.14
(b) A = 0.68 and a = 0.32
(c) A = 0.63 and a = 0.36
(d) A = 0.32 and a = 0.68
(e) A = 0.36 and a = 0.63

26. Assuming Hardy-Weinberg equilibrium, if the frequency of the two alleles at the gene being studied are 0.6 and 0.4, the genotypic frequency of heterozygotes will be

(a) 0.80 (b) 0.64
(c) 0.48 (d) 0.32
(e) 0.16

27. In shorthorn cattle, we find red, white and roan colour phenotypes. Suppose that 12 in 230 cattle are white, assume Hardy-Weinberg equilibrium in the population. The frequency of the allele found in red and roan individuals would be

(a) .814 (b) .772
(c) .228 (d) .052
(e) none of the above

28. The frequency of roan individuals in the above example would be

(a) .596 (b) .352
(c) .176 (d) .052
(e) none of the above

29. The following numbers of individuals in a population have the corresponding genotypes. AA = 108, Aa = 144, aa = 48. Based on the Hardy-Weinberg equation and its corresponding five assumptions, the expected numbers for each genotype would be

(a) AA = 108, Aa = 144, aa = 48
(b) AA = 123, Aa = 138, aa = 39
(c) AA = 104, Aa = 146, aa = 50
(d) AA = 48, Aa = 108, aa = 144
(e) none of the above

30. Factors which tend to change gene frequencies in a population are

(a) migration and crossing over (recombination)
(b) random mating
(c) natural selection and mutation
(d) both a and c
(e) none of the above

31. Which of these is not a mode of natural selection?

(a) Stabilizing selection
(b) Disruptive selection
(c) Operational selection
(d) Directional selection

32. Selection coefficient

(a) relates to the effect of an allele on an individual
(b) measures the selection against a particular genotype
(c) can be calculated from the variation from the expected Hardy-Weinberg equilibrium
(d) all of these
(e) none of these

33. In a balanced polymorphism

(a) selection against a homozygous recessive condition may not lead to a reduction in allele frequency
(b) migration between members of a diverse population counteracts directional selection
(c) increased reproductive success of heterozygous individuals may not change allele frequencies
(d) all of these
(e) none of these

34. Which of these illustrates genetic load in population?

(a) Individuals homozygous for a recessive lethal allele do not survive to reproductive age

(b) A native species of tree from Florida is unlikely to survive after being transplanted to Wisconsin

(c) Allele frequencies are expected to remain constant in the absence of selection

(d) All of these

(e) None of these

CHANGING ALLELE FREQUENCIES

35. A ______ occurs when many members of a group die and only a few are left, by chance, to replenish the numbers

(a) population bottleneck

(b) geographical isolation

(c) founder effect

(d) natural selection

36. The collection of deleterious alleles in populations is called

(a) genetic drift (b) selection

(c) genetic load (d) migration

37. Sickle cell disease illustrates balanced polymorphism because carriers are resistant to

(a) malaria

(b) spontaneous abortion

(c) tuberculosis

(d) diarrheal disease

38. Deleterious alleles can be maintained in a population when heterozygotes have a reproductive advantage. This situation is described as

(a) inbreeding

(b) geographical isolation

(c) a population bottleneck

(d) a balanced polymorphism

39. Which factor has the least influence on disrupting Hardy-Weinberg equilibrium?

(a) Nonrandom mating

(b) Migration

(c) Mutation

(d) Genetic drift

40. Different allele frequencies from one geographic area to an adjacent area constitute

(a) founder effects

(b) bottlenecks

(c) clines

(d) balanced polymorphisms

41. Worldwide, about 1/3 of all marriages occur between people who were born fewer than ten miles apart. This is an example of

(a) natural selection (b) genetic drift

(c) nonrandom mating (d)migration

42. Which form of selection will most effectively remove a recessive disease-causing allele from a population?

(a) Selection against a dominant phenotype

(b) Selection against a recessive phenotype

(c) Selection against heterozygotes

(d) Selection against homozygotes

43. For Hardy-Weinberg equilibrium to be maintained, mutation must be

(a) occurring at a very low rate

(b) occurring in some individuals but not others

(c) absent

(d) mutation does not play a role in this situation

44. Consider a gene in a population where the dominant allele G occurs in 56% of the gametes. What is the frequency of the recessive allele?

(a) 56%

(b) 44%

(c) 0%

(d) Cannot be determined

45. Assuming Hardy-Weinberg equilibrium, what percentage of individuals are heterozygous if $p = 0.6$?

(a) 16% (b) 24%
(c) 35% (d) 48%

46. Approximately, 1/2000 individuals have a recessive genetic disorder. What is the frequency of the recessive allele?

(a) 0.005 (b) 0.995
(c) 0.978 (d) 0.022

47. Which of the following represents the proportion of individuals within a population displaying a dominant phenotype?

(a) p^2 (b) $2pq$
(c) $p^2 + 2pq$ (d) $p^2 + 2pq + q^2$

48. Assume that the frequency of PKU (a recessive disorder) in your state is 1/2500. What is the frequency of the PKU allele in this population?

(a) 0.0004 (b) 0.0008
(c) 0.02 (d) 0.98

49. Assume that the incidence of an X-linked recessive disorder is 1 in 200 male births. What is the frequency of the mutant allele?

(a) 0.000025 (b) 0.005
(c) 0.071 (d) 0.995

50. Again assuming that an X-linked recessive disorder occurs in 1 in 200 male births, what is the frequency of affected females?

(a) 0.000025 (b) 0.005
(c) 0.071 (d) 0.995

51. Assume that the incidence of an X-linked recessive disorder is 1 in 200 female births. What is the frequency of the mutant allele?

(a) 0.000025 (b) 0.005
(c) 0.071 (d) 0.995

52. Assume that you encounter a very large population of mice that have an unusual mating system: individuals with a streak of white fur between the eyes mate only with individuals lacking this marking. Is this population likely to be in equilibrium? Why or why not?

(a) Yes, the population is large
(b) Yes, individuals with the trait preferentially mate with those lacking the trait
(c) No, mating is non-random
(d) No, mutation has occurred in this population resulting in the white streak trait

53. ______ is the source of new alleles in a population

(a) Genetic drift (b) Mutation
(c) Selection (d) Nonrandom mating

54. In a population in Hardy-Weinberg equilibrium, the frequencies of a recessive allele will ______ over time

(a) increase (b) decrease
(c) remain the same (d) vary over time

55. Unlike prokaryotes, the control of transcription by eukaryotes is designed to react to change by

(a) changing
(b) ignoring change
(c) remaining constant
(d) changing the environment

56. Thickness of back fat in a certain breed of swine has been estimated to have a heritability of 80%. Suppose the average back fat thickness of this breed is 1.2 inches, and the average of individuals selected from this population to be the parents of the next generation is 0.8 inch. What is the expected average of the next generation?

(a) .32 (b) .40
(c) .60 (d) .88
(e) 1.20

57. The average yearly milk production of a herd of cows is 18,000 pounds. The average milk production of the individuals selected to be the parents of next generation is 20,000 pounds. The average milk production of the offspring generation is 18,440 pounds. The heritability of milk production in this population would be

(a) .087 (b) .22
(c) 4.55 (d) 34.32
(e) none of the above

58. Body weight in laboratory albino rats is under polygenic control. Suppose that 4 pairs of genes contribute with equal and cumulative effects to the phenotype. How many phenotypes are possible in populations of these mice?

(a) 4 (b) 5
(c) 11 (d) 17
(e) None of the above

59. Members of the same species which are capable of interbreeding is best described as a(n)

(a) community (b) population
(c) ecosystem (d) biosphere

60. If 16% of the persons in a population show a recessive trait, what is the allelic frequency for the dominant allele?

(a) 4% (b) 16%
(c) 84% (d) 96%

61. For a particular human population, if the allelic frequency of the O allele for blood type was 0.1, and the frequency for the B allele was 0.5, what would be the allelic frequency for the A allele?

(a) 0.1 (b) 0.2
(c) 0.5 (d) 0.4

62. In the following population, what would be the allelic frequency for the dominant allele? 20 homozygous recessives; 320 homozygous dominants; 160 heterozygotes?

(a) 80% (b) 60%
(c) 10% (d) 20%

63. If four per cent of a population shows a recessive trait, what will be the frequency of carriers in the following?

(a) 8% (b) 16%
(c) 32% (d) 64%

64. If there is only one allele for a gene in a population, that gene is referred to as

(a) monoallelic (b) fixed
(c) common (d) monocistronic

65. Which of the following would cause deviation from the Hardy-Weinberg equilibrium?

(a) Small population
(b) Isolated
(c) Random mating
(d) Lack of selection pressure

66. If 36% of the population is heterozygous for a certain gene, what per cent of the population will show the recessive phenotype in the next generation?

(a) 4% (b) 8%
(c) 16%
(d) need more information to determine

67. Which of the following formulas lets you predict the genotypic frequency of the next generation?

(a) $p + q + 1$
(b) $p^2 + 2pq + q^2$
(c) $e + mc^2$
(d) d = 0.5 lambda / n * sin (theta)

68. The total aggregate of alleles in a population is referred to as

(a) gene pool (b) allelic frequency
(c) genotypic frequency (d) none of these

69. Which of the following is not a necessary condition of Hardy-Weinberg equilibrium?

(a) No natural selection
(b) Random mating
(c) No mutations
(d) Migration of individuals

70. Which statement best describes the Hardy-Weinberg principle?

(a) Recessive alleles eventually disappear in large populations
(b) When a population is large, the allele frequency will change over time
(c) Dominant alleles become more prevalent in large populations
(d) When there is a large population, the mechanism of inheritance does not change the allele frequencies

71. Genetic drift can be defined as

(a) gene frequencies change over time because of random effects due to a large population in size
(b) gene frequencies change over time because of random effects due to a small population size
(c) gene frequencies stay the same over time because of random effects due to a small population size
(d) gene frequencies change over time because of predicted effects due to a small population size

72. In a population of 10 million individuals birth rate is 19 per 1000 and the death rate is 14 per 1000. The annual rise in the population would be

(a) 50,000 (b) 500,000
(c) 14,000 (d) 5,000

73. If the frequency of recessive allele causing disease in the homozygous recessive condition in a population of 10,000 is 0.04, then the number of people affected by the disease will be

(a) 400 (b) 3600
(c) 496 (d) 16

74. If all organisms in a population are triploid, then Hardy-Weinberg theorem applicable will be

(a) $(p + q)^2$ (b) $(p + q + r)^2$
(c) $(p + q + r)^3$ (d) $(p + q)^2$

75. Which of the following statement is correct about a population showing evolution?

(a) Individuals will be homozygous
(b) Will follow Hardy-Weinberg equilibrium
(c) Will not follow Hardy-Weinberg equilibrium
(d) Individuals will be in stressful condition

76. Consider that two populations are growing exponentially with the initial difference in growth rate of 10%. After 10 generations the difference between population size would be

(a) 2:1 (b) 10:1
(c) 4:1 (d) 1:1

77. What type of genetic drift is characterized by a small subgroup of a population leaving and forming a new population?

(a) Gene flow (b) Bottleneck effect
(c) Sexual selection (d) Founders effect

78. Which is the effect of change in the gene frequency?

(a) Gene flow (b) Genetic drift
(c) Natural selection (d) All of the above

79. What is the mechanism for change in the allele frequency?

(a) Gene flow (b) Natural selection
(c) Genetic drift (d) All of the above

80. The Founder effect is caused by

(a) disasters (b) disease
(c) migration (d) all of the above

81. The bottleneck effect is caused by

(a) disasters (b) migration
(c) colonization (d) all of the above

82. What is the best explanation for a population being described as an evolutionary unit?

(a) Population can evolve, not individuals
(b) Natural selection only involves individuals, not populations
(c) Genetic changes occur only in populations
(d) A population's gene pool remains the same throughout the time

83. When a population is in Hardy-Weinberg equilibrium, what is not happening in the species?

(a) Survival (b) Reproduction
(c) Evolution (d) Death

84. Mutations are important because they bring about

(a) death of the organism
(b) genetic variation needed for a population to evolve
(c) benefits for the individual, not for the population
(d) Hardy-Weinberg equilibrium within a population

85. In certain grasses the ability to grow in soils contaminated with the toxic metal nickel is determined by a dominant allele. 78% of the seeds of the grass species *Agrostis tenuis* were able to germinate and grow on contaminated soil. What proportion of the plants is heterozygous?

(a) 0.28 (b) 0.32
(c) 0.50 (d) 0.64

86. On what does natural selection act?

(a) Phenotype
(b) Genotype
(c) A population's gene pool
(d) Homozygous dominant and heterozygous individuals

87. What is the effect produced when a bee carries pollen from one population to another?

(a) Founder effect
(b) Gene flow
(c) Assortative mating
(d) Diversifying selection

88. Which of the following defines the Hardy-Weinberg equilibrium?

(a) Constant gene frequencies which do not change from generation to generation
(b) Heterozygosity at all loci
(c) Elimination of all lethal alleles
(d) Elimination of genetic drift

89. Which of the following would be expected to have the smallest proportion of heterozygous gene loci?

(a) An individual from an inbred population of vertebrates
(b) An individual from an outbred population of vertebrates
(c) An individual from an outbred population of invertebrates
(d) An island population

90. In tropical areas where malaria is prevalent, people who have one allele for beta thalassemia have a selective advantage over people who have no or two alleles for beta thalassemia. What is this an example of?

(a) Frequency dependent selection
(b) Diversifying selection
(c) Hybrid vigour
(d) Heterozygous advantage

91. Approximately 4% of the turtle in the pond shows the recessive phenotype long nose (nn). What is the frequency of the dominant allele (N) in the population?

(a) 0.16 (b) 0.20
(c) 0.40 (d) 0.80

92. Approximately 4% of the turtle population in the pond shows the recessive phenotype long nose (nn). What is the frequency of heterozygotes in the population?

(a) 0.08 (b) 0.24
(c) 0.32 (d) 0.48

93. Within the squirrel population at park, 16% show the recessive phenotype of a curled tail (tt). What is the frequency of the dominant allele (T) in the population?

(a) 0.40 (b) 0.16
(c) 0.26 (d) 0.60

94. If in a population, 1 in 2500 babies is affected by a recessive condition (cystic fibrosis), then what is the frequency of the dominant allele?

(a) 0.02 (b) 0.36
(c) 0.56 (d) 0.98

95. A population has 36% of homozygous recessive genotype (aa). Then the frequency of allele 'a' is

(a) 0% (b) 20%
(c) 60% (d) 70%

96. 360 out of 1000 individuals in a population have a genotype AA while 480 have Aa genotype. The rest 160 have aa. Then what is the frequency of the allele A in this population?

(a) 0.7 (b) 0.6
(c) 0.5 (d) 0.4

97. 25 individuals in a population are homozygous dominant, then the individuals that are expected to be homozygous recessive are

(a) 100 (b) 75
(c) 50 (d) 25

MARK TRUE OR FALSE (T/F)

1. If the value of fitness is unity, the survival would be zero
2. The word "population" was given by Johannsen
3. Sandler and Novitski had no idea about meiotic drive
4. The term "genetic drift" was coined by Wright
5. Hardy-Weinberg law operates with multilines
6. A random mating population or a panmictic population mean the same thing
7. Zygotic frequency is also known as genotypic frequency
8. Fitness does not give selective advantage
9. Meiotic drive and segregation distortion mean the same thing
10. Random genetic drift is the change in gene frequency due to sampling error
11. 100% survival will result if the value of W is 1
12. Hardy belonged to England, whereas Weinberg belonged to Germany
13. Random genetic drift is a directional force of evolution
14. Gene pool is the sum total of genes in a population
15. Mutation rates are generally too low to have a significant effect on allele frequencies
16. The gene pool is the variety of alleles of a particular gene present in a given species
17. In most natural populations, many genes are polymorphic
18. Most mutations do not alter the phenotype
19. Some mutations can increase an individual's chance of survival
20. Mutational analysis in various populations indicates that PKU originated only once
21. Natural selection results in differential survival based on phenotype

22. Frequencies of different mutations in different populations provide information on the natural history of alleles
23. Genetic drift is a random process
24. Consanguinity increases the proportion of heterozygotes in the population
25. One of the conditions that must be met for Hardy-Weinberg equilibrium is that organisms must be free to move from population to population
26. Albinism is not common in India but affects a particular community. A particular reason for this is nonrandom mating
27. Genetic drift is the collection of deleterious alleles in populations
28. Most of the mutations alter the phenotype
29. Some mutations can increase a person's survival chances
30. Natural selection results in differential survival based on phenotype
31. Migration has the least disrupting influence on Hardy-Weinberg equilibrium
32. Some genetic disorders are more common in Jews because they are a more variable group
33. Majority of marriages take place between people who live very closely to each other. This is an example of nonrandom mating
34. Selection against heterozygote will most effectively remove a recessive disease-causing allele from a population
35. Mutation does not play a role in maintaining Hardy-Weinberg equilibrium
36. For Hardy-Weinberg equilibrium, organisms should move from population to population
37. Weinberg was a German physician
38. P + q is always equal to 1
39. Genotype frequency and zygotic frequency are not the same thing
40. Artificial selection favors characters that are disadvantageous for the survival of the individual
41. Selection coefficient is also known as selective advantage
42. If the value of S is 1, then there is no survival
43. Segregation distortion and meiotic drive are the same thing
44. The term "genetic load" was coined by Hardy in 1950
45. Isozymic studies can detect polymorphic alleles
46. Adaptive value of a population decreases by genetic polymorphism
47. A small sample size would have more genetic drift
48. Hardy-Weinberg law does not operate in self pollinated crops
49. Random mating does not occur in synthetic varieties of maize
50. The term "genetic homeostasis" was coined by Lerner

19

Tissue Culture

MULTIPLE-CHOICE QUESTIONS

1. **Removing the cell walls from two different strains of organisms and then allowing the membrane bound cells to combine with one another best describes**

   (a) genetic fusion (b) protoplast fusion

   (c) cell fusion (d) DNA fusion

2. **Increased genetic diversity following extended time in a tissue culture is a problem called**

   (a) gene alteration

   (b) temporal modification

   (c) somaclonal variation

   (d) culture shock

3. **A mass of dividing, undifferentiated cells in a tissue culture is called**

   (a) a shield (b) a callus

   (c) an embryoid (d) an aggregate

   (e) a plasmodium

4. **Callus is a disorganized mass of plant cells. In tissue culture, callus can be forced to form roots by adding**

   (a) abscisic acid (b) auxin

   (c) nitrogen (d) agar

5. **Light that shines on one side of an upright stem causes more auxin to move to the**

   (a) bottom of the stem (b) top of the stem

   (c) darker side (d) lighted side

6. **This hormone is produced in the roots and promotes the outgrowth of axillary buds**

   (a) auxin (b) cytokinin

   (c) gibberellic acid (d) ethylene

7. **When the ratio of auxin to cytokinin in tissue culture is**

   (a) low, rooting can be induced in an explant

   (b) high, rooting can be induced in callus

   (c) low, shooting can be induced in callus

   (d) intermediate, cell division is promoted in explants to produce callus

8. Which of the following is not correct? Plant secondary metabolites

(a) perform a vital physiological function
(b) ward off potential predators
(c) attract pollinators
(d) combat infectious diseases

9. If humans had a shoot apical meristem then

(a) we would increase in girth (diameter)
(b) all the cells in our body would divide
(c) new sets of organs such as arms would be continually produced
(d) we would get lignified and have to worry about woodpeckers

10. To produce plants that are homozygous for all traits, the best choice is

(a) cell suspension culture
(b) callus culture
(c) anther / pollen culture
(d) plant organ culture
(e) protoplast culture

11. Cell suspension cultures require

(a) organogenesis (b) electroporation
(c) differentiation (d) aggregation
(e) disaggregation

12. If you want to use a plant tissue culture as a chemical factory for vitamins, choose

(a) suspension cultures
(b) callus cultures
(c) organ cultures
(d) anther pollen cultures
(e) protoplast cultures

13. The fastest way to a ripe tomato using tissue culture is by

(a) anther/pollen culture
(b) plant organ culture
(c) protoplast culture
(d) callus culture
(e) cell suspension culture

14. Unlike the somatic cells of animals, plant cells can be grown in tissue culture and regenerate new plants

(a) because each cell contains the entire genome
(b) because plant cells can dedifferentiate and revert back to seeds
(c) because plant cells are able to express genes that weren't previously expressed
(d) both (a) and (b)
(e) both (b) and (c)

15. Which of the following are mismatched?

(a) Cell suspension culture—somatic cell embryogenesis
(b) Protoplast isolation—hybrids
(c) Homozygous plants—anther/pollen culture
(d) Callus culture—differentiated tissues regenerate
(e) All are correctly matched

16. The composition of agar is

(a) agarose
(b) agarose plus agaropectin
(c) agaropectin
(d) none of these

17. The father of plant tissue culture is

(a) G. Haberlandt (b) E. C. Cocking
(c) R. J. Gautheret (d) P. R. White

18. Among the given auxins, which one is the most frequently used in plant tissue culture?

(a) 2,4-D (b) IBA
(c) NAA (d) IAA

19. In general, callus cultures are sub-cultured after every

(a) 2-3 weeks (b) 8-10 weeks
(c) 4-6 weeks (d) 6-8 weeks

20. Distant crosses may fail due to

(a) inability of pollen to germinate
(b) failure of the pollen tubes to grow
(c) degeneration of endosperm
(d) all of the above

21. Anther culture is ordinarily used for the production of

(a) diploid plants (b) polyploid plants
(c) haploid plants (d) all of the above

22. Somaclonal variation arises due to

(a) gene mutation, gene amplification and transposable elements
(b) deletion and duplication
(c) changes in chromosome number and DNA methylation
(d) all of the above

23. In 1981, the terms "somaclonal variation" and "somaclone" were coined by

(a) Larkin and Scowcroft
(b) Evans and Sharp
(c) Skirvin
(d) Vasil

24. For long-term storage of germplasm, which of the following is used?

(a) Liquid oxygen
(b) Mineral oil
(c) Carbon dixoide
(d) Liquid nitrogen

25. The technique of cryopreservation involves

(a) freezing and storage
(b) thawing and reculture
(c) freezing and reculture
(d) both a and b

26. Among the given compounds, the one which is commonly used for fusing protoplasts is

(a) glycerol (b) proline
(c) sorbitol (d) DMSO

27. Among the given treatments, which one is used for protoplast DNA uptake?

(a) High pH (10.5) and high Ca^{++} concentration (50 m mol/l)
(b) Polythylene glycol
(c) High voltage electric current
(d) All of the above

28. Protoplast fusion is induced by treatment with

(a) high pH (10.5) and high Ca^{++} concentration (50 m mol/l)
(b) high voltage electric current
(c) polyethylene glycol
(d) all of the above

29. Tissue culture refers to

(a) pollen culture (b) protoplast culture
(c) ovule culture (d) all of these

30. Naked cell is called

(a) chromoplast (b) protoplast
(c) cytoplast (d) proplastid

31. The plant part that is used for regeneration is called

(a) clone (b) explant
(c) callus (d) endosperm

32. A mass of unorganized regenerated cells in culture medium is called

(a) embryoid (b) callus
(c) somatic cell (d) all of these

33. The process of differentiation of root and shoot from somatic embryos in culture medium is called

(a) gametogenesis (b) organogenesis
(c) embryogenesis (d) all of these

34. Hybrid cell involving protoplast of two different species is called

(a) homokaryon (b) eukaryon
(c) heterokaryon (d) all of these

35. Organ culture refers to

(a) anther culture (b) embryo culture
(c) ovule culture (d) all of these

36. Callus refers to a mass of

(a) cells (b) organized cells
(c) unorganized cells (d) none of these

37. Allotetraploids can be produced in a single step by

(a) anther culture
(b) somatic hybridization
(c) cloning
(d) none of these

38. Somatic hybridization is useful in producing

(a) allotetraploids (b) distant hybrids
(c) transgenics (d) all of these

39. Multiple identical copies of a gene can be obtained by

(a) gene cloning
(b) gene splicing
(c) chromosome cloning
(d) gene sequencing

40. The term "somaclonal variation" was first used by

(a) Maheshwari
(b) Larkin and Scowcroft
(c) Murashige
(d) Gamborg

41. The anther culture technique was first developed by

(a) Gamborg
(b) Guha and Maheshwari
(c) Larkin
(d) Maheshwari

42. Guha and Maheshwari developed anther culture technique working with

(a) *Brassica* (b) *Datura*
(c) wheat (d) rice

43. The nutrient medium for tissue culture was first developed by

(a) Gamborg *et al.*
(b) Maheshwari
(c) White
(d) Murashige and Scoog

44. Murashige and Scoog first developed nutrient medium for tissue culture in

(a) 1952 (b) 1962
(c) 1942 (d) 1932

45. Micropropagation is widely used in

(a) horticulture (b) forestry
(c) floriculture (d) all of these

46. In vegetatively propagated species, somaclonal variation is

(a) low (b) high
(c) very high (d) not seen

47. The examples of secondary metabolites are

(a) mint oil (b) quinine
(c) morphine (d) caffeine
(e) all of the above

48. Meristem culture can be used for

(a) eliminating pathogens
(b) germplasm collection
(c) cryopreservation
(d) mass cloning of plants
(e) all of the above

49. Cryopreservation

(a) is done at –198°C in liquid ozone
(b) is done at –196°C in liquid nitrogen
(c) is done at –196°C in liquid ozone
(d) is done at –198°C in liquid nitrogen

50. Which one of the following is not a synthetic auxin?

(a) IAA (b) IBA
(c) NAA (d) 2, 4-D

51. The reasons for the escape of the meristem from virus invasion is

(a) viruses move readily in a plant body through the vascular system, which is absent in meristem
(b) mitosis in the meristem cells competes with virus multiplication
(c) a virus 'inactivating system' has highest activity in the meristem
(d) there is high auxin level in the meristem that may inhibit virus multiplication
(e) tissue injury caused by excision of the meristem may result in virus degradation
(f) all of the above

52. Out of the following, which one is not the basic component of culture media used for plant cultivation?

(a) Complex mixture of salts
(b) Amino acids
(c) Serum albumin
(d) Sugar/sucrose

53. Mark the incorrect statement about agar, a gelling agent in plant tissue culture medium

(a) not digested by plant enzymes
(b) it is not used in micropropagation work
(c) it does not react with media constituents
(d) it remains stable at incubation temperature

54. Which one of them is not the main effect of polyamines in the tissue culture system?

(a) Promotion of tuber and bulb formation
(b) Adventitious root formation
(c) Promotion of shoot formation
(d) Somatic embryogenesis

55. Media room of a plant tissue culture lab should consist of the following except

(a) pH meter
(b) autoclave machine
(c) analytical balance
(d) biosafety cabinet

56. In growth room, humidifier serves as

(a) containment reducer
(b) humidity reducer
(c) medium drying preventer
(d) temperature control

57. The instrument necessary for drying the washed glassware is

(a) vacuum pump (b) hot air oven
(c) heater (d) autoclave

58. The commonly used cytokinin in meristem culture is

(a) Zeatin (b) NAA
(c) BAP (d) 2,4 D

59. Coconut milk in combination with gibberellic acid is highly suitable for the growth of

(a) shoot apices (b) root tip
(c) stem (d) leaf part

60. What is the first formation of callus tissue for outcome of cells?

(a) Cell division (b) Cell elongation
(c) Cell expansion (d) Cell stringent

61. The production of ethylene is inhibited by specific antisense gene, namely

(a) glyphoshate (b) ACC synthase
(c) ACC synthetase (d) lyase

62. Which of the following technique is used to produce Flavr Savr tomato?

(a) rDNA technology
(b) Transgenesis
(c) Antisense RNA technology
(d) rRNA technology

63. Who reported the suspension cultures from carrot root explant?

(a) Watson and Crick
(b) Steward and Shantz
(c) Benthaman and Hook
(d) Lederber and Tatum

64. The developmental pathway of numerous well organized small embryoids is defined as

(a) organogenesis
(b) micropropagation
(c) somatic embryogenesis
(d) suspension culture

65. Artificial seed production helps to study the role of

(a) endocarp (b) endosperm
(c) pericarp (d) mesocarp

66. Microspore behaving like a zygote and undergoing change to form embryoid is known as

(a) direct androgenesis
(b) indirect androgenesis
(c) anther culture
(d) pollen culture

67. Somatic embryogenesis is

(a) germ line cells developing into embryos
(b) non-germ line cells developing into embryos
(c) embryos developing from zygotes
(d) embryonic tissue becoming somatic

68. The carbon source used mainly in plant tissue culture is

(a) sucrose (b) mannose
(c) glucose (d) lactose

69. The chemical compounds produced in plants are known as

(a) cytochemicals
(b) histochemicals
(c) phytochemicals
(d) secondary metabolites

70. The auxins inhibit the production of certain secondary metabolites by the action of

(a) IAA (b) 2,4-D
(c) NAA (d) Kinetin

71. Plant growth regulators influence growth metabolism and ______ of cultured cells

(a) differentiation (b) elongation
(c) enlargement (d) transgenesis

72. The optimal pH for plant tissue cultures is in the range of

(a) 2-3 (b) 3-5
(c) 4-5 (d) 5-6

73. The plant tissue culture medium can be sterilized in an autoclave at ______ degree Celsius

(a) 131 (b) 121
(c) 141 (d) 111

74. The process for the fusion of a normal protoplast with an enucleated protoplast is

(a) hybridization (b) cybridization
(c) rDNA technology (d) transgenesis

75. ______ plants can be developed from ovary culture

(a) Diploid (b) Haploid
(c) Monoploid (d) Dicot

76. Protoplast fusion can be done by

(a) polyethylene glycol
(b) glycerol
(c) ethylene
(d) nitrogen

77. Solid carbon dioxide is used as a cryoprotectant at ______ °C

(a) – 191 (b) – 155
(c) – 80 (d) – 76

78. Slow freezing method of cryopreservation is done at ______ °C/min

(a) 0.5 – 5.0 (b) 0.4 – 5.0
(c) 0.3 – 5.0 (d) 0.2 – 5.0

79. Which one of the following is used as a cryoprotectant?

(a) DMSO (b) Glycerate
(c) Ethyl acetate (d) Calcium ions

80. Which techniques mostly related to protoplasts that can be regenerated to viable plants?

(a) Electroporation (b) Gene gun
(c) Microinjection (d) Liposome mediated

81. The phenomenon of mature cells in meristematic state to produce callus is

(a) dedifferentiation
(b) redifferentiation
(c) shoot-bud differentiation
(d) meristem differentiation

82. The enzyme that can easily release the individual cells from the leaf tissues is

(a) macerozyme (b) lysozyme
(c) zymogen (d) chymotrypsin

83. The ability of callus cells to differentiate into a plant organ is called

(a) dedifferentiation
(b) redifferentiation
(c) shoot-bud differentiation
(d) meristem differentiation

84. What is plant tissue culture?

(a) The technique of *in vitro* maintaining and growing cells
(b) The technique of *in vivo* growing cells
(c) The technique of growing plants in gardens
(d) The technique of cutting plants

85. Name the type of culture that involves the addition of fresh nutrient medium and draining out the unused medium?

(a) Batch (b) Continuous
(c) Discontinuous (d) Open continuous

86. Virus infections of crops may result in retarded cell division is referred to as

(a) hyperplasia (b) hypoplasia
(c) necrosis (d) all of the above

87. Virus infections of crops may result in excessive cell division is referred to as

(a) hyperplasia (b) hypoplasia
(c) necrosis
(d) endometrial hyperplasia

88. Increased genetic diversity following extended time in a tissue culture is called

(a) gene alteration
(b) temporal modification
(c) somaclonal variation
(d) culture shock

89. The culture used in plants tissue culture as a chemical factory for vitamins is

(a) suspension (b) callus
(c) organ (d) anther

90. Which of the following are mismatched?

(a) Cell suspension culture somatic cell embryogenesis
(b) Protoplast isolation-hybrids
(c) Homozygous plants-anther/pollen culture
(d) Callus culture-differentiated tissues regenerate

91. Plant transformation is

(a) plant growth in culture generates increased genetic variation
(b) plant cells in suspension cultures from individual embryos that can grow into plants
(c) the incorporation of foreign DNA into the plant genome
(d) dedifferentiation callus cells develop into tissue that is different from the original source tissue

92. What technique is used to introduce genes into dicots?

(a) Electroporation
(b) Particle bombardment
(c) Microinjection
(d) Ti plasmid infection

93. The delayed ripening tomato was created by ______ gene

(a) altered (b) silenced
(c) replaced (d) relocated

94. Antisense technology

(a) alters or transfers cells
(b) combines genetic material from different species
(c) combines organelles and cells
(d) selectively blocks expression of a gene

95. Which plant can die easily from Ti plasmid infection?

(a) Wheat (b) Corn
(c) Tomato (d) Millet

96. Transposons are

(a) mobile genetic elements between homologous chromosomes
(b) mobile genetic elements between non-homologous chromosomes
(c) non-mobile genetic elements
(d) recombinant genetic elements

97. Ti plasmid type of gene transfer method works with

(a) fungi (b) dicots only
(c) animals (d) bacteria

98. Ti plasmid naturally occurs in

(a) *Agrobacterium tumefaciens*
(b) *Bacillus* species
(c) *Rhizobium* species
(d) *Nitrobacteria* species

99. The plasmid that can resist ampicillin is

(a) pBR 327 (b) pBR 456
(c) pUC 10 (d) Ti plasmid

100. Asynchronous growth refers to cultured cells that can be varying in

(a) size (b) structure
(c) growth (d) cell division

101. Who reported cell cultures and protoplast cultures in cereals?

(a) I. K. Vasil and V. Vasil
(b) Haberlandt
(c) Robbins
(d) Schenk

102. The concept of plants regeneration from single cell was given by

(a) Haberlandt and Hanning
(b) Skoog and Miller
(c) Vasil and Haberlandt
(d) White

103. The concept of isolating protoplasts using enzymes was reported by

(a) Cocking (b) Murashige
(c) Skoog (d) Bhojwani

104. What type of glassware can be used in the plant tissue culture work?

(a) Borosilicate (b) Plastic
(c) Aluminium (d) Metallic

105. The optimum relative humidity of plant tissue cultures is_____%

(a) 20-98 (b) 30-98
(c) 40-98 (d) 50-98

106. The optimum condition of autoclaving in plant tissue culture is_____ degree C, _____ psi, _____ min

(a) 123, 15, 15 (b) 121, 17, 15
(c) 121, 15, 25 (d) 121, 15, 15

107. The solution used to sanitize clean surfaces in food and dairy industries is

(a) hypochlorite solution
(b) hypochloric acid
(c) sodium hydrochloride
(d) chlorine

108. Which scientists first developed anther and pollen culture for the production of haploid plants?

(a) Skoog
(b) Hilderbrandt
(c) Stewart and Reinert
(d) Maheshwari and Guha

109. Which enzyme can degrade middle lamella of plant cells?

(a) Zymogen (b) Cellulase
(c) Macerozyme (d) Pectinase

110. Which type of continuous cultures is highly useful for studies related to cytodifferentiation and production of secondary metabolites?

(a) chemostat (b) closed
(c) turbidostat (d) batch

111. The culture in which cell cycles for majority of cultured cells occur simultaneously is called ______ culture

(a) batch (b) synchronous
(c) asynchronous (d) suspension

112. The measurement of viability of cultured cells is identified by

(a) fluorescent microscopy
(b) trypan blue stain
(c) fluorescein diacetate method
(d) binocular dissected method

113. What suppresses somatic embryogenesis?

(a) Zinc
(b) Ethyl acetate
(c) Dimethyl sulfoxide
(d) Cytokinin

114. Encapsulated embryoids behave like true seeds that can grow in soil are called

(a) natural (b) hybrid
(c) artificial (d) cybrid

115. The fusion of normal protoplast with enucleated protoplast results in the formation of

(a) cybrid
(b) hybrid
(c) cytoplasmic hybrids
(d) both (a) and (c)

116. The viability of protoplasts can be checked by

(a) dimethyl sulfoxide
(b) phenosafranin stain
(c) trypan blue
(d) iodine

117. Which of the following statements is correct?

(a) Agar is not extracted from marine algae such as seaweeds
(b) Callus undergoes differentiation and produces somatic embryoids
(c) Surface sterilization of explants is done by using mercuric bromide
(d) pH of the culture medium is 5.0 to 6.0

118. Protoplasts can be produced from suspension cultures, callus tissues or intact tissues by enzymatic treatment with

(a) catalytic enzymes
(b) pectolytic enzymes
(c) both cellulolytic and pectolytic enzymes
(d) proteolytic enzymes

119. Which method of plant propagation involves the use of girdling?

(a) Grafting (b) Cuttings
(c) Layering (d) Micropropagation

120. Which one of the following is used in the culture of regenerating protoplasts, single cells or very dilute cell suspensions?

(a) Nurse medium
(b) Nurse or feeder culture
(c) Both (a) and (b) (d) None of these

121. Subculturing is similar to propagation by cuttings because

(a) it separates multiple micro shoots and places them in the medium
(b) it uses scions to produce new micro shoots
(c) both use *in vitro* growing conditions
(d) all of the above

122. When plated only in nutrient medium, how much time is required for the protoplast to synthesize new cell wall?

(a) 2-5 days (b) 5-10 days
(c) 10-15 days (d) 15-17 days

123. The problem of necrosis and gradual senescence while performing tissue culture can be overcome by

(a) spraying auxins (b) spraying cytokinins
(c) suspension culture
(d) subculture

124. The production of secondary metabolites requires the use of

(a) protoplast (b) cell suspension
(c) meristem (d) auxillary buds

125. Synthetic seed is produced by encapsulating somatic embryos with

(a) sodium chloride (b) sodium alginate
(c) sodium acetate (d) sodium nitrate

126. DMSO (dimethyl sulfoxide) is used as

(a) gelling agent (b) alkylating agent
(c) chelating agent (d) cryoprotectant

127. The most widely used chemical for protoplast fusion, as fusogen, is

(a) mannitol
(b) sorbitol
(c) mannol
(d) poly ethylene glycol (PEG)

128. Cybrids are produced by

(a) fusion of two different nuclei from two different species
(b) fusion of two same nuclei from same species
(c) nucleus of one species but cytoplasm from both the parent species
(d) none of the above

129. Part of plant used for culturing is called

(a) scion (b) explant
(c) stock (d) callus

130. A medium which is composed of chemically defined compound is called

(a) natural media (b) synthetic media
(c) artificial media (d) none of these

131. Somaclonal variations are

(a) caused by mutagens
(b) produced during tissue culture
(c) caused by gamma rays
(d) induced during sexual embryogeny

132. Which vector is mostly used in crop improvement?

(a) Plasmid (b) Cosmid
(c) Phasmid (d) *Agrobacterium*

133. To obtain a virus free plant, what can be used as an explant in micropropagation?

(a) Apical meristem
(b) Either apical or axillary meristem
(c) Axillary meristem
(d) Embryo

134. Somaclones are obtained by

(a) plant breeding (b) genetic engineering
(c) tissue culture (d) irradiation

135. In virus-infected plants, the meristematic tissues in both apical and axillary buds are free of virus because

(a) the dividing cells are virus resistant
(b) meristems have antiviral compounds
(c) cell division of meristems is faster than rate of viral multiplication
(d) viruses cannot multiply within meristem cell(s)

136. What is the first indication for formation of callus tissue for outcome of cells?

(a) Cell division (b) Cell elongation
(c) Cell expansion (d) Cell stringent

137. Which plant growth hormone is mainly required for cell division?

(a) Gibberellin (b) Auxin
(c) Cytokinin (d) Ethylene

138. Callus is yellow in colour due to synthesis of ______ pigments

(a) carotenoid (b) anthocyanin
(c) chlorophyll (d) phycocyanin

139. A single cell or small aggregates of cells can be easily multiplied by

(a) micropropagation
(b) organogenesis
(c) cell culture (d) suspension culture

140. The production of ethylene is inhibited by specific antisense gene, namely

(a) glyphosate (b) ACC synthase
(c) ACC synthetase (d) lyase

141. Which of the following is responsible for ripening?

(a) Glyphosate
(b) ACC synthase
(c) ACC synthetase
(d) Polygalacturonidase

142. Which of the following technique is used to produce Flavr Savr tomato?

(a) rDNA technology
(b) Transgenesis
(c) Antisense RNA technology
(d) rRNA technology

143. The developmental pathway of numerous well organized small embryoids is defined as

(a) organogenesis
(b) micropropagation
(c) somatic embryogenesis
(d) suspension culture

144. Artificial seed production helps to study the role of

(a) endocarp (b) endosperm
(c) pericarp (d) mesocarp

145. The *in vitro* development of haploid plants is called

(a) organogenesis (b) androgenesis
(c) embryogenesis (d) micropropagation

146. Microspore behaves like a zygote and undergoes change to form embryoid is known as

(a) direct androgenesis
(b) indirect androgenesis
(c) anther culture
(d) pollen culture

147. The precursors for the synthesis of nopalines in Ti plasmid is

(a) phosphoenolpyruvate + amino acid
(b) pyruvate + amino acid
(c) alpha-ketoglutarate + amino acid
(d) oxalate + amino acid

148. Which of the following statements is TRUE regarding transposons?

(a) They are sequences of mRNA that can move around in the genome
(b) They exist in wheat but are not found in the human genome
(c) They are the most abundant type of repeat in the genome
(d) All of the above are true regarding transposons

149. The gene transfer technique involves a tiny needle that is used to inject DNA into a cell lacking that DNA sequence is known as

(a) electroporation
(b) liposome transfer
(c) microinjection
(d) particle bombardment

150. The gene transfer technique involves the use of a fatty bubble to carry a gene into a somatic cell is

(a) electrofusion (b) liposome transfer
(c) laser transfection (d) biolistics

151. The broad spectrum herbicide is

(a) gluphosate
(b) sulfonyl urea
(c) phosphoinothricin
(d) imidazollinones

152. Which amino acid is a derivative of glyphosate?

(a) Alanine (b) Serine
(c) Valine (d) Glycine

153. The carbon source used mainly in plant tissue culture is

(a) sucrose (b) mannose
(c) surcose (d) lactose

154. The chemical compounds that are produced by the plants are known as

(a) cytochemicals
(b) histochemicals
(c) phytochemicals
(d) secondary metabolites

155. Evans blue dye stains cell which are

(a) dead (b) live
(c) dividing (d) expanding

156. Somaclones are produced by

(a) Micropropagation
(b) Mutation
(c) Polyploidy
(d) Hybridisation

157. The length of Ti plasmid is ______ kilobytes

(a) 20 (b) 200
(c) 2 (d) 2000

158. Which technique is mostly related to protoplasts that can be regenerated to viable plants?

(a) Electroporation (b) Gene gun
(c) Microinjection (d) Liposome mediated

159. Which region codes for proteins involved in the uptake and metabolism of opines in Ti plasmids?

(a) Promoter (b) Vir
(c) Selectable marker (d) Opine catabolism

160. Which plants have been developed for expressing antigens derived from animal viruses?

(a) Tomato (b) Tobacco
(c) Potato (d) Corn

161. Name the type of culture that involves the addition of fresh nutrient medium and drawing out the used medium?

(a) Batch (b) Continuous
(c) Discontinuous (d) Open continuous

162. A characteristic feature of the chloroplast genome is the presence of two

(a) simple tandem arrays
(b) repeat interspersions
(c) compound tandem arrays
(d) identical inverted repeats

163. The optimum relative humidity of plant tissue culture is ______%

(a) 20-98 (b) 30-98
(c) 40-98 (d) 50-98

164. Which enzyme can degrade middle lamella and cell wall of plant cells?

(a) Zymogen (b) Cellulases
(c) Macerozyme (d) Pectinase

165. Which type of continuous culture is highly useful for studies related to cytodifferentiation and production of secondary metabolites?

(a) Chemostat (b) Closed
(c) Turbidostat (d) Batch

166. The physical treatment method of synchronous culture is

(a) cold treatment (b) chemical inhibition
(c) colchicine (d) starvation

167. Which chemical suppresses the somatic embryogenesis?

(a) Zinc
(b) Ethyl acetate
(c) Dimethyl sulfoxide
(d) Cytokinin

168. The viability of protoplasts can be checked by

(a) dimethyl sulfoxide
(b) phenosafranine stain
(c) tryphan blue
(d) iodine

MARK TRUE OR FALSE (T/F)

1. Tissue culture is the way of growing plants as isolated differentiated cells
2. Plant tissue culture refers to cultivation of explants *in vivo*
3. Adventitious refers to development of organs or embryos from unusual points of origin, including callus

4. Agar is a vegetable product made from fungi
5. Aseptic means free from all microorganisms
6. In an autoclave, sterilization is done at 126 degrees centigrade
7. IAA is a synthetic auxin
8. Zeatin is an auxin
9. BAP is a synthetic cytokinin
10. IBA is a natural auxin
11. Callus is an actively dividing organized tissue
12. Cell culture is the group of cells *in vitro*
13. A clone is always homogeneous
14. Cytokinins decrease apical dominance
15. Auxins often induce adventitious roots
16. Dedifferentiation reverts meristematic to differentiated cells
17. In embryogenesis, an embryo develops from a fertilized egg cell or asexually from a single or group of cells
18. An adventitious embryo developing *in vitro* by vegetative means is known as an embryoid
19. Gibberellins induce root formation
20. Magnesium is a macro-element
21. Manganese is a micro-element
22. Vegetative propagation of plants *in vivo* is known as micropropagation
23. Plasmid is a chromosomal, autonomously replicating element
24. A plant cell without a cell membrane is known as protoplast
25. Increase of genetic variability in higher plants, which takes place *in vitro* culture, is known as somaclonal variation
26. Growth of cells in a solid medium is called suspension culture
27. Growth of a tissue or a plant in a test tube is *in vivo*
28. *In situ* and *in vivo* means the same thing
29. First attempt at plant tissue culture was made by Haberlandt
30. Skoog used coconut milk for the culture of Datura embryos
31. Movel and Martin produced virus free Dahlia by meristem culture in 1952
32. Cocking reported that it is the ratio of auxin to cytokinin, which is responsible for organ formation
33. First book on Plant Tissue Culture was written by Gautheret in 1959
34. In 1960, Cocking isolated protoplasts by enzymatic method
35. Murashige and Skoog produced the famous MS media for plant tissue culture in 1952
36. DNA sequencing method was given by Carlson
37. Vasil coined the term 'Somaclonal Variation'
38. The first genetically transformed products were released by Calgene
39. Bollguard cotton was released by Monsanto
40. Yield Guard cotton was released by Ciba seeds
41. Roundup Ready is Canola with herbicide resistance
42. Endless summer is a transgenic tomato
43. Penicillin was discovered by Flemming
44. In tissue culture, the smaller the explant, the less likelihood of transmitting endogenous infestations
45. Plants that are easy to propagate by conventional cuttings, culture with difficulty
46. Shoot tips and most recent flushes of growth are more suitable for tissue culture
47. The main approach for the elimination of a virus is the use of heat therapy
48. Ethanol in tissue culture may prevent the production of exudates
49. Polyvinyl pyrrolidine is an important adsorbent against exudates in tissue culture
50. Gelrite is a synthetic product, which has the advantage of producing a clear gel rather than opaque like agar

51. Agar is a fungal extract
52. pH of the tissue culture medium is most commonly adjusted to 6.5 at the time of preparation
53. The greatest potential of clonal multiplication is through somatic embryogenesis
54. Induction of embryogenesis does not require an auxin
55. Agar is a seaweed derivative that can be used as a gelling agent
56. The agar concentration used for tissue culture is in the range of 0.4% to 1.0%
57. Synthetic gells are known to cause vitrification, which is a physiological problem occurring during tissue culture of many species
58. Agar gel and agar are the same things
59. In tissue culture, a concentration of 1-5% sucrose is usually used *in vitro*
60. If pH of the nutrient medium is higher than 6.0, the medium may become too soft
61. Auxins should be dissolved in I N HCl
62. Gibberellins are dissolved in water with alcohol
63. Synthetic auxins are less active than IAA
64. Synthetic auxins are more effective, as they are not degraded by the enzymes present in the plant tissues
65. Cytokinins are not heat stable, so they cannot be added to the medium prior to autoclaving
66. Gibberellins are heat labile and cannot be autoclaved, so they must be added to the medium after autoclaving using millipore filtration
67. Abscisic acid is regarded as being a growth inhibitor
68. Abscisic acid is found to stimulate embryoid development from callus
69. Abscisic acid has the ability to modify cytokinin synthesis and act as a gibberellin antagonist
70. Ethylene production by tissues grown in the dark is more than if tissues are grown in light
71. Most plants are not able to synthesize vitamins *in vitro,* so it is necessary to add them to *in vitro* culture
72. Activated charcoal absorbs toxic gases such as ethylene produced by some cultures
73. MS medium has a lower concentration of salts and nitrate as compared to other media
74. MS medium has been used successfully with a wide variety of dicotyledonous plants
75. For callus initiation, 2, 4–D is added to the medium
76. Organic stocks are more stable than inorganic stocks
77. Precipitated stock solutions cannot be used by the plants
78. If the gel consistency is too soft, the pH of the medium could be low
79. If fructose is used in the medium, the gel may be softer
80. Naphthalene acetic acid is an auxin
81. Naphthalene acetic acid is not autoclavable
82. Abscisic acid is a cytokinin
83. Spraying with fungicide or pesticide can be carried out during acclimatization
84. The advantage of filter sterilization is that thermolabile substances can pass through the filter unchanged
85. Virus particles cannot pass through the filter
86. Irradiation sterilization of nutrient media is very cheap
87. Carbon dioxide is a far better carbon source than sucrose for *in vitro* culture
88. When a weak current is passed between the tissue and the culture medium, increase in callus growth can be observed
89. Process whereby tissues, cells or callus may be induced to form shoots and complete plants is called organogenesis

90. Organogenesis can be initiated without hormones
91. Embryogenesis is a process whereby a plant is formed from one cell in a tissue, or callus by the normal zygotic pathway
92. Embryogenesis can be initiated with or without hormones
93. Somatic embryogenesis as a means of propagation is commonly used
94. Somatic embryogenesis is used to produce mutant plants or somaclones
95. Somaclonal variation is tissue specific
96. 2, 4-D can cause somaclonal variation
97. Anoxia may cause mitotic abnormalities in growing tissues
98. *In ovulo* culture can include anything from the culture of individual ovules to whole ovaries or even whole flowers
99. Viruses move readily in a plant body through the vascular system, which is absent in the meristem
100. There is low auxin level in the meristem, which may inhibit virus multiplication
101. Agar is a polysaccharide with a high molecular mass

20

DNA Biotechnology

MULTIPLE-CHOICE QUESTIONS

TECHNIQUES AND ANALYSIS

1. **Cloning a mammal by somatic nuclear transfer involves all of the following except**
   (a) artificial doubling of the haploid chromosome number of an egg cell
   (b) removal of a somatic cell from an adult
   (c) harvesting egg cells from a female
   (d) removal of the nucleus from an egg cell
   (e) placing the developing embryo into the uterus of a foster mother

2. **The size of DNA fragment (gene) that can be cloned in plasmid is about**
   (a) 15 kb (b) 45 kb
   (c) 200 kb (d) 150 kb

3. **Dolly, the sheep, was cloned from**
   (a) an embryonic cell
   (b) a fetal cell
   (c) a mammary gland cell
   (d) an artificial cell

4. **What is genetic engineering?**
   (a) Making of new genes
   (b) Making of new nucleotides
   (c) Transfer of DNA between living cells
   (d) Transfer of mature nuclei between cells

5. **Which of the following is not needed in a PCR reaction?**
   (a) DNA polymerase
   (b) Primase
   (c) Primers
   (d) Deoxynucleoside triphosphates
   (e) DNA

6. **To reduce the non-specific priming in a PCR one may**
   (a) increase the magnesium concentration
   (b) make the last six bases at the primer 3′ ends GC-rich
   (c) allow the polymerase to mix the reactants after the tube becomes hot
   (d) lower the annealing temperature

7. The number of amplified pieces of DNA equals ______ after five cycles of PCR

(a) 5 (b) 10
(c) 25 (d) 32

8. Current applications of gene cloning include

(a) cleaning up toxic waste
(b) manufacturing human growth hormone
(c) instilling pest resistance in plants
(d) a and c only
(e) a, b, and c

9. Is it possible to use PCR to produce many copies of all DNA of one chromosome?

(a) Yes, if the correct primers are available
(b) Yes, if the telomeres are present
(c) No, PCR cannot copy DNA, only RNA
(d) No, PCR copies short sequences of DNA only

10. Place in order the following steps involved in PCR: (1) newly synthesized strands act as templates, (2) temperature lowered; DNA primers and polymerase added, (3) heat separates strands of target DNA, (4) complementary base pairing between primers and template, (5) DNA nucleotide bases added; new strand synthesized

(a) 1 - 2 - 3 - 4
(b) 3 - 5 - 4 - 2 - 3 - 1
(c) 3 - 2 - 4 - 5 - 3 - 1
(d) 2 - 3 - 4 - 5 - 2 - 1

11. PCR replicates the

(a) plants (b) species
(c) DNA (d) age
(e) blood vessels

12. What is DNA fingerprinting used for?

(a) Identification (b) Law and justice
(c) Paternity (d) All of the above

13. What is the main problem with DNA fingerprinting?

(a) Inaccuracy
(b) Time consuming
(c) Not an exact match, more like a probability
(d) All of the above

14. What is the main point behind DNA fingerprinting?

(a) Everyone's DNA is alike
(b) DNA can be found easily
(c) Everyone's DNA is complex and unique
(d) None of the above

15. Where do they get the patterns for DNA fingerprinting?

(a) Introns (b) Exons
(c) Ribosomes (d) Chromosomes

16. Where can DNA be obtained for DNA fingerprinting?

(a) Blood (b) Hair
(c) Sperm (d) All of the above

17. In step 1 of PCR amplification, denature means

(a) stirring DNA together in a test tube
(b) heating blood vessels to boiling
(c) breaking the hydrogen bonds that hold DNA strands together
(d) refrigerating the DNA until it freezes
(e) waiting one week for the DNA to separate into many strands

18. Which of the following lab techniques would show the amount and size of RNA?

(a) Southern blot (b) PCR
(c) Western blot (d) DNA sequencing
(e) Northern blot

19. Large triplet repeat expansions can be detected by

(a) polymerase chain reaction
(b) single strand conformational polymorphism analysis
(c) Southern blotting
(d) Western blotting

20. Which of the following techniques produces lots of a specific segment of DNA?

(a) Southern blot (b) PCR
(c) Western blot (d) DNA sequencing
(e) Northern blot

21. A Northern blot is used to separate and study

(a) genomic DNA (b) cDNA
(c) RNA (d) short polypeptides
(e) proteins

22. Tools to detect polymorphism in plants are ______ maps

(a) RFLP and QTL
(b) AFLP and PCR
(c) PCR and QTL
(d) RFLP and AFLP
(e) AFLP and QTL

23. The PCR technique involves the use of

(a) synthesized oligonucleotide primers
(b) cloned probes
(c) DNA polymerase
(d) metaphase chromosomes
(e) a and c

24. Northern blot is used to

a) test polymorphism in linkage analysis
b) analyze protein variation
c) analyze DNA sequence
d) analyze gene expression in different tissues
e) analyze a Southern blot that has mistakenly been run upside down

25. Which of the following is a plasmid-encoded trait?

(a) Transduction (b) Transformation
(c) Translocation (d) Conjugation
(e) Mutation

26. Plasmid is

(a) a mutant plastid
(b) a piece of DNA that replicates freely in the environment
(c) the causative agent transduction
(d) transferred from parent to offspring at division
(e) unable to replicate autonomously within its host

27. Bacterial insertion sequence (IS) elements

(a) do not begin and end with inverted repeat sequences
(b) are not the sites of elevated recombination
(c) do not encode their own transposase enzyme
(d) do not have the potential to interrupt genes
(e) are not components of larger simple transposons

28. Introduction of a tobacco mosaic virus transgene into plants in 1986 was used to demonstrate

(a) cross-expression (b) co-inoculation
(c) co-transformation (d) cross-protection
(e) cross-inoculation

29. Restriction endonuclease is used to cleave

(a) DNA into nucleotides
(b) DNA at specific places
(c) RNA into nucleotides
(d) RNA at specific places

30. Cutting genomic DNA with a single restriction enzyme will result in DNA fragments that

(a) are all of the same length
(b) all end with the same base sequence pattern
(c) all migrate the same distance on a gel
(d) all have the same molecular weight
(e) all contain the same genes

31. Which of the following is most likely to be present in a BAC?

(a) cDNA (b) EST
(c) LB, RB (d) UTR
(e) Opine genes

32. Which of the following is present on a Ti plasmid, but not on any component of a binary vector system?

(a) Vir genes (b) GUS genes
(c) LB, RB (d) MCS
(e) Opine genes

33. Whole genome shotgun sequencing involves

(a) "shooting" contents of entire nuclei into DNA sequencer and obtaining a readout
(b) random sequencing of DNA clones followed by clone alignment based on overlap
(c) shotgun mutagenesis, mapping and sequencing of newly discovered single genes
(d) alignment of clones based on overlap of known landmarks followed by sequencing
(e) probing the genome with known sequences, PCR-amplification and sequencing

34. Why might you find two kanamycin resistance genes on different parts of a T-DNA plasmid?

(a) One of the genes could be used for positive selection, and one could be used for negative selection
(b) One of the genes could be used for selection in plants, and one could be used for selection in bacteria
(c) This arrangement facilitates site-specific recombination for marker-free selection
(d) Each gene might have been introduced by an independent co-transformation event
(e) Each gene might have been introduced by an independent member of a binary vector system

35. Why have been transgenic proteins, present in crops, often tested in the presence of stomach acid before the plants were released?

(a) To see whether the protein will be mutated into a more harmful protein (e.g., prions)
(b) To see whether the protein can be digested to provide substantially equivalent nutrients
(c) To see whether the protein will be digestible by an average consumer
(d) To see whether the protein will persist long enough to cause an allergic reaction
(e) To see whether latent activities in the protein (e.g., phosphatases) will be activated

36. Star Link is most closely associated with which of the following terms?

(a) Glufosinate (b) Event 176
(c) Cry 9 (d) Cry 1
(e) Glyphosate

37. Which of the following accurately describes the role of restriction enzymes in genetic engineering?

(a) Cutting sequences of double-stranded DNA into fragments
(b) Opening holes in the membranes of the target cells
(c) Making multiple copies of gene sequences of single-stranded DNA
(d) Removing the nucleus of a cell and replacing it with another

38. A gene library is a

(a) collection of genes from different organisms
(b) collection of clones carrying different DNA segments
(c) collection of organisms, all carrying the same gene
(d) bacterial strain carrying lots of genes
(e) cloned gene that has been replicated many thousands of times

39. DNA from an organism can be incorporated into a vector using the enzyme

(a) DNA polymerase
(b) RNA polymerase
(c) ligase
(d) restriction endonuclease

40. DNA ligase carries out which of the following?

(a) Causes DNA to replicate
(b) Causes DNA transcription
(c) Joins DNA fragments to combine
(d) Breaks DNA at specific points

41. Which of the following is not an example of a vector which can transport DNA from one cell to another?

(a) Plasmid (b) Cosmid
(c) Primer (d) Phagemids

42. In gene technology, fragments of DNA can be separated according to their size by the technique of

(a) gel electrophoresis
(b) chromatography
(c) polymerase chain reaction
(d) ultracentrifugation

43. The difference between a simple tandem array and a compound tandem array is

(a) the frequency of different sequences
(b) the direction the sequences face (left or right)
(c) the number of different sequences involved
(d) the number of repetitions of sequences

44. In the creation of a microarray (biochip), fragments of DNA are placed on a

(a) microscope slide (b) circuit board
(c) silicone chip (d) membrane

45. Proteomics is the study of

(a) all proteins in an organism
(b) gene-transcribing proteins
(c) structural proteins of a cell
(d) regulating proteins in humans

46. Proteomics

(a) is another term for genomics in humans
(b) is the study of the collection of proteins produced in a particular cell
(c) is the study of proteins produced by a particular gene
(d) proves that a single gene codes for only one protein

47. Electroporation is a technique used with

(a) calluses (b) pollen
(c) protoplasts (d) organs
(e) cell suspensions

48. The restriction enzyme produced by a bacterium does not cut its own DNA because the

(a) enzyme is found in a different cellular organelle from the DNA
(b) recognition sequence does not occur in the bacterium's DNA
(c) DNA is protected from the enzyme by bound histones
(d) DNA is protected from the enzyme by modification of certain bases
(e) enzyme is not active until released from the bacterium

49. Genetic engineering has modified ____ for the creation of mono-unsaturated fatty acids

(a) PCR denaturase (b) QTL polymerase
(c) LCP lipase (d) QLR esterase
(e) ACP desaturase

50. A gene can be isolated from

(a) mRNA using reverse transcriptase
(b) genomic library
(c) chemical synthesis
(d) all of the above

51. Vectors can be used for cloning of DNA molecules up to

(a) 50 kbp (b) 25 kbp
(c) 100 kbp (d) 75 kbp

52. The presence of transgene/ DNA segment into transformed cells can be detected by

(a) Southern hybridization
(b) PCR amplification
(c) dot blot assay
(d) all of the above

53. T-DNA is flanked on both the sides by direct repeat sequences of

(a) 24 bp (b) 15 bp
(c) 35 bp (d) 45 bp

54. Binary vector PGV 3850 was developed after fusion of the vector

(a) Ti plasmid and pBR 327
(b) Ti plasmid and pBR 322
(c) Ti plasmid and pUC 11
(d) Ti plasmid and EMBL 3

55. Stable integration of T-DNA has been reported in

(a) *Petunia* and tobacco
(b) cotton and tomato
(c) sunflower and *Brassica*
(d) all of the above

56. PEG-induced DNA uptake by protoplasts and genetic transformation has been reported in

(a) *Triticum monococcum*
(b) *Oryza sativa*
(c) *Saccharum* sp.
(d) all of the above

57. Transformation through electroporation has been reported in

(a) rice (b) wheat
(c) tobacco (d) all of the above

58. Among the given scorable markers, which one is generally used?

(a) Luciferase (lux)
(b) β-glucourinidase (Gus)
(c) Octopine synthase (ocs)
(d) Nopaline synthase (nos)

59. Crystal proteins are proteolytically processed in the insect midgut to yield a toxic core fragment of

(a) 80 kDa (b) 60 kDa
(c) 70 kDa (d) 50 kDa

60. The Cry II B protein is specific to

(a) coleoptera (b) diptera
(c) lepidoptera (d) orthopoda

61. Among the given proteins, which has been evaluated for insect control?

(a) Cowpea trypsin inhibitor and serine protease inhibitor
(b) Cystein protease inhibitor and proteinase inhibitor II
(c) Lectin and aprotinin
(d) All of the above

62. The slow ripening transgenic tomato Flavr Savr was developed in USA by using

(a) antisense RNA technology
(b) ribozyme technology
(c) co-suppression approach
(d) transgene silencing approach

63. The barnase and barstar genes were isolated from

(a) *Agrobacterium rhizogenes*
(b) *Bacillus thuringiensis*
(c) *Bacillus amyloliquefaciens*
(d) *Bacillus subtilis*

64. Of the given reognition sites, which one is recognised by *EcoRI*?

(a) AAG/CTT TTC/GAA
(b) A/GATCT TCTAG/A
(c) CC/CGGG GGGC/CC
(d) G/AATTC CTTAA/G

65. Control of Plant Gene Expression was dubbed as "terminator technology" by

(a) United States Department of Agriculture, USA
(b) Delta and Pine Land Company
(c) Rural Advancement Foundation International
(d) DBT, New Delhi

66. Yield Guard, and Maximizer are transgenic varieties of

(a) cotton (b) soybean
(c) tobacco (d) maize

67. Soybean transgenic variety "Roundup Ready" is resistant to

(a) glyphosate (b) atrazine
(c) phosphinothricin (d) yellow mosaic

68. Potato transgenic variety "New Leaf" is resistant to

(a) late blight (b) potato virus
(c) frost (d) Colorado beetle

69. Tomato transgenic line 'Endless Summer' has the feature of

(a) early ripening
(b) high TSS
(c) delayed ripening
(d) bacterial wilt resistance

70. Vitrification of cultures may not be reduced by

(a) higher agar concentration
(b) growth retardants
(c) agar hydrolysate
(d) gibberellic acid

71. Which of the following restriction enzymes has a four-base recognition sequence?

(a) *Hpa* II (b) *Hpa* I
(c) *Hind* III (d) *Eco* RI

72. Which of the following restriction enzymes has a six-base recognition sequence?

(a) *Hin* P II (b) *Hpa* II
(c) *Hin* FI (d) *Bgl* II

73. Bt gene is isolated from

(a) plant (b) bacterium
(c) fungi (d) virus

74. Golden rice is rich in

(a) vitamin A (b) β-carotene
(c) thiamine (d) vitamin C

75. Flavr Savr tomato is developed for increasing

(a) flavour of tomato (b) acidity
(c) shelf-life (d) aroma

76. Genetic engineering has succeeded in modifying canola oil to replace

(a) yogurt
(b) coconut oil
(c) palm oil
(d) cocoa butter
(e) margarine

77. Genome sequencing has been done in which of the following crops?

(a) Rice (b) Corn
(c) Barley (d) Wheat
(e) All of the above

78. Pores in protoplasts may be opened to DNA by the application of

(a) magnetism (b) light
(c) enzymes (d) ultrasound
(e) electricity

79. Plant transformation is

(a) when a plant grown in culture generates increased genetic variation
(b) when plant cells in suspension cultures form individual embryos that can grow into plants
(c) the incorporation of foreign DNA into the plant genome
(d) when dedifferentiated callus cells develop into tissue that is different from the original source tissue
(e) none of the above

80. In recombinant DNA technology, which enzyme is used to join fragments that have been cut by restriction enzymes?

(a) EcoRI
(b) DNA methylases
(c) DNA polymerase
(d) DNA ligase

81. Suppose ENZ-1 and ENZ-2 are two different restriction enzymes. If various pieces of DNA are cut with either of these enzymes, which of the following cut DNA molecules would join together easily to form recombinant DNA molecules?

(a) Human DNA cut with ENZ-1 and gorilla DNA cut with ENZ-2
(b) Human DNA cut with ENZ-1 and human DNA cut with ENZ-2
(c) Human DNA cut with ENZ-2 and bacterial DNA cut with ENZ-2
(d) Bacterial DNA cut with ENZ-1 and gorilla DNA cut with ENZ-2

82. Molecular mapping of genes involves associating phenotypes through linkage with

(a) restriction fragment length polymorphisms (RFLPs)
(b) single nucleotide polymorphisms (SNPs)
(c) minisatellite markers or variable number of tandem repeats (VNTRs)
(d) minisatellite markers (dinucleotide repeats)
(e) all of the above

83. First generation of transgenic plants is called

(a) TO (b) T2
(c) T (d) T1

84. Foreign genes (transgenes) can be transferred by

(a) plasmid method
(b) micro-injection
(c) particle bombardment
(d) all of these

85. Maximum transgenic plants have been released in

(a) rapeseed (b) rice
(c) tomato (d) wheat

86. In cotton, resistance to *Helicoverpa* has been transferred from

(a) *Bacillus thuringiensis*
(b) *Rhizobium*
(c) fish
(d) *Pseudomonas*

87. In tomato, antifreezing gene has been transferred from

(a) *Arabidopsis* (b) polar bear
(c) fish (d) none of these

88. In tobacco, cold resistance has been transferred from

(a) barley (b) finger millet
(c) *Arabidopsis* (d) none of these

89. In tobacco, protein quality has been improved by transferring glutenin gene from

(a) wheat (b) rice
(c) maize (d) barley

90. In maize, resistance to European corn borer has been transferred from

(a) *Arabidopsis* (b) wheat
(c) soyabean (d) Bt

91. In wheat, herbicide resistance to glufosinate has been transferred from

(a) *Arabidopsis* (b) *Streptomyces*
(c) soyabean (d) Bt

92. Which of the following techniques can be utilized most efficiently for map-based gene cloning?

(a) Chromosome walking
(b) Chromosome landing
(c) Chromosome banding
(d) Chromosome painting

93. Barnase/ barstar system of male sterility was initially demonstrated in

(a) *B. napus* (b) *O. sativa*
(c) *T. aestivum* (d) *Z. mays*

94. The most often used promoter for gene transfer in plants is

(a) *nos promoter*
(b) *Adh* 1 promoter
(c) *35 S* promoter
(d) SV40 early promoter

95. Restriction enzymes are needed for which of the following?

(a) RAPDs
(b) Nick translation
(c) AFLP
(d) Dot blot hybridization

96. Which of the following transformation techniques is the least likely to lead to rearrangements of the DNA inserts?

I. *Agrobacterium*-mediated
II. particle gun
III. electroporation

(a) I (b) III
(c) II (d) II and III

97. The controversial terminator technology seeks to provide

(a) protection to transgenes from piracy
(b) selective termination of crop diseases
(c) hybrid seed fit for consumption but not for use as seed
(d) transgenic varieties that can be grown by farmers generation after generation

98. Which of the following produces blunt ends?

(a) *Alu* I (b) *Hind* III
(c) *Hin P* II (d) *Eco*RI

99. Which of the following cleaves outside the target site?

(a) *Hpa* II (b) *Sau* 3A
(c) *Taq* I (d) *Bam* HI

100. Which of the following does not have a 6-base target sequence?

(a) *Eco* RI (b) *Hind* III
(c) *Hin* f 1 (d) *Bam* HI

101. Which of the following is not the characteristic of C_4 plant?

(a) There are two CO_2 acceptors, namely PEP and RUBP
(b) RUBP carboxylase is present in the mesophyll
(c) The first stable product is a 4-carbon compound
(d) Oxygen does not have any inhibitory effect on the process

102. Laurical is a transgenic variety of

(a) *Brassica napus* (b) soybean
(c) flax (d) coconut

GENOMICS

103. The human genome project began as researchers' mapped ______ and sites of cytogenetic abnormalities

(a) lods (b) RFLPs
(c) PCRs (d) VNTRs

104. Which genetic map is the most detailed?

(a) Cytogenetic (b) Linkage
(c) Physical (d) Sequence

105. In the Sanger method of DNA sequencing, DNA synthesis ______ when a dideoxy base is encountered

(a) commences (b) continues
(c) stops (d) increases

106. The first organism to have its genome sequenced was

(a) *Haemophilus influenzae*
(b) *Escherichia coli*
(c) *Mycoplasma genitalium*
(d) *Saccharomyces cerevisiae*

107. About ______ of the genes in *Saccharomyces cerevisiae* have counterparts among mammals

(a) 1/4 (b) 1/3
(c) 1/2 d) 2/3

108. Chromosomal and linkage maps are generated by

(a) family data (b) RFLP's
(c) positional cloning (d) none of the above

109. The Human Genome Project officially began in

(a) 1988 (b) 1990
(c) 1992 (d) 1995

110. Funding for the Human Genome Project comes from

(a) the NIH (National Institute of Health, USA)
(b) the DOE (Department of Energy, USA)
(c) the NIH and the DOE
(d) the NIH, the DOE and ELSI (Ethical, Legal, and Social Issues, USA)

111. Of the two groups who worked on the first draft sequence of the human genome

(a) Francis Collins and the International Consortium skipped the BAC stage
(b) Francis Collins led the effort by Celera Genomics
(c) Craig Venter's group shotgunned multiple copies of entire genomes into small pieces and used a computer program to assemble the overlaps into larger pieces
(d) all of the above are true

112. The "Bermuda rules" stated that

(a) researchers had to release new DNA sequences to the public database within 24 hours
(b) microarray technology could not be used for bioterrorism
(c) the human genome data would be posted on the internet
(d) GenBank would be in charge of organizing data regarding the human genome

113. Louise Brown, the first test-tube baby, was conceived using which assisted reproductive technology?

(a) Artificial insemination
(b) Intracytoplasmic sperm injection
(c) *In vitro* fertilization
(d) Gamete intrafallopian transfer

AGRICULTURAL BIOTECHNOLOGY

114. Which technique is used to introduce genes into dicots?

(a) Electroporation (b) Particle acceleration
(c) Microinjection (d) Ti plasmid infection

115. Plants containing genes encoding cytokines and blood clotting factors are used in

(a) nutrition improvement
(b) pharmaceutical production
(c) vaccine production
(d) textile production

116. Which cell-based plant technology involves the combining of two cells without cell walls from different species?

(a) Clonal propagation
(b) Cybridization (c) Protoplast fusion
(d) Mutant selection

117. If the goal were to create a plant resistant to an insecticide, which cell-based plant technology would be most effective?

(a) Clonal propagation
(b) Cybridization (c) Protoplast fusion
(d) Mutant selection

118. The delayed ripening tomato was created by a biotechnology that ______ a gene

(a) altered (b) silenced
(c) replaced (d) relocated

119. A ______ is a re creation of a portion of an ecosystem in a laboratory

(a) microcosm (b) mibridization
(c) bioremediation (d) rhizosecretion

120. Two genes from a bacterium (*Alcaligenes eutrophus*) and a cotton gene produce

(a) a plastic
(b) a vaccine against the bacterium
(c) a pharmaceutical product
(d) herbicide resistance

121. Assume that you are the president of a plant biotechnology company and you want to offer your customers a new variety of cucumber that tastes great, lasts longer on the shelf, and is less susceptible to insect damage. Which method will be the most precise and produce plants with the desired characteristics quicker?

(a) Traditional plant breeding
(b) Genetic modification through genetic engineering
(c) Neither, the president wants too much
(d) Neither, research efforts have not focused on creating organisms with specific combinations of characteristics

122. A researcher identifies a naturally occurring variant possessing characteristic of interest. This plant is selectively bred. This is an example of

(a) traditional plant breeding
(b) transgenic technology
(c) mutant selection
(d) none of the above

123. Antisense technology

(a) selectively blocks expression of a gene
(b) combines genetic material from different species
(c) combines organelles and cells
(d) alters or transfers cells

124. The first field tests were of which genetically altered organism?

(a) Bt corn
(b) Vaccinia virus containing a gene from the rabies virus
(c) The "flavr savr" tomato
(d) Strawberry seedlings sprayed with "ice-minus" bacteria

125. Which of the following dies from Ti plasmid infection?

(a) Rice (b) Corn
(c) Sorghum (d) All of the above

126. Which of the agricultural challenges below cannot be solved with transgenic techniques?

(a) Crops are damaged by frost
(b) Crops are killed by a virus
(c) Public concern about safety of synthetic pesticides
(d) Public preference for organic vegetables

127. Transplastomics

(a) targets genes in the chloroplast
(b) provides exceptionally low yields of protein products
(c) produces genes that are released in pollen
(d) offers little opportunity for practical use

128. Given the DNA sequence ATTAAGGC, which sequence would be used by researchers as an antisense molecule?

(a) AUUAAGGC (b) UAAUUCCG
(c) CGGAATTA (d) TAATTCCG

129. Which of the following statements is true regarding genomics?

(a) Plant genomics lags behind similar efforts in animals and microorganisms
(b) Researchers can make use of genomic information even if the entire genome of an organism is not known
(c) Researchers are busy trying to determine the genome of the potato plant
(d) All of the above are true

130. Plants derived sexually from the same plant are ______, while those from somatic tissue from the same plant are ______

(a) identical, different
(b) different, also different
(c) different, identical
(d) plants cannot be derived from somatic tissue

131. Cytologists can use which of the following to describe locations of a gene at a specific place on the chromosome?

(a) DNA sequence of a chromosomal region
(b) Protein expression from a chromosomal region
(c) Banding pattern of stained chromosomes
(d) Comparison to markers located within a few thousand bp

132. Cytogenetic mapping

(a) requires that the gene should be cloned if *in situ* hybridization is to be used
(b) is a high resolution method of gene localization
(c) can be used to determine relative order of genes located very close to each other
(d) all of these
(e) none of these

133. Which of the following questions could be easily answered by FISH?

(a) How often does recombination occur between the ebony and sepia loci in *Drosophila*?
(b) In a particular family affected with Becker muscular dystropy, is the mutation due to the deletion of the entire gene?
(c) How large a piece of DNA would you need to clone in order to clone the group of human globin genes from chromosome 11?
(d) All of these
(e) None of these

134. Which of these is a key characteristic of a molecular marker?

(a) It is a known gene
(b) It is located at a known site on the chromosome
(c) It is only useful for linkage and physical mapping studies
(d) None of these

135. A molecular marker which is amplified by PCR and is polymorphic by length is a(n)

(a) restriction fragment length polymorphism (RFLP)
(b) variable number of tandem repeats (VNTR)
(c) amplified fragment length polymorphism (AFLP)
(d) single nucleotide polymorphism (SNP)

136. A polymorphism is

(a) any change in the DNA sequence
(b) the most common variation of a gene or marker sequence
(c) the least common variation of a gene or marker sequence
(d) a variation of gene or marker sequence present in > 1% of the population
(e) none of these

137. Which of these statements regarding RFLP analysis is correct?

(a) RFLP analysis requires Southern blotting for detection of fragments
(b) RFLPs can identify single base pair changes at any site in the chromosome
(c) An RFLP typically produces several different alleles
(d) All of these are correct
(e) None of these are correct

138. A monomorphic DNA segment is

(a) a segment of DNA that exists in many forms in the population
(b) a segment of DNA that controls a single gene function
(c) a segment of DNA inherited in a dominant fashion
(d) a segment of DNA shared by over 99% of the population
(e) all of these

139. Linkage mapping can determine the distance between which of the following pairs of DNA sequence?

(a) AFLPs and RFLPs
(b) Two AFLPs
(c) Two known genes
(d) A known gene and any type of molecular marker
(e) All of these

140. Which of the following would be reasonable use of an RFLP map?

(a) Identification of the exact location of an unknown gene along the chromosome
(b) Description of the size of DNA fragment required to clone the region containing an unknown gene
(c) Identification of the region in which an unknown gene is located
(d) All of these
(e) None of these

141. Which of these genetic markers is most likely to be highly polymorphic (have many different alleles)?

(a) An RFLP
(b) A microsatellite
(c) An SNP
(d) All of these are equally polymorphic
(e) None of these are likely to be polymorphic

142. Why might the use of microsatellites in genetic mapping studies be an advantage over RFLPs?

(a) Microsatellites are easier to detect
(b) Microsatellites are more abundant than RFLPs
(c) Microsatellites have more potential alleles than RFLPs
(d) All of these
(e) None of these

143. How are individual chromosomes identified in chromosome sorting techniques?

(a) Relative level of fluorescence when stained with a dye mixture
(b) Level of charge relative to size
(c) Size of the molecule
(d) All of these
(e) None of these

144. Which of the following would not be a critical characteristic of a YAC vector?

(a) Telomeric sequences
(b) A gene encoding a required structural protein
(c) An origin of replication
(d) A centromere
(e) All of these are critical characteristics of a YAC

145. The collection of proteins that can be produced by a given species is

(a) considered that species' genetic complement
(b) correlated with the size of the organism
(c) called the proteome
(d) all of these (e) none of these

146. A cDNA library

(a) can also be called an expressed sequence tag (EST) library
(b) consists of coding sequences from genes that are expressed
(c) is specific to the set of conditions under which the original mRNA was generated
(d) all of these
(e) none of these

147. Which of these might be an advantage to genetic testing of individuals via microarrays?

(a) Many different potential mutations in a single gene could be tested at once
(b) Expression patterns of many different genes can be analyzed simultaneously
(c) Microarray analysis can provide information on relative levels of expression of particular genes
(d) All of these (e) None of these

148. Which of the following statements regarding the proteome is the most correct?

(a) A large proportion of the proteome is expressed by each cell of a species
(b) Levels of gene expression at the mRNA level generally correlate highly with levels of functional protein
(c) The proteins produced by a specific cell depend on cell type and environmental conditions
(d) All of the above
(e) None of the above

149. If computers were not able to access the entire genomic sequence of an organism, which of the following techniques might allow determination of the gene sequence that encodes a particular protein?

(a) PCR amplification of related gene sequence
(b) Hybridization of a genomic library with a degenerate probe
(c) Production of synthetic peptides
(d) All of these
(e) None of these

150. Which of these concerns would apply to functional protein microarrays but not antibody microarrays?

(a) Antibodies recognize relatively short peptide sequences from a protein, and presence of the same peptide sequence in several proteins is possible
(b) Three-dimensional structure of a protein is essential for correct function, and the process of microarray preparation may interfere with this structure
(c) Certain functions, such as structural support of a cell, may not be amenable to analysis on a microarray
(d) All of these apply to functional protein

GENOME ANALYSIS

151. Human genes are not always readily produced by bacteria. Which of the following modifications can be useful?

(a) Inserting a cDNA sequence rather than the entire gene
(b) Inserting a synthetic DNA sequence if the coding region is very short
(c) Production of a hybrid or fusion protein
(d) All of these
(e) None of these

152. Prior to production of recombinant human insulin, diabetic patients could use insulin isolated from cattle. Which of the listed items would not be a drawback to this procedure?

(a) Insulin from cattle is slightly different from human insulin, potentially leading to allergic reactions
(b) Members of some religions consider cattle sacred and thus are unable to use insulin isolated from cattle
(c) Infectious diseases may be transferred in the isolated insulin
(d) Despite the relatively stable supply of cattle pancrease from slaughter houses, insulin isolated from cattle is still relatively expensive and in somewhat limited supply
(e) None of these; all are drawbacks of the use of cattle insulin

153. Bacteria that allow the formation of ice crystals have been engineered. Commercial fruit farmers can spray this bacterial strain on their fruit plants and reduce frost damage. This is an example of

(a) bioremediation (b) biological control
(c) biodegradation (d) bioeradication

154. Which of these is an example of bio-degradation?

(a) A strain of bacteria chemically captures heavy metal ions into chemical compounds
(b) A population of microorganisms metabolized toluene from a massive leak of fuel into carbon dioxide and other small molecules, reducing toluene levels
(c) Naturally occurring microorganisms are able to dechlorinate common industrially produced contaminants such as trichloroethane
(d) All of these are biodegradation
(e) None of these are biodegradation

155. In gene knockout technology

(a) a gene is inserted by nonhomologous recombination
(b) a mutant gene is replaced by a functional copy
(c) a functional gene is replaced by a mutant copy
(d) a functional gene is inserted in addition to the mutant copy

156. Production of transgenic plants is easier than the production of transgenic animals because

(a) plant cells can grow in cell culture
(b) plant cells have a lower number of potentially lethal genes
(c) plant cells are totipotent
(d) production of mutant plants poses less ethical dilemmas than production of mutant animals
(e) none of these

157. Which of the following groups of individuals could be considered to be clones?

(a) Fraternal twins
(b) Several strawberry plants that grew from runners from the same parent
(c) Littermates from an inbred strains of mice
(d) All of these
(e) None of these

158. What process causes shortening of telomeres during cell division?

(a) DNA synthesis
(b) Exonuclease removal of primers
(c) Ligation of DNA fragments
(d) Telomerase activity

159. Identify the best description of a stem cell

(a) a cell that has differentiated into a specialized cell type
(b) a cell that is capable of division
(c) a cell that remains undifferentiated
(d) a cell that can grow in cell culture

160. Which of these is an example of an adult stem cell?

(a) A red blood cell
(b) A neuron
(c) A cell from a blastocyst
(d) Skin cell that produce new epithelial layers

161. Which of these uses of transgenic technology is not directly relevant to agricultural application?

(a) Production of a pharmaceutical protein in goat's milk
(b) Production of salmon that grow all year round instead of just in warm weather
(c) Production of soybean plants that are resistant to herbicides
(d) Production of "super mice" that carry the human growth hormone gene

162. How many different bands would you expect an individual to have in a VNTR test?

(a) Two (b) Between 20 and 40
(c) Up to 100 (d) Thousands

163. How many different bands are expected in an individual for a particular STR?

(a) One (b) Two
(c) Up to 20 (d) 20 to 100

164. Which of these is an accurate description of gene therapy?

(a) A form of site directed mutagenesis
(b) Introduction of cloned genes into living cells to cure disease
(c) Cloning of a disease gene in order to understand the disease
(d) All of these
(e) None of these

165. Diseases amenable to treatment by gene therapy

(a) must be relatively mild
(b) must be caused by a defect in cells that are clinically accessible
(c) must have other types of treatments available in case gene therapy fails
(d) all of these
(e) none of these

GENE THERAPY AND GENETIC COUNSELING

166. Germline therapy is

(a) heritable
(b) not heritable
(c) sometimes heritable
(d) unrelated to heritability

167. The first gene therapy used cells altered outside the recipient's body and is called ______ gene therapy

(a) *in situ* (b) *in vivo*
(c) *ex vivo* (d) vaccine

168. Which of the following is not a vector used in gene therapy?

(a) AAV (b) Herpes
(c) Retrovirus (d) HIV

169. A transgenic mouse is an example of

(a) germline gene therapy
(b) heritable gene therapy
(c) constitutional gene therapy
(d) somatic gene therapy

170. Germline gene therapy could potentially correct a genetic defect in a(n)

(a) affected individual only
(b) affected individual and his or her offspring only
(c) affected individual and all of his or her descendants
(d) parent of an affected child

171. Which cell type would not be a direct target for gene therapy?

(a) Red blood (b) Muscle
(c) Liver (d) Endothelium

172. Which of the following is a preferred vector for transferring genes to nerve cells?

(a) AAV (b) Herpes
(c) Retrovirus (d) HIV

173. Enabling tumour cells to produce immune system biochemicals is an approach called

(a) cancer surgery (b) a cancer vaccine
(c) a cancer target (d) none of the above

174. Gene therapy targets

(a) genotypes
(b) phenotypes
(c) either a or b depending on the application
(d) both genotypes and phenotypes

175. Why are neurons difficult targets for gene therapy?

(a) They are not easily accessible
(b) They are small
(c) They do not divide
(d) They lack a nucleus

176. About one-half of current gene therapy trials target

(a) cystic fibrosis (b) cancer
(c) ADA deficiency (d) sickle cell disease

177. Melanoma is amenable to ______ treatment

(a) chimeraplasty (b) protein based
(c) suicide gene (d) vaccine

178. Which vector used in gene therapy infects nerve cells and can be used to treat brain tumours?

(a) Adeno-associated virus
(b) Adenovirus
(c) Herpes virus
(d) Retrovirus

179. Which vector used in gene therapy has proved useful in the treatment of sickle cell disease?

(a) Adeno-associated virus
(b) Adenovirus
(c) Herpes virus
(d) Retrovirus

180. Hydroxyurea has been useful in the treatment of sickle cell disease because it

(a) destroys sickled blood cells
(b) raises fetal haemoglobin levels
(c) raises stem cell numbers
(d) transfers new genes to red blood cells

181. A man and woman, each with a family history of sickle cell disease and no children would benefit most by

(a) prenatal screening
(b) carrier screening
(c) inherited predisposition screening
(d) no screening because they already know their status

182. A nasal spray containing adenovirus carrying a functional human CFTR gene is used to treat cystic fibrosis. This is an example of ______ gene therapy

(a) *in situ* (b) *in vivo*
(c) *ex vivo* (d) vaccine

183. Gene therapy would have to "fix" ______ % of the cells in the liver to be effective

(a) 1 (b) 5
(c) 10 (d) 50

GENETICALLY MODIFIED ORGANISMS

184. The use or alteration of cells or biochemicals to provide a useful product describes

(a) recombinant DNA technology
(b) transgenic technology
(c) biotechnology
(d) gene targeting

185. Which of the technologies listed below is a valuable method for mass-producing drugs and other useful proteins?

(a) Recombinant DNA technology
(b) Transgenic technology
(c) Biotechnology
(d) Gene targeting

186. Manufacturing recombinant DNA molecules involves cutting a gene from its normal location, inserting it into a circular piece of DNA from a bacterial cell, and then transferring the circle of DNA to cells of another species. Which of the tools below is used to cut the gene from its normal location?

(a) Restriction enzyme
(b) Plasmid
(c) Bacteriophage
(d) Vector

187. Manufacturing recombinant DNA molecules involves cutting a gene from its normal location, inserting it into a circular piece of DNA from a bacterial cell, and then transferring the circle of DNA to cells of another species. Which of the statements below describe the circular piece of DNA from a bacterial cell?

(a) Restriction enzyme
(b) Plasmid
(c) Bacteriophage
(d) Vector

188. Which gene transfer technique involves a tiny needle that is used to inject DNA into a cell lacking that DNA sequence?

(a) Electroporation
(b) Liposome transfer
(c) Microinjection
(d) Particle bombardment

189. The process of ______ involves the introduction of a gene into a cell where it exchanges places with its counterpart in the host cell

(a) transgenic technology
(b) gene targeting
(c) knockout technology
(d) recombinant DNA technology

190. A multicellular organism that carries a specific genetic change in each cell because of an intervention at the fertilized egg stage is a

(a) transversion (b) transition
(c) transgenic (d) transformation

191. The first drug produced using recombinant DNA technology is used to treat

(a) hemophilia (b) dwarfism
(c) heart attack (d) diabetes

192. Genetic engineering manipulates gene products at the level of the

(a) protein (b) amino acid
(c) DNA (d) RNA

193. A knockout mouse is so named because

(a) it contains aggression genes
(b) it contains multiple copies of a human gene
(c) it contains an activated human gene
(d) none of the above

194. The first patent for a transgenic organism was awarded in 1988. Which organism was patented?

(a) Yeast used in industrial processes
(b) A bacterium able to metabolize components of crude oil
(c) A mouse that manufactures human protein in its milk
(d) Life forms cannot be patented

195. Palindromic sequences in DNA

(a) form "blunt" ends when cut by restriction enzymes
(b) reflect the same sequence on two sides
(c) are not useful in recombinant DNA experiments
(d) all of the above

196. A cDNA version of a gene includes

(a) codons for a mature mRNA
(b) sequences corresponding to promoters
(c) sequences corresponding to introns
(d) both b and c

197. Which of the following transgenic pharming products is incorrectly paired with the host organism that produces it?

(a) Haemoglobin—rabbit
(b) Human growth hormone—rat
(c) Lactoferrin—cows
(d) Alpha-1-antitrypsin—sheep

198. Swapping an inactivated allele for a gene of interest produces a ______ mouse while replacing a gene with another that has an altered function creates a ______ mouse

(a) knockout, knockout
(b) knockout, gene targeted
(c) knockout, knockin
(d) gene targeted, knockin

199. Gene targeting is done on a(n)

(a) sperm cell
(b) egg cell
(c) fertilized ovum
(d) early embryonic cell

200. ______ consist of recombinant cells containing different fragments of a foreign genome

(a) DNA probes
(b) Homologous recombinants
(c) Genomic libraries
(d) Knockout organisms

201. Recombinant DNA technology methods began in the

(a) 1950's (b) 1960's
(c) 1970's (d) 1980's

202. ______ are used to select genes of interest from a genomic library

(a) Restriction enzymes
(b) Cloning vectors
(c) DNA probes
(d) Gene targets

203. For the same gene, it is possible to patent

(a) expressed sequence tags
(b) cDNA
(c) SNPs
(d) all of the above

204. Which gene transfer technique involves the use of a fatty bubble to carry a gene into a somatic cell?

(a) Electroporation
(b) Liposome transfer
(c) Microinjection
(d) Particle bombardment

205. "Naked" DNA

(a) is free of nucleic acids
(b) is free of the cell
(c) is free of protein
(d) contains just the sugar-phosphate backbone

206. Which of the following gene-targeted mice have shown that a gene product once thought important is not vital for survival?

(a) Neurofibromatosis
(b) X collagen
(c) SCID
(d) Sickle-cell

207. The first drug produced using recombinant DNA technology was

(a) streptokinase (b) tPA
(c) insulin (d) penicillin

208. A highly variable gene variant or DNA sequence present in more than 1% of a population is called

(a) polymorphism (b) VNTR
(c) STR (d) RFLP

209. The differences in DNA fragment sizes resulting from differences in restriction enzyme cutting sites are called

(a) polymorphisms (b) VNTRs
(c) STRs (d) RFLPs

210. Short sequences of DNA are amplified by ______ before they are analyzed

(a) RFLP (b) STR
(c) PCR
(d) small sequences are not used in DNA analysis

211. Northern blots probe

(a) DNA and RNA (b) RNA and proteins
(c) RNA (d) proteins
(e) DNA

212. Which is the most specific recombinant DNA library?

(a) genomic (b) chromosomal
(c) cRNA (d) cDNA
(e) protein

213. Recombinant DNA research is dependent on

(a) vectors (b) hosts
(c) restriction endonucleases
(d) cloning (e) all of the above

214. The polymerase chain reaction is a technique that

(a) probes DNA
(b) selectively replicates RNA
(c) probes and selectively replicates DNA
(d) probes RNA
(e) selectively replicates DNA

215. A "YAC" is a useful

(a) probe (b) host
(c) vector (d) screen
(e) library

DNA BIOTECHNOLOGY: APPLICATIONS

216. VNTRs are

(a) tandem repeats
(b) DNA sequences
(c) variable in number
(d) used in DNA fingerprinting
(e) all of the above

217. How many base pairs are present in the human genome?

(a) 3×10^6 (b) 3×10^3
(c) 3×10^9 (d) 3×10^8
(e) 3×10^7

218. In positional cloning, the starting point is knowledge of

(a) amino acid sequence of the protein
(b) DNA sequence of the gene
(c) insertion of the gene into a vector
(d) isolation of the gene
(e) RNA sequence of the transcript

219. Restriction enzymes typically recognize

(a) sequences in three-fold symmetry
(b) single-stranded DNA only
(c) several nucleotide sequences simultaneously
(d) specific palindromic sequences
(e) all of the above

220. A variety of *E. coli* clones have been isolated. The DNA has been extracted, digested with restriction enzymes, denatured, separated by gel electrophoresis, and transferred to nylon membrane by the Southern blot procedure. A radioactive probe is used that hybridizes with a gene of interest. The DNA corresponding to a single clone yields a single DNA band after probing the blot. Based on this information only,

(a) all of the clones tested, except the one described, have the gene of interest
(b) only the one clone described has the gene of interest
(c) the gene of interest is located entirely on the DNA band visualized
(d) the part of the gene recognized by the probe is located on the DNA band visualized
(e) both b and d

221. Using the techniques of genetic engineering, you design a cytoplasmic protein you want to accumulate within the ER of yeast cells. To accomplish this goal, you need to

(a) incorporate appropriate lipid groups
(b) do nothing; all proteins go through the ER
(c) incorporate appropriate DNA sequence to create signal sequences into mature peptide
(d) incorporate appropriate mannose-6-phosphate groups
(e) incorporate radioactive amino acids into the protein

222. RFLPs are not

(a) cut by restriction endonucleases
(b) used to construct linkage maps
(c) used as genetic markers
(d) used in DNA fingerprinting
(e) polymorphic DNA sequences

223. The most prevalent transgenic organisms are

(a) animals (b) bacteria
(c) viruses (d) yeast
(e) plants

224. Assume that you are trying to insert a gene into a plasmid and someone gives you a preparation of DNA cut with restriction enzyme X. The gene you wish to insert has sites on both ends for cutting by restriction enzyme Y. You have a plasmid with a single site for Y, but not for X. Your strategy should be to

(a) cut the plasmid with restriction enzyme X and insert the fragments cut with Y into the plasmid
(b) insert the fragments cut with X directly into the plasmid without cutting the plasmid
(c) cut the DNA again with restriction enzyme Y and insert these fragments into the plasmid cut with the same enzyme
(d) cut the plasmid twice with restriction enzyme Y and ligate the two fragments onto the ends of the human DNA fragments cut with restriction enzyme X
(e) cut the plasmid with enzyme X and then insert the gene into the plasmid

225. How does a bacterial cell protect its own DNA from restriction enzymes?

(a) By reinforcing bacterial DNA structure with covalent phosphodiester bonds
(b) Using DNA ligase to seal the bacterial DNA into a closed circle
(c) Adding histones to protect the double-stranded DNA
(d) By forming "sticky ends" of bacterial DNA to prevent the enzyme from attaching
(e) By adding methyl groups to adenines and cytosines

226. Bacteria containing recombinant plasmids are often identified by which process?

(a) Producing antibodies specific for each bacterium containing a recombinant plasmid
(b) Examining the cells with an electron microscope
(c) Removing the DNA of all cells in a culture to see which cells have plasmids
(d) Exposing the bacteria to an antibiotic that kills the cells lacking the plasmid
(e) Using radioactive tracers to locate the plasmids

227. Use the following information to answer the question below.

A eukaryotic gene has "sticky ends" produced by the restriction endonuclease EcoRI. The gene is added to a mixture containing EcoRI and a bacterial plasmid that carries two genes, which make it resistant to ampicillin and tetracycline. The plasmid has one recognition site for EcoRI located in the tetracycline resistance gene. This mixture is incubated for several hours and then added to bacteria growing in nutrient broth. The bacteria are allowed to grow overnight and are streaked on a plate using a technique that produces isolated colonies that are clones of the original. Samples of these colonies are then grown in four different media: nutrient broth plus ampicillin, nutrient broth plus tetracycline, nutrient broth plus ampicillin and tetracycline, and nutrient broth containing no antibiotics. The bacteria containing the engineered plasmid would grow in the

(a) nutrient broth, the ampicillin broth, and the tetracycline broth
(b) nutrient broth and the tetracycline broth only
(c) nutrient broth only
(d) ampicillin broth and the nutrient broth
(e) ampicillin and tetracycline broth only

228. Probes are short, single-stranded DNA or RNA segments that are used to identify DNA fragments with a particular sequence. Before the probe can identify a specific restriction fragment, what must be done?

(a) The fragments must be treated with heat or chemicals to separate the strands of the double helix
(b) The fragments must be separated by electrophoresis
(c) The probe must be hybridized with the fragment
(d) a and b only
(e) (a), (b), and (c)

229. The principal problem with inserting an unmodified mammalian gene into the bacterial chromosome, and then getting that gene expressed is that

(a) prokaryotes use a different genetic code from that of eukaryotes
(b) bacteria translate polycistronic messages only
(c) bacterial DNA is not found in a membrane-enclosed nucleus and is therefore incompatible with mammalian DNA
(d) bacterial RNA polymerase cannot make RNA complementary to mammalian DNA
(e) bacteria cannot remove eukaryotic introns

230. Which one of the following enables one to create complementary DNA (cDNA) from mRNA; results in a smaller gene product (RNA processed; no introns) that is more easily translated by bacteria?

(a) Restriction enzyme
(b) Gene cloning
(c) DNA ligase
(d) Gel electrophoresis
(e) Reverse transcriptase

231. Which of the following is least related to the others?

(a) Nucleic acid probe
(b) Southern blotting
(c) DNA microarray assays
(d) Nucleic acid hybridization
(e) Denaturation

232. Proteomics presents a particular challenge because

(a) a cell's proteins differ with cell type
(b) proteins are extremely varied in structure and chemical properties
(c) the number of proteins in humans probably exceeds the number of genes
(d) a and b are true
(e) a, b, and c are true

MARK TRUE OR FALSE (T/F)

1. PCR requires knowledge about parts of a target DNA sequence to be amplified
2. A gene can have different functions in different tissues at different times in development
3. The Human Genome Project is limited to the study of humans
4. With the advent of genomics, the concept of gene is now clearly defined
5. Genome information will affect your everyday life in many ways
6. The consequences of genetic manipulations are always obvious after extensive laboratory and field testing
7. Until the advent of Bt corn, Bt toxin was not used as a pest control method
8. Using biotechnology to increase the use of insecticides will not encourage the persistence of pests that are resistant to the chemicals
9. *In situ* hybridization is done on fragments of specific chromosomes
10. Changes in restriction enzyme sites can be used as polymorphic markers

11. An AFLP is an example of a sequence tagged site
12. RFLPs are inherited in a simple Mendelian fashion and display codominance
13. Isolation of individual chromosomes can be used to map genes
14. One of the goals of the Human Genome Project is to address ethical issues arising from use of the information gathered
15. A single microarray may have a surface area of less than three square inches, yet may contain unique spots of tens of thousands of gene sequences
16. Functional protein microarrays can identify protein functions only if their sequence is known
17. A computer program must be written in a specific language in order for the computer to understand what needs to be done
18. Recombinant microorganisms are fundamentally different from nonrecombinant strains
19. Transgenic organisms contain recombinant DNA integrated into their genome
20. The ability to grow embryonic stem cells in the laboratory has made gene replacement technology in mammals feasible
21. Knockout mice can serve as model organisms for study of human disease
22. DNA fingerprinting provides information about predisposition for genetic disease
23. Gene therapy by gene addition is best able to treat diseases in which a gene function is missing
24. Human proteins can be produced in the milk or semen of farm animals.
25. The genetic engineering of crop plants can make them healthier and more beneficial to humans
26. Restriction endonucleases cut DNA into small fragments
27. A DNA sequencing machine sorts pieces of DNA according to their size
28. RFLPs show individual variation
29. RFLPs can be used to determine the position of specific genes
30. RFLPs are produced by enzymes, which cleave DNA at specific sites
31. RFLPs can be used for prenatal diagnosis
32. RFLPs have no known useful function
33. Particle gun is suitable for the transformation of embryogenic callus
34. Streptomycin phosphotransferase is the most commonly used selectable marker
35. Cry I protein is specific for Coleoptera
36. The bar gene confers resistance to phosphinothricin
37. The bar gene has been isolated from *Agrobacterium*
38. The cry IA gene has been transferred into onion
39. Carlson *et al.* produced the first somatic hybrid
40. Indirect selection for polygenic traits cannot be done with RFLP
41. A cultivar can be identified with RFLP
42. Silver nitrate is a very good surface sterilizing agent
43. About 100 F_2 plants are required for the study of inheritance of an RFLP marker and a linked trait
44. *Eco* PI is a Type III restriction endonuclease
45. Polymerase chain reaction technique was developed by Gilbert
46. TA 29 promoter is light-responsive
47. Suspension cultures do not show somaclonal variation
48. Solanaceae is not a good material for somatic hybridization
49. Suspension cultures are good for long term *in vitro* storage of germplasm

50. Plasmid is a circular DNA molecule, which is capable of self replication in the host
51. ELISA test is a serological test, which uses antibodies and enzymes, for the detection of viruses in plant material
52. When viral genome is integrated within T-DNA and introduced into plant cells, it is known as agroinfection
53. Restriction enzymes cleave DNA molecule within sites with any base sequence
54. Acetosyringone is a phenolic compound produced by monocots at wound sites and it acts as a signal molecule for the expression of *vir* operons of Ti plasmid
55. Transformation is the process by which isolated DNA enters a cell and a portion of it gets integrated into the cell chromosome by recombination
56. A small DNA, which is used to identify a complementary DNA sequence, is known as a probe
57. A DNA molecule, which can self propagate in the host and is suitable for DNA cloning, is known as a plasmid
58. DNA sequencing is the determination of nucleotide sequence of a DNA molecule
59. An endonuclease cuts DNA molecules at internal sites
60. Reverse transcriptase is an RNA-dependent DNA polymerase used to obtain complementary RNA from mRNA
61. Gene or DNA cloning is the introduction of a recombinant DNA molecule into a suitable host to produce multiple copies of the recombinant DNA
62. Antisense RNA is the RNA produced by transcription of the antisense strand of a gene
63. When DNA is introduced into protoplasts by exposing them for a very short duration to a high voltage electric current, it is called electroporation
64. If the expression of a transgene disappears in a few generations, it is called gene silencing
65. Reporter genes produce an enzyme that allows the selection of the cells expressing this gene
66. Reporter gene that allows the selection of only those cells, which express this gene, is known as a promoter gene
67. Expression vector is a vector which is designed for the expression of the DNA inserts
68. Promoter is the DNA sequence to which RNA polymerase binds during transcription initiation
69. A vector that is able to replicate in the cells of two different organisms is known as a shuttle vector
70. Ti plasmid is involved in the production of crown gall in many monocot species
71. Cycloheximide acts as an anti-fungal agent
72. Gene amplification means increasing the number of copies of a gene in the genome
73. Plasmid vectors are generally used for the cloning of relatively large (100-1000 kbp) DNA segments
74. Type III restriction endonuclease is most commonly used in gene cloning
75. Cosmids can be used for the cloning of 80-90 kbp DNA fragments
76. The *barstar* gene can restore the male sterility induced by barnase
77. Vectors can be classified into cloning and expression vectors
78. *Barnase* gene has been successfully transferred in maize for producing male sterility
79. *Agrobacterium* rhizogenes causes hairy root disease
80. The Cry IV proteins are specific for Diptera
81. Acetosyringone can activate *vir* operons
82. The crystal proteins are soluble in the acidic environment of the insect midgut

83. The *vir* region has five operons
84. The *vir* operons are activated by alcohols
85. The *cry* genes code for proteins of any length
86. Tobacco was the first crop in which genetic transformation through direct DNA uptake by protoplasts was reported for the first time
87. Serological tests are not able to classify *Bacillus thuringiensis* strains
88. Selectable marker npt II is generally used in plants
89. The Ri plasmid is involved in the disease of hairy root of monocot species
90. Most of the restriction endonucleases produce staggered cuts
91. *Eco* I was the first restriction endonuclease to be isolated
92. 'Flavr Savr' is a tomato transgene in which antisense technology has been used
93. Khorana *et al.* (1970) synthesized the gene for Alanyl-tRNA of fungi
94. Maximizer transgenic of maize is resistant to herbicides
95. Polymerase chain reaction is known as People's choice reaction
96. 'Yield Guard' maize transgenic is resistant to corn borer
97. The annealing temperature range in a PCR is generally 40-60 degrees centigrade
98. The right temperature for DNA denaturation in a PCR is 90-98 degrees centigrade
99. RAPD is a PCR based codominant marker
100. Yeast artificial chromosomes are used for cloning of DNA fragments
101. Viruses are the hosts of choice for DNA cloning
102. The *E. coli* strain K 12 is the most commonly used for cloning experiments
103. Plasmids that are integrated into the bacterial chromosome are called episomes
104. F plasmids are not responsible for conjugation
105. R plasmids carry genes for resistance to antibiotic
106. Colicins are the proteins that kill sensitive *E. coli* cells
107. Degradative plasmids enable the host bacterium to metabolize unusual molecules like toluene
108. Ti plasmid is not a virulence plasmid
109. The replication control of single copy plasmid is different from that of its bacterial host
110. The replication control of multicopy plasmid is the same as that of its bacterial host cells
111. A module may be regarded as a DNA segment or sequence performing a specific function
112. Each module can consist of only one gene
113. In plasmid vector *p*BR322, *p* signifies plasmid, B is for Boliver and R is for Rogers
114. Plasmid *p*UC gets its name from the University of California
115. Cosmids are essentially plasmids that contain a maximum of 250 base pairs of lambda DNA
116. A plasmid vector that contains origin of replication from a phage, in addition to that of the plasmid, is called phagemid
117. Phasmid vectors are lambda insertion vectors
118. Artificial chromosomes are only circular vectors that are suitably maintained in, usually, 1 to 2 copy per cell
119. BAC vectors have the origin of replication of *E. coli* F factor
120. Shuttle vectors can replicate in cells of any number of species
121. Yeast episomal plasmid is a replicative plasmid vector
122. Yeast replicative plasmid is not an ARS (autonomously replicating sequence) vector
123. Plant cells normally contain plasmids
124. A selectable marker governs a feature, which enables only such cells that possess it to survive under the selective conditions

125. Genes conferring resistance to kanamycin is a good scorable marker
126. Examples of commonly used selectable markers are gus, lux, ocs and noc
127. A strong promoter supports a high transcription rate
128. If a foreign gene has introns, it cannot be expressed in *E. coli* or any other prokaryotic host
129. The technique of DNA-DNA hybridization is known as Southern blotting
130. Sequencing technique with an enzymatic procedure was developed by Maxam and Gilbert
131. In restrictive gels, the size of the molecule has a major influence on the result of separation
132. In nonrestrictive gels, the frictional resistance of gels is kept negligibly low. As a result, the electrophoretic mobility of the molecules being separated depends only on their net charge
133. Nonrestrictive gels have concentrations of 0.2 to 0.5%, and have a small pore size
134. Horizontal agarose gells are used for the separation of high molecular weight proteins
135. Agarose gells above 1% concentration are cloudy
136. DNA chips cannot be used for the detection of genetic diseases
137. In dot blot assay, test DNAs or RNAs are immobilized on a membrane and a labeled probe is hybridized with them to detect the presence of complementary sequences
138. In microarrays, a series of probes are immobilized on a glass slide as microdots, which are then hybridized with a mixture of test DNA sequences that are lasbelled with a fluorochrome
139. RT-PCR means PCR can be used to produce cDNA copies of mRNA
140. An amplicon is the RNA sequence that is amplified by PCR
141. PCR amplification is not sensitive to inhibitors like phenolics present in the DNA
142. In a physical map, distances between genes are shown in base pairs rather than map units
143. Biotechnology is the controlled use of biological agents, such as microorganisms or cellular components, for beneficial use
144. DNA cloning and gene cloning are two different things
145. A chimaeric gene consists of a gene from one organism joined to regulatory sequences from another organism
146. Restriction exonucleases which cut DNA at specific sites are called molecular scissors
147. A suitable organism that serves as a host for propagation of the recombinant DNA, i.e. vector containing the DNA fragment to be cloned is called the DNA insert
148. A lambda exonuclease removes nucleotides from the 3' ends
149. *E. coli* exonuclease III removes nucleotides from 3' end
150. Restriction endonucleases are dispensible for DNA cloning and sequencing
151. Type I restriction endonucleases have recognition sequences of about 80 bp
152. *Hinf* III is a type III restriction endonuclease
153. Adaptors are short, chemically synthesized DNA double strands, which have no sticky ends
154. A cDNA is the copy or complementary DNA produced by using mRNA as a template
155. Use of cDNA is essential when the expression of an eukaryotic gene is required in a prokaryote
156. A good vector should be ideally less than 50 kb in size
157. An ideal vector should not have more than 1-2 unique target sites

158. A vector used for propagation of DNA inserts in a suitable host is called an expression vector
159. Before RNA can be studied by PCR (polymerase chain reaction), it has to be translated into complementary DNA
160. Western blotting is used to detect specific protein in a mixture of protein
161. Northern blotting is used to detect DNA sequence
162. Southern blotting is primarily used to detect DNA sequence
163. Gel electrophoresis is used in both Southern and Northern blottings
164. The polymerase chain reaction produces multiple copies of DNA
165. The polymerase chain reaction requires oligonucleotide primers
166. The polymerase chain reaction has a high specificity but low sensitivity
167. The polymerase chain reaction requires the use of heat
168. The polymerase chain reaction can be used to detect RNA virus
169. Proto-oncogenes regulate the normal cell division
170. Mutated proto-oncogenes are associated with cancer
171. Gene translocation can transform proto-oncogenes
172. Viral insertion can disrupt normal proto-oncogenes
173. *Ras* oncogenes are the most commonly observed oncogenes in human tumours

21

Genetics of Cancer and Immunology

MULTIPLE-CHOICE QUESTIONS

1. **Oncogenes**
   (a) are derived from proto-oncogenes
   (b) induce uncontrolled cell proliferation
   (c) are derived from proto-oncogenes and induce uncontrolled cell proliferation
   (d) are viral genes
   (e) are tumour suppressor genes

2. **The function of the *ras* gene family involves**
   (a) chromatin condensation
   (b) signal transduction
   (c) cell cycle control
   (d) tumour suppression
   (e) chromosome segregation

3. **A predisposition to cancer usually implies the presence of**
   (a) an extended cell cycle
   (b) a germline (gametic) mutation
   (c) a viral infection a somatic cell mutation
   (d) a fragile chromosome

4. **Cancer is best described as**
   (a) an environmental disease at the somatic cell level
   (b) a bacterial disease at the somatic cell level
   (c) a genetic disease at the gametic cell level
   (d) a genetic disease at the somatic cell level
   (e) an environmental disease at the gametic cell level

5. **Apoptosis represents genetically programmed**
   (a) differentiation (b) cell death
   (c) proto-oncogene conversion
   (d) determination
   (e) tumour suppression

6. **Which of the following is not one of the ways in which antibodies inactivate antigens?**
   (a) Carry viral antigens to the surface of the infected cell to allow recognition by killer T cells
   (b) Clump the antigen-antibody complex tagging the antigen for destruction
   (c) Interact with antigens to form antigen-antibody complexes
   (d) React with viral attachment proteins, thereby inactivating them
   (e) Activate a proteolytic system that lyses invading bacterial cells

7. Generation of a secondary immune response requires which of the following?

(a) The release of perforins by B cells
(b) The production of B and T memory cells during first exposure to the antigen
(c) The rapid mobilization of naive lymphocytes
(d) The activation of the secondary immune system
(e) Recombinant DNA vectors to carry the primary antigen

8. During the formation of the DNA segments encoding a human kappa light chain and the subsequent transcription, mRNA splicing, translation, and posttranslational processing, which of the following would not typically occur?

(a) An L segment will recombine to be adjacent to a V segment
(b) The J region will be spliced to be adjoining the C region during the maturation of the initial RNA transcript
(c) Somatic recombination brings a J region to be contiguous with an L-V segment
(d) All of these are necessary for kappa light chain formation

9. Evidence that RAG-1 and RAG-2 directly participate in the somatic recombination events in maturing cells of the immune system include which of the following?

(a) Transfer of RAG-1 or RAG-2 into fibroblasts results in V(D)J recombination
(b) RAG-1 or RAG-2 deficient mice make T cells but not B cells
(c) RAG-1 and RAG-2 are normally expressed in lymphocytes only in those stages of maturation when V(D)J recombination is taking place
(d) Two of the above
(e) All of the above

10. The iso-agglutinin gene (I) does not

(a) produce proteins that can have an effect on B-cell response to blood transfusions
(b) have a non-lethal null genotype
(c) code for proteins that are targeted to the surface of RBCs
(d) have a codominant relationship among two of its alleles
(e) underlie an important component of blood type

11. Hemolytic disease of the newborn (HDN) is prevented by providing an Rh^- mother of an Rh^+ foetus with a preparation of antibodies against the Rh antigen because

(a) the mother's Rh^- cells will be neutralized by the antibodies against Rh that she is given
(b) the foetus' Rh antibodies must be eliminated
(c) HDN is caused by the Rh^- mother's inability to make a necessary attack on the Rh antigen
(d) the antibodies protect the mother from attack by Rh^+ cells of the foetus
(e) antibodies against the Rh^- antigen bind to fetal cells that have entered the maternal circulation before the maternal immune system has a chance to mount a full immune response to the Rh antigen

12. Which of the following is not true about HLA genes?

(a) The array of alleles of the four closely linked HLA genes define one haplotype
(b) HLA genes are highly polymorphic
(c) The glycoproteins encoded by the HLA genes are found only on cells of the immune system such as B-lymphocytes, T-lymphocytes, and macrophages
(d) The HLA genes are homologous to the mouse MHC genes
(e) Siblings have approximately a one-in-four chance of sharing the same combination of HLA haplotypes

13. Which of the following hypotheses have been advanced to explain the correlation between HLA genotype and diseases such as ankylosing spondylitis and Reiter's syndrome?

(a) A nearby locus outside the HLA complex carries an allele conferring susceptibility to a disease and is typically inherited along with the particular HLA haplotype
(b) Particular HLA alleles confer susceptibility to specific diseases
(c) All of the above
(d) Particular HLA alleles may interact with environmental factors (such as infection), which then together give rise to a disease
(e) None of the above

14. Severe combined immunodeficiency syndrome (SCID) is all of the following except

(a) a recessive genetic disease
(b) a good candidate for gene therapy
(c) genetically homogeneous
(d) characterized by an absence of functional T cells
(e) capable of being caused by a deficiency of adenosine deaminase

15. In Acquired Immune Deficiency Syndrome (AIDS), the Human Immunodeficiency Virus (HIV)

(a) is able to remain latent in a host cell for years
(b) passes from donor to host as an RNA virus in a protein capsid enveloped in a coat derived from the plasmid membrane of a T helper cell
(c) infects a T helper cell, integrating into its genome, and destroying it when the infected cell is called upon to participate in an immune response
(d) reduces the T4 cell population to a point where it can no longer mount an adequate immune response
(e) all of the above

16. A(n) ______ is a multisubunit protein produced by B cells that binds to foreign substances and alters the components of immune system

(a) antibody (b) cytokine
(c) antigen (d) none of the above

17. T cells provide the ______ response

(a) humoral immune (b) cellular immune
(c) inherited immune
(d) progressive immune

18. A transplant that occurs between species, such as human and a pig, is called a(n)

(a) autograft (b) isograft
(c) allograft (d) xenograft

19. Which blood type can be transfused to an individual whose blood type is unknown?

(a) AB^+ (b) AB^-
(c) O^+ (d) O^-

20. A couple expecting their second child is worried about Rh incompatibility. Their first child was Rh^+. They have their blood typed. Which result could be the cause for alarm?

(a) Both parents are Rh^-
(b) Both parents are Rh^+
(c) Man Rh^- and woman Rh^+
(d) Man Rh^+ and woman Rh^-

21. Allergens stimulate the production of ______ antibodies that bind to mast cells, causing them to release allergy mediators

(a) IgA (b) IgD
(c) IgE (d) IgG

22. Which antibody type protects against bacteria, viruses, and toxins, especially in secondary immune responses?

(a) IgA (b) IgD
(c) IgE (d) IgG

23. Severe combined immune deficiencies affect which branch of the immune system?

(a) Humoral (b) Cellular
(c) Both (d) Neither

24. Humoral immunity can be boosted using

(a) monoclonal antibody technology
(b) treatment with interferon
(c) treatment with interleukin-2
(d) treatment with cytokines

25. Which of the following is not an HLA-linked disease?

(a) Narcolepsy
(b) Ankylosing spondylitis
(c) Reiter's disease
(d) All of the above are HLA-associated

26. Which of the following is not part of the nonspecific, innate defense?

(a) phagocytosis
(b) unbroken skin
(c) inflammatory response
(d) fever

27. ______ are cytokines that cause fever, temporarily maintaining a higher body temperature that directly kills some infecting bacteria and viruses

(a) Interferons
(b) Interleukins
(c) Tumour necrosis factors
(d) Collectins

28. The specific parts of the antibody molecule that bind the antigen are called

(a) interleukins
(b) heavy chains
(c) antigen binding sites
(d) idiotypes

29. Helper T cells secrete ______ which stimulate white blood cells to mature in bone marrow

(a) interleukins
(b) interferons
(c) colony stimulating factors
(d) tumour necrosis factors

30. ______ cells coordinate innate and acquired immune responses

(a) Helper T (b) Cytotoxic T
(c) Gamma-delta T (d) B

31. Mutations encoding ______ cause inherited immune deficiencies

(a) cytokine genes (b) T cell receptors
(c) antibody genes (d) all of the above

32. People who cannot produce a complete ______ protein resist HIV infection

(a) CD4 (b) CCR5
(c) cytotoxin (d) AIDS

33. A transplant that occurs between identical twins is called a(n)

(a) autograft (b) isograft
(c) allograft (d) xenograft

34. Bioweapons

(a) have been used for centuries
(b) employ pathogens to harm innocent people
(c) are inexpensive and fairly easy to produce
(d) All of the above are true regarding bioweapons

35. Which of the below provide evidence suggesting that allergies may be a holdover of an immune function that was important in the past?

(a) People with allergies have higher levels of eosinophils
(b) People with allergies have higher levels of T cells
(c) People with allergies have lower levels of eosinophils
(d) People with allergies have lower levels of T cells

36. The polio vaccine uses

(a) an attenuated pathogen
(b) an inactivated toxin
(c) part of the pathogen surface
(d) "naked" DNA from the pathogen

37. Monoclonal antibodies are produced by a fused cell consisting of

(a) a B cell and a T cell
(b) a B cell and a cancer cell
(c) a mast cell and a macrophage
(d) none of the above

38. B cells secrete

(a) cytokines (b) antibodies
(c) antigens (d) helper T cells

39. A major advancement in transplantation technology occurred in 1984 when ______ was transplanted into "Baby Fae"

(a) a baboon liver
(b) baboon bone marrow
(c) a baboon heart
(d) a pig liver

40. Which of the following statements concerning chromosomes is not correct?

(a) Their number is normally 46
(b) Mosaicism is the coexistence of cells with different number of chromosomes within the same organism
(c) They are always identical in cells of the same phenotype
(d) Nondisjunction must be followed by translocation
(e) They can be used as tumour markers

41. Which of the following statements is wrong? Nephroblastoma

(a) is a malignancy of childhood
(b) distant metastases develop rapidly
(c) it may be present with systemic hypertension
(d) if the tumour is localized to the kidney, a nephrectomy is indicated
(e) it causes hypercalcemia

42. Which of the following conditions is not associated with true hematuria?

(a) Urinary tract tuberculosis
(b) Acute cystitis
(c) Malignant hypertension
(d) Renal infarction

43. Which of the following statements about anthrax is not correct?

(a) It is an occupational disease
(b) Woolsorter's disease develops following the inhalation of the causative microorganism
(c) More than 90% of patients exhibit skin lesions
(d) The malignant pustula is very painful

44. Which of the following states predispose an affected person to colon carcinoma?

(a) Ulcerative colitis
(b) Chronic giardiasis
(c) Crohn's disease
(d) Hirschsprung's disease

45. Which of the following is not a predisposing factor for thromboembolic disorders

(a) carcinoma of the pancreas
(b) a type O blood group
(c) oral contraceptives
(d) obesity
(e) myocardial infarction

46. Which of the following is not true?

(a) Fever development is attributed to an increased production of interleukin-1
(b) Fever slows down the growth of certain tumours
(c) Fever is advantageous in patients with rickettsial infections
(d) Fever unfavourably increases viral infections by promoting viral proliferation
(e) Fever is advantageous in neurosyphilis

47. In chronic lymphocytic leukemia

(a) an absolute lymphocytosis is observed
(b) thrombocytosis is observed
(c) splenomegaly is always present
(d) the development of an acute blastic crisis is possible

48. Clubbing of the fingers is observed in which of the following conditions?

(a) Chronic meningococcal meningitis
(b) Rheumatoid arthritis
(c) Schistosomiasis
(d) Carcinoma of the lung

49. Which of the following statements about chronic lymphocytic lymphoma is correct?

(a) Irradiation preceding the onset is an etiological factor
(b) In 50% of the cases the onset is before the age of 30
(c) A painful enlargement of the spleen develops
(d) A Coombs negative hemolytic anemia is observed

50. The most common solid tumours – breast, colon, etc., arise in ______ cells.

(a) epithelial (b) mesothelial
(c) nerve cells (d) muscle cells

51. Leukemias usually arise from

(a) epithelial cells
(b) neurons
(c) blood-forming tissues
(d) epidermal cells

52. Which of the following is a test for detecting precancerous cells?

(a) MRI (b) CT Scan
(c) Pap smear (d) Endoscopy

53. Proto-oncogenes are possessed by the

(a) RNA virus
(b) DNA virus
(c) Cells themselves
(d) Pathogenic bacteria

54. The first tumour-suppressor gene to be studied is associated with

(a) myeloma (b) sarcoma
(c) retinoblastoma (d) carcinoma

55. p53 is a

(a) translation factor (b) polymerase
(c) endonuclease (d) transcription factor

56. p53 is capable of binding to which family of proteins?

(a) Bcl – 1 (b) Bcl – 2
(c) Bcl – 3 (d) Bcl – 4

57. About how many types of cancer are there?

(a) Roughly 50 types
(b) More than 100 types
(c) About 300 types
(d) More than 1000 types

58. Across the globe, ______ is the most common type of cancer that kills men.

(a) lung cancer (b) stomach cancer
(c) liver cancer (d) oesophageal cancer

59. Worldwide, ______ is the most common cancer that kills women.

(a) lung cancer (b) stomach cancer
(c) breast cancer (d) cervical cancer

60. ______ is the most common form of cancer in all humans.

(a) brain cancer (b) leukemia
(c) skin cancer (d) colon cancer

61. Which of the viruses below cause cancer resulting from chronic infection?

(a) Herpes simplex viruses (HSV)
(b) Human papilloma virus (HPV)
(c) Hepatitis B virus (HBV)
(d) B and C

62. What kinds of foods are linked to colon cancer?

(a) Processed meats
(b) Microwaveable foods
(c) Foods with salt substitutes
(d) Shellfish

63. ______ is the most deadly of all cancers of the female reproductive system

(a) Uterine cancer (b) Vaginal cancer
(c) Cervical cancer (d) Ovarian cancer

64. Cancer cells

(a) are not stimulated to enter into the "cell cycle" and thus never reproduce
(b) age faster than normal cells causing premature cell death
(c) have acquired a specific set of capabilities and characteristics due to genetic changes
(d) stop dividing when they come in contact with normal cells

65. Cancer cells do not have the ability to initiate death via ______ and may divide indefinitely

(a) mitotic catastrophe b) spindle chaos
(c) apoptosis d) evasion

66. Cancer cells are said to "break all the rules" because they

(a) kill the organism in which they live
(b) do not grow through mitosis
(c) grow much larger than normal cells, creating tumours
(d) divide without appropriate external signals

67. Which of the following is true of normal adult cells but not cancer cells?

(a) Division in the presence of external growth signals
(b) Contact with other cells increases the likelihood of division
(c) Cell death after a fixed number of cell divisions
(d) Large amount of telomerase present

68. Which of the following contribute to the metastatic spread of cancer cells?

(a) Cytoskeletal changes and cell adhesion/motility
(b) Increased enzyme production
(c) Pseudopod formation
(d) All of the above are correct

69. Name the cancer that starts in the skin or the tissues that line other organs?

(a) Carcinoma (b) Pancreas
(c) Leukemia (d) None of the above

70. The abnormal growth of cells in the body is known as

(a) cancer (b) totipotency
(c) malignancy (d) both (a) and (c)

71. Name the most common cancer in the world, due to which women die?

(a) Rectal cancer (b) Vaginal cancer
(c) Breast cancer (d) Ovarian

72. Stomach cancer is also known as .

(a) diaphragm cancer
(b) duodenum cancer
(c) oesophageal cancer
(d) gastric cancer

73. Which cancer is known as the Silent Killer?

(a) Brain cancer
(b) Liver cancer
(c) Stomach cancer
(d) Lung cancer

74. What process distinguishes malignant tumours from benign tumours?

(a) Rate of tumour growth
(b) Metastasis
(c) Size of tumour
(d) Location of the tumour

75. Which of these "superfoods' have been associated with a reduction in cancer risk?

(a) Kale
(b) Garlic
(c) Brocolli
(d) No scientific evidence to support 'super-foods' reduce cancer risk

76. What types of cancers are more likely to be altered by chemotherapy?

(a) Slow growing cancers
(b) Localized cancers
(c) Thyroid cancers
(d) Fast growing cancers

77. Name the process by which a malignant cell spreads throughout the normal cells?

(a) Invasiveness (b) Metastasis
(c) Progression (d) Transformation

78. What is the origin of the cancerous cells?

(a) Stem cells (b) Mesodermal cells
(c) Polyclonal cells (d) Monoclonal cells

79. Which of the following is the characteristic of a cancer cell?

(a) Apoptosis
(b) Density dependent inhibition
(c) Contact inhibition
(d) Loss of anchorage dependence

80. Name the genes which directly inhibit cell growth or promote cell death.

(a) Caretaker genes
(b) Checkpoint genes
(c) Transcription factor genes
(d) Gatekeeper genes

81. If DNA is damaged, which of the following genes arrest cell cycle?

(a) p 16 (b) p 43
(c) p 53 (d) p 33

82. Name the chemical carcinogen which causes prostate cancer?

(a) Arsenic (b) Asbestos
(c) Magnesium (d) Cadmium

83. Which of these factors increases the risk for cancer of the oesophagus?

(a) Salt (b) Processed meat
(c) Alcohol (d) Vegetables

84. Which of these factors increases the risk of cancer of the stomach?

(a) Obesity
(b) Sugar
(c) Salt and salt-preserved foods
(d) Dietary fibre

85. Which of these factors reduces the risk of cancer of the colorectum?

(a) Vitamin C (b) Dietary fibre
(c) Alcohol (d) Oestrogen

86. Which of these factors is associated in the risk for prostate cancer?

(a) Insulin-like growth factor – 1
(b) Dietary fat
(c) Alcohol
(d) Salt

87. Which of these increases the risk for lung cancer?

(a) Saturated fat
(b) Obesity
(c) High dose of Beta-carotene supplements
(d) Alcohol

88. The stimulation of antigen specific T cells by appropriately presented antigen alone results in

(a) Cytotoxicity (b) Allergy
(c) Cell division (d) Production of IL – 3

89. Select the wrong statement from the following regarding the receptors of innate immune system

(a) They are included in the Toll family of receptors
(b) They include MHC complexes
(c) They recognize the molecular patterns
(d) They include scavenger receptors

90. A cytokine which can increase the body temperature directly is

(a) IL – 2 (b) IL – 3
(c) IL – 5 (d) IL – 6

91. Which of the following statement is true about IgM of human?

(a) IgM can cross the placenta
(b) IgM is produced by high affinity plasma cells
(c) IgM is primarily restricted in the circulation
(d) IgM can protect mucosal surface

92. The heavy chain of immunoglobulin molecules are

(a) Encoded by a constant region exon
(b) Expressed by T cells
(c) Not glycosylated
(d) Heavily phosphorylated

93. Presence of ______ can be used to separate helper T cells from cytotoxic T cells.

(a) Class II MHC (b) CD – 2
(c) CD – 3 (d) CD – 4

94. A chemokine with indirect antiviral activity

(a) TNF (b) TGF
(c) INF (d) IL

95. High tillers of antinuclear antibodies indicate

(a) oncogene inactivation
(b) fungal disease
(c) autoimmune disease
(d) inactivation of tumour suppressor gene

96. Which of the following is an autoimmune disease?

(a) Hemophilia A
(b) Type 2 diabetes mellitus
(c) Hemophilia B
(d) Type 1 diabetes mellitus

97. Which of the following vaccine will not pose any problems in immune compromised person?

(a) BCG (b) Mumps
(c) Pneumococcal (d) Measles

98. Which is least likely to occur for the removal of cancerous cells in our body?

(a) Autophagy
(b) Phagocytosis
(c) T-cell based cytotoxicity
(d) Complement fixation

99. Naturally acquired immunity would be most likely acquired through which of the following processes?

(a) Infection with disease causing organism followed by recovery
(b) Vaccination
(c) Natural birth
(d) Drinking colostrum

100. B and T cells are produced by stem cells that are formed in

(a) the spleen (b) the liver
(c) circulatory system (d) bone marrow

101. Which of the following substances will not stimulate an immune response unless they are bound to a larger molecule?

(a) Antibody (b) Virus
(c) Antigen (d) Hapten

102. Which of the following immune cells or molecules are most effective in destroying intracellular pathogens?

(a) Antibodies (b) T cytolytic cells
(c) T helper cells (d) B cells

103. B cells that produce and release a large amount of antibody are called

(a) Plasma cells (b) Memory cells
(c) Killer cells (d) Neutrophils

104. In agglutination reactions, the antigen is a ______ and in precipitation reactions, the antigen is a

(a) soluble molecule/whole cell
(b) whole cell/soluble molecule
(c) protein/carbohydrates
(d) protein/antibody

105. Monoclonal antibodies recognize a single

(a) epitome (b) bacterium
(c) virus (d) antigen

106. B cells are activated by

(a) interferon (b) hybridoma
(c) lymphoma (d) antigen

107. Fusion between a plasma cell and a tumour cell creates a

(a) lymphoma (b) myeloma
(c) hybridoma (d) killer cell

MARK TRUE OR FALSE (T/F)

1. Apoptosis is a normal self-destruction mechanism that eliminates damaged and potentially harmful cells
2. Normal cell proliferation is modulated by cell cycle regulation
3. Signaling systems do not permit proliferation and apoptosis to be coordinated within a population of cells
4. In cancer, cells proliferate out of control and avoid fail-safe destruction mechanisms through the accumulation of a series of special mutations in the same somatic cell
5. Many classes of genes that are mutated to cause cancers are important components of the cell that directly or indirectly contribute to growth control and differentiation
6. It is a non-lethal event if mitosis occurs before DNA replication is completed
7. When DNA is damaged during G_1 by X irradiation, cyclin-dependent protein kinase (CDK) activity of CDK-cyclin complexes is activated
8. Cysteine-containing aspartate-specific proteases (caspases) are the engines of cell construction in cells
9. In normal cells, each caspase is present in an enzymatically inactive state, called the zymogen form
10. Many forms of cellular damage trigger leakage of mitochondria, which somehow induces the apoptotic response
11. A molecule called ligand is produced by secretion from signaling cells
12. Cell division is inhibited by the action of mitogens, which are polypeptide ligands released usually from a paracrine source
13. Negative secreted factors that are necessary to block activation of the apoptosis pathway are known as survival factors
14. Tumour-promoting mutant alleles of tumour-suppressor genes mutationally activate the proteins that they encode
15. Cancer is a genetic disease
16. Certain cancers are inherited as highly penetrant simple Mendelian traits
17. Most carcinogenic agents are not mutagenic
18. Various oncogenes have been isolated from tumour viruses
19. Dominant oncogenes have been isolated from tumour viruses
20. Certain cancers are highly correlated to specific chromosomal rearrangements
21. The blood streams of an individual may contain many different kinds of antibodies
22. Antigens are known as agglutinin
23. Antibody is known as agglutinogen
24. Antibody-producing cells in vertebrates arise in the bone marrow
25. Antibody-producing cells become T and B lymphocytes
26. The term 'vaccine' is derived from vaccinia virus, which has been used as a live vaccine for small pox
27. Conventional vaccines are always dead vaccines
28. Live vaccines are inactivated pathogens
29. An ideal vaccine is toxic

30. Killed pathogen vaccines may sometimes be ineffective
31. Conventional vaccines may sometimes revert to virulence after replication in the vaccinated individuals
32. Tumour cells are immortalized and transformed
33. Transforming viruses carry oncogenes
34. Retroviruses deactivate cellular genes
35. Quantitative or qualitative changes cannot explain oncogenicity
36. Nondefective retroviruses activate proto-oncogenes
37. Proto-oncogenes can be activated by translocation
38. Growth factor receptor kinases can be mutated to oncogenes
39. Oncoproteins may not regulate gene expression
40. p53 is not a DNA-binding protein
41. p53 is activated by modifications of amino acids
42. Telomere shortening causes cell senescence
43. p53 may affect aging
44. Defects in repair systems cause mutations to accumulate in tumours
45. T cell receptors have no relationship to immunoglobins
46. The primary response to an antigen is mounted by B cells that do not survive beyond the response period
47. B cell differentiation is not responsible for acquired immunity
48. B cell development proceeds through sequential stages
49. T cell development does not proceed through sequential stages
50. Class II proteins are involved in interactions between T cells

22
Biochemistry

MULTIPLE-CHOICE QUESTIONS

1. Melvin Calvin and his colleagues used which of the following to deduce the steps in the Calvin Cycle?
(a) Radioactive phosphate
(b) Radioactive sulfate
(c) Algae
(d) SDS PAGE electrophoresis
(e) Ultracentrifugation

2. Energy is important for life forms because
(a) it is required to do work
(b) it is required to make specific alterations in the cell
(c) all life forms require a continuous supply of it
(d) both (a) and (b)
(e) choices (a), (b), and (c)

3. Which of the following statements is not true of the value D*H*?
(a) D*H* is change in enthalpy
(b) D*H* = D*E* + D(*PV*)
(c) D*H* is change in heat content
(d) A reaction with a positive D*H* value is exothermic
(e) In biology, D*H* is basically the same as D*E*

4. Which of the following is defined as "heat content or total energy content?"
(a) Enthalpy
(b) kcal/kJ multiplied by the Keq
(c) Gibb's free energy
(d) Entropy
(e) Flouresence

5. The statement "Energy is neither created nor destroyed" describes
(a) the first law of thermodynamics
(b) the second law of thermodynamics
(c) the law of conservation of energy
(d) enthalpy
(e) both (a) and (c)

6. Fireflies and certain types of bacteria have the ability to convert the energy stored in ATP into light. Which of the following types of work is performed by the firefly?
(a) Electrical (b) Bioluminescence
(c) Mechanical and synthetic
(d) Heat (e) Concentration

7. Substrate activation may involve

(a) accepting or donating protons by the enzyme
(b) temporary covalent bonds
(c) a change in enzyme conformation induced by substrate binding
(d) nucleophilic substitution
(e) all of the above

8. A sick person often has a fever. Which of the following statements best explains why this occurs?

(a) Enzymes do not function as well at temperatures other than the optimal temperature
(b) Sweating removes prosthetic groups from biological systems
(c) Bacteria and viruses reproduce more rapidly at higher body temperature
(d) The higher temperature increases the activity of lysases
(e) Both (a) and (b)

9. The work of James B. Sumner was to

(a) isolate urease
(b) disprove "vitalism"
(c) crystallize a common animal protein
(d) originate the term *ferments* to describe enzymes
(e) both (a) and (b)

10. Why is the Lineweaver-Burk plot important in enzyme kinetics?

(a) It reveals the presence of organic prosthetic groups in enzymes
(b) It is a single-reciprocal plot
(c) It makes it easier to determine V_{max}
(d) It illustrates enzyme specificity
(e) Actually the Lineweaver-Burk plot is not important

11. Which of the following variables is not part of the Michaelis-Menten equation?

(a) AEG (b) Km
(c) [S] (d) V_{max}
(e) v

12. The equation $v = V_{max}$ [S] / (Km + [S]) is part of which of the following plots?

(a) Lineweaver-Burk (b) Michaelis-Menten
(c) Eadie-Hofstee (d) Both a and b
(e) None of the above

13. A means of detecting the presence of specific carbohydrate moieties on glycoproteins is

(a) photobleaching
(b) liposome formation
(c) SDS PAGE
(d) the freeze fracture technique
(e) ferritin conjugated lectins

14. Cholesterol

(a) destabilizes the cell membrane
(b) intercalates between the fatty acid chain within the bilayer
(c) is found in abundance in prokaryotic cell membranes
(d) increases permeability for small cations
(e) all of the above

15. Starting with shredded spinach leaves, you follow a procedure that allows for separation of cellular organelles. You are specifically looking for the fraction that contains the mitochondria. To identify this fraction you should test for the

(a) general presence of enzymes
(b) presence of enzymes associated with cellular respiration
(c) polysaccharides that specifically surround the mitochondria
(d) phospholipids unique to the mitochondrial membrane
(e) phospholipids unique to intracellular membranes

16. Which of the following molecules would not readily cross an intact cell membrane by simple diffusion?

(a) Water (b) Fatty acids
(c) Ethanol (d) Glucose
(e) Oxygen

17. Cystic fibrosis is the result of malfunction of the cell in transporting which of the following ions?

(a) Na^+ (b) OH^-
(c) K^+ (d) Cl^-
(e) Glucose

18. You wish to dehydrate a piece of meat using solutions of varying salt concentrations. The best concentration to use would be

(a) 0.01% (b) 0.09%
(c) 0.9% (d) 1%
(e) 10%

19. Ionophores are

(a) the gating mechanisms associated with the transport of ions
(b) intrinsic proteins that passively transport ions
(c) chemicals that form pores in the plasma membrane and allow ions to cross
(d) intrinsic proteins that actively transport ions
(e) membrane proteins that allow for the movement of small-molecular-weight compounds

20. Which of the following best describes the special "high-energy" bond of ATP?

(a) Hydrogenation (b) Phosphoester
(c) Ionic (d) Phosphoanhydride
(e) Hydrogen

21. Oxidation in biological systems is accompanied by

(a) hydrogenation
(b) resonance stabilization
(c) repulsion
(d) dehydrogenation
(e) all of the above

22. Glucose is transported in the bloodstream to cells in all parts of your body. In body cells, glucose has four main fates. Which of the following is not one of those fates?

(a) Glucose is transformed into sucrose
(b) Glucose is used to synthesize glycogen
(c) Glucose is converted to acetyl CoA to make body fat
(d) Glucose is converted to lactate
(e) Glucose is catabolized to carbon dioxide and water

23. At which enzymatic step of glycolysis is water a product?

(a) 3 (b) 5
(c) 6 (d) 9
(e) 10

24. During the first phase of glycolysis, ATP is used to form which type of bond with glucose?

(a) Dehydrogenation
(b) Hydrogenation
(c) Phosphoanhydride
(d) Substrate-level phosphorylation
(e) Phosphoester

25. Within animal cells, glycolysis and gluconeogenesis must not occur at the same time. Therefore, regulation is important. Which of the following molecules is least important in the regulation of glycolysis and gluconeogenesis?

(a) ATP/ADP
(b) Acetyl CoA
(c) NADH
(d) Fructose-2,6-bisphosphate
(e) Phosphofructokinase-2

26. The enzyme used to break down fructose-1,6-bisphosphate into two trioses is called

(a) phosphoglucoisomerase
(b) enolase
(c) aldolase
(d) triose phosphate isomerase
(e) hexokinase

27. During strenuous exercise, you may notice that your muscles burn. Which of the following statements best explains this phenomenon?

(a) Proteins are being digested to provide energy
(b) Carbon dioxide is building up in muscle and changing the pH
(c) ADP is accumulating, which produces a burning sensation
(d) Without oxygen, pyruvate is being converted to lactic acid
(e) All of the above

28. β–oxidation

(a) is a process used to oxidize fatty acids
(b) is the second step in the oxidation of glucose
(c) is a process used to digest some polysaccharides
(d) occurs in the cytoplasm
(e) both (b) and (c)

29. NADH concentrations serve to regulate oxidative decarboxylation and TCA cycle. Which of the following enzymes is not regulated by NADH?

(a) α–ketoglutarate dehydrogenase
(b) Pyruvate dehydrogenase
(c) Succinate dehydrogenase
(d) Malate dehydrogenase
(e) Isocitrate dehydrogenase

30. Of the carrier molecules in the electron transport chain, which has heme as part of its prosthetic group?

(a) Flavoproteins
(b) Cytochromes
(c) Copper containing cytochromes
(d) Iron sulfur proteins
(e) Coenzyme Q

31. The sequential process of fatty acid catabolism to acetyl CoA is called

(a) oxidative deamination
(b) β oxidation
(c) the Cori cycle
(d) the glyoxylate cycle
(e) transamination

32. Carboxypeptidase

(a) is an endopeptidase
(b) removes amino acids from the amino terminus
(c) removes amino acids from the carboxy terminus
(d) is the same as an aminopeptidase
(e) both a and d

33. Which of the numbered respiratory complexes is not correctly paired with its name?

(a) Complex II—succinate-coenzyme Q oxido-reductase complex
(b) Complex I—NADH dehydrogenase complex
(c) Complex III—coenzyme Q-cytochrome *c* oxidoreductase complex
(d) Complex IV—cytochrome *c* reductase complex
(e) None of the above

34. Transamination

(a) can involve only a small number of amino acids
(b) involves the amination of an alpha keto acid
(c) liberates a free ammonia molecule
(d) involves transfer of amino groups from an amino acid to another amino acid
(e) none of the above

35. Bacteriochlorophyll differs from chlorophyll *a* and *b* in structure and function. Which of the following statements correctly contrasts these types of chlorophyll?

(a) Bacteriochlorophyll has a saturated carbon-carbon bond at one location in the porphyrin ring, whereas chlorophyll does not
(b) Chlorophyll has a methyl group attached to the porphyrin ring, whereas bacteriochlorophyll has a formyl group
(c) Chlorophyll has a phytol side chain, but bacteriochlorophyll does not
(d) Bacteriochlorophyll has a porphyrin ring, whereas chlorophyll does not
(e) Both a and d correctly contrast these types of chlorophyll

36. In the Calvin cycle, the enzyme that catalyzes the capture of carbon dioxide and the formation of 3-phosphoglycerate is

(a) phosphoglycerokinase
(b) glyceraldehyde-3-phosphate dehydrogenase
(c) ribulose-5-phosphate kinase
(d) triose phosphate isomerase
(e) ribulose bisphosphate carboxylase/oxygenase (rubisco)

37. The regeneration of which molecule allows for continuous carbon assimilation in the Calvin cycle?

(a) Ribulose 1,5-bisphosphate
(b) 3-phosphoglycerate
(c) Dihydroxyacetone phosphate
(d) Glycerate 1,3-bisphosphate
(e) Glyceraldehyde 3-phosphate

38. Which of the following is not an essential feature of electron transfer from water to $NADP^+$?

(a) Plastocyanin (PC)
(b) Coenzyme Q
(c) Photosystem II complex
(d) Photosystem I complex
(e) Cytochrome *b6/f* complex

39. A house plant seems to be growing slowly and lacks its normal bright green colour. You call a botanist for advice. She suggests that the plant may be deficient in magnesium (Mg^{++}). Why these symptoms are associated with Mg^{++} deficiency?

(a) Mg^{++} is an important component of chlorophyll
(b) Lack of Mg^{++} in the soil allows the pathogenic bacteria to grow
(c) Enzymes used in the Calvin cycle require a large amount of Mg^{++}
(d) Mg^{++} is important for the structure of many amino acids
(e) Mg^{++} is required before NADPH can function

40. Which of the following statements correctly characterizes the relationship between $NADP^+$/NADPH and NAD^+/NADH?

(a) $NADP^+$/NADPH is used primarily for catabolic reactions
(b) Only NAD^+/NADH is used to transport electrons and protons
(c) Neither are helpful for oxygenic phototrophs
(d) $NADP^+$/NADPH has an extra phosphate compared to NAD^+/NADH
(e) Both are used extensively during photosynthesis in oxygenic phototrophs

41. *Aerobic* refers to which property of chemotrophs?

(a) Heat losses occur in the presence of oxygen
(b) Chemotrophs remove carbon dioxide from the air
(c) Chemotrophs require oxygen to produce energy
(d) Chemotrophs use, but do not require oxygen
(e) Fermentation releases great amounts of gas, but only in chemotrophs

42. Matter and energy flow through the biosphere. The flow of matter, however, differs from the flow of energy. Which of the following statements accurately describes these differences?

(a) Matter flows in cycles, whereas energy flows in one direction
(b) Energy flows from chemotrophs to phototrophs, whereas matter flows from phototrophs to chemotrophs
(c) Energy flows as organic molecules are reduced to inorganic molecules, but matter does not
(d) Matter does not accompany energy as it enters the biosphere, but it does flow with energy from the biosphere
(e) Both a and b

43. In a chemical reaction, the standard free energy change ($\Delta G0°$) is calculated to be -283.67 cal/mol. What can be said of the chemical reaction?

(a) The reaction is not spontaneous under standard conditions
(b) The reaction violates the second law of thermodynamics
(c) Products predominate over reactants at equilibrium under standard conditions
(d) The reaction goes spontaneously to the right under standard conditions
(e) Both c and d

44. Photosynthesis is an important process that

(a) is performed by heterotrophs
(b) is performed by organisms living near deep-ocean thermal vents
(c) uses water and carbon dioxide as reactants
(d) produces oxidized products
(e) none of the above

45. Covalent modification

(a) affects the activity of an enzyme by adding or removing a chemical group
(b) can involve the addition of phosphate groups
(c) produces modifications that cannot be reversed
(d) is a means of regulation like allosteric regulation
(e) all of the above

46. Hopanoids

(a) function in signal transduction mechanisms
(b) are found in eukaryotes only
(c) are examples of sterols
(d) none of the above

47. With regard to the semipermeable nature of the plasma membrane, which of the following would readily cross without the aid of a transport protein?

(a) Glucose (b) Amino acids
(c) Water (d) Calcium ions
(e) DNA

48. You are experimenting with a variety of lipids to determine their efficacy for use as drug delivery system liposomes. What is one feature of the individual lipid that would best ensure the use of a lipid for this purpose?

(a) It should be exclusively hydrophilic
(b) It must be composed entirely of unsaturated fatty acids
(c) It should be exclusively hydrophobic
(d) It must have a structure similar to cholesterol
(e) It should be amphipathic

49. You want to modify plant cells. With the procedure you are using, the plant cells must be in a plasmolyzed state. This means that the plant cells must be placed in a(n)

(a) acid solution (b) hypertonic solution
(c) basic solution (d) hypotonic solution
(e) isotonic solution

50. In the kidney, the specialized transport proteins that allow for very rapid fluid movement into or out of cells are known as

(a) osmosins
(b) porins
(c) ionophores
(d) anion exchange proteins
(e) aquaporins

51. The type of ATPases associated with the integral binding of ATP as part of the transport process is the

(a) ABC type (b) V type
(c) F type (d) P type

52. Which of the following is true of NAD^+?

(a) It is a coenzyme
(b) It releases an adenosine to become NADH
(c) NAD^+ serves as an electron source for biological oxidation
(d) It is derived from vitamin E
(e) All of the above

53. The negatively charged phosphates of ATP influence one another by

(a) dehydrogenation
(b) charge repulsion
(c) resonance hybridization
(d) resonance stabilization
(e) all of the above

54. The *gross* output of ATP from glycolysis is ______, whereas the *net* output of ATP is

(a) 2; 4 (b) 4; 2
(c) 6; 4 (d) 4; 1
(e) 2; 1

55. Which of the following statements is not true of the TCA cycle?

(a) Acetate enters the TCA cycle and joins a four-carbon acceptor molecule to form citrate
(b) ATP/GTP is generated at one point by substrate-level phosphorylation
(c) FAD is an electron acceptor in the cycle
(d) Decarboxylation occurs at two locations in the TCA cycle
(e) Oxidation occurs at three steps in the TCA cycle

56. Which of the following is not a product of the TCA cycle?

(a) Carbon dioxide (CO_2)
(b) NADH
(c) $FADH_2$
(d) ATP
(e) Acetyl CoA

57. The Hatch-Slack cycle occurs in which of the following types of plants?

(a) CAM plants (b) C3 plants
(c) Tropical grasses (d) C4 plants
(e) Both c and d

58. The relationship between photosystem I (PSI) and photosystem II (PSII) is correctly described by which of the following statements?

(a) PSI absorbs only short wavelengths of light
(b) Electrons are excited by PSI or PSII, but not both
(c) The absorption maximum of PSII is 700 nm
(d) PSI is designated P700, whereas PSII is designated P680
(e) The absorption maximum of PSI is 680 nm

59. The polymerization of macromolecules is similar in many respects. Which of the following principles below is *least* likely to be common to all methods of polymerization of macromolecules?

(a) The polymer is directional
(b) As monomers are added to the polymer, water is removed from the macromolecule
(c) To be added to the polymer, the monomer must be activated
(d) Macromolecules are synthesized by the addition of monomers
(e) Polymerization is passive, requiring little ATP

60. Which branch of chemistry deals specifically with living systems?

(a) Organic chemistry
(b) Inorganic chemistry
(c) Biochemistry
(d) Biological chemistry
(e) Both c and d

61. Which of the following is not true of phospholipids?

(a) A basic component in phospholipids is phosphatidic acid
(b) Sphingolipids are the predominant phospho-lipids in membranes
(c) Phospholipids are amphipathic
(d) Phospholipids are important in membrane structure
(e) Serine is a molecule that may be part of a phosphoglyceride

62. A negative free energy change indicates that

(a) the reaction is not possible under any conditions
(b) the reaction is exergonic
(c) the reaction has no equilibrium under any conditions
(d) enthalpy must be added to the reaction before it can proceed
(e) the reactant is predominant at equilibrium

63. The active site for carboxypeptidase

(a) involves only six out of a total of 307 amino acids
(b) contains a glutamate residue at position 69
(c) uses iron as the prosthetic group
(d) contains amino acids that are contiguous to one another along the primary sequence of the protein
(e) both c and d

64. While examining glucose transport into a cell, the immediate phosphorylation of glucose following its entry into the cell

(a) allows the cell to maintain higher levels of glucose outside the cell
(b) puts glucose into a form for use in cellular respiration
(c) puts glucose into a form to be stored
(d) keeps the glucose from being transported back out of the cell
(e) all of the above

65. There are 10 enzymatic reactions that convert glucose to pyruvate. Steps ______ and ______ are the steps in which ATP is consumed, whereas______ and ______ are the reactions that produce ATP

(a) 1; 2; 9; 10　　(b) 1; 5; 6; 8
(c) 1; 3; 7; 10　　(d) 2; 4; 7; 10
(e) 2; 3; 7; 8

66. In electron transport, which respiratory complex is not involved in the flow of electrons from NADH?

(a) Complex I　　(b) Complex II
(c) Complex III　　(d) Complex IV
(e) All of the above

67. Which of the following is true of enzymes?

(a) Enzymes may function separately from cells
(b) Enzymes were originally known as "ferments"
(c) An enzyme is a specific biological catalyst
(d) Both a and c
(e) Choices a, b, and c

68. A hypothetical automobile has 100 parts that are to be assembled by four workers. During the car's assembly, each worker constructs 25 parts individually, and then the four resulting subcomponents are assembled together. The manner in which the car was assembled is much like which cellular strategy?

(a) Assisted self-assembly
(b) Electrostatic assembly
(c) Renaturation
(d) Hierarchical assembly
(e) Self-assembly

69. Which of the following is a terpene?

(a) Glycerol　　(b) Phenanthrene
(c) Testosterone　　(d) Vitamin D
(e) Dolichol

70. An allosteric inhibitor

(a) increases the rate of substrate binding
(b) binds at the allosteric site
(c) is identical to the active site
(d) binds and activates the high-affinity state of the enzymes
(e) all of the above

71. Which of the following is not a characteristic of active transport?

(a) Exclusively move one molecule at a time in a unidirectional manner
(b) sensitive to metabolic poisons
(c) can be coupled with passive transport to generate the energy necessary for active transport
(d) can work as symports or antiports
(e) all of the above

72. In the first step of glycolysis, glucose can be phosphorylated because
(a) the transfer of a phosphate from ATP to glucose is exergonic
(b) a phosphoanhydride bond has higher energy than a phosphoester bond
(c) both the number 2 and 3 carbons can be spontaneously phosphorylated
(d) the ketosugar is rapidly phosphorylated at the carbon 1 hydroxyl group
(e) both a and b

73. During which of the following stages of the TCA cycle does substrate-level phosphorylation take place?
(a) TCA-2 (b) TCA-3
(c) TCA-4 (d) TCA-5
(e) TCA-6

74. The plants referred to as C3 and C4 plants get this designation based on the number of carbons in the first detectable product of carbon dioxide fixation. The C3 product is _______, whereas the C4 product is
(a) 3-phosphoglycerate; malate
(b) glycerol; malate
(c) triose phosphate; oxaloacetate
(d) 3-phosphoglycerate; oxaloacetate
(e) ribose; phosphoenolpyruvate

75. Which of the following is an alkaloid?
(a) Geraniol (b) Caffeic acid
(c) Azadirachtin (d) Quinine

76. Shikimic acid pathway is involved in the synthesis of
(a) phenolics (b) terpenes
(c) alkaloids (d) steroids

77. An alkaloid that is useful in the treatment of cancer is
(a) quinine (b) vinblastine
(c) morphine (d) reserpine

78. β-Carotene is a
(a) monoterpene (b) diterpene
(c) triterpene (d) tetraterpene

79. Azadirachtin is used for the control of
(a) bacterial disease (b) insects
(c) fungal disease (d) rodents

80. Which is the one major use of gel electrophoresis?
(a) Electricity conductor
(b) DNA fingerprinting
(c) Pre-natal testing
(d) Artificial incrimination
(e) Detecting unhealthy bone marrow

81. In which material is gel electrophoresis usually performed?
(a) Red blood cells (b) Syrup
(c) Agarose (d) Milk
(e) Ethanol

82. What happens during gel electrophoresis?
(a) Molecules are broken
(b) Cells are matched with one another
(c) Molecules are separated based on physical characteristics
(d) Unhealthy cells die
(e) The DNA cells fall apart

83. During gel electrophoresis, which molecules move the farthest?
(a) Large ones (b) Slippery ones
(c) Thin ones (d) Small ones
(e) Oblong-shaped ones

84. In which science is gel electrophoresis not used?
(a) Biochemistry (b) Molecular biology
(c) Microbiology (d) Genetics
(e) Physics

MECHANISM OF SELECTED REACTIONS

85. Light reaction is the process in which

(a) chemical energy is converted into carbohydrates
(b) oxidative phosphorylation occurs
(c) light energy is converted into chemical energy
(d) no phosphorylation takes place

86. The other name of Hatch-Slack pathway is

(a) Calvin cycle (b) C3 pathway
(c) C4 pathway (d) CAM pathway

87. Which one of the following enzymes is bifunctional?

(a) Phosphoribulokinase
(b) GAP dehydrogenase
(c) Ribose phosphate isomerase
(d) RUBP carboxylase

88. Cyclic photophosphorylation involves

(a) PSI (b) PSII
(c) PSI and PSII (d) none of the above

89. One turn of the TCA cycle

(a) produces 2 $FADH_2$ molecules
(b) requires 3 NADH molecules
(c) releases 2 CO_2 molecules
(d) produces 1 ADP molecule

90. The following is a substrate-level phosphorylation reaction

(a) fructose 1,6-bisphosphate ————> DHAP + glyceraldehyde-3 phosphate
(b) 1,3 bisphosphoglycerate + ADP <========> 3-P-glycerate + ATP
(c) malate + NAD+ ————————> oxaloacetate + NADH + H+
(d) pyruvate + CoA-SH + NAD ———————> acetyl-CoA + NADH + CO_2
(e) fumarate + H_2O ———————— malate

91. For every glucose oxidized by the central pathways (glycolysis / PDH / TCA cycle), how many NADH are produced?

(a) 5 (b) 10
(c) 15 (d) 20
(e) 25

92. For every one molecule of acetyl CoA oxidized by the citric acid cycle, how many ATP (or equivalents) are produced?

(a) 6 (b) 12
(c) 18 (d) 24
(e) 36

93. The conversion of succinate into fumarate is catalyzed by

(a) synthase (b) synthetase
(c) dehydrogenase (d) kinase
(e) carboxylase

94. The following are electron carriers except

(a) coenzyme A
(b) cytochrome a
(c) nonheme iron protein
(d) Co Q
(e) NADH

95. The following is a mobile electron carrier in the electron transport chain?

(a) complex I (b) complex II
(c) complex III (d) cytochrome c
(e) all of the above

96. There are ______ irreversible reactions in glycolysis

(a) 1 (b) 2
(c) 3 (d) 4
(e) 5

97. There are ______ substrate level phosphorylation reaction(s) in the TCA cycle

(a) 1 (b) 2
(c) 3 (d) 4
(e) 5

98. The conversion of pyruvate to acetyl CoA, isocitrate to alpha-ketoglutarate, and alpha-ketoglutarate to succinyl CoA have the following in common

(a) they are carboxylation reactions
(b) they occur in the cytoplasm
(c) they involve oxidation and decarboxylation and are thus called oxidative decarboxylation
(d) they are reactions of the TCA cycle
(e) they produce ATP

99. The following vitamin is needed for the decarboxylation of an alpha-keto acid

(a) thiamine (B1) (b) niacin
(c) riboflavin (d) biotin
(e) vitamin A

100. The following lipoprotein is predominantly composed of triglycerides and disappears from blood a few hours after a meal

(a) LDL (b) HDL
(c) VLDL (d) chylomicrons

101. Glycogen is mostly stored in the

(a) liver and red blood cells
(b) kidney
(c) heart
(d) liver and skeletal muscles
(e) adipose tissue

102. Which of the following is a catabolic pathway for lipids?

(a) Glycogenesis (b) Gluconeogenesis
(c) Beta-oxidation (d) Urea cycle
(e) Embden Meyerhoff pathway

103. Which of the following carbons is the most reduced?

(a) Carbon with four hydrogens
(b) Carbon with an alcohol group
(c) Carbon dioxide
(d) Carbon of a ketone
(e) Carbon of a carboxylic acid

104. The enzyme catalyzing the reaction S + ATP $\longrightarrow$ S-P + ADP is a

(a) carboxylase (b) kinase
(c) dehydrogenase (d) isomerase
(e) synthetase

105. The following group is not found in CoA

(a) phosphate (b) sulfhydryl
(c) ribose (d) amide
(e) pyridine

106. The poison cyanide affects

(a) glycolysis
(b) TCA cycle
(c) electron transport chain
(d) substrate level phosphorylation
(e) none of the above

GLYCOGEN METABOLISM

107. Which of the following statements about glycogen metabolism is false?

(a) Unlike the liver, skeletal muscles do not have glucose 6-phosphatase; thus skeletal muscles do not export their glycogen derived glucose to other tissues
(b) Glycogenolysis occurs at the non-reducing end of the glycogen chain.
(c) In glycogenesis, glucose activation is carried out by reaction with a nucleotide, UTP
(d) The alpha 1,4 glycosidic linkages in glycogen is broken down by the enzyme pyrophosphorylase
(e) Glycogen synthesis requires energy

108. Gluconeogenesis requires

(a) biotin (b) bicarbonate
(c) PEP carboxykinase
(d) ATP
(e) all of the above

109. In humans, glucose can be made from all of the following except

(a) lactate (b) pyruvate
(c) acetyl-CoA (d) glycerol
(e) some amino acids (glucogenic amino acids)

110. The oxidative phase of HMS produces

(a) $FADH_2$ (b) NADH
(c) CoA-SH (d) NADPH
(e) glucose

PENTOSE PHOSPHATE PATHWAY

111. Which of the following is a function of the pentose phosphate pathway?

(a) It produces ribose 5-P required for DNA, RNA synthesis
(b) It produces a reducing agent required to keep red blood cells flexible
(c) It produces sugars with various number of carbon atoms
(d) It oxidizes glucose
(e) All of the above

112. Gluconeogenesis occurs predominantly in the

(a) spleen (b) skeletal muscles
(c) liver (d) RBC
(e) adipose tissue

113. Which of the following atoms is not found in biotin?

(a) N (b) S
(c) P (d) O
(e) H

LIPID METABOLISM

114. The quantum of energy produced when the same weight of lipid and hydrated glycogen oxidized is

(a) equal
(b) six times higher for lipid
(c) six times higher for hydrated glycogen
(d) two times higher for lipid

115. The enzyme which catalyzes the hydrolysis of the fatty acids in the 2 or â-position of phospholipids is

(a) phospholipase A (b) phospholipase B
(c) phospholipase C (d) phospholipase D

116. The fatty acid oxidation pathway in which oxidation results in the removal of one carbon at a time is

(a) β-oxidation (b) ω-oxidation
(c) α-oxidation (d) decarboxylation

117. Triacylglycerols are synthesized through

(a) reversal of lipolysis
(b) reversal of β-oxidation pathway
(c) glycerol and fatty acid activation
(d) ω-oxidation

118. Fatty acid with 18-carbon atoms are synthesized with the help of

(a) fatty acid synthase complex
(b) elongase
(c) fatty acid synthase complex plus elongase
(d) desaturase

119. The reducing agent used in fatty acid synthesis is

(a) $FADH_2$ (b) NADH
(c) CoA-SH (d) NADPH
(e) hydrogen

120. The conversion of aceto acetate into acetone during ketone body formation is a ______ reaction

$$CH_3\,CO\,CH_2\,COO \longrightarrow CO_2 + CH_3\,CO\,CH_3$$

(a) redox
(b) isomerization
(c) carboxylation
(d) decarboxylation of alpha-keto acid
(e) none of the above (it is actually the decarboxylation of a beta-keto acid!)

121. In beta-oxidation, fatty acids are converted into their

(a) phosphates (b) esters
(c) thioesters (d) anhydrides
(e) none of the above

122. Which of the following pathways occurs in the mitochondria?

(a) Glycogenesis
(b) Glycogenolysis
(c) Fatty acid synthesis
(d) Beta-oxidation of fatty acids
(e) HMS

123. Fatty acid oxidation produces

(a) $FADH_2$ (b) NADH
(c) Acetyl CoA (d) all of the above

124. Which of the following is a product when CH_3 CH_2 CH_2 CH_2 COO undergoes fatty acid oxidation?

(a) Butyl CoA (b) Propionyl CoA
(c) Hexyl CoA (d) Methane
(e) None of the above

125. How many acetyl CoA molecules are produced when

CH_3 CH_2 CH_2 CH_2 CH_2 COO undergoes beta-oxidation?

(a) 1 (b) 2
(c) 3 (d) 4
(e) 5

126. How many high energy bonds are hydrolyzed when the fatty acid CH_3 CH_2 CH_2 CH_2 CH_2 COO undergoes beta-oxidation?

(a) 1 (b) 2
(c) 3 (d) 4
(e) 5

127. How many net ATPs are produced when the fatty acid

CH_3 CH_2 CH_2 CH_2 CH_2 COO undergoes beta-oxidation?

(a) 4 (b) 6
(c) 36 (d) 46
(e) 44

128. Fatty acid synthesis requires

(a) biotin (b) malonyl CoA
(c) acetyl CoA (d) ATP
(e) all of the above

129. The following are ketone bodies except

(a) acetyl CoA
(b) beta-hydroxybutyrate
(c) acetoacetate
(d) acetone

130. Acetyl CoA is an important reactant/ product or intermediate for the following metabolic pathways except

(a) fatty acid synthesis
(b) cholesterol synthesis
(c) beta-oxidation
(d) gluconeogenesis
(e) none of the above

131. HMG-CoA is converted into mevalonate during cholesterol synthesis by the enzyme

(a) oxidase (b) isomerase
(c) reductase (d) phosphorylase
(e) kinase

132. Fatty acid transport into mitochondria is carried out by

(a) creatine (b) carnitine
(c) ornithine (d) creatinine

133. The fatty acid *CH_3-CH_2-CH_2-CH_2-CH_2-CH_2-COOH (the asterisk * represents a radioactive label) is fed to a human. After half-hour where would the label be found?

(a) Acetyl-CoA
(b) Propionyl-CoA
(c) Malonyl-CoA
(d) Both acetyl and propionyl-CoA

REGULATION OF METABOLISM

134. Which enzyme in gluconeogenesis is regulated by fructose 2,6-bisphosphate?

(a) Fructose 1,6-bisphosphatase
(b) PEP carboxykinase
(c) Pyruvate carboxylase
(d) Glucose g-phosphatase

135. Glucagen

(a) stimulates glycogenolysis
(b) inhibits glycogenesis
(c) slows down glycolysis
(d) stimulates gluconeogenesis
(e) all of the above

136. The process whereby the catalytic activity of an enzyme is increased or decreased by the covalent attachment of a group such as phosphate to the enzyme is called

(a) induction
(b) allosteric control
(c) covalent modification
(d) repression
(e) feedback inhibition

137. Which of the following is an important intrinsic control of beta-oxidation?

(a) AMP (b) ADP
(c) Acetyl CoA (d) Fatty acyl CoA
(e) Malonyl CoA

138. The intracellular messenger that mediates the action of epinephrine and glucagons is

(a) ATP (b) acetyl CoA
(c) cyclic AMP (d) AMP
(e) Pi

139. The key control point in glycolysis is the enzyme

(a) PFK-1 (b) PFK-2
(c) glucokinase (d) hexokinase
(e) isomerase

140. Which of the following regulator inhibits glycolysis and TCA cycle intrinsically?

(a) Cyclic AMP (b) AMP
(c) ATP (d) NADH
(e) FAD

141. Which of the following is not true in late starvation?

(a) Skeletal proteins are broken down into amino acids, some of which are used by the liver to make glucose
(b) Most cells resort to fatty acid oxidation to make ATP for their energy needs
(c) Beta-hydroxybutyrate and acetoacetate concentrations in the blood becomes elevated
(d) Blood insulin level is low
(e) Glycogen is broken down to stabilize blood glucose

PROTEINS AND AMINO ACID METABOLISM

142. Which of the following amino acids is optically inactive?

(a) Alanine (b) Glycine
(c) Leucine (d) Aspartic acid

143. The reagent that is used for quantitative determination of amino acids is

(a) Sanger's (b) Molisch's
(c) Benedict's (d) Ninhydrin

144. The protein with quarternary structure is

(a) insulin (b) myoglobin
(c) haemoglobin (d) keratin

145. The interaction, which is involved in the secondary structure of protein, is

(a) hydrogen bond
(b) hydrophobic
(c) van der Waals force
(d) ionic bond

146. The bond, which is not disturbed during denaturation of protein, is

(a) covalent bond
(b) hydrogen bond
(c) ionic bond
(d) van der Waals force

147. The quarternary structure of proteins is represented by

(a) amino acid sequence
(b) arrangement of subunits
(c) alpha-helix
(d) three-dimensional conformation
(e) beta pleated sheats

148. Alkaptonuria is a metabolic disorder that results in the accumulation of

(a) phenylalanine
(b) phenylalanine hydroxylase
(c) homogentisic acid
(d) phenylpyruvate
(e) tyrosine

149. The synthesis of dipeptide represents a reaction described as

(a) catabolic (b) dehydration
(c) hydrolysis (d) anabolic
(e) both anabolic and dehydration

150. In *Neurospora*, a mutation was induced that causes the loss of function of an enzyme essential for the biosynthesis of vitamin, pyrodoxine. On which medium will such organisms not grow?

(a) Minimal
(b) Complete
(c) Minimal + all vitamins
(d) Minimal + pyridoxine
(e) Neither minimal nor minimal + pyridoxine

151. Ehlers-Danlos syndrome is due to a mutation affecting

(a) haemoglobin (b) collagen
(c) actin and myosin (d) phenylalanine
(e) histones

152. Principal classes of membrane proteins include all of the following except

(a) receptors
(b) cell surface markers
(c) spectrins
(d) transport proteins

153. An enzyme synthesized in the laboratory is found to have little activity when compared to the enzyme extracted from a cell culture. Both enzymes were examined and have identical amino acid composition. Which is the best explanation for the lack of activity of the synthesized enzyme?

(a) The primary amino acid sequence was altered while the composition was not altered
(b) The van der Waals radius was altered during laboratory synthesis
(c) The synthesized enzyme was not folded correctly because molecular chaperones were not present
(d) The ATP required for self-assembly was present in the cell extract, but not in the laboratory synthesis
(e) Denaturation of the synthesized enzyme was not complete

154. The enzyme that aids our body in digesting starch is

(a) maltase (b) cellulase
(c) amylase (d) lactase

155. β-sheets are stabilized by

(a) hydrophobic bonds
(b) ionic bonds
(c) hydrogen bonds
(d) covalent bonds

156. Chaperons are involved in

(a) translation
(b) transcription
(c) mRNA processing
(d) polypeptide folding

157. The amino acid sequence of a polypeptide chain comprises the ______ structure of the protein

(a) primary (b) secondary
(c) tertiary (d) quaternary

158. Electrophoresis separates DNA fragments of different sizes with ______ fragments moving closer to the ______ pole

(a) shorter, negative (b) shorter, positive
(c) longer, negative (d) longer, positive

159. In two-dimensional gel electrophoresis

(a) different forms of the same protein will tend to migrate at the same position
(b) up to about a hundred different proteins can be distinguished from each other
(c) proteins with similar functions will be located near each other
(d) all of these
(e) none of these

160. Antibodies are

(a) proteins produced by the immune system
(b) able to bind specifically to a single antigen
(c) an example of proteins with quaternary structure
(d) all of the above
(e) none of the above

161. All of the following are true of protein denaturation except that it

(a) is a shape change
(b) is always irreversible
(c) may be caused by a pH change
(d) could result from a temperature change

162. There are several levels of protein structure, the most complex of which is

(a) primary (b) secondary
(c) tertiary (d) quaternary

163. The functional group-NH_2 is a(n)

(a) carboxyl group (b) amino group
(c) hydroxyl group (d) phosphate group
(e) carbonyl group

164. The sequence of amino acids in a polypeptide is called the

(a) primary structure
(b) secondary structure
(c) tertiary structure
(d) quaternary structure

165. The globular shape of a protein is called the

(a) primary structure
(b) secondary structure
(c) tertiary structure
(d) quaternary structure

166. In proteins, elements of secondary structure combine to form a(n)

(a) domain (b) motif
(c) alpha helix (d) beta sheet
(e) chaperone

167. At what level(s) of protein structure would you expect to find disulfide bridges?

(a) Primary (b) Secondary
(c) Tertiary (d) Quarternary
(e) Only in (b) and (c)

168. Polymerization reactions in which polysaccharides are synthesized from monosaccharides or proteins are synthesized from amino acids

(a) result in the formation of water
(b) are hydrolysis reactions
(c) release energy
(d) result in the formation of covalent bonds between monomers called peptide bonds
(e) all of the above

169. Which of the following is a characteristic of proteins?

(a) Some may enhance the rate of specific chemical reactions
(b) They may form either long, thin fibrous molecules, or compact, rounded globular molecules
(c) They store genetic information for cellular metabolism
(d) They form through hydrolysis reactions
(e) (a) and (b)

170. Many surface proteins are anchored by
(a) polar amino acids
(b) hydrogen bonding amino acids
(c) nonpolar fatty acids
(d) nonpolar amino acids
(e) polar fatty acids

171. Transmembrane proteins are
(a) always fixed in position
(b) always abundant
(c) often not fixed in position
(d) never abundant
(e) none of the above

172. Metabolism is determined by
(a) size of proteins in the cell
(b) availability of amino acids
(c) proteins formed as dictated by the genetic material
(d) protein composition of the DNA
(e) activity of the enzymes produced in the nucleus

173. The principal contractile proteins found in the skeletal muscle are
(a) actin and troponin
(b) actin and myosin
(c) troponin and tropomyosin
(d) myosin and tropomyosin
(e) actin and tropomyosin

174. Which of the following is not an amino acid?
(a) Glutamic acid (b) Aspartic acid
(c) Glutamine (d) Palmitic acid
(e) Leucine

175. What type of covalent bonds link the amino acids in proteins?
(a) Peptide bonds (b) Hydrogen bonds
(c) Ionic bonds (d) Glycosidic bonds
(e) Ester bonds

176. Which of the following is an amino acid found in proteins?
(a) Adenosine (b) Adenine
(c) Alanine (d) Linoleic acid
(e) Creatine

177. Which of the following can affect enzyme activity?
(a) Temperature (b) pH
(c) The presence of certain metal ions
(d) The addition or removal of phosphate
(e) All of the above

178. Prosthetic groups are
(a) required by all enzymes in the cells
(b) loosely bound to enzymes via hydrogen bonds
(c) sites on the enzyme molecule that permit allosteric modification of enzyme activity
(d) linked to phosphate groups
(e) tightly bound to enzymes and are required for their activity

179. The initial rate of an enzyme catalyzed reaction depends on
(a) the concentration of the enzyme
(b) the concentration of the substrate
(c) the affinity of the enzyme for its substrate
(d) all of the above
(e) none of the above

180. Which of the following statements is false?
(a) After a resistance training session, the rate of protein synthesis in the exercised muscles is increased
(b) After a resistance training session, the rate of protein breakdown in the exercised muscles is increased
(c) Both a and b
(d) Protein cannot be used as a fuel for exercise
(e) Exercise increases the rate of secretion of the growth hormone

181. Trypsin catalyzes the hydrolysis of a peptide bond on the carboxyl side of
(a) arginine (b) proline
(c) leucine (d) phenylalanine

182. The source for bromelain is

(a) human (b) bacteria
(c) fungi (d) pineapple

183. The amino acids are attached to the tRNA through

(a) 3′OH group of terminal adenosine
(b) 5′OH group of terminal adenosine
(c) 3′OH group of terminal cytosine
(d) 5′OH group of terminal cytosine

184. High fidelity of protein synthesis is maintained by

(a) peptidyl transferase
(b) amino acyl tRNA synthetase
(c) terminating codons
(d) elongation factors

185. Tetracycline inhibits binding of amino acyl tRNA to the

(a) A site on the prokaryotic ribosome
(b) A site on the eukaryotic ribosome
(c) P site on the eukaryotic ribosome
(d) P site on the prokaryotic ribosome

186. A common reaction in amino acid metabolism between an amino acid and a keto-acid is

(a) transamination (b) redox
(c) addition/elimination
(d) phosphorylation
(e) hydrolysis

187. THF is derived from

(a) riboflavin (b) pantothenic acid
(c) folic acid (d) citric acid
(e) ascorbic acid

188. THF carries the following one carbon groups except

(a) $-CH_3$ (b) $-CH_2$
(c) -CH=O (d) CO_2

189. The nitrogens in urea are derived from aspartic acid and

(a) ala (b) gly
(c) ammonium (d) citrulline
(e) arg

190. In amino acid catabolism, the amino group is carried in the blood as

(a) glu (b) gln
(c) NH_3 (d) lys
(e) asp

191. The carbon skeletons from glucogenic amino acids are converted into all of the following except

(a) oxaloacetate (b) fumarate
(c) succinyl CoA (d) alpha-ketoglutarate
(e) pyruvate
(f) acetyl CoA

192. The carbon skeletons required for amino acid synthesis are derived from all of the following except

(a) alpha-ketoglutarate
(b) oxaloacetate
(c) pyruvate
(d) fumarate
(e) PEP

193. The following coenzyme is required by transaminases

(a) SAM (b) TPP
(c) biotin (d) PLP
(e) THF

194. What is required for this reaction?

$R-NH_3$ ——————————> $R-N(CH_3)^3$

(a) SAM (b) TPP
(c) biotin (d) PLP
(e) THF

195. Phenylalanine is catabolized to fumarate and acetoacetate and is therefore

(a) ketogenic
(b) glucogenic
(c) ketogenic and glucogenic
(d) androgenic
(e) none of the above

196. Pyridoxal phosphate has

(a) a thiol
(b) a quaternary nitrogen
(c) a ketone group
(d) a carboxyl group
(e) none of the above

197. The following are intermediates of the urea cycle except

(a) ornithine
(b) carbamoyl phosphate
(c) citrulline
(d) arginine
(e) succinate

198. The reaction in which SAM is formed from met and ATP involves the attack of the sulfur atom of met on the ______ atom of ATP

(a) alpha-phosphorus
(b) beta-phosphorus
(c) gamma-phosphorus
(d) C-1'
(e) C-5'

199. In lead poisoning, the heme biosynthesis enzyme ______ is affected

(a) ALA synthase
(b) PBG synthase
(c) ferrochelatase
(d) uroporphyrinogen III synthase
(e) none of the above

200. Which of the following about heme metabolism is false?

(a) Uroporphyrinogen III is a cyclic compound
(b) Bilirubin is a cyclic, colourless breakdown product of heme
(c) The conversion of heme into biliverdin releases CO
(d) ALA synthase requires PLP

LIPIDS AND MEMBRANES

201. Which of the following is true of fatty acids?

(a) They are polar molecules
(b) They are aldehydes
(c) Lecithin is a fatty acid
(d) Prostaglandins are derived from fatty acid

202. The following does not contain sphingosine

(a) cerebroside
(b) ganglioside
(c) ceramide
(d) phosphatidylcholine

203. Identify the polyunsaturated fatty acid from the following

(a) palmitoleic (b) oleic
(c) linoleic (d) stearic

204. Which of the following is not a component of glycerophospholipid

(a) fatty acid (b) choline
(c) glycerol (d) sphingosine

205. The lipid that can serve as cellular energy source is

(a) triacylglycerol (b) waxes
(c) bile acids (d) sterols

206. The fatty acid present in butter that contributes to the off-flavour during storage is

(a) lauric (b) stearic
(c) butyric (d) myristic

207. Erucic acid is present in

(a) palm oil (b) mustard oil
(c) rice bran oil (d) soybean oil

CARBHOHYDRATES

208. Non-reducing sugar from the following is

(a) maltose (b) lactose
(c) sucrose (d) glucose

209. Which of the following is levorotatory?

(a) Glucose (b) Mannose
(c) Sucrose (d) Fructose

210. The epimer of glucose is

(a) galactose (b) fructose
(c) arabinose (d) ribose

211. Identify the aldopentose from the following

(a) xylulose (b) ribulose
(c) ribose (d) erythrose

212. An example of heteropolysaccharide is

(a) amylose (b) hemicellulose
(c) cellulose (d) amylopectin

GLYCOGEN METABOLISM

213. Which of the following pathway produces NADPH?

(a) Glycolysis (b) TCA cycle
(c) Glyoxylate cycle (d) HMP shunt

214. ATP molecule is formed during the conversion of phosphoenol pyruvate to pyruvate in

(a) oxidative phosphorylation
(b) phosphorylation
(c) substrate level phosphorylation
(d) product phosphorylation

215. The reaction, which is irreversible in TCA cycle, is

(a) isocitrate to α- ketoglutarate
(b) α-ketoglutarate to succinyl CoA
(c) succinyl CoA to succinate
(d) malate to oxaloacetate

216. Glyoxysomes contain the enzyme

(a) Isocitrate lyase
(b) Succinate dehydrogenase
(c) Fumarase
(d) Malate dehydrogenase

217. Which of the following compounds is uncoupler of oxidative phosphorylation

(a) 2, 4-dinitrophenol
(b) cyanide
(c) rotenone
(d) antimycin A

ENZYMES, VITAMINS AND COENZYMES

218. The competitive inhibitor for succinate dehydrogenase is

(a) malic acid (b) malonic acid
(c) citric acid (d) ascorbic acid

219. Which of the following statements is not true with respect to non-competitive inhibition?

(a) Inhibitors bind to a site other than the active site
(b) ES complex does not decompose at the normal rate to yield products
(c) Inhibition is not reversed by increasing the substrate concentration
(d) Inhibition is reversed by increasing the substrate concentration

220. Km is expressed as

(a) mole/ litre (b) mole
(c) mg (d) no units

221. At maximal velocity, the reaction follows the kinetics of

(a) zero order (b) first order
(c) second order (d) mixed order

222. Which of the following is an iron-containing enzyme?

(a) Carbonic anhydrase
(b) Pyruvate kinase
(c) Hexokinase
(d) Cytochrome oxidase

223. The coenzyme form of pantothenic acid is

(a) acetyl CoA
(b) coenzyme A
(c) cofactor A
(d) pantothenyl phosphate

224. The coenzyme involved in transamination reaction is

(a) pyridoxal phosphate
(b) thiamine pyrophosphate
(c) flavin monophosphate
(d) biocytin

225. Which of the following is not the active form of pyridoxine?

(a) Pyridoxol (b) Pyridoxal
(c) Pyridoxamine (d) Pyridine

226. The active ring system involved in the functioning of TPP is

(a) pyrimidine (b) thiazole
(c) pyridine (d) imidazole

227. Para amino benzoic acid (PABA) is a constituent of

(a) folic acid (b) coenzyme A
(c) lipoic acid (d) cyanocobalamin

MARK TRUE OR FALSE (T/F)

LIPIDS

1. Carbon 1 in palmitic acid is also called the alpha carbon
2. A triglyceride rich in oleic acid is a liquid at room temperature
3. The "head" of PE is hydrophobic
4. In a cerebroside, the polar head is a sugar
5. Cholesterol esters are made up of a steroid and a fatty acid
6. Sphingomyelin can function as a detergent
7. When a triglyceride is saponified with potassium hydroxide, soaps are formed
8. Cholesterol dissolves in water easily
9. Linoleic acid is polyunsaturated fatty acid
10. Sphingosine is not a component of glycerophospholipid
11. The lipid that can serve as a cellular energy source is triacylglycerol
12. Lauric acid in butter is responsible for its off-flavour during storage
13. Soybean oil contains erucic acid
14. Fatty acid with 18 carbons and three double bonds is linolenic
15. The hydroxyl fatty acid present in castor oil is stearic acid
16. Jojoba oil is an example of liquid wax
17. Cerebrosides are composed of choline
18. Saponification is the process of alkali hydrolysis of oil
19. The product of linoleic acid with bromine is tetrabromo octadecanoic acid
20. The product of linoleic acid with hydrogen is oleic acid
21. The product of linoleic acid with aqueous KOH solution is soap
22. Crude oil mainly contains alkanes
23. Essential oils contain mono- and sesquiterpenes
24. Triacylglycerols undergo hydrolysis by the enzyme lipase to form glycerol and fatty acids
25. Fatty acids are transported across the inner mitochondrial membrane with the help of carnitine
26. Oxidation of fatty acids occur in the organelle chloroplast matrix
27. The reductant in fatty acid synthesis is NADP
28. The ATP yield from the complete oxidation of one molecule of stearic acid is 120
29. Fats are mostly in non-oxidised state with only carboxyl group
30. Glycogen is extensively oxygenated product and hence it produces more energy

CARBHOHYDRATES

31. Sucrose is a non-reducing sugar
32. Glucose is levorotatory
33. Galactose is the epimer of glucose
34. Ribulose is an aldopentose
35. Amylose is an example of heteropolysaccharide
36. There are 5 asymmetric carbons present in alpha-D-glucopyranose
37. Dihydroxyacetone is optically inactive
38. Starch and glycogen are polymers of alpha-D-glucopyranose

39. N-acetyl glucosamine is the repeating unit in chitin
40. Acid catalysed dehydration of pentose yields furfural
41. On hydrolysis of one molar solution of sucrose using hydrochloric acid, molarity of glucose and fructose would be 1 M each
42. Human beings can digest cellulose
43. Sucrose can mutarotate
44. Glucose is dextrorotatory
45. One mole of glucose oxidized by HMS produces one mole of CO_2, one mole of pentose, and two moles of NADPH
46. One of the substrates for glycogen synthase is glucose
47. TPP is required for transaldolase
48. Glycolysis produces NADPH
49. Oxidative phosphorylation produces ATP molecule during the conversion of phosphoenol pyruvate to pyruvate
50. Conversion of alpha-ketoglutarate to succinyl Co A is irreversible in TCA cycle
51. Fumarase enzyme is present in glyoxysomes
52. 2,4-dinitrophenol is an uncoupler of oxidative phosphorylation

AMINO ACIDS AND PROTEINS

53. PLP is derived from vitamin B_6
54. One of the nitrogen atoms in urea is derived from an amino acid
55. One of the first reaction in the breakdown of amino acids is transamination
56. Synthesis of glycine from serine requires THF
57. Delta-ALA is formed from gly and succinyl-CoA
58. THF contains a pteridine ring, PABA and glu
59. When THF donates its one-carbon moiety in a reaction, it always becomes oxidized to DHF
60. Glycine is optically inactive
61. Benedict's reagent is used for quantitative determination of amino acids
62. The protein with quarternary structure is myoglobin
63. Covalent bond is not disturbed during denaturation of proteins
64. The decarboxylated product of histamine is histidine
65. Below isoelectric point, proteins possess a negative charge
66. Peptide bond is not broken during the denaturation of proteins
67. Casein is the phosphoprotein present in milk
68. High fidelity in protein synthesis is maintained by elongation factors
69. Pineapple is the source of bromelain
70. Trypsin hydrolysis is a peptide bond on the amino side of proline
71. A protein has 33 amino acids. The bases present in the reading frame would be 99
72. Assume that the protein folds into a three-dimensional shape. The protein thus has a primary, secondary, tertiary and quaternary structure
73. Pro is an imino acid
74. Pro has an indole side chain
75. When oxygen binds haemoglobin, BPG (formerly called DPG) is expelled
76. When oxygen binds haemoglobin, electrostatic bonds are broken
77. When oxygen binds haemoglobin, its quaternary structure is altered
78. When oxygen binds haemoglobin, the Fe atom moves into the porphyrin's plane
79. Val and ile branch at the beta-carbon
80. Myoglobin is a fibrous protein
81. Polyglutamic acid at pH 7 will exist as an alpha-helix
82. PITC is a chemical used in the identification of the N-terminal amino acid
83. All but one of the common amino acids have the same general structure
84. All amino acids have an amine group attached to a central carbon atom
85. Amino acids are the monomers used to build polypeptides and proteins
86. Some of the R-groups on some of the amino acids are hydrophilic

87. Peptide bond is the name given to the group of atoms that hold the R-groups onto the amino acid central carbon atom
88. Polypeptides are chains of amino acids
89. Polypeptides can be linear or branched chains
90. The primary sequence of a polypeptide chain is the location where the branch points occur
91. Hydrophilic amino acid R-groups are always found on the inside of the molecule after it has folded into its tertiary structure
92. All proteins have quaternary structure but not necessarily any secondary structure
93. Enzymes are amino acids found in proteins that regulate chemical reactions
94. Amino acids and proteins are ionized at typical biological pH such that both the amino group and the carboxyl group gain hydrogen ions to become $-NH_3^+$ and -COOH, respectively
95. A protein with quaternary structure contains four domains
96. Tandem mass spectrometry can be used to determine the specific amino acid sequence of a protein
97. Western blotting of 2D gel electrophoresis would be a high resolution method of demonstrating a change in a particular protein as a result of mutation
98. All enzymes are proteins
99. Enzymes may have one or more polypeptide chains
100. In order to function, some enzymes require biomolecules which are not proteins
101. Vitamins A, D, E and K function as cofactors for allosteric enzymes
102. Enzymes do not have disulfide linkages in their chemical structure
103. Sodium ion (Na +) is a coenzyme for some enzymes
104. In the reaction A $\longrightarrow$ B, the amount of B formed in one minute is the rate of the reaction
105. In a reaction X$\longrightarrow$ Y, the energy of the product (Y) is higher than that of the reactant - this reaction is easily catalyzed by an appropriate enzyme
106. Reaction 1 has an activation energy of 11 kcal/mol, while reaction 2 has an activation energy of 22 kcal/mol. Reaction 1 therefore is much slower than reaction 2.
107. The graph between velocity and [S] for an allosteric enzyme is hyperbolic
108. Km is the rate at which the substrate concentration is half maximum

ENZYMES, VITAMINS AND COENZYMES

109. The graph between pH and enzyme function is bell shaped
110. Citric acid is the competitive inhibitor of succinate dehydrogenase
111. Cytochrome oxidase is not an iron-containing enzyme
112. Inhibitors bind to a site other than the active site
113. Inhibition is reversed by increasing the substrate concentration
114. Km is expressed as Mole/litre
115. A coenzyme that is covalently bound to the enzyme protein is not the prosthetic group
116. Active enzyme concentration increases in the presence of non-competitive inhibitor
117. The enzyme protease fails to work in boiling water, as it is denatured and becomes inactive
118. Pyridoxal is not the active form of pyridoxine
119. The coenzyme form of vit B_6 is pyridine phosphate
120. The coenzyme form of folic acid is THF
121. The coenzyme required for transketolase is TPP

23
Forestry

MULTIPLE-CHOICE QUESTIONS

1. Which of the following is the richest country, in terms of plant wealth, having over 55,000 species

(a) Colombia (b) China
(c) Brazil (d) India

2. Centre of diversity of teak is

(a) USA (b) India
(c) Australia (d) China

3. In terms of species diversity, India's ranking in world is

(a) tenth (b) third
(c) 24th (d) 45th

4. The country with one of the largest assemblages of woody plant species is

(a) India (b) Pakistan
(c) Colombia (d) Canada

5. The maximum number of species in Indian forests, which are of some food value, is of

(a) flowers (b) leaves
(c) stem tubers (d) edible fruits

6. The timber, wolves, rabbits and vegetation in a forest together constitute part of a

(a) population (b) community
(c) species (d) genus

7. Which of the following methods of reforestation has the lowest direct cost but is also the slowest method and the least reliable?

(a) Natural seeding (b) Direct seeding
(c) Planting seedlings (d) Planting cuttings

8. What is a coniferous tree?

(a) A tree that does not loose the needles in winter (evergreen)
(b) A tree that has cones (e.g., pine cones)
(c) A tree that looses its leaves in winter
(d) A tree that does not have cones

9. What is a riparian zone?

(a) An area where logging occurs
(b) A type of road
(c) An area that is influenced by water (i.e., an area along a river, stream or lake)
(d) An old growth forest

10. What is Silviculture?

(a) It is art and science of harvesting forests
(b) It is the science of tree identification
(c) It is the growing of seedling for tree planting
(d) It is the art and science of growing, harvesting, and regenerating forests

11. What does biodiversity mean?

(a) It is the study of biology
(b) It refers to the biology of plant and animals
(c) It refers to the plants, animals and other living organisms
(d) It is the study of animals in the forest

12. What does the term "old growth forest" refer to?

(a) It refers to forests that have not been logged
(b) It refers to forests, which exhibit characteristics of being old (e.g., having numerous standing, dead trees within the forest)
(c) It refers to forests over 100 years old
(d) It refers to forests that have not been burned

13. What is meant by the term "natural regeneration after logging"?

(a) This refers to how natural an area looks after it has been logged
(b) This refers to growing seedling in a tree nursery from the seed found in the area harvested
(c) This refers to reforesting an area by planting new trees after logging
(d) This refers to a method that allows a new forest to grow back naturally after harvesting from the seed of the previous forest and the remaining forest, without having a plant

14. What is an ecosystem?

(a) A forest that is made up of the same species of trees
(b) A system of classifying the plants and animals
(c) A group of animals, all living in the same general area
(d) A complex system of plants, animals, fungi, and microorganisms together with their environment (soil, water, air and nutrients) that function together in some manner

15. How do you define Sustainable Forest Management?

(a) The harvesting of forest land in a manner, which ensures that those forests will grow back so that future harvesting can be sustained
(b) The development of forests to meet current needs without jeopardizing the forests' future productivity, ecological diversity, or capacity for regeneration
(c) Managing a forest in a way that accounts for all the values found within that forest
(d) Ensuring that all forests that are harvested are reforested promptly

16. What are the main components of a Silviculture system?

(a) Harvesting and planting
(b) Harvesting, site preparation, regeneration and planting
(c) Harvesting, site preparation, and thinning
(d) Harvesting, site preparation, regeneration and stand lending

17. What is meant by AAC?

(a) Actual Allowable Cut
(b) Annual Aspen Cut
(c) Annual Allowable Cut
(d) Annual Allowable Conifers

18. What is a shade tolerant tree species?

(a) A species that cannot grow in the shade
(b) A species that requires open, sunny conditions for optimal growth
(c) Tree species that can only grow in the shade
(d) Tree species that have evolved to grow well in shade

19. When a plantation has been declared "free-to-grow", what does this indicate?

(a) Planted trees are free from tree-to-tree and tree-to-other species competition threatening their survival
(b) There is no longer any money required for Silviculture treatments to ensure that trees survive to maturity
(c) The trees in the plantation have become established and are not likely to die
(d) Planted trees have become large enough that they are now free from the threat of insects and disease
(e) All of the above

20. Why do foresters sometimes prescribe "spacing"?

(a) If the forest is considered crowded, which can result in slow tree growth or very small trees
(b) In order to increase the amount of nutrients available to residual trees, thereby increasing either the rate of growth or the size
(c) To remove less vigorous trees that would otherwise die off on their own
(d) All of the above

21. "Pioneer tree species" are generally

(a) shade tolerant
(b) shade intolerant
(c) sun tolerant
(d) neither

22. What does "serotinous cones" mean?

(a) These are cones that produce seed only once every five years
(b) These are the male cones on a tree
(c) These are cones that require direct sunlight to open and release their seed
(d) These are cones that open to release seed only when stimulated by the heat of a fire or intense heat from the sun

23. What are the major harvesting/regeneration systems available for foresters to prescribe?

(a) Clear cutting systems and selective logging systems
(b) Clear cutting systems and shelter wood systems
(c) Clear cutting systems, selection systems, seed tree systems and shelter wood systems
(d) Clear cutting systems, variable retention systems, and selective logging

24. Which harvesting/regeneration system is the most appropriate to manage an uneven-aged stand?

(a) Selection (b) Clear cut
(c) Seed tree (d) Shelter wood

25. What is the difference between "spacing" and "commercial thinning"?

(a) Trees are generally bigger in commercial thinning
(b) Spacing is carried out on over crowded forests, while commercial thinning is only carried out on mature well-spaced forests
(c) Spacing involves removing less vigorous trees at a given interval, while thinning also removes less vigorous trees but at no set interval
(d) With commercial thinning the thinned (harvested) trees are older/bigger and are utilized in a manufacturing facility

26. What is a "Duff"?

(a) The layer of loosely compacted, decaying debris underlying the little layer on the forest floor
(b) A type of planting shovel
(c) A common herb found in pine forests
(d) None of the above

27. All the plants, animals and protists living in a forest make-up a

(a) population (b) community
(c) species (d) phylum

28. Gene bank is best maintained as

(a) DNA bank (b) seed bank
(c) field bank (d) shoot-tip bank

29. Recalcitrant seeds are produced by

(a) mango and rubber
(b) cocoa and coconut
(c) coffee and oil palm
(d) all of these

30. Adventive embryos occur naturally in

(a) mango and citrus
(b) guava and citrus
(c) mango and apricot
(d) citrus and apple

31. Diocious condition occurs in

(a) pistachio and hemp
(b) papaya and hemp
(c) date palm and pistachio
(d) all of the above

32. In the gametophytic system, self-incompatibility is usually the consequence of

(a) pollen-stigma interaction
(b) pollen tube-ovule interaction
(c) pollen tube-style interaction
(d) both a and b above

33. The phenomenon of crossing over occurs during

(a) leptotene (b) zygotene
(c) pachytene (d) diplotene

34. Mather divided phenotypic variance into

(a) additive, dominance and epistatic
(b) additive, epistatic and environmental
(c) additive, dominance, epistatic and environmental
(d) additive, dominance and environmental

35. From the replicated data, which of the following can be calculated?

(a) Phenotypic variance
(b) Genotypic variance
(c) Environmental variance
(d) All of the above

36. The wood of which one of the following trees is used for making musical instruments

(a) *Artocarpus integrifolia*
(b) *Acacia catechu*
(c) *Dalbergia latifolia*
(d) *Quercus floribundas*

37. Which of the following is a medicinal plant of India

(a) *Ephedra* species
(b) *Calamus viminalis*
(c) *Anthocephalus chinensis*
(d) *Xylia xylocarpa*

38. *Ammit majus* is used for

(a) synthesis of steroidal drugs
(b) colic pain
(c) heart treatment
(d) treatment of leukoderma

39. *Casuarina junghuniana,* an important exotic tree in India, has been introduced in India from

(a) Indonesia (b) Malaysia
(c) Australia (d) China

40. The most common types of orchards used worldwide are

(a) clonal seed orchards
(b) seedling-seed orchards
(c) extensive seedling seed orchards
(d) all of the above

41. Ramet is

(a) member of inbred lines
(b) member of self-pollinated crops
(c) member of grafted plants
(d) member of a clone

42. When we alternate the two selected clones in each row and column of the orchard, the design is known as

(a) completely random block
(b) chess- board
(c) fixed block
(d) balanced incomplete block

43. The spacing of trees in the seed orchard should be

(a) 3 meters (b) 5 meters
(c) 10 meters (d) 15 meters

44. The first step in genetic improvement of a plant species is

(a) domestication
(b) germplasm collection
(c) selection
(d) hybridization

45. In most of the breeding programmes, the main aim is to develop a variety with

(a) high yielding ability
(b) disease resistance
(c) change in maturity date
(d) improved quality

46. Which is a prerequisite for crop improvement?

(a) Genetic variation
(b) Sex reproduction
(c) Easy pollination control
(d) Cytoplasmic male sterility

47. The first Director General and Vice-President of ICAR was

(a) Dr. M.S. Swaminathan
(b) Dr. B.P. Pal
(c) Dr. M.S. Randhawa
(d) Diwan Bahadur Sir Vijay Raghavacharya

48. National Bureau of Plant Genetic Resources was established in

(a) 1966 (b) 1976
(c) 1979 (d) 1972

49. Indian Grassland and Fodder Research Institute was established in

(a) 1972 (b) 1962
(c) 1970 (d) 1972

50. Breeder seed has genetic purity of

(a) 98% (b) 99%
(c) 100% (d) 95%

51. Seed viability is tested by

(a) 2,3,5-triphenyl tetrazolium chloride
(b) 2,3,5-triphenyl tetrazolium bromide
(c) GRODEX
(d) all of these

52. Tag of which colour is issued for breeder seed?

(a) Yellow/ golden (b) White
(c) Blue (d) Green

53. Staggered planting means sowing of two strains

(a) at different dates
(b) at different locations
(c) in alternate rows
(d) in different blocks

54. Centre for DNA fingerprinting and Diagnostics (CDFD) is located at

(a) New Delhi (b) Hyderabad
(c) Bangalore (d) Calcutta

55. The concept of "centers of origin of crop plants" was proposed by

(a) N.I. Vavilov (b) C. Linnaeus
(c) J.R. Harlan (d) J.B. Hutchinson

56. In India, exotic collections of germplasm carry the prefix

(a) EC (b) IC
(c) IW (d) EG

57. The introduction of rubber trees in India was arranged by

(a) East India Company
(b) Forest Research Institute
(c) Botanical survey of India
(d) Kew Botanic Gardens

58. Forest Research Institute, Dehradun, has a plant introduction organization that looks after which of the following aspect of forest tree germplasm?

(a) Introduction
(b) Collection and maintenance
(c) Evaluation and maintenance
(d) All of these

59. Exploration would be the most successful if it is targeted at

(a) farmer's field

(b) a primary center of origin

(c) a microcenter

(d) a secondary center of origin

60. Kanyakumari represents

(a) arid zone (b) subtropical zone

(c) tropical zone (d) temperate zone

61. The Royal Botanic Garden is located at

(a) Kew (England) (b) Ontario (Canada)

(c) Senegal (Africa) (d) Florida (USA)

62. India's first National Forest Policy was formulated in

(a) 1904 (b) 1950

(c) 1952 (d) 1976

63. The National Commission on Agriculture was constituted in

(a) 1950 (b) 1952

(c) 1970 (d) 1976

64. Tassar and silk worm/cocoons are reared on the leaves of

(a) Arjun (b) *Sesbania*

(c) *Mahua* (d) *Saijna*

65. Rotation through a species, which retains satisfactory vigor of growth and reproduction on a given site, is known as

(a) physical rotation

(b) technical rotation

(c) silvicultural rotation

(d) financial rotation

66. The rotation period of Deodar Working Circle-Chakrata Forest Division is

(a) 20 years (b) 100 years

(c) 150 years (d) 160 years

67. A perennial plant with a woody stem, usually not more than six meters in height and having branches from the base is known as

(a) herb (b) bush

(c) shrub (d) tree

68. The shape of a pine or deodar tree is

(a) conical (b) cylindrical

(c) flat-topped (d) normal

69. The deciduous trees are

(a) *Pinus* and *Dalbergia*

(b) *Bombax* and *Mangifera*

(c) *Abies* and *Mallotus*

(d) *Acacia* and *Terminalia*

70. Outgrowths on the lower part of the stem, generally vertically above the lateral roots, thus connecting the base of the stem in the roots are known as

(a) epicornic branches (b) buttresses

(c) forking (d) fluting

71. Roots produced from the lower bole of a tree are known as

(a) lateral roots (b) prop roots

(c) stilt roots (d) pneumatophores

72. The flowering time of *Dalbergia sissoo* is

(a) June to September (b) February to April

(c) May to June (d) March to Mid-May

73. Time period between pollination and seed ripening of *Pinus roxburghii* is

(a) 6-7 months (b) 24-26 months

(c) 2-3 months (d) 15-17 months

74. Canopy density of 0.4 - 0.6 of a forest is known as

(a) thin (b) dense

(c) open (d) closed

75. Canopy class comprising of the middle storey of a multi-layered or storeyed forest is known as

(a) Groundcover (b) Underwood
(c) Overwood (d) Undergrowth

76. A species capable of persisting and developing under shade conditions called shade bearer is

(a) *Taxus baccata* (b) *Mallotus*
(c) *Abies pindrow* (d) *Derbergia latifolia*

77. Frost, which occurs as a result of cold air brought in from elsewhere, is known as

(a) advective frost (b) pool frost
(c) radiation frost (d) none of the above

78. Which of the following is frost hardy?

(a) *Zizyphus jujuba* (b) *Tectonia grandis*
(c) *Cedrus deodara* (d) *Acacia arabica*

79. Which of the following is a tropical forest?

(a) dry evergreen forest
(b) pine forest
(c) dry deciduous forest
(d) sub-alpine forest

80. Which of the following species shows seed dispersal by water?

(a) Teak (b) *Populus*
(c) *Salix* (d) *Bombax*

81. Which of the following species shows seed dispersal by birds and animals?

(a) Walnut (b) Mulberry
(c) *Acacia* (d) *Dalbergia*

82. The maximum number of seeds per kg out of the following species is reported in

(a) *Cedrus deodara* (b) *Tectonia grandis*
(c) *Eucalyptus* (d) *Albizzia lebbek*

83. The 'Taungya' system, as a mode of replanting vast teak areas, was evolved in 1850's in

(a) Brazil (b) California
(c) Burma (d) India

84. Root nodules are not formed in

(a) *Albizzia* (b) *Dalbergia*
(c) *Laucaena* (d) *Tectona*

85. Which of the following is not a major insect pest of Indian forests?

(a) Neem shoot borer (b) Teak defoliator
(c) Deodar defoliator (d) Toon shoot borer

86. The form of plant succession, which is initiated under extremely dry conditions, is known as

(a) secondary succession
(b) hydrarch succession
(c) xerarch succession
(d) primary succession

87. Which of the following terms regarding classification of forest types pertains to the natural features of the land on which the forest grows?

(a) Physiography (b) Physiognomy
(c) Floral composition (d) Habitat conditions

88. Northern Tropical wet evergreen forest is found in

(a) Karnataka (b) Punjab
(c) Orissa (d) Uttar Pradesh

89. Which of the following countries has the maximum percentage of land areas under forests?

(a) Russia (b) Canada
(c) India (d) Japan

90. The chemical, TTZ, used for testing seed viability stains living tissues

(a) yellow (b) blue
(c) red (d) brown

91. The seeds of which species looses viability within a month?

(a) *Morus indica* (b) *Acacia catechu*
(c) *Albizzia chinensis* (d) *Tectona grandis*

92. Which of the following seeds have a very poor germination capacity?

(a) *Dalbergia sissoo* (b) *Albizzia lebbek*
(c) *Pinus* (d) *Prunus*

93. Which of the following is not a disease of polythene bag plants?

(a) Collar rot (b) Root-rots
(c) Foliage diseases (d) Nematode diseases

94. The percentage of forest area to geographical area is maximum in

(a) Mizoram
(b) Andaman and Nicobar Islands
(c) Manipur
(d) Tripura

95. Forest lands owned by the government but not constituted into Reserved, Protected or Village Forests are known as

(a) valuable forests (b) inaccessible forests
(c) un-classed forests (d) minor forests

96. The Head of the State Forest Department is designated as

(a) Divisional Forest Officer
(b) Chief conservator of forests
(c) Forest Ranger
(d) Section Officer

97. A felling area, usually one of an annual series unless otherwise stated, preferably numbered with Roman numerals I, II, III, etc. is known as

(a) felling series
(b) working circles
(c) coupe
(d) age-class distribution

98. Which is not a type of rotation recognized in forestry

(a) physical rotation
(b) silvicultural rotation
(c) tree rotation
(d) technical rotation

99. The total increment of a crop, up to a given age divided by that age is known as

(a) mean annual increment
(b) periodic annual increment
(c) current annual increment
(d) final mean annual increment

100. All material from thinning or operations preceding the main felling in a regular forest, or its cash equivalent is known as

(a) final yield
(b) intermediate yield
(c) normal yield
(d) sustained yield

101. In relation to crop composition, which of the following statements is wrong?

(a) 75% and over teak may be classified as pure teak
(b) 50-75% teak may be classified as semi-pure teak
(c) 25-50% teak may be classified as mixed teak
(d) less than 25% may be classified as miscellaneous with some teak

102. The sum (by numbers or volume) of all the trees growing in the forest, or a specified part of it is known as

(a) normal growing stock
(b) growing stock
(c) sample plot measurement
(d) clear felling system

103. *Taungya* is

(a) an Burmese word which means cultivation in the hill
(b) a Burmese word which means cultivation in the plains
(c) a Chinese word which means cultivation in the hill
(d) an Indian word which means cultivation in the hill

104. Which one of the following is correct?

(a) *Albizzia* spp. grow very slowly
(b) *Albizzia* spp. grow very fast
(c) The seeds of *Albizzia* are spread by water
(d) The seeds of *Albizzia* are spread by insects

105. Which one of the following is correct?

(a) *Tectona grandis* does not coppice
(b) *Morus alba* can coppice strongly
(c) *Morus alba* can coppice poorly
(d) None of the above

106. Which one of the following is correct?

(a) Pigs do not damage sal species
(b) Pigs do not damage teak species
(c) Pigs damage sal species but not teak species
(d) Pigs damage both sal and teak species

107. Which one of the following is correct?

(a) The forests cover more than 25% of the geographical area of India
(b) The forests cover less than 25% of the geographical area of India
(c) The forests cover more than 27% of the geographical area of India
(d) The forests cover more than 29% of the geographical area of India

108. Which one of the following is correct?

(a) Porcupines in forests destroy seedlings of bamboo
(b) Giraffes feed on *Ficus* spp. in forests
(c) Porcupines in forests do not destroy seedlings of bamboo
(d) Elephants do not feed on *Ficus* spp. in forests

109. Which one of the following is correct?

(a) *Dioscorea* is not a climber
(b) *Ipomaea* is also not a climber
(c) *Lantana camara* is a climber
(d) Both *Dioscorea* and *Ipomaea* are climbers

110. Which one of the following is correct?

(a) *Santalum album* is an epiphyte
(b) *Ficus bengalensis* is not an epiphyte
(c) Epiphyte is plant which is nourished by another plant
(d) *Ficus bengalensis* is an epiphyte

111. The commonly used weedicide in the forests is

(a) GA_3 (b) IAA
(c) 2, 4-D (d) Abscicic acid

112. Which one of the following is correct?

(a) *Taxus baccata* grows in tropical forest
(b) *Quercus* grows in tropical wet evergreen forest
(c) *Shorea robusta* is a tree of subtropical forest
(d) *Dalbergia sissoo* grows in tropical moist deciduous forest

113. Which one of the following is correct?

(a) In Deodar, male and female flowers come together
(b) Trees have mostly unisexual flowers
(c) Deodar flowers from June to October
(d) Taxus has monoecious flowers

114. Which one of the following is correct?

(a) Conifers are pollinated by wind (Anemophily)
(b) Teak shows pollination by birds (Zoophily)
(c) *Bombax* is pollinated by insects (Entomophily)
(d) None of the above

115. Which one of the following is wrong?

(a) Mycorrhiza is found in *Eucalyptus*
(b) Mycorrhiza is believed to fix nitrogen from raw humus
(c) Mycorrhiza is a structure produced from the combination of the modified rootlet with fungal tissue
(d) In endotrophic mycorrhiza fungi usually belong to *Ascomycetes*

116. Which one of the following is correct?

(a) *Ficus bengalensis* has stilt roots
(b) Stilt roots are not adventitious roots
(c) Prop-roots are produced by branches which reach the ground and get fixed in the soil
(d) None of the above

117. Which one of the following is wrong?

(a) *Acacia catechu* is a deciduous tree
(b) In an evergreen tree the old leaves never fall
(c) *Mangifera indica* is an evergreen tree
(d) None of the above

118. Which one of the following is correct?

(a) The crown is conical in shape in chir and deodar
(b) The crown is the upper branchy part of a tree below the bole
(c) The crown has no fixed shape in trees
(d) None of the above

119. Which one of the following is correct?

(a) Silviculture has no relation with economics
(b) Shrub is an annual plant with a woody stem
(c) The maximum height of teak is more than that of a deodar tree
(d) Silviculture is the art and science of cultivating forest crops

120. Which of the following is a new development in forestry?

(a) Keeping communities away from forests
(b) Scientific forestry
(c) Conservation of forests
(d) Collecting timber

121. Who among the following was the first Inspector General of Forestry in India?

(a) Nagurunderi (b) John Dawson
(c) Dietrich Brandis (d) None of the above

122. According to the Forest Act, 1878, which of the following were called the best forests?

(a) Village forest (b) Protected forest
(c) Reserved forest (d) None of the above

123. Which of the following is not a local name of shifting cultivation?

(a) Kumri (b) Podu
(c) Rai (d) Dhya

124. Who among the following were a community of skilled wood cutters and shifting cultivators?

(a) Gonds (b) Kalangs
(c) Halbas (d) Dhuruvas

125. Java is famous for

(a) huge population (b) rice production
(c) mining industries (d) flood and famines

126. Forests of which trees were preferred by the forest department?

(a) Forests having soft wood
(b) Forests with trees suitable for building homes
(c) Forests with trees suitable for building railways and ships
(d) Forests with trees which provided fuel, fodder and leaves

127. Five hundred plant species can be found in one forest patch in

(a) Chhattisgarh
(b) Eastern Ghats
(c) South Brazilian plains
(d) Amazon

128. Why did colonists need durable timber?

(a) For furniture
(b) To build ships for the Royal Navy
(c) To construct bridges
(d) To build homes

129. Which of the following was not a feature of "scientific forestry"?

(a) Natural forests were left untouched
(b) Natural forests were cleared to make way
(c) Tribals were encouraged to settle in forest villages
(d) Lands used for cultivation of food crops were converted into timber plantations

130. Which of the following is not a feature of shifting cultivation?

(a) Single crop is grown in these plots
(b) Plots cleared are cultivated for a few years and then left fallow
(c) Seeds are sown in the ashes
(d) Parts of the forest are cut and burnt in rotation

131. Which of the following species of trees were suited for building ships and railways?

(a) Rosewood and Sal
(b) Sal and Semur
(c) Teak and Mahogany
(d) Teak and Sal

132. Which among the following is the main reason for survival of some forests in India?

(a) Environmentalists
(b) Conservationists
(c) Villages protected them as sacred grooves
(d) Scientific forestry

133. Deforestation refers to

(a) Planting of trees
(b) Cultivation of crops
(c) Disappearance of forests
(d) Depletion of forests

134. Logging is effected by

(a) Lean of trees (b) Wind fallen trees
(c) Defect (d) All of the above

135. Which of the following types of vegetation has commercially important trees like ebony, mahogany, rosewood and rubber?

(a) Tropical rainforests
(b) Montane forests
(c) Tropical thorn forests
(d) Tropical deciduous forests

136. Which one of the following types of vegetation does rubber belong to?

(a) Himalayan (b) Tropical evergreen
(c) Tundra (d) None of the above

137. Which of the following trees is used for treating blood pressure?

(a) Sarpaganda (b) Kachnaar
(c) Neem (d) Jamun

138. In which of the following states of India evergreen forests are found?

(a) Odisha (b) Rajasthan
(c) Punjab (d) Assam

139. Which medicinal plant has high antibiotic and antibacterial properties?

(a) Kachnaar (b) Babool
(c) Sarpagandha (d) Neem

140. A very large ecosystem on land having distinct type of vegetation and wildlife is called

(a) biodiversity (b) biome
(c) ecology (d) biosphere reserve

141. Which of the following trees is found in tropical rainforests?

(a) Sal (b) Mahogany
(c) Teak (d) Peepal

142. Which part of Himalayas is covered with dense forests?

(a) Western (b) Northern
(c) Eastern (d) Southern

143. Edaphic factor is due to

(a) herbivores (b) soil
(c) man (d) temperature

144. Environment planning organisation is

(a) CPHERI (b) CSIR
(c) NEERI (d) ICAR

145. Competition is more severe between

(a) closely related species growing in the same habitat
(b) distantly related species growing in different habitat
(c) differently related species growing in different habitat
(d) closely related species growing in the same niche

146. Water holding capacity is highest in

(a) mesophytes (b) halophytes
(c) xerophytes (d) lithophytes

147. Waterlogging occurs

(a) in sandy soils (b) in clay soils
(c) in loamy soil (d) on gravels

148. Sunken stomata are found in the leaves of

(a) nerium (b) hydrilla
(c) peepal (d) guava

149. Species which are only found in some particular areas isolated by geographical barriers are called

(a) endemic species (b) rare species
(c) extinct species (d) none of the above

150. Extensive planting of a single commercially valuable species is called

(a) mixed farming
(b) enrichment plantation
(c) jhumming
(d) intensive subsistence farming

151. Chir Pine plantations in the Himalayas have replaced the

(a) Himalayan oak (b) teak
(c) babul (d) eucalyptus

152. Reserved and protected forests are also referred to as

(a) mangrove forest
(b) open forest
(c) unclassed forest
(d) permanent forest estate

153. Sacred groves are

(a) places for grazing animals
(b) forests earmarked for commercial felling of trees
(c) parts of large forests that have been left untouched by the people
(d) forests used for planting trees with medicinal properties

MARK TRUE OR FALSE (T/F)

1. Shrub is an annual plant with a woody stem
2. Tree is a large woody perennial plant
3. The maximum height of teak is more than that of a Deodar tree
4. Silviculture is the art and science of cultivating forest crops
5. Silviculture has no relation with economics
6. Exotic means not native to the area
7. Indigenous means it has been introduced to a region
8. Conifer is an angiosperm
9. Maximum age of teak is about 100 years
10. The crown is conical in shape in Chir and Deodar
11. The lower side of leaf in trees is often darker than the upper side
12. The crown is the upper branchy part of a tree below the bole
13. A monocotyledonous tree producing timber is usually known as 'hard wood'
14. In an evergreen tree the old leaves never fall
15. *Acacia catechu* is a deciduous tree
16. *Mangifera indica* is an evergreen tree
17. Buttresses are formed in the basal portion of the stem

18. Fluting is irregular involutions and swellings on the bole just below the basal swelling
19. In bamboos, the roots are produced from the underground stem called rhizome
20. The roots in bamboos are adventitious
21. *Ficus bengalensis* has stilt roots
22. Prop-roots are produced by branches, which reach the ground and get fixed in the soil
23. Stilt roots are not adventitious roots
24. Pneumatophore is a spike-like projection of the roots of swamp tree
25. *Rhizophora* has pneumatophores
26. Mycorrhiza is a structure produced from the combination of the modified rootlet with fungal tissue
27. In ectotrophic mycorrhiza, fungi usually belong to *Basidiomycetes*
28. In endotrophic mycorrhiza, fungi usually belong to *Ascomycetes*
29. Mycorrhiza is found in *Eucalyptus*
30. Mycorrhiza is not found in *Populus*
31. Mycorrhiza is believed to fix nitrogen from raw humus
32. Lignotubers are over ground swellings found on most species of *Eucalyptus*
33. Root nodules contain *Rhizobium* bacteria
34. *Rhizobium* is present in Malvaceae family
35. *Rhizobium* are absent in *Crotolaria*
36. Deodar flowers from June to October
37. In Deodar, male and female flowers come together
38. Trees have mostly unisexual flowers
39. *Taxus* has monoecious flowers
40. *Salix* has dioecious flowers
41. Conifers are pollinated by wind (Anemophily)
42. Teak shows pollination by birds (Zoophily)
43. *Bombax* is pollinated by insects (Entomophily)
44. Ecology is the study of plants and/ or animals in relation to their environment
45. Coppice forests are those which are regenerated by some vegetative method
46. High forests are regenerated from seed
47. All trees which form the upper most leaf canopy and have their leading shoots free are called dominated trees
48. Stomata help in perspiration and photosynthesis
49. Short days may cause dormancy in *Populus*
50. *Taxus baccata* grows in moist temperate forest
51. *Quercus* grows in tropical wet evergreen forest
52. *Shorea robusta* is a tree of subtropical forest
53. *Dalbergia sissoo* grows in tropical moist deciduous forest
54. Stand density index is the number of trees corresponding to a given standard diam
55. 2,4-D is the commonly used weedicide in the forests
56. Afforestation of railways strips is often done with mango trees
57. Under-planting is defined as sowing or planting under an existing stand
58. *Ricinus communis* are introduced in sal *taungyas* as frost protection crops
59. Some hill species like walnut are planted in winter after snowfall
60. *Tamarix* can be used for making baskets
61. *Terminalia* seeds show fast germination
62. *Albizzia* has soft coated seeds
63. Shifting cultivation is a constructive method of cultivation
64. Teak is an Indian exotic for Uttar Pradesh
65. *Eucalyptus* is a foreign exotic
66. *Cuscuta reflexa* is a total parasite common in forest areas
67. Partial parasites draw a part of their nourishment from host
68. *Viscum* occurring on oaks and walnuts is a total parasite

69. Sandal tree is a stem parasite
70. Epiphyte is plant growing on, but not nourished by another plant
71. *Santalum album* is an epiphyte
72. *Ficus bengalensis* is not an epiphyte
73. Large woody climbers in tropical areas are also called *liane* or *liana*
74. *Dioscorea* is a climber
75. *Ipomaea* is also a climber
76. *Lantana camara* is an obnoxious weed
77. Sal borer or *Hoplocerambyx* is a useful insect found in forests
78. Pigs do not damage sal and teak species
79. Porcupines in forests destroy seedlings of bamboo
80. Elephants feed on *Ficus* spp. in forests
81. The forests cover more than 25% of the geographical area of India
82. Feeding on twigs or shoots, with or without attached leaves, of shrubs, trees or woody climbers by animals is known as browsing
83. The seeds of *Dalbergia sissoo* are spread by birds
84. The seeds of *Albizzia* are spread by wind
85. Physiognomy means the general appearance of a forest community
86. Floristics refers to the species present in a particular forest
87. Physiography refers to the natural features of the forest type
88. *Cassia fistula* requires light for germination
89. In shelterwood system, the mature crop is removed in a series of operations, the last of which is the seedling felling
90. *Morus alba* can coppice strongly
91. *Tectona grandis* does not coppice
92. *Albizzia* spp. grow very fast
93. *Taungya* is a Burmese word, which means cultivation in the hill
94. Pruning of the dead branches is known as green pruning
95. Girdling is cutting through bark and outer living layers of wood in a continuous incision all round the bole of a tree
96. Thinning cycle is the planned interval that elapses between successive thinning in the same area
97. Stand density index is the weight of the trees corresponding to a given standard diameter
98. Crown thinning is not suitable for areas where there is demand for only relatively big-sized timber
99. The trees of the inferior species are often girdled so that they may gradually die
100. The crown has no fixed shape in trees

SECTION-II

ANSWERS

Answers

CHAPER 1: GENERAL

1.1 MULTIPLE-CHOICE QUESTIONS

1. c					
2. b	23. a	44. d	65. d	86. a	107. b
3. e	24. b	45. a	66. c	87. a	108. d
4. c	25. c	46. e	67. d	88. d	109. a
5. e	26. c	47. b	68. c	89. b	110. d
6. e	27. a	48. a	69. a	90. a	111. a
7. e	28. d	49. d	70. a	91. c	112. d
8. c	29. c	50. d	71. d	92. c	113. b
9. b	30. a	51. c	72. b	93. a	114. d
10. b	31. d	52. e	73. e	94. c	115. a
11. c	32. b	53. a	74. b	95. a	116. a
12. e	33. c	54. a	75. d	96. c	117. d
13. b	34. c	55. c	76. a	97. b	118. b
14. a	35. a	56. a	77. a	98. a	119. d
15. e	36. a	57. d	78. c	99. b	120. c
16. a	37. a	58. e	79. c	100. b	121. d
17. a	38. d	59. d	80. c	101. c	122. b
18. a	39. c	60. a	81. a	102. a	123. d
19. b	40. c	61. c	82. b	103. a	124. a
20. b	41. d	62. a	83. a	104. c	125. d
21. a	42. a	63. a	84. d	105. b	126. a
22. a	43. b	64. e	85. c	106. a	127. d

128. a
129. c
130. c
131. b
132. d
133. a
134. d
135. d
136. a
137. d
138. d
139. b
140. c
141. b
142. a
143. d
144. a
145. c
146. d
147. c
148. d
149. a
150. b
151. d
152. c
153. d
154. d
155. c
156. a
157. b
158. c
159. a
160. c
161. a
162. d
163. b
164. d
165. a
166. c
167. c
168. a
169. e
170. b
171. e
172. a
173. a
174. d
175. d
176. c
177. c
178. a
179. a
180. d
181. a
182. d
183. b
184. e
185. c
186. b
187. c
188. a
189. b
190. d
191. c
192. b
193. c
194. b
195. a
196. d
197. e
198. d
199. c
200. a
201. a
202. e
203. c
204. d
205. e
206. c
207. c
208. d
209. d
210. d
211. d
212. d
213. c
214. b
215. a
216. b
217. a
218. d
219. a
220. b
221. b
222. b
223. d
224. b
225. a
226. a
227. d
228. d
229. a
230. c
231. d
232. a
233. c
234. b
235. d
236. a
237. a
238. c
239. b
240. c
241. b
242. b
243. d
244. b
245. c
246. b
247. d
248. c
249. b
250. b
251. c
252. b
253. a
254. a
255. d
256. b
257. b
258. c
259. c
260. a
261. a
262. d
263. c
264. c
265. a
266. c
267. a
268. b
269. a
270. a
271. c
272. c
273. c
274. b
275. a
276. a
277. c

1.2 MARK TRUE OR FALSE

1. F
2. F
3. T
4. F
5. T
6. T
7. F
8. F
9. F
10. F
11. F
12. T
13. F
14. T
15. F
16. F
17. F
18. F
19. F
20. F
21. F
22. F
23. T
24. F
25. T
26. F
27. F
28. F
29. T
30. T
31. F
32. T
33. T
34. F
35. F
36. T
37. F
38. F
39. T
40. T
41. T
42. F
43. F
44. F
45. T
46. T
47. T
48. F
49. T
50. T
51. F
52. F
53. T
54. T
55. F
56. T
57. F
58. T
59. F
60. T
61. T
62. T
63. F
64. F
65. T

CHAPTER 2: NATURAL SELECTION, GENETICS AND EVOLUTION

2.1 MULTIPLE-CHOICE QUESTIONS

1. a	21. c	41. a	61. a	81. a	101. b
2. c	22. e	42. c	62. d	82. c	102. b
3. c	23. c	43. a	63. c	83. a	103. c
4. d	24. d	44. e	64. c	84. c	104. b
5. d	25. c	45. d	65. c	85. b	105. a
6. d	26. b	46. c	66. c	86. b	106. c
7. b	27. b	47. a	67. b	87. b	107. a
8. c	28. b	48. b	68. a	88. c	108. d
9. d	29. a	49. a	69. a	89. d	109. a
10. c	30. b	50. b	70. c	90. b	110. b
11. d	31. c	51. b	71. b	91. b	111. a
12. d	32. b	52. a	72. e	92. c	112. d
13. b	33. d	53. b	73. a	93. d	113. b
14. a	34. d	54. a	74. c	94. a	114. d
15. b	35. d	55. a	75. b	95. a	115. d
16. a	36. a	56. b	76. d	96. d	116. a
17. c	37. b	57. c	77. b	97. d	117. c
18. c	38. d	58. c	78. a	98. b	118. d
19. d	39. c	59. a	79. d	99. b	119. a
20. e	40. b	60. b	80. e	100. c	

2.2 MARK TRUE OR FALSE

1. F	13. T	25. T	37. F	49. F	61. T
2. F	14. F	26. T	38. F	50. T	62. T
3. F	15. F	27. T	39. F	51. T	63. F
4. F	16. T	28. F	40. T	52. T	64. F
5. T	17. F	29. T	41. T	53. F	65. F
6. T	18. F	30. T	42. F	54. T	66. T
7. T	19. T	31. F	43. T	55. F	67. T
8. T	20. F	32. F	44. T	56. F	68. F
9. T	21. T	33. T	45. F	57. T	69. T
10. T	22. T	34. T	46. T	58. T	70. F
11. F	23. F	35. F	47. F	59. F	
12. F	24. F	36. F	48. T	60. F	

CHAPTER 3: GENERAL GENETICS

3.1 MULTIPLE-CHOICE QUESTIONS

1. b
2. b
3. d
4. b
5. a
6. d
7. a
8. e
9. b
10. d
11. d
12. c
13. a
14. a
15. b
16. d
17. c
18. b
19. a
20. b
21. b
22. a
23. d
24. c
25. a
26. c
27. b
28. a
29. d
30. d
31. d
32. d
33. b
34. a
35. b
36. d
37. c
38. a
39. d
40. b
41. a
42. b
43. a
44. d
45. a
46. d
47. b
48. d
49. b
50. c
51. a
52. d
53. b
54. d
55. d
56. b
57. c
58. b
59. b
60. c
61. c
62. d
63. b
64. c
65. e
66. a
67. c
68. c
69. d
70. c
71. a
72. d
73. d
74. d
75. b
76. a
77. b
78. d
79. c
80. b
81. c
82. a
83. b
84. a
85. a
86. c
87. a
88. d
89. a
90. d
91. a
92. e
93. e
94. d
95. b
96. b
97. c
98. d
99. c
100. b
101. c
102. b
103. a
104. c
105. d
106. b
107. b
108. b
109. c
110. d
111. c
112. d
113. d
114. b
115. a
116. c
117. c
118. c
119. a
120. d
121. c
122. d
123. a
124. c
125. d
126. d
127. b
128. d
129. c
130. d
131. b
132. c
133. d
134. d
135. b
136. a
137. e
138. d
139. d
140. d
141. e
142. b
143. e
144. e
145. a
146. e
147. d
148. b
149. d
150. b
151. e
152. a
153. e
154. e
155. a
156. b
157. b
158. d
159. a
160. a
161. a
162. b
163. a
164. b
165. c
166. a
167. b
168. c
169. a
170. d
171. a
172. b
173. a
174. d
175. a
176. d
177. a
178. d
179. a
180. b
181. a
182. c
183. d
184. a
185. c
186. b
187. d
188. b
189. b
190. b
191. b
192. a
193. b
194. d
195. d
196. b
197. a
198. d
199. d
200. c
201. b
202. a
203. d
204. d
205. d
206. b
207. b
208. b
209. d
210. d
211. d
212. a
213. b
214. d
215. b
216. d
217. a
218. b
219. d
220. d
221. c
222. d
223. b
224. a
225. d
226. d
227. b
228. d
229. a
230. c
231. b
232. d
233. a
234. a

235. b
236. b
237. b
238. a
239. b
240. d
241. a
242. c
243. b
244. a
245. d
246. d
247. c
248. d
249. d
250. a
251. d
252. d
253. a
254. d
255. d
256. d
257. b
258. d
259. b
260. d
261. c
262. a
263. c
264. b
265. a
266. c
267. d
268. d
269. d
270. d
271. d
272. c
273. c
274. d
275. d
276. c
277. c
278. d
279. b
280. d
281. a
282. b
283. b
284. d
285. d
286. c
287. c
288. d
289. c
290. a
291. b
292. a
293. a
294. c
295. d
296. d
297. e
298. d
299. c
300. d
301. d
302. d
303. c
304. b
305. e
306. c
307. b
308. d
309. b
310. d
311. d
312. d
313. c
314. d
315. c
316. b
317. c
318. b
319. e
320. c
321. b
322. d
323. b
324. e
325. a
326. d
327. d
328. b
329. a
330. d
331. a
332. a
333. e
334. a
335. d
336. d
337. b
338. b
339. a
340. e
341. b
342. b
343. b
344. a
345. a
346. e
347. e
348. a
349. a
350. e
351. a
352. c
353. b
354. c
355. a
356. e
357. a
358. b
359. e
360. e
361. b
362. d
363. a
364. a
365. c
366. a
367. c
368. c
369. c
370. a
371. b
372. a
373. d
374. b
375. c
376. a
377. a
378. a
379. a
380. c

3.2 MARK TRUE OR FALSE

1. F
2. T
3. T
4. T
5. T
6. F
7. T
8. T
9. F
10. F
11. F
12. T
13. T
14. T
15. F
16. F
17. T
18. T
19. T
20. F
21. F
22. F
23. T
24. T
25. F
26. F
27. T
28. F
29. F
30. T
31. T
32. T
33. T
34. T
35. F
36. F
37. F
38. F
39. T
40. T
41. F
42. T
43. F
44. T
45. T
46. T
47. F
48. T
49. F
50. T
51. T
52. T
53. F
54. F
55. T
56. F
57. F
58. T
59. T
60. F
61. F
62. T
63. T
64. F
65. T
66. F
67. T
68. F
69. T
70. T
71. T
72. T
73. T
74. T
75. F
76. F
77. T
78. F
79. T
80. F
81. T
82. T
83. F
84. F
85. T
86. T
87. F
88. F
89. T
90. T

91. T	94. F	97. T	100. T	103. T	105. F
92. F	95. T	98. T	101. T	104. T	106. T
93. F	96. T	99. F	102. F		

CHAPTER 4: MICROSCOPY

4.1 MULTIPLE-CHOICE QUESTIONS

1. c	15. c	29. c	43. a	57. a	71. c
2. a	16. b	30. b	44. a	58. b	72. b
3. c	17. c	31. d	45. c	59. c	73. c
4. a	18. d	32. c	46. a	60. c	74. d
5. a	19. a	33. b	47. b	61. c	75. b
6. d	20. c	34. e	48. b	62. d	76. c
7. b	21. a	35. d	49. c	63. c	77. b
8. a	22. d	36. c	50. d	64. c	78. d
9. a	23. d	37. a	51. b	65. b	79. b
10. d	24. b	38. a	52. d	66. d	80. c
11. c	25. c	39. c	53. c	67. d	81. d
12. a	26. a	40. c	54. c	68. c	82. d
13. a	27. b	41. d	55. c	69. a	83. c
14. a	28. d	42. b	56. a	70. d	

4.2 MARK TRUE OR FALSE

1. F	13. T	25. F	37. T	49. T	61. T
2. F	14. T	26. F	38. T	50. T	62. T
3. F	15. F	27. T	39. T	51. T	63. F
4. F	16. T	28. F	40. F	52. F	64. T
5. T	17. T	29. T	41. F	53. T	65. T
6. T	18. F	30. F	42. T	54. T	66. F
7. F	19. T	31. T	43. T	55. T	67. T
8. T	20. F	32. T	44. F	56. F	68. F
9. T	21. F	33. T	45. T	57. T	69. T
10. F	22. T	34. F	46. T	58. T	70. T
11. F	23. F	35. F	47. F	59. F	71. T
12. F	24. T	36. F	48. T	60. F	

CHAPTER 5: CELL AND CELL STRUCTURE

5.1 MULTIPLE-CHOICE QUESTIONS

1. a	3. b	5. b	7. d	9. d	11. c
2. c	4. a	6. b	8. a	10. b	12. b

13. a
14. c
15. b
16. d
17. a
18. b
19. a
20. a
21. c
22. e
23. c
24. e
25. c
26. c
27. a
28. c
29. b
30. b
31. e
32. a
33. b
34. e
35. b
36. d
37. c
38. b
39. b
40. d
41. a
42. b
43. c
44. a
45. d
46. b
47. c
48. d
49. d
50. c
51. b
52. c
53. c
54. a
55. b
56. e
57. a
58. a
59. b
60. b
61. c
62. b
63. a
64. d
65. a
66. d
67. b
68. d
69. b
70. c
71. c
72. d
73. c
74. a
75. e
76. e
77. b
78. d
79. d
80. b
81. d
82. a
83. e
84. c
85. c
86. e
87. b
88. c
89. c
90. e
91. c
92. b
93. c
94. d
95. b
96. e
97. d
98. a
99. c
100. d
101. e
102. c
103. a
104. e
105. b
106. c
107. b
108. e
109. d
110. d
111. c
112. a
113. d
114. b
115. e
116. a
117. d
118. e
119. b
120. b
121. a
122. c
123. c
124. c
125. d
126. c
127. b
128. c
129. a
130. a
131. c
132. b
133. c
134. d
135. b
136. b
137. d
138. b
139. c
140. a
141. c
142. b
143. b
144. a
145. b
146. c
147. d
148. b
149. c
150. d
151. d
152. b
153. a
154. b
155. a
156. a
157. e
158. e
159. a
160. a
161. b
162. c
163. b
164. b
165. d
166. e
167. b
168. c
169. b
170. b
171. c
172. b
173. d
174. c
175. b
176. a
177. b
178. c
179. a
180. b
181. c
182. b
183. b
184. c
185. b
186. a
187. c
188. a
189. d
190. c
191. a
192. a
193. e
194. a
195. e
196. d
197. c
198. c
199. d
200. d
201. c
202. a
203. d
204. a
205. a
206. b
207. d
208. b
209. d
210. a
211. b
212. a
213. d
214. b
215. b
216. b
217. a
218. a
219. a
220. b
221. a
222. b
223. a
224. d
225. d
226. d
227. d
228. c
229. b
230. d
231. d
232. a
233. a
234. c
235. d
236. d
237. a
238. b
239. c
240. c
241. a
242. b
243. d
244. a
245. a
246. b
247. b
248. a
249. c
250. d
251. b
252. b
253. b
254. a
255. b
256. b
257. d
258. a
259. d
260. d
261. b
262. c
263. c
264. c
265. c
266. b
267. d
268. b
269. b
270. b
271. c
272. d
273. c
274. b
275. c
276. b

277. c	295. b	313. c	331. d	349. a	367. b
278. c	296. b	314. d	332. d	350. c	368. b
279. d	297. a	315. b	333. c	351. b	369. d
280. c	298. c	316. b	334. d	352. a	370. b
281. c	299. c	317. d	335. d	353. a	371. d
282. b	300. c	318. a	336. c	354. c	372. c
283. b	301. c	319. d	337. c	355. c	373. b
284. d	302. c	320. b	338. b	356. b	374. d
285. a	303. c	321. d	339. c	357. c	375. a
286. b	304. d	322. d	340. d	358. d	376. d
287. b	305. d	323. c	341. a	359. b	377. c
288. b	306. d	324. b	342. c	360. a	378. d
289. d	307. d	325. b	343. a	361. d	379. a
290. b	308. c	326. d	344. a	362. c	380. d
291. b	309. c	327. c	345. c	363. d	381. b
292. b	310. a	328. c	346. b	364. c	382. c
293. c	311. b	329. d	347. d	365. b	
294. c	312. b	330. c	348. c	366. b	

5.2 MARK TRUE OR FALSE

1. F	10. F	19. F	28. T	37. F	46. T
2. F	11. F	20. T	29. F	38. T	47. T
3. T	12. F	21. F	30. T	39. T	48. T
4. T	13. T	22. T	31. F	40. F	49. F
5. F	14. T	23. T	32. F	41. T	50. F
6. T	15. F	24. F	33. F	42. T	
7. T	16. F	25. F	34. T	43. T	
8. T	17. T	26. T	35. F	44. F	
9. T	18. T	27. T	36. T	45. F	

CHAPTER 6: CELL DIVISION

6.1 MULTIPLE-CHOICE QUESTIONS

1. a	7. a	13. b	19. b	25. a	31. b
2. c	8. c	14. d	20. d	26. a	32. a
3. b	9. a	15. d	21. c	27. d	33. d
4. b	10. d	16. c	22. b	28. a	34. c
5. e	11. a.	17. d	23. c	29. b	35. a
6. e	12. a	18. c	24. b	30. a	36. b

37. c
38. d
39. a
40. d
41. a
42. b
43. b
44. a
45. c
46. b
47. a
48. c
49. b
50. c
51. b
52. c
53. d
54. d
55. c
56. a
57. c
58. a
59. b
60. c
61. a
62. a
63. c
64. e
65. e
66. a
67. a
68. b
69. c
70. d
71. d
72. d
73. b
74. a
75. d
76. e
77. d
78. a
79. b
80. b
81. e
82. d
83. d
84. b
85. e
86. e
87. a
88. a
89. a
90. d
91. d
92. c
93. c
94. b
95. b
96. a
97. c
98. a
99. d
100. b
101. a
102. a.
103. c
104. c
105. d
106. a
107. d
108. d
109. d
110. b
111. b
112. b
113. d
114. a
115. b
116. d
117. a
118. b
119. d
120. b
121. a
122. a
123. b
124. a
125. e
126. e
127. b
128. b
129. b
130. d
131. d
132. a
133. c
134. c
135. d
136. d
137. c
138. b
139. a
140. d
141. d
142. d
143. d
144. c
145. c
146. a
147. d
148. d
149. c
150. c
151. d
152. d
153. b
154. b
155. c
156. b
157. d
158. c
159. d
160. d
161. b
162. a
163. d
164. a
165. d
166. b
167. d
168. a
169. d
170. a
171. d
172. c
173. a

6.2 MARK TRUE OR FALSE

1. T
2. T
3. F
4. F
5. F
6. T
7. F
8. T
9. F
10. T
11. T
12. F
13. F
14. T
15. T
16. T
17. T
18. F
19. T
20. F
21. F
22. T
23. T
24. F
25. F
26. T
27. F
28. T
29. T
30. T
31. F
32. T
33. T
34. T
35. T
36. T
37. F
38. F
39. F
40. T
41. T
42. F
43. T
44. T
45. F
46. T
47. T
48. F
49. T
50. F
51. F

CHAPTER 7: MENDELISM

7.1 MULTIPLE-CHOICE QUESTIONS

1. b
2. a
3. c
4. d
5. c
6. c
7. a
8. e
9. b
10. e
11. b
12. b
13. a
14. a
15. a
16. c
17. b
18. d
19. a
20. d
21. c
22. e
23. d
24. a

25. c	47. d	69. d	91. c	113. b	135. b
26. a	48. d	70. d	92. d	114. c	136. c
27. d	49. b	71. a	93. b	115. c	137. c
28. d	50. g	72. a	94. b	116. c	138. a
29. b	51. b	73. b	95. d	117. c	139. c
30. b	52. c	74. b	96. d	118. c	140. b
31. d	53. c	75. a	97. c	119. d	141. b
32. d	54. b	76. a	98. b	120. d	142. e
33. b	55. b	77. e	99. b	121. b	143. b
34. a	56. d	78. b	100. e	122. b	144. c
35. c	57. a	79. b	101. e	123. d	145. c
36. b	58. b	80. b	102. b	124. c	146. e
37. d	59. b	81. a	103. e	125. c	147. e
38. c	60. d	82. c	104. c	126. e	148. a
39. b	61. b	83. d	105. a	127. c	149. b
40. d	62. c	84. b	106. b	128. a	150. c
41. d	63. c	85. a	107. e	129. d	151. c
42. a	64. a	86. c	108. a	130. d	152. c
43. d	65. c	87. e	109. b	131. e	153. b
44. b	66. c	88. c	110. b	132. b	154. d
45. d	67. c	89. d	111. b	133. c	155. d
46. a	68. b	90. a	112. b	134. e	156. d

7.2 MARK TRUE OR FALSE

1. T	13. T	25. T	37. T	49. F	61. T
2. F	14. F	26. F	38. T	50. F	62. T
3. T	15. T	27. T	39. F	51. T	63. F
4. F	16. T	28. F	40. T	52. F	64. F
5. T	17. T	29. F	41. F	53. T	65. F
6. T	18. T	30. F	42. F	54. F	66. F
7. T	19. F	31. T	43. T	55. F	67. F
8. T	20. T	32. F	44. F	56. F	68. T
9. T	21. T	33. F	45. T	57. F	
10. F	22. F	34. T	46. F	58. F	
11. F	23. F	35. T	47. F	59. T	
12. T	24. T	36. F	48. T	60. F	

CHAPTER 8: SEX DETERMINATION AND SEX LINKAGE

8.1 MULTIPLE-CHOICE QUESTIONS

1. c	4. a	7. a	10. d	13. b	16. b
2. e	5. b	8. b	11. c	14. e	17. a
3. a	6. a	9. e	12. e	15. d	18. e

19. b	33. b	47. d	61. c	75. d	89. d
20. d	34. c	48. a	62. b	76. b	90. c
21. b	35. b	49. d	63. a	77. d	91. b
22. b	36. c	50. d	64. a	78. c	92. a
23. b	37. b	51. d	65. d	79. c	93. c
24. c	38. c	52. a	66. d	80. d	94. a
25. c	39. c	53. d	67. b	81. d	95. b
26. a	40. c	54. a	68. c	82. a	96. b
27. b	41. a	55. b	69. c	83. b	97. a
28. a	42. d	56. a	70. d	84. c	98. a
29. c	43. d	57. a	71. d	85. d	
30. a	44. d	58. c	72. b	86. a	
31. b	45. d	59. a	73. b	87. b	
32. c	46. a	60. d	74. c	88. d	

8.2 MARK TRUE OR FALSE

1. F	13. F	25. F	37. T	49. F	61. T
2. T	14. T	26. T	38. T	50. F	62. T
3. F	15. F	27. F	39. F	51. T	63. T
4. F	16. T	28. T	40. T	52. F	64. F
5. T	17. T	29. T	41. T	53. T	65. F
6. F	18. F	30. F	42. T	54. T	66. F
7. T	19. T	31. T	43. F	55. T	67. T
8. T	20. F	32. T	44. T	56. F	68. F
9. T	21. T	33. F	45. F	57. F	69. F
10. F	22. T	34. T	46. T	58. T	70. F
11. T	23. T	35. T	47. F	59. T	71. T
12. F	24. F	36. T	48. F	60. F	72. T

CHAPTER 9: EXTRANUCLEAR INHERITANCE

9.1 MULTIPLE-CHOICE QUESTIONS

1. b	11. d	21. c	31. a	41. a	51. a
2. e	12. a	22. d	32. b	42. d	52. b
3. d	13. c	23. d	33. a	43. a	53. c
4. a	14. c	24. a	34. d	44. d	54. c
5. c	15. b	25. b	35. b	45. d	55. b
6. d	16. d	26. c	36. a	46. c	56. c
7. c	17. b	27. a	37. a	47. c	57. c
8. a	18. d	28. b	38. d	48. c	58. a
9. d	19. d	29. d	39. d	49. c	59. c
10. d	20. d	30. d	40. d	50. c	60. b

61. b	64. c	67. a	70. a	73. a	76. d
62. c	65. d	68. c	71. c	74. c	77. d
63. d	66. a	69. a	72. b	75. a	

9.2 MARK TRUE OR FALSE

1. F	10. T	19. F	28. T	36. F	44. T
2. F	11. F	20. T	29. F	37. T	45. T
3. T	12. T	21. T	30. T	38. F	46. F
4. F	13. F	22. F	31. T	39. T	47. T
5. F	14. F	23. T	32. T	40. T	48. T
6. F	15. T	24. F	33. T	41. F	49. T
7. T	16. F	25. T	34. T	42. T	50. F
8. T	17. T	26. T	35. F	43. T	
9. F	18. F	27. T			

CHAPTER 10: QUANTITATIVE GENETICS

10.1 MULTIPLE-CHOICE QUESTIONS

1. e	13. c	25. e	37. d	49. c	61. a
2. c	14. b	26. b	38. d	50. d	62. b
3. a	15. b	27. a	39. a	51. a	63. a
4. d	16. d	28. d	40. c	52. d	64. d
5. c	17. d	29. d	41. b	53. c	65. a
6. d	18. d	30. d	42. d	54. d	66. b
7. d	19. a	31. a	43. d	55. a	67. b
8. d	20. e	32. d	44. b	56. a	68. b
9. c	21. d	33. a	45. b	57. c	
10. b	22. b	34. d	46. d	58. b	
11. a	23. b	35. b	47. c	59. a	
12. c	24. a	36. c	48. d	60. c	

10.2 MARK TRUE OR FALSE

1. F	10. F	19. F	28. F	37. F	46. F
2. F	11. F	20. F	29. F	38. F	47. F
3. T	12. T	21. F	30. T	39. F	48. T
4. F	13. F	22. F	31. F	40. T	49. T
5. F	14. T	23. F	32. T	41. T	50. T
6. T	15. F	24. F	33. F	42. F	
7. F	16. F	25. F	34. T	43. F	
8. T	17. T	26. T	35. F	44. F	
9. F	18. F	27. T	36. F	45. T	

CHAPTER 11: CYTOLOGY AND CYTOGENETICS

11.1 MULTIPLE-CHOICE QUESTIONS

1. c
2. e
3. a
4. e
5. b
6. a
7. d
8. e
9. d
10. c
11. c
12. b
13. c
14. c
15. c
16. c
17. e
18. b
19. e
20. b
21. b
22. c
23. b
24. d
25. d
26. c
27. c
28. c
29. d
30. e
31. b
32. d
33. b
34. d
35. e
36. a
37. c
38. d
39. b
40. c
41. d
42. a
43. d
44. e
45. d
46. d
47. a
48. b
49. c
50. a
51. e
52. c
53. b
54. a
55. c
56. b
57. b
58. a
59. d
60. b
61. d
62. d
63. d
64. a
65. a
66. b
67. a
68. c
69. b
70. b
71. d
72. c
73. d
74. b
75. d
76. d
77. c
78. e
79. d
80. b
81. b
82. c
83. b
84. a
85. c
86. a
87. b
88. b
89. b
90. e
91. a
92. b
93. c
94. c
95. a
96. a
97. b
98. c
99. d
100. d
101. d
102. b
103. e
104. d
105. d
106. c
107. b
108. c
109. b
110. c
111. b
112. d
113. b
114. c
115. a
116. a
117. c
118. d
119. c
120. c
121. b
122. d
123. c
124. a
125. b
126. d
127. d
128. a
129. d
130. a
131. d
132. b
133. d
134. b
135. c
136. a
137. b
138. c
139. b
140. b
141. c
142. a
143. c
144. b
145. a
146. c
147. c
148. a
149. a
150. a
151. a
152. d
153. c
154. b
155. a
156. a
157. c
158. b
159. a
160. d
161. a
162. b
163. b
164. b

11.2 MARK TRUE OR FALSE

1. F
2. T
3. F
4. T
5. F
6. T
7. F
8. T
9. F
10. T
11. F
12. F
13. T
14. T
15. F
16. T
17. F
18. T
19. F
20. T
21. F
22. T
23. T
24. F
25. F
26. T
27. F
28. T
29. F
30. T
31. T
32. F
33. F
34. T
35. F
36. T
37. T
38. T
39. F
40. T
41. T
42. F
43. T
44. F
45. T
46. T
47. T
48. T
49. T
50. T

CHAPTER 12: LINKAGE AND RECOMBINATION

12.1 MULTIPLE-CHOICE QUESTIONS

1. a
2. d
3. b
4. b
5. b
6. a
7. d
8. d
9. b
10. b
11. d
12. b
13. b
14. d
15. c
16. b
17. d
18. b
19. e
20. a
21. a
22. a
23. a
24. b
25. d
26. b
27. a
28. b
29. a
30. c
31. a
32. a
33. c
34. b
35. d
36. a
37. d
38. b
39. c
40. c
41. b
42. d
43. c
44. c
45. c
46. c
47. b
48. a
49. c
50. c
51. c
52. c
53. d
54. e
55. a
56. e
57. e
58. a
59. c
60. b
61. d
62. d
63. b
64. b
65. c
66. d
67. c
68. d
69. d
70. d
71. b
72. b
73. c
74. a
75. c
76. c
77. c
78. b
79. b
80. d
81. b
82. b
83. d
84. c
85. c
86. b
87. b
88. c
89. c
90. a
91. c
92. d
93. b
94. a
95. d
96. a
97. a
98. c
99. b
100. a
101. d

12.2 MARK TRUE OR FALSE

1. T
2. F
3. T
4. F
5. F
6. T
7. T
8. T
9. F
10. T
11. T
12. F
13. T
14. T
15. F
16. F
17. T
18. F
19. T
20. F
21. T
22. F
23. T
24. F
25. F
26. F
27. F
28. T
29. T
30. T
31. F
32. F
33. T
34. T
35. F
36. F
37. T
38. F
39. T
40. T
41. F
42. F
43. T
44. F
45. F
46. F
47. T
48. F
49. T
50. T

CHAPTER 13: CHROMOSOMAL ABERRATIONS

13.1 MULTIPLE-CHOICE QUESTIONS

1. d
2. b
3. a
4. c
5. c
6. a
7. b
8. a
9. d
10. d
11. a
12. d
13. b
14. b
15. c
16. c
17. b
18. d
19. b
20. b
21. c
22. d
23. b
24. a
25. c
26. d
27. d
28. b
29. b
30. a
31. a
32. c
33. d
34. d
35. b
36. a
37. d
38. b
39. a
40. d
41. d
42. b

43. b
44. d
45. b
46. c
47. d
48. d
49. d
50. d
51. d
52. b
53. d
54. a
55. b
56. d
57. d
58. a
59. d
60. d
61. e
62. e
63. d
64. c
65. c
66. d
67. d
68. b
69. c
70. b
71. e
72. d
73. b
74. e
75. e
76. d
77. c
78. b
79. b
80. a
81. d
82. a
83. d
84. d
85. b
86. d
87. d
88. b
89. a
90. a
91. a
92. a
93. a
94. a
95. e
96. a
97. d
98. e
99. e
100. e
101. c
102. e
103. e
104. e
105. c
106. e
107. a
108. c
109. c
110. a
111. e
112. d
113. a
114. d
115. c
116. e
117. a
118. a
119. d
120. b
121. c
122. c
123. b
124. b
125. e
126. c
127. d
128. a
129. a
130. d
131. c
132. d
133. e
134. d
135. d
136. c
137. b
138. b
139. a
140. c
141. d
142. c
143. d
144. d
145. d
146. b
147. c
148. b
149. e
150. a
151. c
152. c
153. d
154. b
155. a
156. c
157. c
158. c
159. d
160. d
161. c
162. d
163. b
164. d
165. b
166. c
167. b
168. d
169. b
170. b
171. c
172. c
173. b
174. a
175. c
176. a
177. b
178. a
179. a

13.2 MARK TRUE OR FALSE

1. F
2. F
3. T
4. T
5. F
6. F
7. F
8. T
9. T
10. F
11. T
12. F
13. T
14. F
15. T
16. F
17. T
18. T
19. F
20. T
21. F
22. T
23. T
24. F
25. F
26. F
27. T
28. T
29. T
30. T
31. T
32. T
33. F
34. F
35. T
36. F
37. T
38. F
39. T
40. T
41. F
42. T
43. F
44. T
45. F
46. T
47. F
48. T
49. T
50. F
51. T
52. T
53. T
54. T
55. F
56. T
57. T
58. T
59. T
60. F
61. F
62. T
63. T
64. T
65. F
66. T
67. F
68. T
69. F
70. F
71. F
72. T
73. T
74. T
75. F
76. F
77. T
78. T
79. F
80. T
81. T
82. T
83. F
84. T
85. T
86. T
87. F
88. F
89. T
90. T
91. F
92. F
93. F
94. T
95. T
96. T
97. T
98. F
99. T
100. F
101. T
102. F
103. T
104. T
105. F
106. F
107. T
108. T
109. F
110. T
111. F
112. T
113. F

CHAPTER 14: GENETICS OF BACTERIA AND BACTERIOPHAGES

14.1 MULTIPLE-CHOICE QUESTIONS

1. a	19. e	37. b	55. c	73. b	91. a
2. d	20. c	38. c	56. a	74. a	92. a
3. a	21. b	39. d	57. c	75. d	93. a
4. e	22. c	40. e	58. a	76. b	94. a
5. d	23. d	41. e	59. c	77. a	95. a
6. d	24. b	42. a	60. a	78. d	96. a
7. c	25. d	43. a	61. c	79. c	97. c
8. a	26. b	44. b	62. c	80. d	98. c
9. b	27. d	45. a	63. c	81. c	99. b
10. d	28. d	46. a	64. c	82. b	100. b
11. e	29. d	47. a	65. c	83. b	101. c
12. c	30. b	48. b	66. c	84. c	102. a
13. a	31. c	49. b	67. c	85. a	103. b
14. b	32. d	50. b	68. b	86. b	104. a
15. a	33. e	51. b	69. d	87. b	105. d
16. a	34. b	52. b	70. b	88. b	
17. b	35. a	53. b	71. d	89. d	
18. c	36. b	54. c	72. b	90. a	

14.2 MARK TRUE OR FALSE

1. T	10. F	19. T	28. T	37. T	46. F
2. F	11. T	20. F	29. T	38. F	47. T
3. F	12. T	21. T	30. F	39. F	48. T
4. T	13. F	22. F	31. T	40. T	49. F
5. F	14. F	23. F	32. F	41. T	50. F
6. F	15. T	24. T	33. T	42. F	
7. T	16. T	25. T	34. F	43. T	
8. T	17. F	26. T	35. T	44. F	
9. T	18. T	27. F	36. T	45. T	

CHAPTER 15: GENE MUTATIONS

15.1 MULTIPLE-CHOICE QUESTIONS

1. b	10. d	19. a	28. c	37. b	46. d
2. d	11. d	20. c	29. a	38. c	47. d
3. a	12. c	21. c	30. c	39. b	48. e
4. c	13. d	22. a	31. c	40. c	49. a
5. d	14. c	23. c	32. d	41. d	50. d
6. b	15. c	24. b	33. d	42. c	51. b
7. b	16. d	25. b	34. a	43. c	52. b
8. a	17. a	26. b	35. c	44. a	53. b
9. d	18. a	27. a	36. b	45. b	54. c

55. e	69. b	83. d	97. b	111. b	125. d
56. b	70. b	84. c	98. a	112. b	126. c
57. d	71. b	85. d	99. a	113. a	127. c
58. a	72. c	86. d	100. d	114. b	128. b
59. c	73. a	87. d	101. c	115. c	129. a
60. b	74. d	88. c	102. b	116. c	130. d
61. c	75. d	89. b	103. d	117. c	131. d
62. e	76. d	90. a	104. a	118. d	132. b
63. d	77. b	91. b	105. a	119. d	133. a
64. d	78. b	92. a	106. c	120. c	134. a
65. d	79. b	93. c	107. a	121. c	135. b
66. b	80. b	94. d	108. a	122. a	136. c
67. c	81. a	95. c	109. d	123. a	137. c
68. d	82. d	96. a	110. d	124. a	138. d

15.2 MARK TRUE OR FALSE

1. T	13. T	25. T	37. F	49. F	61. F
2. F	14. T	26. F	38. T	50. F	62. T
3. T	15. T	27. T	39. T	51. T	63. T
4. T	16. F	28. F	40. F	52. T	64. F
5. T	17. T	29. T	41. T	53. T	65. F
6. F	18. T	30. F	42. F	54. T	66. F
7. T	19. F	31. F	43. F	55. F	67. F
8. F	20. F	32. T	44. T	56. T	
9. T	21. F	33. T	45. F	57. T	
10. F	22. T	34. F	46. T	58. T	
11. F	23. T	35. T	47. T	59. T	
12. T	24. T	36. T	48. T	60. T	

CHAPTER 16: GENETIC MATERIAL (DNA AND RNA)

16.1 MULTIPLE-CHOICE QUESTIONS

1. c	14. b	27. b	40. a	53. a	66. c
2. b	15. a	28. d	41. d	54. b	67. b
3. c	16. e	29. c	42. d	55. c	68. c
4. a	17. c	30. b	43. d	56. b	69. c
5. d	18. b	31. a	44. d	57. a	70. b
6. d	19. d	32. a	45. e	58. d	71. c
7. a	20. a	33. b	46. d	59. b	72. c
8. c	21. d	34. c	47. b	60. c	73. a
9. d	22. c	35. d	48. d	61. b	74. e
10. b	23. d	36. d	49. c	62. c	75. c
11. d	24. d	37. d	50. b	63. b	76. d
12. b	25. b	38. d	51. c	64. c	77. d
13. a	26. b	39. a	52. c	65. b	78. b

79. b
80. c
81. a
82. d
83. c
84. c
85. b
86. d
87. c
88. b
89. b
90. b
91. d
92. b
93. c
94. a
95. a
96. d
97. b
98. b
99. a
100. e
101. c
102. b
103. c
104. a
105. b
106. d
107. d
108. b
109. a
110. e
111. b
112. d
113. e
114. a
115. b
116. d
117. b
118. c
119. a
120. c
121. e
122. e
123. e
124. b
125. a
126. b
127. d
128. c
129. c
130. a
131. c
132. b
133. b
134. d
135. b
136. b
137. d
138. c
139. b
140. c
141. b
142. b
143. b
144. c
145. b
146. b
147. c
148. b
149. e
150. c
151. a
152. c
153. b
154. b
155. b
156. e
157. e
158. e
159. b
160. d
161. a
162. d
163. b
164. a
165. e
166. b
167. b
168. e
169. b
170. b
171. c
172. d
173. a
174. b
175. b
176. d
177. a
178. b
179. b
180. b
181. c
182. b
183. b
184. d
185. d
186. d
187. b
188. b
189. a
190. b
191. d
192. d
193. e
194. c
195. e
196. d
197. e
198. a
199. e
200. d
201. c
202. b
203. a
204. b
205. d
206. d
207. e
208. c
209. b
210. d
211. e
212. e

16.2 MARK TRUE OR FALSE

1. T
2. T
3. T
4. T
5. F
6. T
7. T
8. F
9. F
10. F
11. T
12. T
13. T
14. T
15. F
16. T
17. T
18. T
19. T
20. F
21. T
22. T
23. T
24. T
25. T
26. F
27. T
28. F
29. F
30. T
31. T
32. F
33. T
34. T
35. F
36. T
37. T
38. T
39. T
40. T
41. T
42. T
43. F
44. T
45. T
46. F
47. F
48. T
49. T
50. F
51. T
52. T
53. T
54. T
55. T
56. F
57. F
58. T
59. F
60. F
61. T
62. T
63. F
64. F
65. T
66. F
67. T
68. T
69. T
70. F
71. F
72. F
73. F
74. F
75. F
76. T
77. F
78. T
79. F
80. F
81. F
82. F
83. T
84. F
85. T
86. F
87. T
88. T
89. F
90. F
91. T
92. T
93. T
94. F
95. T
96. F
97. F
98. T
99. T
100. F
101. T
102. F
103. T
104. T
105. F
106. F
107. T
108. T
109. F
110. F
111. T
112. T
113. F
114. T
115. F

CHAPTER 17: GENETICS OF DEVELOPMENT AND BEHAVIOUR

17.1 MULTIPLE-CHOICE QUESTIONS

1. e	18. b	35. c	52. c	69. c	86. b
2. c	19. d	36. a	53. b	70. a	87. c
3. c	20. a	37. c	54. a	71. b	88. c
4. b	21. a	38. d	55. b	72. b	89. a
5. c	22. a	39. b	56. d	73. b	90. d
6. a	23. d	40. c	57. d	74. b	91. d
7. d	24. a	41. a	58. b	75. c	92. b
8. d	25. c	42. c	59. c	76. b	93. d
9. e	26. c	43. c	60. b	77. d	94. d
10. e	27. b	44. b	61. c	78. a	95. d
11. c	28. d	45. d	62. a	79. b	96. a
12. c	29. a	46. d	63. b	80. b	97. c
13. e	30. c	47. b	64. b	81. c	98. c
14. a	31. a	48. c	65. d	82. c	99. b
15. a	32. b	49. c	66. b	83. c	100. c
16. c	33. a	50. d	67. b	84. b	101. d
17. b	34. d	51. a	68. d	85. a	102. b

17.2 MARK TRUE OR FALSE

1. T	7. T	13. T	19. F	25. T	31. F
2. F	8. T	14. T	20. T	26. F	32. T
3. T	9. T	15. F	21. T	27. T	33. T
4. F	10. F	16. F	22. T	28. F	34. F
5. T	11. T	17. T	23. T	29. T	35. T
6. T	12. F	18. T	24. F	30. F	36. T

CHAPTER 18: POPULATION GENETICS

18.1 MULTIPLE-CHOICE QUESTIONS

1. a	12. b	23. b	34. e	45. d	56. d
2. c	13. c	24. d	35. a	46. d	57. b
3. c	14. d	25. b	36. c	47. c	58. e
4. b	15. d	26. c	37. a	48. c	59. b
5. d	16. a	27. b	38. d	49. b	60. d
6. a	17. c	28. b	39. c	50. c	61. d
7. d	18. e	29. a	40. c	51. c	62. a
8. e	19. d	30. c	41. c	52. b	63. c
9. a	20. e	31. c	42. a	53. b	64. b
10. b	21. c	32. b	43. c	54. c	65. a
11. c	22. d	33. d	44. b	55. c	66. d

67. b	72. a	77. d	82. a	87. b	92. c
68. a	73. d	78. d	83. c	88. a	93. d
69. d	74. b	79. d	84. b	89. b	94. d
70. d	75. c	80. c	85. d	90. d	95. c
71. b	76. b	81. a	86. a	91. d	96. c
					97. d

18.2 MARK TRUE OR FALSE

1. F	10. T	19. T	28. F	37. T	46. F
2. T	11. T	20. F	29. T	38. T	47. T
3. F	12. T	21. T	30. T	39. F	48. T
4. T	13. F	22. T	31. F	40. F	49. F
5. F	14. T	23. T	32. F	41. F	50. T
6. T	15. T	24. F	33. T	42. T	
7. T	16. F	25. F	34. F	43. T	
8. F	17. T	26. T	35. F	44. F	
9. T	18. T	27. F	36. F	45. T	

CHAPTER 19: TISSUE CULTURE

19.1 MULTIPLE-CHOICE QUESTIONS

1. b	23. a	45. d	67. b	89. a	111. b
2. c	24. d	46. c	68. a	90. d	112. c
3. b	25. d	47. e	69. c	91. c	113. d
4. b	26. d	48. e	70. a	92. d	114. c
5. c	27. d	49. b	71. a	93. b	115. d
6. b	28. d	50. a	72. d	94. d	116. b
7. b	29. d	51. f	73. b	95. b	117. b
8. a	30. b	52. c	74. b	96. b	118. c
9. c	31. b	53. b	75. b	97. b	119. c
10. c	32. b	54. a	76. a	98. a	120. c
11. e	33. b	55. d	77. c	99. a	121. a
12. a	34. c	56. c	78. a	100. a	122. b
13. b	35. d	57. b	79. a	101. a	123. b
14. c	36. c	58. c	80. a	102. c	124. b
15. d	37. b	59. a	81. a	103. a	125. b
16. b	38. d	60. c	82. a	104. a	126. d
17. a	39. a	61. b	83. b	105. a	127. d
18. a	40. b	62. c	84. a	106. d	128. c
19. c	41. b	63. b	85. b	107. a	129. b
20. d	42. b	64. c	86. b	108. d	130. b
21. c	43. d	65. b	87. a	109. c	131. b
22. d	44. b	66. a	88. c	110. b	132. d

133. b
134. c
135. c
136. c
137. c
138. a
139. d
140. b
141. d
142. c
143. c
144. b
145. b
146. a
147. c
148. c
149. c
150. b
151. c
152. d
153. a
154. c
155. a
156. a
157. b
158. a
159. d
160. a
161. b
162. d
163. a
164. c
165. b
166. a
167. d
168. b

19.2 MARK TRUE OR FALSE

1. F
2. F
3. T
4. F
5. T
6. F
7. F
8. F
9. T
10. F
11. F
12. T
13. F
14. T
15. T
16. F
17. T
18. T
19. F
20. T
21. T
22. F
23. F
24. F
25. T
26. F
27. F
28. T
29. T
30. F
31. T
32. F
33. T
34. T
35. F
36. F
37. F
38. F
39. T
40. F
41. T
42. T
43. T
44. T
45. F
46. T
47. T
48. F
49. T
50. T
51. F
52. F
53. T
54. F
55. T
56. F
57. T
58. F
59. T
60. F
61. F
62. T
63. F
64. T
65. F
66. T
67. T
68. T
69. T
70. F
71. F
72. T
73. F
74. T
75. T
76. F
77. T
78. T
79. T
80. T
81. F
82. F
83. F
84. T
85. F
86. F
87. F
88. T
89. T
90. F
91. T
92. T
93. F
94. T
95. F
96. T
97. T
98. T
99. T
100. F
101. T

CHAPTER 20: DNA BIOTECHNOLOGY

20.1 MULTIPLE-CHOICE QUESTIONS

1. a
2. a
3. c
4. c
5. b
6. c
7. d
8. e
9. d
10. c
11. c
12. d
13. c
14. c
15. a
16. d
17. c
18. d
19. c
20. b
21. c
22. d
23. e
24. d
25. b
26. d
27. e
28. d
29. b
30. b
31. d
32. e
33. b
34. b
35. d
36. c
37. a
38. b
39. c
40. c
41. c
42. a
43. c
44. a
45. a
46. b
47. c
48. d
49. e
50. d
51. b
52. d
53. a
54. b
55. d
56. b
57. b
58. b
59. b
60. b
61. d
62. a
63. c
64. d
65. c
66. d
67. a
68. d
69. c
70. d
71. a
72. d
73. b
74. b
75. c
76. d
77. e
78. e
79. c
80. d
81. c
82. e
83. a
84. d

85. a
86. a
87. c
88. c
89. a
90. d
91. b
92. a
93. a
94. c
95. c
96. a
97. a
98. a
99. b
100. c
101. d
102. a
103. b
104. b
105. c
106. a
107. a
108. a
109. b
110. c
111. c
112. a
113. c
114. d
115. b
116. c
117. d
118. b
119. a
120. a
121. b
122. a
123. a
124. d
125. b
126. d
127. a
128. a
129. d
130. c
131. c
132. a
133. b
134. b
135. c
136. d
137. a
138. d
139. e
140. c
141. b
142. b
143. a
144. b
145. c
146. d
147. d
148. c
149. b
150. c
151. d
152. c
153. b
154. b
155. c
156. c
157. b
158. b
159. c
160. d
161. d
162. b
163. b
164. b
165. b
166. a
167. c
168. d
169. a
170. c
171. a
172. b
173. b
174. a
175. c
176. b
177. d
178. c
179. a
180. b
181. b
182. b
183. b
184. c
185. a
186. a
187. b
188. c
189. b
190. c
191. d
192. c
193. c
194. c
195. b
196. a
197. a
198. c
199. d
200. c
201. c
202. c
203. d
204. b
205. c
206. b
207. c
208. a
209. d
210. c
211. c
212. d
213. e
214. e
215. c
216. e
217. c
218. d
219. d
220. e
221. c
222. d
223. e
224. c
225. e
226. d
227. e
228. e
229. e
230. e
231. c
232. e

20.2 MARK TRUE OR FALSE

1. T
2. F
3. F
4. F
5. F
6. F
7. F
8. F
9. F
10. F
11. T
12. T
13. T
14. T
15. T
16. F
17. T
18. F
19. T
20. T
21. T
22. F
23. T
24. T
25. T
26. T
27. F
28. T
29. T
30. T
31. T
32. F
33. T
34. F
35. F
36. T
37. F
38. F
39. T
40. F
41. T
42. F
43. F
44. T
45. F
46. F
47. F
48. F
49. F
50. T
51. T
52. T
53. F
54. F
55. T
56. T
57. F
58. T
59. T
60. F
61. T
62. F
63. T
64. T
65. T
66. F
67. T
68. T
69. T
70. F
71. F
72. T
73. F
74. F
75. F
76. T
77. T
78. T
79. T
80. T
81. T
82. F
83. F
84. F
85. F
86. T
87. F
88. T
89. F
90. T
91. F
92. T
93. F
94. F
95. T
96. T
97. T
98. T
99. F
100. T
101. F
102. T

103. T	115. F	127. T	139. T	151. F	163. T
104. F	116. T	128. T	140. F	152. T	164. T
105. T	117. T	129. T	141. F	153. F	165. T
106. T	118. F	130. F	142. T	154. T	166. F
107. T	119. T	131. T	143. T	155. T	167. T
108. F	120. F	132. T	144. F	156. F	168. T
109. F	121. T	133. F	145. T	157. F	169. T
110. F	122. F	134. T	146. F	158. F	170. T
111. T	123. F	135. T	147. T	159. T	171. T
112. F	124. T	136. F	148. F	160. T	172. T
113. F	125. F	137. T	149. T	161. F	173. T
114. T	126. F	138. T	150. F	162. T	

CHAPTER 21: GENETICS OF CANCER AND IMMUNOLOGY

21.1 MULTIPLE-CHOICE QUESTIONS

1. c	19. d	37. b	55. a	73. b	91. c
2. b	20. d	38. b	56. b	74. b	92. a
3. b	21. c	39. c	57. b	75. d	93. d
4. d	22. d	40. e	58. a	76. d	94. c
5. b	23. c	41. e	59. c	77. a	95. c
6. a	24. a	42. c	60. c	78. d	96. b
7. b	25. b	43. e	61. d	79. d	97. c
8. a	26. b	44. a	62. a	80. d	98. a
9. d	27. b	45. b	63. d	81. c	99. a
10. c	28. c	46. d	64. c	82. d	100. d
11. e	29. c	47. a	65. c	83. c	101. d
12. c	30. c	48. d	66. d	84. c	102. b
13. c	31. d	49. d	67. c	85. b	103. a
14. c	32. d	50. b	68. d	86. a	104. b
15. e	33. b	51. a	69. a	87. c	105. a
16. a	34. b	52. c	70. d	88. b	106. d
17. b	35. a	53. c	71. c	89. b	107. c
18. d	36. a	54. b	72. d	90. a	

21.2 MARK TRUE OR FALSE

1. T	10. T	19. T	28. T	37. T	46. T
2. T	11. T	20. T	29. F	38. T	47. F
3. F	12. F	21. T	30. T	39. F	48. T
4. T	13. T	22. F	31. T	40. F	49. F
5. T	14. F	23. F	32. T	41. T	50. T
6. F	15. T	24. T	33. T	42. T	
7. F	16. T	25. T	34. F	43. T	
8. F	17. F	26. T	35. F	44. T	
9. T	18. T	27. F	36. T	45. F	

CHAPTER 22: BIOCHEMISTRY

22.1 MULTIPLE-CHOICE QUESTIONS

1. c
2. e
3. d
4. a
5. e
6. b
7. e
8. a
9. e
10. c
11. a
12. b
13. e
14. b
15. b
16. d
17. d
18. e
19. c
20. d
21. d
22. a
23. d
24. e
25. c
26. c
27. d
28. a
29. c
30. b
31. b
32. c
33. d
34. b
35. a
36. e
37. a
38. b
39. a
40. d
41. c
42. a
43. a
44. c
45. e
46. e
47. c
48. e
49. b
50. e
51. a
52. a
53. b
54. b
55. e
56. e
57. e
58. d
59. e
60. e
61. b
62. b
63. a
64. e
65. c
66. b
67. e
68. d
69. e
70. b
71. a
72. e
73. d
74. d
75. d
76. a
77. b
78. d
79. b
80. b
81. c
82. c
83. d
84. e
85. c
86. c
87. d
88. a
89. c
90. b
91. b
92. b
93. c
94. a
95. d
96. c
97. a
98. c
99. a
100. d
101. d
102. c
103. a
104. b
105. e
106. c
107. d
108. e
109. c
110. d
111. e
112. c
113. c
114. d
115. a
116. c
117. c
118. c
119. d
120. e
121. c
122. d
123. d
124. b
125. c
126. b
127. e
128. e
129. a
130. d
131. c
132. b
133. b
134. a
135. e
136. d
137. e
138. c
139. a
140. c
141. e
142. b
143. d
144. c
145. a
146. a
147. b
148. c
149. e
150. a
151. b
152. c
153. c
154. c
155. c
156. d
157. a
158. b
159. e
160. d
161. b
162. d
163. b
164. a
165. c
166. b
167. e
168. a
169. e
170. d
171. e
172. c
173. b
174. d
175. a
176. c
177. e
178. e
179. d
180. d
181. a
182. d
183. a
184. b
185. a
186. a
187. c
188. d
189. c
190. b
191. f
192. d
193. d
194. a
195. c
196. b
197. e
198. e
199. b
200. b
201. d
202. d
203. c
204. d
205. a
206. c
207. b
208. c
209. d
210. a
211. c
212. b
213. d
214. c
215. b
216. a
217. a
218. b
219. d
220. a
221. a
222. d
223. b
224. a
225. d
226. b
227. a

22.2 MARK TRUE OR FALSE

1. F	23. T	45. T	67. T	89. F	111. F
2. T	24. T	46. F	68. F	90. F	112. T
3. F	25. T	47. F	69. T	91. F	113. F
4. T	26. F	48. F	70. F	92. F	114. T
5. T	27. F	49. F	71. T	93. F	115. F
6. T	28. F	50. T	72. F	94. F	116. F
7. T	29. T	51. F	73. T	95. F	117. T
8. F	30. F	52. T	74. F	96. F	118. F
9. T	31. T	53. T	75. T	97. T	119. F
10. T	32. F	54. T	76. T	98. F	120. T
11. T	33. T	55. T	77. T	99. T	121. T
12. F	34. F	56. T	78. T	100. T	
13. F	35. F	57. T	79. T	101. F	
14. T	36. T	58. T	80. F	102. F	
15. F	37. T	59. F	81. F	103. F	
16. T	38. F	60. T	82. T	104. T	
17. F	39. T	61. F	83. T	105. F	
18. T	40. T	62. F	84. T	106. F	
19. T	41. T	63. T	85. T	107. F	
20. F	42. F	64. F	86. T	108. F	
21. T	43. F	65. F	87. F	109. T	
22. T	44. T	66. T	88. T	110. F	

CHAPTER 23: FORESTRY

23.1 MULTIPLE-CHOICE QUESTIONS

1. c	16. d	31. d	46. a	61. a	76. d
2. b	17. c	32. c	47. b	62. c	77. a
3. a	18. d	33. c	48. b	63. c	78. a
4. a	19. a	34. c	49. b	64. a	79. c
5. d	20. d	35. d	50. c	65. c	80. a
6. b	21. b	36. c	51. d	66. d	81. b
7. a	22. d	37. a	52. a	67. c	82. d
8. b	23. c	38. d	53. a	68. a	83. c
9. c	24. a	39. a	54. b	69. d	84. d
10. d	25. d	40. a	55. a	70. b	85. a
11. c	26. a	41. d	56. a	71. c	86. c
12. b	27. b	42. b	57. d	72. d	87. a
13. d	28. b	43. c	58. d	73. b	88. c
14. d	29. d	44. a	59. c	74. a	89. d
15. b	30. a	45. a	60. c	75. b	90. c

91. a	102. b	113. c	124. b	135. a	146. c
92. d	103. a	114. a	125. b	136. b	147. b
93. d	104. b	115. d	126. c	137. a	148. a
94. b	105. b	116. c	127. d	138. d	149. a
95. c	106. d	117. b	128. b	139. d	150. b
96. b	107. b	118. a	129. b	140. b	151. a
97. c	108. a	119. d	130. a	141. b	152. d
98. c	109. d	120. c	131. d	142. d	153. c
99. a	110. d	121. c	132. c	143. b	
100. b	111. c	122. c	133. c	144. a	
101. b	112. d	123. a	134. d	145. a	

23.2 MARK TRUE OR FALSE

1. F	18. F	35. F	52. F	69. T	86. F
2. T	19. T	36. T	53. T	70. F	87. T
3. F	20. T	37. F	54. T	71. F	88. F
4. T	21. F	38. F	55. T	72. T	89. T
5. F	22. T	39. F	56. F	73. T	90. F
6. T	23. F	40. T	57. T	74. T	91. T
7. F	24. T	41. T	58. F	75. T	92. T
8. F	25. F	42. F	59. T	76. F	93. F
9. F	26. T	43. F	60. F	77. F	94. T
10. T	27. T	44. T	61. F	78. T	95. T
11. F	28. F	45. T	62. F	79. T	96. F
12. F	29. T	46. T	63. T	80. F	97. F
13. F	30. F	47. F	64. T	81. T	98. T
14. F	31. T	48. F	65. T	82. F	99. T
15. T	32. F	49. T	66. T	83. T	100. F
16. T	33. T	50. T	67. F	84. T	
17. T	34. F	51. F	68. F	85. T	

SECTION-III

APPENDICES

Appendix 1

Glossary of Genetics and Plant Breeding

Acentric chromosome. Chromosome fragment lacking a centromere.

Acclimatization. The adaptation of an individual to a changed climate, or the adjustment of a species or a population to a changed environment over a number of generations.

Acrocentric. A chromosome or chromatid that has its centromere near the end.

Adenine. A purine base found in RNA and DNA.

A-DNA. A right-handed DNA double helix that has 11 base pairs per turn. DNA exists in this form when partially dehydrated.

Agglutinin. An antibody in blood plasma that brings about clumping (agglutination) of blood cells that carry an incompatible agglutinogen.

Agglutinogen. An antigen carried by red blood cells that reacts with a specific agglutinin in the plasma and causes clumping of the cells. When a specific antigen is injected into an animal body, it stimulates the production of a corresponding antibody.

Albinism. Absence of pigment in skin, hair, and eyes of an animal. Absence of chlorophyll in plants.

A-Line. The male sterile parent line in a cross being made to produce hybrid seed. Commonly used with reference to hybrid sorghum, hybrid wheat, etc.

Alkaptonuria. An inherited metabolic disorder. Alkaptonurics excrete excessive amounts of homogentisic acid (alkapton) in the urine.

Alkylating agent. A chemical agent that can add alkyl groups (for example, ethyl or methyl groups) to another molecule; many mutagens act through alkylation.

Allele. One of a pair, or series, of alternative forms of a gene that occur at a given locus in a chromosome.

Allele frequency. The proportion of one allele relative to all alleles at a locus in a population.

Allopolyploid. A polyploidy having chromosome sets from different species.

Allotetraploid. An organism with four genomes derived from hybridization of different species. Usually, in forms that become established, two of the four genomes are from one species and the two from another species.

Alternate segregation. In a reciprocal translocation, the passage of both normal chromosomes to one pole and both translocated chromosomes to the other pole.

Alternation of generations. The alternation of gametophyte and sporophyte stages in the life cycle of a plant.

Amber codon. The codon UAG, a nonsense codon.

Amino acid. A peptide; the basic building block of proteins (or polypeptides).

Amorph. A mutation that obliterates gene function; a null mutation.

Amphidiploid. A species or type of plant derived from doubling the chromosomes in the F_1 hybrid of two species; an allopolyploid. In an amphidiploid the two species are known, whereas in other allopolyploids they may not be known.

Amplification. The production of many DNA copies from one master region of DNA.

Anaphase. The stage of mitosis or meiosis during which the daughter chromosomes pass from the equatorial plate to opposite poles of the cell (toward the ends of the spindle). Anaphase follows metaphase and precedes telophase.

Aneuploid (heteroploid). An organism or cell having a chromosome number that is not an exact multiple of the monoploid (n) with one genome, that is, a hyperploid has a higher number (e.g., $2n + 1$) and a hypoploid has a lower number (e.g., $2n - 1$). Also applied to cases where a part of the chromosome is duplicated or deficient.

Antibody. Substance in a tissue or fluid of the body that acts in antagonism to a foreign substance (antigen).

Anticoding strand. The strand of the DNA double helix that is actually transcribed. Also known as the antisense or template strand.

Anticodon. Three bases in a transfer RNA molecule that are complementary to the three bases of a specific codon in messenger RNA.

Antigen. A substance, usually a protein, introduced into a living organism that elicits antibody formation.

Antiparallel. A term used to describe the opposite orientation of the two strands of a DNA double helix; the 5' end of one strand aligns with the 3' end of the other strand.

Antisense DNA. 1. The strand of chromosomal DNA that is transcribed. 2. A DNA sequence that is complementary to all or part of an mRNA molecule.

Antisense gene. A gene that produces a transcript (mRNA) that is complementary to the pre-mRNA or mRNA of a normal gene (usually constructed by inverting the coding region relative to the promoter).

Antisense RNA. RNA that is made from the DNA strand that is complementary to the sense strand of the DNA.

Apomixis. Reproduction from an unfertilized egg or from somatic cells associated with the egg.

Asynapsis. The failure or partial failure in the pairing of the homologous chromosomes during the meiotic prophase.

Atavism. Reappearance of an ancestral trait after several generations because of recessiveness or other masking effects.

ATP. Adenosine triphosphate. An energy-rich compound that promotes certain activities in the cell.

Autogamy. A process of self-fertilization within one undivided cell, resulting in homozygosity e.g. in *Paramecium*.

Autopolyploid. A polyploidy that has multiple and identical or nearly identical sets of chromosomes (genomes). A polyploid species with genomes derived from the same original species.

Autoradiogram. A pattern of dark spots in a developed photographic film or emulsion, in the technique of autoradiography.

Autoradiography. A process in which radioactive materials are incorporated into cell structures, which are then placed next to a film or photographic emulsion, thus forming a pattern on the film corresponding to the location of the radioactive compounds within the cells.

Autosome. Any chromosome that is not a sex chromosome.

Autozygote. A diploid individual in which the two genes of a locus are identical by descent from an ancestral gene.

Auxotroph. A mutant microorganism that will not grow on a minimal medium but that requires the addition of some compound such as amino acid or a vitamin.

Backcross. The cross of an F_1 hybrid to one of the parental types.

Back mutation. A second mutation at the same site in a gene as the original mutation. The second mutation restores the wild-type nucleotide sequence.

Bacteriophage. Virus that attacks bacteria. Such viruses are called bacteriophages because they destroy their bacterial hosts.

Balanced lethal. Lethal mutations in different genes on the same pair of chromosomes that remain in repulsion because of close linkage or crossover suppression.

Barr body. A condensed mass of chromatin found in the nuclei of placental mammals that contains one or more X chromosomes. Named for its discoverer Murray Barr.

Base analog. Unnatural purine or pyrimidine base, differing slightly from the normal base that can be incorporated into nucleic acid.

BC_1, BC_2, etc. Symbols used to designate the first backcross generation, the second backcross generation, etc.

Biometry. The science dealing with the application of statistical methods to biological problems.

Biotype. A population in which all individuals have an identical genotype.

Bivalent. A pair of synapsed or associated homologous chromosomes that have undergone the duplication process to form a group of four chromatids.

B-Line. The fertile counterpart of the A-line. The B-line does not have fertility restoring genes and is used as the male parent to maintain the A-line.

Brachydactyly. A human phenotype of unusually short digits, generally inherited as an autosomal dominant.

Breeder Seed. Seed (or vegetative propagating material) increased by the originating, or sponsoring, plant breeder or institution and which is used as the source for the increase of foundation seed.

Callus. An undifferentiated clone of plant cells.

Candidate gene. A gene whose function suggests that it may be involved in the genetic variation observed for a particular trait, e.g., the gene for growth hormone is a candidate gene for body weight.

Cap. The structure found on the 5′-end of eukaryotic mRNA, and consisting of an inverted, methylated guanosine residue.

Cap site. The site in a gene where translation is initiated.

Carcinogen. A substance capable of inducing cancer in an organism.

Carrier. An individual who carries a recessive allele that is not expressed.

Catabolite repression. Glucose-mediated reduction in the rates of transcription of operons that encode enzymes involved in catabolic pathways (such as the *lac* operon).

Cell cycle. The set of events that take place in the divisions of mitotic cells. The cell cycle oscillates between mitosis (M phase) and interphase. Interphase can be subdivided in order into G_1, S phase, and G_2. DNA synthesis occurs during S phase. The length of the cell cycle is regulated through a special option in G_1, in which G_1 cells can enter a resting phase called G_0.

Cell division. The process by which two cells are formed from one.

Central dogma. The hypothesis that information flows only from DNA to RNA to protein; although some exceptions are now known, the rule is generally valid.

Centriole. An organelle in many animal cells that appears to be involved in the formation of the spindle during mitosis.

Centromere. Spindle-fibre attachment region of a chromosome.

Certified Seed. The progeny of foundation, registered, or certified seed, produced and handled so as to maintain satisfactory genetic identity and purity, and approved and certified by an official certifying agency.

Chain terminator. Codons which do not code for an amino acid. They signal ribosomes to terminate protein synthesis. The codons are UAA, UAG and UGA, and have been termed ochre, amber and opal, respectively. Also known as stop codons or termination codons. Often two of these codons are found together at the end of a coding sequence of RNA.

Character. One of the many details of structure, form, substance, or function that make up an individual organism.

Chi-square (X^2) test. A statistical test used to determine the probability of obtaining observed proportions by chance, under a specific hypothesis.

Chiasma (pl., chiasmata). A visible change of partners or a crossover in two of a group of four chromatids during the first meiotic prophase. In the diplotene stage of meiosis, the four chromatids of a bivalent are associated in pairs, but in such a way that one part of two chromatids is exchanged. This point of "change of partners" is the chiasma.

Chimera (plant). Part of a plant with a genetically different constitution as compared with other parts of the same plant. It may result from different zygotes that grow together or from artificial fusion (grafting).

Chloramphenicol. An antibiotic that interferes with protein synthesis.

Chromatid. In mitosis or meiosis, one of the two identical strands resulting from self-duplication of a chromosome.

Chromatin. The deoxyribonucleohistone in chromosomes; originally named because of the readiness with which it stains with certain dyes.

Chromocenter. Body produced by the fusion of the heterochromatic regions of the chromosomes in the polytene tissues (e.g., the salivary glands) of certain Diptera.

Chromomeres. Small bodies that are identified by their characteristic size and linear arrangement along a chromosome.

Chromonema (pl., chromonemata). An optically single thread forming an axial structure within each chromosome.

Chromosome aberration. Abnormal structure or number of chromosomes; includes deficiency, duplication, inversion, translocation, aneuploidy, polyploidy, or any other change from the normal pattern.

Chromosome banding. Staining of chromosomes in such a way that light and dark areas occur along the length of the chromosomes. Lateral comparisons identify pairs. Each human chromosome can be identified by its banding pattern.

Chromosomes. Darkly staining nucleoprotein bodies that are observed in cells during division. Each chromosome carries a linear array of genes.

Cistron. A unit of function in DNA. One cistron specifies one polypeptide chain in protein synthesis.

Clone. All the individuals derived by vegetative propagation from a single original individual.

Code dictionary. A listing of the 64 possible codons and their translational meanings (the corresponding amino acids).

Coding. The specification of a peptide sequence, by the code contained in DNA molecules.

Coding sequence. That portion of a gene which directly specifies the amino acid sequence of its protein product. Non-coding sequences of genes include control regions, such as promoters, operators and terminators, as well as the intron sequences of certain eukaryotic genes.

Coding strand. The strand of duplex DNA which contains the same base sequence (after substituting U for T) found in the mRNA molecule resulting from transcription of that segment of DNA. Also known as Sense strand. The mRNA molecule is transcribed from the other strand, known as the template or antisense strand.

Codominant alleles. Alleles that produce independent effects when heterozygous.

Codon. A set of three adjacent nucleotides in an mRNA molecule that specifies the incorporation of an amino acid into a polypeptide chain or that signals the end of polypeptide synthesis.

Coincidence. The ratio of the observed frequency of double crossovers to the expected frequency, where the latter is calculated by assuming that the two crossover events occur independently of each other.

Colchicine. An alkaloid derived from the autumn crocus that is used as an agent to arrest spindle formation and interrupt mitosis.

Combining Ability, General. The average or over-all performance of a genetic strain in a series of crosses.

Combining Ability, Specific. The performance of specific combinations of genetic strains in crosses in relation to the average performance of all combinations.

Competent. Able to take up exogenous DNA and thereby be transformed.

Complementarity. The relationship between the two strands of a double helix of DNA. Thymine in one strand pairs with adenine in the other strand, and cytosine in one strand pairs with guanine in the other strand.

Complementary DNA (cDNA). Synthetic DNA transcribed from a specific RNA through the action of the enzyme reverse transcriptase.

Complementary entity. One of a pair of nucleotide bases that form hydrogen bonds with each other. Adenine (A) pairs with thymine (T) [or with Uracil (U) in RNA], and guanine (G) pairs with cytosine (C).

Complementary genes. Two or more interdependent genes, such that (in the case of dominant complementarity) the dominant allele from either gene can only produce an effect on the phenotype of an organism if the dominant allele from the other gene is also present; or (in the case of recessive complementarity) only double homozygous recessive show the effect.

Complementary RNA (cRNA). Synthetic RNA produced by transcription from a specific DNA single-stranded template.

Complementation. The production of a wild-type phenotype when two different mutations are combined in a diploid or a heterokaryon.

Complementation test (cis-trans test). Introduction of two recessive mutations in the same cell but on different chromosomes to determine whether they are alleles of the same gene, that is, whether they affect the same genetic function. If the mutations are allelic, the genotype m_1 +/+ m_2 will exhibit a mutant phenotype, whereas if they are nonallelic, it will exhibit the wild phenotype.

Conditional lethal mutation. A mutation that is lethal under one set of environmental conditions - the restrictive conditions - but is viable under another set of environmental conditions - the permissive conditions, e.g., temperature-sensitive mutations.

Conjugation. The union of two bacterial cells, during which chromosomal material is transferred from the donor to the recipient cell.

Constitutive enzyme. An enzyme that is synthesized continually regardless of growth conditions.

Constitutive gene. A gene that is continually expressed in all cells of an organism.

Constitutive promoter. An unregulated promoter that allows for continual transcription of its associated gene.

Constitutive synthesis. Continual production of RNA or protein by an organism.

Constitutive. An organism is said to be constitutive for the production of an enzyme or other protein if that protein is always produced by the cells under all physiological conditions.

Controlling element. In maize, a transposable element such as Ac or Ds that is capable of influencing the expression of a nearby gene.

Correlation. A statistical association between variables. A mutual relationship between two things such that an increase or decrease of one is generally associated with an increase or decrease of the other. Linear correlation is measured by the correlation coefficient, which may range in value from -1 to +1.

Contig. A set of ordered overlapping clones that constitute a chromosomal region or a genome.

Cosmid. A cloning vector that can replicate autonomously like a plasmid and be packaged into a phage.

Coupling (cis-arrangement). The condition in which a double heterozygote has received two linked mutations from one parent and their wild-type alleles from the other parent, e.g., a b/a b x + +/+ + produces a b/+ +.

cpDNA. Chloroplast DNA.

Crisscross inheritance. Transmission of a gene from a male parent to a female child to male grandchild-for example, X-linked inheritance.

Crossing-over. A process in which chromosomes exchange material through the breakage and reunion of their DNA molecules.

Crossover unit. A measure of distance on genetic maps that is based on the average number of crossing-over events that take place during meiosis. A map interval that is one crossover unit in length (sometimes called a centimorgan) implies that only one in every hundred chromatids recovered from meiosis will have undergone a crossing-over event in this interval.

Cultivar. A variety.

Culture. Tissue or cells multiplying by asexual division, grown for experimentation.

Cytogenetics. Area of biology concerned with chromosomes and their implications in genetics.

Cytokinesis. Cytoplasmic divisions and other changes exclusive of nuclear division that are a part of mitosis or meiosis.

Cytology. The study of the structure or function of the cells.

Cytoplasm. The protoplasm of the cell outside the nucleus in which cell organelles (mitochondria, chloroplasts, etc.) reside. All living parts of the cell except the nucleus.

Cytoplasmic inheritance. Hereditary transmission dependent on the cytoplasm or structures in the cytoplasm rather than the nuclear genes; extrachromosomal inheritance.

Cytosine. A pyrimidine base found in RNA or DNA.

Cytosol. The fluid part of the cytoplasm, outside the organelles.

Deficiency (deletion). Absence of a segment of a chromosome, reducing the number of loci.

Degeneracy. An aspect of the genetic code in which a particular amino acid is encoded by more than one codon.

Denaturated DNA. Duplex DNA that has been converted to single strands by breaking the hydrogen bonds of complementary nucleotide pairs. Usually achieved by heating.

Denaturation. Loss of native configuration of a macro-molecule (protein or nucleic acid) by physical or chemical means, usually accompanied by loss of biological activity. Denatured proteins often unfold their polypeptide chains and express changed properties of solubility. The separation of duplex nucleic acid molecules into single strands.

Denature. To induce structural alterations that disrupt the biological activity of a molecule. Often refers to breaking hydrogen bonds between base pairs in double-stranded nucleic acid molecules to produce single-stranded polynucleotides, or altering the secondary and tertiary structure of a protein, destroying its activity.

De novo. From the Latin, meaning arising anew, afresh, once more.

Deoxyribonuclease (DNAse). Any enzyme that hydrolyses DNA.

Deoxyribonucleic acid. DNA.

Determinate. Descriptive of an inflorescence in which the terminal flower opens first, thus arresting the prolongation of the floral axis. Example, a cyme.

Deviation. As used in statistics, a departure from an expected value.

Diakinesis. A stage of meiosis just before metaphase I in which the bivalents are shortened and thickened.

Dicentric chromosome. One chromosome having two centromeres.

Di-deoxynucleotide. A deoxynucleotide that lacks a 3′- hydroxyl group, and is thus unable to form the 3′-5′ phospho-diester bond necessary for chain elongation. Di-deoxynucleotides are used in DNA sequencing and the treatment of viral diseases.

Dihybrid. An individual that is heterozygous for two pairs of alleles. The progeny of a cross between homozygous parents differing in two respects.

Diploid. An organism or cell with two sets of chromosomes (2n) or two genomes. Somatic tissue of higher plants and animals are ordinarily diploid in chromosome constitution in contrast with the haploid (monoploid) gametes.

Diplonema (adj., diplotene). That stage in prophase of meiosis I following the pachytene stage, but preceding diakinesis, in which the chromosomes of bivalents separate from each other at or around their centromeres.

Direct repeat. Two or more stretches of DNA within a single molecule which have the same nucleotide sequence in the same orientation. Direct repeats may be either adjacent to one another or far apart on the same molecule.

Directed mutagenesis. The process of generation of nucleotide changes in cloned genes by any one of several procedures, including site-specific and random mutagenesis. Also called *in vitro* mutagenesis.

Discontinuous variation. Phenotypic variability involving distinct classes such as red versus white or tall versus dwarf.

Disjunction. Separation of homologous chromosomes during anaphase of mitotic or meiotic divisions.

DNA. Deoxyribonucleic acid; the information-carrying genetic material that comprises the genes.

DNA amplification. Multiplication of a piece of DNA in a test-tube into many thousands of millions of copies. The most commonly used process is the polymerase chain reaction (PCR) system.

DNA fingerprint. The autoradiographic banding pattern produced when DNA is digested with a restriction enzyme that cuts outside a family of VNTRs and a Southern blot of the electrophoretic gel is probed with a VNTR-specific probe. Unlike true fingerprints, these patterns are not unique to each individual.

DNA helicase (gyrase). An enzyme that catalyses the unwinding of the complementary strands of a DNA double helix.

DNA hybridization. The pairing of two DNA molecules, often from different sources, by hydrogen bonding between complementary nucleotides. This technique is frequently used to detect the presence of a specific nucleotide sequence in a DNA sample.

DNA ligase. An enzyme that catalyses a reaction that links two DNA molecules via the formation of a phospho-diester bond between the 3′ hydroxyl and 5′ phosphate of adjacent nucleotides. It plays an important role in DNA repair and replication.

DNA polymerase. An enzyme that catalyses the synthesis of double-stranded DNA, using single-stranded DNA as a template.

DNA polymorphism. The existence of two or more alternative forms (alleles) of a chromosomal locus that differ in nucleotide sequence or have variable numbers of repeated nucleotide units.

DNA primase. An enzyme that catalyses the synthesis of short strands of RNA that initiate the synthesis of DNA strands.

DNA repair. A variety of mechanisms that repair errors that occur during DNA replication.

DNA repair enzymes. Enzymes that catalyse the repair of DNA.

DNA replication. The process whereby DNA makes exact copies itself, under the action of and control of DNA polymerase.

DNase (deoxyribonuclease). An enzyme that catalyses the cleavage of DNA. DNase I is a digestive enzyme secreted by the pancreas, that degrades DNA into shorter nucleotide fragments. Many other endonucleases and exonucleases are involved in DNA repair and replication.

Dominance. A condition in which one member of an allelic pair is manifested to the exclusion of the other.

Double helix. The structure of DNA first proposed by Watson and Crick, with two interlocking helices joined by hydrogen bonds between paired bases.

Double-stranded complementary DNA (dscDNA). A double-strand DNA molecule created from a cDNA template.

Down syndrome. An abnormal human phenotype, including mental retardation, due to a trisomy of chromosome 21; more common in babies born to older mothers.

dsDNA. Double-stranded DNA.

Duplex DNA. Double-stranded DNA.

Duplicate Genes. Two or more pairs of genes that produce identical effects, whether alone or together.

Duplication. The occurrence of a segment more than once in the same chromosome or genome. Also, the multiplication of cells.

Dyad. A pair of sister chromatids joined at the centromere, as in the first division of meiosis.

Electrophoresis. The migration of suspended particles in an electric field.

Electroporation. A process whereby cell membranes are made permeable to DNA by applying an intense electric current.

Embryo. An organism in the early stages of development.

Embryo-sac. A large, thin-walled space within the ovule of the seed plant in which the egg and, after fertilization, the embryo develop; the mature female gametophyte in higher plants.

Encode. To specify, after decoding by transcription and translation, the sequence of amino acids in a protein.

5′ end. The phosphate group that is attached to the 5′ carbon atom of a sugar (ribose or deoxyribose) of the terminal nucleotide of a nucleic acid molecule.

End-labelling. The introduction of a radioactive atom at the end of a DNA or RNA molecule. A commonly used method is to use T4 polynucleotide kinase to introduce a ^{32}P atom onto the end of a DNA molecule.

Endomitosis. Duplication of chromosomes without division of the nucleus, resulting in increased chromosome number within a cell. Chromosome strands separate but the cell does not divide.

Endonuclease. An enzyme that breaks strands of DNA at internal positions; some are involved in recombination of DNA.

Endopolyploidy. A state in which the cell of a diploid organism contains multiples of the diploid chromosome number (i.e., 4n, 8n; etc.).

Endosperm. Nutritive tissue that develops in the embryo sac of most angiosperms. It usually forms after the fertilization of the two fused primary endosperm nuclei of the embryo sac with one of the two male gamete nuclei. In most diploid plants, the endosperm is triploid (3n).

End-product inhibition. The inhibition of an enzyme by a metabolite. The enzyme is sometimes the first enzyme in a biosynthetic pathway, and the metabolite is generally the product of the last step in the pathway.

Enucleate cell. A cell having no nucleus.

Enzyme. A protein that accelerates a specific chemical reaction in a living system.

Episome. A genetic element in bacteria that can replicate free in the cytoplasm or can be inserted into the main bacterial chromosome and replicate with the chromosome.

Epistasis. Interactions between products of nonallelic genes. Genes suppressed are said to be hypostatic. Dominance is associated with members of allelic pairs, whereas epistasis is interaction among products of nonalleles.

Epitope. A part of an antigen molecule that is recognized by a specific immunoglobulin.

Equational division. Mitotic-type division that is usually the second division in the meiotic sequence; somatic mitosis and the nonreductional division of meiosis.

Equatorial plate. The figure formed by the chromosomes in the center (equatorial plane) of the spindle in mitosis.

Euchromatin. Genetic material that is not stained so intensely by certain dyes during interphase and that comprises many different kinds of genes.

Eugenics. State-controlled human breeding in an attempt to improve future generations.

Eukaryote. A member of the large group of organisms that have nuclei enclosed by a membrane within their cells.

Eukaryotic cell. A cell containing a nucleus.

Euploid. An organism or cell having a chromosome number that is an exact multiple of the monoploid (x) or haploid number.

Excision repair. The repair of a DNA lesion by removal of the faulty DNA segment and its replacement with a wild-type segment.

Exon. Any non-intron section of the coding sequence of a gene; together, the exons constitute the messenger RNA and are translated into protein.

Exonuclease. An enzyme that digests DNA or RNA, beginning at the ends of the strands.

Expression library. A population of different DNA molecules encoding peptides, that has been cloned into one kind of expression vector.

Expressivity. Degree of expression of a trait controlled by a gene. A particular gene may produce different degrees of expression in different individuals.

Extrachromosomal. Structures that are not a part of the chromosomes; DNA units in the cytoplasm that control cytoplasmic inheritance.

F^- cell. In *E. coli*, a cell having no fertility factor; a female cell.

F^+ cell. In *E. coli,* a cell having a free fertility factor; a male cell.

F factor (fertility factor). A bacterial episome whose presence confers donor ability (maleness).

F' factor. A fertility factor into which a part of the bacterial chromosome has been incor-porated.

F_1. The first filial generation. The first generation of descent from a given mating.

F_2. The second filial generation produced by crossing *inter se* or by self-pollinating the F_1.

Feulgen's test. A histochemical test in which the distribution of DNA in the chromosomes of dividing cell nuclei can be observed. A tissue section is first treated with dilute hydrochloric acid to remove the purine bases of the DNA, thus exposing the aldehyde groups of the sugar deoxyribose. The section is then immersed in Schiff's reagent, which combines with the aldehyde groups to form a magenta-coloured compound.

Fingerprint. The characteristic spot pattern produced by electrophoresis of the polypeptide fragments obtained through denaturation of a particular protein with a proteolytic enzyme.

First-division segregation pattern. A linear pattern of spore phenotypes within the ascus for a particular allele pair, produced when the alleles go into separate nuclei at the first meiotic division, showing that no crossover has occurred between the allele pair and the centromere.

Forward mutation. A mutation that converts a wild-type allele into a mutant allele.

Foundation seed. Seed stocks increased from breeder seed, and so handled as to closely maintain the genetic identity and purity of a variety. Production of foundation seed is carefully supervised or approved by representatives of an agricultural experiment station. Foundation seed is the source of certified seed, either directly or through registered seed.

Frame-shift mutation. The insertion or deletion of a nucleotide pair or pairs, causing a disruption of the translational reading frame.

Functional genomics. Studying patterns of gene expression and interaction in the genome as a whole.

G_0 phase. The resting phase that can occur in G_1 of interphase of the cell cycle.

G_1 phase. The part of interphase of the cell cycle that precedes S phase.

G_2 phase. The part of interphase of the cell cycle that follows S phase.

Gamete. A mature male or female reproductive cell (sperm or egg).

Gametogenesis. The formation of gametes.

Gametophyte. The phase of the plant life cycle that bears the gametes; the cell have n chromosomes.

G cap. The 5′-terminal methylated guanine nucleoside that is present on many eukaryotic mRNAs; it is joined, after transcription, to the mRNA.

Gene. A hereditary determinant of a specific biological function; a unit of inheritance (DNA) located on a fixed position on the chromosome. The fundamental physical and functional unit of heredity, which carries information from one generation to the next; a segment of

DNA, composed of a transcribed region and a regulatory sequence that make transcription possible.

Gene amplification. The process by which the number of copies of a chromosomal segment is increased in a somatic cell.

Gene conservation; genetic resources conservation. The conservation of species, populations, individuals or parts of individuals, by *in situ* or *ex situ* methods, to provide a diversity of genetic materials for present and future generations.

Gene conversion. A process, often associated with recombination, during which one allele is replicated at the expense of another, leading to non-Mendelian segregation ratios. In whole tetrads, for example, the ratio may be 6:2 or 5:3 instead of the expected 4:4.

Gene flow. The spread of genes from one breeding population to another by migration, possibly leading to allele frequency changes.

Gene Interaction. Modification of gene action by a nonallelic gene.

Gene mutation. A point mutation that results from changes within the structure of a gene.

Gene pool. The sum total of all different alleles in the breeding members of a population at a given time.

Genetic code. The set of correspondences between nucleotide pair triplets in DNA and amino acids in proteins.

Genetic complementation. When two DNA molecules that are in the same cell together produce a function that neither DNA molecule can supply on its own.

Genetic equilibrium. Condition in a group of interbreeding organisms in which the allele frequencies remain constant over time.

Genetic load. The proportion by which the fitness of the optimum genotype is decreased by deleterious genes, as expressed in lethal equivalents or 'genetic deaths".

Genetic map. The linear array of genes on a chromosome, based on recombination frequencies (linkage map) or physical location (physical or chromosomal map).

Genetic mapping. Determining the linear order of genes and/or DNA markers along a chromosome.

Genetic markers. Alleles used as experimental probes to keep track of an individual, a tissue, a cell, a nucleus, a chromosome, or a gene.

Genetics. The science of heredity and variation.

Genome. A complete set (n) of chromosomes (hence, of genes) inherited as a unit from one parent.

Genomic library. A library encompassing the entire genome.

Genomics. The cloning and molecular characterization of entire genomes.

Genotype. The genetic constitution of an organism.

Genus. A somewhat arbitrary group of closely related species, where perceived relationship is typically based on physical resemblance.

Germplasm. The hereditary material transmitted to the offspring through the germ cells.

Gram-negative organism. Any prokaryotic organism that does not retain the first stain (crystal violet) used in Gram's staining technique. It does retain the second stain (safranin O) and therefore has a pink colour when viewed under a light microscope. Retention of the stain is due to the structure of the cell wall.

Gram-positive organism. Any prokaryotic organism that retains the first stain used in the Gram technique, which gives a purple-black colour when viewed under a light microscope. Retention of the stain is due to the structure of the cell wall.

Gram staining. A technique to distinguish between two major bacterial groups, based on stain retention by their cell walls. Bacteria are heat-fixed, then stained with crystal violet, followed by iodine solution, and then rinsed with alcohol or acetone. Gram-positive bacteria are stained bright purple, while Gram-negative bacteria decolourise.

Green Revolution. Name given by William Goud to the dramatic increase in crop productivity during the third quarter of the 20th century, as a result of integrated advances in genetics and plant breeding, agronomy, and pest and disease control.

Guanine. A purine base found in DNA or RNA.

Gynandromorph. An individual in which one part of the body is female and another part is male; a sex mosaic.

Haploid (monoploid). An organism or cell having only one complete set (n) of chromosomes or one genome.

Haploidization. Production of a haploid from a diploid by progressive chromosome loss.

Haplotype. A group of alleles, each from a different locus in the same region of a chromosome, that exist in the same double helix.

Hemizygous. The condition in which only one allele of a pair is present, as in sex linkage or as a result of deletion.

Haemoglobin. Conjugated protein compound containing iron, located in erythrocytes of vertebrates; important in the transportation of oxygen to the cells of the body.

Hemophilia. A bleeder's disease; tendency to bleed freely from even a slight wound; hereditary condition dependent on a sex-linked recessive gene.

Heredity. Resemblance amongst individuals related by descent; transmission of traits from parents to offspring.

Heritability. Degree to which a given trait is controlled by inheritance.

Hermaphrodite. An individual with both male and female reproductive organs.

Heteroalleles. Mutations that are functionally allelic but structurally non-allelic; mutations at different sites in a gene.

Heterochromatin. Chromatin staining darkly even during interphase, often containing repetitive DNA with few genes.

Heterogeneous nuclear RNA (hnRNA). Large RNA molecules, which are unedited mRNA transcripts, or pre-mRNAs found in the nucleous of a eukaryotic cell.

Heterokaryon. A cell containing two or more different nuclei.

Heterologous. From a different source, as in heterologous DNA.

Heterologous probe. A DNA probe that is derived from one species and used to screen for a similar DNA sequence from another species.

Heteroploid (aneuploid). An organism characterized by a chromosome number other than the true haploid (monoploid) or diploid number (2n+1 or 2n-1).

Heteropyknosis. Property of certain chromosomes, or of their parts, to remain more dense and to stain more intensely than other chromosomes or parts during the cell cycle.

Heterosis. Superiority of heterozygous genotypes in respect to one or more traits in comparison with corresponding homozygotes.

Heterozygote. An organism with unlike members of any given pair or series of alleles that consequently produces unlike gametes.

Histones. Group of proteins rich in basic amino acids. They function in the coiling of DNA in chromosomes and in the regulation of gene activity.

"Holandric" gene. A gene carried on the Y chromosome and therefore transmitted from father to son.

Homeologous chromosome. Partly homologous chromosomes, usually indicating some original ancestral homology.

Homeotic mutation. A mutation that causes a body part to develop in an inappropriate position in an organism, such as the mutation in *Drosophila* that causes legs to develop on the head in place of antennae.

Homoalleles. Mutations that are both functionally and structurally allelic; mutations at the same site in the same gene.

Homodimer. A protein with two identical polypeptide chains.

Homokaryon. Cell with two or more identical nuclei as a result of fusion. Opposite: heterokaryon.

Homologous chromosomes. Chromosomes that pair with each other at meiosis or chromosomes in different species that have retained most of the same genes during their evolution from a common ancestor.

Homopolymer. A nucleic acid strand that is composed of one kind of nucleotide, e.g., GGGGGGGG.

Homozygote. An individual having a homozygous gene pair.

Homozygous gene pair. A gene pair having identical alleles in both copies.

Hybrid. An offspring of homozygous parents differing in one or more genes; more generally, an offspring of a cross between unrelated strains.

Hybridization. The crossing of individuals of unlike genetic constitution.

Hybridize. To produce hybrids by crossing individuals with different genotypes.

Hydroponics. The growing of plants in aerated water containing all the essential mineral nutrients, with no soil. Also called soilless gardening or cultivation.

Hyperploid. Aneuploid containing a small number of extra chromosomes.

Hypoploid. Aneuploid with a small number of chromosomes missing.

I_1, I_2, etc. Symbols used to designate the first inbred generation, second inbred generation, etc.

Inbred Line. (1) a pure line usually originating by self-pollination and selection; (2) the product of inbreeding.

Inbreeding. Matings between related individuals.

Inbreeding coefficient. The probability of homozygosity that results because the zygote obtains copies of the *same* ancestral gene.

Incompatibility. Failure to obtain fertilization and seed formation after self-pollination, usually due to slow pollen tube growth in the stylar tissue.

Incomplete dominance. Expression of two alleles in a heterozygote that allows the heterozygote to be distinguished from either of its homozygous parents.

Independent assortment. The random distribution of alleles to the gametes that occurs when genes are located in different chromosomes. The distribution of one pair of alleles is independent of other genes located in nonhomologous chromosomes.

Indeterminate. Descriptive of an inflorescence in which the terminal flower is last to open. The flowers arise from axillary buds, and the floral axis may be indefinitely prolonged by a terminal bud. Example, a raceme.

Inducer. A low-molecular-weight compound or a physical agent that is bound by a repressor so as to produce a complex that can no longer bind to the operator; thus, the presence of the inducer turns on the expression of the gene(s) controlled by the operator.

Inducible. A gene or gene-product is said to be inducible if its transcription or synthesis is increased by exposure of the cells to an effector. Effectors are usually small molecules whose effects are specific to particular operons or groups of genes.

Inducible enzyme. An enzyme that is synthesized only in the presence of the substrate that acts as an inducer.

Inducible gene. A gene that is expressed only in the presence of a specific metabolite, the inducer.

Induction. Act or process of causing to occur; process whereby a cell or tissue influences neighbouring cells or tissues. Turning on transcription of a specific gene or operon. Getting an organism to make a protein by exposing it to some stimulus.

Initiation codon; initiator. The codon AUG which specifies the first amino acid methionine of a polypeptide chain. In bacteria, the initiation codon is either AUG, which is translated as *n*-formyl methionine or, rarely, GUG (valine). In eukaryotes, the initiation codon is always AUG and is translated as methionine. The term is also used to describe the corresponding sequence in DNA, namely ATG.

In situ. From the Latin, meaning "in the natural place". Refers to experimental treatments performed on cells or tissues rather than on extracts from them.

Interference. Crossing-over at one point that reduces the chance of another crossover nearby.

Interphase. The stage in the cell cycle when the cell is not dividing.

Introns. Intervening sequences of DNA bases within eukaryotic genes that are not represented in the mature RNA transcript because they are spliced out of the primary RNA transcript.

Inversion. A rearrangement that reverses the order of the linear array of genes in a chromosome.

Inverted repeat. A sequence present twice in a DNA molecule, but in reverse orientation.

In vitro. From the Latin, meaning "within glass"; biological processes made to occur experimentally outside the organism in a test tube or other container.

In vivo. From the Latin, meaning "within the living organism".

Isoagglutinogen. An antigen such as A or B blood type factor, that occurs normally.

Isoalleles. Different forms of a gene that produce the same phenotype or very similar phenotypes.

Isochromosome. A chromosome with two identical arms and identical genes. The arms are mirror images of each other.

Isozyme. A variant of a particular enzyme. In general, all the isozymes of a particular enzyme have the same function and sometimes the same activity, but they differ in amino-acid sequence. With the help of isozyme analysis, based on electrophoresis techniques that can separate the different variants, related species or cultivars can be distinguished.

Karyogram. A diagram representing the characteristic features of the chromosomes of a species.

Karyotype. The chromosome constitution of a cell or an individual; chromosomes arranged in order of length and according to position of the centromere.

Kharif. The summer season.

Kilobase. 1000 nucleotide pairs.

Kinetochore. A complex of proteins to which a nuclear spindle fibre attaches.

Klinefelter syndrome. An abnormal human male phenotype due to an extra X chromosome (XXY).

Lagging strand. The strand of DNA that is synthesized discontinuously during replication (because DNA synthesis can proceed only in the 5′ to 3′ direction).

Lampbrush chromosomes. Large diplotene chromosomes present in oocyte nuclei, particularly conspicuous in amphibians.

LD_{50} (lethal dose$_{50\%}$). The amount of a chemical required to kill 50% of the test population. The higher the LD_{50}, the lower the presumed toxicity of the chemical.

Leader sequence. A sequence of nucleotides at the 5′ end of an mRNA that is not translated into protein.

Leading strand. The strand of DNA that is synthesized continuously during replication.

Leptonema (adj., leptotene). Stage in meiosis immediately preceding synapsis in which the chromosomes appear as single, fine threadlike structures.

Lethal allele. An allele that renders an organism or a cell possessing it inviable.

Ligase. An enzyme that joins the ends of two strands of nucleic acid.

Ligation. The joining of two or more DNA molecules by covalent bonds.

Line. A group of individuals from a common ancestry. A more narrowly defined group than a strain or variety.

Linkage. A relationship among genes in the same chromosomes; such genes tend to be inherited together.

Linkage Group. A group of genes arranged in a linear order on a chromosome.

Linkage map. A linear or circular diagram that shows the relative positions of genes on a chromosome as determined by genetic analysis.

Locus. A fixed position on a chromosome that is occupied by a given gene or one of its alleles.

Lysogenic. A type or phase of the virus life cycle during which the virus integrates into the host chromosome of the infected cell, remaining essentially dormant for some period of time.

Lysogenic bacteria. Bacteria harbouring temperate (non-virulent, lysogenic) bacteriophages.

Lysogeny. A condition in which a bacteriophage genome (pro-phage) survives within a host bacterium, either as part of the host chromosome or as part of an extrachro-mosomal element, and does not initiate lytic functions.

Lytic. A phase of the virus life cycle during which the virus replicates within the host cell, releasing a new generation of viruses when the infected cell lyses.

Lytic cycle. The steps in viral production that usually lead to cell lysis.

Lysosome. A membrane-bound sac within the cytoplasm of animal cells that contains enzymes responsible for the digestion of material in food vacuoles, the dissolution of foreign particles entering the cell and, on the death of the cell, the breaking down of all cell structures. The digestive system of the cell.

M_1, M_2, etc. Symbols used to designate the first generation, second generation, etc. following exposure to mutagenic agents (ionizing radiations, chemical mutagens, etc.)

M phase. The mitotic phase of the cell cycle.

Male Sterility. A condition in which pollen is absent or nonfunctional in flowering plants.

Map unit. The "distance" between two linked gene pairs where 1 per cent of the products of meiosis are recombinant; a unit of distance in a linkage map.

Mass Selection. A system of breeding in which seed from individuals selected on the basis of phenotype is composited and used to grow the next generation.

Maternal effect. Trait controlled by a gene of the mother but expressed in the progeny.

Maternal inheritance. Inheritance controlled by extra-chromosomal (i.e., cytoplasmic) factors that are transmitted through the egg.

Mean. The arithmetic average.

Medium. Any material on which experimental cultures are grown.

Meiosis. The process by which the chromosome number of a reproductive cell becomes reduced to half the diploid (2n) or somatic number; results in the formation of gametes in animals or spores in plants; important source of variability through recombination.

Mendel's first law. The two members of a gene pair segregate from each other in meiosis; each gamete has an equal probability of obtaining either member of the gene pair.

Mendel's second law. The law of independent assortment; unlinked or distantly linked segregating gene pairs assort independently at meiosis.

Merozygote. Partial zygote produced by a process of partial genetic exchange, such as transformation in bacteria.

Messenger RNA (mRNA). RNA that carries information necessary for protein synthesis from the DNA to the ribosomes.

Metacentric chromosome. A chromosome with the centromere near the middle and the two arms of about equal length.

Metafemale (superfemale). In Drosophila, abnormal female; usually sterile, with an excess of X chromosomes compared with sets of autosomes (e.g., XXX; AA).

Metaphase. The stage of cell division in which the chromosomes are most discrete and arranged in an equatorial plate; stage following prophase and preceding anaphase.

Methylation. Modification of a molecule by the addition of a methyl group.

Micron; micrometre. A unit of distance: 10^{-6} m; 0.001 mm.

Microsatellite DNA. A type of repetitive DNA based on very short repeats such as dinucleotides.

Midparent value. The mean of the values of a quantitative phenotype for two specific parents.

Minimal medium. A medium containing only inorganic salts, a carbon source, and water.

Missense mutation. A mutation that alters a codon in such a way that it encodes a different amino acid.

Mitosis. Disjunction of duplicated chromosomes and division of the cytoplasm to produce two genetically identical daughter cells.

Monohybrid. An offspring of two homozygous parents that differ from one another by the alleles present at only one gene locus.

Monohybrid cross. A cross between parents differing in only one trait or in which only one trait is being considered.

Monoploid (haploid). Organism or cell having a single set of chromosomes or one genome (chromosome number n).

Monosome. A chromosome which has no homolog present. A haploid chromosome in an otherwise normal diploid individual.

Monosomic. A diploid organism lacking one chromosome of its proper complement (2n-1); an aneuploid. Monosome refers to the single chromosome, disome to two chromosomes of a kind, and trisome to three chromosomes of a kind.

Monozygotic twins. One egg or identical twins.

Mosaic. A chimera; a tissue containing two or more genetically distinct cell types or an individual composed of such tissues.

Multiple alleles. A condition in which a particular gene occurs in three or more allelic forms in a population of organisms.

Multiple Genes. Two or more independent pairs of genes which produce complementary or cumulative effects upon a single character of the phenotype.

Mutant. An organism which has acquired a heritable variation as a result of mutation.

Mutation. A change in the DNA at a particular locus in an organism. The term is used loosely to include point mutations involving a single gene change as well as a chromosomal change.

Muton. The smallest part of a gene that can be involved in a mutation event; now known to be a nucleotide pair.

Noblization. A term used in sugarcane breeding to denote the crossing of *Saccharum officinarum* with related species, followed by one or more backcrosses to *S. officinarum*.

Nondisjunction. Failure of disjunction or separation of homologous chromosomes in mitosis or meiosis, resulting in too many chromosomes in some daughter cells and too few in others.

Nonrecurrent parent. Parent which is not involved in a backcross.

Nucleic acid. A macromolecule composed of phosphoric acid, pentose sugar and organic bases; DNA and RNA.

Nucleoid. A DNA mass within a chloroplast or mitochondrian.

Nucleolar organizer. A chromosomal segment containing genes that control the synthesis of ribosomal RNA, located at the secondary constriction of some chromosomes.

Nucleolus. An RNA-rich, spherical sac in the nucleus of metabolic cells; associated with the nucleolar organizer; storage place for ribosomes and their precursors.

Nucleoprotein. Conjugated protein composed of nucleic acid and protein; the material of which the chromosomes are made.

Nucleoside. A nitrogen base bound to a sugar molecule. A core particle consisting of an octamer of histones and 146 nucleotide- pairs.

Nucleotide. A unit of DNA and RNA molecules containing a phosphate, a sugar, and an organic base.

Nucleosome (Nu body). Spherical subunits of eukaryotic chromatin that are composed of nucleus. The part of the eukaryotic cell that contains the chromosomes; separated from the cytoplasm by a membrane.

Null mutation. A mutation that abolishes the expression of a gene.

Nullisomic. An otherwise diploid cell or organism lacking both members of a chromosome pair (2n-2).

Octoploid. Cell or organism with eight genomes or sets of chromosomes (chromosome number 8n).

Okazaki fragment. Since DNA can be replicated in only one direction, i.e., nucleotides can be added only at the 3′ end, only one of the two strands of a double helix can be replicated continuously. The other strand is replicated in small segments (Okazaki fragments) that are subsequently joined together by DNA ligase.

Oligomer. A molecule formed from a small number of monomers.

Oligonucleotide. A short molecule (usually 6 to 100 nucleotides) of single-stranded DNA.

Oligonucleotide. A short segment of synthetic DNA.

Oncogene. A gene that can cause neoplastic transformation in animal cells growing in culture and tumour formation in animals themselves.

Operator. The region of DNA that is upstream from a gene or genes and to which one or more regulatory proteins (repressor or activator) bind to control the expression of the gene(s).

Operon. A functionally integrated genetic unit for the control of gene expression in bacteria. It consists of one or more genes that encode one or more polypeptide(s) and the adjacent site (promoter and operator) that controls their expression by regulating the transcription of the structural genes.

Organogenesis. The production of organ systems in animal embryogenesis.

Ovary. The enlarged basal portion of the pistil, in which the seeds are borne.

Overdominance. A condition in which heterozygotes are superior to either of the associated homozygotes.

Ovule. The structure which bears the female gamete and becomes that seed after fertilization.

Pachynema. A midprophase stage in meiosis immediately following zygonema and before diplonema. Under the microscope, the chromosomes are visible as long, paired threads. Rarely, four chromatids are detectable.

Palindrome. A segment of DNA in which the base-pair sequence reads the same in both directions from a point of symmetry.

Panmictic population. A population in which mating occurs at random. Random mating in a population.

Panmixis. Paracentric inversion. An inversion that is entirely within one arm of a chromosome and does not include the centromere.

Paracentric inversion. An inversion not involving the centromere.

Parthenocarpy. The production of fruits without fertilization and, normally, with seeds.

Parthenogenesis. The development of a new individual from an egg without fertilization.

Partial Dominance. Lack of complete dominance; the production of a hybrid intermediate between the parental types.

Pathogen. An organism that causes a disease.

Pathogenicity. The ability of an organism to incite a disease.

Pedigree. A table, chart, or diagram representing the ancestry of an individual.

Penetrance. The percentage of individuals that show a particular phenotype among those capable of showing it.

Peptide. A compound containing amino acids. A breakdown or buildup unit in protein metabolism.

Pericentric inversion. An inversion including the centromere, hence involving both arms of a chromosome.

Phenotype. The observable characteristics of an organism.

Photoreactivation. A DNA repair process that is light dependent.

Physiologic Race. Pathogens of the same species and variety, which are structurally similar but which differ in physiological and pathological characteristics, especially in ability to parasitize varieties of a particular host.

Plasmagene. A cytoplasmic-borne unit of heredity.

Plasmid. Autonomously replicating extra chromosomal DNA molecule.

Pleiotropy (adj., pleiotropic). Condition in which a single gene influences more than one trait.

Ploidy. The number of chromosome sets.

Point mutation. A mutation that can be mapped to one specific locus.

Polydactyly. The occurrence of more than the usual numbers of fingers or toes.

Polygene. One of many genes involved in quantitative inheritance.

Polymerase. An enzyme that catalyzes the formation of DNA or RNA.

Polymerase chain reaction (PCR). A procedure involving multiple cycles of denaturation, renaturation, and polynucleotide synthesis that amplifies a particular DNA sequence.

Polymorphism. Two or more kinds of individuals maintained in a breeding population.

Polynucleotide. A linear sequence of joined nucleotides in DNA or RNA.

Polypeptide. A linear molecule with two or more amino acids and one or more peptide groups. They are called dipeptides, tripeptides, and so on, according to the number of amino acids present.

Polyploid. An organism with more than two sets of chromosomes (2n diploid) or genomes e.g., triploid (3n), tetraploid (4n), etc.

Polytene chromosomes. Giant chromosomes produced by interphase replication without division and consisting of many identical chromatids arranged side-by-side in a cable-like pattern.

Population. Entire group of organisms of one kind; an interbreeding group of plants or animals.

Position effect. A difference in phenotype that is dependent on the position of a gene or group of genes, often caused by heterochromatin that is nearby.

Primer. A short nucleotide sequence with a reactive 3'-OH that can initiate DNA synthesis along a template.

Prion. Proteinaceous infectious particle that causes degenerative disorders of the central nervous system, such as "scrapie" in sheep.

Probe. Defined nucleic acid segment that can be used to identify specific DNA molecules bearing the complementary sequence, usually through autoradiography.

Prokaryote. A member of a large group of organisms (including bacteria and blue-green algae) that lacks true nuclei in their cells and that do not undergo meiosis.

Prophase. The stage of mitosis between interphase and metaphase. During this phase, the centriole divides and the two daughter centrioles move apart. Each sister DNA strand from interphase replication becomes coiled and the chromosome is longitudinally double except in the region of the centromere. Each partially separated chromosome is called a chromatid. The two chromatids of a chromosome are sister chromatids.

Promoter. A nucleotide sequence of DNA to which RNA polymerase binds and initiates transcription. It usually lies upstream of (5′ to) a coding sequence. A promoter sequence aligns the RNA polymerase so that transcription will initiate at a specific site.

Promoter sequence. A regulatory DNA sequence that initiates the expression of a gene.

Pro-phage. The genome of a temperate bacteriophage integrated into the chromosome of a lysogenic bacterium and replicated along with the host chromosome.

Proteinaceous infectious particle; prion. An abnormal form of a normal cell protein, with no detectable nucleic acid, found in the brain of mammals and believed to be the agent responsible for the class of diseases called spongiform encephalopathies, including scrapie in sheep and bovine spongiform encephalopathy (mad cow disease) in cattle.

Proteome. The complete set of protein-coding genes in a genome.

Protoplast. A plant or bacterial cell from which the wall has been removed.

Prototroph. An organism such as a bacterium that will grow on a minimal medium.

Provirus. A viral chromosome that has integrated in a host genome.

Pseudodominance. The sudden appearance of a recessive phenotype in a pedigree, due to deletion of a masking dominant gene.

Pseudogene. An inactive but stable component of a genome resembling a gene; apparently derived from active genes by mutation.

Pure Line. A strain in which all members have descended by self-fertilization from a single homozygous individual. A pure line is genetically pure (homozygous).

Quantitative Character. A character that is influenced by a series of independent genes which are cumulative in their effect.

R_1, R_2, etc. *Symbols* used to designate the first generation, second generation, etc. following exposure of seeds or plants to ionizing radiations.

Reading frame. A series of triplets beginning from a specific nucleotide. Each triplet is represented by a single amino acid in the protein synthesized. The reading frame defines which sets of three nucleotides are read as triplets in the DNA, and hence as codons in the corresponding mRNA; this is determined by the initiation codon, AUG. Thus the sequence AUGGCAAAAUUUCCC would read as AUG/GCA/AAA/UUU/CCC/ and not as A/UGC/CAA/AAU/UUC/CC. Depending on where one begins, each DNA strand contains three different reading frames.

Recessive. Applied to one member of an allelic pair lacking the ability to manifest itself when the other or dominant member is present.

Reciprocal crosses. Crosses between different strains with the sexes reversed; for example, female A x male B and male A x female B are reciprocal crosses.

Reciprocal recurrent selection. A recurrent selection breeding system in which genetically different groups are maintained, and in each selection cycle, individuals are mated from the different groups to test for combining ability.

Recombination. The production of gene combinations not found in the parents by the assortment of nonhomologous chromosomes and crossing-over between homologous chromosomes during meiosis. For linked genes, the frequency of recombination can be used to estimate the genetic map distance; however, high frequencies (approaching 50 per cent) do not yield accurate estimates.

Recombinant DNA. A novel DNA sequence formed by the combination of two nonhomologous DNA molecules.

Recon. A region of a gene within which there can be no crossing-over; now known to be a nucleotide pair.

Recurrent Parent. Parent to which hybrid material is crossed in a backcross.

Recurrent Selection. A breeding system designed to increase the frequency of favorable genes for yield or other characteristics by repeated cycles of selection.

Reduction division. Phase of meiosis in which the paternal and maternal chromosomes of the bivalent separate.

Registered seed. The progeny of foundation or registered seed produced and handled so as to maintain satisfactory genetic identity and purity, and approved and certified by an official certifying agency. Registered seed is normally grown for the production of certified seed.

Replication. A duplication process that is accomplished by copying from a template.

Reporter gene. A gene that encodes a product that can readily be assayed. Thus, reporter genes are used to determinate whether a particular DNA construct has been successfully introduced into a cell, organ or tissue.

Repressible enzyme. An enzyme whose synthesis is diminished by a regulatory molecule.

Repression. Inhibition of transcription by preventing RNA polymerase from binding to the transcription initiation site: a repressed gene is "turned off."

Repressor. A protein which binds to a specific DNA sequence (the operator) upstream from the transcription initiation site of a gene or operon and prevents RNA polymerase from commencing mRNA synthesis. Examples of repressors are the C_1 protein of bacteriophage and the *lac*1 protein of the *lac* operon.

Repulsion (trans-arrangement). The condition in which a double heterozygote has received a mutant and a wild-type allele from each parent; for example, a + / a + x + b / + b produces a + / + b.

Restriction enzyme. An endonuclease that recognizes a specific short sequence in DNA and cleaves the DNA molecule.

Reverse transcriptase. An enzyme that catalyses the synthesis of DNA using an RNA template.

Reversion. Restitution of a mutant gene to the wild-type condition, or at least to a form that gives the wild type phenotype. More generally, the appearance of the trait expressed by a remote ancestor; a throwback; atavism.

RFLP (Restriction fragment length polymorphism). A genetic difference among individuals that is detected by comparing DNA fragments released by digestion with one or more restriction enzymes.

Rh factor. Antigen in the red blood corpuscles of certain people. A pregnant Rh-negative woman carrying an Rh-positive child may develop antibodies, causing the child to develop a hemolytic disease.

S_0. Symbol used to designate the original selfed plant.

S_1, S_2, etc. Symbols for designating first selfed generation (progeny of S_0 plant), second selfed generation (progeny of S_1 plant), etc.

Satellite DNA. That portion of the DNA in plant and animal cells consisting of highly repetitious sequences (millions of copies) typically in the range from 5 to 500 bases. Thousands of copies occur tandemly (end-on-end) at each of many sites. It can be isolated from the rest of the DNA by density gradient centrifugation.

Satellite RNA. A small, self-splicing RNA molecule that accompanies several plant viruses, including tobacco ringspot virus.

Semi-conservative replication. During DNA duplication, each strand of a parent DNA molecule is a template for the synthesis of its new complementary strand. Thus, one half of a pre-existing DNA molecule is conserved during each round of replication.

Sense RNA. A primary transcript (RNA) that contains a coding region (contiguous sequence of codons) that is translated to produce a polypeptide.

Sequence hypothesis. Francis Crick's seminal concept that genetic information exists as a linear DNA code; DNA and protein sequence are collinear.

S phase. The part of interphase of the cell cycle in which DNA synthesis occurs.

Second-division segregation pattern. A pattern of ascospore genotypes for a gene pair showing that the two alleles separate into different nuclei only at the second meiotic division, as a result of a crossover between that gene pair and its centromere; can be detected only in a linear ascus.

Seed. A mature ovule with its normal coverings. A seed consists of the seed coat, embryo, and, in certain plants, an endosperm.

Segregation. The separation of paternal and maternal chromosomes from each other at meiosis; the separation of alleles from each other in heterozygotes; the occurrence of different phenotypes among offspring, resulting from chromosome or allele separation in their heterozygous parents. Mendel's first principal of inheritance.

Selection. (1) any process, natural or artificial, which permits an increase in the proportion of certain genotypes or groups of genotypes in succeeding generations; (2) a plant, line, or strain which originated by a selection process.

Self-Fertile. Capable of fertilization and setting seed after self-pollination.

Self-Sterility. Failure to complete fertilization and obtain seed after self-pollination.

Sex-influenced dominance. A dominant expression that depends on the sex of the individual (e.g., horns in sheep are dominant in males and recessive in females).

Sex-limited. Expression of a trait in only one sex. Examples: Milk production in mammals; egg production in chickens.

Sex-linkage. Association or linkage of a hereditary trait with sex; the gene is in a sex chromosome, usually the X; often used synonymously with X-linkage.

Sexduction. Sexual transmission of donor *E. coli* chromosomal genes on the fertility factor.

Silent mutation. Mutation in which the function of the protein product of the gene is unaltered.

Single-cell protein (SCP). Protein produced by micro-organisms. The dried mass of a pure sample of a protein-rich-micro-organism, which may be used either as feed (for animals) or as a food (for humans).

Single copy. A gene or DNA sequence which occurs only once per (haploid) genome. Most structural genes, those encoding functional proteins, are single-copy genes.

Somatic-cell. A cell that is a component of the body, in contrast with a germ cell that is capable, when fertilized, of reproducing the organism.

Southern blot. The transfer of DNA fragments from an electrophoretic gel to a cellulose or nylon membrane by capillary action.

Species. Interbreeding, natural populations that are reproductively isolated from other such groups.

Splicing. The process that covalently joins exon sequences of RNA and eliminates the intervening intron sequences.

Standard deviation. A measure of variability in a set of data. The square root of the variance.

Statistic. A value based on a sample or samples of a population from which estimates of a population value or parameter may be obtained.

Strain. A group of individuals from a common origin. Generally, a more narrowly defined group than a variety.

Structural gene. A gene that specifies the synthesis of a polypeptide.

Supercoiled plasmid. The predominant *in vivo* form of plasmid, in which the plasmid is coiled around histone-like proteins. Supporting proteins are stripped away during extraction from the bacterial cell, causing the plasmid molecule to supercoil around itself *in vitro*.

Supergene. A group of neighbouring genes on a chromosome that tend to be inherited together and sometimes are functionally related.

Synapsis. The pairing of homologous chromosomes in the meiotic prophase.

Synaptinemal complex. A ribbon like structure formed between synapsed homologues at the end of the first meiotic prophase, binding the chromatids along their length and facilitating chromatid exchange.

Synthetic Variety. Advanced generations of open-pollinated seed mixtures of a group of strains, clones, or inbreds, or of hybrids among them.

TATA box. A conserved adenine- and thymine-rich promoter sequence located 25-30 bp upstream of a gene, which is the binding site of RNA polymerase.

Tautomeric shift. The transfer of a hydrogen atom from one position in an organic molecule to another position.

Tautomerism. A type of isomerism in which the two isomers are in equilibrium.

Telomere. The tip of a chromosome.

Telophase. The last stage in each mitotic or meiotic division in which the chromosomes are assembled at the poles of the division spindle. Terminalization. Repelling movements of the centromeres of bivalents in the dipolotene stages of the meiotic prophase that tends to move the visible chiasmata toward the ends of the bivalents.

Template. An RNA or single-stranded DNA molecule upon which a complementary nucleotide strand is synthesized. A pattern or mould. DNA stores coded information and acts as a model or template from which information is copied into complementary strands of DNA or transcribed into mRNA.

Template strand. The polynucleotide strand that a polymerase uses for determining the sequence of nucleotides during the synthesis of a new nucleic acid strand.

Testcross. Backcross to the recessive parental type, or a cross between genetically unknown individuals with a fully recessive tester to determine whether an individual in question is heterozygous or homozygous for a certain allele. Also used as a test for linkage.

Tetrad. The four cells arising from the second meiotic division in plants (pollen tetrads) or fungi (ascospores). The term is also used for the four chromatids formed by the association of duplicated homologous chromosomes during meiosis.

Tetrasomic. Pertaining to a nucleus or an organism with four members of one of its chromosomes whereas the remainder of its chromosome complement is diploid. (Chromosome formula: $2n+2$.)

Three-point testcross. A testcross in which one parent has three heterozygous gene pairs.

Thymine. A pyrimidine base found in DNA. The other three organic bases- adenine, cytosine, and guanine- are found in both RNA and DNA, but in RNA, thymine is replaced by uracil.

Ti plasmid. A circular plasmid of *Agrobacterium tumifaciens* that enables the bacterium to infect plant cells and produce a tumour.

Top Cross. An outcross of selections, clones, lines, or inbreds, to a common pollen parent. In maize, commonly an inbred-variety cross.

Totipotent cell (or nucleus). An undifferentiated cell (or nucleus) such as blastomere that when isolated or suitably transplanted can develop into a complete embryo.

Transcription. Process through which mRNA is formed along a DNA template. The enzyme RNA polymerase catalyzes the formation of RNA from ribonucleotide triphosphates.

Transduction. The movement of genes from a bacterial donor to a bacterial recipient with the use of a phage as the vector.

Transfection. The process by which exogenous DNA in solution is introduced into cultured cells.

Transformation. (1). The directed modification of a genome by the external application of DNA from a cell of different genotype. (2). Conversion of normal higher eukaryotic cells in tissue culture into a cancer-like state of uncontrolled division.

Transgene. A gene that has been modified by externally applied recombinant DNA techniques and reintroduced into the genome by germ-line transformation.

Transgenic. A term applied to organisms that have been altered by introducing DNA molecules into them.

Transgressive Segregation. The segregation of individuals, in the F_2 or a later generation of a cross, which show a more extreme development of a character than either parent.

Transgressive variation. The appearance in the F_2 (or a later) generation of individuals showing more extreme development of a trait than either of the original parents.

Transition. A mutation caused by the substitution of one purine by another purine or one pyrimidine by another pyrimidine in DNA or RNA.

Translation. Protein (polypeptide) synthesis directed by a specific messenger RNA; occurs on ribosomes.

Translocation. Change in position of a segment of a chromosome to another part of the same chromosome or to a different chromosome.

Transposons. DNA elements that can move from one position in a DNA molecule to another.

Transversion. A mutation caused by the substitution of a purine for a pyrimidine or a pyrimidine for a purine in DNA or RNA.

Trihybrid. The offspring from homozygous parents differing in three pairs of genes.

Trisomic. An otherwise diploid cell or organism that has an extra chromosome of one pair. (Chromosome formula 2n+1)

Turner syndrome. An abnormal human female phenotype produced by the presence of only one X chromosome (XO).

Unequal crossing-over. Crossing-over between repeated DNA sequences that have paired out of register, creating duplicated and deficient products.

Univalent. An unpaired chromosome at meiosis.

Uracil. A pyrimidine base found in RNA but not in DNA. In DNA, uracil is replaced by thymine.

Variance. A measure of variation in a population. The square of the standard deviation.

Variance, Environmental. The variance resulting from environmental or nongentic causes.

Variance, Genetic. The variance resulting from genetic causes.

Variance, Phenotypic. The total variance, the sum of the environmental and the genetic variance.

Variation. In biology, the occurrence of differences among individuals.

Variegation. The occurrence within a tissue of sectors with differing phenotypes.

Variety. A subdivision of a species. An agricultural variety is a group of similar plants which by structural features and performance can be identified from other varieties within the same species.

Vector. A plasmid or viral chromosome that may be used to construct recombinant DNA molecules for introduction into living cells.

Vernalization. The treatment of seeds before sowing to hasten flowering. Vernalization may be accomplished in certain species by exposure of germinating seeds to temperatures slightly above freezing.

Virulent phage. A phage (virus) that destroys the host (bacterial) cell.

Western blot. The transfer of proteins from an electrophoretic gel to a cellulose or nylon membrane by means of an electric force.

Wild type. The customary phenotype or standard for comparison.

W/v. Weight per volume; the weight of a constituent in 100 cm^3 of solution, expressed as a percentage.

Wobble hypothesis. An explanation of how one tRNA may recognize more than one codon. The first two bases of the mRNA codon and anticodon pair properly, but the third base in the anticodon has some wobble that permits it to pair with more than one base.

X chromosome. A chromosome associated with sex determination. In most animals, the female has two and the male has one X chromosome.

Xenia. Hereditary influence from the pollen parent to the endosperm in the seed in certain plants.

Y chromosome. The partner of the X chromosome in the male of many animal species.

Z-DNA; zig-zag DNA. A form of DNA duplex in which the double helix is wound in a left-hand, instead of a right-hand, manner. DNA adopts the Z configuration when purines and pyrimidines alternate on a single strand, e.g.,

5′CGCGCGCG3′ or 5′CACACACACA3′
3′GCGCGCGC5′ 3′GTGTGTGTGT5′

Zygonema. Stage in meiosis during which synapsis occurs; after the leptotene stage and before the pachytene stage in the meiotic prophase.

Appendix 2
Glossary of Tissue Culture

Abscisic acid. A plant growth regulator involved in abscission, dormancy, stomatal opening/ closure, and inhibition of seed germination. It also affects the regulation of somatic cell embryogenesis in some plant species.

Acclimatization. The adaptation of a living organism (plant, animal or micro-organism) to a changed environment that subjects it to physiological stress. Acclimatization should not be confused with adaptation.

Activated charcoal; activated carbon. Charcoal which has been treated to remove hydrocarbons and to increase its adsorptive properties. It acts by condensing and holding a gas or solute onto its surface; thus inhibitory substances in nutrient medium may be adsorbed to charcoal included in the medium.

Adenine. A white crystalline purine base. A constituent of DNA and RNA and nucleotides such as ADP and ATP. It is added to some tissue culture media, as adenine sulphate, to promote shoot formation and for its weak cytokinin effect.

Adsorbent. A substance to which compounds adhere. In tissue culture, an adsorbent is added to the culture medium to adsorb compounds released by cultured cells or tissues, thus minimizing any adverse effect on the subsequent growth in culture. A common adsorbent in tissue culture is *activated charcoal*.

Adventitious. Developing from unusual points of origin, such as shoots or root tissues from callus or embryos from sources other than zygotes.

Agar. A polysaccharide solidifying agent used in nutrient media preparations and obtained from certain types of red algae (*Rhodophyta*).

Agarose. The main constituent of agar.

Alginate. Polysaccharide gelling agent.

Ampicillin. A penicillin-derived antibiotic that prevents bacterial growth by interfering with synthesis of the cell wall.

Anaerobe. An organism that can grow in the absence of oxygen.

Anaerobic. An environment or condition in which molecular oxygen is not available for chemical, physical or biological processes.

Anther culture. The aseptic culture of anthers for the production of haploid plants from microspores.

Anther. Microsporangium bearing microspores which develop into pollen (microgametophytes). The upper part of a stamen, containing pollen sacs within which are numerous pollen grains.

Anthesis. The flowering period. Anthesis is the time of full bloom, which lasts till fruit set.

Antiauxin. A chemical that interferes with the auxin response. Antiauxin may or may not involve prevention of auxin transport or movement in plants. Some antiauxins are said to promote morphogenesis *in vitro,* such as 2,3,5-tri-iodobenzoate, or 2,4,5-trichlorophenoxyacetate which stimulate the growth of some cultures.

Antibiotic. A class of natural and synthetic compounds that inhibit the growth of or kill some micro-organisms.

Antibiotic resistance. The ability of a micro-organism to produce a protein that disables an antibiotic or prevents transport of the antibiotic into the cell.

Antiseptic. Any substance that kills or inhibits the growth of disease-causing micro-organism (a micro-organism capable of causing sepsis), but is essentially non-toxic to cells of the body.

Antioxidant solution. Pre-treatment solution (e.g., Vitamin C) that retards senescence and browning of tissue.

Antioxidant. Compound that slows the rate of oxidation reactions.

Apical dominance. The phenomenon of inhibition of growth of lateral (axillary) buds in a plant by the presence of the terminal (apical) bud on the branch, due to auxins produced by the apical bud.

Apical meristem. A region of the tip of each shoot and root of a plant in which cell division is continually occurring to produce new stem and root tissue, respectively.

Apoenzyme. Inactive enzyme that has to be associated with a specific organic molecule called a co-enzyme in order to function. The apoenzyme/co-enzyme complex is called a holoenzyme.

Apoptosis. The process of cell death, which occurs naturally as a part of normal development, maintenance and renewal of tissue in an organism. Apoptosis differs from necrosis, in which cell death is caused by a toxic substance.

Artificial seed. Encapsulated or coated somatic embryos (embryoids) that are planted and treated like seed.

Ascorbic acid. A water-soluble vitamin present naturally in some plants, and also synthetically produced. Aside from its role as a vitamin, it is used as an antioxidant in plant tissue culture.

Asexual embryogenesis. The sequence of events whereby embryos develop from somatic cells. Also known as Somatic cell embryogenesis.

Assay. To test or evaluate.

Asepsis. Without infection or contaminating microorganisms.

Aseptic technique. Procedures used to prevent the introduction of fungi, bacteria, viruses, mycoplasma or other microorganisms into cell, tissue and organ culture.

Assay. To test or evaluate.

Autoclave. An enclosed chamber in which substances are heated under pressure to sterilize utensils, liquids, glassware, etc., using steam. The routine method uses steam pressure of 103.4×10^3 Pa at 121°C for 15 minutes, or longer to allow large volumes to reach the critical temperature.

Autologous cells. Cells that are taken from an individual, cultured (or stored), and, possibly, genetically manipulated before being infused back into the original donor.

Autolysis. The process of self destruction of a cell, cell organelle, or tissue. It occurs by the action of lysosomic enzymes.

Auxin. A group of plant growth regulators (natural or synthetic) which stimulate cell division, enlargement, apical dominance, root initiation, and flowering. One naturally produced auxin is indole-acetic acid (IAA).

Auxotroph. A mutant cell or micro-organism lacking the capacity to form an enzyme or metabolite present in the parental strain, and that consequently will not grow on a minimal medium, but requires the addition of some compound such as an amino acid or a vitamin for growth.

Axenic culture. A culture without foreign or undesired life forms. An axenic culture may include the purposeful co-cultivation of different types of cells, tissues or organisms.

Axillary bud. A bud found at the axil of a leaf (synonymous with lateral bud).

Axillary bud proliferation. Propagation in culture using protocols and media which promote axillary (lateral shoot) growth.

Browning. Discoloration due to phenolic oxidation of freshly cut surfaces of explant tissue. In later stages of culture, such discolouration may indicate a nutritional or pathogenic problem, generally leading to necrosis.

Callus. An unorganized, proliferative mass of differentiated plant cells; a wound response.

Cell culture. Term used to denote the maintenance or cultivation of cells *in vitro* including the culture of single cells. In cell cultures, the cells are no longer organized into tissues.

Cell fusion. Formation of a single hybrid cell from two cells of different species, cultured *in vitro*. The cells fuse and coalesce, but their nuclei may remain separated. During subsequent cell division, a single spindle is formed so that each daughter cell has a single nucleus containing sets of chromosomes from each parental line. Subsequent divisions often result in the loss of chromosomes and therefore of genes.

Cell generation time. The interval between consecutive divisions of a cell.

Cell hydridization. The fusion of two or more dissimilar cells leading to the formation of a synkaryon.

Cell line. A cell line arises from a primary culture at the time of the first successful subculture. The term "cell line" implies that cultures from it consist of lineages of cells originally present in the primary culture.

Cell strain. A cell strain is derived either from a primary culture or a cell line by the selection or cloning of cells having specific properties or markers.

Cell suspension. Cells in culture in moving or shaking liquid medium, often used to describe suspension cultures of single cells and cell aggregates.

Charcoal. The black porous residue of partly burnt wood, bones, etc; a form of carbon. When treated to purify it and increase its adsorptive power, it is called activated charcoal, in which form it is added to nutrient medium in order to prevent or decrease the effect of browning.

Chelate. Complex organic molecule that can combine with cations and does not ionize. Chelates can supply micronutrients to plants at slow, steady rates. Usually used to supply iron to plant cells.

Clonal propagation. Asexual reproduction of plants that are considered to be genetically uniform and originated from a single individual or explant.

Clone. In animal cell culture terminology a population of cells derived from a single cell by mitoses. A clone is not necessarily homogeneous and , therefore, the terms *clone* and *cloned* do not indicate homogeneity in a cell population, genetic or otherwise. In plant culture terminology, the term may refer to a culture derived as above or it may refer to a group of plants propagated only be vegetative and asexual means, all members of which have been derived by repeated propagation from a single individual.

Cloning efficiency. The percentage of cells plated (seeded, inoculated) that form a clone. One must be certain that the colonies formed arose from single cells in order to properly use this term.

Coconut milk. Liquid endosperm of the coconut often used to supply organic nutrients to cultured cells and tissues.

Colchicine. An alkaloid obtained from *Colchicum autumnale* or autumn crocus, which inhibits spindle formation in cells during mitosis, so that chromosomes cannot separate during anaphase, thus inducing multiple sets of chromosomes.

Competent. A competent cell is capable of developing into a fully functional embryo. The opposite is non-competent.

Complementation. The ability of two different genetic defects to compensate for one another.

Contaminant. Bacterial, fungal or algal micro-organism accidentally introduced into a culture or culture medium.

Continuous cell culture. A culture which is apparently capable of an unlimited number of population doublings; often referred to as immortal cell culture.

Conversion. The development of a somatic embryo into a plant.

Crown gall. A bulbous growth that occurs at the base of certain plants as a result of infection, especially by *Agrobacterium tumefaciens*; a bacterial gene carried by the Ti plasmid is transferred by the bacteria into a higher plant cell, where it causes a tumour-like growth.

Crown. The region at the base of the stem of cereals and forage species from which tillers or branches arise. In woody plants, the root-stem junction. In forestry, the top portions of the tree.

Cryopreservation. Ultra-low temperature storage of cells, tissues, embryos or seeds. This storage is usually carried out using temperatures below -100°C.

Cryoprotectant. Compound preventing cell damage during freezing and thawing processes. Cryoprotectants are agents with high water solubility and low toxicity. Two types of cryoprotectant agent are commonly used: permeating (glycerol and DMSO) and non-permeating (sugars, dextran, ethylene glycol, polyvinyl pyrolidone and hydroxyethyl starch).

Culture. A population of plant or animal cells or micro-organisms that is grown under controlled conditions.

Culture medium. Any nutrient system for the cultivation of cells of plants, bacteria or other organisms; usually a complex mixture of organic and inorganic nutrients.

Culture room. Room for maintaining cultures and often in a controlled environment of light, temperature and humidity.

Cybrid. The viable cell resulting from the fusion of a cytoplast with a whole cell, thus creating a cytoplasmic hybrid.

Cyclic AMP (cyclic adenosine monophosphate). A "messenger" that regulates many intracellular reactions by transducing signals from extracellular growth factors to cellular metabolic pathways.

Cytokinin. Plant growth regulators (hormones) characterized as substances that induce cell division and cell differentiation (e.g., BA, kinetin, and 2-ip). In tissue culture, these substances are associated with enhanced callus and shoot development. The compounds are derivatives of adenine.

Cytoplast. The intact cytoplasm remaining following the enucleation of a cell.

Cytoplasmic hybrid. Synonymous with "cybrid".

Cytoplasmic inheritance. Inheritance attributable to extranuclear genes; for example genes in cytoplasmic organelles such as mitochondria or chloroplasts, or in plasmids, etc.

Cytosine. A pyrimidine base found in DNA and RNA.

Cytosol. The fluid portion of the cytoplasm, i.e., the cytoplasm minus its organelles.

Density-dependent inhibition of growth. Mitotic inhibition correlated with increased cell density.

Death phase. The final growth phase, during which nutrients have been depleted and cell number decreases.

De-differentiation. The process by which cells lose their specialization and proliferate by cell division to form a mass of cells which, in response to appropriate stimuli, may later differentiate again to form either the same cell type or a different one. De-differentiation occurs in response to wounding and in tissue cultures.

De-ionized water. Water which is free of most inorganic and organic compounds.

***De novo*.** Arising anew, afresh.

Determinate growth. Growth determined and limited in time, as in most floral meristems and leaves. The differentiation process is irreversibly established. Determinate growth contrasts with the usual culture growth, which is infinite and indeterminate.

Determination. Process by which undifferentiated cells in an embryo become committed to develop into specific cell types, such as neurons, fibroblasts or muscle cells.

Determined. Describing embryonic tissue at a stage when it can develop only as a certain kind of tissue.

Differentiated. Cells that maintain, in culture, all or much of the specialized structure and function typical of the cell type *in vivo*.

Diploid. The state of the cell in which all chromosomes, except sex chromosomes, are two in number and are structurally identical with those of the species from which the culture was derived.

Direct embryogenesis. Embryoids form directly in culture, without an intervening callus phase, on the surface of zygotic or somatic embryos or on explant tissues (leaf section, root tip, etc.).

Direct organogenesis. Formation of organs directly on the surface of cultured intact explants. The process does not involve callus formation.

Donor plant (mother plant). An explant, graft or cutting used as a source of plant material for micro-propagation purposes.

Electroporation. Creation, by means of an electrical current, of transient pores in the plasmalemma usually for the purpose of introducing exogenous material, especially DNA, from the medium.

Embryo culture. *In vitro* development or maintenance of isolated mature or immature embryos.

Embryogenesis. The process of embryo initiation and development.

Embryoid. An embryo-like body developing *in vitro*. It forms a complete, self-contained platelet with no vascular connection with the callus.

Embryonic stem cells. Cells of the early embryo that can give rise to all differentiated cells, including germ line cells.

Epigenetic event. Any change in a phenotype which does not result from an alteration in DNA sequence. This change may be stable and heritable and includes alteration in DNA methylation, transcriptional activation, translational control and post-translational modifications

Epigenetic variation. Phenotypic variability which has a nongenetic basis.

Ethylene. A gaseous plant growth regulator regulating various aspects of vegetative growth, fruit ripening and abscission of plant parts.

Euploid. The situation which exists when the nucleus of a cell contains exact multiples of the haploid number of chromosomes.

Explant. Tissue taken from its original site and transferred to an artificial medium for growth or maintenance.

Explant culture. The maintenance or growth of an explant in culture.

Exponential phase. The growth stage where cells undergo their maximum rate of cell division. The exponential phase follows the lag phase, and precedes the linear growth phase.

***Ex vitro* (L. "from glass").** Organisms removed from tissue culture and transplanted; generally plants to soil or potting mixture.

Finite cell culture. A culture which is capable of only a limited number of population doubling after which the culture ceases proliferation.

Friability. A term indicating the tendency for plant cells to separate from one another.

Friable. A term commonly used to describe a crumbling or fragmenting callus. A friable callus is easily dissected and readily dispersed into single cells or clumps of cells in solution.

Gall. A tumourous growth in plants.

Gametoclonal variation. Variation in phenotype, either genetic or epigenetic in origin, expressed by gametoclones.

Gametoclone. Plants regenerated from cell cultures derived from meiospores, gametes or gametophytes.

Gelatin. A glutinous, proteinaceous gelling and solidifying agent. Gelatin is produced by boiling animal connective tissues, which partially hydrolyses the collagen. Gelatin is used to gel or solidify nutrient solutions for tissue culture.

Gelrite. The brand name of a *Pseudomonas*-derived refined polysaccharide used as a gelling agent and agar substitute.

Gibberellins. Plant growth regulators involved in elongation, enhancement of flower, fruit and leaf size, germination, vernalization and other processes.

Growth inhibitor. Any substance inhibiting the growth of an organism.Two plant growth regulators that may act as inhibitors are ethylene and abscisic acid.

Habituation. The acquired ability of a population of cells to grow and divide independently of exogenously supplied growth regulators.

Hardening off. Adapting plants to outdoor conditions by gradually withholding water, lowering the temperature, increasing light intensity, or reducing the nutrient supply. The hardening-off process conditions plants for survival when transplanted outdoors.

HEPA filter (High efficiency particulate air filter). A filter capable of screening out particles larger than 0.3 μm. HEPA filters are used in laminar air flow cabinets (hoods) for sterile transfer work.

Heterokaryon. A cell possessing two or more genetically different nuclei in a common cytoplasm, usually derived as a result of cell-to-cell fusion.

Heteroploid. The term given to a cell culture when the cells comprising the culture possess nuclei containing chromosome numbers other than the diploid number. Thus, a heteroploid culture would be one which contains aneuploid cells.

Homokaryon. A cell possessing two or more genetically identical nuclei in a common cytoplasm, derived as a result of cell-to-cell fusion.

Hybrid cell. The term used to describe the mononucleate cell which results from the fusion of two different cells, leading to a formation of a synkaryon.

Hybridoma. The cell which results from the fusion of an antibody producing tumour cell (myeloma) and an antigenically-stimulated normal plasma cell. Such cells are constructed because they produce a single antibody directed against the antigen epitope which stimulated the plasma cell. This antibody is referred to as a monoclonal antibody.

Indirect embryogenesis. Embryo formation on callus tissues derived from zygotic or somatic embryos, seedling plant or other tissues in culture.

Indirect organogenesis. Organ formation on callus tissues derived from explants.

Induction. Initiation of a structure, organ or process *in vitro.*

Inoculate. Deliberately introduce something into. The process is inoculation. Not the same as *contamination.* In bacteriology, tissue culture, etc., placing inoculum into (or onto) medium to initiate a culture.

Inoculation cabinet. Small room or cabinet for inoculation (of tissue or micro-organism cultures) operations, often with a current of sterile air to carry contaminants away from the work area.

Inoculum. A small piece of tissue cut from callus, or an explant from a tissue or organ, or a small amount of cell material from a suspension culture, transferred into fresh medium for continued growth of the culture.

***In situ* (Latin for "in place").** Meaning in the natural place or in the original place.

***In vitro* (Latin for "in glass").** Living in test tubes, outside the organism or in an artificial environment, typically in glass vessels in which cultured cells, tissues, organs or whole plants may reside.

***In vitro* propagation.** Propagation of plants in a controlled, artificial environment, using plastic or glass culture vessels, aseptic techniques and a defined growth medium.

***In vitro* transformation.** A heritable change, occurring in cells in culture, either intrinsically or from treatment with chemical carcinogens, oncogenic viruses, irradiation, transfection with oncogenes, etc. and leading to the acquisition of altered morphological, antigenic, neoplastic, proliferative or other properties.

***In vivo* (Latin for "in living").** The natural conditions in which organisms reside.

Juvenile. A phase in the sexual cycle of a plant characterized by differences in appearance from the adult and which lacks the ability to respond to flower-inducing stimuli,

Kanamycin. An antibiotic of the aminoglycoside family that poisons translation by binding to the ribosomes.

Karyoplast. A cell nucleus, obtained from the cell by enucleation, surrounded by a narrow rim of cytoplasm and a plasma membrane.

Kinetin. One of the cytokinins, a group of growth regulators that characteristically promote cell division in plants.

Liposome. A closed lipid vesicle surrounding an aqueous interior; may be used to encapsulate exogenous materials for ultimate delivery of these into cells by fusion with the cell.

Lux (symbol: lx). The unit of measurement for luminance (i.e., the amount of illumination) impinging upon a surface. 1 lx is the luminance impinging upon a surface of 1 m^2, each point of which is at a distance of 1 m away from a uniform point source of light of 1 cd (candela).

Lysis. The destruction or breakage of cells either by viruses or by chemical or physical treatment.

Macropropagation. Production of plant clones from growing parts.

Meristem. Undifferentiated but determined tissue, the cells of which are capable of active cell division and differentiation into specialized and permanent tissue such as shoots and roots.

Meristem culture. *In vitro* culture of a generally shiny, dome-like structure measuring less than 0.1 mm in length when excised, most often excised from the shoot apex.

Meristem tip. An explant comprising the meristem (meristematic dome) and usually one pair of leaf primordia. Also refers to explants originating from apical meristem tip or lateral or axillary meristem tip. Do not confuse the meristem tip with the term "shoot tip," which is much larger and usually has more immature leaves and stem tissue.

Micropropagation. Miniaturized *in vitro* multiplication and/or regeneration of plant material under aseptic and controlled environmental conditions on specially prepared media that contain substances necessary for growth; used for three general types of tissue: excised embryos (= embryo culture); shoot-tips (= meristem culture or mericloning); and pieces of tissue that range from bits of stems to roots.

Minitubers. Small tubers (5-15 mm in diameter) formed on shoot cultures or cuttings of tuber-forming crops, such as potato.

Morphogen. A substance that stimulates the development of form or structure in an organism.

Morphogenesis. (a) The evolution of a structure from an undifferentiated to a differentiated state. (b) The process of growth and development of differentiated structures.

Morphogenic response. The effect on the developmental history of a plant or its parts exposed to a given set of growth conditions or to a change in the environment.

Morphogenesis. (a) The evolution of a structure from an undifferentiated to a differentiated state. (b) The process of growth and development of differentiated structures.

Mutant. A phenotypic variant resulting from a changed or new gene.

Opine. The condensation product of an amino acid with either a keto-acid or a sugar, produced by the crown gall tissues. Opine synthesis is a unique characteristic of tumour cells.

Organ culture. The maintenance or growth of organ primordia or the whole or parts of an organ *in vitro* in a way that may allow differentiation and preservation of the architecture and/or function.

Organized. Arranged into definite structures.

Organogenesis. The evolution, from dissociated cells, of a structure which shows natural organ form or function or both.

Pathogen free. Free from specific organisms based on specific tests for the designated organisms.

Petri dish. Flat round dish with a matching lid, made of glass or plastic material, and used for culturing organisms.

pH. A measure of acidity and alkalinity. Equal to the log of the reciprocal of the hydrogen ion concentration of a solution, expressed in grams per litre. A reading of 7 is neutral (e.g., pure water), whereas below 7 is acid and above 7 is alkaline.

Phenols. Compounds with hydroxyl group(s) attached to the benzene ring, forming esters, ethers and salts.

Phytohormone. A substance that stimulates growth or other processes in plants. They include auxins, abscissic acid, cytokinins, gibberellins and ethylene.

Photoperiod. The length of day or period of daily illumination provided or required by plants for reaching the reproductive stage.

Photoperiodism. The response of an organism to changes in day length.

Phytochrome. A reversible pigment system of a protein nature, found in the cytoplasm of green plants.

Plaque. A clear spot on an otherwise opaque culture plate of bacteria or cultured bacteria cells, showing where cells have been lysed by viral infection.

Plating efficiency. The percentage of inoculated cells which give rise to cell colonies when seeded into culture vessels.

Polyethylene glycol (PEG). A polymer having the general formula: $HOCH_2(CH_2OCH_2)XCH_2OH$ and available in a range of molecular weights from *ca* 1000 to *ca* 6000. It is commonly used to promote cell or protoplast fusion, and to facilitate DNA uptake in the transformation of organisms such as yeast.

Polyvinylpyrrolidone (PVP). An occasional constituent of plant tissue culture isolation media. PVP is of variable molecular weight and has antioxidant properties, so is used to prevent oxidative browning of explanted tissues.

Precocious germination. Premature germination of the embryo, prior to completion of embryogenesis.

Plant tissue culture. The growth or maintenance of plant cells, tissues, organs or whole plants *in vitro.*

Population density. The number of cells per unit area or volume of a culture vessel. Also the number of cells per unit volume of medium in a suspension culture.

Protoplast. A cell from which the entire cell wall has been removed. This term is used to describe such plant, bacterial or fungal cells.

Protoplast fusion. Technique in which protoplasts are fused into a single cell.

Primary culture. A culture started from cells, tissues or organs taken directly from organisms. A primary culture may be regarded as such until it is sub-cultured for the first time. It then becomes a cell line.

Primary meristem. Meristem of the shoot or root tip giving rise to the primary plant body.

Primary tissue. A tissue that has differentiated from a primary meristem.

Primordium. A group of cells which gives rise to an organ.

Pro-embryo. A group of cells arising from the division of the fertilized egg cell or somatic embryo before those cells which are to become the embryo are recognizable.

Protoclone. Regenerated plant derived from protoplast culture or a single colony derived from protoplasts in culture.

Protocol. The step-by-step experiments proposed to describe or solve a scientific problem, or the defined steps of a specific procedure.

Protoderm. A primary meristem tissue that gives rise to epidermis.

Protoplast culture. The isolation and culture of plant protoplasts by mechanical means or by enzymatic digestion of plant tissues or organs, or cultures derived from these.

Protoplast fusion. The coalescence of the plasmalemma and cytoplasm of two or more protoplasts in contact with one another.

Prototroph. An organism such as a bacterium that will grow on a minimal medium.

Quiescent. Quiet, at rest, but not necessarily dormant, and having the potential for resumed activity; can apply to non-meristematic cells.

Recalcitrant. Of seeds: unable to survive drying and subsequent storage at low temperature.

Reculture. The process by which a cell monolayer or a plant explant is transferred, without subdivision, into fresh medium.

Regeneration. In plant cultures, a morphogenetic response to a stimulus that results in the production of organs, embryos or whole plants.

Shoot apical meristem. Undifferentiated tissue, located within the shoot tip, generally appearing as a shiny dome-like structure distal to the youngest leaf primordium and measuring less than 0.1 mm in length when excised.

Shoot differentiation. The development of growing points, leaf primordia and finally shoots from a shoot tip, axial bud, or even a callus surface.

Shoot tip (apex) culture. A structure consisting of the shoot apical meristem plus one to several primordial leaves, usually measuring from 0.1-1.0 mm in length; in instances where more mature leaves are included, the structure can measure up to several centimeters in length.

Somaclonal variation. Phenotypic variation, either genetic or epigenetic in origin, displayed among somaclones.

Somaclone. Plants derived from any form of cell culture involving the use of somatic plant cells.

Somatic cell hybrid. The cell or plant resulting from the fusion of animal cells or plant protoplasts, respectively, derived from somatic cells which differ genetically.

Somatic cell genetics. The study of genetic phenomena of somatic cells. The cells under study are most often cells grown in culture.

Somatic cell hybridization. The *in vitro* fusion of animal cells or plant protoplasts derived from somatic cells which differ genetically.

Somatic embryo. An organized embryonic structure morphologically similar to a zygotic embryo but initiated from somatic (non-zygotic) cells.

Somatic embryogenesis. In plant culture, the process of embryo initiation and development from vegetative or nongametic cells.

Stage I. A step in *in vitro* propagation characterized by the establishment of an aseptic tissue culture of a plant.

Stage II. A step in *in vitro* plant propagation characterized by the rapid numerical increase of organs and other structures.

Stage III. A step in *in vitro* plant propagation characterized by preparation of propagules for successful transfer to soil, a process involving rooting of shoot cuttings, hardening of plants and initiating the change from the heterotrophic to the autotrophic state.

Stage IV. A step in *in vitro* plant propagation characterized by the establishment in soil of a tissue culture derived plant, either after undergoing a Stage III pre-transplant treatment or, in certain species, after the direct transfer of plants from Stage II into soil.

Sterile. Without Life.

Sterile room. Operation room for performing inoculations under aseptic conditions; usually now replaced by use of laminar air-flow cabinets, in which filtered air is blown from the inside to the outside.

Subculture. With plant cultures, this is the process by which the tissue or explant is first subdivided, then transferred into fresh culture medium.

Substrain. A substrain can be derived from a strain by isolation of a single cell or groups of cells having properties or markers not shared by all cells of the parent strain.

Suspension culture. A type of culture in which cells, or aggregates of cells, multiply while suspended in liquid medium.

Synchronous culture. A culture in which the majority of the cells are dividing at the same time or are at a specific phase of the cell cycle.

Synkaryon. A hybrid cell which results from the fusion of the nuclei it carries.

Tissue culture. The maintenance or growth of tissues, *in vitro*, in a way that may allow differentiation and preservation of their architecture and/or function.

Totipotent cell; totipotent nucleus. An undifferentiated cell (or nucleus), such as a blastomere, that, when isolated or suitably transplanted, can develop into a complete embryo.

Totipotency. A cell characteristic in which the potential for forming all the cell types in the adult organism is retained.

Transfection. The transfer, for the purpose of genomic integration, of naked, foreign DNA into cells in culture.

Transformation. In plant cell culture, the introduction and stable genomic integration of foreign DNA into a plant cell by any means, resulting in a genetic modification.

Type I callus. A type of adventive embryogenesis found with gramineous monocots, which has been induced on an explant where the somatic embryos are arrested at the coleptilar or scutellar stage of embryogeny. The embryos are often fused together especially at the coleorhizal end of the embryo axis. This tissue can be subcultured and maintains this morphology.

Type II callus. A type of adventive embryogenesis found with gramineous monocots, which has been induced on an explant where the somatic embryos are arrested at the globular stage of embryogeny. The globular embryos often arise individually from a common base. The tissue can be subcultured and maintains this morphology.

Undifferentiated. With plant cells, existing in a state of cell development characterized by isodiametric cell shape, very little or no vacuole, and a large nucleus, and exemplified by cells comprising an apical meristem or embryo. With animal cells, this is the state wherein the cell in culture lacks the specialized structure and/or function of the cell type *in vivo*.

Unorganized growth. *In vitro* formation of tissues with few differentiated cell types and no recognizable structure.

Variant. A culture exhibiting a stable phenotypic change, whether genetic or epigenetic in origin.

Vegetative propagation. Reproduction of plants using a nonsexual process involving the culture of plant parts such as stem and leaf cuttings.

Vermiculite. Coarse aggregate material made from expanded mica having a high cation exchange capacity and high water-holding capacity and used as a rooting medium and a soil additive.

Virus-free. Free from specified viruses based on tests designed to detect the presence of the organisms in question.

Appendix 3

Glossary of Biotechnology

Adaptor. A synthetic double-stranded oligonucleotide that has a blunt end, while the other end has a nucleotide extension that can base pair with a cohesive end created by cleavage of a DNA molecule with a specific type II restriction endonuclease.

Aerobe. A micro-organism that grows in the presence of oxygen.

Aflatoxin. Toxic compounds, produced by moulds (fungi) of the *Aspergillus flavus* group, that bind to DNA and prevent replication and transcription.

Agarose gel electrophoresis. A process in which a matrix composed of a highly purified form of agar is used to separate larger DNA and RNA molecules.

Agrobacterium. A genus of bacteria that includes several plant pathogenic species, causing tumour-like symptoms.

Agrobacterium tumefaciens. A bacterium that causes crown gall disease in some plants.

AIDS (acquired immunodeficiency syndrome). The usually fatal human disease in which the immune system is destroyed by a retrovirus (Human Immunodeficiency Virus, HIV).

Alternative mRNA splicing. The inclusion or exclusion of different exons to form different mRNA transcripts.

Alu sequences. A family of 300-bp sequences occurring nearly a million times in the human genome.

Aminoacyl site; A-site. One of two sites on ribosomes to which the incoming aminoacyl tRNA binds.

Aminoacyl tRNA synthetase. Enzyme that attaches each amino acid to its specific tRNA molecule.

Amplified fragment length polymorphism (AFLP). A type of DNA marker, generated by digestion of genomic DNA with two restriction enzymes to create many DNA fragments, ligation of specific sequences of DNA (called adaptors) to the ends of these fragments, amplification of the fragments via PCR (using a set of primers with sequences corresponding to the adapters, plus various random combinations of three additional bases at the end), and visualization of fragments via gel electrophoresis.

Amplify. To increase the number of copies of a DNA sequence, either *in vivo* by inserting into a cloning vector that replicates within a host cell, or *in vitro* by polymerase chain reaction (PCR).

Anneal. The pairing of complementary DNA or RNA sequences, via hydrogen bonding, to form a double-stranded polynucleotide.

Annealing. The process of heating (de-naturing step) and slowly cooling (re-naturing step) double-stranded DNA to allow the formation of hybrid DNA or complementary strands of DNA or of DNA and RNA.

Antibody. An immunological protein (called an immunoglobulin, Ig) produced by certain white blood cells (lymphocytes) of the immune system of an organism in response to a contact with a foreign substance (antigen).

Antibody class. The class to which an antibody belongs, depending on the type of heavy chain present. In mammals, there are five classes of antibodies: iga, igd, ige, igg, and igm.

Antibody structure. Antibodies have a well-defined structure. Each antibody has two identical "light" chains and two identical "heavy" chains. Each chain comprises a constant region, i.e., a region that is the same between antibodies of the same class and sub-class, and a variable region that differs between.

Antigen. A compound that elicits an immune response by stimulating the production of antibodies.

Antigenic determinant. A surface feature of a micro-organism or macromolecule, such as a glycoprotein, that elicits an immune response.

Antiserum. The fluid portion of the blood of an animal (after coagulation of the blood), containing antibodies.

Arabidopsis. A genus of flowering plants in the Cruciferae. *A. thaliana* is used in research as a model plant because it has a small genome (5 pairs of chromosomes; 2n = 10) and can be cultured easily, with a generation time of two months.

Attenuated vaccine. A virulent organism that has been modified to produce a less virulent form, but nevertheless retains the ability to elicit antibodies against the virulent form.

Attenuation. A mechanism for controlling gene expression in prokaryotes that involves premature termination of transcription.

Attenuator. A nucleotide sequence in the 5′ region of a prokaryotic gene (or in its RNA) that causes premature termination of transcription, possibly by forming a secondary structure.

Autonomous. A term applied to any biological unit that can function on its own, i.e., without the help of another unit, such as a transposable element that encodes an enzyme for its own transposition.

Autoradiograph. A picture prepared by labeling a substance such as DNA with a radioactive material such as tritiated thymidine and allowing the image produced by decay radiation to develop on a film over a period of time.

Autoradiography. A technique that captures the image formed in a photographic emulsion as a result of the emission of either light or radioactivity from a labeled component that is placed next to unexposed film.

BAC (bacterial artificial chromosome). A cloning vector constructed from bacterial fertility (F) factors; like YAC vectors, they accept large inserts of size 200 to 500 kb.

Bacillus. A rod-shaped bacterium.

***Bacillus thuringiensis* (Bt).** A bacterium that kills insects; a major component of the microbial pesticide industry.

Bacterial toxin. A toxin produced by a bacterium, such as Bt toxin by *Bacillus thuringiensis*.

Bacteriophage. A virus that infects bacteria. Also called phage.

Binary vector system. A two-plasmid system in *Agrobacterium tumefaciens* for transferring into plant cells a segment of T-DNA that carries cloned genes. One plasmid contains the virulence gene (responsible for transfer of the T-DNA), and another plasmid contains the T-DNA borders, the selectable marker and the DNA to be transferred.

Biocontrol. The control of living organisms (especially pests) by biological means.

Bioconversion. Conversion of one chemical into another by living organisms, as opposed to their conversion by enzymes (which is biotransformation) or by chemical processes.

Biodegradation. The breakdown by living organisms of a compound to its chemical constituents.

Bio-enrichment. Adding nutrients or oxygen to increase microbial breakdown of pollutants.

Biofuel. A gaseous, liquid or solid fuel that contains energy derived from a biological source. For example, rapeseed oil can be used in place of diesel fuel in modified engines.

Biogas. A mixture of methane and carbon dioxide resulting from the anaerobic decomposition of waste such as domestic, industrial and agricultural sewage.

Bioinformatics. The use and organization of information of biological interest. In particular, it is concerned with organizing bio-molecular databases, in getting useful information out of such databases, in utilizing powerful computers for analysing such information, and in integrating information from disparate biological sources.

Biolistics. A technique to insert DNA into cells. The DNA is mixed with small metal particles, usually tungsten or gold. These are then fired into a cell at very high speed. They puncture the cell and carry the DNA into the cell. Also known as Microprojectile bombardment.

Biopesticide. A compound that kills organisms by virtue of specific biological effects rather than as a broader chemical poison. Specific types include bio-insecticides and bio-fungicides. Bio-pesticides differ from biocontrol agents in that bio-pesticides are passive agents, whereas biocontrol agents are active, seeking out the pest to be destroyed. There are some extremely attractive anti-pest materials, such as *Bacillus thuringiensis* (Bt) toxin, which specifically interferes with the absorption of food from the guts of some insects but is harmless to mammals.

Biotechnology. The use of biological processes or organisms for the production of materials and services of benefit to humankind. Biotechnology includes the use of techniques for the improvement of the characteristics of economically important plants and animals and for the development of micro-organisms to act on the environment.

B lymphocytes; B cells. An important class of lymphocytes that mature in bone marrow (in mammals), that are largely responsible for the antibody-mediated or humoral immune response; they give rise to the antibody-producing plasma cells and some other cells of the immune system.

Blunt end. The end of a DNA duplex molecule in which neither strand extends beyond the other. Also known as Flush end.

Broad-host-range plasmid. A plasmid that can replicate in a number of different bacterial species.

Bud sport. A somatic mutation arising in a bud and producing a genetically different shoot. Bud sport includes changes due to gene mutation, somatic reduction, chromosome deletion or polyploidy.

Buffer. A solution that resists change in pH when an acid or alkali is added, or when solutions are diluted.

Buoyant density. The intrinsic density which a molecule, virus or sub-cellular particle has when suspended in an aqueous solution of a salt, such as caesium chloride, or a sugar, such as sucrose. DNA from different species has a characteristic buoyant density, which reflects the proportion of G=C base pairs. The greater the proportion of G=C, the greater the buoyant density of the DNA.

CAAT box (also CAT box). A conserved sequence found within the promoter region of the protein-encoding genes of many eukaryotic organisms. It has the consensus sequence GGCCAATCT; it occurs around 75 bases prior to the transcription initiation site; and it is one of several sites for recognition and binding of regulatory proteins called transcription factors.

Capsid. The protein coat of a virus. The capsid often determines the shape of the virus.

Carcinoma. A malignant tumour derived from epithelial tissue, which forms the skin and the outer cell layers of internal organs.

Catalyst. A substance that promotes a chemical reaction by lowering the activation energy of a chemical reaction, without itself undergoing any permanent chemical change. The process is catalysis.

cDNA; complementary DNA. The double-stranded DNA complement of an mRNA sequence; synthesized *in vitro* from a mature RNA template using reverse transcriptase (to create a single strand of DNA from the RNA template) and DNA polymerase (to create the double-stranded DNA).

cDNA clone. A double-stranded DNA molecule that is carried in a vector and was synthesized *in vitro* from an mRNA sequence by using reverse transcriptase and DNA polymerase.

cDNA library. A collection of cDNA clones that were generated *in vitro* from the mRNA sequences isolated from an organism or a specific tissue or cell type or population of an organism.

Chimeric DNA. A recombinant DNA molecule containing unrelated genes.

Chimeric gene. A semi-synthetic gene, consisting of the coding sequence from one organism, fused to promoter and other sequences derived from a different gene.

Chromatography. A method for separating and identifying the components of mixtures of molecules having similar chemical and physical properties.

Chromosome jumping. A technique that allows two segments of duplex DNA that are separated by thousands of base pairs (about 200 kb) to be cloned together.

Chromosome walking. A technique that identifies overlapping cloned DNA fragments that form one continuous segment of a chromosome.

Cloning vector. A small, self-replicating DNA molecule - usually a plasmid or viral DNA chromosome - into which foreign DNA is inserted in the process of cloning genes or other DNA sequences of interest. It can carry inserted DNA and be perpetuated in a host cell. Also called a cloning vehicle, vector, or vehicle.

Co-integrate vector system. A two-plasmid system for transferring cloned genes to plant cells. The cloning vector has a T-DNA segment that contains cloned genes. After introduction into *Agrobacterium tumifaciens*, the cloning vector DNA undergoes homologous recombination with a resident disarmed Ti plasmid to form a single plasmid carrying the genetic information for transferring the genetically engineered T-DNA region to plant cells.

Co-integrate. A DNA molecule formed by the fusion of two different DNA molecules, usually mediated by a transposable element.

Competence. Ability of a bacterial cell to take up DNA molecules and become genetically transformed.

Copy number. The average number of molecules of a plasmid or gene per genome contained in a cell.

Cosmid. A plasmid vector which contains the two cos (cohesive) ends of phage lambda and one or more selectable markers such as an antibiotic resistance gene.

Curing. The elimination of a plasmid from its host cell. Many agents which interfere with DNA replication, e.g., ethidium bromide, can cure plasmids from either bacterial or eukaryotic cells.

Cut. To make a double-stranded break in DNA, usually with a type II restriction endonuclease.

Density gradient centrifugation. High-speed centrifugation in which molecules "float" at a point where their density equals that in a gradient of caesium chloride or sucrose.

Differential centrifugation. A method of separating sub-cellular particles according to their sedimentation coefficients, which are roughly proportional to their size.

Differentially permeable. Referring to a membrane, through which different substances diffuse at different rates; some substances may be unable to diffuse through such a membrane.

Disarm. To delete from a plasmid or virus genes that are cytotoxic or tumour inducing.

DNA construct. A DNA molecule inserted into a cloning vector, usually a plasmid.

DNA diagnosis. The use of DNA polymorphisms to detect the presence of a specific allele (often associated with a disease or syndrome) or DNA sequence.

DNA fingerprint. The unique pattern of DNA fragments identified originally by Southern hybridization (using a probe that binds to a polymorphic region of DNA) or now by polymerase chain reaction (PCR) (using primers flanking the polymorphic region).

DNA micro-array. A small glass surface to which has been fixed an array of DNA fragments, each with a defined location. A typical DNA chip would contain 10,000 discrete spots (each containing a different DNA fragment) in an area of just a few square centimetres. When a solution of fluorescently labelled DNA fragments is hybridized to the chip, spots to which hybridization occurs are visible as fluorescence. If the spots on the chip are genes, hybridization with cDNA from a particular tissue shows which genes are expressed in that tissue.

DNA probe. A labelled (tagged) segment of DNA that is able, after a DNA hybridization reaction, to detect a specific DNA sequence in a mixture of sequences. If the tagged sequence is complementary to any one in the mixture, the two sequences will form a double helix.

DNA sequencing. Procedures for determining the nucleotide sequence of a DNA fragment. There are two common methods for doing this. The Maxam and Gilbert technique (chemical degradation), that uses different chemicals to break the DNA into fragments at specific bases; or the Sanger technique (called the dideoxy or chain-terminating method) uses DNA polymerase to make new DNA chains, with dideoxy nucleotides (chain terminators) to stop the chain randomly as it grows. In both cases, the DNA fragments are separated according to length by polyacrylamide gel electrophoresis, enabling the sequence to be read directly from the gel.

Dolly. The name of the first mammal to be created by cloning a cell from an adult animal. In this particular case, the cell came from the mammary tissue of an adult ewe.

Dominant selectable marker gene. A gene that allows the host cell to survive under conditions where it would otherwise die.

Electro-blotting. The electrophoretic transfer of macromolecules (DNA, RNA or protein) from a gel, in which they have been separated, to a support matrix, such as a nitrocellulose sheet. A transfer usually used in techniques such as Southern and Northern blotting.

Electrophoresis. A technique that separates charged molecules such as DNA, RNA or protein, on the basis of relative migration in an appropriate matrix (such as agarose gel or polyacrylamide gel) subjected to an electric field.

Electroporation. An electrical treatment of cells that induces transient pores, through which DNA can enter the cell.

ELISA (enzyme-linked immunosorbent assay). A sensitive technique for accurately determining specific molecules in a mixed sample. The amount of protein or other antigen in a given sample is determined by means of an enzyme-catalysed colour change, avoiding both the hazards and expense of radioactive techniques.

Elongation factors. Soluble proteins that are required for polypeptide chain elongation.

Empirical. Relating to or based upon practical experience, trial and error, direct observation or observation alone, without benefit of scientific method, knowledge or theory.

Encapsulation. Any method of getting something, usually an enzyme or bacterium, into a small package or capsule while it is still working or alive. It is a method for immobilizing cells for use in a bioreactor.

Encapsulating agents. Anything which forms a shell around an enzyme or bacterium, although the agents used are usually polysaccharides such as alginate or agar.

Episome. A genetic extrachromosomal element (e.g., the fertility factor (F) in *Escherichia coli*) which replicates within a cell independently of the chromosome and is able to integrate into the host chromosome.

Epitope. A specific chemical domain on an antigen that stimulates the production of, and is recognized by, an antibody.

Ethylenediamine tetraacetic acid (EDTA). A chelating compound. In tissue culture it is used to keep nutrients, such as iron, bound in a form that leaves them still available to the plant but which prevents them from precipitating out.

Exogenous DNA. DNA that has been derived from a source organism and has been cloned into a vector and introduced into a host cell. Also referred to as foreign DNA or heterologous DNA.

Expression vector. A cloning vector that has been constructed in such a way that, after insertion of a DNA molecule, its coding sequence is properly transcribed and the RNA is translated.

F factor. A bacterial episome that confers the ability to function as a genetic donor in conjugation; the fertility factor in bacteria.

False-negative. A negative assay result that should have been positive.

False-positive. A positive assay result that should have been negative.

Feedback inhibition. The process by which the accumulated end product of a biochemical pathway stops synthesis of that product.

Fermentation. The anaerobic breakdown by micro-organisms of complex organic substances, especially carbohydrates like glucose. The process is energy-yielding.

F factor. A bacterial episome that confers the ability to function as a genetic donor in conjugation; the fertility factor in bacteria.

Flanking region. The DNA sequences extending either side of a specific sequence.

Fluorescence *in situ* hybridization (FISH). Hybridization of cloned DNA to intact chromosomes, where the cloned DNA has been labelled with a fluorescent dye.

Fluorescence-activated cell sorting (FACS). The use of laser beams to detect differences in fluorescence between different types of cells in a mixture, and the subsequent deflection of cells into separate bins corresponding to each type of cell in the mixture.

Flow cytometry. A technique used to sort cells or other biological materials by means of flow through apertures of defined size or by laser sorting.

Foreign DNA. A DNA molecule that is incorporated into either a cloning vector or a chromosomal site.

Four-base cutter. A type II restriction endonuclease that binds (and subsequently cleaves) DNA at sites that contain a sequence of four nucleotide pairs that is uniquely recognised by that enzyme.

Fusion gene. A hybrid gene created by joining portions of two different genes (to produce a new protein) or by joining a gene to a different promoter (to alter or regulate gene transcription).

GC island. A segment of DNA that is rich in G=C base pairs and often precedes a transcribed gene in the genomes of vertebrate organisms.

Gel. A lyophilic colloid that has coagulated to a rigid or jelly-like solid. It is used for the electrophoretic separation of nucleic acids or proteins, and for encapsulation.

Gel electrophoresis. An analytical method for separating molecules according to their size. Samples are put at one end of a slab of polymer gel; an electric field across the gel pulls the molecules through it; the smaller molecules pass more easily and so move towards the other end faster; the various sizes of molecules end up at different positions according their size.

Gene cloning. The process of synthesizing multiple copies of a particular DNA sequence using a bacteria cell or another organism as a host. The gene of interest is inserted into a self-replicating DNA molecule (DNA vector, often a plasmid) and the resulting recombinant DNA molecule is amplified in an appropriate host cell. Used in genetic engineering.

Gene insertion. The incorporation of one or more copies of a gene into a chromosome.

Gene library. Collection of cloned DNA fragments that ideally includes all the genetic information of an organism. If the original source of the DNA is the genomic DNA from an organism, then it is called a genomic library; if the DNA is from cDNA made by enzymatic copying of RNA, then the library includes representative fragments from all genes that were being expressed at the time the RNA was sampled, and would be called a cDNA library.

Gene probe. A single-stranded DNA or RNA fragment used in genetic engineering to search for a particular gene or other DNA sequence. The probe has a base sequence complementary to the target sequence and will thus attach to it by base pairing. By labelling the probe, it can be identified after subsequent separation and purification.

Gene splicing. A stage in the processing of mRNA, occurring only in eukaryote cells, in which intervening sequences (introns) are removed from the primary RNA transcript (hnRNA), and the coding exons are joined together to form the mature mRNA molecule.

Gene therapy. The treatment of inherited diseases by introducing into the cells of affected individuals the wild-type copies of the defective gene causing the disorder. If reproductive cells are modified, the procedure is called germ-line or heritable gene therapy. If cells other than reproductive cells are modified, the procedure is called somatic-cell or non-inheritable gene therapy.

Genetically engineered organism (GEO). Sometimes used for genetically modified organism.

Genetically modified organism (GMO). An organism that has been modified by the application of recombinant DNA technology.

Genetic engineering. Changes in the genetic constitution of cells (apart from selective breeding) resulting from the introduction or elimination of specific genes through modern molecular biology techniques. This technology is based on the use of a vector for transferring useful genetic information from a donor organism into a cell or organism that does not possess it.

Genetic fingerprinting. A technique in which an individual's DNA is analysed to reveal the pattern of repetition of particular nucleotide sequences throughout the genome.

Genetic transformation. The transfer of extra-cellular DNA among and between species by using bacterial or viral vectors.

Genomic DNA library; genomic library. A collection of clones containing the genomic DNA sequences of an organism. Typically, these molecules are propagated in bacteria or phage.

GM food. Food that comprises, in whole or in part, material that has been modified by the application of recombinant DNA technology.

HIV. Human immunodeficiency virus. The retrovirus that causes AIDS in humans.

Hybridoma. A hybrid cell, derived from a B (antibody producing) lymphocyte fused to a tumour cell, which grows indefinitely in tissue culture and is selected for the secretion of the specific antibody produced by that B cell.

Immobilized cells. Cells entrapped in matrices such as alginate, polyacrylamide and agarose designed for use in membrane and filter bioreactors.

Immune response. The processes, including the synthesis of antibodies, that are used by vertebrates to respond to the presence of a foreign antigen.

Immunity. The state of relative insusceptibility of an animal or plant to infection by disease-producing organisms or to the harmful effects of their poisons.

Immunization. The production of immunity in an individual by artificial means. Active immunization involves the introduction, either orally or by infection, of specially treated bacteria, viruses or their toxins so as to stimulate the production of antibodies.

Inactivated agent. A virus, bacterium or other organism that has been treated to prevent it from causing a disease.

Insert. A DNA molecule that is incorporated into a cloning vector.

Insertion element. Generic term for DNA sequences found in bacteria capable of genome insertion.

Insertion site; cloning site. A unique restriction site in a vector DNA molecule into which foreign DNA can be inserted.

Integrating vector. A vector that is designed to integrate cloned DNA into the host cell chromosomal DNA.

Integration. The recombination process which inserts a small DNA molecule (usually by homologous recombination) into a larger one. If the molecules are circular, integration involves only a single crossing-over; if linear, then two crossings-over are required.

Interferon. A family of small proteins that stimulate viral resistance in cells.

IS element (insertion sequence). A short (800-1400 nucleotide pairs) DNA sequence found in bacteria that is capable of transposing to a new genomic location.

Live vaccine. A living, non-virulent form of a micro-organism or virus that is used to elicit an antibody response that will protect the inoculated organism against infection by a virulent form of the micro-organism or virus. Also a living, non-virulent micro-organism or virus that expresses a foreign antigenic protein and is used to inoculate humans or animals. The latter organisms are also called a live recombinant vaccines.

Long template. A DNA strand that is synthesized during the polymerase chain reaction and has a primer sequence at one end but is extended beyond the site that is complementary to the second primer at the other end.

M 13. A single-stranded DNA bacteriophage used as a vector for DNA sequencing.

Marker. An identifiable DNA sequence that facilitates the study of inheritance of a trait or a gene. Such markers are used in mapping the order of genes along chromosomes and in following the inheritance of particular genes: genes closely linked to the marker will generally be inherited with it.

Marker-assisted selection (MAS). The use of DNA markers to increase the response to selection in a population. The markers will be closely linked to one or more quantitative trait loci.

Marker gene. A gene of known function and known location on the chromosome.

Microprojectile bombardment. A procedure for modifying cells by shooting DNA-coated metal (tungsten or gold) particles into them.

Microsatellite. A form of VNTR. Specifically, a segment of DNA characterized by the occurrence of a variable number of copies (from a few up to 30 or so) of a sequence of around 5 or fewer bases (called a repeat unit).

Mini-prep. A small-scale (mini-) preparation of plasmid or phage DNA. Used to analyse DNA in a cloning vector after a cloning experiment.

Minisatellite. A form of VNTR in which the repeat units typically range from 10 to 100 bases. They are usually detected by Southern hybridization, using a probe comprising a clone of the repeat unit.

Molecular cloning. The biological amplification of a specific DNA sequence through mitotic division of a host cell into which it has been transformed or transfected.

Molecular genetics. The area of knowledge concerned with the genetic aspects of molecular biology, especially with DNA, RNA and protein molecules.

Monoclonal antibody (mab). A single type of antibody that is directed against a specific epitope (antigen, antigenic determinant) and is produced by a single clone of B cells or a single hybridoma cell line, which is formed by the fusion of a lymphocyte cell with a myeloma cell.

Multi-copy. Describing plasmids which replicate to produce many plasmid molecules per host genome, e.g., pBR322 is a multi-copy plasmid, there are usually 50 pBR322 molecules (or copies) per *E. coli* genome.

Northern blot. A cellulose or nylon membrane to which RNA molecules have been attached by capillary action. The transferred RNA is hybridized to single-stranded DNA probes. Northern blot technique is often used to measure expression (transcription) of a gene for which a specific cDNA is available for use as a probe.

Northern blotting. Similar to Southern blotting, except that RNA is transferred onto a matrix and the presence of a specific RNA molecule is detected by DNA-RNA hybridization.

Northern hybridization. Hybridization of a labelled DNA probe to RNA fragments that have been transferred from an agarose gel to a nitrocellulose filter.

Open reading frame (ORF). A sequence of nucleotides in a DNA molecule that has the potential to encode a peptide or protein: it starts with a start triplet (ATG), is followed by a string of triplets each of which encodes an amino acid, and ends with a stop triplet (TAA, TAG or TGA).

Palindrome. Originally a word, sentence or verse that reads the same from right to left as it does from left to right. In biotechnology, the term is applied to a segment of DNA in which the base-pair sequence reads the same in both directions from a central point of symmetry.

Palindromic sequence. A segment of duplex DNA whose 5′-to-3′ sequence is identical on each DNA strand. The sequence is the same when one strand is read left-to-right and the other strand is read right-to-left.

Partial digest. Addition of a restriction enzyme to a DNA sample under particular conditions or for a limited period, such that only a proportion of the target sites in any individual molecule are cleaved.

pBR322. One of the first plasmid vectors widely used; especially used for cloning DNA in *E. coli*.

Phagemids. Cloning vectors that contain components derived from both phage chromosomes and plasmids.

Physical map. A map showing physical locations on a DNA sequence, such as restriction sites and sequence-tagged sites. Also a diagram of a chromosome or a karyotype, showing the location of loci (genes and markers).

Polyacrylamide gel electrophoresis (PAGE). A method for separating nucleic acid or protein molecules according to their molecular size. The molecules migrate through the inert gel matrix under the influence of an electric field. In the case of protein PAGE, detergents such as sodium dodecyl sulphate (SDS) are often added to ensure that all molecules have a uniform charge.

Polyadenylation. Post-transcriptional addition of a polyadenylic acid tail to the 3′ end of eukaryotic mRNAs. Also called poly-(A) tailing. The adenine-rich 3′ terminal segment is called a poly (A) tail.

Polyclonal antibody. A serum sample that contains a mixture of immunoglobulin molecules secreted against a specific antigen, each recognizing a different epitope, some antibodies of which bind to different antigenic determinants of one antigen.

Polymerase chain reaction (PCR). A procedure that amplifies a particular DNA sequence. It involves multiple cycles of *denaturation*, *annealing* to oligonucleotide primers, and *extension* (polynucleotide synthesis), using a thermostable DNA polymerase, deoxyribonucleotides, and primer sequences in multiple cycles of denaturation-renaturation-DNA synthesis.

Polymerase. An enzyme that catalyses the formation of polymeric molecules from monomers. A DNA polymerase synthesizes DNA from deoxynucleoside triphosphates using a complementary DNA strand and a primer. An RNA polymerase synthesizes RNA from monoribonucleoside triphosphates and a complementary DNA strand.

Polymerization. Chemical union of two or more molecules of the same kind such as glucose or nucleotides to form a new compound (starch or nucleic acid) having the same elements in the same proportions but a higher molecular weight and different physical properties.

Primer. A short DNA or RNA fragment annealed to a template of single-stranded DNA, providing a 3′ hydroxyl end from which DNA polymerase extends a new DNA strand to produce a duplex molecule.

Primer DNA polymerase. DNA polymerase that provides primers for the DNA polymerization. Unlike RNA polymerase, DNA polymerase is unable to initiate the *de novo* synthesis of a polynucleotide chain. DNA polymerase can only add nucleotides to a free 3′ hydroxyl group at the end of a pre-existing chain. A short oligonucleotide, known as a primer, is therefore needed to supply such a hydroxyl group for the initiation of DNA synthesis.

Primer walking. A method for sequencing long (>1 kb) cloned pieces of DNA. The initial sequencing reaction reveals the sequence of the first few hundred nucleotides of the cloned DNA. On the basis of these data, a primer containing about 20 nucleotides and complementary to a sequence near the end of sequenced DNA is synthesized, and is then used for sequencing the next few hundred nucleotides of the cloned DNA. This procedure is repeated until the complete nucleotide sequence of the cloned DNA is determined.

Probe. For diagnostic tests, the agent that is used to detect the presence of a molecule in a sample or a DNA or RNA sequence labelled or marked with a radioactive isotope or that is used to detect the presence of a complementary sequence by hybridization with a nucleic acid sample.

Probe DNA. A labelled DNA molecule used to detect complementary-sequence nucleic acid molecules by molecular hybridization.

Protein sequencing. The process of determining the amino-acid sequence of a protein or its component polypeptides.

Quantitative trait locus (QTL). A locus that affects a quantitative trait. The plural form (quantitative trait loci) is also abbreviated as QTL.

Random amplified polymorphic DNA (RAPD; pronounced 'rapid'). A technique using single, short (usually 10-mer) synthetic oligonucleotide primers for PCR. The primer, whose sequence has been chosen at random, initiates replication at its complementary sites on the DNA, producing fragments up to about 2 kb long, which can be separated by electrophoresis and stained with ethidium bromide. A primer can exhibit polymorphism between individuals, and polymorphic fragments can be used as markers.

Recombinant DNA. The result of combining DNA fragments from different sources.

Recombinant DNA technology. A set of techniques which enable one to manipulate DNA. One of the main techniques is DNA cloning.

Recombinant protein. A protein whose amino acid sequence is encoded by a cloned gene.

Recombinant RNA. A term used to describe RNA molecules joined *in vitro* by T4 RNA ligase.

Recombinant toxin. A single multifunctional toxic protein that has been created by combining the coding regions of various genes.

Recombinant vaccine. A vaccine produced from a cloned gene.

Relaxed plasmid. A plasmid that replicates independently of the main bacterial chromosome and is present in 10-500 copies per cell.

Re-naturation. The re-association of two nucleic acid strands after denaturation.

Repeat unit. A sequence of bases that occurs repeatedly in the genome, often end-on-end, i.e., tandemly.

Repetitive DNA. DNA sequences that are present in a genome in multiple copies, sometimes a million times or more.

Replica plating. A procedure for duplicating the bacterial colonies growing on agar medium in one Petri plate to agar medium in another Petri plate.

Replicative form (RF). The molecular configuration of viral nucleic acid that is the template for replication in the host cell.

Restriction endonuclease. A class of endonucleases that cleaves DNA after recognizing a specific sequence. There are three types of restriction endonuclease enzymes: Type I: Cuts non-specifically a distance greater than 1000 bp from its recognition sequence and contains both restriction and methylation activities. Type II: Cuts at or near a short, and often palindromic, recognition sequence. A separate enzyme methylates the same recognition sequence. They may make the cuts in the two DNA strands exactly opposite one another and generate blunt ends, or they may make staggered cuts to generate sticky ends.

The type II restriction enzymes are the ones commonly exploited in recombinant DNA technology. Type III: Cuts 24-26 bp down-stream from a short, asymmetrical recognition sequence. Requires ATP and contains both restriction and methylation activities.

Restriction exonuclease. A class of nucleases that degrades DNA or RNA, starting from an end either 5′ or 3′.

Restriction fragment. A fragment of DNA produced by cleaving (digesting, cutting) a DNA molecule with one or more restriction endonucleases.

Restriction fragment length polymorphism (RFLP). The occurrence of variation in the length of DNA fragments that are produced after cleavage with a type II restriction endonuclease. The differences in DNA lengths are due to the presence or absence of recognition site(s) for that particular restriction enzyme. RFLPs were initially detected using hybridization with DNA probes after separation of digested genomic DNA by gel electrophoresis (Southern analysis). Now they are typically detected by electrophoresis of digested PCR product.

Restriction map. The linear array of restriction endonuclease sites on a DNA molecule.

Restriction nuclease. A bacterial enzyme that cuts DNA at a specific site.

Restriction site. The specific nucleotide sequence in DNA that is recognized by a type II restriction endonuclease and within which it makes a double-stranded cut. Restriction sites usually comprise four or six base pairs that typically are palindromic.

Retrovirus. A class of eukaryotic RNA viruses that can form double-stranded DNA copies of their genomes by using reverse transcription; the double-stranded forms integrate into chromosomes of an infected cell.

Ri plasmid. A class of large conjugative plasmids found in the soil bacterium *Agrobacterium rhizogenes*. Ri plasmids are responsible for hairy root disease of certain plants.

Sequence-tagged site (STS). Short, unique DNA sequence (usually 200 to 500 bp) that, by being able to be amplified by PCR, is uniquely "tagged" to the site on the chromosome from which it was amplified.

Sequencing. The determination of the order of nucleotides in a DNA or RNA molecule, or that of amino acids in a polypeptide chain.

Single-nucleotide polymorphism (SNP; pronounced "snip"). A polymorphism at a particular base site in a coding sequence.

Single-strand-DNA-binding protein. A protein that coats DNA single strands, keeping them in an extended state.

Single-stranded. A term used to describe nucleic acid molecules consisting of only one polynucleotide chain.

Six-base cutter. A type II restriction endonuclease that binds (and subsequently cleaves) DNA at sites that contain a sequence of six nucleotide pairs that is uniquely recognized by that enzyme.

Small nuclear ribonucleoprotein (snrnp; pronounced snurp). A compound comprising small nuclear RNA and nuclear protein, that is heavily involved in the post-transcriptional processing of mRNA, especially the removal of introns.

Small nuclear RNA (snRNA). Short RNA transcripts of 100-300 bp that associate with proteins to form small nuclear ribonucleoprotein particles.

Southern blot. A cellulose or nylon membrane to which DNA fragments previously separated by gel electrophoresis have been transferred by capillary action.

Southern blotting. A technique for transferring denatured DNA molecules that have been separated electrophoretically, from a gel to a matrix (such as a nitrocellulose membrane) on which a hybridization assay can be performed.

Southern hybridization. A procedure in which a cloned, labelled segment of DNA is hybridized to DNA restriction fragments on a Southern blot.

Splicing. During the maturation of eukaryotic mRNA, the process that eliminates intervening intron sequences and covalently joins exon sequences of RNA.

Split genes. In eukaryotes, structural genes are typically divided (split) by a number of non-coding regions called introns.

Staggered cuts. Symmetrically cleaved phosphodiester bonds that lie on both strands of duplex DNA but are not opposite one another.

Sticky ends; cohesive ends. The single-stranded nucleotide sequence left on a restriction fragment by type II restriction enzymes that cut each strand at a separate location.

Stringent plasmid. A plasmid that only replicates along with the main bacterial chromosome and is present as a single copy, or at most several copies, per cell.

Sub-clone. A method in which smaller DNA fragments are cloned from a large insert which has already been cloned in a vector.

Superbug. Bacterial strain of *Pseudomonas* developed by Chakrabarty, who combined hydrocarbon-degrading genes carried on different plasmids into one organism.

***Taq* polymerase.** A heat-stable DNA polymerase isolated from the thermophilic bacterium *Thermus aquaticus,* and used in PCR.

T-DNA. The segment of DNA in the Ti plasmid of *Agrobacterium tumefaciens* that is transferred to plant cells and inserted into the chromosomes of the plant.

Ti plasmid. Tumour-inducing plasmid. A giant plasmid of *Agrobacterium tumefaciens* that is responsible for the induction of tumours in infected plants. Ti plasmids are used as vectors to introduce foreign DNA into plant cells.

Transformant. In prokaryotes, a cell that has been genetically altered through the uptake of foreign DNA. In higher eukaryotes, a cultured cell that has acquired a malignant phenotype.

Transformation. The uptake and establishment of DNA in a bacterium or yeast cell, in which the introduced DNA often changes the phenotype of the recipient organism.

Transformation efficiency. The number of cells that take up foreign DNA as a function of the amount of added DNA; expressed as transformants per microgram of added DNA.

Transgene. A gene from one genome that has been incorporated into the genome of another organism. Often refers to a gene that has been introduced into a multicellular organism.

Transgenic. An organism in which a foreign gene (a transgene) is incorporated into its genome. The transgene is present in both somatic and germ cells, is expressed in one or more tissues, and is inherited by offspring in a Mendelian fashion.

Transposition. The process whereby a transposon or insertion sequence inserts itself into a new site on the same or another DNA molecule.

Transposon. A transposable or movable genetic element. A relatively small DNA segment that has the ability to move (mobile genetic element) from one chromosomal position to another.

Transposon tagging. The insertion of a transposable element into or nearby a gene, thereby marking that gene with a known DNA sequence.

Vector. A plasmid or phage that is used to deliver selected foreign DNA for cloning and in gene transfer.

***Vir* genes.** A set of genes on a Ti plasmid that prepare the T-DNA segment for transfer into a plant cell.

Virion. An infectious virus particle. A plant pathogen that consists of a naked RNA molecule of approximately 250-350 nucleotides, whose extensive base pairing results in a nearly correct double helix.

Viroid. An infectious entity similar to a virus but smaller, consisting only of a strand of nucleic acid without the protein coat characteristic of a virus.

Virulence. The degree of ability of an organism to cause disease. The relative infectiousness of a bacterium or virus, or its ability to overcome the resistance of the host metabolism.

Virulent phage. A phage (virus) that destroys the host (bacterium).

Virus. An infectious particle composed of a protein capsule and a nucleic acid core (DNA or RNA), which is dependent on a host organism for replication.

VNTR. Variable number tandem repeat. A short DNA sequence that is present as tandem repeats and in highly variable copy number.

Western blot. A technique in which protein is transferred from an electrophoretic gel to a cellulose or nylon support membrane following electrophoresis. A particular protein molecule can then be identified by probing the blot with a radio-labelled antibody which binds only the specific protein to which the antibody was prepared.

YAC. Yeast artificial chromosome, used as a vector system for cloning DNA fragments that can be hundreds of kilobases long. Linear cloning vectors constructed from essential elements of yeast chromosomes. They can accommodate foreign DNA inserts of 200 to 500 kb.

Yeast cloning vectors. The yeasts, and especially *Saccaromyces cerevisiae*, are favourite organisms in which to clone and express DNA. They are eukaryotes, and so can splice out introns, the non-coding sequences in the middle of many eukaryotic genes.

Appendix 4
Glossary of Biochemistry

Acidic amino acids. Those whose side chains can carry a negative charge at certain pH values, e.g., aspartic acid and glutamic acid.

Active site. The site on an enzyme molecule where the substrate molecule binds and where its reaction is facilitated.

Active transport. Transport of a substance across a membrane against an electrochemical gradient; requires the expenditure of metabolic energy.

Alginate. Component of the cell walls of many rhodophytes and kelps. Alginates have an affinity for water, and so help to slow desiccation when the algae are exposed to the air; they are commercially important in the production of paper, toothpaste, beer, and frozen foods.

Alkaloid. One of a group of nitrogenous basic substances found in plants. It may have a bitter taste; many are pharmacologically active.

Allosteric. An effect that affects the activity of one part of an enzyme (such as an active site) by the binding of a molecule at a different site (regulatory site), at a different location on the enzyme.

Alpha-helix. Frequently highly stable protein chain conformation stabilized by hydrogen bonding between peptide groups and having side chains projecting outwards in a spiral (3.6 residues per turn). One of the classic "secondary" structures.

Amino acid. Unit molecule from which proteins are constructed by polymerization.

Amino acid analyzer. Automated machine that determines amino acid composition of a protein.

Amino acid sequencer. Automated machine that determines linear order of amino acids in a protein chain (i.e. the protein's primary structure).

Amino acid synthesizer. Automated machine capable of synthesizing polypeptide chains by solid phase method.

Amino acid side chain. That portion of the amino acid that extends beyond the alpha-carbon and gives the amino acid its unique chemical character.

Amino acid residue. The portion of the amino acid that remains after incorporation into a polypeptide chain. Includes the alpha-carbon and the nitrogen/carbonyl moieties.

Amino peptidase. Enzyme that cleaves amino acid residues from a protein chain commencing at the n-terminal.

Amphipathic. Having both hydrophobic and hydrophilic regions in a single molecule.

Anabolism. All metabolisms in which complex biomolecules are built up from simpler ones. These processes usually require cellular energy.

Antibodies. Proteins involved in recognizing bacteria, viruses, toxins, etc. as part of the immune defense system; circulate in blood/ lymph systems.

Apoenzyme. Enzyme lacking correct cofactor/ coenzyme and hence unable to function correctly.

Apolipoproteins. The protein portion of lipoproteins (without the lipid).

Aromatic amino acids. Those with aromatic side chains, e.g. tyrosine, phenylalanine, tryptophane and histidine.

Asymmetric carbon. A carbon that carries four different substituents and therefore acts as a center of chirality.

ATP. "Adenosine triphosphate". A relatively stable, high energy molecule used to fuel chemical reactions within cells.

Attenuation. A mechanism for regulating prokaryotic gene expression in which the synthesis of a nascent RNA transcript is terminated before RNA polymerase has reached the structural genes.

Basic amino acids. Those whose side chains can carry a positive charge at certain pH values e.g. lysine, arginine and histidine.

B- DNA. A DNA duplex with a right-hand helical structure; the usual form of DNA *in vivo*.

Beta-conformation. Stable "zig-zag" conformation of protein chain which can align with sections of chain in same conformation and cross-link efficiently via hydrogen bonds between the peptide linkages. One of the classic "secondary" structures.

Beta sheet. Two or more sections of protein chain in beta conformation that have become aligned and linked by hydrogen bonding. Effectively form a twisted sheet with side chains projecting above and below plane of sheet.

Beta turn. Defined 90 or 180 degree turn in a protein chain stabilized by a hydrogen bond across the turn between peptide units.

Biochemistry. The study of those molecules which are used and manufactured by living things.

Bioinformatics. As applied to proteins, typically the use of theoretical computational techniques to classify, group, align, store, access and interpret protein sequence/3D data. Major application is in the prediction of protein shape, properties and function from primary sequence data alone.

Bioluminescence. The production of light by a chemical reaction within an organism. The process occurs in many bacteria and protists, as well as certain animals and fungi.

Blood group antigens. Oligosaccharides that are carried in the form of glycoproteins and glycolipids on the outside of blood cell membranes.

Bohr effect. The effect of protons on the binding of oxygen to haemoglobin; promotes both the release of oxygen from haemoglobin in the tissues and the release of carbon dioxide from the blood in the lungs.

C-terminus. That end of a protein chain which carries a free α-carboxyl group.

Carbohydrates. Class of biochemical compounds which includes sugars, starch, chitin, and steroids.

Carboxypeptidase. Enzyme that cleaves amino acids from a protein chain commencing at the c-terminal.

Cellulose. Carbohydrate polymer of the simple sugar glucose.

Chaperonins. Proteins that facilitate the proper folding of other proteins.

Chiral. A molecule that is not superimposable on its mirror image. A carbon with four different substituents is called a chiral atom or center of chirality.

Chitin. A carbohydrate polymer found in the cell walls of fungi and in the exoskeletons of arthropods, which provides strength for support and protection.

Chlorophyll. The green-coloured pigment that absorbs light during photosynthesis, often found in plants, algae, and some bacteria; it includes a porphyrin ring, and often has a long hydrophobic tail.

Chromatography. General term for related techniques to purify the components of peptide/ protein mixtures according to molecular size, polarity, charge and recognition properties, etc.

Chromophore. A chemical group that absorbs light of characteristic wavelengths.

Coenzyme. A small organic molecule that binds to an enzyme and is essential for its activity but is not permanently altered by the reaction. Many coenzymes are derived from vitamins.

Collagen. Long proteins whose structure is wound into a triple helix. The resulting fibres have a high tensile strength. Collagen is a primary component of mammalian hair.

Conformational change. Large, medium or small adjustment to the molecular shape/dynamics of a protein that may follow a change in environment or the specific recognition of another molecule.

Consensus sequence. Nucleotide or amino acid sequences that show significant similarity but are not identical.

Curie. A unit of radioactivity equal to 2.22 x 1012 disintegrations per minute.

Denaturation. Loss of a protein's typical conformation and activity through extreme alterations to its environment (e.g. changes in pH and temperature, etc.).

Disulfide bridge. Covalent linkage between 2 cysteine side chains formed when they come in close proximity in the fold and there is an oxidizing environment. Play a critical role in holding together the folds of many proteins and enhancing the stability under hostile conditions.

DNA. "Deoxyribonucleic acid". The nucleic acid which carries the genetic code of an organism. It is the primary component of chromosomes.

Electron microscopy. Very high resolution form of microscopy, capable of visualizing the smallest organisms and the organization of macromolecular protein complexes.

Electrophoresis. Experimental technique by which a mixture of peptides/proteins can be separated on the basis of their molecular charge.

Electrospray mass spectrometry. Useful method for analyzing the composition of peptide mixtures according to their molecular weight.

Endonuclease. An enzyme that cleaves a nucleic acid chain at an internal phosphodiester bond.

Endopeptidase. Enzyme that can cleave peptide bonds within the body of a protein chain.

Enthalpy. A thermodynamic quantity equal to the internal energy of a system plus the product of the pressure and volume. It is equal to the heat change in constant-pressure reactions (most biological reactions).

Entropy. A thermodynamic quantity that expresses the degree of disorder or randomness in a system. The entropy of an open system tends to increase unless energy is expended.

Enzyme. Complex protein which helps to speed biochemical reactions. Enzymes are important in the construction and degradation of other molecules.

Episomes. Plasmids that can undergo integration into the bacterial chromosome.

Epitope. Part of a protein's surface area liable to be recognized and bound to by an appropriate antibody.

Essential amino acids. Those required in the human diet.

Eukaryotes. Organisms whose cells are compartmentalized by internal cellular membranes to produce a nucleus and organelles.

Exon. A region in the coding sequence of a gene that is translated into protein.

Exopeptidase. Enzyme that cleaves amino acid residues from one or other end of a protein chain.

Fluid mosaic model. The model of membranes in which proteins are embedded in a phospholipid bilayer and are free to move in the plane of the membrane.

Functional genomics. The development and application of global (i.e. genome-wise or biosystem-wise) experimental approaches for monitoring and quantifying gene function, using the molecular structure/function knowledge and reagents provided by structural genomics.

Gel electrophoresis. Electrophoresis in which the supporting medium is a gel (usually agarose or acrylamide); used for separating proteins and nucleic acids base on net charge and size.

Globular proteins. Proteins whose three-dimensional folded shape is relatively compact.

Glucogenic. Compounds, such as certain amino acids that can be used by cells for the biosynthesis of glucose.

Glucose. Simple sugar and the primary product of photosynthesis. It is polymerized to make cellulose and chitin.

Glycoprotein. A membrane-bound protein which has attached branching carbohydrates.

Haemoglobin. Protein complex found in the blood of most chordates and the roots of certain legumes. It binds oxygen molecules, and in chordates serves as the means by which the oxygen is supplied to the cells of the body.

Histones. Small, basic proteins that bind DNA to form the nucleosome.

Homologous recombination. Genetic recombination that requires extensive sequence homology between the recombining DNA molecules. Meiotic recombination by crossing over in eukaryotes is an example.

HPLC. High performance liquid chromatography. Versatile method for the separation of peptide/ protein mixtures, usually on the basis of relative hydrophobicity.

Hydrophilic. The property of a molecule that produces attractive interactions with water molecules.

Hydrophobic. The property of having no attractive interactions with water. Hydrophobic substances are nonpolar.

Hydrophobic effect. The stabilization of tertiary and quaternary protein structures which result from the packing of hydrophobic side chains in the interior of the protein.

Hypochromism. The reduction in the absorbance at 260 nm that accompanies the transition from random-coil DNA to a double-strand helix.

Imino acid. Contains secondary instead of primary amine function.

Indole. Side chain group of amino acid tryptophan.

Inhibitor. Molecule capable of preventing an enzyme working, frequently by binding in or near the catalytic site and blocking the usual interaction with substrate.

Intercalation. Refers to the inter-leafing of a small molecule between adjacent bases in a DNA helix.

Intron. The portion of the coding sequence of a gene that is not translated into protein.

Ion. An atom or small molecule which carries a positive or negative charge.

Isoelectric point (pi). The pH at which a peptide/ protein carries no overall charge.

Joule (j). A unit for energy (or work), defined as the work done by a force of 1 Newton when the object it acts on moves 1 meter.

Keratin. Structural protein found in skin, hair, horns, hooves, feathers and fur.

Lagging strand. The daughter DNA strand that is synthesized in the opposite direction to the direction of movement of the replication fork; it is synthesized as a series of fragments that are subsequently joined.

Leading strand. The daughter DNA strand that is synthesized in the same direction as the direction of movement of the replication fork; it is synthesized continuously rather than in fragments.

Ligand. A molecule that binds specifically to a protein. The term can also be used to mean a chemical substance that forms a coordination complex with a transition metal ion.

Lipids. A class of biochemical compounds which includes fats, oils, and waxes.

Lipid bilayer. A membrane structure that consists of two back-to-back layers of lipids, in each of which the polar head groups on each side face the water and the nonpolar tails lie in the center of the membrane.

Luciferase. Enzyme which activates luciferin to produce bioluminescence.

Luciferin. Compound whose activated form emits light.

Metabolism. The totality of the chemical reactions that occur in an organism.

Micelles. Solid spherical bodies that form when an amphipathic substance is added to water and shaken. The amphipathic molecules are arranged with their polar head groups facing out toward the water and their nonpolar tails facing toward the center.

Molecular chaperone. A molecule (often a protein itself) that may assist another protein in the attainment and/or performance of the latter's function, e.g. assistance in reaching the final folded state or guidance to an interactive site.

Motif. A frequently observed 3D pattern of assemblage of secondary structures seen within different protein molecules, sometimes called a "supersecondary" structure.

Luciferin. Compound whose activated form emits light.

Noncompetitive inhibitor. An inhibitor of an enzyme-catalyzed reaction that acts by binding to a site on the enzyme different from the active site and reducing the enzyme's catalytic efficiency (Vmax).

N-terminus/terminal. That end of a protein chain that carries the free α-amino group.

NMR. Nuclear magnetic resonance. Technique for determining protein 3D structures in solution, detecting secondary structures and measuring conformational changes.

Okazaki fragments. Small fragments of DNA that are synthesized on the lagging strand during DNA replication. They are later joined to form a continuous strand by DNA polymerase I and DNA ligase.

Oligopeptide. An imprecise term used to describe a peptide of around 6-10 residues.

Oncogene. A gene that codes for a protein that is receptor or a part of a signal transduction pathway for a cellular growth factor. A mutated oncogene can transform a normal cell to a cancer cell.

Open reading frame. A DNA sequence that is bounded by start and stop codons; it may represent the coding sequence for a polypeptide.

Operator. DNA site located between a promoter site and the structural genes of an operon. A repressor protein binds to this sequence of DNA and blocks the initiation of transcription.

Operon. A set of contiguous prokaryotic structural genes that are transcribed as a unit, plus the adjacent regulatory elements that control their expression.

Palindrome. A sequence of DNA that is the same on one strand read right to left as on the other strand read left to right, that is, a back-to-back pair of inverted repeats.

Peptide bond. The covalent bond that links successive amino acids; it consists of an amide bond between the alpha carboxyl-group of one amino acid and the alpha-amino group of the next.

Peptidoglycan. Carbohydrate polymer cross-linked by proteins. It is found in the cell wall of gram positive bacteria, where it stains with the dye crystal-violet.

Phenotype. The measurable characteristic of an organism that results from the interaction of its genetic makeup with the environment.

Phosphate. An ion consisting of a phosphorus atom and four oxygen atoms. Among other things, it is used in the construction of nucleic acids.

Photoreactivation. A repair mechanism for DNA in which an enzyme uses light energy to break cyclobutane-linked pyrimidine dimers. These dimers are created by UV irradiation of DNA.

Plasmid. A small, circular DNA, extrachromosomal in location, found in many bacteria; replicates independently of chromosomal DNA and may occur in multiple copies per cell.

Polymer. A molecule that is made by covalently linking a number of smaller molecular units (monomers) those are similar or identical to each other.

Polymerase chain reaction (PCR). A powerful technique for synthesizing a large amount of DNA from very small amounts of DNA having a specific sequence. This is accomplished through repeated cycles of denaturation, primer annealing, and replication (extension) using a heat-resistant DNA polymerase. Is also used in DNA sequencing.

Primary structure. The linear sequence of nucleotides or amino acids in the polynucleotide (RNA or DNA) or polypeptide (protein).

Primer. A short sequence of DNA or RNA that base-pairs with a DNA template strand and provides a free 3' -OH end from which a DNA polymerase can extend a DNA strand.

Processivity. The degree to which a DNA or RNA polymerase remains bound to its template during a polymerization reaction.

Prokaryotes. Single-celled organisms that are not compartmentalized by internal cellular membranes; includes the eubacteria and archaebacteria.

Promoter. The DNA sequence to which RNA polymerase binds to initiate transcription of RNA.

Prosthetic group. A metal ion or small molecule (other than an amino acid) that associates with a protein and is essential to its biochemical functioning; its attachment to the protein may be either covalent or noncovalent.

Protein. Class of biochemical compounds constructed from amino acids. Proteins may be structural, such as those that make up hair and cartilage, or they may be reactive, such as the enzymes.

Protein engineering. The non-natural production of new protein variants, either as a result of modifying existing proteins or their genes, or *de novo* design.

Proteinase. Enzyme capable of hydrolysing certain peptide bonds in protein chains.

Proteome. An all-embracing term (covering quantity, range and type) to describe the population of protein molecules output by the genome of an organism, or, in the context of a multicellular organism, the population of protein molecules output by a specific type of tissue or differentiated cell.

Proteomics. The use of quantitative techniques to measure changes in the population of proteins output by an organism's genome during normal biological processes, disease states or in response to drugs. General aim is to relate gene expression to the characterization and control of biological processes.

Pseudogene. A DNA sequence that bears strong similarity to a functioning gene, but whose protein product is not very likely to be biologically active.

Quarternary structure. The level of structure that results when separate, folded polypeptide chains (subunits) associate in a specific way to produce a complete oligomeric protein.

Random coil. A linear polymer that has no secondary or tertiary structure but instead has randomly varying geometries. This is the state of a denatured protein or nucleic acid.

Receptor. A protein that upon binding a specific molecule (can be a small molecule or a macromolecule) initiates a biological response.

Recombinant DNA molecule. A DNA molecule that is constructed from segments of two or more precursor DNA molecules. Used as a tool in biotechnology and in many areas of biochemistry and molecular genetics.

Repressor. A protein that inhibits the transcription of a gene (or genes) by binding to an operator sequence of DNA.

Restriction endonucleases. Enzymes that catalyze the double-strand cleavage of DNA at the sites of specific sequences.

Reverse transcriptase. An enzyme found in retroviruses that synthesizes a double-strand DNA molecule from a single-strand RNA template.

Ribosome. A very large protein-RNA complex that catalyzes the synthesis of polypeptides based on the sequence of an mRNA.

RNA. "Ribonucleic acid". The nucleic acid which carries the DNA message into parts of the cell where it is interpreted and used.

Rubisco. Protein which fixes carbon in photosynthetic organisms. It binds molecules of carbon dioxide to a five-carbon molecule. Rubisco is the most common protein on earth.

Secondary structure. The first level of actual folding of the backbone of a linear polymer to form a regular, repeating structure. Examples are the B- and Z-helical forms of DNA and the alpha-helix and beta-sheet structures of polypeptides.

Second-order reaction. A reaction in which two reactant molecules must come together for the reaction to occur. The reaction is called second-order because the reaction rate depends on the product of two reactant concentrations.

Sedimentation coefficient (s). A measure of the velocity at which particular particles will sediment during centrifugation; it depends on the density of the medium and the size, shape, and mass of the particle.

Signal recognition particles (srps). Proteins that bind to a specific n-terminal signal sequence on nascent polypeptides being formed on ribosomes; they assist in docking these ribosomes on the surface of the endoplasmic reticulum.

Site-specific mutagenesis. Alteration of a protein primary structure by artificial means (usually via the gene) to test mechanistic hypotheses or to alter activity.

Southern blotting. A hybridization technique for detecting the presence of a specific DNA sequence in a genome. The DNA is extracted, cleaved into fragments, separated by gel electrophoresis, denatured, and blotted onto a nitrocellulose filter. The filter is incubated under annealing conditions with a radio labeled DNA probe, and the presence of bands of DNA containing the sequence of interest is detected by radioaudiography.

Specificity. Frequently applied to enzymes as a descriptor of the limited range of substrates upon which the enzyme will act.

Starch. A complex polymer of glucose, used by plants and green algae to store surplus sugar for later use.

Structural genomics. As arising from the genome sequencing projects, the drive to elucidate the 3 D structure, function and mechanism of the proteins produced from the genes in order to apply the knowledge. Goals include: the determination of the shapes and actions of all human proteins, or of the complete sets of proteins in particular functional classes, such as all enzymes or all cell-surface receptors.

Substrate. Typically the molecule(s) that will be transformed by the catalytic action of an enzyme.

Sugar. Any of several small carbohydrates, such as glucose, which are "sweet" to the taste.

Supercoiling. Turns of the two helical DNA strands around each other that are either larger or smaller than the number of turns in the most stable linear helical conformation that would occur in a free solution. Only a helix that is circular or else bound at both ends can maintain supercoiling.

Suppression. A mutation that restores the wild-type phenotype, but it occurs at a second site on the DNA that is outside of the gene containing the original mutation.

Svedberg unit (s). The unit of the sedimentation coefficient, which is equal to 10^{-13} seconds.

Telomerase. A DNA polymerase that adds a short repeating sequence to the 3' strand at either end of a linear chromosomal DNA molecule, thereby creating a single-strand overhang. This permits DNA replication of the full length of the chromosome.

Tertiary structure. The folding of the elements of secondary structure, such as alpha helices and beta-sheet.

Topoisomerase. An enzyme that changes the super coiling of DNA helices by either allowing the super helical torsion to relax (reducing the super coiling) or adding more twists and increasing the super coiling.

Transcription. Synthesis of a messenger RNA molecule that has a sequence complementary to that of a strand of DNA.

Transition state. The highest energy state (and the molecular configuration that corresponds to it) that exists between reactant and product in a chemical reaction.

Translation. Synthesis of a sequence of amino acids in a polypeptide based on the sequence information in mRNA.

Turnover number. The number of substrate molecules that one enzyme molecule can convert to product (turn over) per second when the enzyme is saturated with substrate.

Twist. The total number of times the two strands of a DNA helix cross over each other, excluding writhing.

Vector. A DNA molecule that can be used to introduce a DNA sequence into a cell. The vector, which is usually plasmid or viral DNA, must be capable of being replicated by the cell.

X-ray crystallography. Important technique for the deduction of protein 3D structure. Requires crystals of pure protein.

X-ray diffraction. A technique used to determine the three-dimensional structure of molecules, including macromolecules. A crystal of the substance is illuminated with a beam of x-rays, and the repeating elements of the crystal scatter the x-rays to form a diffraction pattern that gives information on the location of atoms in the molecule (requires resolution of the phase problem).

Z-DNA. A duplex of DNA with a specific left-handed helical structure.

Zwitterion. Natural state of free amino acids in which α-amino group is protonated giving a positive charge and a carboxyl group is deprotonated giving a negative charge.

Appendix 5
Glossary of Forestry

Acre. An area of land measuring 43,560 square feet.

Angiosperm. A plant that has true flowers and bears its seeds in fruits. In temperate zones, many angiosperms are deciduous trees, while in tropical zones, many are evergreen trees.

Annual ring. The combination of one early wood layer (light coloured) and one latewood layer (dark coloured) seen in a cross-section of a tree. One annual ring usually represents one year of growth.

Artificial regeneration. The growth of new trees through seeding and planting.

Association. A collection of plants with ecologically similar requirements, including one or more dominant species from which the group derives a definite character.

Bark. The tough exterior covering of a woody root or stem that protects the tree from injury caused by insects and other animals, by other plants, by disease and by fire.

Basal area (of a tree). The cross-sectional area of the trunk four and a half feet above the ground; (per acre) the sum of the basal areas of the trees on an acre; used as a measure of forest density.

Best Management Practice. Forest management practices that reduce erosion and prevent or control water pollution.

Biltmore stick. A tool calibrated to measure the diameter of a tree at breast height. Biltmore sticks are calibrated with different scales depending on the users' arm length.

Biodiversity. The variety of life forms in a given area; can be categorized in terms of number of species, variety of plant and animal communities, genetic variability or some combination of these categories.

Blaze. To mark a tree, usually by painting or cutting the bark. Forest properties often are delineated by blazing trees along the boundary lines.

Board Foot. A unit of measure equal to a board that is 1 inch thick, 12 inches long and 12 inches wide, or 144 cubic inches.

Bole. The main trunk of a tree.

Breast height. Four and a half feet above ground level.

Broad leaf. A class of trees that have broad, flat leaves of many different shapes; most are deciduous; also called hardwood because most broad-leaved trees have harder wood than do conifers.

Browse. Parts of woody plants, including twigs, shoots, and leaves, eaten by forest animals.

Buck. To cut trees into shorter lengths, such as logs or cordwood.

Buffer strip. A narrow zone or strip of land, trees or vegetation bordering an area. Common examples include visual buffers, which screen the view along roads, and streamside buffers, which are used to protect water quality. Buffers may also be used to prevent the spread of forest pests.

Butt log. A log cut from the bole immediately above the stump.

Caliper. A tool to measure the diameter of a tree.

Cambium. A thin layer of specialized cells within a tree's trunk that divide to produce new inner bark cells to the outside and new sapwood cells to the inside. The narrow band of cells that is responsible for the tree's growth in circumference.

Canopy. The "roof" of the forest formed by the crowns of the tallest trees.

Cellulose. The scientific name for wood fibre.

Chain. A distance of 66 feet.

Clearcut. A harvesting and regeneration method that removes all trees within a given area.

Clinometer. An instrument that is held at eye level to read stump height and merchantable or total height when standing 50 and 66 feet from the base of the tree. The difference between the two readings yields the height.

Codominant tree. A tree that extends its crown into the canopy and receives direct sunlight from above but limited sunlight from the sides. One or more sides of a codominant tree are crowded by the crowns of dominant trees.

Competition. The struggle between trees to obtain sunlight, nutrients, water and growing space. Every part of the tree, from the roots to the crown, competes for space and food.

Conifer. A class of trees that are evergreen, have needle or scalelike foliage and conelike fruit; often called softwood. Examples include pine, cedar and cypress.

Conservation. Planned management and wise use of natural resources for present and future generations.

Cord. A standard unit of measure equivalent to 128 cubic feet of round or split wood. A standard cord measures 4 feet by 4 feet by 8 feet. A face cord or short cord is 4 feet by 8 feet by any length of wood under 4 feet.

Cord wood. Small diameter or low quality wood suitable for firewood, pulp, or chips.

Cover. Any plant that intercepts rain drops before they reach the soil or that holds soil in place.

Crook. A tree defect characterized by a sharp bend in the main stem.

Crop tree. A young tree of a desirable species with certain characteristics desired for timber value, water quality enhancement, or wildlife or aesthetic uses.

Crown. The branches and foliage at the top of a tree.

Cruise. A survey or inventory of forestland to locate timber and estimate its quantity by species, products, size, quality or other characteristics.

Cull. A saw timber sized tree that has no timber value as a result of poor shape or damage from injury, insects or disease.

Cutting cycle. The period of time between major harvests in a stand.

Deciduous. A group of trees that lose all of their leaves every year.

Decomposition. The process by which organic material such as leaves and branches are broken down by bacteria, fungi, protozoans and the many different kinds of animals that live in the soil.

Den tree. A tree with cavities suitable for birds or mammals to nest in.

Dendrology. The study of trees; tree identification.

Diameter at Breast Height (DBH). Tree diameter measured at 4.5 feet above ground level.

Earlywood. Wood cells produced at the beginning of a tree's growing season that are generally light in colour. Also called springwood.

Ecology. The science or study of the relationships between organisms and their environment.

Ecological succession. The gradual change of plant and animal communities over time.

Ecosystem. A loosely defined area consisting of numerous habitats.

Edge. The transition between two different types or ages of vegetation.

Endangered species. Any species or subspecies in immediate danger of becoming extinct throughout all or a significant portion of its range.

Environment. The sum of all external living and non-living conditions and influences that affect the development and survival of an organism.

Erosion. The wearing away or removal of land or soil by the action of wind, water, ice or gravity.

Even-Aged Management. A forest management method used to produce stands that are all the same age or nearly the same age by harvesting all trees in an area at one time or in several cuttings over a short time.

Evergreen. A group of trees that do not lose all of their leaves every year but go through a gradual replacement by dropping only their oldest leaves each year. Instead of being bare in winter, these trees have leaves all year.

Felling. The cutting of standing trees.

Fire shelter. Firefighters use this personal protection as a last resort if a wildfire traps them and they cannot escape. Firefighters can get into the tent-like shelter, made of heat reflective material, in about 25 seconds.

Foliage. The leaves of a tree or other plant.

Forage. Vegetation such as leaves, stems, buds and some types of bark, that can be eaten for food and energy.

Forb. Any herb other than grass.

Forest. A biological community dominated by trees and other woody plants.

Forest Floor. The lowest level of the forest that is made up of tree seedlings, dead leaves and needles, grasses, ferns, flowers, fungi, and decaying plants and logs.

Forest management. Caring for a forest so that it stays healthy and vigorous and provides the products and values the landowner desires.

Forest type. A designation or name given to a forest based on the most abundant tree type or types in the stand; groups of tree species commonly growing in the same stand because their environmental requirements are similar. Examples of forest types include (a) pine; (b) mixed hardwood; (c) cypress; and (d) oak.

Forestry. The art and science of managing forests to produce various products and benefits including timber, wildlife habitat, clean water, biodiversity and recreation.

Frilling. The method of killing trees by inflicting a series of cuts around the bole and applying an herbicide to the wounds. Frilling or girdling can be used to reduce the density of a stand or to kill individual undesirable trees.

Fuel loading. A buildup of easily ignited leaves, pine straw, branches and trees on the forest floor.

Girdling. A method of killing trees by cutting through the stem, thus interrupting the flow of water and nutrients.

Growth rings. The layers of wood a tree adds each season; also called annual rings. These rings frequently are visible when a tree is cut and can be used to estimate its age and growth rate.

Gymnosperm. A plant whose seeds are not enclosed in flowers. Most gymnosperms produce their seeds on the surface of the scales of female cones and are pollinated by wind. Conifers are the most common type of gymnosperm.

Habitat. An area in which a specific plant or animal naturally lives, grows and reproduces; the area that provides a plant or animal with adequate food, water, shelter and living space.

Hardwoods. Trees with broad, flat leaves as opposed to coniferous or needled trees. Wood hardness varies among the hardwood species, and some are actually softer than some softwoods.

Heartwood. The central core of a tree, which is made up of dense, dead wood and provides strength to the tree.

Herbaceous vegetation. Low-growing, non-woody plants, including wildflowers and ferns, in a forest understory.

High-grading. A harvesting technique that removes only the biggest and most valuable trees from a stand and provides high returns at the expense of future growth potential.

Hypsomete. Any device used for measuring tree height.

Improvement cut. A weeding done in stands of pole-size or larger trees.

Increment borer. A hollow auger-like tool with a screw bit used to remove core samples from trees.

Industrial forester. A professional employed by a wood-using industry, usually a sawmill, who purchases timber from private woodland owners.

Intermediate crown class. Trees with crowns that extend into the canopy with dominant and codominate trees. These trees receive little direct sunlight from above and none from the sides. Crowns generally are small and crowded on all sides.

Intermediate tolerance. A characteristic of certain tree species that allows them to survive, though not necessarily thrive, in relatively low light conditions.

Intolerance. A characteristic of certain tree species that does not permit them to survive in the shade of other trees.

Introduced species. A non-native species that was intentionally or unintentionally brought into an area by humans.

Latewood. Wood cells produced at the end of the growing season that make up the darker section of an annual ring. Also called summerwood.

Landing. A cleared area within a timber harvest where harvested logs are processed, piled, and loaded for transport to a sawmill or other facility.

Limiting factor. Any requirement for wildlife survival that is in limited supply, brought into an area by humans.

Logger. An individual who harvests timber for a living.

Lopping. Cutting tree tops to a maximum specified height above the ground after a tree is felled.

Lump-sum sale. A timber sale in which an agreed-on price for marked standing trees is set before the wood is removed (as opposed to a unit sale).

Marking timber. Indicating by paint or other means which trees are to be cut or otherwise treated. It is advisable to mark trees to be harvested twice-once at eye level and once on the stump.

Mast. Fruits or nuts used as a food source by wildlife. Soft mast includes most fruits with fleshy coverings, such as black gum seed. Hard mast refers to nuts such as acorns and beech.

Merritt Hypsomete. A scale that measures the number of 16-foot logs in a tree.

Multiple-Use Management- The management of land or forest for more than one purpose, such as wood production, water quality, wildlife, recreation, aesthetics and clean air.

Natural regeneration. The growth of new trees in one of the following ways without human assistance: (a) from seeds carried by wind or animals, (b) from seeds stored on the forest floor, or (c) from stumps that sprout.

Niche. The physical and functional "address" of an organism within an ecosystem; or, where a living thing is found and what it does there.

Nongame wildlife. Wildlife species that are protected by state wildlife laws and cannot be hunted.

Non-industrial private forestland (NIPF). Forestland owned by a private individual, group, or corporation not involved in wood processing.

Old-growth forest. A wooded area, usually greater than 200 years of age, that has never been altered or harvested by humans.

Overmature. A quality exhibited by trees that have declined in growth rate because of old age and loss of vigor.

Overstocked. The situation in which trees are so closely spaced that they compete for resources and do not reach full growth potential.

Patch cut. A clearcut on a small area.

Phloem. The part of a tree that carries sap from the leaves to the rest of the tree. Also called inner bark.

Photosynthesis. The process by which a plant or tree combines water and carbon dioxide with energy from the sun to make glucose and oxygen.

Plant Succession. The progression of plants from bare ground to mature forest.

Prescribed Burning. The practice of using regulated fires to reduce or eliminate material on the forest floor, for seedbed preparation or to control competing vegetation.

Pruning. The act of sawing or cutting branches from a living tree. In forest management, pruning is done to promote the growth of clear, valuable wood on the tree bole.

Pulpwood. Wood used in the manufacture of paper, fibreboard or other wood fibre products. Pulpwood-sized trees are usually a minimum of 4 inches in diameter.

Regeneration. The process by which a forest is reseeded and renewed. Advanced regeneration refers to regeneration that is established before the existing forest stand is removed.

Regeneration cut. A timber harvest designed to promote natural establishment of trees.

Reforestation. Re-establishing a forest by planting or seeding an area from which forest vegetation has been removed.

Release. To free a tree from competition with its immediate neighbors by removing the surrounding trees. This occurs naturally and artificially.

Renewable resource. A naturally occurring raw material or form of energy that has the capacity to replenish itself through ecological cycles and sound management practices.

Residual stand. The trees remaining intact following any cutting operation.

Resin. A group of sticky liquid substances secreted by plants that appear on the plant's external surface after a wound.

Rot. A tree defect characterized by woody decay in a standing tree or log.

Rotation. The number of years required to establish and grow trees to a specified size, product or condition of maturity. A pine rotation may range from as short as 20 years for pulpwood to more than 60 years for saw timber.

Silviculture. The art and science of growing forest trees.

Sapling. A tree at least four and a half feet tall and up to 4 inches in diameter.

Sawlog. A log large enough to be sawed economically on a saw mill. Saw logs are usually at least 8 inches in diameter at the small end.

Saw timber. Wood of large enough size to be used to produce lumber for construction and furniture.

Seed tree. A mature tree left uncut to provide seed for regeneration of a harvested stand.

Seed tree cut. A harvesting method in which a few scattered trees are left in the area to provide seeds for a new forest stand.

Seed-tree harvest. The felling of all the trees in an area except for a few desirable individuals that provide seed for the next forest.

Selection harvest. The harvest of all individual trees or small groups at regular intervals to maintain an uneven-aged forest. Selection harvests are used to manage species that do not need sunlight to survive.

Selective cutting. The periodic removal of individual trees or groups of trees to improve or regenerate a stand.

Shade-intolerant species. Trees that require full sunlight to thrive and cannot grow in the shade of larger trees.

Shade-tolerant species. Trees that have the ability to grow in the shade of other trees and in competition with them.

Shelterwood cut. Removing trees in the harvest area in a series of two or more cuttings so that new seedlings can grow from the seeds of older trees. This method produces an even-aged forest.

Shelterwood harvest. The harvest of all mature trees in an area in a series of two or more cuts, leaving enough trees of other sizes to provide shade and protection for forest seedlings.

Silviculture. The art, science and practice of establishing, tending and reproducing forest stands of desired characteristics. It is based on knowledge of species' characteristics and environmental requirements.

Slash. Branches and other woody material left on a site after logging.

Snag. A standing dead or dying tree.

Softwood. A tree belonging to the order Coniferales. Softwood trees are usually evergreen, bear cones and have needles or scale like leaves. Examples include pines, spruces, firs and cedars.

Species. A group of related organisms having common characteristics and capable of interbreeding.

Sprout. A tree growing from a cut stump or previously established root system.

Stand density. The quantity of trees per unit area, usually evaluated in terms of basal area, crown cover and stocking.

Stand. A group of trees that are sufficiently the same in species composition and arrangement of age classes and condition so that they can be managed as a unit.

Stand density. The quantity of trees per unit area, usually evaluated in terms of basal area, crown cover and stocking.

Stocking. The number and density of trees in a forest stand. Stands are often classified as under stocked, well-stocked or overstocked.

Stratification. Division of a forest, or any ecosystem, into separate layers of vegetation that provide distinct niches for wildlife.

Streamside Management Zone (SMZ). An area adjacent to a stream in which vegetation is maintained or managed to protect water quality.

Stumpage. The value of standing trees in a forest.

Stumpage price. The price paid for standing forest trees.

Stump height. The distance from the ground to the top of the stump. Good logging practice dictates that stumps be as low as possible (preferably as low as 12 inches) to reduce waste, to minimize visual impact on the logging site, and to promote resprouting of trees.

Sustained yield. An ideal forest management objective in which the volume of wood removed equals growth within the total forest.

Sweep. A tree defect characterized by a gradual curve in the main stem.

Thinning. A tree removal practice that reduces tree density and competition between trees in a stand.

Timber stand improvement (t.s.i.). Any practice that increases the value or rate of value growth in a stand of potential sawtimber trees. Pruning and thinning are considered t.s.i.

Tolerance. A tree species' capacity to grow in shade.

Transpiration. The loss of water through leaves.

Turpentine. A distilled chemical produced from tapping into a living pine and harvesting the sap.

Understocked. A stand of trees so widely spaced, that even with full growth potential realized, crown closure will not occur.

Under story. The area below the forest canopy that comprises shrubs, snags and small trees. Because the under story receives little light, many of the plants at this level tolerate shade and will remain part of the under story. Others will grow and replace older trees that fall.

Unit sale. A timber sale in which the buyer makes regular (weekly, monthly) payments based on mill receipts. Unit sales are useful when the amount of timber sold is so large that a pre-harvest, lump-sum payment would be prohibitive.

Veneer log. A high-quality log of a desirable species suitable for conversion to veneer. Veneer logs must be large, straight, of minimum taper, and free from defects.

Virgin forest. An area of old-growth trees that has never been harvested by humans.

Watershed. A region defined by patterns of stream drainage. A watershed includes all the land that contributes water to a particular stream or river.

Well-stocked. The situation in which a forest stand contains trees spaced widely enough to prevent competition yet closely enough to utilize the entire site.

Wild life. A broad term that includes nondomesticated vertebrates, especially mammals, birds and fish.

Wildlife habitat. The native environment of an animal. Habitats ideally provide all the elements needed for life and growth: food, water, cover and space.

Wind throw. A tree felled by wind. Wind throws, also known as blow downs, are common among shallow-rooted species and in areas where cutting has reduced stand density.

Wood. The solid interior of a tree.

Wood chemicals. Chemicals that are found naturally in the various parts of a tree.

Xylem. The part of a tree that transports water and nutrients up from the roots to the leaves. Older xylem cells become part of the heartwood. Also called sapwood.

Appendix 6
Nobel Prize

This award is given for outstanding achievement in physics, chemistry, physiology or medicine, peace, or literature. These awards were established by the will of Alfred Nobel, who left a large amount of money for annual prizes. These prizes were given for the first time in 1901. The Bank of Sweden Prize in Economic Sciences in the memory of Alfred Nobel was established in 1968 and the funds for this were provided by the Swedish National bank known as Sveriges Riksbank, and was first awarded in 1969. The Nobel Prizes are awarded without regard to nationality. The judges are from the Royal Swedish Academy of Sciences for physics and chemistry, as well as economic science awards; the Swedish Royal Caroline Medico-Surgical Institute for physiology or medicine, the Swedish Academy for literature, and a committee elected by the Norwegian parliament for the peace award. The awards are presented on Dec. 10, which is the anniversary of Nobel's death. The Peace Prize is presented in Oslo and the others are presented in Stockholm. A prize is sometimes shared. Many times the Nobel Peace Prize has been given to an organization.

Appendix 7
All Nobel Prizes in Chemistry

The Nobel Prize in Chemistry has been awarded 114 times to 191 Nobel laureates between 1901 and 2022. Fredrick Sanger received it twice in 1958 and 1980 and Barry Sharpless also twice in 2001 and 2022. This means that a total of 189 individuals have received the Nobel Prize in Chemistry.

2022. Carolyn R. Bertozzi, USA, **Morten Meldal**, Denmark and **Barry Sharpless**, USA — For the development of click chemistry and bioorthogonal chemistry.

2021. Benjamin List, Germany and **David W. C. MacMillan,** USA — For the development of asymmetric organocatalysis.

2020. Emmanuelle Charpentier, Germany and **Jennifer, A. Doudna**, USA — For development of a method for genome editing.

2019. John B. Goodenough, USA, **M. Stanley Whittingham, U.K.** and **Akira Yoshino**, Japan — For the development of lithium-ion batteries.

2018. Frances H. Arnold, USA, — For the directed evolution of enzymes, **George P. Smith** and **Sir Gregory P. Winter** — For the phage display of peptides and antibodies.

2017. Jacques Dubochet, Switzerland, **Joachim Frank**, USA/Germany and **Richard Henderson**, U.K. — For developing cryo-electron microscopy for the high-resolution structure determination of biomolecules in solution.

2016. Jean-Pierre Sauvage, France, **Sir J. Fraser Stoddart**, U.K./USA and **Bernard L. Feringa**, Netherlands — For the design and synthesis of molecular machines.

2015. Tomas Lindahl, Sweden/USA and **Paul Modrich**, USA and **Aziz Sancar**, USA/Turkey — For mechanistic studies of DNA repair.

2014. Eric Betzig, USA, **Stefan W. Hell**, Germany/Romania and **William E. Moerner**, USA — For the development of super-resolved fluorescence microscopy.

2013. Martin Karplus, USA/Austria, **Michael Levitt**, USA/U.K./Israel and **Arieh Warshel** USA/Israel — For the development of multiscale models for complex chemical systems.

2012. Robert J. Lefkowitz, USA and **Brian K. Kobilka**, USA — For studies of G-protein-coupled receptors.

2011. Dan Shechtman, Israel/USA — For the discovery of quasicrystals.

2010. Richard F. Heck, USA, **Ei-ichi Negishi**, Japan and **Akira Suzuki**, Japan — For palladium-catalysed cross couplings in organic synthesis.

2009. Venkatraman Ramakrishnan, USA/India/U.K., **Thomas A. Steitz**, USA and **Ada E. Yonath**, Israel — For studies of the structure and function of the ribosome.

2008. Osamu Shimomura, Japan, **Martin Chalfie**, USA and **Roger Y. Tsien**, USA — For the discovery and development of the green fluorescent protein, GFP.

2007. Gerhard Ertl, Germany — For his studies of chemical processes on solid surfaces.

2006. Roger D. Kornberg, USA — For his studies of the molecular basis of eukaryotic transcription.

2005. Yves Chauvin, France, **Robert H. Grubbs**, USA and **Richard R. Schrock**, USA — For the development of the metathesis method in organic synthesis.

2004. Aaron Ciechanover, Israel, **Avram Hershko**, Israel and **Irwin Rose**, USA — For the discovery of ubiquitin-mediated protein degradation.

2003. Peter Agre, USA — For the discovery of water channels in cell membranes. **Roderick Mackinnon**, USA — For structural and mechanistic studies of ion channels in cell membranes.

2002. John B. Fenn, USA and **Koichi Tanaka**, Japan — For their development of soft desorption ionization methods for mass spectrometric analyses of biological macromolecules. **Kurt Wüthrich**, Switzerland — For his development of nuclear magnetic resonance spectroscopy for determining the three-dimensional structure of biological macromolecules in solution.

2001. William S. Knowles, USA and **Ryoji Noyori**, Japan — For their work on chirally catalysed hydrogenation reactions. **K. Barry Sharpless**, USA — For his work on chirally catalysed oxidation reactions.

2000. Alan J. Heeger, USA, **Alan G. Macdiarmid**, USA and **Hideki Shirakawa**, Japan — For the discovery and development of conductive polymers.

1999. Ahmed H. Zewail, USA / Egypt — For his studies of the transition states of chemical reactions using femtosecond spectroscopy.

1998. Walter Kohn, USA — For his development of the density-functional theory. **John A. Pople**, United Kingdom/USA — For his development of computational methods in quantum chemistry.

1997. Paul D. Boyer, USA and **John E. Walker**, United Kingdom — For their elucidation of the enzymatic mechanism underlying the synthesis of adenosine triphosphate (ATP). **Jens C. Skou**, Denmark — For the first discovery of an ion-transporting enzyme, Na^+, K^+-ATPase.

1996. Robert F. Curl, Jr., USA, **Sir Harold W. Kroto**, United Kingdom and **Richard E. Smalley**, USA — For their discovery of fullerenes.

1995. Paul Crutzen, Netherlands, **Mario Molina**, Mexico and **Frank Sherwood Rowland**, USA — For their work in atmospheric chemistry, particularly concerning the formation and decomposition of ozone.

1994. George A. Olah, USA — Carbocations.

1993. Kary Banks Mullis, USA — Invention of the polymerase chain reaction (PCR). **Michael Smith**, Canada — Development of site-specific mutagenesis.

1992. Rudolph A. Marcus, USA — Theories of electron transfer.

1991. Richard Robert Ernst, Switzerland — Development of high-resolution nuclear magnetic resonance spectroscopy (NMR).

1990. Elias James Corey, USA — Development of novel methods for the synthesis of complex natural compounds (retrosynthetic analysis).

1989. Sidney Altman, Canada and **Thomas Robert Cech**, USA — Discovery of the catalytic properties of ribonucleic acid (RNA).

1988. Johann Deisenhofer, Germany, **Robert Huber**, Germany and **Hartmut Michel**, Germany — Determination of the three-dimensional structure of a photosynthetic reaction center.

1987. Donald J. Cram, USA, **Charles J. Pedersen**, USA and **Jean-Marie Lehn**, France — Development of molecules with structurally specific interaction of high selectivity.

1986. John C. Polanyi, Canada, **Dudley R. Herschbach**, USA and **Yuan Tseh Lee**, USA — Dynamics of chemical elementary processes.

1985. Herbert A. Hauptman, USA and **Jerome Karle**, USA — Development of direct methods for the determination of crystal structures.

1984. Robert Bruce Merrifield, USA — Method for the preparation of peptides and proteins.

1983. Henry Taube, Canada — Reaction mechanisms of electron transfer, especially with metal complexes.

1982. Aaron Klug, United Kingdom — Development of crystallographic methods for the elucidation of biologically important nucleic acid protein complexes.

1981. Kenichi Fukui, Japan and **Roald Hoffmann**, USA — Theories on the progress of chemical reactions (frontier orbital theory).

1980. Paul Berg, USA — Studies on the biochemistry of nucleic acids, particularly hybrid DNA (technology of gene surgery). **Walter Gilbert**, USA and **Frederick Sanger**, United Kingdom — Determination of base sequences in nucleic acids.

1979. Georg Wittig, Germany and **Herbert C. Brown**, USA — Development of (organic) boron and phosphorous compounds.

1978. Peter D. Mitchell, United Kingdom — Studies of biological energy transfer, development of the chemiosmotic theory.

1977. Ilya Prigogine, Belgium — Contributions to the thermodynamics of irreversible processes, particularly to the theory of dissipative structures.

1976. William N. Lipscomb, USA — Structure of boranes and problems of chemical bonding.

1975. John W. Cornforth, United Kingdom — Stereochemistry of enzyme catalysis reactions. **Vladimir Prelog**, Switzerland/Yugoslavia — Studies on the stereochemistry of organic molecules and reactions.

1974. Paul J. Flory, USA — Physical chemistry of macromolecules.

1973. Ernst Otto Fischer, Germany and **Geoffrey Wilkinson**, United Kingdom — Chemistry of metal-organic sandwich compounds.

1972. Christian B. Anfinsen, USA — Studies on ribonuclease. **Stanford Moore**, USA and **William H. Stein**, USA — Studies on the active center of ribonuclease.

1971. Gerhard Herzberg, Canada — Electron structure and geometry of molecules, particularly of free radicals (molecular spectroscopy).

1970. Luis F. Leloir, Argentina — Discovery of sugar nucleotides and their role in the biosynthesis of carbohydrates.

1969. Odd Hassel, Norway and **Derek H. Barton**, United Kingdom — Development of the concept of conformation.

1968. Lars Onsager, USA, Norway — Studies on the thermodynamics of irreversible processes.

1967. Manfred Eigen, Germany, **George Porter**, United Kingdom and **Ronald G. W. Norrish**, United Kingdom — Investigations of extremely fast chemical reactions.

1966. Robert S. Mulliken, USA — Studies on chemical bonds and the electron structure of molecules by means of the orbital method.

1965. Robert Burns Woodward, USA — Syntheses of natural products.

1964. Dorothy Crowfoot-Hodgkin, United Kingdom — Structure determination of biologically important substances by means of X-rays.

1963. Giulio Natta, Italy and **Karl Ziegler**, Germany — Chemistry and technology of high polymers.

1962. John Cowdery Kendrew, United Kingdom and **Max Ferdinand Perutz**, United Kingdom/Austria — Studies on the structures of globulin proteins.

1961. Melvin Calvin, USA — Studies on the assimilation of carbonic acid by plants (photosynthesis).

1960. Willard F. Libby, USA — Application of carbon 14 for age determinations (radiocarbon dating).

1959. Jaroslav Heyrovský, Czechoslovakia — Polarography.

1958. Frederick Sanger, United Kingdom — Structure of proteins, especially of insulin.

1957. Sir Alexander R. Todd, United Kingdom — Studies on nucleotides and their coenzymes.

1956. Sir Cyril N. Hinshelwood, United Kingdom and **Nikolai N. Semjonow**, Soviet Union — Mechanisms of chemical reactions.

1955. Vincent Du Vigneaud, USA — Synthesis of a polypeptide hormone.

1954. Linus Carl Pauling, USA — Studies on the nature of the chemical bond (molecular structure of proteins).

1953. Hermann Staudinger, Germany — Discoveries in the area of macromolecular chemistry.

1952. Archer J. P. Martin, United Kingdom and **Richard L. M. Synge**, United Kingdom — Invention of distribution chromatography

1951. Edwin M. Mcmillan, USA and **Glenn Seaborg**, USA — Discoveries in the chemistry of transuranium elements.

1950. Kurt Alder, Germany and **Otto P. H. Diels**, Germany — Development of the diene synthesis.

1949. William F. Giauque, USA — Contributions to chemical thermodynamics, properties at extremely low temperatures (adiabatic demagnetization).

1948. Arne W. K. Tiselius, Sweden — Analysis by means of electrophoresis and adsorption, discoveries about serum proteins.

1947. Sir Robert Robinson, United Kingdom — Studies on alkaloids.

1946. John H. Northrop, USA and **Wendell M. Stanley**, USA — Preparation of enzymes and virus proteins in pure form. **James B. Sumner**, USA — Crystallizability of enzymes.

1945. Artturi I. Virtanen, Finland — Discoveries in the area of agricultural and food chemistry, method of preservation of fodder.

1944. Otto Hahn, Germany — Discovery of the nuclear fission of atoms.

1943. George De Hevesy, Hungary — Application of isotopes as indicators in the investigation of chemical processes.

1942. No Nobel Prize was awarded this year. The prize money was with 1/3 allocated to the Main Fund and with 2/3 to the Special Fund of this prize section.

1941. No Nobel Prize was awarded this year. The prize money was with 1/3 allocated to the Main Fund and with 2/3 to the Special Fund of this prize section.

1940. No Nobel Prize was awarded this year. The prize money was with 1/3 allocated to the Main Fund and with 2/3 to the Special Fund of this prize section.

1939. Adolf F. J. Butenandt, Germany — Studies on sexual hormones. **Leopold Ruzicka**, Switzerland — Studies on polymethylenes and higher terpenes.

1938. Richard Kuhn, Germany — Studies on carotenoids and vitamins.

1937. Sir Walter N. Haworth, United Kingdom and **Paul Karrer**, Switzerland — Studies on carotenoids and flavins and vitamins A and B_2.

1936. Peter J. W. Debye, Germany/Netherlands — Studies on dipole moments and the diffraction of X rays and electron beams by gases.

1935. Frédéric Joliot, France and **Irène Joliot-Curie**, France — Syntheses of new radioactive elements (artificial radioactivity).

1934. Harold C. Urey, USA — Discovery of heavy hydrogen (deuterium).

1933. No Nobel Prize was awarded this year. The prize money was with 1/3 allocated to the Main Fund and with 2/3 to the Special Fund of this prize section.

1932. Irving Langmuir, USA — Surface chemistry.

1931. Friedrich Bergius, Germany and **Carl Bosch**, Germany — Development of chemical high-pressure processes.

1930. Hans Fischer, Germany — Studies on blood and plant pigments, synthesis of hemin.

1929. Hans Von Euler-Chelpin, Sweden/Germany and **Arthur Harden**, United Kingdom — Studies on fermentation of sugars and enzymes.

1928. Adolf Windaus, Germany— Study of sterols and their relation with vitamins (vitamin D).

1927. Heinrich O. Wieland, Germany — Constitution of bile acids.

1926. Theodor Svedberg, Sweden — Disperse of systems (ultracentrifuge).

1925. Richard A. Zsigmondy, Germany/Austria — Colloid chemistry (ultramicroscope).

1924. No Nobel Prize was awarded this year. The prize money was allocated to the Special Fund of this prize section.

1923. Fritz Pregl, Austria — Microanalysis of organic compounds.

1922. Francis W. Aston, United Kingdom — Discovery of a large number of isotopes, mass spectrograph.

1921. Frederick Soddy, United Kingdom — Chemistry of radioactive substances, occurrence and nature of the isotopes.

1920. Walther H. Nernst, Germany — Studies on thermodynamics.

1919. No Nobel Prize was awarded this year. The prize money was allocated to the Special Fund of this prize section.

1918. Fritz Haber, Germany — Synthesis of ammonia from its elements.

1917. No Nobel Prize was awarded this year. The prize money was allocated to the Special Fund of this prize section.

1916. No Nobel Prize was awarded this year. The prize money was allocated to the Special Fund of this prize section.

1915. Richard Willstätter, Germany — Investigation of plant pigments, particularly of chlorophyll.

1914. Theodore W. Richards, USA — Determination of atomic weights.

1913. Alfred Werner, Switzerland — Bonding relations of atoms in molecules (inorganic chemistry).

1912. Victor Grignard, France — Grignard's reagent. **Paul Sabatier**, France — Hydrogenation of organic compounds in the presence of finely divided metals.

1911. Marie Curie, France, Poland — Discovery of radium and polonium.

1910. Otto Wallach, Germany — Alicyclic compounds.

1909. Wilhelm Ostwald, Germany — Catalysis, chemical equilibria and reaction rates.

1908. Sir Ernest Rutherford, United Kingdom — Decay of the elements, chemistry of radioactive substances.

1907. Eduard Buchner, Germany — Biochemical studies, discovery of fermentation without cells.

1906. Henri Moissan, France — Investigation and isolation of the element fluorine.

1905. Adolf Von Baeyer, Germany — Organic dyes and hydroaromatic compounds.

1904. Sir William Ramsay, United Kingdom — Discovery of the indifferent gaseous elements in air (noble gases).

1903. Svante A. Arrhenius, Sweden — Theory of electrolytic dissociation.

1902. Emil H. Fischer, Germany — Synthetic studies in the area of sugar and purine groups.

1901. Jacobus Henricus Van't Hoff, Netherlands — Discovery of the laws of chemical dynamics and of the osmotic pressure in solutions.

Appendix 8
All Nobel Prizes in Physiology or Medicine

2022. Svanto Paabo, Sweden — For his discoveries concerning the genomes of extinct hominins and human evolution.

2021. David Julius, USA and **Ardem Patapoutian,** USA — For their discoveries of receptors for temperature and touch.

2020. Harvey J. Alter, USA, **Michael Houghton,** U.K. and **Charles M. Rice**, USA — For the discovery of Hepatitis C Virus.

2019. William G. Kaelin Jr, USA, **Sir Peter J. Ratcliffe**, UK and **Gregg L. Semenza**, USA — For their discoveries of how cells sense and adapt to oxygen availability.

2018. James P. Allison, USA and **Tasuku Honjo**, Japan — For their discovery of cancer therapy by inhibition of negative immune regulation.

2017. Jeffrey C. Hall, USA, **Michael Rosbash**, USA and **Michael W. Young**, USA — For their discoveries of molecular mechanisms controlling the circadian rhythm.

2016. Yoshinori Ohsumi, Japan — For his discoveries of mechanisms for autophagy.

2015. William C. Campbell, Ireland/USA and **Satoshi Ōmura**, Japan — For their discoveries concerning a novel therapy against infections caused by roundworm parasites. **Tu Youyou**, China — For her discoveries concerning a novel therapy against Malaria.

2014. John O'Keefe, USA/UK, **May-Britt Moser**, **Norway and Edvard I. Moser**, Norway — For their discoveries of cells that constitute a positioning system in the brain.

2013. James E. Rothman, USA, **Randy W. Schekman**, USA and **Thomas C. Südhof**, USA/Germany — For their discoveries of machinery regulating vesicle traffic, a major transport system in our cells.

2012. Sir John B. Gurdon, UK and **Shinya Yamanaka**, Japan — For the discovery that mature cells can be reprogrammed to become pluripotent.

2011. Bruce A. Beutler, USA and **Jules A. Hoffmann**, France — For their discoveries concerning the activation of innate immunity.

2010. Robert G. Edwards, U.K. — For the development of *in vitro* fertilization.

2009. Elizabeth H. Blackburn, USA/Australia, **Carol W. Greider**, USA and **Jack W. Szostak**, USA — For the discovery of how chromosomes are protected by telomeres and the enzyme telomerase.

2008. Harald zur Hausen, Germany — For his discovery of human papilloma viruses causing cervical cancer, **Françoise Barré-Sinoussi**, France and **Luc Montagnier**, France — For their discovery of human immunodeficiency virus.

2007. Mario R. Capecchi, USA, **Sir Martin J. Evans,** UK and **Oliver Smithies,** USA — For their discoveries of principles for introducing specific gene modifications in mice by the use of embryonic stem cells.

2006. Andrew Z. Fire, USA and **Craig C. Mello,** USA — For their discovery of RNA interference - gene silencing by double-stranded RNA.

2005. Barry J. Marshall, Australia and **J. Robin Warren,** Australia — For their discovery of the bacterium *Helicobacter pylori* and its role in gastritis and peptic ulcer disease.

2004. Richard Axel, USA and **Linda B. Buck,** USA — For their discoveries of odorant receptors and the organization of the olfactory system.

2003. Paul C. Lauterbur, USA and **Sir Peter Mansfield,** UK — For their discoveries concerning magnetic resonance imaging.

2002. Sydney Brenner, UK, **H. Robert Horvitz,** USA and **John E. Sulston,** UK —For their discoveries concerning genetic regulation of organ development and programmed cell death.

2001. Leland H. Hartwell, USA, **R. Timothy Hunt,** UK and **Paul M. Nurse,** UK — For their discoveries of "key regulators of the cell cycle".

2000. Arvid Carlsson, Sweden, **Paul Greengard,** USA and **Eric Kandel,** USA — For their discoveries concerning signal transduction in the nervous system.

1999. Günter Blobel, USA — For the discovery that proteins have intrinsic signals that govern their transport and localization in the cell.

1998. Robert F. Furchgott, USA, **Louis J. Ignarro,** USA and **Ferid Murad,** USA — For their discoveries concerning nitric oxide as a signaling molecule in the cardiovascular system.

1997. Stanley B. Prusiner, USA — For his discovery of Prions - a new biological principle of infection.

1996. Peter C. Doherty, Australia and **Rolf M. Zinkernagel,** Switzerland — For their discoveries concerning the specificity of the cell mediated immune defense.

1995. Edward B. Lewis, USA — Christiane Nüsslein-Volhard, Federal Republic of Germany. **Eric F. Wieschaus,** USA — For their discoveries concerning the genetic control of early embryonic development.

1994. Alfred G. Gilman, USA and **Martin Rodbell,** USA — For their discovery of G-proteins and the role of these proteins in signal transduction in cells.

1993. Richard J. Roberts, UK and **Phillip A. Sharp,** USA — For their independent discoveries of split genes.

1992. Edmond H. Fischer, Switzerland/USA and **Edwin G. Krebs,** USA — For their discoveries concerning reversible protein phosphorylation as a biological regulatory mechanism.

1991. Erwin Neher, Federal Republic of Germany and **Bert Sakmann,** Federal Republic of Germany — For their discoveries concerning the function of single ion channels in cells.

1990. Joseph E. Murray, USA and **E. Donnall Thomas,** USA — For their discoveries concerning organ and cell transplantation in the treatment of human disease.

1989. J. Michael Bishop, USA and **Harold E. Varmus,** USA — For their discovery of the cellular origin of retroviral oncogenes.

1988. Sir James W. Black, UK, **Gertrude B. Elion,** USA and **George H. Hitchings,** USA — For their discoveries of important principles for drug treatment.

1987. Susumu Tonegawa, Japan — For his discovery of the genetic principle for generation of antibody diversity.

1986. Stanley Cohen, USA and **Rita Levi-Montalcini,** Italy / USA — For their discoveries of growth factors.

1985. Michael S. Brown, USA and **Joseph L. Goldstein,** USA — For their discoveries concerning the regulation of cholesterol metabolism.

1984. Niels K. Jerne, Denmark, **Georges J. F. Köhler,** Federal Republic of Germany and **César Milstein,** Argentina / UK — For theories concerning the specificity in development and control of the immune system and the discovery of the principle for production of monoclonal antibodies.

1983. Barbara McClintock, USA — For her discovery of mobile genetic elements.

1982. Sune K. Bergström, Sweden, **Bengt I. Samuelsson,** Sweden and **Sir John R. Vane,** UK — For their discoveries concerning prostaglandins and related biologically active substances.

1981. Roger W. Sperry, USA — For his discoveries concerning the functional specialization of the cerebral hemispheres. **David H. Hubel,** USA and **Torsten N. Wiesel,** Sweden — For their discoveries concerning information processing in the visual system.

1980. Baruj Benacerraf, USA, **Jean Dausset,** France and **George D. Snell,** USA — For their discoveries concerning genetically determined structures on the cell surface that regulate immunological reactions.

1979. Alan M. Cormack, USA and **Sir Godfrey N. Hounsfield,** UK — For the development of computer assisted tomography.

1978. Werner Arber, Switzerland, **Daniel Nathans,** USA and **Hamilton O. Smith,** USA —For the discovery of restriction enzymes and their application to problems of molecular genetics.

1977. Roger Guillemin, USA and **Andrew V. Schally,** USA — For their discoveries concerning the peptide hormone production of the brain. **Rosalyn Yalow,** USA — For the development of radioimmunoassay of peptide hormones.

1976. Baruch S. Blumberg, USA and **D. Carleton Gajdusek,** USA — For their discoveries concerning new mechanisms for the origin and dissemination of infectious diseases.

1975. David Baltimore, USA, **Renato Dulbecco,** USA and **Howard Martin Temin,** USA — For their discoveries concerning the interaction between tumour viruses and the genetic material of the cell.

1974. Albert Claude, Belgium, **Christian De Duve,** Belgium and **George E. Palade,** USA — For their discoveries concerning the structural and functional organization of the cell.

1973. Karl Von Frisch, Federal Republic of Germany, **Konrad Lorenz,** Austria and **Nikolaas Tinbergen,** USA — For their discoveries concerning organization and elicitation of individual and social behavior patterns.

1972. Gerald M. Edelman, USA and **Rodney R. Porter,** UK — For their discoveries concerning the chemical structure of antibodies.

1971. Earl W. Jr. Sutherland, USA — For his discoveries concerning the mechanisms of the action of hormones.

1970. Sir Bernard Katz, UK, **Ulf Von Euler,** Sweden and **Julius Axelrod,** USA — For their discoveries concerning the humeral transmitters in the nerve terminals and the mechanism for their storage, release and inactivation.

1969. Max Delbrück, USA, **Alfred D. Hershey,** USA and **Salvador E. Luria,** USA — For their discoveries concerning the replication mechanism and the genetic structure of viruses.

1968. Robert W. Holley, USA, **Har Gobind Khorana,** USA and **Marshall W. Nirenberg,** USA — For their interpretation of the genetic code and its function in protein synthesis.

1967. Ragnar Granit, Sweden, **Haldan Keffer Hartline,** USA and **George Wald,** USA — For their discoveries concerning the primary physiological and chemical visual processes in the eye.

1966. Peyton Rous, USA — For his discovery of tumour inducing viruses. **Charles Brenton Huggins,** USA — For his discoveries concerning hormonal treatment of prostate cancer.

1965. François Jacob, France, **André Lwoff,** France and **Jacoues Monod,** France — For their discoveries concerning genetic control of enzyme and virus synthesis.

1964. Konrad Bloch, USA and **Feodor Lynen,** Federal Republic of Germany — For their discoveries concerning the mechanism and regulation of the cholesterol and fatty acid metabolism.

1963. Sir John Carew Eccles, Australia, **Sir Alan Lloyd Hodgkin,** UK and **Sir Andrew Fielding Huxley,** UK — For their discoveries concerning the ionic mechanisms involved in excitation and inhibition in the peripheral and central portions of the nerve cell membrane.

1962. Francis Harry Compton Crick, UK, **James Dewey Watson,** USA and **Maurice Hugh Frederick Wilkins,** UK/New Zealand —For their discoveries concerning the molecular structure of nuclear acids and its significance for information transfer in living material.

1961. Georg von Békésy, USA — For his discoveries of the physical mechanism of stimulation within the cochlea.

1960. Sir Frank Macfarlane Burnet, Australia, **Sir Peter Brian Medawar,** UK — For discovery of acquired immunological tolerance.

1959. Severo Ochoa, USA and **Arthur Kornberg,** USA — For their discovery of the mechanisms in the biological synthesis of ribonucleic acid and deoxyribonucleic acid.

1958. George Wells Beadle, USA and **Edward Lawrie Tatum,** USA — For their discovery that genes act by regulating definite chemical events.

Joshua Lederberg, USA — For his discoveries concerning genetic recombination and the organization of the genetic material of bacteria.

1957. Daniel Bovet, Italy — For his discoveries relating to synthetic compounds that inhibit the action of certain body substances, and especially their action on the vascular system and the skeletal muscles.

1956. André Frédéric Cournand, USA, **Werner Forssmann,** Federal Republic of Germany and **Dickinson W. Richards,** USA — For their discoveries concerning heart cauterization and pathological changes in the circulatory system.

1955. Axel Hugo Theodor Theorell, Sweden — For his discoveries concerning the nature and mode of action of oxidation enzymes.

1954. John Franklin Enders, USA, **Thomas Huckle Weller,** USA and **Frederick Chapman Robbins,** USA — For their discovery of the ability of poliomyelitis viruses to grow in cultures of various types of tissue.

1953. Sir Hans Adolf Krebs, UK — For his discovery of the citric acid cycle. **Fritz Albert Lipmann,** USA — For his discovery of co-enzyme A and its importance for intermediary metabolism.

1952. Selman Abraham Waksman, USA — For his discovery of streptomycin, the first antibiotic effective against tuberculosis.

1951. Max Theiler, Union of South Africa — For his discoveries concerning yellow fever and how to combat it.

1950. Edward Calvin Kendall, USA, **Tadeus Reichstein,** Switzerland and **Philip Showalter**

Hench, USA — For their discoveries relating to the hormones of the adrenal cortex, their structure and biological effects.

1949. Walter Rudolf Hess, Switzerland — For his discovery of the functional organization of the interbrain as a coordinator of the activities of the internal organs. **Antonio Caetano De Abreu Freire Egas Moniz,** Portugal — For his discovery of the therapeutic value of leucotomy in certain psychoses.

1948. Paul Hermann Müller, Switzerland — For his discovery of the high efficiency of DDT as a contact poison against several arthropods.

1947. Carl Ferdinand Cori, USA and **Gerty Theresa Cori,** USA — For their discovery of the course of the catalytic conversion of glycogen. **Bernardo Alberto Houssay,** Argentina — For his discovery of the part played by the hormone of the anterior pituitary lobe in the metabolism of sugar.

1946. Hermann Joseph Muller, USA — For the discovery of the production of mutations by means of X-ray irradiation.

1945. Sir Alexander Fleming, UK, **Sir Ernst Boris Chain,** UK and **Lord Howard Walter Florey,** Australia — For the discovery of penicillin and its curative effect in various infectious diseases.

1944. Joseph Erlanger, USA and **Herbert Spencer Gasser,** USA — For their discoveries relating to the highly differentiated functions of single nerve fibres.

1943. Henrik Carl Peter Dam, Denmark — For his discovery of vitamin K. **Edward Adelbert Doisy,** USA — For his discovery of the chemical nature of vitamin K.

1942-1940. The prize money was allocated to the Main Fund (1/3) and to the Special Fund (2/3) of this prize section.

1939. Gerhard Domagk, Germany — For the discovery of the antibacterial effects of prontosil. (Caused by the authorities of his country to decline the award, but later received the diploma and the medal.)

1938. Corneille Jean François Heymans, Belgium — For the discovery of the role played by the sinus and aortic mechanisms in the regulation of respiration.

1937. Albert Szent-Györgyi Von Nagyrapolt, Hungary — For his discoveries in connection with the biological combustion processes, with special reference to vitamin C and the catalysis of fumaric acid.

1936. Sir Henry Hallett Dale, UK and **Otto Loewi,** Austria — For their discoveries rela-ting to chemical transmission of nerve impulses.

1935. Hans Spemann, Germany — For his discovery of the organizer effect in embryonic development.

1934. George Hoyt Whipple, USA, **George Richards Minot,** USA and **William Parry Murphy,** USA — For their discoveries concerning liver therapy in cases of anemia.

1933. Thomas Hunt Morgan, USA — For his discoveries concerning the role played by the chromosome in heredity.

1932. Sir Charles Scott Sherrington, UK and **Lord Edgar Douglas Adrian,** UK — For their discoveries regarding the functions of neurons.

1931. Otto Heinrich Warburg, Germany — For his discovery of the nature and mode of action of the respiratory enzyme.

1930. Karl Landsteiner, Austria — For his discovery of human blood groups.

1929. Christiaan Eijkman, The Netherlands — For his discovery of the antineuritic vitamin. **Sir Frederick Gowland Hopkins,** UK — For his discovery of the growth-stimulating vitamins.

1928. Charles Jules Henri Nicolle, France — For his work on typhus.

1927. Julius Wagner-Jauregg, Austria — For his discovery of the therapeutic value of malaria inoculation in the treatment of dementia paralytica.

1926. Johannes Andreas Grib Fibiger, Denmark — For his discovery of the *Spiroptera* carcinoma.

1925. The prize money for 1925 was allocated to the Special Fund of this prize section.

1924. Willem Einthoven, Netherlands — For his discovery of the mechanism of the electro-cardiogram.

1923. Sir Frederick Grant Banting, Canada and **John James Richard Macleod,** Canada — For the discovery of insulin.

1922. Sir Archibald Vivian Hill, UK — For his discovery relating to the production of heat in the muscle. **Otto Fritz Meyerhof,** Germany — For his discovery of the fixed relationship between the consumption of oxygen and the metabolism of lactic acid in the muscle.

1921. The prize money for 1921 was allocated to the Special Fund of this prize Section.

1920. Schack August Steenberger Krogh, Denmark — For his discovery of the capillary motor regulating mechanism.

1919. Jules Bordet, Belgium — For his discoveries relating to immunity.

1918-1915. The prize money for 1918-1915 was allocated to the Special Fund of this prize section.

1914. Robert Bárány, Austria — For his work on the physiology and pathology of the vestibular apparatus.

1913. Charles Robert Richet, France — In recognition of his work on anaphylaxis.

1912. Alexis Carrel, France — In recognition of his work on vascular suture and the transplantation of blood-vessels and organs.

1911. Allvar Gullstrand, Sweden — For his work on the dioptrics of the eye.

1910. Albrecht Kossel, Germany — In recognition of the contributions to our knowledge of cell chemistry made through his work on proteins, including the nucleic substances.

1909. Emil Theodor Kocher, Switzerland — For his work on the physiology, pathology and surgery of the thyroid gland.

1908. Ilya Ilyich Mechnikov, Russia and **Paul Ehrlich,** Germany — In recognition of their work on immunity.

1907. Charles Louis Alphonse Laveran, France — In recognition of his work on the role played by protozoa in causing diseases.

1906. Camillo Golgi, Italy and **Santiago Ramon Cajal,** Spain — In recognition of their work on the structure of the nervous system.

1905. Robert Koch, Germany — For his investigations and discoveries in relation to tuberculosis.

1904. Ivan Petrovich Pavlov, Russia — In recognition of his work on the physiology of digestion, through which knowledge on vital aspects of the subject has been transformed and enlarged.

1903. Niels Ryberg Finsen, Denmark — In recognition of his contribution to the treatment of diseases, especially *Lupus vulgaris,* with concentrated light radiation, whereby he has opened a new avenue for medical science.

1902. Sir Ronald Ross, UK — For his work on malaria, by which he has shown how it enters the organism and thereby has laid the foundation for successful research on this disease and methods of combating it.

1901. Emil Adolf von Behring, Germany — For his work on serum therapy, especially its application against diphtheria, by which he has opened a new road in the domain of medical science and thereby placed in the hands of the physician a victorious weapon against illness and deaths.

Appendix 9
All Nobel Peace Prizes

The Nobel Peace Prize has been awarded 103 times to 140 Nobel Laureates between 1901 and 2022, 110 individuals and 30 organizations. Since the International Committee of the Red Cross has been awarded the Nobel Peace Prize three times (in 1917, 1944 and 1963), and the Office of the United Nations High Commissioner for Refugees has been awarded the Nobel Peace Prize two times (in 1954 and 1981), there are 30 individual organizations which have been awarded the Nobel Peace Prize.

2022. Alex Byalyatski, Belarus — Russian rights group Memorial and Ukraine Center for Civil Liberties amid a war in their region that is the worst conflict in Europe since World War II.

2021. Maria Ressa, Philippines and **Dmitry Muratov**, Russia — For their efforts to safeguard freedom of expression which is a precondition for democracy and lasting peace.

2020. World Food Programme (founded in 1961) by the Norwegian Nobel Committee.

2019. Abiy Ahmed Ali, Ethiopia — For his efforts to achieve peace and international cooperation, and in particular for his decisive initiative to resolve the border conflict with neighbouring Eritrea.

2018. Denis Mukwege, DRC and **Nadia Murad**, Iraq — For their efforts to end the use of sexual violence as a weapon of war and armed conflict.

2017. International Campaign to Abolish Nuclear Weapons (ICAN) — For its work to draw attention to the catastrophic humanitarian consequences of any use of nuclear weapons and for its ground-breaking efforts to achieve a treaty-based prohibition of such weapons.

2016. Juan Manuel Santos, Colombia — For his resolute efforts to bring the country's more than 50-year-long civil war to an end.

2015. National Dialogue Quartet — For its decisive contribution to the building of a pluralistic democracy in Tunisia in the wake of the Jasmine Revolution of 2011.

2014. Kailash Satyarthi, India and **Malala Yousafzai**, Pakistan — For their struggle against the suppression of children and young people and for the right of all children to education.

2013. Organisation for the Prohibition of Chemical Weapons (OPCW) — For its extensive efforts to eliminate chemical weapons.

2012. European Union (EU) — For over six decades contributed to the advancement of peace and reconciliation, democracy and human rights in Europe.

2011. Ellen Johnson Sirleaf, Liberia, **LeymahGbowee**, Liberia and **Tawakkol Karman**, Yemen — For their non-violent struggle for the safety of women and for women's rights to full participation in peace-building work.

2010. Liu Xiaobo, China — For his long and non-violent struggle for fundamental human rights in China.

2009. Barack H. Obama, USA — For his extraordinary efforts to strengthen international diplomacy and cooperation between peoples.

2008. Martti Ahtisaari, Finland — For his important efforts, on several continents and over more than three decades, to resolve international conflicts.

2007. Intergovernmental panel on climate change (IPCC), Switzerland and **Albert Arnold (Al) Gore Jr.,** USA — For their efforts to build up and disseminate greater knowledge about man-made climate change, and to lay the foundations for the measures that are needed to counteract such change.

2006. Muhammad Yunus, Bangladesh and **Grameen Bank,** Bangladesh — For their efforts to create economic and social development from below.

2005. International Atomic Energy Agency, Austria and **Mohamed Elbaradei,** Egypt — For their efforts to prevent nuclear energy from being used for military purposes and to ensure that nuclear energy for peaceful purposes is used in the safest possible way.

2004. Wangari Maathai, Kenya — For her contribution to sustainable development, democracy and peace.

2003. Shirin Ebadi, Iran — For her efforts for democracy and human rights.

2002. Jimmy Carter Jr., USA, Former President of the United States of America, for his decades of untiring effort to find peaceful solutions to international conflicts, to advance democracy and human rights.

2001. United Nations, New York, USA and **Kofi Annan,** Ghana — United Nations Secretary General.

2000. Kim Dae Jung, South Korea — For his work for democracy and human rights in South Korea and in East Asia in general, and for peace and reconciliation with North Korea in particular.

1999. Doctors Without Borders, Brussels, Belgium.

1998. John Hume, Northern Ireland and **David Trimble,** Northern Ireland — For their efforts to find a peaceful solution to the conflict in Northern Ireland.

1997. International campaign to ban landmines (ICBL) and **Jody Williams,** USA — For their work for the banning and clearing of anti-personnel mines.

1996. Carlos Felipe Ximenes Belo, East Timor and **Jose Ramos-Horta,** East Timor — For their work towards a just and peaceful solution to the conflict in East Timor.

1995. Joseph Rotblat, Poland/UK and **Pugwash Conferences on Science and World Affairs** — For their efforts to diminish the part played by nuclear arms in international politics and in the longer run to eliminate such arms.

1994. Yasser Arafat, Palestine — Chairman of the Executive Committee of the PLO. President of the Palestinian National Authority. **Shimon Peres,** Israel, Foreign Minister of Israel and **Yitzhak Rabin,** Israel, Prime Minister of Israel — For their efforts to create peace in the Middle East.

1993. Nelson Mandela, South Africa, Leader of the ANC and **Fredrik Willem De Klerk.** President of the Republic of South Africa.

1992. Rigoberta Menchu Tum, Guatemala — Campaigner for human rights, especially for indigenous peoples.

1991. Aung San Suu Kyi, Burma — Oppositional leader, human rights advocate.

1990. Mikhail Sergeyevich Gorbachev, Russia — President of the USSR who helped to bring the Cold War to an end.

1989. The 14th Dalai Lama (Tenzin Gyatso), Tibet — Religious and political leader of the Tibetan people.

1988. The United Nations Peace Keeping Forces New York, NY, U.S.A.

1987. Oscar Arias Sanchez, Costa Rica — President of Costa Rica. Initiator of peace negotiations in Central America.

1986. Elie Wiesel, U.S.A — Chairman of 'The President's Commission on the Holocaust'.

1985. International Physicians for the Prevention of Nuclear War, Boston, U.S.A.

1984. Desmond Mpilo Tutu, South Africa — Bishop of Johannesburg, former Secretary General South African Council of Churches (S.A.C.C.). for his work against apartheid.

1983. Lech Walesa, Poland — Founder of Solidarity, campaigner for human rights.

1982. Alva Myrdal, Sweden — Former Cabinet Minister and diplomat. Delegate to United Nations General Assembly on Disarmament. **Alfonso García Robles,** Mexico — diplomat, delegate to the United Nations General Assembly on Disarmament, former Secretary for Foreign Affairs.

1981. Office of the United Nations High Commissioner for Refugees, Geneva, Switzerland.

1980. Adolfo Perez Esquivel, Argentina — Architect, sculptor and human rights leader.

1979. Mother Teresa, India — Leader of the Order of the Missionaries of Charity.

1978. Mohamed Anwar Al-Sadat, President of the Arab Republic of Egypt and **Menachem Begin,** Prime Minister of Israel — For jointly negotiating peace between Egypt and Israel.

1977. Amnesty International London, Great Britain — A worldwide organization for the protection of the rights of prisoners of conscience.

1976. Betty Williams, Northern Ireland and UK and **Mairead Corrigan,** Northern Ireland and UK — Founders of the Northern Ireland Peace Movement.

1975. Andrei Dmitrievich Sakharov, Russia-Soviet nuclear physicist. Campaigner for human rights.

1974. Seán Mac Bride, Ireland — President of the International Peace Bureau, Geneva, and the Commission of Namibia, United Nations, New York and **Eisaku Sato,** Prime Minister of Japan.

1973. Henry A. Kissinger — Secretary of State, State Department, Washington and **Le Duc Tho,** Democratic Republic of Viet Nam (Declined the prize.) — For jointly negotiating the Vietnam peace accord in 1973.

1972. The prize money for 1972 was allocated to the Main Fund.

1971. Willy Brandt, Federal Republic of Germany — Chancellor of the Federal Republic of Germany.

1970. Norman Borlaug, USA — Led research at the International Maize and Wheat Improvement Center, Mexico City.

1969. International Labour Organization (I.L.O.), Geneva.

1968. René Cassin, France — President of the European Court for Human Rights.

1967-1966. The prize money was allocated to the Main Fund (1/3) and to the Special Fund (2/3) of this prize section.

1965. United Nations Children's Fund (UNICEF), New York — Founded by U.N. in 1946. An international aid organization.

1964. Martin Luther King Jr., USA — Leader of the Southern Christian Leadership Conference and campaigner for civil rights.

1963. International Committee of the Red Cross, Geneva, founded in1863. League of Red Cross Societies, Geneva.

1962. Linus Carl Pauling, USA — California Institute of Technology. Campaigner for an end to nuclear weapons tests.

1961. Dag Hjalmar Agne Carl Hammarskjöld, Sweden — Secretary General of the United Nations (awarded the Prize posthumously).

1960. Albert John Lutuli, Rhodesia, South Africa — President of the South Africa liberation movement, the African National Congress.

1959. Philip J. Noel-Baker, Great Britain — Member of Parliament, life long worker for international peace and co-operation.

1958. Georges Henri Pire, Belgium — Father of the Dominican Order, Leader of the relief organization for refugees, l'Europe du Coeur au Service du Monde.

1957. Lester Bowles Pearson, Canada — A Former Secretary of State for External Affairs of Canada.

1956-1955. The prize money was allocated to the Main Fund (1/3) and to the Special Fund (2/3) of this prize section.

1954. Office of the United Nations High Commissioner for Refugees, Geneva — An international relief organization, founded by U.N. in 1951.

1953. George Catlett Marshall, USA — President of American Red Cross, ex-Secretary of State and of Defense and a Delegate to the U.N.

1952. Albert Schweitzer, Germany/Gabon — Missionary surgeon. Founder Lambaréné Hospital in République du Gabon.

1951. Léon Jouhaux, France — President of the International Committee of the European Council and a delegate to the UN.

1950. Ralph Bunche, USA — Professor Harvard University, Cambridge. Acting Mediator in Palestine 1948.

1949. Lord John Boyd Orr of Brechin, Scotland/ UK — Physician, Politician, prominent organizer and Director General Food and Agricultural Organization, President National Peace Council and World Union of Peace Organizations.

1948. The prize money was allocated to the Main Fund (1/3) and to the Special Fund (2/3) of this prize section.

1947. The Friends Service Council (The Quakers), London. Founded in 1647. — **The American Friends Service Committee** (The Quakers), Washington. The society's first official meeting was held in 1672.

1946. Emily Greene Balch, USA — Former Professor of History and Sociology and Honorary International President of Women's International League for Peace and Freedom. **John Raleigh Mott,** USA — Chairman of the first International Missionary Council, President of the World Alliance of Young Men's Christian Associations.

1945. Cordell Hull, USA — Former Secretary of State and one of the initiators of the United Nations.

1944. International Committee of the Red Cross, Geneva.

1943-1939. The prize money was allocated to the Main Fund (1/3) and to the Special Fund (2/3) of this prize section.

1938. Nansen International Office for Refugees — An international relief organization in Geneva started by F. Nansen in 1921.

1937. Cecil of Chelwood, Viscount, UK — Writer and Founder and President of the International Peace Campaign.

1936. Carlos Saavedra Lamas, Argentina — Foreign Minister and President of the League of Nations).

1935. Carl Von Ossietzky, Germany — A Journalist.

1934. Arthur Henderson, UK — A Former Foreign Secretary and Chairman of the League of Nations Disarmament Conference 1932-1934.

1933. Sir Norman Angell (Ralph Lane), UK — A Writer and Member of the Commission Executive Committee of the League of Nations and the National Peace Council.

1932. The prize money for 1932 was allocated to the Special Fund of this prize section.

1931. Jane Addams, USA — A Sociologist and International President of the Women's International League for Peace and Freedom. **Nicholas Murray Butler,** USA — President of Columbia University. Promoter of the Briand-Kellogg Pact.

1930. Lars Olof Nathan (Jonathan) Söderblom, Sweden — An Archbishop.

1929. Frank Billings Kellogg, USA — A Former Secretary of State who Negotiated the Briand-Kellogg Pact.

1928. The prize money for 1928 was allocated to the Special Fund of this prize section.

1927. Ferdinand Buisson, France — A Former Professor at the Sorbonne University, Paris and Founder and President of the League for Human Rights. **Ludwig Quidde,** Germany — He was a Historian and Professor at Berlin University. Member of Germany's constituent assembly 1919.

1926. Aristide Briand, France — He was the Foreign Minister and Negotiator of the Locarno Treaty and the Briand-Kellogg Pact and **Gustav Stresemann,** Germany — A Former Lord High Chancellor (Reichs-kanzler), Foreign Minister and Negotiator of the Locarno Treaty.

1925. Sir Austen Chamberlain, UK — He was the Foreign Minister and Negotiator of the Locarno Treaty. **Charles Gates Dawes,** USA — He was the Vice-President of the United States of America.

1924-1923. The prize money for 1924-1923 was allocated to the Special Fund of this prize section.

1922. Fridtjof Nansen, Norway — A Scientist and Explorer.

1921. Karl Hjalmar Branting, Sweden — He was the Prime Minister and Swedish Delegate to the Council of the League of Nations and **Christian Lous Lange,** Norway — He was the Secretary General of the Inter-Parliamentary Union, Brussels.

1920. Léon Victor Auguste Bourgeois, France — A Former Secretary of State and President of the Parliament (Sénat).

1919. Thomas Woodrow Wilson, USA — He was the President of the United States of America and Founder of the League of Nations.

1918. The prize money for 1918 was allocated to the Special Fund of this prize section.

1917. International Committee of The Red Cross, Geneva.

1916-1914. The prize money for 1916-1914 was allocated to the Special Fund of this prize section.

1913. Henri La Fontaine, Belgium — A Member of the Belgian Parliament and President of the Permanent International Peace Bureau, Berne.

1912. Elihu Root, USA — A Former Secretary of State and Initiator of several arbitration agreements.

1911. Tobias Michael Carel Asser, The Netherlands — A Cabinet Minister and Member of the Privy Council. Initiator of the International Conferences of Private Law at the Hague. **Alfred Hermann Fried,** Austria — He was a Journalist and Founder of the peace journal *Die Waffen Nieder*.

1910. Bureau International Permanent De La Paix (Permanent International Peace Bureau), Bern.

1909. Auguste Marie François Beernaert, Belgium — He was a Former Prime Minister and Member of the Belgian Parliament and **Paul Henribenjamin Balluet D'estournelles De Constant, Baron De Constant De Rebecque,** France — He was a Member of the French Parliament (Sénateur). Founder and President of the French parliamentary group for international arbitration.

1908. Klas Pontus Arnoldson, Sweden — He was a Writer and Former Member of the Swedish Parliament and Founder of the Swedish Peace and Arbitration League and **Fredrik Bajer,** Denmark — Member of the Danish Parliament. Honorary President of the Permanent International Peace Bureau, Berne.

1907. Ernesto Teodoro Moneta, Italy — He was the President of the Lombard League of Peace and **Louis Renault,** France — He was a Professor of International Law at Sorbonne University, Paris.

1906. Theodore Roosevelt, USA — He was the President of the United States of America and one of the signatories of 1905 peace treaty between Russia and Japan.

1905. Baroness Bertha Sophie Felicita Von Suttner, Austria — She was the Honorary President of the Permanent International Peace Bureau, Berne and author of *Die Waffen Nieder* (Lay Down Your Arms).

1904. Institute of International Law, Gent, Belgium — A scientific society.

1903. Sir William Randal Cremer, Great Britain — He was the member of the British Parliament.

1902. Elie Ducommun, Switzerland — He was the Honorary Secretary of the Permanent International Peace Bureau, Berne and **Charles Albert Gobat,** Switzerland — He was the Secretary General of the Inter-Parliamentary Union and the Honorary Secretary of the Permanent International Peace Bureau, Berne.

1901. Jean Henri Dunant, Switzerland — He was the founder of the International Committee of the Red Cross, Geneva and **Frédéric Passy,** France — He was the founder and President of the first French peace society.

Appendix 10

List of Indian/India Born Nobel Prize Winners

NOBEL PRIZE IN LITERATURE

1. Rabindranath Tagore (1861-1941) was a Bengali poet, philosopher, playwright, composer, and a novelist. He became Asia's first Nobel laureate when he won the 1913 Nobel Prize in Literature. Tagore was born in Calcutta. He was a Bengali Brahmin by birth. Tagore began writing poems at the age of eight and wrote his first short stories and dramas when he was sixteen years old. His major works included *Gitanjali*, *Gora*, and *Ghare-Baire*. Two of his songs are now the national anthems of Bangladesh and India, i.e., the *Amar Shonar Bangla* and the *Jana Gana Mana*, respectively.

2. Sir Vidiadhar Surajprasad Naipaul (1932-2018) was a novelist from Trinidad. He descended from Hindu Indians who immigrated to Trinidad. Naipaul left Trinidad in 1950 to attend Oxford University and settled in England. He won critical recognition with *A House for Mr. Biswas* (1961). Other novels written by him include, *In a Free State* (1971, Booker Prize), *Guerrillas* (1975), and *A Bend in the River* (1979). He also wrote *The Enigma of Arrival* (1987) and *Half a Life* (2001). Naipaul was awarded the Nobel Prize for Literature in 2001.

NOBEL PRIZE IN PHYSICS

1. Sir Chandrasekhara Venkata Raman (1888-1970). He was born in Trichinopoly and died in Bangalore. He received a Nobel Prize in 1930 for discovering that when light passes through a transparent material, some of the light that emerges at a right angle to the original beam is of other frequencies (Raman frequencies) characteristic of the material.

2. Subrahmanyan Chandrasekhar (1910-1995). He was born in Lahore and died in Chicago. He left the University of Cambridge to join the staff of the University of Chicago in 1938. He reported that following its red giant phase, a star with a remaining mass greater than 1.4 times that of the Sun (the Chandrasekhar limit) collapses and becomes a neutron star during a supernova explosion. Stellar remnants more massive than about three solar masses collapse even further to become black holes. He shared a 1983 Nobel Prize with W. A. Fowler.

NOBEL PRIZE IN PHYSIOLOGY OR MEDICINE

1. Har Gobind Khorana (1922-2011). He was born in Raipur. He obtained his PhD from the University of Liverpool and later taught in Canada and the US, from 1970 at MIT. He shared 1968 Nobel Prize with M. W. Norenberg and R. W. Holley for research that helped show how the cell nucleus controls the synthesis of proteins. In 1970 he prepared the first artificial copy of a yeast gene.

NOBEL PRIZE IN CHEMISTRY

1. Venkatraman Radhakrishnan (1952-), Tamil Nadu born received the 2009 Nobel Prize in Chemistry "for the structure and function of the ribosome". He shared the award with Thomas A. Steitz and Ada E. Yonath. He was working with MRC Laboratory of Molecular Biology in Cambridge when he received the honour. He grew up in a family of academics. While his father, C. V. Ramakrishnan, got his Post-Doctoral Fellowship in Madison, Wisconsin, his mother, R. Rajalakshmi, obtained a McGill University Fellowship to do PhD in Psychology, which she finished in 18 months.

Vital functions of an organisms are managed by complex protein molecules produced in the cell's ribosomes. Along with other researchers, Venkataraman Ramakrishnan used X-Ray crystallography in 2000 to determine the structure of ribosomes, which is made up of hundreds of thousands of atoms. Among other applications, Nobel Prize website mentioned that Ramakrishnan's research has been vital in the production of antibiotics.

NOBEL PRIZE IN ECONOMICS

1. Amartya Sen (1933-). He was born at Santiniketan, India. He was awarded the 1998 Nobel Prize in Economics for his work in welfare economics and social choice. Sen is well known for his work on the causes of famine and his research led to the development of solutions for limiting the effects of food shortages. After studying at Presidency College in Calcutta he went to the University of Cambridge. He taught in the universities of Jadavpur from 1956–58 and Delhi from 1963–71, the London School of Economics from 1971–77, the University of Oxford from 1977–88, and Harvard University from 1988–98. He wrote *Poverty and Famines: An Essay on Entitlement and Deprivation* (1981) which showed that declining wages, unemployment, rising food prices, and inefficient food distribution could lead to starvation.

2. Abhijit Vinayak Banerjee (1961-), Mumbai born economist made the country proud as he became the 10th Indian and the sixth laureate with the Calcutta chromosome, to win a Nobel Prize in Economic Sciences. He shared the prestigious global award with his economist-wife, Esther Duflo and another US-based economist Michael Kremer. The Swedish Academy announced 2019 Sveriges Riksbank Prize in Economic Sciences in memory of Alfred Nobel for the economists approach to alleviating global poverty. Born in 1961, the half-Bengali and half-Konkani lived his early life in West Bengal and studied at the University of Calcutta. Later he received his post-graduate degree in Economics from New Delhi's Jawaharlal Nehru University in 1983. He went on to obtain his PhD in Economics from the Harvard University in 1988. Currently he is the Ford Foundation Professor of Economics at Massachusetts Institute of Technology in Cambridge, shared his views on India's economic showdown. He warned the Indian economy is going into 'a tailspin' and his solution is for the Indian Government to focus on an increasing demand, rather than on deficits or stability.

NOBEL PEACE PRIZE

1. Mother Teresa (1910 –1997) won the Nobel Peace Prize in 1979. She was born Agnes Gonxha Bojaxhiu in Skopje, Macedonia, on August 26, 1910. Her family was of Albanian descent. At the age of twelve, she felt strongly the call of God. She knew she had to be a missionary to spread the love of Christ. At the age of eighteen she left her parental home in Skopje and joined the Sisters of Loreto, an Irish community of nuns with missions in India. After a few months' training in Dublin she was sent to India, where on May 24, 1931, she took her initial vows as a nun. From 1931 to 1948 Mother Teresa taught at St. Mary's High School in Calcutta, but the suffering and poverty she glimpsed outside the convent walls made such a deep impression on her that in 1948 she received permission from her superiors to leave the convent school and devote herself to working among the poorest of the poor in the slums of Calcutta. Although she had no funds, she depended on Divine Providence, and started an open-air school for slum children. Soon she was joined by voluntary helpers, and financial support was also forthcoming. This made it possible for her to extend the scope of her work. On October 7, 1950, Mother Teresa received permission from the Holy See to start her own order, "The Missionaries of Charity", whose primary task was to love and care for those persons nobody was prepared to look after. In 1965 the Society became an International Religious Family by a decree of Pope Paul VI. Today the order comprises Active and Contemplative branches of Sisters and Brothers in many countries. In 1963 both the Contemplative branch of the Sisters and the Active branch of the Brothers was founded. In 1979 the Contemplative branch of the Brothers was added, and in 1984 the Priest branch was established.The Society of Missionaries has spread all over the world, including the former Soviet Union and Eastern European countries. They provide effective help to the poorest of the poor in a number of countries in Asia, Africa, and Latin America, and they undertake relief work in the wake of natural catastrophes such as floods, epidemics, and famine, and for refugees. The order also has houses in North America, Europe and Australia, where they take care of the shut-ins, alcoholics, homeless, and AIDS sufferers. The Missionaries of Charity throughout the world are aided and assisted by Co-Workers who became an official International Association on March 29, 1969. By the 1990s there were over one million Co-Workers in more than 40 countries. Along with the Co-Workers, the lay Missionaries of Charity try to follow Mother Teresa's spirit and charisma in their families. Mother Teresa's work has been recognised and acclaimed throughout the world and she has received a number of awards and distinctions, including the Pope John XXIII Peace Prize (1971) and the Nehru Prize for her promotion of international peace and understanding (1972). She also received the Balzan Prize (1979) and the Templeton and Magsaysay awards.

2. Kailash Satyarthi (1954-), along with Malala Yousafzai, received the Nobel Peace Prize in 2014 "for their struggle against the suppression of children and young people, and for the right of all children to education". He taught children in Vidisha, a small town in Madhya Pradesh, where he grew up. He had acquired his degree in Electrical Engineering, but decided to be a teacher. In 1980, he left teaching and founded "Bachpan Bachao Andolan", an organization that worked towards freeing children from slave-like conditions. He has been active for the fight against child labour and children's rights to education in a wide range of other organizations. To achieve a peaceful world, following the tradition of Mahatama Gandhi, the Indian activist has been working towards ending child labour, exploitation, and encouraging them to attend School. He also contributed to the development of international conventions on the rights of children, according to the Swedish Academy. As a mentor of UNESCO body, he works towards providing "Education for All". After his Nobel win, he made it to the Fortune "World's Greatest Leaders" list in 2015. Satyarthi is married to Sumedha, and has two children—a son and a daughter.

Appendix 11

State Agricultural Universities in India

1. Acharya NG Ranga Agricultural University, Rajendra Nagar, Hyderabad-500030, Andhra Pradesh
2. Agriculture University, Mandor, Jodhpur-342304
3. Agriculture University Borkhera, Kota-324001
4. Anand Agricultural University, Anand-388110, Gujarat
5. Assam Agricultural University, Jorhat-785013, Assam
6. Bidhan Chandra Krishi Viswavidyalaya, Mohanpur, Nadia-741252, West Bengal
7. Bihar Agricultural University, Bhagalpur-813210, Bihar
8. Birsa Agricultural University, Kanke, Ranchi-834006, Jharkhand
9. Chandra Shekhar Azad University of Agriculture & Technology, Kanpur-208002, Uttar Pradesh
10. Chaudhary Charan Singh Haryana Agricultural University, Hisar-125004, Haryana
11. Chhattisgarh Kamdhenu Vishwavidyalaya, Anjora, Durg, Chhattisgarh
12. CSK Himachal Pradesh Krishi Vishvavidyalaya, Palampur-176062, Himachal Pradesh
13. Dr Balasaheb Sawant Konkan Krishi Vidyapeeth, Dapoli Distt, Ratnagiri 415712, Maharashtra
14. Dr Panjabrao Deshmukh Krishi Vidyapeeth, Krishinagar, Akola-444104, Maharashtra
15. Dr YSP Horticultural University Solan, Nauni-173230, Himachal Pradesh
16. Dr YSR Horticultural University, West Godavari Dist., Tadepalligudem-534101, Andhra Pradesh
17. Govind Ballabh Pant University of Agriculture & Technology, Pantnagar-263145, Dist. Udham Singh, Nagar, Uttarakhand
18. Guru Angad Dev Veterinary and Animal Science University, Ludhiana-141004, Punjab
19. Indira Gandhi Krishi Vishwavidyalaya, Krishak Nagar, Raipur-492006, Chhattisgarh
20. Jawaharlal Nehru Krishi Viswavidyalaya, Krishi Nagar, Adhartal, Jabalpur-482004, Madhya Pradesh

21. Junagadh Agricultural University, Univ. Bhavan, Motibagh, Junagadh-362001, Gujarat
22. Karnataka Veterinary, Animal and Fisheries Sciences University, Nandinagar, PB No. 6, Bidar 585401, Karnataka
23. Kamdhenu University, Karmayogi Bhavan, Block-1, B1-wing, 4th Floor, Room No. 414, Sector 10-A, Gandhinagar-382010
24. Kerala Agricultural University, Vellanikara, Trichur-680656, Kerala
25. Kerala University of Fisheries & Ocean Studies, Papangad, Kochi-682506, Kerala
26. Kerala Veterinary and Animal Sciences University, Pattom, Thiruvananthapuram-695004, Kerala
27. Lala Lajpat Rai University of Veterinary & Animal Sciences, Hisar, Haryana
28. Nanaji Deshmukh Veterinary Science University, South Civil Lines, Jabalpur-482001, Madhya Pradesh
29. Navsari Agricultural University, Navsari-396450 Gujarat
30. Maharana Pratap Univ. of Agriculture & Technology, Udaipur-313001, Rajasthan
31. Maharashtra Animal Science & Fishery University, Seminary Hills, Nagpur-440006, Maharashtra
32. Mahatma Phule Krishi Vidyapeeth, Rahuri-413722, Maharashtra
33. Manyavar Shri Kanshiram Ji University of Agriculture and Technology, Banda - 210001, Uttar Pradesh
34. Narendra Deva University of Agriculture & Technology, Kumarganj, Faizabad-224229, Uttar Pradesh
35. Orissa Univ. of Agriculture & Technology, Bhubaneshwar-751003, Orissa
36. Prof. Jayashankar Telangana State Agricultural University, Admn. Office: Rajendranagar, Hyderabad-500030
37. Punjab Agricultural University, Ludhiana-141004, Punjab
38. Rajasthan University of Veterinary and Animal Sciences, Bikaner-334006, Rajasthan
39. Rajendra Agricultural University, Pusa, Samastipur-848125, Bihar
40. Rajmata Vijayraje Scindia Krishi Vishwa Vidyalaya, Race Course Road, Gwalior-474002, Madhya Pradesh
41. Sardar Vallabhbhai Patel University of Agriculture and Technology, Modipuram, Meerut-250110, Uttar Pradesh
42. Sardarkrushinagar-Dantiwada Agricultural University, Sardar Krushinagar, Dist. Banaskantha-385506, Gujarat
43. Sher-E-Kashmir Univ. of Agricultural Sciences & Technology, Railway Road, Jammu-180009, Jammu and Kashmir
44. Sher-E-Kashmir Univ. of Agricultural Sciences & Technology of Kashmir, Shalimar Campus, Srinagar-191121, Jammu & Kashmir
45. Sri Karan Narendra Agriculture University, Jobner-303329
46. Sri Konda Laxman Telengana State Horticultural, Rajendra Nagar Campus, Hyderabad
47. Sri Venkateswara Veterinary University, Admn office, Regional Library Building, Tirupati-517502
48. Swami Keshwanand Rajasthan Agricultural University, Bikaner-334006, Rajasthan
49. Tamil Nadu Agricultural University, Coimbatore-641003, Tamil Nadu
50. Tamil Nadu Fisheries University, Nagapattinam– 611003, Tamil Nadu
51. Tamil Nadu Veterinary & Animal Science University, Chennai-600051, Tamil Nadu
52. University of Agricultural Sciences, Bangalore, Shimoga Karnataka

53. University of Agricultural Sciences, Dharwad-580005, Karnataka
54. University of Horticultural Sciences, Sector No. 60 Navanagar, Bagalkot-587102, Karnataka
55. UP Pandit Deen Dayal Upadhaya Pashu Chikitsa Vigyan Vishwa Vidhyalaya evam Go Anusandhan Sansthan, Mathura-281001, Uttar Pradesh
56. Uttar Banga Krishi Viswavidyalaya, P.O. Pundibari, Dist. Cooch Bihar-736165, West Bengal
57. Uttarakhand University of Horticulture and Forestry, Pauri Garhwal, Uttarakhand
58. Vasantrao Naik Marathwada Agricultural University, Parbhani-431402, Maharashtra
59. West Bengal University of Animal & Fishery Sciences, 68 KB Sarani, Kolkata-700037, West Bengal

Appendix 12
Merits & Awards, ICAR 2017

The Indian Council of Agricultural Research, New Delhi announced the following ICAR Awards:

1. ICAR Challenge Award 2017

To find a solution for any immediate or long-standing problem, or limitation in agriculture, which is coming in the way of agricultural development and/or enhancing productivity in any major agricultural, horticultural or animal/fish product, ICAR has instituted a Challenge Award. The award carries a cash prize of ₹ 10.00 lakh, a citation, in addition to a share in the income generated by ICAR from the commercialization of the technology/product/process developed by the scientist while solving any of the given challenges as per ICAR rules and norms. The list of "Challenges" can be obtained either from the Award Cell of ICAR or can be down loaded from ICAR website. Any scientist or group of scientists may, at any time, file a claim of having solved any one of the listed "challenges".

2. Sardar Patel Outstanding ICAR Institution Award 2017

In order to recognize outstanding performance by the ICAR institutes, DUs of ICAR, CAU and State Agricultural Universities, three Awards of ₹ 10.00 lakh each, a citation and a plaque will be given to two ICAR Institutes/NRC/Project Directorates National Bureaus (a large and a small institute each) and one State Agricultural University/DUs/CAU.

3. Chaudhary Devi Lal Outstanding All India Coordinated Research Project Award 2017

In order to recognize outstanding performance of the AICRP and its cooperating centres and to provide incentive for outstanding performance in terms of linkages and research output and its impact, one annual award of ₹ 3.00 lakh (₹ 2.00 lakh for the main coordinating unit and ₹ 1.00 lakh for the best coordinating centre) in cash, a citation and a plaque is to be given to the selected AICRP. All the All India Coordinated Research Projects, which have been in operation for at least 10 years can apply for the award. Forwarding authority may give a clear-cut recommendation regarding the most significant achievements made in the AICRP and the best coordinating centre.

4. Jawaharlal Nehru Award For P.G. Outstanding Doctoral Thesis Research in Agricultural and Allied Sciences, 2017

In order to promote high quality doctoral thesis research in priority/frontier areas of agriculture and allied sciences, ICAR has instituted 18 awards of ₹ 50,000/- in cash plus a citation and silver medal (gold polished) each to be awarded annually for the outstanding original research work in agriculture and allied sciences. This award is meant exclusively for the doctoral thesis related to agricultural sciences from Indian Universities. The Ph.D. degree/provisional degree for this award must have been awarded during the year preceding the year of the award, i.e., 2016. A thesis will be considered only once for this award. Applicant must have evidence of publication of his/her work in the form of published/accepted form of at least one good research paper in a reputed journal having NAAS rating of ≥ 6 from the research work done for the Ph.D. thesis. The forwarding authority may give clear cut recommendation highlighting the merit of the research work.

5. Panjabrao Deshmukh Outstanding Woman Scientist Award 2017

All women scientists engaged in research in agricultural and allied subjects /extension in a recognized institutions are eligible for this award. The award consists of ₹ 1.00 lakh in cash and citation along with provision of equal amount of ₹ 1.00 lakh for motivating woman scientists and female students across the country including travel within a year of receiving the award. The awards are exclusively meant for individual women scientists. The forwarding authority may give clear cut recommendation highlighting the most significant achievements made by the scientists.

6. Vasantrao Naik Award for Outstanding Research Application in Dry Land Farming Systems 2017

In order to promote outstanding research and application in priority aspects of dry land farming systems & water conservation, an Annual Award of ₹ 1.00 lakh is to be awarded to an outstanding scientist or extension worker. All agricultural and allied scientists engaged in research/technology application work in dry land farming in India are eligible for the award. The award is also open to small interdisciplinary team of the scientists comprising up to six scientists/team of scientists. The forwarding authority may give clear cut recommendation highlighting the most significant achievements made by the scientists/ team of scientists.

7. Jagjivan Ram Abhinav Kisan Puruskar/ Jagjivan Ram Innovative Farmer Award (National/Zonal) 2017

In order to recognize the outstanding contributions of innovative farmers for initiatives in development adoption, modification and dissemination of improved technology and practices for increased income with sustainability, following National and Zonal Awards are announced:

(i) National: One annual national award of ₹ **1.00 lakh** each in any of the areas of agriculture and allied sciences + equal amount of travel grant across the country to promote his achievement are to be given to farmers at national level. Agricultural Production Commissioners/ Secretaries/Directors of Agril./Hort./A.H./ Fisheries/Sericulture, Vice-Chancellors of Agricultural Universities/Directors of ICAR Institute will identify and nominate the farmers in their areas of jurisdiction and forward the authentic information to the Council.

(ii) Zonal: Eleven annual awards of ₹ **0.50** lakh each + equal amount of travel grant to promote his/her achievement and motivate farmers in his/her perspective zone. All the KVKs in the country are divided zone wise. There are eight zones in the country and each zone is headed by Zonal Project Director. The geographical area of each zone is given in the guidelines of award. Agricultural Production Commissioners/ Secretaries/Directors of Agril./Hort/A.H./ Fisheries/Sericulture, Vice-Chancellors of agricultural universities/ Directors/ Joint Directors of ICAR Institutes and Directors of ATARIs/

NGOs, shall identify and nominate the farmers in their respective areas of jurisdiction and forward the authenticated nomination form to the Council. Nominating authority may put on record a clear cut recommendation highlighting the contributions made by the nominee and giving full justification for the nomination.

8. N.G. Ranga Farmer Award for Diversified Agriculture 2017

In order to recognize outstanding contribution of innovative farmers for diversified agriculture, one annual award of ₹ **1.00 lakh** in any of the areas of Diversified Agriculture is given by ICAR. Agricultural Production Commissioners /Secretaries/Directors of Agril./Hort./A.H./ Fisheries/Sericulture Vice-Chancellors of AUs/ Directors of ICAR Instt./Zonal Directors of KVKs/NGOs, other organizations connected with plant and animal sciences will identify and nominate the farmers in their area of jurisdiction and forward the nomination after proper authentication to the Council. All farmers selected for National/Zonal Award and meeting the criteria of this award are also eligible. Nominating authority may put on record a clear cut recommendation highlighting the contributions made by the nominee and giving full justification for the nomination.

9. Pandit Deen Dayal Upadhyay Antyodaya Krishi Puruskar 2017 (National & Zonal)

In order to recognize the contributions of marginal, small and landless farmers for developing sustainable integrated models of farming, the ICAR has instituted Pandit Deen Dayal Upadhyay Antyodaya Krishi Puruskar (National & Zonal) annually. For National level there is one award comprising of ₹ **1,00,000/-** (Rupees One Lakh only) and Award Certificate to be given annually. At zonal level there are total eleven awards: one for each zone of ATARIs comprising of ₹ **50,000/-** (Rupees Fifty Thousand only). Nominating authority may put on record a clear cut recommendation highlighting the contributions made by the nominee and giving full justification for the nomination.

10. Haldhar Organic Farmer Award 2017

In order to recognize outstanding contribution of organic farmers ICAR has instituted an award titled Haldhar Organic Farmer Award. The award consists of ₹ **1,00,000/-** (Rupees One Lakh only). The award is annual in nature. Any farmer involved in organic farming/activities in the area of field crop/horticultural crops/medicinal crops/ milk products, etc., with an experience of 10 years is eligible. Applications must be submitted in the recommended format and should be duly authenticated and forwarded by the competent forwarding authority.

11. Chaudhary Charan Singh Award For Excellence in Journalism in Agricultural Research and Development 2017

Six annual awards carrying cash award of ₹ **1,00,000/-** (One Lakh only) and a certificate are to be given to journalists for Print Media [Hindi Journalism/ English Journalism/ Journalism in Regional languages (four awards)] and Electronic media (two awards). The contribution made by the journalists would be judged on the basis of the articles/success stories published in Hindi/English/Regional languages Newspapers/ Magazines/Journals/electronic media in India during the preceding three years. The applications shall be submitted in the proper format only and shall be submitted through proper channel and authenticated by their competent supervising authority.

12. Fakhruddin Ali Ahmed Award for Outstanding Research in Tribal Farming Systems 2017

The award is primarily meant for any person or team (with two or three associates, if any) engaged in applied research and its applications in tribal areas of the country aimed at improving the biological resources and livelihoods or in original work directly applicable to tribal farming system. Two awards each with the value of ₹ **1.00 lakh** in cash and citation + provision of equal amount for study on related subject in geographical area of work for a year. The forwarding authority may give clear cut recommendation regarding the most significant contributions made by the concerned scientist/ team of scientists.

13. Bharat Ratna Dr C. Subramaniam Award for Outstanding Teachers 2017

In order to provide recognition to outstanding teachers and to promote quality teaching in the field of agriculture, four outstanding teacher awards are given annually. Each award consists of ₹ **1.00 lakh** in cash + travel grant of ₹ **1.00 lakh** to promote innovation in teaching. The applications through proper channel in respect of the eligible teachers are invited from SAUs, CAUs and DUs. The forwarding authority may give clear cut recommendation highlighting the most significant contributions made by the concerned teacher.

14. Pandit Deen Dayal Upadhyay Krishi Vigyan Protsahan Puraskar (National & Zonal) 2017

These awards promote healthy competition among Krishi Vigyan Kendras (KVKs) at Zonal and National Level for application of science and technology in agriculture. All KVKs are eligible to submit the application for these awards in the prescribed format duly forwarded and authenticated by the competent forwarding authority. For competition at national level, there is one award having prize money of ₹ **25.0 lakh** (₹ **20.00 lakh** for infrastructural development + ₹ **1.0 lakh** for sharing among staff + ₹ **4.0 lakh** for training of KVK staff). At zonal level there are a total of eleven awards: one for each zone of KVKs. Each award consists of ₹ **2.25 lakh** (₹ **1.50 lakh** for purchase of office/farm equipment + ₹ **0.75 lakh** for training of KVK staff). The Directors/Joint Directors of ICAR institutes/Vice-chancellors/Directors of Extension of Agricultural Universities/Directors of ATARIs may forward the applications in their respective areas of operations. The forwarding authority may give a 1-2 page note on the specific and most significant contributions made by the concerned KVK.

15. Dr Rajendra Prasad Puruskar for technical books in Hindi in Agricultural and Allied Sciences 2017

These awards recognize to authors of original Hindi Technical books in agriculture and allied sciences & incentivize Indian writers to write original standard works in agricultural and allied sciences in Hindi. The award is meant for individuals as well as teams of authors. An individual award consists of ₹ **1.00 lakh** in cash and a citation. There are four awards, one each in the Crop/Horticultural Sciences; NRM/Agricultural Engineering, Animal/Fisheries Sciences and Social Sciences. All original Hindi technical books in the designated subject areas of agriculture and allied sciences written by Indian authors, including editors of multi-author books in which the editor also has himself contributed substantially, are eligible. The author/editor must have had a substantial and active involvement in the relevant field of agriculture and allied sciences. The publication must be free from any infringement of copy rights. The publication must have been written and published during preceding year of the award. The forwarding authority may give clear cut recommendation on the originality and technical quality of the publication.

16. Lal Bahadur Shastri Outstanding Young Scientist Award 2017

In order to recognize the talented young scientists who have shown extraordinary originality and dedication in their research programmes, four individual awards are to be given annually. An individual award of ₹ **1.00 lakh** in cash and a citation and a challenge project for three years with budgetary provision of ₹ **10.00 lakh** per year+ ₹ **5.00 lakh** for foreign training (up to 3 months), if deemed necessary by the ICAR. The challenge project and foreign training will be administered/monitored by Division of Agricultural Education of ICAR. All young scientists who possess a doctoral degree and are below forty years of age (on 31st Dec.2016) and hold a regular teaching, research, extension education job in the ICAR-SAU system of institutions and engaged in research in agricultural and allied sciences for at least five years continuously are eligible for consideration. The forwarding authority may give clear cut recommendation regarding the most significant contributions made by the concerned scientist.

17. Rafi Ahmed Kidwai Award for Outstanding Research in Agricultural Sciences 2017

In order to recognize outstanding research in agricultural and allied sciences & provide incentives for excellence in agricultural research, this award is to be given to agricultural scientists for outstanding contribution in specified areas. A total of four awards are provided under the award. Each award carries a cash prize of ₹ **5.00 lakh** in addition to the citation. All Indian scientists engaged in agricultural research and overseas Indian scientists working in the areas relevant to Indian agriculture are eligible for these awards. The forwarding authority may give clear cut recommendation regarding the most significant contributions made by the concerned scientist.

18. Swami Sahajanand Saraswati Outstanding Extension Scientist Award 2017

The award is exclusively meant for individual extension scientist/teacher for excellence in agricultural extension methodology and education work. Two individual awards have been provided. An individual award would consist of ₹ **1.00 lakh** in cash and a citation. Two awards have been assigned across the disciplines in agriculture & allied sciences. Applications must be submitted in the recommended format and should be duly authenticated and forwarded by the competent forwarding authority.

19. NASI-ICAR Award for Innovation and Research on Farm Implements - 2017

In order to reduce drudgery of farm women by development of farm implements and to encourage researchers and innovators to develop farm implements for farm women, ICAR and NASI have instituted the NASI-ICAR Award For Innovation and Research on Farm Implements. The award consists of ₹ **1.00 lakh** in cash, citation and certificate. The award is annual in nature. All Scientists/Engineers/Innovators engaged in research in agricultural farm implements are eligible. Applications must be submitted in the recommended format and should be duly authenticated and forwarded by the competent forwarding authority.

20. ICAR Award for Outstanding Interdisciplinary Team Research in Agricultural and Allied Sciences 2015-16

In order to recognize, encourage and promote the understanding that practical and useful research would normally have to be interdisciplinary in approach, the ICAR has constituted the ICAR Award for Outstanding Interdisciplinary Team Research in Agricultural and Allied Sciences. The award is biennial in nature. All agricultural scientists engaged in interdisciplinary team research in India in the specified subject areas are eligible. The team must have scientist-level representation from a minimum of three well-recognized disciplines and may also have technical officers (T6 and above). They must have been working on an integrated research project dealing with an inherently interdisciplinary problem in a system based, problem solving mode. The final phase of the research work including its field validation must have been completed during the five years preceding the year of the award. Each member of the team must have remained its active member continuously for at least three years preceding the year of the award. Documentary evidence should be provided that the project has been running/ has run continuously for at least five years at that time of submission of the application. The award is not limited to NARS, i.e., Agricultural Scientists outside NARS are also eligible if they meet the eligibility criteria as mentioned above. There would be maximum 4 awards, and each award would be of ₹ **5,00,000/-** (Rupees Five Lakh only). Not more than one award will be given in any discipline.

Cash Award Scheme for Administrative/ Technical/Supporting category employees of ICAR Research Institutes/NRCs/Bureaus/ZCUs has been instituted by the ICAR in order to recognize the excellence in performance. Three annual awards of ₹ **51,000/-** (Rupees Fifty One Thousand only) are to be given to the awardees, selected among applications received from the regular employees of ICAR. The forwarding authority may provide a detailed note on the most significant activities made by the employee in his/ her service career.

Appendix 13

Institutions under ICAR – 64

1. ICAR-Central Island Agricultural Research Institute, Port Blair
2. ICAR-Central Arid Zone Research Institute, Jodhpur
3. ICAR-Central Avian Research Institute, Izatnagar
4. ICAR-Central Inland Fisheries Research Institute, Barrackpore
5. ICAR-Central Institute Brackishwater Aquaculture, Chennai
6. ICAR-Central Institute for Research on Buffaloes, Hisar
7. ICAR-Central Institute for Research on Goats, Makhdoom
8. ICAR-Central Institute of Agricultural Engineering, Bhopal
9. ICAR-Central Institute for Arid Horticulture, Bikaner
10. ICAR-Central Institute of Cotton Research, Nagpur
11. ICAR-Central Institute of Fisheries Technology, Cochin
12. ICAR-Central Institute of Freshwater Aquaculture, Bhubaneshwar
13. ICAR-Central Institute of Research on Cotton Technology, Mumbai
14. ICAR-Central Institute of Subtropical Horticulture, Lucknow
15. ICAR-Central Institute of Temperate Horticulture, Srinagar
16. ICAR-Central Institute on Postharvest Engineering and Technology, Ludhiana
17. ICAR-Central Marine Fisheries Research Institute, Kochi
18. ICAR-Central Plantation Crops Research Institute, Kasargod
19. ICAR-Central Potato Research Institute, Shimla
20. ICAR-Central Research Institute for Jute and Allied Fibres, Barrackpore
21. ICAR-Central Research Institute of Dryland Agriculture, Hyderabad
22. ICAR-National Rice Research Institute, Cuttack
23. ICAR-Central Sheep and Wool Research Institute, Avikanagar, Rajasthan
24. ICAR-Central Sheep and Wool Research Institute, Dehradun
25. ICAR-Central Soil Salinity Research Institute, Karnal
26. ICAR-Central Tobacco Research Institute, Rajamundry

27. ICAR-Central Tuber Crops Research Institute, Trivandrum
28. ICAR-ICAR Research Complex for Eastern Region, Patna
29. ICAR-ICAR Research Complex for NEH Region, Barapani
30. ICAR-Central Coastal Agricultural Research Institute, Ela, Old Goa, Goa
31. ICAR-Indian Agricultural Statistics Research Institute, New Delhi
32. ICAR-Indian Grassland and Fodder Research Institute, Jhansi
33. ICAR-Indian Institute of Agricultural Biotechnology, Ranchi
34. ICAR-Indian Institute of Horticultural Research, Bengaluru
35. ICAR-Indian Institute of Natural Resins and Gums, Ranchi
36. ICAR-Indian Institute of Pulses Research, Kanpur
37. ICAR-Indian Institute of Soil Sciences, Bhopal
38. ICAR-Indian Institute of Spices Research, Calicut
39. ICAR-Indian Institute of Sugarcane Research, Lucknow
40. ICAR-Indian Institute of Vegetable Research, Varanasi
41. ICAR-National Academy of Agricultural Research & Management, Hyderabad
42. ICAR-National Institute of Biotic Stresses Management, Raipur
43. ICAR-National Institute of Abiotic Stress Management, Malegaon, Maharashtra
44. ICAR-National Institute of Animal Nutrition and Physiology, Bengaluru
45. ICAR-National Institute of Research on Jute & Allied Fibre Technology, Kolkata
46. ICAR-National Institute of Veterinary Epidemiology and Disease Informatics, Hebbal, Bengaluru
47. ICAR-Sugarcane Breeding Institute, Coimbatore
48. ICAR-Vivekananda Parvatiya Krishi Anusandhan Sansthan, Almora
49. ICAR-Central Institute for Research on Cattle, Meerut, Uttar Pradesh
50. ICAR-National Institute of High Security Animal Diseases, Bhopal
51. ICAR-Indian Institute of Maize Research, New Delhi
52. ICAR- Central Agroforestry Research Institute, Jhansi
53. ICAR-National Institute of Agricultural Economics and Policy Research, New Delhi
54. ICAR- Indian Institute of Wheat and Barley Research, Karnal
55. ICAR- Indian Institute of Farming Systems Research, Modipuram
56. ICAR- Indian Institute of Millets Research, Hyderabad
57. ICAR- Indian Institute of Oilseeds Research, Hyderabad
58. ICAR- Indian Institute of Oil Palm Research, Pedawegi, West Godaw
59. ICAR- Indian Institute of Water Management, Bhubaneswar
60. ICAR-Indian Institute of Rice Research, Hyderabad
61. ICAR- Central Institute for Women in Agriculture, Bhubaneswar
62. ICAR-Central Citrus Research Institute, Nagpur
63. ICAR-Indian Institute of Seed Research, Mau
64. ICAR-Indian Agricultural Research Institute, Hazaribagh, Jharkhand

Appendix 14

Deemed Universities (as on 23rd June, 2008)

1. Gandhi Institute of Technology and Management, Andhra Pradesh, Visakhapatnam
2. Koneru Lakshmaiah Education Foundation, Andhra Pradesh, Vaddeswaram
3. Vignan's Foundation for Science, Technology & Research, Andhra Pradesh, Guntur
4. Sri Sathya Sai Institute of Higher Learning, Andhra Pradesh, Anantapur
5. North Eastern Regional Institute of Science and Technology, Arunachal Pradesh, Itanagar
6. Nava Nalanda Mahavihara, Bihar, Nalanda
7. Punjab Engineering College, Chandigarh
8. Indian Agricultural Research Institute, New Delhi
9. Indian Institute of Foreign Trade, New Delhi
10. Indian Law Institute, New Delhi
11. Institute of Liver and Biliary Sciences, New Delhi
12. Jamia Hamdard, New Delhi
13. National Museum Institute of the History of Art, Conservation and Museology, New Delhi
14. National Institute of Educational Planning and Administration, New Delhi
15. TERI School of Advanced Studies, New Delhi
16. Gujarat Vidyapith, Faridabad, Haryana
17. Sumandeep Vidyapeeth, Gujarat, Waqhodia
18. Lingaya's Vidyapeeth, Faridabad, Haryana
19. Maharishi Markandeshwar (Deemed to be University), Ambala, Haryana
20. Manav Rachna International Institute of Research and Studies, Faridabad, Haryana
21. National Brain Research Centre, Manesar, Haryana
22. National Dairy Research Institute, Karnal, Haryana
23. Birla Institute of Technology, Mesra, Ranchi, Jharkhand
24. BLDE (Deemed to be University), Bijapur, Karnataka
25. Indian Institute of Science, Bangalore, Karnataka
26. International Institute of Information Technology, Bangalore, Karnataka
27. JSS Academy of Higher Education & Research, Mysore, Karnataka

28. Jain (Deemed to be University), Bangalore, Karnataka
29. Jawaharlal Nehru Centre for Advanced Scientific Research, Bangalore, Karnataka
30. KLE Academy of Higher Education & Research, Belgaum, Karnataka
31. Manipal Academy of Higher Education, Manipal, Karnataka
32. NITTE (Deemed to be University), Magalore, Karnataka
33. Sri Devaraj Urs Academy of Higher Education and Research, Kolar, Karnataka
34. Sri Siddhartha Academy of Higher Education, Tumkur, Karnataka
35. Swami Vivekananda Yoga Anusandhana Samsthana, Bangalore, Karnataka
36. Yenepoya (Deemed to be University), Mangalore, Karnataka
37. Indian Institute of Space Science and Technology, Thiruvanthapuram, Kerala
38. Kerala Kalamandalam, Thrissur, Kerala
39. Lakshmibai National Institute of Physical Education, Gwalior, Madhya Pradesh
40. Bharati Vidyapeeth, Pune, Maharashtra
41. Central Institute of Fisheries Education, Mumbai, Maharashtra
42. D. Y. Patil Education Society, Kolhapur, Maharashtra
43. Datta Meghe Institute of Medical Sciences, Wardha, Maharashtra
44. Deccan College Post-Graduate and Research Institute, Pune, Maharashtra
45. Defence Institute of Advanced Technology, Pune, Maharashtra
46. Dr. D. Y. Patil Vidyapeeth, Pune, Maharashtra
47. Gokhale Institute of Politics and Economics, Pune, Maharashtra
48. Homi Bhabha National Institute, Mumbai, Maharashtra
49. Indira Gandhi Institute of Development Research, Mumbai, Maharashtra
50. Institute of Chemical Technology, Mumbai, Maharashtra
51. International Institute for Population Sciences, Mumbai, Maharashtra
52. Krishna Institute of Medical Sciences, Satara, Maharashtra
53. MGM Institute of Health Sciences, Navi Mumbai, Maharashtra
54. NarseeMonjee Institute of Management Studies, Mumbai, Maharashtra
55. Pravara Institute of Medical Sciences, Ahmednagar, Maharashtra
56. Symbiosis International, Pune, Maharashtra
57. Tata Institute of Fundamental Research, Mumbai, Maharashtra
58. Tata Institute of Social Sciences, Mumbai, Maharashtra
59. Tilak Maharashtra Vidyapeeth, Pune, Maharashtra
60. Kalinga Institute of Industrial Technology, Bhubaneswar, Odisha
61. Siksha 'O' Anusandhan, Bhubaneswar, Odisha
62. Sri Balaji Vidyapeeth, Pondicherry, Puducherry
63. Thapar Institute of Engineering and Technology, Patiala, Punjab
64. Banasthali Vidyapith, Tonk, Rajasthan
65. Birla Institute of Technology and Science, Pilani, Rajasthan
66. IIS (Deemed to be University), Jaipur, Rajasthan
67. Institute of Advanced Studies in Education, Churu, Rajasthan
68. Jain Vishva Bharati Institute, Ladnun, Rajasthan
69. Janardan Rai Nagar Rajasthan Vidyapeeth, Udaipur, Rajasthan
70. LNM Institute of Information Technology, Jaipur, Rajasthan
71. Academy of Maritime Education and Training, Chennai, Tamil Nadu

72. Amrita Vishwa Vidyapeetham, Coimbatore, Tamil Nadu
73. Avinashilingam Institute for Home Science and Higher Education for Women, Coimbatore, Tamil Nadu
74. B.S. Abdur Rahman Crescent Institute of Science and Technology, Chennai, Tamil Nadu
75. Bharath Institute of Higher Education and Research, Chennai, Tamil Nadu
76. Chennai Mathematical Institute, Siruseri, Tamil Nadu
77. Chettinad Academy of Research and Education, Chengalpattu, Tamil Nadu
78. Dr. M.G.R. Educational and Research Institute, Chenni, Tamil Nadu
79. Gandhigram Rural Institute, Dindigul, Tamil Nadu
80. Hindustan Institute of Technology and Science, Chennai, Tamil Nadu
81. Kalasalingam Academy of Research and Education, Krihnakoil, Tamil Nadu
82. Karpagam Academy of Higher Education, Coimbatore, Tamil Nadu
83. Karunya Institute of Technology and Sciences, Coimbatore, Tamil Nadu
84. Meenakshi Academy of Higher Education and Research, Chennai, Tamil Nadu
85. Noorul Islam Centre for Higher Education, Kumarakovil, Tamil Nadu
86. Periyar Maniammai Institute of Science & Technology, Vallam, Tamil Nadu
87. Ponnaiyah Ramajayam Institute of Science and Technology, Thanjavur, Tamil Nadu
88. Sathyabama Institute of Science and Technology, Chennai, Tamil Nadu
89. Saveetha Institute of Medical and Technical Sciences, Chennai, Tamil Nadu
90. Shanmugha Arts, Science, Technology & Research Academy, Thanjuvar, Tamil Nadu
91. Sri Chandrasekharendra Saraswathi Viswa Mahavidyalaya, Kanchipuram, Tamil Nadu
92. Sri Ramachandra Medical College and Research Institute, Chennai, Tamil Nadu
93. SRM Institute of Science and Technology, Kanchipuram, Tamil Nadu
94. St. Peter's Institute of Higher Education and Research, Chennai, Tamil Nadu
95. Vel Tech Rangarajan Dr. Sagunthala R&D Institute of Science and Technology, Chennai, Tamil Nadu
96. Vels Institute of Science, Technology & Advanced Studies, Chennai, Tamil Nadu
97. Vinayaka Mission's Research Foundation, Salem, Tamil Nadu
98. Vellore Institute of Technology, Vellore, Tamil Nadu
99. ICFAI Foundation for Higher Education, Hyderabad, Telengana
100. International Institute of Information Technology, Hyderabad, Telengana
101. Bhatkhande Music Institute, Lucknow, Uttar Pradesh
102. Central Institute of Higher Tibetan Studies, Varanasi, Uttar Pradesh

Deemed universities under "de-novo" category

1. Central Institute of Buddhist Studies, Leh, Ladakh
2. Chinmaya Vishwavidyapeeth, Ernakulam, Kerala
3. National Institute of Food Technology Entrepreneurship and Management, Sonipat, Haryana
4. Indian Association for the Cultivation of Science, Kolkata, West Bengal
5. National Rail and Transportation Institute, Vadodra, Gujarat
6. Kalinga Institute of Social Sciences, Bhubaneswar, Odisha

Appendix 15
National Research Centres (NRC)

1. ICAR-National Research Centre for Banana, Trichi
2. ICAR-National Research Centre for Grapes, Pune
3. ICAR-National Research Centre for Litchi, Muzaffarpur
4. ICAR-National Research Centre for Pomegranate, Solapur
5. ICAR-National Research Centre on Camel, Bikaner
6. ICAR-National Research Centre on Equines, Hisar
7. ICAR-National Research Centre on Meat, Hyderabad
8. ICAR-National Research Centre on Mithun, Medziphema, Nagaland
9. ICAR-National Research Centre on Orchids, Pakyong, Sikkim
10. ICAR-National Research Centre on Pig, Guwahati
11. ICAR-National Research Centre on Plant Biotechnology, New Delhi
12. ICAR-National Research Centre on Seed Spices, Ajmer
13. ICAR-National Research Centre on Yak, Dirang, West Kameng, Arunachal Pradesh
14. ICAR-National Centre for Integrated Pest Management, New Delhi
15. National Research Centre on Integrated Farming (ICAR-NRCIF), Motihari

Appendix 16
Institutes

1. **Central Agricultural Research Institute (CARI),** Post Box No. 181, Andaman Nicobar & Lakshwadeep Group of Islands Port Blair-744101
   Email: pblcarian@sancharnet.in
2. **Central Arid Zone Research Institute (CAZRI),** Jodhpur, Rajasthan-342003
   Email: nljoshi@cazri.raj.nic.in
   Website: www.icar.org.in/cazri.htm
3. **Central Avian Research Institute (CARI),** Izatnagar, Uttar Pradesh-243122
   Email: cavri@x400.nicgw.nic.in
4. **Central Inland Fishries Research Institute (CIFRI),** Barrackpore, West Bengal-743101
   Email: info@cifri.gov.in
   Website: www.cifri.com
5. **Central Institute for Sub-Tropical Horticulture (CISTH),** Rae Bareli Road, P.O. Dilkusha, Lucknow, Uttar Pradesh-226002
   Email: cisth@x400.nicgw.nic.in
6. **Central Institute for Research on Baffaloes (CIRB),** Sirsa Road, Hisar, Haryana-125001
   Email: cirb@x400.nicgw.nic.in
7. **Central Institute for Research on Cotton Technology (CIRCOT),** Adenwala Road, Matunga, Mumbai, Maharashtra-400019
   Email: circot@vsnl.com
   Website: education.vsnl.com/circot
8. **Central Institute for Cotton Research (CICR),** P.O. No. 225, G.P.O., Panjari, Wardha Road, Nagpur, Maharashtra-440010
9. **Central Institute for Freshwater Aquaculture (CIFA),** P.O. Kausalyaganga, Bhubaneshwar, Orissa-751002
   Email: cifa@ori.nic.in
10. **Central Institute of Post Harvest Engineering & Technology (CIPHET),** PAU Campus, Ludhiana, Punjab-141004
    Email: ciphet@satyam.net.in
    Website: http://www.icar.org.in/ciphet.html
11. **Central Institute of Agricultural Engineering (CIAE),** Nabibagh, Berasia Road, Bhopal, Madhya Pradesh
    Email: director@ciae.mp.nic.in
    Website: www.mp.nic.in/ciae
12. **Central Institute of Arid Horticulture (CIAE),** Beechwal, Ganganagar Road, Bikaner, Rajasthan
    Email: ciah@hub.nic.in
    Website: www.icar.org.in/ciah/ciah.htm
13. **Central Institute of Brakishwater Aquaculture (CIBA),** 141, Marshal's Road, Egmore, Chennai, Tamil Nadu
    Email: ciba@tn.nic.in
    Website: www.ciba.tn.nic.in

14. **Central Institute of Fisheries Education (CIFE),** Jaiprakash Road, Seven Bungalows, Versova, Mumbai, Maharashtra-400061
Email: director.cife@gmail.com
Website: www.cife.edu.in
15. **Central Institute of Fisheries Technology (CIFT),** Willingdon Island, P.O. Matsyapuri, Cochin, Kerala-682029
Email: root@cift.ker.nic.in
16. **Central Institute of Temperate Horticulture (CITH),** P.O. Sanatnagar, Srinagar, J&K-190005
Email: cith@hub1.nic.in
17. **Central Marine Fisheries Research Institute (CMFRI),** P.O. No. 1603, Ernakulam, Cochin, Kerala-682014
Email: mdcmfri@md2.vsnl.net.in
Website: www.cmfri.com
18. **Central Plantation Crops Research Institute (CPCRI),** Kasaragod, Kerala 670124 Email: cpcri@md3.vsnl.net.in
Website: cpcri.nic.in
19. **Central Potato Research Institute (CPRI),** Shimla, Himachal Pradesh-171001
Email: director@cpri.ernet.in
20. **Central Research Institute for Jute & Allied Fibres (CRIJAF),** 24 Paraganas, Barrackpore, West Bengal-743101
Email: crijaf@cal2.vsnl.net.in
21. **Central Research Institute for Dryland Agriculture (CRIDA),** Santosh Nagar, P.O. Saidabad, Hyderabad, Andhra Pradesh-500659
Email: hpsingh@crida.ap.nic.in
22. **Central Rice Research Institute (CRRI),** Cuttack, Orissa-753006
Email: root@crri.ori.nic.in
23. **Central Sheep & Wool Research Institute (CSWRI),** Avikanagar, Tehsil Malpura, Tonk, Rajsthan-304501
Email: root@cswri.raj.nic.in
24. **Central Soil & Water Conservation Research & Training Institute (CSWCRTI),** 218, Kaulagarh Road, Dehradun, Uttar Pradesh-248195
Email: cswcrti@cswcrti.up.nic.in
25. **Central Soil Salinity Research Institute (CSSRI),** Rajahmundri, Andhra Pradesh-533105
Email: gbsing@cssri.ernet.in
Website: www.cssri.org
26. **Central Tabacco Research Institute (CTRI),** Rajahmundri, Andhra Pradesh-533105
Email: ctri@pol.net.in
27. **Central Tuber Crops Research Institute (CTCRI),** Sreekartiyam, Thiruvananthapuram, Trivandrum, Kerala-695017
Email: ctcri@x400.nicgw.nic.in
28. **ICAR Research Complex for Goa (ICARRCG),** Ela Old Goa, Goa-403402
Email: director@icargoa.res.in
Website: icargoa.res.in
29. **ICAR Research Complex for NEH Region (ICARRCNEHR),** Umroi Road, Barapani, Meghalaya-793103
Email: root@icarneh.ren.nic.in
30. **Indian Lac Research Institute (ILRI),** Namkum, Ranchi, Jharkhand-834010
Email: ilri@bih.nic.in
31. **Indian Veterinary Research Institute (IVRI),** Izatnagar, Uttar Pradesh-243122
Email: singh@wiprobt.ems.vsnl.net.in
32. **Indian Agricultural Research Institute (IARI),** Pusa, Dr. K. S. Krishnan Marg, New Delhi-110012
Email: root@iari.ernet.in
Website: www.iari.res.in
33. **Indian Agricultural Statistics Research Institute (IASRI),** Library Avenue, Pusa, New Delhi-110012
Email: iasri@iasri.res.in
Website: www.iasri.res.in

34. **Indian Grassland & Fodder Research Institute (IGFRI),** Pahuj Dam, Jhansi-Gwalior Road, Jhansi, Uttar Pradesh-284003
Email: igfri@igfri.up.nic.in
35. **Indian Institute of Pulses Research (IIPR),** Kalyanpur, Kanpur, Uttar Pradesh-208024
Email: root@iipr.up.nic.in
Website: http://iipr.up.nic.in
36. **Indian Institute of Horticulture Research (IIHR),** Hassaraghatta, Lake Post, Bangalore, Karnataka-560089
Email: root@iihr.res.in
Website: www.iihr.res.in
37. **Indian Institute of Soil Sciences (IISS),** Nabi Bagh, Berasia Road, Bhopal, Madhya Pradesh-462038
Email: director@iiss.ernet.in.
asrao@iiss.ernet.in and iiss@iiss.ernet.in
38. **Indian Institute of Spices Research (IISR),** P.O. No. 1701, Marikannu P.O., Calicut, Kerala-673012
Email: nrcp@ren.nic.in
39. **Indian Institute of Sugarcane Research (IISR),** Rae Bareli Road, P.O. Dilkusha, Lucknow, Uttar Pradesh-226002
Email: iisrin@lw1.vsnl.net.in
40. **Indian Institute of Vegetable Research (PDV),** Gandhinagar, Naira, P.O. Varanasi, Uttar Pradesh-221005
Email: pdveg@x400.nicgw.nic.in
41. **National Academy of Agricultural Research Management (NAARM),** Rajendranagar, Hyderabad Andhra Pradesh-500030
Email: sptiwari@naarm.ernet.in
42. **National Dairy Research Institute (NDRI),** Karnal, Haryana
Email: root@ndri.hry.nic.in
43. **National Institute for Research on Jute Allied Fibres Technology (NIRJAFT),** 12, Regent Park, Calcutta, West Bengal
Email: nirjaft@wb.nic.in
44. **National Institute of Animal Nutrition & Physiology (NIANP),** NDRI Campus, Adugodi, Bangalore, Karnataka-560030
Email: director@nainpbng.kar.nic.in
Website: http://www.nianp.res.in
45. **Sugarcane Breeding Institute (SBI),** Coimbatore, Tamil Nadu-641007
Email: sugaris@md3.vsnl.net.in
46. **Vivekanand Parvatiya Krishi Anusandhan Shala (VPKAS),** Almora, Uttarakhand
Email: vpkas@hub1.nic.in
Website: http://vpkas.nic.in

Appendix 17
National Bureaus

1. ICAR-National Bureau of Plant Genetics Resources, New Delhi
2. ICAR-National Bureau of Agriculturally Important Microorganisms, Mau, Uttar Pradesh
3. ICAR-National Bureau of Agricultural Insect Resources, Bengaluru
4. ICAR-National Bureau of Soil Survey and Land Use Planning, Nagpur
5. ICAR-National Bureau of Animal Genetic Resources, Karnal
6. ICAR-National Bureau of Fish Genetic Resources, Lucknow

Appendix 18

Total Number of Varieties Released from Department of Genetics & Plant Breeding, G.B. Pant University of Agriculture & Technology, Pantnagar, Uttarakhand, India

Crop	No. of varieties released	Names
Wheat	32	Kalyan sona (AS 227), Sonalika (R.R.21), UP 301, UP 310, UP 319, UP 215, UP 262, UP 368, UP 115, UP 2003, UP 2121, UP 2113, UP 1109, UP 2338, UP 2382, UP 2425, UP 2565, UP 2526, UP 2554, UP 2572, UP 2584, UP 2628, UP 2684, UP 2748, UP 2784, UP 2785, UP 2855, UP 2844, UP 2865, UP 2903, UP 2938, UP 2944
Rice	27	IR 24, Prasad, Govind, Pant Dhan 4, Manahar, Pant Dhan 6, Pant Dhan 10, Pant Dhan 11, Pant Dhan 12, Pant Sankar Dhan 1, Pant Majhera 7, Pant Dhan 16, Pant Sugandh Dhan 15, Pant Sugandh Dhan 17, Pant Sankar Dhan 3, Pant Dhan 18, Pant Dhan 19, Pant Sugandh Dhan 21, Pant Dhan 22, Pant Dhan 23, Pant Sugandh Dhan 25, Pant Sugandh Dhan 27, Pant Basmati 1, Pant Basmati 2, Pant Dhan 24, Pant Dhan 26, Pant Dhan 28

Maize	17	Protina, Tarun, Navin, Sweta, Kanchan, D 765, Surya, Gaurav (D 981), Amar, Pragati (D 994), Pant Sankar Makka 1, Pant Sankar Makka 2, Pant Sankar Makka 3, Pant Sankar Makka 4, Pant Sankar Makka 5, Pant Sankar Makka 6, Pant Popcorn 1
Barley	03	UPB 1008, PRB 502, PRB 701
Pulses		
Arhar	05	UPAS 120, Pant Arhar 291, Pant Arhar 3, Pant Arhar 6, Pant Arhar 7
Chickpea	06	Pant G 114, Pant G 186, Sadbhawana, Surya, WCG 10, Pant Kabuli Channa
Lentil	09	Pant L. 406, Pant L. 234, Pant L. 639, Pant L. 4, Pant L. 5, Pant L. 6, Pant L. 7, Pant L. 8, Pant L. 9
Moong	09	Pant Moong 1, Pant Moong 2, Pant Moong 3, Pant Moong 4, Pant Moong 5, Pant Moong 6, Pant Moong 7, Pant Moong 8, Pant Moong 9
Urdbean	11	Pant Urd 19, Pant Urd 30, Pant Urd 31, Pant Urd 35, Manikya, Pant Urd 40, Pant Urd 6, Pant Urd 7, Pant Urd 8, Pant Urd 9, Pant Urd 10
Field pea	13	Pant P 5, Pant P 13, Pant P 14, Pant P 25, Pant P 42, Pant P 74, Pant P 86, Pant P 108, Pant P 155, Pant P 157, Pant P 243, Pant P 250, Pant P 347
Rice bean	02	PRR 1, PRR 2
Grain Cowpea	06	Pant Lobiya 1, Pant Lobiya 2, Pant Lobiya 3, Pant Lobiya 4, Pant Lobiya 5, Pant Lobiya 6
Soybean	19	Bragg, Ankur, Alankar, Shilajeet, PK N262, PK 327, PK 308, PK 416, PK 472, PK 564, Pant Soybean 1024, Pant Soybean 1042, Pant Soybean 1029, Pant Soybean1092, Pant Soybean1241, PRS 1, Pant Soybean 1347, Pant Soybean 1225, Pant Soybean 19, Pant Soybean 20, Pant Soybean21, Pant Soybean 22, Pant Soybean 23, Pant Soybean 24, Pant Soybean 25, Pant Soybean 26
Rapeseed Mustard		
Toria	06	PT 30, PT 303, PT 507, PT 2002-25 (Uttara), Pant Hill Toriya 1, PT 508

Yellow Sarson	03	Pant Pili Sarson 1, Pant Sweta, Pant Girija
Indian-Mustard	05	Kranti, Krishna, Pant Rai 19, Pant Rai 20, Pant Rai 21
Karan Rai	01	Kiran
Millets		
Ragi-Mandua	05	PES 176, PES 110, Pant Mandua 3, PRM 1, PRM 2
Foxtail Millet	02	Pant Sataria 4, PRK 1 (Himadri)
Grain Amaranth	03	PRA 1, PRA 2, PRA 3
Jhangora	01	PRJ 1
Proso Millet	01	PRC 1
Buck wheat	01	PRB 1
Fodder Crops		
Sorghum	20	UP Chari 1, UP Chari 2, UP Chari 3, UP Chari 4, UP Chari 5, UP Chari 6, UP Chari 7, UP Chari 8, UP Chari 9, UP Chari 10, UP Chari 11, CSV 35 F, Pant Chari 12, Pant Chari 13, Pant Chari 14, Pant Chari 15, CSH 20 (M.F.), CSH 24 (M.F.), CSH 40 (M.F.), CSH 44 (M.F.)
Forage cowpea	12	UPS 5286, UPC 5287, UPC 287, UPC 4200, UPC 8705, UPC 9202, UPC 607, UPC 618, UPC 622, UPC 621, UPC 625, UPC 628
Oat	02	UPO 94, UPO 212
Berseem	01	UPB 110
Sugar Crops		
Sugarcane	09	Co Pant 84211, Co Pant 84212, Co Pant 90223, Co Pant 94211, Co Pant 96219, Co Pant 97222, Co Pant 99214, Co Pant 3220, Co Pant 05224,
Sugarbeet	01	Pant S 10
Cotton	03	Shyamali, Pramukh, Lohit
Dhaincha	01	Pant SES 1
Poplar	01	Pant Poplar 5
Total	**247**	

Appendix 19

List of Released Varieties from Central Agricultural University, Imphal

Crops	No. of varieties released	Names
Rice	04	CAU-R1, CAU-R2, CAU-R3, CAU-R4
Paphiopedilum	01	SHEETAL-1
Total	**05**	